W9-AYY-788

DISTRIBUTED COMPUTING

A Practical Synthesis of Networks, Client-Server Systems, Distributed Applications, and Open Systems

Amjad Umar, Ph.D.

Bell Communications Research (Bellcore)
Piscataway, New Jersey

P T R Prentice-Hall
Englewood Cliffs, New Jersey 07632

Library of Congress Cataloging-in-Publication Data

Umar, Amjad
Distributed computing : a practical synthesis / Amjad Umar.
p. cm.
Includes bibliographical references and index.
ISBN 0-13-036252-2
I. Electronic data processing--Distributed processing
2. Computer networks. I. Title.
QA76.9.D5U4 1993 92-38284
004'.35--dc20 CIP

Acquisitions editor: Paul Becker
Editorial/production supervision: Inkwell Publishing Services
Cover design: Eloise Starkweather
Buyer: Mary McCartney

© 1993 by Bellcore
Published by P T R Prentice-Hall, Inc.
A Simon & Schuster Company
Englewood Cliffs, New Jersey 07632

All rights reserved. No part of this book may be reproduced, in any form or by any means, without permission in writing from the publisher.

Printed in the United States of America

10 9 8 7 6 5 4 3 2 1

The publisher offers discounts on this book when ordered in bulk quantities. For more information, write:

Special Sales/College Marketing
Prentice-Hall, Inc.
College Technical and Reference Division
Englewood Cliffs, NJ 07632

ISBN 0-13-036252-2

Prentice-Hall International (UK) Limited, *London*
Prentice-Hall of Australia Pty. Limited, *Sydney*
Prentice-Hall Canada, Inc., *Toronto*
Prentice-Hall Hispanoamericana, S.A., *Mexico*
Prentice-Hall of India Private Limited, *New Delhi*
Prentice-Hall of Japan, Inc., *Tokyo*
Simon & Schuster Asia Pte. Ltd., *Singapore*
Editora Prentice-Hall do Brasil, Ltda., *Rio de Janeiro*

Dedicated to my family:
my loving wife Dolorese, fond memories of my parents,
and the rest of the gang.

About the Author: Dr. Umar has over 20 years of experience in database/data communications, which includes 10 years in technical support and development of networks and databases, five years in management of distributed computing, and five years of university teaching and research in networks, databases, and software engineering. Currently a project manager in Bell Communications Research, he teaches seminars and graduate courses as an adjunct at Stevens Institute of Technology, Fordham University, and Columbia University. Before joining Bellcore, he was on the faculty at the University of Michigan (Dearborn and Ann Arbor Campuses) where he received the Distinguished Faculty award. His work and consulting assignments include the telecommunications industry, manufacturing organizations, educational institutions, and organizations in England, Singapore, and China. He has an M.S. in Computer, Information, and Control Engineering and Ph.D. in Industrial and Operations Engineering (major in information systems) from the University of Michigan. His Ph.D. dissertation is on distributed systems design. He has authored several technical papers and is a member of the IEEE Computer Society and ACM.

Trademarks

The following list recognizes the commercial and intellectual property of the trademark holders whose products are mentioned in this book. Omission from this list is inadvertent:

AIX—Trademark of IBM Corporation
AS/400—Trademark of IBM Corporation
AT & T—Trademark of AT&T
ATLAS—Trademark of UNIX International
DB2—Trademark of IBM Corporation
DEC—Trademark of Digital Equipment Corporation
DECnet—Trademark of Digital Equipment Corporation
Encina—Trademark of Transarc Corp.
Encompass—Trademark of Tandem Computers
Ethernet—Trademark of Xerox Corporation
HP—Trademark of Hewlett-Packard Company
IBM—Trademark of International Business Corporation
IBM PC, IBM PS/2 —Trademarks of International Business Corporation
IMS, DB2, CICS—Trademarks of International Business Corporation
Information Warehouse—Trademark of IBM Corporation
Kerberos—Trademark of the Massachusetts Institute of Technology
Macintosh—Trademark of Apple Computers, Inc.
MS-DOS—Trademark of Microsoft Corporation
MVS, MVS/ESA, MVS/XA—Trademarks of International Business Corporation
Netview—Trademark of IBM Corporation
Netware—Trademark of Novell Corporation
Network File System —Trademark of Sun Microsystems, Inc.
NFS —Trademark of Sun Microsystems, Inc.
OS/2 —Trademark of IBM Corporation
OSCA Architecture—Trademark of Bellcore
Quest—Trademark of Gupta Technologies
RS6000—Trademark of IBM Corporation
Topend—Trademark of NCR
Tuxedo—Trademark of Unix Systems Laboratories
SQL Windows—Trademark of Gupta Technologies
SNA, VTAM, NCP, SDLC—Trademarks of International Business Corporation
Sunnet Manager—Trademark of Sun Microsystems
Supra—Trademark of Cincom Corporation
ULTRIX—Trademark of Digital Equipment Corporation
Unix—Trademark of Unix Systems Laboratories, Inc.
VAX—Trademark of Digital Equipment Corporation
VMS—Trademark of Digital Equipment Corporation
X/Open—Trademark of X/Open Company Ltd.
XWindow—Trademark of the Massachusetts Institute of Technology

Disclaimer

This book presents a broad picture of computer and information systems as they relate to distributed computing. The material has been compiled and prepared to be used as a graduate/senior level text for computer and information systems students and as a reference for information systems practitioners and managers. Its scope, precision, and insight are intended to make it a useful text and reference guide. None of the material is intended for use as design requirements for communication products. The material presented represents its status at the time of final preparation. Trends are noted where they are evident.

The views and opinions presented in this book are solely those of the author and do not represent the views of Bellcore, his current employer. No Bellcore material described in this book is intended to be or shall be construed to be an approval, certification, or endorsement of the book or its contents by Bellcore. The book is primarily based on lecture notes and technical reports compiled and prepared by the author before he joined Bellcore.

Contents

List of Acronyms

ACM	Association of Computing Machinery
ACSE	Association Control Service Elements
AI	Artificial Intelligence
AIA	Application Integration Architecture
APPC	Advanced Program to Program Communications
ANSI	American National Standards Institute
BISDN	Broadband Integrated Services Digital Network
BSP	Business System Planning
CAD	Computer Aided Design
CAM	Computer Aided Manufacturing
CBX	Computerized Branch Exchange
CCITT	The International Telegraph and Telephone Consultative Committee
CICS	Customer Information Control System—an IBM mainframe transaction manager
CIM	Computer Integrated Manufacturing
CLNP	Connectionless Mode Network Protocol
CLNS	Connectionless Mode Network Service
CMIP	Common Management Information Protocol
CMIS	Common Management Information Service
CMISE	Common Management Information Service Element
CMOT	Common Management Information Services and Protocol Over TCP/IP
CPU	Central Processing Unit
CSMA/CD	Carrier Sense Multiple Access/Collision Detect
DAF/ODP	Distributed Application Framework/Open Distributed Processing
DAS	Distributed Application System
DBMS	Database Management System
DCP	Distributed Computing Platform
DCRM	Distributed Computing Reference Model
DCS	Distributed Computing System
DDBM	Distributed Database Manager
DDBMS	Distributed Database Management System
DDL	Data Definition Language
DDTMS	Distributed Data and Transaction Management System
DFM	Distributed File Manager
DIS	Draft International Standard
DISOS	Distributed Operating System
DML	Data Manipulation Language
DNA	Digital Network Architecture from DEC
DOD	Department of Defense
DQDB	Distributed Queue Dual Bus
DRDA	Distributed Relational Database Architecture (from IBM)
DS	Directory Services
DTM	Distributed Transaction Manager
DTMS	Distributed Transaction Management System
ES-IS	End System to Intermediate System
FAP	File Allocation Program (Procedure)
FDM	Frequency Division Multiplexing
FDDI	Fiber Distributed Data Interface
FEP	Front End Processor
FMS	Flexible Manufacturing System
FTAM	File Transfer, Access, and Management
FTP	File Transfer Protocol
GUI	Graphical User Interface

IEEE	Institute for Electrical and Electronic Engineers
I/O	Input/Output
IMS	Information Management System—IBM DB/DC system on mainframes
IP	Internet protocol
IPC	Interprocess Communication
ISDN	Integrated Services Digital Network
ISO	International Organization for Standardization
IT	Information Technology
LAN	Local Area Network
LDBMS	Local Database Management System
LLC	Logical Link Control
LU	Logical Unit—an endpoint in the IBM SNA environment
MAN	Metropolitan Area Network
MAC	Medium Access Control
MAP	Manufacturing Automation Protocol
Mbps	Million bits per second
MHS	Message Handling Service
MIPS	Million instructions per second
MMS	Manufacturing Messaging Specification
MVS	Multiple Virtual System—operating system on IBM's mainframes
MUX	Multiplexor
NAS	Network Application Support—DEC's open architecture
NBS	National Bureau of Standards
NCP	Network Control Program—a component of IBM's SNA
NFS	Network File Services—SUN Microsystem's File System for Networks
NIST	National Institute of Standards and Technology
NLM	Network Loadable Module (A Novell Netware feature)
NM	Network Management
NMS	Network Management System
ODIF	Office Document Interchange Format
OODBMS	Object-Oriented Database Management System
OOPL	Object-Oriented Programming Language
OSF	Open Software Foundation
OSF-DCE	OSF Distributed Computing Environment
OSF-DME	OSF Distributed Management Environment
OSI	Open System Interconnection
PBX	Private Branch Exchange
PCM	Pulse Code Modulation
PU	Physical Unit (used in IBM's SNA)
RDA	Remote Database Access
RTS	Reliable Transfer Service
RPC	Remote Procedure Call
SAA	System Application Architecture, IBM's "Open" Environment
SDLC	Synchronous Data Link Control—Layer 2 Protocol in IBM's SNA
SQL	Structured Query Language
SMDS	Switched Multimegabit Data Service
SNA	System Network Architecture—IBM's Network Architecture
SNMP	Simple Network Management Protocol—TCP/IP Network Management Protocol
SONET	Synchronous Optical Network
TCP/IP	Transmission Control Protocol/Internet Protocol
TCP	Transmission Control Protocol
TDM	Time Division Multiplexing
TOP	Technical and Office Protocol
UDP	User Datagram Protocol
VT	Virtual Terminal
VTAM	Virtual Telecommunications Access Method—a component of IBM's SNA
WAN	Wide Area Network

Preface

Book Objectives and Highlights

The objective of this book is to serve as a tutorial on the technical as well as the management aspects of distributed computing. The emphasis is on interrelationships between networks, client-server systems, distributed applications, and open system standards. Unnecessary formulas and formality are actively avoided in order to answer questions such as:

- What exactly is distributed computing, and what are its advantages/disadvantages over the conventional centralized computing environments?
- What are the underlying technologies in distributed computing, and what approaches can be used to develop/acquire, utilize, support, and manage these technologies?
- What is the necessary vocabulary needed to understand distributed computing, and how do the terms and concepts interrelate?
- What are the key issues in network management and distributed application management?
- What is the role of open systems in the current and future technologies?

The reader of this book should be able to plan and architect distributed computing services that combine networks, databases, user interfaces, application systems, and management services to meet the enterprise needs. Particular attention is paid to heterogeneous environments that involve different technologies from different suppliers (e.g., TCP/IP, SNA, LU6.2, MVS, UNIX, X.25, OSI, relational and object-oriented databases). The key features of this book are:

- Synthesis of rapidly advancing fields such as networks, client-server systems, distributed databases, distributed transaction processing, distributed operating systems, distributed applications, and open systems standards.
- State-of-the-art, state-of-the-market and state-of-the-practice discussion for a realistic coverage.
- Self-contained tutorials on the subject matter in each chapter with several references for additional studies.
- Different levels of discussion in each chapter for different audiences (conceptual overviews, management summaries, trends, and technical details).
- A single case study, which is developed throughout the book. Hints and sketchy solutions are suggested for the case study.

Book Organization and Contents

The book is organized into the following four parts:[1]

- Part I defines the basic terms and introduces a framework for distributed computing, which is used throughout the book. This part consists of Chapter 1 (Introduction).
- Part II focuses on networks. This part consists of three chapters. Chapter 2 (Communication Network Technologies) describes LANs, MANs, WANs, and high-speed networks. Chapter 3 (Network Architectures and Network Interconnectivity) introduces the OSI Model, compares network architectures, and describes network interconnectivity devices and open networking. Chapter 4 (Network Management) discusses network management standards and tools such as OSI-CMIP, TCP/IP-SNMP, and IBM-Netview.
- Part III concentrates on the application support services needed in distributed computing. This part also consists of three chapters. Chapter 5 (Client-Server Systems and Application Interconnectivity) gives numerous examples of client-server systems and discusses services such as RPCs, APPC, Sockets, and ROSE. Chapter 6 (Distributed Data and Transaction Management) explains distributed database management, with a discussion of standards such as RDA, OSI TP, and distributed transaction processing. Chapter 7 (Distributed Operating Systems and Distributed Computing Platforms) gives examples of a few evolving systems such as Amoeba and Athena.
- Part IV highlights the architectural and management aspects of distributed applications and distributed computing. The three chapters in this section include:
- Chapter 8 (Distributed Applications and Application Downsizing/Rightsizing) introduces a methodology for developing distributed applications; Chapter 9 (Open Systems) defines open systems and gives examples of emerging standards based environments such as OSI DAF/ODP, OSF-DCE, UI-ATLAS, IBM's SAA, and DEC's NAS; and Chapter 10 (Management and Support Considerations) describes the management issues of planning, staffing, organizing, and monitoring of distributed computing technologies.
- The appendices include five short tutorials on special topics such as communication protocols and the OSI Stack (Appendix A), TCP/IP (Appendix B), SNA and LU6.2 (Appendix C), MAP/TOP (Appendix D), and database technologies and SQL (Appendix E).

Intended Audience and Recommended Usage

The primary audience of this book is the information technology (IT) practitioners/managers and the students in information systems. It can be used in academic courses or in corporate training, or as a self-learning tool and as a reference. Here are some suggestions and examples based on my own experience.

[1] The acronyms used here are explained in the book.

Academic use. Table 1a shows a sample academic course outline that I have used, with slight modifications, more than 10 times at different universities since 1986.[2] The course, intended to go beyond the traditional data communication courses, was initially taught as a special topics course at the University of Michigan (Dearborn), and has since been packaged and taught as industrial seminars in the United States and overseas. The academic course, usually taught to evening graduate students, has been attended by the information system (IS) majors from management, computer science, and industrial engineering departments. Ideally, the students should have a basic understanding of database and data communication technologies. However, many IS majors with no prior training in these fields also have done quite well. (Many IS students at present are exposed to database/data communication concepts in introductory IS courses, and have some hands-on experience in this field.)

The course is roughly organized in three modules, one module per month: networks (Part II of the book), connectivity (Part III of the book), and applications/management (Part IV of the book). I have found that three projects and one examination works well. The projects are flexible, to facilitate students with different backgrounds. Here is an example. The first project involves networks (case study problems at the end of Chapters 2 and 3). The second concentrates on application interconnectivity (case study problems at the end of Chapters 5 and 6), and the third is a "free for all" (students choose a topic of their interest from Chapters 7 to 10 and the appendices). I have been very pleasantly surprised by the reception of this course as evidenced by student enrollments, course evaluations, and requests to repeat this course in different universities and the industry (in many cases, to my own surprise, there was a waiting list). The feedback has repeatedly indicated that combining networks, databases, and applications is the main strength of the course.

The preceding suggested outline can be customized for different audiences. Consider, for example, a technical audience with good preparation in networks and data communications (perhaps they have taken a university course in data communications). On three different occasions when I taught such a course, I spent the first month to refresh, illustrate, and expand network concepts. For example, I used this time to discuss emerging high-speed networks (Section 2.7, Chapter 2), network interconnectivity (Section 3.5, Chapter 3), network management (Chapter 4), and network architecture examples such as OSI, TCP/IP, SNA and MAP (Appendices A to D). This allowed us to tie loose ends in networking. Chapter 5 through 10 were covered in detail in the next two months. The project assignments were also modified to include a LAN set-up and implementation of a client-server application on a LAN.

There is enough material in this book to satisfy different academic needs in this interesting and rapidly advancing field. As discussed before, the book material has been used as an introductory course (which may or may not be followed by in-depth courses in different topics) or as a "capstone" course. The case study described in this book, with hints included to enhance learning, has served effectively for classroom

[2] Details of the early course offerings can be found in A. Umar, "Balancing Practice and Theory in an Interdisciplinary Course in Networks and Distributed Computers," Proceedings of the Information Systems Education Conference, Atlanta, October 1987.

TABLE 1 Sample Course Outlines

a. **University Course**: Introduction to Distributed Computing
Audience: Information systems majors in management, computer science and industrial engineering
Prerequisite: Database and data communications concepts

Week	*Course Topic*	*Reading*
1	Introduction	Ch. 1 (Sections 1.1-1.9)
2	Network technologies, WANs	Ch. 2 (Sections 2.1-2.3)
3	LANs, MANs, network trends	Ch. 2 (Sections 2.4-2.7)
4	Network architectures & OSI	Ch. 3 (Sections 3.1-3.3)
5	Network interconnectivity	Ch. 3 (Sections 3.4-3.5)
6	Application connectivity	Ch. 5 (Sections 5.1-5.2)
7	Client-server systems	Ch. 5 (Sections 5.3-5.5)
8	Database review and distributed databases	Appendix E, Ch. 6 (Sections 6.1-6.3)
9	Distributed transaction Mgmt	Ch. 6 (Sections 6.4-6.9)
10	Examination	
11	Distributed operating systems	Ch. 7 (Sections 7.1-7.4)
12	Distributed applications	Ch. 8 (Sections 8.1-8.5)
13	Open systems	Ch. 9 (Sections 9.1-9.6)
14	Management of networks	Ch. 4 (Sections 4.1-4.2, 4.7)
	Organizational issues	Ch. 10 (Sections 10.1-10.5)
15	Wrap-ups, special topics	Appendix Tutorials

Sample Projects:
Project 1: Networks technologies and architectures (Chs. 2, 3)
Project 2: Client-server and distributed management (Chs. 5, 6)
Project 3: "Free for all" (a topic from Chs. 7 to 10 and appendices)

b. **Industrial Training Seminar**: Distributed Computing: Networks, Databases and Applications

Day	*Hours*	*Topic*	
1	1	Introduction	Ch. 1 (Sections 1.1-1.2, 1.8)
	2	Network technologies, WANs	Ch. 2 (Sections 2.1-2.3)
	3	LANs, MANs, ISDN, B-ISDN	Ch. 2 (Sections 2.4-2.7)
2	2	Network architectures & OSI	Ch. 3 (Sections 3.1-3.3)
	2	Network interconnectivity	Ch. 3 (Sections 3.4-3.5)
	2	TCP/IP	Appendix B
3	2	SNA & LU6.2	Appendix C
	2	MAP/TOP & more on OSI	Appendix D and A
	2	Management of networks	Ch. 4 (Sections 4.1-4.5)
4	2.5	Client-server systems	Ch. 5 (Sections 5.1-5.4)
	2.5	Distributed databases	Ch. 6 (Sections 6.1-6.6)
	1	Distributed operating system	Ch. 7 (Sections 7.1-7.4, 7.7)
5	2	Distributed applications	Ch. 8 (Sections 8.1-8.3)
	2	Open systems	Ch. 9 (Sections 9.1-9.4)
	2	Organizational issues	Ch. 10 (Sections 10.1-10.5)

projects. This case study can be modified, or case studies of other companies can be used instead for future courses. (It is recommended to develop network and application connectivity for another company in the first two projects and then merge the new company with XYZCORP in Project 3 to illustrate integration across enterprises.) It depends on the interest and imagination of the instructors to properly position a course. At present, many universities do not offer a course in distributed systems despite pressing industrial need. We hope that this will change with time.

Industrial training and self-study. Table 1b shows a sample five-day industrial seminar outline I have used several times for the Society of Manufacturing Engineers (SME) and Frost & Sullivan (England). These seminars were attended by manufacturing engineers, network planners, systems analysts, application developers, CIM (computer integrated manufacturing) managers, CIM planners, process engineers, and information technology managers. These seminars were usually offered as two modules: three days on networks and two days on higher-level issues (distributed databases, client-server computing, and distributed applications). This allowed people to choose one or both modules (the higher-level seminars usually drew more attendees). I used the case study described in this book for group projects.

In addition to the university courses and industrial seminars, this book can also be used for self-study by information technology (IT) practitioners and managers. Here are some suggestions.

IT managers should read Chapter 1 for an overview of the subject matter and then read the overviews and management summaries/trends in each chapter for an overall understanding of the subject matter. The chapters on open systems, network management, and management/support issues should be of particular interest to most IT managers. Technical discussion of some topics may be of interest to managers in some areas. For example, database administrators should review the chapter on data and transaction management, managers of application development should read the chapter on distributed applications, and managers of technical support should read the three chapters in Part III.

Network professionals may skip Part II (they should know this material anyway) and may concentrate on Parts III and IV to understand how networks relate to distributed databases, client/server systems, distributed applications, and open systems.

Application designers who have to develop applications in distributed environments should find the chapters on client-server, distributed data and transaction management, and distributed applications of particular interest. The overview of networks will help them in developing some background on the delivery mechanisms on which the distributed applications run. The new employees (fresh university graduates) may find this coverage a good training tool in understanding how the distributed databases, distributed applications, and management roles interplay in organizations.

Due to the heavy leaning towards practical corporate aspects, some computer scientists (especially those who love algorithms) probably will not find this book very useful. In addition, managers not directly involved in IT may find this material to be too technical and dense.

Acknowledgments

Many colleagues and friends have helped in the preparation of this book. Many of my university colleagues read early drafts and made numerous suggestions. Professors Vic

Streeter and Daniel Teichroew of the University of Michigan, Professor Lynda Joe Callaway of Fordham Graduate School of Business and Professor Peter Jurkat of the Stevens Institute of Technology gave valuable suggestions about different topics. My longtime friends and colleagues from my early days in the industry, Warner Mach and John Gruber, were "surprisingly insightful" (they really know what I know). I should not forget the contribution of many students at the University of Michigan (Dearborn), University of Michigan (Ann Arbor), Stevens Institute of Technology, and Fordham who "suffered" through very rough drafts of many chapters. The list of topics included in this book is based on extensive discussions with the attendees of my seminars on networks and distributed databases in the United States, England, and Singapore.

I have greatly benefitted from the Bellcore peer review process. I asked many of my colleagues to review specific chapters for content and/or style. Here is an alphabetical list of the reviewers who commented on at least one chapter (some reviewed four to five): Lawrence Chin, Balakrishnan Dasarathy, Judith DeVries, Al Dickman, Cedric Druce, Frank Farbanec, Gene Geer, Frank Gratzer, Jim Hand, Khalid Khalil, Al Lang, Reva Leung, Al Lucas, Don Mahler, Frank Marchese, Malesh Mariswamy, John Mills, Kathy McEnerney, Henry Nghiem, Terry Peaks, Marc Pucci, Cho-Wei Sit, Suresh Subramaniam, Leon Theisen, Gomer Thomas, and Mike Tyrrell. I really feel fortunate to have access to so many experts for sanity checking (some of them did say that I was insane). The review process resulted in many interesting debates, some of which I lost. I have made many friends in this process and have gained valuable insights.

I want to express my gratitude towards my management at Bellcore (Pete Georges, Bill Lundy, and John Witsken) for their support and understanding.

Personal Comments

In the Winter of 1989, while I was on the faculty at the University of Michigan, a "friend" suggested that I should develop my course packs, transparencies, and technical reports into a book. His argument: Many books cover network technologies but no book ties networks to higher-level issues of databases and applications (I had realized this myself when I was preparing course material). I looked at my material and thought, "Why not? It should not take more than a year." So here I am, years later, completely exhausted and wondering why I ever undertook this project. (This tells you how good I am at predictions.) Anyway, most of this material has been written deep into nights and weekends while I have been working fulltime at Bellcore. The writing process has been interrupted many times due to work assignments and life in general.

I have done my best to emphasize the real problems of development, deployment and management of distributed computing. The practical flavor reflects my many years of hands-on experience in this field (my friends in academia contend that I have been irreversibly contaminated by reality). Undoubtedly, I have missed a few topics and have not covered several topics in sufficient detail. Why? Three reasons: lack of time, lack of space (book size), and lack of energy. My extremely patient wife, Dolorese, knows this better than anyone else.

Amjad Umar
Piscataway, New Jersey

PART ONE

Overview

Chapter 1

Introduction and Overview of Distributed Computing

1.1 Introduction

1.1.1 What Is Distributed Computing?

A distributed computing system (DCS) interconnects many autonomous computers to satisfy the information processing needs of modern enterprises. Basically, distributed computing refers to the services provided by a distributed computing system. Advances in computer and communication technologies have made possible DCSs of different sizes, shapes and forms. Numerous DCSs are currently being used in the banking, government, education, manufacturing, engineering, and medical industries. Here are some examples:

- Banking systems in which each branch office of a bank has a computer for branch office systems. The branch office computers are connected to the head office computer for the interbranch and corporate work.
- University computing systems, where each campus, or department, has its own computer. These computers may be interconnected so that the files and special facilities of some computers can be shared. For example, the statistics department may house an extensive array of statistical packages, which may be used by other departments on an as-needed basis.
- Inventory systems where each plant has its own computer to keep inventory of the local products, with possible access to other plant computers for the products which are not available at the local plant. In some cases, the inventory systems are tied across manufacturers, suppliers and customers for electronic purchase orders, accounts receivable, accounts payable and inventory control. Many of these systems use a standard (called Electronic Data Interchange) for message exchange.
- Financial service systems which enable customers to withdraw cash from computing systems located at different geographical sites.
- Automated tax preparation systems which allow accounting firms and/or individuals to prepare the tax returns in branch offices with a centralized quality assurance check.
- Factory systems where different manufacturing devices such as robots, numerical controllers, and fabrication and assembly systems are interconnected for factory automation. In most cases, the manufacturing activities are grouped into cells where each cell performs one unique operation (e.g., painting). The cells are interconnected into areas, floors, and plants. Such systems are referred to as cellular manufacturing systems.
- Office automation systems which allow users to prepare documents, exchange files and use electronic mail. More recent systems use multimedia systems which allow exchange of voice, data and video for numerous office applications. For example, new teleconferencing systems display text, pictures, and video/voice on different windows of a workstation.
- Cooperative systems formed between different organizations to share information and computing resources. Perhaps the best known cooperative system is the

INTERNET, an outgrowth of the ARPANET (Advanced Research Project Agency Network), which at present connects more than 60,000 computers located at different academic and research centers. Other examples of such systems are Edunet and Tymnet.

- Computer integrated environments which interconnect all enterprise computers to integrate operations at different levels of the enterprise. Examples are the computer integrated manufacturing (CIM) systems, which interconnect the manufacturing, engineering, and administrative computing facilities to support coordination of all activities in manufacturing enterprises.
- Consolidated systems formed due to the business mergers/acquisitions. An example is the EDSNET, which serves all EDS and GM customers. EDSNET is one of the world's largest private network—it took 2000 staff members, over a billion dollars and three years to develop. Another example is the United States Navy's Stock Point Logistics Integrated Environment (SPLICE), which is expected to interconnect more than 60 U.S. Navy and Marine Corps supply bases worldwide.

Due to the relative newness of this field, there are no generally agreed-on definitions as evidenced by the numerous definitions attempted in the last two decades (Bagley gave 50 definitions of distributed processing in 1979 <Bagley 1979>). Our approach is first to present broad definitions of centralization/distribution and DCS, which are refined later.

Simply stated, a system is *centralized* if its components are restricted to one site, *decentralized* if its components are at different sites with no or limited coordination, and *distributed* if its components are autonomous mechanisms which also coordinate their operations through a global mechanism. The notions of autonomous components and coordination are accepted as the basic ingredients of any distributed system <Kleinrock 1985, Enslow 1978>.[1] Examples of distributed systems are human organisms with local muscle movement which are coordinated through the global control of brain signals, and organizations such as the post office and telephone companies with many coordinated local offices. All distributed systems have local as well as global processing capabilities and knowledge.

We will use the following basic definition throughout this book:

A Distributed Computing System (DCS) is a collection of autonomous computers interconnected through a communication network to achieve business functions. Technically, the computers do not share main memory so that the information cannot be transferred through global variables. The information (knowledge) between the computers is exchanged only through messages over a network.

The restriction of no shared memory and information exchange through messages is of key importance because it distinguishes between DCS and shared memory multiprocessor computing systems (see Fig. 1.1). This definition requires that the DCS computers are connected through a network which is responsible for the information exchange between computers. The definition also requires that the computers have to work together and cooperate with each other to satisfy enterprise needs. This

[1]The references cited are not necessarily in alphabetical order.

a. A Shared Memory Multiprocessor Computer (Tightly Coupled)

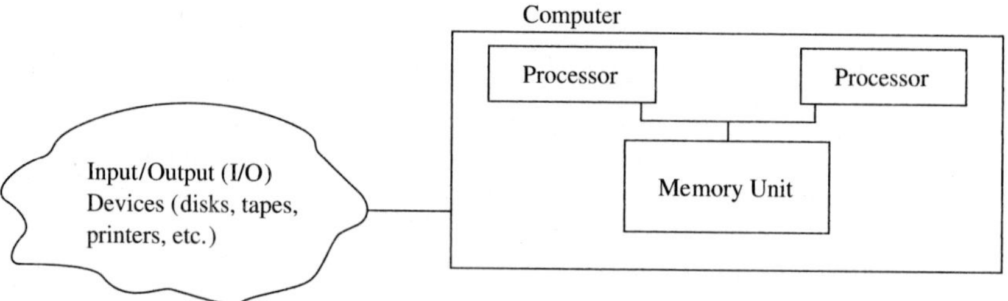

Notes: Shared memory multiprocessor systems consist of many processors which share the same main memory. The memory is accessed through a common bus. The programs in the processors can use the memory to exchange information through global variables. A uniprocessor consists of one processor with one memory unit.

b. Distributed Computing System

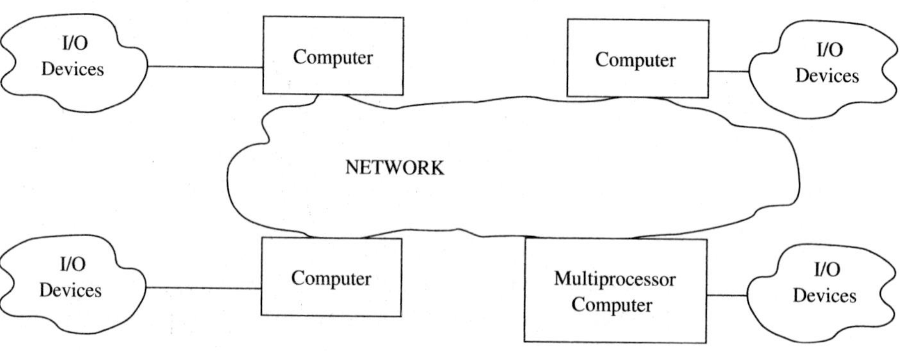

Notes: Many computers, including multiprocessors, are connected through a network. The information exchange between programs at different computers is achieved through messages over the network.

FIGURE 1.1 Distributed Computing versus Multiprocessor Systems

definition conforms to many contemporary definitions <Andrews 1991, Bal 1989, Sloman 1987>.

Most of the computer and information systems literature uses the term *distributed system* instead of distributed computer systems (see for example, the IEEE Transactions of Software Engineering special issue on distributed systems, January, 1987, and the book on distributed systems by Coulouris and Dollimore <Coulouris

1988>). Due to the popularity of this term, we will treat distributed systems and distributed computer systems (DCS) as synonyms in this book.

1.1.2 Why Distributed Computing?

The dramatic growth of DCS is primarily attributed to the availability of very powerful desktop computers which can be interconnected through very fast networks. The desktop computers provide attractive presentation capabilities of graphics, moving videos and sound. The main appeal of DCS is that a user can perform some functions on a local desktop computer, by using suitable presentation tools, while still accessing remotely located databases and computers. Visionary managers have and will exploit these technologies to shape the future of their companies <Keen 1991>. DCS are expected to be one of the best ways to fully utilize the growing processing power of desktop computers—between 40 to 100 million desktop computers are expected to exist in the United States in 1995, with total processor power to exceed 400 million MIPS (million instructions per second) <Gantz 1991>. Many predictions are being made about the expected growth of distributed computing. The following statement by John Donovan <Donovan 1988> typifies the predictions:

> "Decentralized Computing is sweeping business like a wave rolling onto a beach. Its advance is unstoppable — and for some powerful reasons."

The "powerful" reasons presented by Donovan, and others, are as follows:

- *Strategic factors*. Customers, suppliers, and companies are rarely, if ever, at one site. Since most customers, suppliers and companies use computers, the information networks which tie these entities together for interactive processing can give the companies competitive edge.
- *Equipment costs*. The average cost per MIP (million instructions per second), a measure of hardware performance, on a mainframe is almost 100 times more than on a workstation. For example, a 20 MIP mainframe costs about $4 million while a 20 MIP workstation costs less than $10,000. However, it should be noted that mainframes support hundreds of devices and allow thousands of users to share computing resources. The difference in costs is still astounding.
- *User know-how and control*. The users of computing services are becoming increasingly computer literate and competent. These users want to operate their own systems, their own way. They are not content with the control of central sites on what systems are developed and operated when, how and by whom. Distributed/decentralized computing puts data and processing close to the user.
- *Development costs*. Knowledgeable users can practice "end user computing" to build their own systems on their own machines and thus reduce the cost and time to develop software.
- *User interfaces*. The workstations are especially suitable for sophisticated graphical user interfaces (GUI) with pointing devices (mouse) and speech/video systems. This

technology appeals to the users with different cognitive and learning styles who have been generally turned off by the traditional data processing reports.

- *Flexibility and configurability*. Decentralized computing gives many options for improved performance and reliability through redundant data and processing.
- *Exploitation of special hardware*. Workstations and personal computers allow development of specialized software which uses the hardware features of the workstation. For example, specialized graphic devices can be used for computer aided design applications. In addition, each computer can be used as a "server" that satisfies a request from a client. This configuration, commonly known as client-server distributed computing, allows a client (say, a workstation) to request services from print servers, file servers, database servers, directory servers, etc. that are spread across a network.
- *New applications*. Many new realtime applications require processing and data at the point where the requests are generated. For example, it is not possible to run a flexible manufacturing system from a single mainframe.

On the other hand, distributed computing raises several technical and management issues, such as the following:

- *Information islands and lack of standards*. Many incompatible copies of the same application may be created. Development and enforcement of standards for applications, computers and networks developed at different sites by different people at different times is not easy. Lack of standards and tools creates serious compatibility, portability and interconnectivity problems in distributed computing. For example, in the mid 1980s, only 15 percent of the General Motors' shop floor devices communicated with each other <Kaminski 1987>.
- *Difficulties in large application design*. Large application systems may be distributed across many computers. Breaking applications into pieces where each piece can reside on a separate computer is non-trivial. The tradeoffs and the implications of these decisions need careful analysis.
- *Lack of support and management infrastructure*. At present, many of the management and support issues have not been addressed. Examples of the problems are backup/recovery, information system planning in rapidly changing technologies, management of distributed resources and organizational structure design for distributed computing.
- *Concerns for security and integrity control*. Distribution of data and programs to multiple sites opens security and integrity control issues which are not easy to address.
- *Too many options and decisions*. The availability of large number of choices and decisions is both a blessing and a curse. It may take a long time for the developers to wade through the options, understand them and make the best decisions. In addition, the impact of a bad decision at one site may bring misery upon the innocent "neighbors."

1.1.3 Why This Book?

Distributed computing technologies (networks, computers, databases) provide many new opportunities for enterprises. That is the good news. The bad news is that, as noted in the preceding discussion, many of the issues and tradeoffs are not well understood, thus increasing the risk of failures. A particular problem is that a plethora of jargon, interrelationships, models, frameworks, products, and techniques have been introduced (see Fig. 1.2). Information technology practitioners and managers are facing questions such as

- What are all these terms?
- What do they mean?
- How do they interrelate with each other?
- What are the issues and tradeoffs associated with these things?
- Where can I find more information?

The primary objective of this book is to answer these questions and to serve as a tutorial on technical as well as management aspects of distributed computing. Due to the widespread industrial applications and continuing research efforts in this area, our discussion will include

- *State of the Art* approaches, which are prototypes and/or research and development reports and papers
- *State of the Market* information to show commercial availability of the approaches as products
- *State of the Practice* information to show that the approaches/products are being actually used by organizations.

A coverage of all three aspects will give the reader a more realistic view of the subject matter. This is especially important because, due to the delays and filters built in the industry, only a few of the state of the art ideas become state of the market and even fewer become state of the practice. Focus on one area only (e.g., state of the art) may give the reader the wrong impression about the potential impact of the topics discussed. In addition, it is not possible to develop transition strategies from the current to the future environments without an understanding of the current environments ("How can you get there from here if you do not know where you are?").

As stated in the preface, the emphasis is on synthesis and interrelationships and not on detailed technical coverage of one topic. The reader of this book should be able to solve the distributed computing architecture problem shown in Fig. 1.3 (many of the terms used in this figure will be explained later). The book will intentionally cover a great deal of ground so that different views, perspectives and interrelationships of the inputs and outputs shown in Fig. 1.3 can be understood.

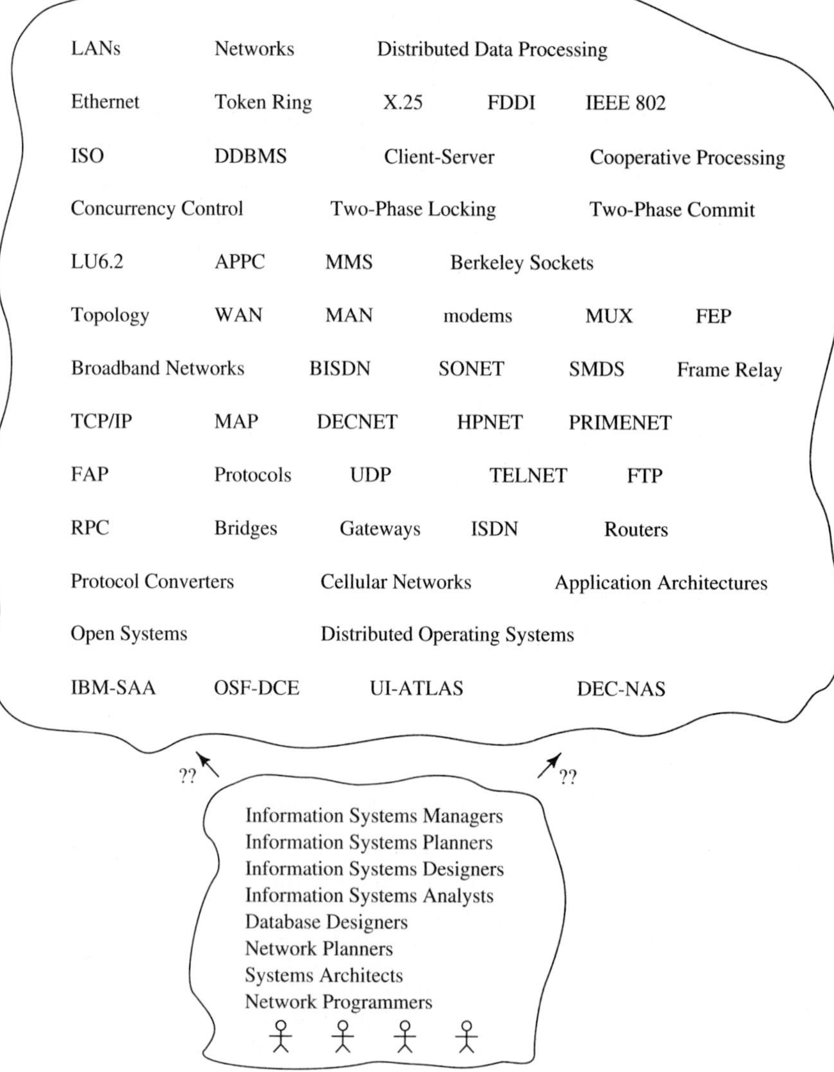

FIGURE 1.2 Jargon/Terms Associated with Distributed Computing

There are usually three different ways of covering a broad subject area like this (see Fig. 1.4):

- A coverage of the terms and concepts only with no detailed discussion. This option is depicted in Fig. 1.4a where the X axis shows the breadth and the Y axis shows the depth of the coverage.
- A very detailed discussion of one topic such as networks with little or no reference to related areas (see Fig. 1.4b)

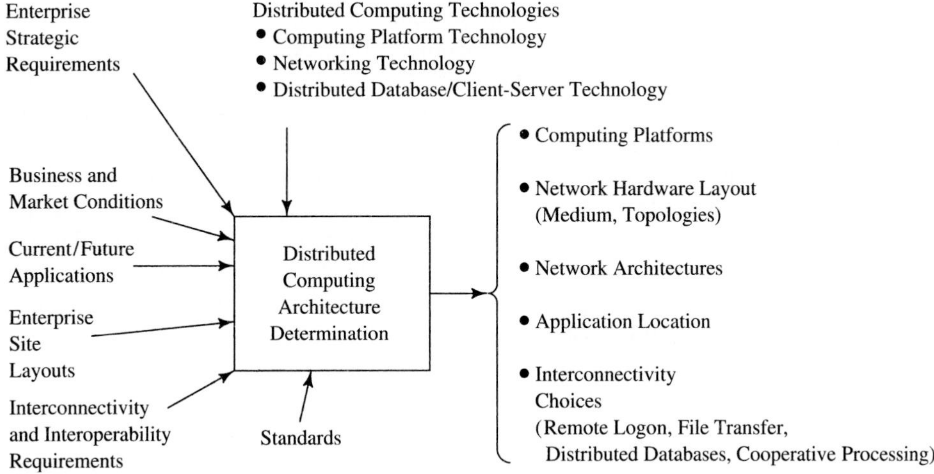

Note: Most of the terms used in this diagram are defined later in this chapter.

FIGURE 1.3 Distributed Computing Architecture Problem

- A coverage of the terms, concepts, building blocks and interrelationships of several related areas (see Fig. 1.4c). This is the approach used in this book.

Each chapter is written as a self contained tutorial on the subject matter. Different levels of discussion are included in each chapter (conceptual overviews, management summaries, trends and technical details) to support different audiences. Numerous references for additional study are provided. To illustrate the key points,

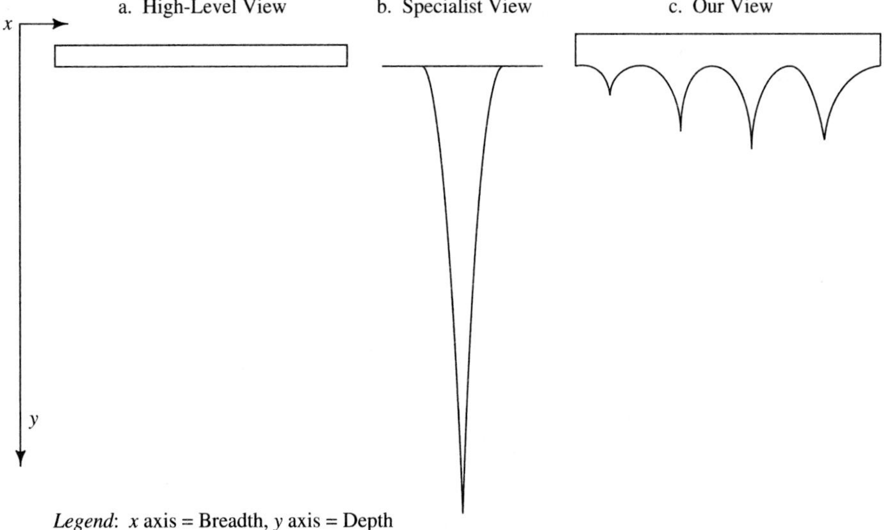

FIGURE 1.4 Coverage of Topics

a single case study about a company that is moving from a centralized to distributed computing environment is used throughout the book.

This chapter is a sneak preview of the coming attractions in this book. We first introduce a framework to establish the interrelationships between distributed computing components such as communication networks, distributed databases, client-server computing, distributed operating systems, and distributed application systems. The framework also includes open systems standards and management/support issues. This framework, introduced in Section 1.2 and reviewed in Sections 1.3 to 1.7, is at the foundation of this book. The desirable goals of distributed computing are reviewed in Section 1.9. The chapter concludes with an outline of a case study which will be used throughout this book to expose the reader to the complex decisions of distributed computing.

1.2 A Distributed Computing Reference Model

1.2.1 Overview of the Reference Model

A reference model is a vision which defines the scope, the structure and the mechanisms of a system. Figure 1.5 shows a Distributed Computing Reference Model which views distributed computing as functional layers of enterprise systems, application systems, and platforms. In addition, management, support, interoperability, portability, and integration issues are introduced at all layers.

At the highest level are the *enterprise systems*, which represent the day-to-day business processes and activities of an enterprise (e.g., car manufacturing, operating an airline, providing mail delivery, teaching students, running a bank, etc.). For example, if you want to open a restaurant, then an enterprise system needs to be established for bringing in the food, storing it, cooking it, etc. These systems establish

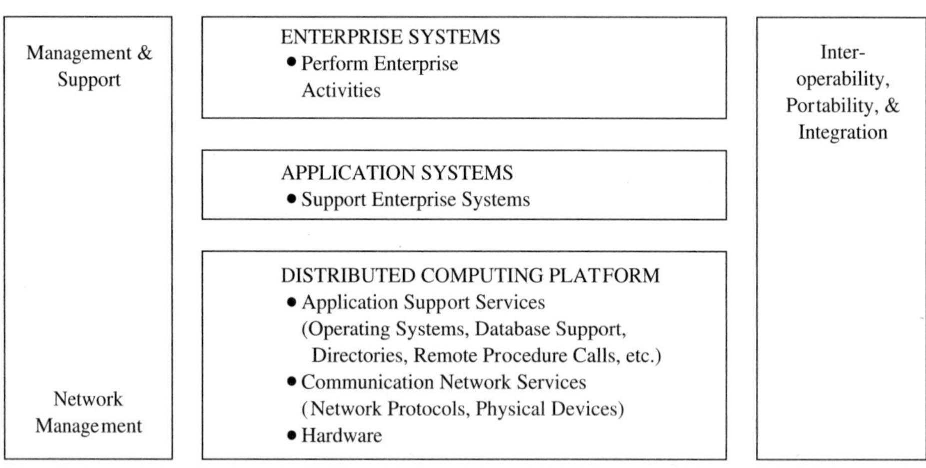

FIGURE 1.5 A Distributed Computing Reference Model

the requirements and the driving forces behind technology utilization because survival of any enterprise depends on the success or failure of enterprise systems. An enterprise system may be centralized or distributed. A *distributed enterprise system (DES)* describes the enterprise activities that are performed at different sites of an organization. Most large organizations are and have been conducting enterprise activities at multiple sites (e.g., cars are designed in one place, assembled in many places, and shipped to dealers at several places).

Application systems provide automated support and facilitate the enterprise systems. These systems use the information technologies to support the enterprise. Examples of application systems are computerized order processing systems, payroll, inventory control, and airline reservation systems. Application systems consist of a user database (a pool of data), a set of programs to access and manipulate the database, and user interfaces to execute the programs. An application system may also be centralized or distributed. A *distributed application system (DAS)* consists of user interface, user data, and programs residing at different computers of the network (see Section 1.5).

Distributed applications rely on several technologies such as computers, networks, distributed databases, and directory services. We will bundle these technologies under the heading of *distributed computing platform (DCP)* (Fig. 1.5). A DCP provides two types of services:

- *Network services* are responsible for the transfer of information between computer systems and applications within the computers. Within the context of distributed computing, networks are primarily delivery vehicles which are used by the applications to deliver messages and responses. In DCS, networks may be small or very large and complex systems. See Section 1.3 for an overview of networks and network services.
- *Application support services* are needed to interconnect and support applications across a network. The services may include directories, facilities to call remotely located procedures, and software to access and manipulate remotely located databases. These services can be provided by a combination of computer operating systems, system software, and computing hardware (see Section 1.4).

Interoperability, portability and integration are concerned with developing the strategies and standards to simplify ("open") the tasks of developing, operating, and accessing the systems. Interoperability means that two systems can work with each other through well-defined interfaces, portability is concerned with moving a system from one environment to another, and integration is concerned with providing a uniform access to the end users. These three issues occur at all levels of the Distributed Computing Reference Model and are laying the foundation of standards for "open systems" (see Section 1.6).

Management and support are concerned with the organizational as well as the technical tools and techniques needed to administer DCS. These services are needed at all layers—the networks need to be managed and supported and so do the application and enterprise systems (see Section 1.7).

1.2.2 Reference Model as a Study Roadmap

Figure 1.6 gives a more detailed view of the Distributed Computing Reference Model (DCRM) and shows how this Model will be used in this book. Basically the book progresses from lower-level issues to higher-level issues of the DCRM.

Part II of this book treats the communication network services. The chapters in this part of the book cover communication networks, network architectures, network interconnectivity and network management. Examples of existing network architectures are included in appendixes to support the discussion in these chapters. Part III concentrates on the application support services needed in distributed computing. The chapters in this part describe the application interconnectivity issues and discuss distributed database managers, client-server support and distributed operating systems. The distributed application architectural and management issues are the focus of Part IV. The chapters in this part include discussion of distributed applications and downsizing, open systems standards for interoperability, portability and integration, and management and support issues.

The layered DCRM view highlights the importance of enterprise systems in relation to the communication network technologies (requirements flow down from

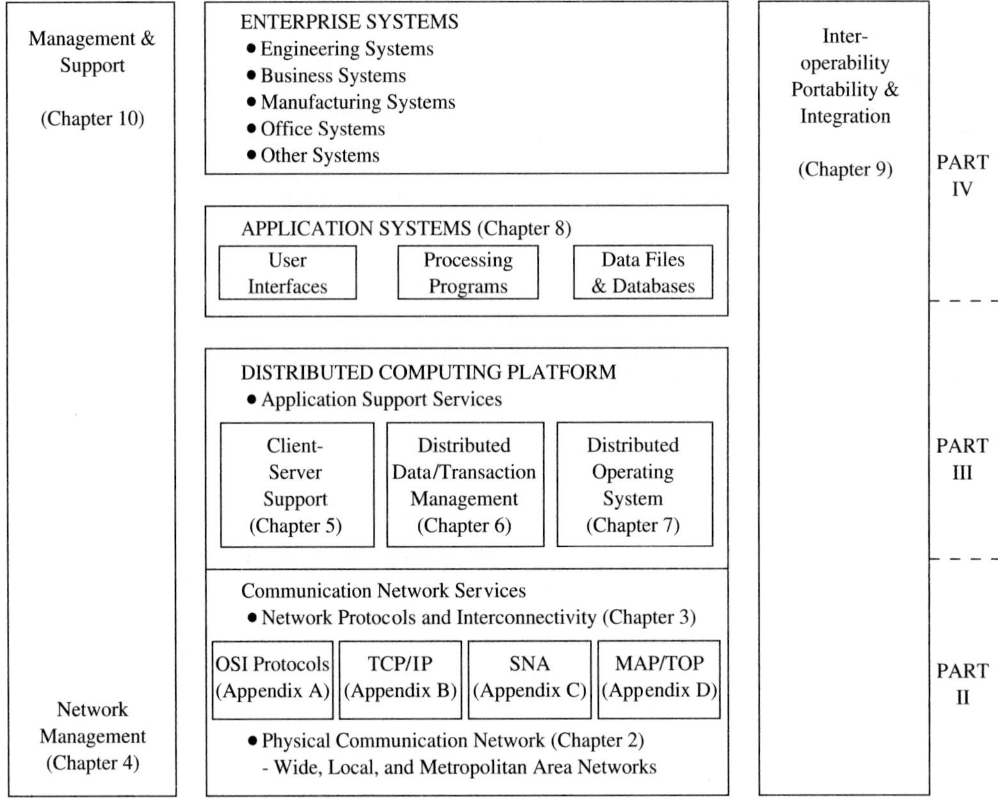

FIGURE 1.6 Distributed Computing Reference Model as a Roadmap

high levels to low levels). Consider, for example, a distributed enterprise system such as a car manufacturing system in which the various enterprise activities (material acquisition, component design, fabrication, molding, assembly, painting, process engineering, etc.) occur at different physical sites. The application system for manufacturing, an automated factory, is a distributed application where the application processes and data exist at various devices that are, one hopes, somehow interconnected. A vision of a completely automated factory imposes certain requirements on the application support and network support services. As more and more sophisticated networks and application support services become commercially available, it is becoming easier to automate several distributed enterprise activities. In essence, higher levels of the DCRM are closer to the business and lower levels are closer to the technology needed to serve the business.

1.3 Overview of Communication Network Services

Communication networks, or just networks, provide the lowest level of service (i.e., information exchange) in distributed computing. In this context, a communication network is a collection of equipment and physical media, viewed as one autonomous whole, that interconnects two or more computers. Figure 1.7 shows some sample network configurations. A wide variety of network configurations are in use; and for one application there may be several viable configurations. For example, a network may consist of three word processors connected through a cable, or it may serve an international airlines reservation system which employs global communication satellites, large processors, and thousands of terminals and workstations. In many organizations, networks are a critical resource (for example, $400 billion a day is moved through the Citicorp networks).

A network can be configured as a wide area network (WAN), which utilizes common carrier facilities for communications; a local area network (LAN), which utilizes vendor supplied cables for connecting computers within a building; a metropolitan area network (MAN) within a region, which may use the communication facilities of cable TV, or a combination of LANs, MANs, and WANs. In addition, the communication between computing devices on a network can use analog or digital data transmission facilities over copper, wireless or fiber optic communication media. The state-of-the-art advancement in network transmission technologies is the development of high-speed local and wide area transmissions, typically in the range of 100 million bits per second (Mbps) or higher. Another area of advancement is the integration of voice, data, and video images for multimedia applications such as teleconferencing and group problem solving, among others. We will discuss the network technologies and configurations in Chapter 2.

A *network architecture* describes the physical components, the functions performed by the components and the interfaces between the components of a network. Network architecture standards are needed to interconnect different networks from different vendors with different capabilities. For example, a Chicago bank which uses a DEC network needs to communicate with a New York bank which uses an IBM network. An Open System Interconnection (OSI) Reference Model has been devel-

a. A Local Area Network (LAN)

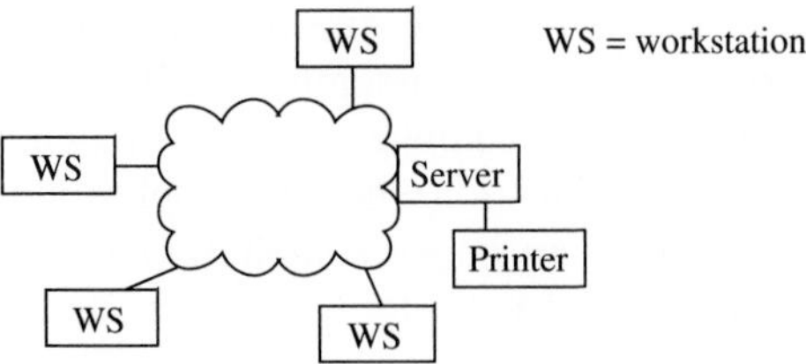

b. A Wide Area Network (Traditional View)

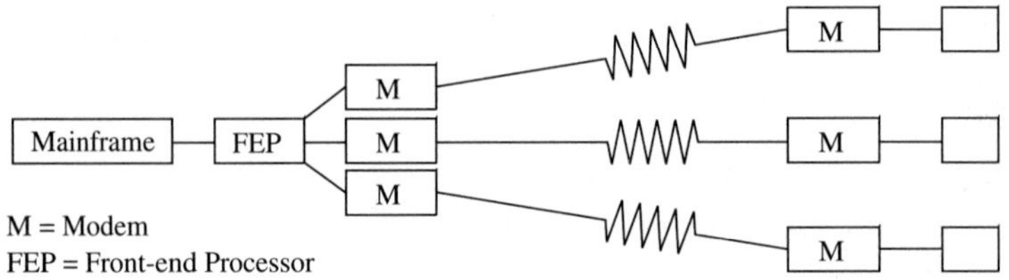

c. A Typical Enterprise Network (LAN + WAN)

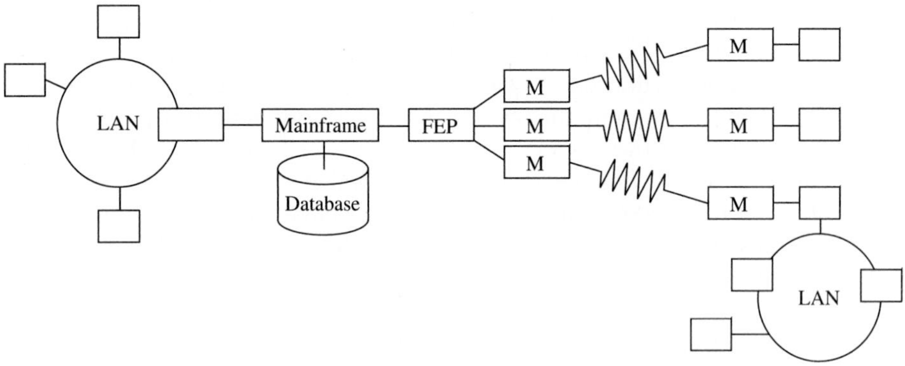

d. A "Supernetwork" (Internet)

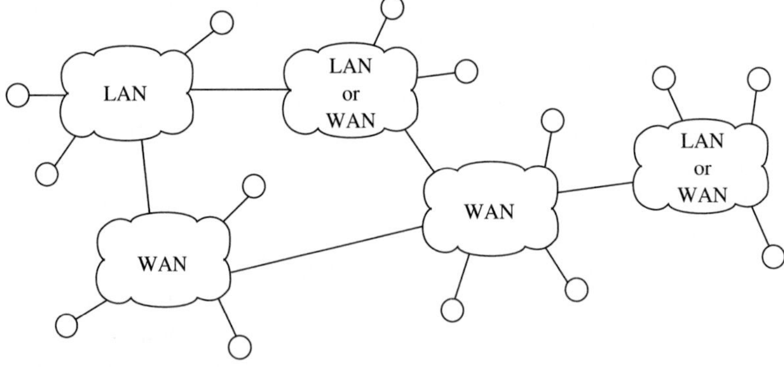

FIGURE 1.7 Examples of Computer Network Configurations

oped to provide standards for networks from different vendors to exchange information freely. The OSI Model casts the functions needed to exchange information between interconnected computers in terms of seven layers (Fig. 1.8). Chapter 3 introduces the OSI Model and shows how it can be used to discuss network interconnectivity. Technical details about this model are given in Appendix A.

Many network architectures have evolved in the last 20 years. Examples of the state-of-the-market/practice network architectures are Department of Defense (DOD) Protocol Suite (called TCP/IP), IBM's System Network Architecture (SNA), DEC's Digital Network Architecture (DNA), and GM's Manufacturing Automation Protocol (MAP). These architectures can be discussed in terms of the seven-layer OSI Model. The tutorials in Appendixes B through D review these network architectures as examples of existing networks which need to be interconnected in organizations.

Due to a growth in the size, complexity, diversity, and organizational reliance on networks, the issue of network management has become an area of strategic importance to many enterprises. *Network management* is concerned with the policies, procedures, and tools needed to manage the performance, faults, security, accounting and configuration of enterprise-wide networks. At present, many state-of-the-market products are available with many state-of-the-practice examples. Increased attention is being paid to managing heterogeneous networks (networks formed by combining networks of different vendors). The network management standards based on the OSI Model have been adopted as the long range network management solutions for large heterogeneous networks. This state-of-the-art as well as state of the market/practice area is discussed in Chapter 4.

1.4 Overview of Application Support Services in Distributed Computing

The application support services are responsible for the higher level issue of application interconnectivity in DCS. For example, after a bank computer in Chicago is connected (network interconnectivity) to a bank computer in New York, how can the money be transferred between two accounts in Chicago and New York? Application support services provide

- Message exchange services between remotely located programs (the program which will debit one account in Chicago to the program which will credit the other account in New York)
- Remote data access and manipulation services (programs in Chicago directly accessing the New York account)
- Naming, security, and administrative services to help locate the resources from authorized users (make sure no one else starts transferring funds to Switzerland).

These services can be accomplished through:

- Terminal emulators and file transfer packages
- Client-server systems

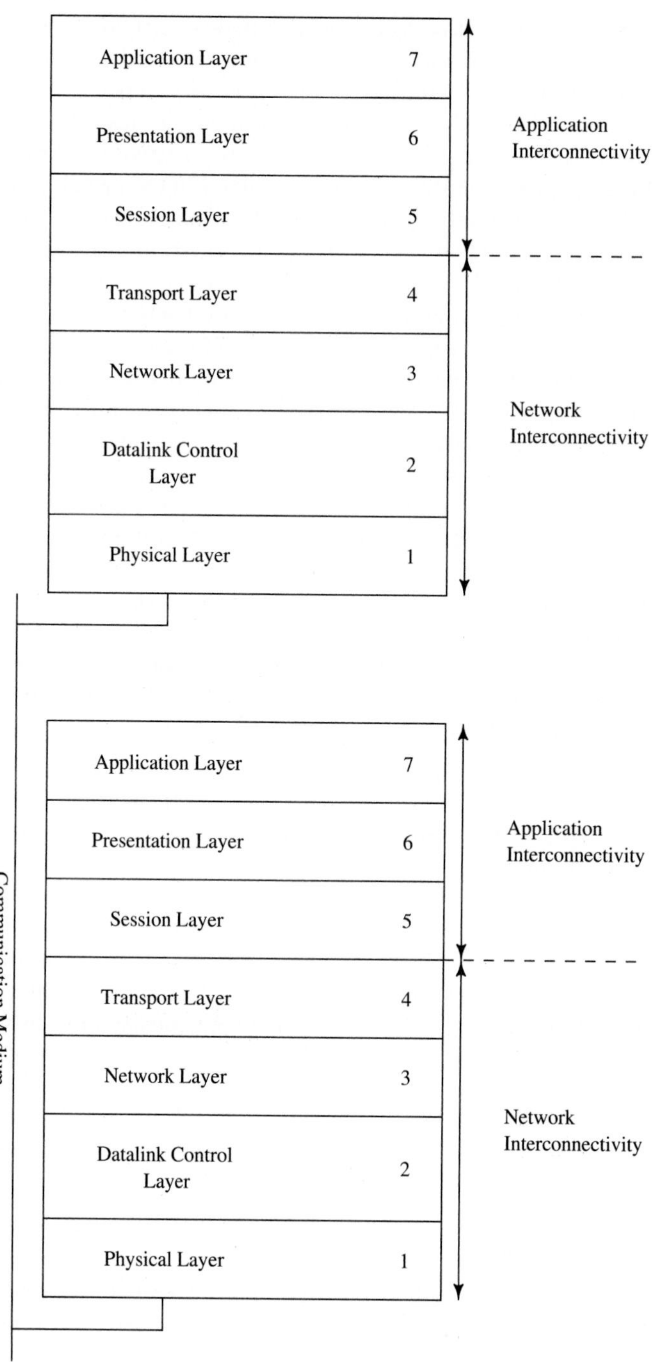

FIGURE 1.8 A Layered View of Networks

- Distributed data and transaction management systems
- Distributed operating systems.

A *terminal emulator* makes a computer look like a terminal which is connected to another computer. Through terminal emulation, a user sitting in Chicago can logon to the New York computer and access the account information. Terminal emulators have been state of the market and state of the practice for almost 20 years, with many products which operate on multiple computer systems (e.g., Kermit, Telnet). A *file transfer package* allows a file to be transferred between different computers (e.g., transfer a customer's credit history from one computer to another). Terminal emulators as well as file transfer packages are location sensitive: The user must know the location and the syntax used at each computer system. Thus if a teller needs to access the accounts of a customer from 10 different banks, he or she will have to explicitly logon to 10 different computers with 10 different passwords (this may take all day). Almost all state-of-the-market/practice computing networks support terminal emulation (remote logon) and file transfer between computers.

A *client-server system* allows remotely located programs to exchange information in realtime. This model allows a service consumer (client) to request a service provider (server) to perform a service. It allows application processes at different sites to interactively exchange messages and is thus a significant improvement over the terminal emulation and file transfer packages. For example, a teller uses a client software at his or her site to access a customer's accounts. The client software retrieves this information by cooperating with servers located at different banks without the need for 10 different logons (you can see some good news and bad news in this). Typically, a user workstation acts as a client issuing service requests to print servers, file servers, and database servers, which may be located at many remote sites. The client-server model provides a foundation for distributed cooperative processing where the processing functions, distributed to many sites, cooperate with each other to solve a problem (see Fig. 1.9). However, development of client-server systems raises many technical and support issues. Remote procedure call (RPC) facilities are the best-known mechanisms to develop client-server systems. "Client-server computing," a recently coined term, refers to distributed computing which utilizes the client-server model. Client-server computing is state of the market but not widely state of the practice at the time of this writing. We will discuss client-server computing in detail in Chapter 5.

A *distributed data and transaction management system (DDTMS)* is a sophisticated version of a client-server system. This system allows a user to store, access, and manipulate data transparently from many computers while maintaining the integrity of data during system failures. (Many client-server systems only support data retrieval and leave the issue of data integrity to application code.) For example, if a failure occurred while money was being transferred between two banks (money transfer is a transaction), then a DDTMS would attempt to roll back the changes made by the failing transaction. The following levels of transparency may be provided by a DDTMS:

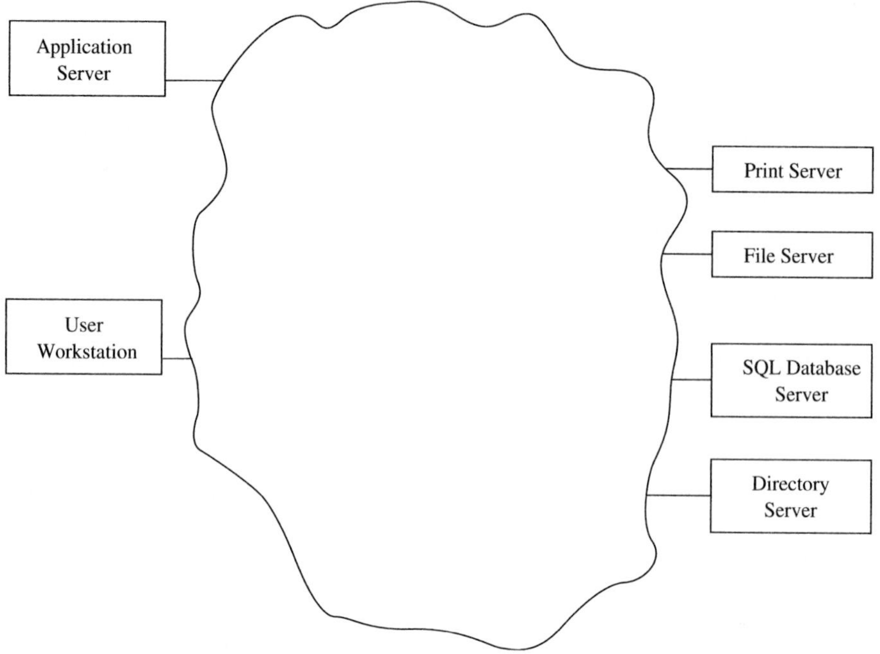

FIGURE 1.9 Example of Client-Server Processing

1. *Read transparency*: The user can read data from any site without knowing the site where the data is located.
2. *Update transparency*: The user can update data that may be duplicated at many sites. This implies that data updated at one site is synchronized with other copies to maintain database consistency and integrity.
3. *Transaction execution transparency*: A transaction (user request) may be decomposed into many subtransactions which may execute at many sites to access distributed data.
4. *Failure transparency*: The user is isolated from site and network failures so that he or she can access the desired data through alternate routes at alternate sites.

Figure 1.10 shows a computing network which supports a DDTMS. The databases D_1 through D_5, residing on computers $C_1, C_2, , , C_5$, respectively, are accessed from workstations W_1, W_2, W_3. Computers C_1, C_2 and C_3 support DDTMS; the workstations W_1, W_2 and W_3 include the DDTMS "front-ends," i.e., the clients. A workstation can read/update the database D_1 by just issuing a query which is routed to C_1 where the database is read/updated. To update the database D_2, the workstation issues the update which is routed to C_2 or C_3, based on a site selection algorithm of a DDTMS, where the database is updated. The DDTMS automatically updates the other copy of D_2. Design and deployment of a DDTMS involves many issues in update synchronization algorithms, global data modeling, deadlock detection and failure handling in distributed systems. Most of the state-of-the-art aspects of DDTMS were

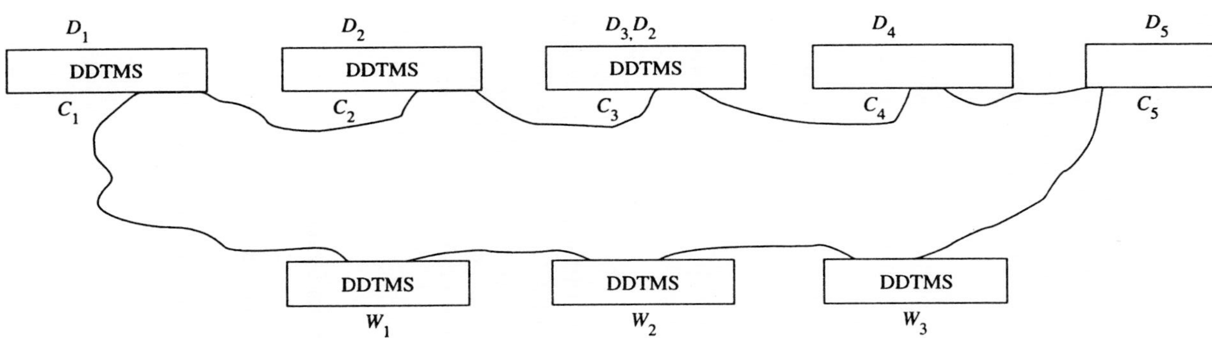

Legend:

- $D_1, D_2, \cdots D_5$ = Databases (e.g., Relational)
- $C_1, C_2, \cdots C_5$ = Large Computer Systems
- DDTMS = Distributed Data and Transaction Management System
- W_1 = Workstations

FIGURE 1.10 Distributed Data and Transaction Management Systems

addressed in the late 1970s and early 1980s. At present, DDTMSs with varying degrees of capabilities are state of the market but not fully state of the practice. DDTMSs are discussed in Chapter 6.

A *distributed operating system (DISOS)* synthesizes and extends the application support services so that a user request arriving at computer C_1 may use any of the resources located anywhere in the network **without** knowledge of their location. Examples of the resources are remote data, CPU, main memory, and a variety of print, file, security, database, and directory services. The functionalities of a distributed operating system include

- Total transparency to the end user so that the entire network appears as one large computing system with all processing, memory units, devices, and services available to the authorized users
- Automatic selection of an appropriate computer system or a server for execution of a request. The selection may be based on criteria such as fastest or cheapest execution.
- Automatic rerouting of a request to an appropriate computing system or a server due to any failures or congestions in the network.

Most of these systems at present are in the state-of-the-art stage (e.g., Amoeba, Tannenbaum 1990) with a few state-of-the-practice cases (e.g., Athena, Champine 1990). Industrial efforts are being directed at building distributed computing platforms (DCPs) which combine all the application support services (terminal emulation, file transfer, DDTMS, client-server systems and DISOS) as options to the users and developers of applications. We will discuss DISOSs and DCPs in Chapter 7.

1.5 Overview of Distributed Application Systems

The purpose of the DCP services (network services and application support services) is to help the most critical aspect of distributed computing—applications. Application systems are crucial to the survival of many organizations in the 1990s. Here are some illustrations <Keen 1991>:

- Between 25 and 80 percent of companies' cash flow is being processed through online processing applications.
- $1.5 trillion of financial transactions flowed through New York City's telecommunications systems each day in 1990 (this number is probably higher now).
- EDI (electronic data interchange) has become a "got to have it" technology for eliminating the paper chase of purchase orders, accounts receivable, accounts payable, delivery notices and so forth. In 1990, the chairman of Sears sent letters to its 5000 suppliers to adopt EDI or be dropped from the Sears suppliers' list.
- Some airlines process ticket orders at about 1500 transactions per second.

- When British Airways acquired British Caledonian, the two airlines' operations were meshed over a weekend because they both used the same information architecture and standards.

Availability of fast networks and application support services which allow applications in different cities to interact with each other in real time will usher a new era of distributed applications. These distributed application systems (DASs), described in Chapter 8, offer many functional, performance, and reliability advantages over the conventional mainframe-oriented applications. For example, the components of a distributed application (data, programs, user interfaces) can be allocated to and accessed from various computers in a network to fit the application needs. In a common DAS configuration shown in Fig. 1.11, the workstations are

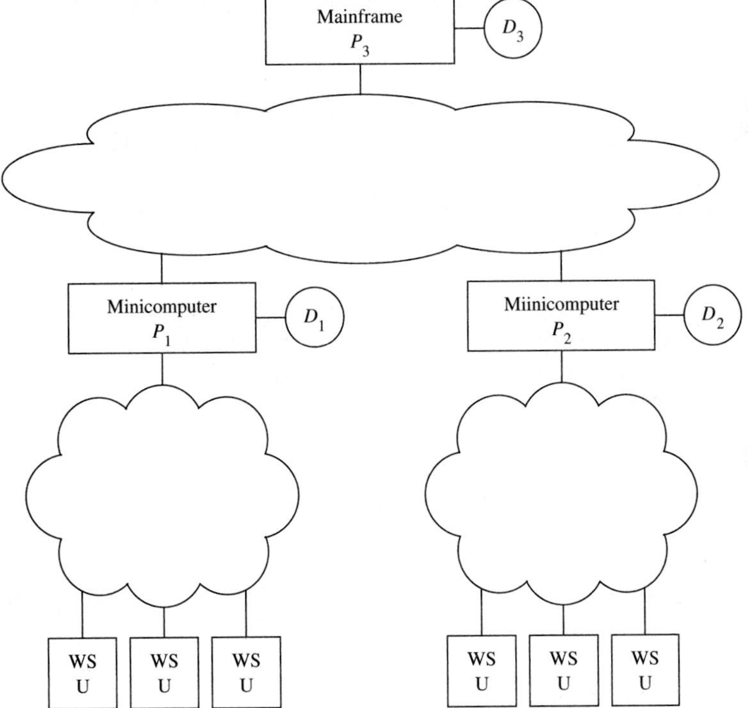
An Application System with
• U = User Interface
• P_1, P_2, P_3 = Programs
• D_1, D_2, D_3 = Databases
Mainframe
P_3
D_3
Minicomputer
P_1
D_1
Miinicomputer
P_2
D_2
WS
U
Comments:
• The user interfaces reside at the workstations. The user can access other programs and data from his or her workstation.
• Some of the programs and databases are at minicomputers for departmental (regional) application services.
• Some programs and databases are at the mainframe for corporate services.

FIGURE 1.11 A Typical Distributed Application System

used for sophisticated user interfaces and mainframes are used for database access and number crunching. A centralized application, by contrast, keeps all data, programs, and user interfaces at one central site, which may become a performance and availability bottleneck.

However, design of distributed applications is a complex task due to too many choices, issues, and interfaces. The growth of the underlying technologies in computing networks and application support services has in fact contributed to the complexity and has introduced many new questions, such as

- What are the factors to be considered in centralization versus distribution of applications?
- How can existing centralized applications be downsized by splitting them into pieces which can be allocated to different sites?
- What are the tradeoffs between using different application support services?
- What are the tradeoffs between performance, availability, security, and complexity of the system? The performance can be improved by locating data at the sites where it is most frequently used, and the availability can be improved by replicating programs and data to more than one site. However, this increases the complexity and the security exposure of the systems.
- How can one ensure the portability and gradual growth of applications that are being split between mainframes, minicomputers and microcomputers?
- Can the established methodologies and tools developed for conventional application development be used for distributed systems? What changes, if any, need to be introduced, and where?

We will discuss distributed application systems (DASs) in Chapter 8 and attempt to answer these questions. We will introduce distributed software engineering, which extends the conventional software engineering technologies for distributed applications. For example, distributed software engineers have to choose the appropriate application support services. The key activity in distributed software engineering is the *distributed application architecture* activity, which identifies the major components of an application system, subdivides and groups these components into fragments (fragmentation), assigns these fragments to computers (allocation), and then interconnects/integrates these components through appropriate application support services. This activity is also of key importance for the currently popular "downsizing/rightsizing" debate. See Chapter 8 for more details.

1.6 Open Systems: Standards in Interoperability, Interconnectivity and Integration

An open system is a vendor transparent environment in which the users can mix and match hardware and software from various vendors on networks from different vendors. Open systems are of crucial importance in distributed computing because the users need to build systems from diverse suppliers of computers, networks, database managers, and software packages. Theoretically, an open system must exhibit interoperability, portability, and integration <Nutt 1992>:

- *Interoperability* means that two systems can work with each other through well-defined interfaces. For example, an application developed on a Unix computer may interact with applications on OS/2 and IBM MVS mainframes. These applications must have well-defined interfaces for information exchange.
- *Portability* means that the applications should be decoupled from the computing platforms and the networks so that changes in the platforms and networks do not necessitate modifications of the application systems. The applications developed on one platform should be transported to and deployed on different platforms.
- *Integration* refers to the ease with which a system can be used. An integrated system basically minimizes the effort needed to use it.

Standards are needed to make open systems a reality. A large number of standards are being developed for interoperability, portability, and integration. The open standards being developed by the International Standards Organization (ISO), the Xopen standards and X Window are examples. Due to the proliferation of standards in distributed computing, many distributed computing architectures are being developed which combine standards into operational systems. These architectures are introduced by standardizing bodies, consortiums and vendors. Examples are Open Software Foundation's Distributed Computing Environment (DCE), ISO's Distributed Application Framework, and IBM's System Application Architecture. We will discuss the open system standards and architectures in Chapter 9.

1.7 Overview of Management and Support of Distributed Systems

Management must address two major issues: (1) how to manage and support the distributed computing technologies (i.e., networks and distributed applications), and (2) how to employ some of these technologies to improve the management processes. These two topics are of crucial importance because as more applications start relying on these technologies, it becomes important to manage these technologies wisely and invest in them as business "insurance."

It is important for upper management to provide a vision for the management and support of distributed computing technologies. The well-known management cycle of planning, organizing/staffing, development/deployment, and monitoring/control can be used as a basis for discussion.

The objective of information system (IS) planning is to exploit the role of technology to shape a company's future. Given a business architecture of an enterprise IS, planning produces a technology architecture IS. Planning must take into account the business growth and strategic business trends plus the technology trends in networks, distributed databases, cooperative processing, open systems and application architectures. Some of the existing planning methodologies need to be reviewed and extended <King 1989, Zachman 1982, Mushet 1985, Nolan 1973, Peck 1988>.

The organizational problems are concerned with establishing the organizational structure to meet the strategic objectives of an organization. Although detailed discussion of these problems is beyond the scope of this book, the centralization/distribution of the enterprise activities and management control are of particular interest to us. Several reference models are being developed, especially in computer integrated manufacturing <Ranky 1986>, for organizations to address the management problems of centralization versus decentralization of activities—see, for example, CIM-OSA <LaVie 1988> and CIMA <Campbell 1988>.

The training and staffing issues are as follows: who needs to know what about distributed computing at what stages in the systems life cycle, how the roles of existing personnel (technical support, computing system specialists, application systems designers, database designers, application systems programmers) are affected, and what the managers need to know about management of distributed computing.

The support of distributed computing involves a wide range of issues in management and support of networks and distributed applications. Examples of these issues are hardware/software selection and ordering (how to select the appropriate hardware/software network/application components); configuration, installation and maintenance of distributed applications; backup and recovery of remotely located files; fault detection and correction in distributed applications; configuration and change management of application components at different sites; and security administration of distributed applications. Comprehensive environments, such as the Open Software Foundation's Distributed Management Environment, are exploiting the networks and database technologies to manage the corporate databases and networks.

Figure 1.12 shows a few typical situations to illustrate the interrelationships between enterprise activities, application activities and application component location. The framework used in Fig. 1.12 considers the centralization/decentralization decisions in terms of three factors:

- Application development, which includes design, construction, modification, testing, and installation activities
- Application operation, which includes the allocation of application system components (data, programs, user interfaces) to different sites
- Enterprise and application management, which includes the planning, organizing, staffing and monitoring/controlling activities.

The main management challenge is to understand the tradeoffs between various options and select the most effective courses of action. Many of the management issues in distributed systems have not been addressed in the literature. In Chapter 10, we will discuss available approaches and outline the areas that need further investigation.

	Payroll	Inventory Control	Order Processing	Manufacturing Resource Planning
Development	C	D	D	C
Operation	C	D	D	D
Management	C	D	C	D

Legend: C = Centralized, D = Decentralized

Discussion:

1. All management activities (planning, organization, staffing, support) as well as the application system development (design, construction, testing) and the operation (location of application components) are centralized. This approach can be used for one application (e.g., payroll in the above matrix) or for all applications. If all applications are centralized and the enterprise management and application development is also restricted to one site, then this approach represents conventional centralized systems. In this case the DCS computers are used as terminals—a typical situation in mainframe-based microcomputer networks. This occurs in enterprises with corporate-wide networks that support most applications at central sites, which can be accessed from remotely located microcomputers or terminals. This configuration is commonly referred to as *centralized data processing*.
2. All development, operation, and mangement activities are distributed. If this approach is adopted for all applications, then this situation represents a completely distributed system, often referred to as a decentralized system. Such systems are common among peer-to-peer computing networks formed among existing independent computing facilities. A well-known example of this configuration is the Advanced Research Project Agency Network (Arpanet).
3. The application and enterprise activities are distributed, but the management control is centralized for standardization and security/police enforcement. This is becoming more and more common in enterprises.
4. The application development is centralized, but the application operation and enterprise management is distributed. This represents a situation whsere a "software house" is used for application development. The developed applications are deployed, operated, and managed at different sites.

FIGURE 1.12 Example of Centralization/Decentralization Decision

1.8 Evolution of Distributed Computing: An Accumulation of Terminology

Distributed computing has evolved in the last twenty years and will continue to evolve for many years to come. During this evolution, we have accumulated many terms such as distributed processing, distributed cooperative processing, distributed data processing, client-server computing, network computing, and supernetwork computing. Let us briefly review the evolution and try to put some of these terms in perspective.

During the 1970s, distributed computing was characterized by mainframes and minicomputers interconnected through wide area networks (WANs). These networks were slow, typically in the range of 2400 to 9600 bits per second (bps), and the computers exchanged information through terminal emulation and file transfer. Typically, minicomputers were emulated as terminals so that data at mainframes could be accessed through terminal emulation. In some cases, files were transferred between mainframes and minicomputers through file transfer packages. Many file transfer and terminal emulation packages were developed in this time period. Although a great deal of research in distributed databases was conducted in this time period (see, for example, Rothnie 1977), this technology did not become state of the market and state of the practice in this time period. Two terms became popular in this stage: (1) Distributed processing which refers to application processes at multiple computers, and (2) distributed data processing which refers to data as well as processes at different computers. Independent of the terms used, the underlying information exchange technologies were file transfer and terminal emulation.

During the 1980s, three fundamental changes took place: proliferation of desktop computers, availability of local area networks (LANs), and common usage of higher data communication rates (4 to 16 million bps for LANs, and 56,000 bps to 1.54 million bps for WANs). Typical DCSs in this time period consisted of mainframes, minicomputers, and desktop computers, interconnected through LANs and WANs. In addition to distributed processing and distributed data processing, the term network computing became popular to underline the role of networks as a value added feature of computers. Although some distributed database and client-server packages became state of the market (see, for example, Rauch-Hinden 1987), the main state-of-the-practice technologies for information exchange in this stage were still terminal emulation and file transfer. Thus the data at a remote computer was still accessed either by remotely logging on to the remote computer or by transferring the files through file transfer packages (many of these systems are operational at present).

During the 1990s, many fundamental changes are taking place: Availability of distributed database and client-server packages for transparent information exchange between remote processes, proliferation of powerful and inexpensive desktop and laptop computers, surge of multivendor products, emphasis on open standards, and commercial availability of high speed networks (100 million bps and higher for LANs, WANs and MANs). Typical DCS in this time period, the focus of this book, consist of many computers of different capabilities from different vendors, which are connected across vast geographical areas over high speed networks from different suppliers. In addition to the earlier terms, the term distributed cooperative processing is in vogue because it underscores the main feature of these systems: They allow processes at different computers to exchange information interactively with each other. Client-server (C-S) computing is the most popular form of distributed cooperative processing. It allows client applications (e.g., spreadsheets, query processors, and user interfaces) to access servers (e.g., database servers, file servers, print servers) transparently across a network. C-S computing is a major step forward from the older terminal emulation and file transfer based distributed computing. C-S computing is currently state of the market and rapidly becoming state of the practice.

The next stage of DCS, expected at the end of this decade, will make the entire computing network appear as a single large computer where different activities will take place seamlessly at different computers. These systems will also include supercomputers tied through Gigabit per second networks, and supervised by distributed workflow managers (distributed operating systems). These high speed computers tied to high speed networks have a great deal of potential. Such systems, called network supercomputing, are state of the art but not state of the market and practice yet. Developments in neural computing are also interesting because they attempt to simulate the physical thought processes of human brain. Basically, one human brain has about 100 billion neurons, where each neuron behaves as a CPU. However, neurons are slow (each neuron operates at 100 Hertz, much slower than the 40 Million Hertz and above of many computer chips). But neurons are interconnected to other neurons through nerve "waves" (each neuron can interact with others through at least 1000 interactions). Thus a human brain can be thought of as a network (a neural network) in which billions of neurons are interconnected in a variety of ways. However, the individual neurons are slow. Very fast computers connected through very fast networks create exciting opportunities for fundamentally new applications in artificial intelligence, medicine, engineering, manufacturing, finance, and management processes, among others.

If all these terms are confusing, just remember one thing: these are all different forms of distributed computing (i.e., a DCS is a collection of autonomous computers interconnected through a communication network to achieve business functions).

1.9 Desirable Goals of Distributed Computing

The preceding evolution of distributed computing has been driven to satisfy the following goals and objectives:

- Support of newer applications
- Increased transparency for the users, developers and managers of distributed computing
- Improved portability and interoperability of applications across computer systems
- Consistency and repeatability of services
- Improved response time and availability of services
- Better management tools and infrastructures.

These goals, discussed next, reflect the driving forces which will shape the nature of distributed computing in the future. Later chapters will describe how exactly these goals are being satisfied.

1.9.1 Support of Newer Applications

The applications in the past could be supported through batch transfer of data between systems. The newer emerging applications require more interactive information exchanges between various remotely located users. Examples of such applications are as follows:

- Sophisticated graphical user interfaces residing on workstations which access remotely located information from many sites
- Multimedia applications which combine data, voice and moving videos on the same workstation. In most cases, the text, the pictures and the moving video/voice appear

on different windows of the same workstation. The information being displayed can be extracted from sources located anywhere in the network

- Image processing applications which require sending, processing and editing of images such as X-rays for the medical industry, photographs used in claims processing for the insurance industry, proofs and advertisements in the publication industry, and visualization of systems dynamics in the aerospace industry
- Realtime applications in manufacturing and aerospace industries, among others, which require exchange of information between geographically distributed processors
- Video conferencing systems and groupware systems which allow remotely located workers to hold meetings, work on joint projects, collaborate on solving problems, and review and critique each other's work. Through text, video and voice, these systems attempt to create an atmosphere where remotely located workers interact with each other as if they were located at one site.
- Future collaborative computing applications which go beyond the computer conferencing and groupware software to cooperatively solve problems. These systems may include high-definition TV and "artificial life" animations. An example is the extensive "decision support systems" which allow location independent teams to work cooperatively as if they were in the same room (talk, see each other, review each other's documents, etc.). It is important to provide all these facilities through one common user interface (i.e., one workstation).

These applications are characterized by a high volume of data that needs to be transmitted interactively across networks. Figure 1.13 shows, for example, the data rates and the average session durations for a few applications. It can be seen that many applications require 100 million bits per second (Mbps) data transfer rates with sessions that can last for several hours. These characteristics impose demands on the networks, computing hardware and the application software. For example, the current voice communication systems used in the telephone industry are based on very slow data rates for an average of three-minute duration.

1.9.2 Transparency

Distributed computing systems must provide as much transparency as possible. We define transparency at the following levels:

- End user transparency
- Developer transparency
- Designer transparency
- Manager transparency.

The end user transparency shows how transparent the user operations are from the underlying networks, operating systems, computer systems and database/transaction managers. Ideally, a 100 percent user transparent system should operate as a single

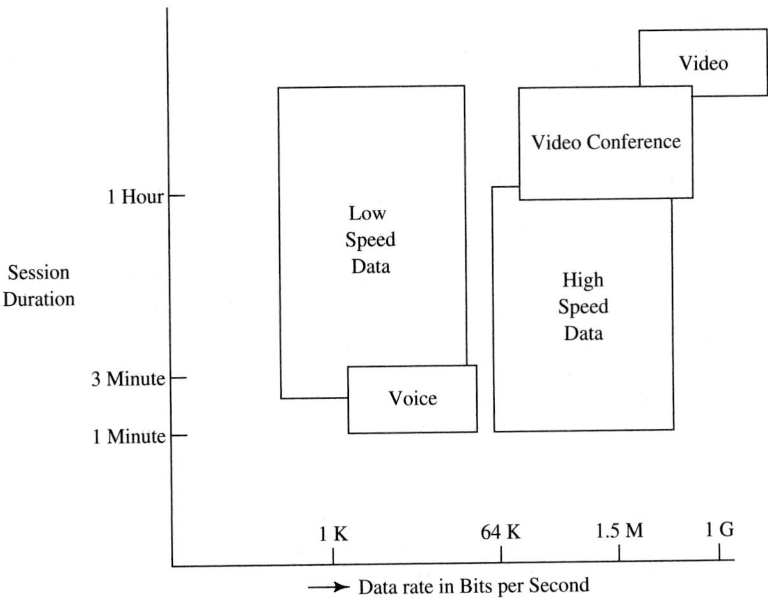

FIGURE 1.13 Information Characteristics of Applications

system in which the user is not aware of what activities are taking place where in the system. The end user transparency can be defined in terms of the following major functional transparencies:

- *Network hardware transparency.* This shows that the end user does not have to know the physical network hardware characteristics of the network.
- *Network services transparency.* This is concerned with providing services such as file transfer transparently on different networks.
- *User location transparency.* This shows that the end user can perform the same operations at any site in the network.
- *Data location transparency.* This allows access, storage, and manipulation of data at any site by using the same commands.
- *Transaction execution transparency.* This indicates that a user does not know how and where his or her transaction will execute. For example, a transaction which needs to access data from three different computers may be decomposed into three different subtransactions and executed in parallel without the knowledge of the user.
- *Processor transparency.* This shows that the user does not know on what computer processor his or her commands are executed.
- *I/O (input/output) device transparency.* This means that the user can use any I/O device such as a printer in the network without having to know the location of the printer.

- *Fault transparency*. This means that any faults in the network components, computing components, I/O devices, or any other components are hidden from the user to minimize impact on the user.

The network software, the distributed application support services and the application systems cooperate in providing these user transparencies. At present, the network hardware and network services transparencies are state of the market with other transparencies gradually becoming state of the market.

In addition to the end user transparency, the application developers can be shielded from the details of different systems while developing applications. In other words, an application system should be portable to different computers interconnected through different networks. Developer transparency (application portability) can be discussed at three levels:

- *User interface transparency*. Same user interface should be portable to different computers.
- *Program code transparency*. Same program code should be portable to different computers.
- *Data transparency*. The database design and access should be portable across all network stations.

Many standards are being developed to support the development transparencies. Examples of the standards are X Window for user interfaces, C for programming and SQL for database accesses.

In addition, the application systems designers should not have to decide at what location the various application systems components should reside. As the distributed computing technologies become more intelligent, the application system components will be moved automatically to appropriate locations for improvements in performance and availability. At present, most of these facilities are not state of the market.

Management transparency means that the management of distributed computing becomes as simple as the management of centralized systems. For example, the security and accounting should be automatic in networks so that different procedures and software would not be needed. A great deal of work is still needed in this area.

We will discuss the issues of transparency in different chapters and will summarize the situation in Chapters 7 and 8.

1.9.3 Consistency and Repeatability of Services

A distributed computing system should be able to maintain the consistency of data and should be able to provide repeatable operations even under network and computing hardware/software failures. The current and future distributed resource managers are increasingly providing these services through distributed data and transaction management systems. We will discuss this in Chapter 6.

1.9.4 Response Time and Availability of Services

The improved speed and reliability of the computer and communication hardware is increasing the response time and availability of the services provided by a distributed computing system. For example, the computing hardware speed is increasing to beyond 50 MIPS (million instructions per second), and the communication data rates in wide as well as local area networks are going beyond 100 Mbps (million bits per second). In addition, the mean time between failures (a measure of hardware reliability) is reportedly more than one year for many devices. On the other hand, the user expectations are also increasing due to increased reliance on these systems and the increased processing and communication requirements of newer applications. For example, multimedia applications with moving color videos require over 500 Mbps communication speeds because each moving video screen represents over 100 million bits of data which needs to be refreshed several times per second <McQuillan 1990>. The advent of high-definition TV is expected to further increase the data bits per screen.

1.9.5 Management Tools and Infrastructures

The issue of network and distributed applications management is of strategic importance to most enterprises. These areas are concerned with the policies, procedures and tools needed to manage the performance, faults, security, accounting and configurations of distributed computing. At present, many state-of-the-market products are available for network management. Increased attention is being paid to managing heterogeneous networks (networks formed by combining networks of different vendors). Network management standards have been adopted for large heterogeneous networks (see Chapter 4 for details). The issue of distributed applications management is still in its infancy and will be discussed in Chapter 10. The main issue is how to manage the performance, faults, security, accounting, and configurations of applications that are split across many computing systems.

1.10 A Case Study

We will use the following case study to illustrate the concepts introduced in this book. This case study is based on the network and application design/management problems of a realistic company.

A company, called XYZCORP, owns several retail electronic device stores to sell microcomputers, televisions, VCRs, radios and calculators. The management of XYZCORP is interested in manufacturing the best-selling products (microcomputers and VCRs) and feels that XYZCORP will have no problem in beating the competition, especially if it makes effective use of CIM. The headquarters of XYZCORP are in Chicago, and 40 appliance stores are located in Pennsylvania, Michigan, Virginia and New Jersey. The manufacturing and engineering plants are in a suburb of Detroit. The plant also includes a warehouse from which all the finished goods will be shipped to the appliance stores. The parts and components will be brought from several locations in the United States.

XYZCORP needs to develop a plan to integrate its business, engineering and manufacturing operations. An enterprise system/information system planning for XYZCORP has been completed. The new corporate headquarters will house the data processing, administration and distribution, and marketing/corporate planning and management offices. The Detroit branch will house the manufacturing plant on the first floor and the research/engineering will be located on the second floor.

The information system planning has produced a list of applications that have been developed to support the business processes (payroll, accounts receivable/ accounts payable, order processing, marketing information systems, and computerized checkout system), engineering processes (CAD, CAE, computer aided process planning) and manufacturing processes (material requirement planning, production scheduling and flexible manufacturing systems). XYZCORP is especially interested in integrating and automating the order processing, CAD/CAM and the "manufacturing" processes of the company products (radios, TVs, VCRs, calculators, IBM PC clones). This system, referred to as the IMCS (integrated manufacturing control system), will receive a customer order and assemble and pack a product for shipping within half an hour of order reception. IMCS consists of many subsystems: an order processing system, which receives customer orders; a CAD/CAE system, which produces the design based on the customer specification; a computer aided process planning (CAPP) system, which creates the manufacturing program; an MRP (material requirement planning) system, which determines the materials needed for the product; and a flexible manufacturing system (FMS), which actually assembles and builds the product. The computing systems for the various offices have been also ordered and are in the process of being installed. Figure 1.14 shows the initial layout of XYZCORP information systems.

The following decisions need to be made in XYZCORP:

- A network layout which shows how the computing devices at various sites will be interconnected and managed. We will make this decision as a series of case study projects in Part II which will involve WAN design, LAN selection and design, network architecture selection, tradeoffs between proprietary and open networks, and network management.
- Evaluation of application support services for applications at different sites to interact with each other. The decisions of DDTMS evaluation/selection, application of client-server systems and distributed operating systems for this enterprise will be made in Part III of this book through a series of case study projects.
- Distributed application architecture which shows how the manufacturing, engineering and engineering applications will be interconnected, integrated, and managed. We will accomplish this in Part IV through a few case study projects.
- Specialized aspects (e.g., network design for different network architectures) will be included in appropriate appendices.

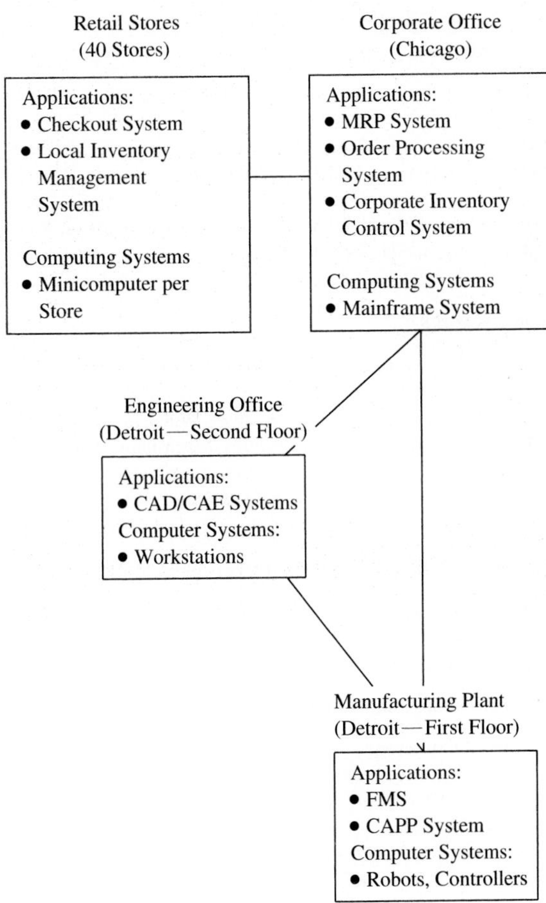

FIGURE 1.14 XYZCORP Initial Layout

This case study will help us to apply the techniques which we will learn in this book to a realistic enterprise.

1.11 Chapter Summary and Suggestions for Further Study

This chapter has presented some definitions and frameworks to establish the interrelationships between networks, application support services, distributed applications, and management of information systems.

Distributed computing is an active area of academic and industrial progress. Different parts of this book introduce the reader to different aspects of this field: networks and network architectures, client-server systems, distributed database management, distributed operating systems, distributed application systems, open systems, and management/support issues. Table 1.1 lists other books and periodicals which may be of benefit to the reader. The books listed are subdivided into distributed computing

TABLE 1.1 Major Sources of Additional Information

Books on Distributed Systems

1. Black, U. D., *Data Communications, Networks and Distributed Processing*, 2nd ed., Reston Publishing Co., 1987.
2. CORNAFION, *Distributed Computing Systems*, Elsevier Science Publishers, 1985.
3. Coulouris, J. and Dollimore, J., *Distributed Systems*, Addison-Wesley, 1988.
4. Duce, D.A., editor, *Distributed Computing Systems Programme*, Peter Peregrinus Ltd, 1984.
5. Mullender, S., editor, *Distributed Systems*, ACM Press, Addison-Wesley, 1989.
6. Sloman, M., and Kramer, J., *Distributed Systems and Computer Networks*, Prentice Hall, 1987.
7. Ziegler, K., *Distributed Computing and the Mainframe*, John Wiley, 1991.

Major Books on Networks

1. Black, U. D., *Data Communications, Networks and Distributed Processing*, 2nd ed., Reston Publishing Co., 1987.
2. Fitzgerald, G., *Business Data Communications*, Wiley, 1989.
3. Stallings, W., *Business Data Communications*, Macmillan, 1990.
4. Stallings, W., *Handbook of Computer Communications Standards*, 3 volumes, Macmillan, 1987.
5. Stallings, W., *Networks and Data Communications*, 3rd ed., Macmillan, 1991.
6. Tannenbaum, A., *Computing Networks*, Prentice Hall, 2nd ed., 1988.

Books on Databases with Some Coverage of Distributed Systems

1. Date, C., *An Introduction to Database Systems*, 5th ed., Addison-Wesley, 1989.
2. Elmasri, R., and Navathe, S., *Fundamentals of Database Systems*, Benjamin-Cummings, 1989.
3. Ozsu, M., and Valduriez, P., *Principles of Distributed Database Systems*, Prentice Hall, 1991.

State-of-the-Art Periodicals and Conference Proceedings

1. The International Conference on Distributed Computing Systems. This conference is held every year. The most recent proceedings are the 8th, 9th, 10th, and 11th conferences (1988 to 1991).
2. *IEEE Network Magazine*
3. *IEEE Computer Magazine*
4. *IEEE Communications Magazine*
5. *IEEE Transaction on Software Engineering*
6. *Information and Management Journal*, North Holland
7. *ACM Computing Surveys*
8. *ACM Communications*

State-of-the-Market/Practice Magazines and Periodicals

1. *Datamation* (Cahners Publication)
2. *Data Communications Magazine* (McGraw-Hill)
3. *Network Computing* (CMP Publication)
4. *Business Communications Review*
5. *Database Management*
6. *Harvard Business Review*
7. *Sloan Management Review*
8. *Enterprise Systems Journal*
9. *Information Week*
10. *Computerworld*, weekly (section on networks and standards)
11. *Infoworld*, weekly (section on networks)
12. *LAN Technology* (M&T Publication)
13. *UNIX World* (special issues on open systems)
14. *Byte Magazine* (special issues on networking)
15. *PC Magazine* (special issues on networking)
16. *PC Computing* (special issues on networking)

books, which cover the various aspects of distributed systems; computer network books, which focus on the lower-level issues of networks (mainly layers 1 to 4, with some discussion of layers 5 to 7); and database books, which cover some aspects of distributed systems such as distributed databases. The periodicals are categorized in terms of state-of-the-art and state-of-the-market/practice emphasis.

Questions and Exercises

1. List five different definitions of distributed systems and distributed computing from the existing literature.
2. Give five examples of distributed systems at the three main levels shown in Fig. 1.5.
3. How does the availability of distributed databases help in the development of distributed applications. Explain through an example.
4. Why is it important to consider the centralization/decentralization of enterprise while designing applications and choosing application systems.
5. Suppose that you are an information systems manager of a company that is migrating from centralized to distributed applications. Use the following table to show who will need to be trained on what aspects of DCS:

Personnel	Training Needed (list topics)
• Database designers	
• Application developers	
• Systems programmers	
• Database administrators	
• Technical support	
• Systems analysts	
• Network designers	

References

Andrews, G.R., "Paradigms for Process Interaction in Distributed Programs," *ACM Computing Surveys*, Mar. 1991, pp. 49–90.

Bagley, T., *SHARE Proceedings*, 1979.

Bal, H., Steiner, J., and Tannenbaum, A., "Programming Languages for Distributed Computing Systems," *ACM Computing Surveys*, Sept. 1989, pp. 261–322.

Bernstein, P., Hadzilacos, and Goodman, N., *Concurrency Control in Database Systems*, Addison-Wesley, 1987.

Blokdijk, A., and Blokdijk, P., "Planning and Design of Information Systems," Academic Press, 1987.

Bray, O., "Integration of Configuration Management, MRPII," *Autofact '88 Proceedings*, SME, 1988, pp. 14.31–14.43.

Byers, TJ, "MAPping the Islands of Automation," *PC World*, Dec. 1986.

Cad, G., "Plant-Wide Communications: A Hierarchical Model and Solution," *Autofact '88 Proceedings*, SME, 1988, pp. 25.31–25.51.

Campbell, R., "An Architecture for Factory Control Automation," *AT&T Technical Journal*, 1988.

Champine, Greer, D., and Ruh, W., "Project Athena as a Distributed Computer System," *IEEE Computer*, Sept. 1990, pp. 41–51.

Chappell, T., "A Case Study in Software Systems Integration," *CIM Review*, Spring 1985.

Chen, B., and Yeh, R., "Formal Specification and Verification of Distributed Systems," *IEEE Transactions on Software Engineering*, Nov. 1983, pp. 710–722.

Coulouris, J., and Dollimore, J., *Distributed Systems*, Addison-Wesley, 1988.

Date, C., *An Introduction to Database Systems*, 3rd ed., Addison-Wesley, 1982.

DeBoever, L., "Emerging Standards in Connectivity," *Software Magazine*, June 1989, pp. 69–75.

Donovan, J., "Beyond Chief Information Officer to Network Manager," *Harvard Business Review*, Sept.-Oct., 1988, pp. 134–140.

Drucker, P., "The Coming of the New Organization," *Harvard Business Review*, Jan.-Feb., 1988.

Elliot, S., "Local Area Network Integration," *Autofact '88*, SME, 1988.

Elmasri, R., and Navathe, S., *Fundamentals of Database Systems*, Benjamin-Cummings, 1989.

Enslow, P. H., "What is a 'Distributed' System?" *IEEE Computer*, Jan. 1978, pp. 13–21.

Gantz, J., "Cooperative Processing and the Enterprise Network," *Networking Management*, Jan. 1991, pp. 25–40.

Graham, G., "Real-World Distributed Databases," *Unix Review*, May 1987.

Gray, J., "An Approach to Decentralized Computer Systems," *IEEE Transactions on Software Engineering*, June 1986, pp. 684-692.

Hsu, C., and Skevington, C., "Integration of Data and Knowledge in Manufacturing Enterprises: A Conceptual Framework," *Journal of Manufacturing Systems*, Vol. 6, No. 4, 1988.

IEEE Transactions of Software Engineering, special issue on distributed systems, Jan., 1987.

Jain, H., "A Comprehensive Model for the Design of Distributed Computer Systems," *IEEE Transactions on Software Engineering*, Oct. 1987, pp. 1092–1104.

Jones, A., and Mclean, C., "A Proposed Hierarchical Control Model for Automated Manufacturing Systems," *Jour. of Manufacturing Systems*, Vol. 5, No. 1, 1987.

Kaminski, M., "Manufacturing Automation Protocol (MAP)—OSI for Factory Communications," in *87 International Symposium on Interoperable Information Systems: ISIS Conf. Proc.*, 1987.

Keen, P., *Shaping the Future: Business Design Through Information Technology*, Harvard Business School Press, 1991.

King, W.R., and Premkumar, G., "Key Issues in Telecommunications Planning," *Information and Management*, Dec. 1989, pp. 255–266.

Kleinrock, L., "Distributed Systems," *Communications of the ACM*, Nov. 1985, Vol. 18, No. 11, pp. 1200–1213.

LaVie, R., "The CIM Integrated Data Processing Environment in the European Open Systems Architecture CIM-OSA," *Engineering Network Enterprise Conference Proceedings*, Baltimore, Md., June 1988, pp. 1–33.

Lew, W., and Machmuller, P., "A Case Study in Database Integration," *CIM Review*, Winter 1985.

Li, R.K., and Bedworth, D., "A Framework for the Integration of Computer-Aided Design and Computer-Aided Process Planning," *Computers and Industrial Engineering*, Vol. 14, No. 4, 1988, pp. 395–413.

Malas, D.E., "Integrating Information Flow in a Discrete Manufacturing Enterprise," *Engineering Network Enterprise Conference Proceedings*, Baltimore, Md., June 1988, pp. 1–113.

Martin, R., "The Standards Test for Portability," *Datamation*, May 15, 1989.

Mcleod, Raymond, "Management Information Systems," *SRA*, 1986.

McQuillan, J., "Broadband Networks," *Data Communications*, June 1990, pp. 76-86.

Moad, J., "Contracting with Integrators," *Datamation*, May 15, 1989.

Mullender, S. (ed.), *Distributed Systems*, ACM Press, Addison-Wesley, 1989.

Mushet, M., "Application Systems Planning," *Information Systems Management*, Winter 1985.

Nolan, R., "Managing the Computer Resource: A Stage Hypothesis," *Communications of the ACM*, Vol. 16, No. 7, July 1973, pp. 399–405.

Nutt, G., *Open Systems*, Prentice Hall, 1992.

Odrey, N., and Nagel, R., "Critical Issues in Integrating Factory Automation Systems," *CIM Review*, Winter 1986, pp. 29–37.

Ozsu, M., and Valduriez, P., "Distributed Database Systems: Where Are We Now?" *IEEE Computer*, Aug. 1991, pp. 68–78.

Peck, R., "Planning Guide," *DataPro*, 1988.

Popek, G., and Walker, B. (eds.), *The LOCUS Distributed System Architecture*, MIT Press, 1985.

Pratt, S., "Applicability of Decentralized/Centralized Control Procedures in Distributed Processing System Development and Operation," *IEEE Trans. on Engineering Management*, Vol. EM32, No. 3, Aug. 1985, pp. 116–123.

Ranky, Paul, *Computer Integrated Manufacturing*, Prentice Hall International, 1986.

Rashid, R., "The Catalyst for Open Systems," *Datamation*, May 15, 1989.

Rauch-Hinden, W., "True Distributed DBMSes Presage Big Dividends," *Mini-Micro Systems*, May and June, 1987.

Rockart, J.F., "Distributed Data Processing Model," *SHARE*, 1979.

Rothnie, J.B., and Goodman, N., "A Survey of Research and Development in Distributed Data Base Management," 3rd Conference on Very Large Data Bases, Tokyo, Oct. 1977, pp. 48–60.

Runyan, L., "The Open Opportunity," *Datamation*, May 15, 1989.

Shatz, S.M., and Wang, J., "Introduction to Distributed Software Engineering," *IEEE Software*, Oct. 1987.

Sloman, M., and Kramer, J., *Distributed Systems and Computer Networks*, Prentice Hall, 1987.

Tannenbaum, A., et al., "Experiences with the Amoeba Distributed Operating Systems," Comm. of ACM, December 1990.

Tannenbaum, A., and Van Renese, R., "Distributed Operating Systems," *ACM Computing Surveys*, December 1985.

Tannenbaum, A., *Computing Networks*, 2nd edition, Prentice Hall, 1989.

Umar, A., and Teorey, T.J., "A Generalized Procedure for Program and Data Allocation," Proceedings of First Pacific Conference on Computer Communications, Seoul, Korea, Oct. 1985.

VanNostrand, R.C., "A User's Perspective on CAD/CAM and MIS Integration," *CIM Review*, Winter 1986.

Wilbur, S., and Bacarisse, B., "Building Distributed Systems with Remote Procedure Call," *Software Engineering Journal*, Sept. 1987, pp. 148–159.

Williams, G., "Integrated Computing Environments," *Datamation*, May 1, 1989.

Zachman, J.A., "Business Systems Planning and Business Information Control Study," *IBM Systems Journal*, Vol. 21, No. 1, 1982, pp.31–53.

PART TWO

Communication Network Services

Chapter 2: Communication Network Technologies
Chapter 3: Network Architectures and Network Interconnectivity
Chapter 4: Network Management

This portion of the book concentrates on the communication network services of the Distributed Computing Reference Model introduced in Chapter 1 (see the highlighted area in the following figure). Chapter 2 introduces the communication network technologies and Chapter 3 presents the network architectures and network interconnectivity issues. The OSI (Open Systems Interface) Model is discussed as a framework for open systems in Chapter 3. Examples of industrial network architectures such as TCP/IP, SNA, MAP, and TOP are included in appendixes to support the discussion. A review of network management concludes this part of the book. After reading these chapters, the reader should be able to discuss, compare and contrast the services provided by the communication networks.

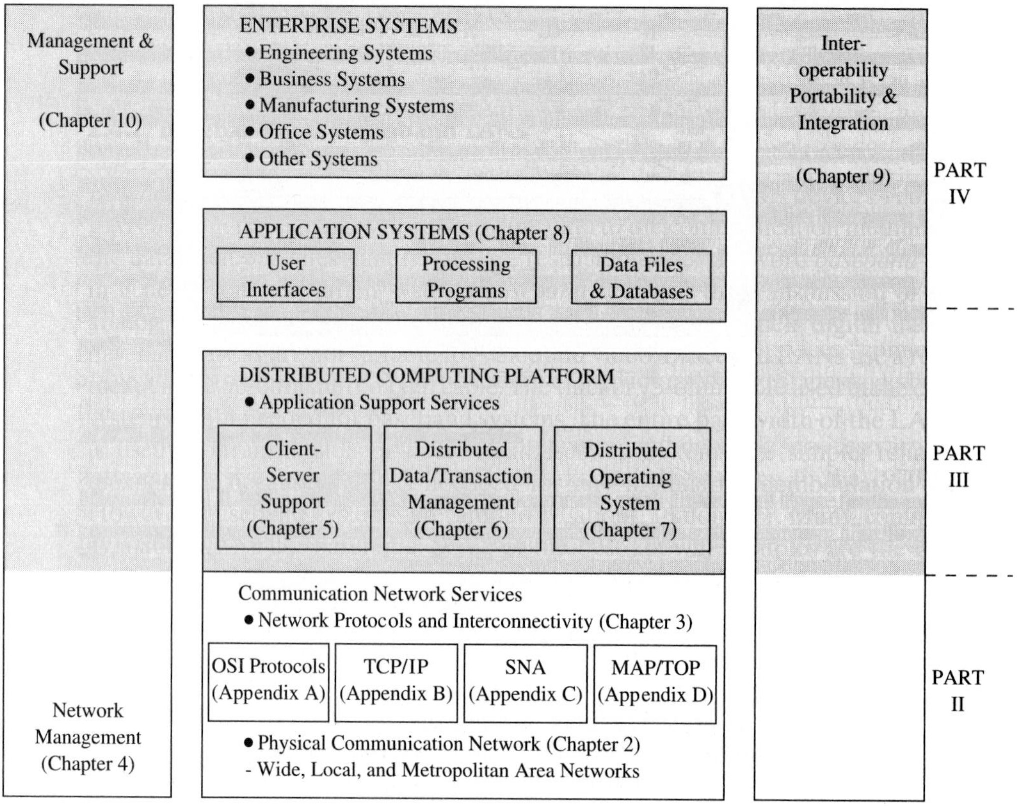

Management & Support

(Chapter 10)

ENTERPRISE SYSTEMS
- Engineering Systems
- Business Systems
- Manufacturing Systems
- Office Systems
- Other Systems

Inter-operability Portability & Integration

(Chapter 9)

PART IV

APPLICATION SYSTEMS (Chapter 8)

User Interfaces | Processing Programs | Data Files & Databases

DISTRIBUTED COMPUTING PLATFORM
- Application Support Services

Client-Server Support (Chapter 5) | Distributed Data/Transaction Management (Chapter 6) | Distributed Operating System (Chapter 7)

PART III

Communication Network Services
- Network Protocols and Interconnectivity (Chapter 3)

OSI Protocols (Appendix A) | TCP/IP (Appendix B) | SNA (Appendix C) | MAP/TOP (Appendix D)

- Physical Communication Network (Chapter 2)
- Wide, Local, and Metropolitan Area Networks

Network Management (Chapter 4)

PART II

Chapter 2

Communication Network Technologies

2.1 Introduction

A *communication network* is a collection of equipment and physical media, viewed as one autonomous whole, that interconnects two or more stations. A *station* is an end-point (source/sink) in a communication network and can be a terminal, computer, sensor or a TV. Communication networks, also referred to as networks in this book, provide the information exchange services in distributed computing. Specifically, they are responsible for three type of services: Delivery, understanding and agreement. Delivery is the physical transport of data between stations. Data, in this context, is anything that conveys meaning to a user (e.g., customer names, bank balances, voice and images). Delivery involves finding a path for the data and sending the data correctly over the selected path. Understanding assures that the data sent is in a format which can be understood by the receiver. Data may need to be translated between senders and receivers. Agreement assures that the data is sent when the receiver is ready to receive it. This means that the rules of exchange (*protocol*) must be established between a sender and a receiver.

This chapter describes the physical aspects of communication networks[1] which are important in studying distributed computing.

[1]Readers familiar with the Open System Interconnection (OSI) Model will recognize that the communication network discussion in this chapter concentrates on layers 1 through 3 of the OSI Model.

Specifically, we will attempt to answer the following questions:

- What is the vocabulary needed to understand communication networks?
- What are the concepts, terms and components of communication networks?
- What are the properties and components of wide area networks, local area networks and metropolitan area networks?
- What are the basic concepts of very fast integrated digital networks which can operate at long and/or short distances to support newer applications such as multimedia, moving video, etc.?
- What are the essential aspects of network performance evaluation which can be used for rough paper and pencil analysis?

The principles of communication network are reviewed in Section 2.2. Networks are generally classified into three categories based on the geographical area covered:

- Local area networks (LANs), which do not use common carrier facilities over short distances with speeds up to 100 Mbps and higher.
- Metropolitan area networks (MANs), which are essentially large LANs that may cover an entire city, perhaps by using cable television facilities
- Wide area networks (WANs), which use common carrier facilities over long distances with speeds up to a few million bits per second (Mbps).

Historically, most WANs were developed in the 1960s, LANs emerged in the late 1970s, and MANs evolved in the late 1980s. These systems are reviewed in Sections 2.3 through 2.5. ISDN (integrated system digital network) is a major step toward providing digital transmission for voice, data, and images. A faster version of ISDN, called Broadband-ISDN (BISDN), is being developed for the end of this century. ISDN and BISDN are discussed in Section 2.6.

A major growth in networking is interconnection and integration of LANs, MANs and WANs into large, high-speed, and intelligent supernetworks (see Fig. 2.1). In these networks, many computers in a building are connected to a LAN, many LANs are interconnected through a MAN, and many MANs are interconnected through WANs at very high speeds. The primary business pressure behind these networks is the large number of LANs which need to exchange information with each other, and the expected growth of multimedia and other sophisticated applications. It is desirable to operate the backbone WAN at 100 million bits per second (Mbps) or higher in order to interconnect the MANs and LANs, which are also operating at these speeds. This provides "wall to wall" 100 Mbps and higher networks. Section 2.7 reviews this important and interesting development area in networks.

A simple procedure for network performance evaluation is introduced in Section 2.8 for quick design tradeoff calculations. The case study at the end of this chapter leads the reader through typical WAN design, LAN layout, and emerging technology selection problems facing an organization.

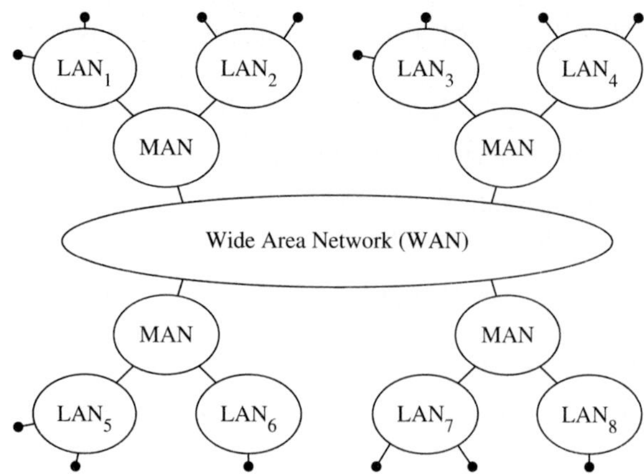

FIGURE 2.1 Networks of the Future

We should indicate here that the discussion of communication network technologies in this chapter reflects the state of the art, state of the market and state of the practice in the free Western world and the Far East (especially Japan, Korea, and Singapore). Many other countries are far behind in utilizing the technologies mentioned here. For example, in Eastern Europe, a potential telephone subscriber has to wait for several *years* to get a telephone line.

The readers familiar with data communications may find Sections 2.2 through 2.6 too basic and may choose to skip these sections. Managers may choose to review the overviews in each section and then read the management summary.

2.2 Communication Network Principles and Concepts

2.2.1 Overview

At the lowest level, a communication network consists of three components (Fig. 2.2a):

- *Data sources/sinks*. These entities generate and receive the data handled by the communication network. Examples of the data are voice, computer bits, and TV patterns.
- *Data/signal converters*. These devices convert the data to signals for transmission on one end and back to data at the other. Data is propagated from one point to another by means of *signals*, which are electromagnetic representation of data. An example of a converter is a modem which converts data bits to continuous signals, which are transmitted across a network. In some networks, called *baseband* networks, the conversions are bypassed by "pressing" the data directly against the communication wire. In these cases, data and signals are the same.
- *Transmitting facilities*. These facilities deliver (transport) the signals across a network. This transport involves finding a path for the signals, sending the signals over

a. Physical View of a Communication Network

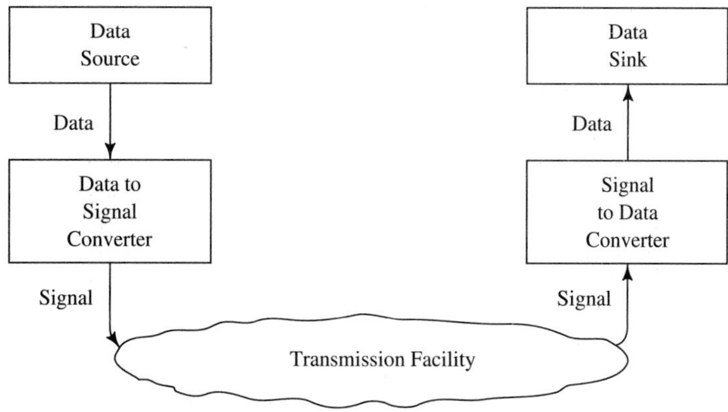

b. Example of a Communication Network

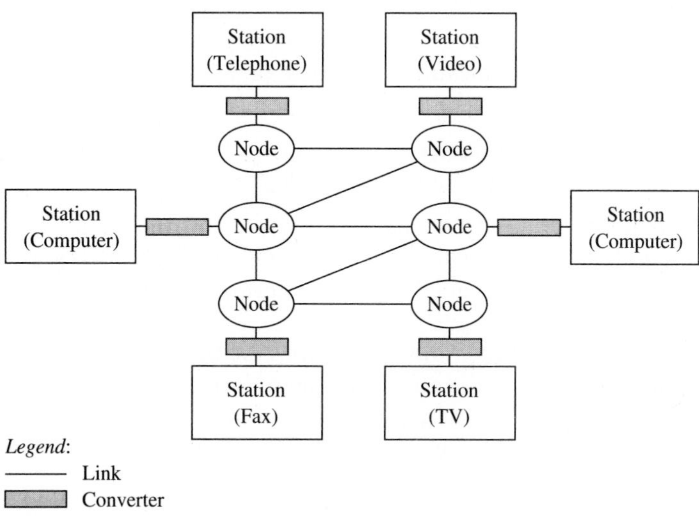

FIGURE 2.2 Views of a Communication Network

the path, and dealing with signal attenuation and distortion over long transmission paths.

Section 2.2.2 discusses the main terms and techniques used in communication networks. A communication network may use analog (continuous) or digital (discrete) data for its inputs and outputs. In digital communication systems, all data is digital (it either comes from digital data sources or is converted to digital format). These systems, discussed in Section 2.2.3, are increasingly being used in most of the current and future distributed applications.

The transmission facilities consist of a wide range of hardware components and software modules. Design of transmission facilities raises questions about what communication medium to use, how to interconnect the various components (network topology), what methods to use for communication between various components, and what techniques to use for data compression and encryption. These issues are discussed in Sections 2.2.4 through 2.2.7.

2.2.2 Physical Communication Characteristics

2.2.2.1 Basic Terms and Definitions

We will use the following terms to refer to the communication network components (see Fig. 2.2b).

- *Station* is an end-point (source/sink) in a communication network. Examples of stations are terminals (text and/or graphics), telephones, sensors (temperature, security), TVs, facsimiles, diskless workstations, personal computers, workstations, minicomputers, or mainframes.
- *Links (communication links)* refer to the physical media that is used to interconnect stations in a communication network. Examples of links are telephone lines, coaxial cables, and fiber cables.
- *Converters* convert different formats of data and signals. Examples are digital to analog converters (modems) and analog to digital converters (codecs).
- *Node* refers to an intermediate system in a communication network. An example of a node is a router which is used to direct traffic from one point to another (see Fig. 2.2b). These are called nodes or intermediate systems.

As mentioned previously, *data* conveys meaning to a user, and a *signal* is an encoding of data in some electromagnetic format. Signals are represented as cyclic waves which may be discrete (digital) or continuous (analog). The following properties characterize cyclic waves (see Fig. 2.3):

- Amplitude, which shows the height of the wave
- Frequency, which shows the cycles per unit time of the wave
- Phase, which shows how far, in degrees, the wave is from its beginning (phase 0).

Data can be digital or analog; signals can also be digital or analog. Figure 2.4 shows the techniques used to convert (encode) data into signals. The technique employed depends on the format of data (analog or digital) and the encoded signal (analog or digital). Figure 2.4 shows that telephones are used to encode analog data to analog signals and digital transmitters are used to encode digital data to digital signals. These conversions can be simple (i.e., a 0 data bit appears as no voltage and a 1 appears as some voltage) or sophisticated (see, for example, Stallings 1991). But how are the digital data bits transmitted by using the analog waves? As shown in Fig. 2.4, modems are used to *modulate* (convert) digital data to analog signals and then demodulate them back to digital data. We will discuss modems in Section 2.2.2.2. Similarly, a codec

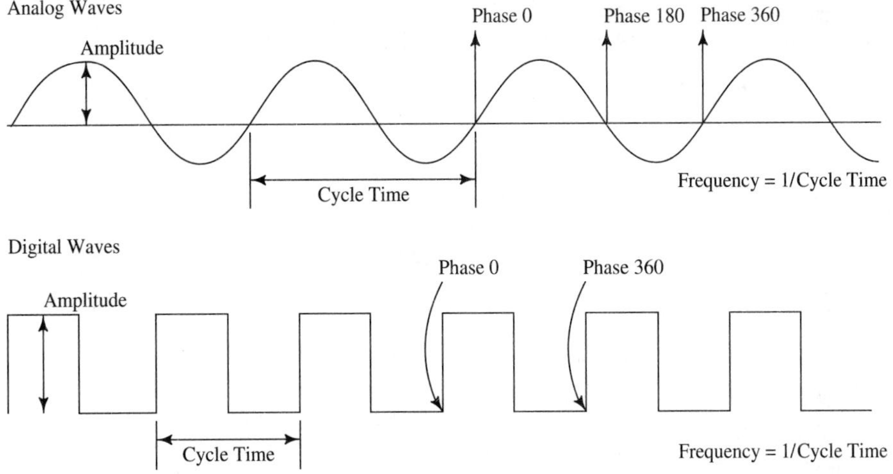

FIGURE 2.3 Cyclic Wave Characteristics

(coder-decoder) is used to convert analog data to digital signals. Codecs are described in Section 2.2.3.2.

After conversion, how are the signals transmitted simultaneously over the same medium? In 1874, Baudot, a French scientist, showed that six users could transmit simultaneously on one wire. This was done by sending information at six different frequencies for the six users and by using filters at the receiving end, which only received unique frequency (see Fig. 2.5a). This experiment is the foundation of what is currently known as frequency division multiplexing (FDM) and is used very widely

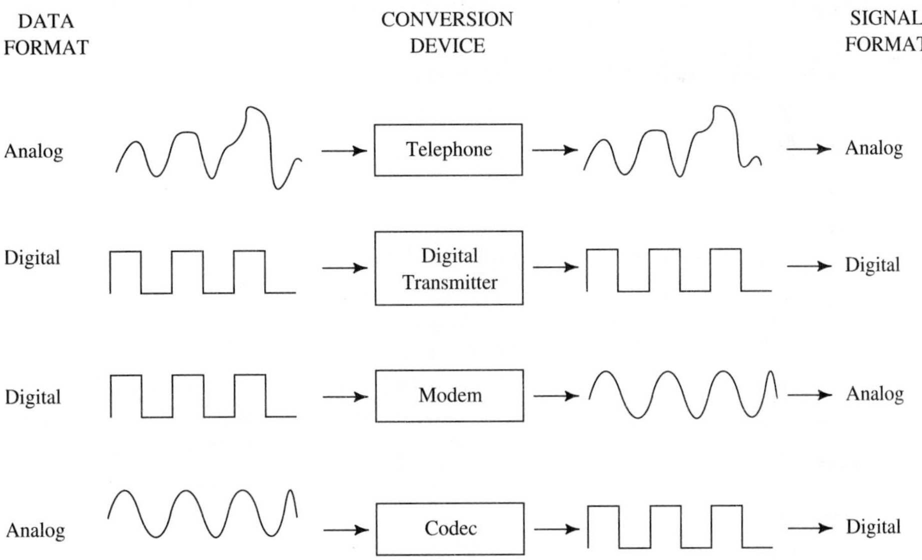

FIGURE 2.4 Examples of Data to Signal Conversion

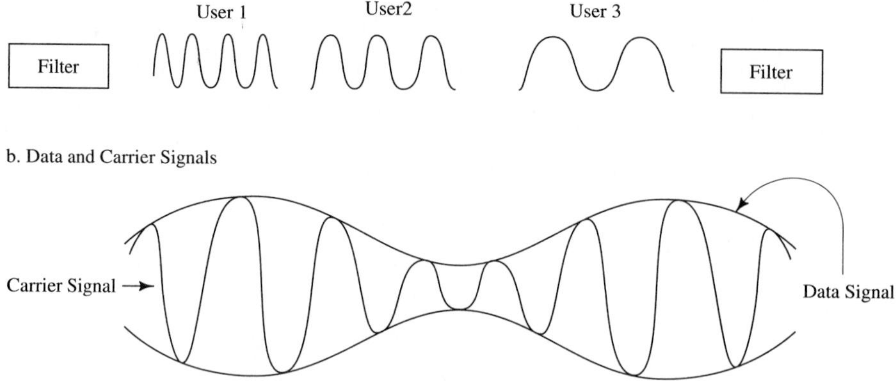

FIGURE 2.5 Frequency Division Multiplexingand Data/Carrier Signals

in communication systems. The six sessions are referred to as the six channels which operate on the same wire. The filters allow the users to "tune" to a particular channel. Notice the similarity of this example to the modern television sets with multiple channels, where each channel represents a frequency range.

The following communication terms are used widely:

- Hertz (Hz) = number of cycles per second
- Baud = number of signal changes per second
- Data rate = number of bits sent per second (bps). Data rate is equal to the baud rate if one bit is carried per signal. In general, data rate = baud rate × data bits per signal.
- Channel = a logical communication path
- Bandwidth = frequency used by a signal (measured in Hz).
- Channel capacity = number of bits that can be transmitted per second. This is the same as data rate.

Let us consider an example to illustrate the basic ideas. Human voice uses frequency ranges from 0 to 4000 Hz, but the commonly available voice graded telephone lines (carriers) use the frequency ranges 300 to 3300 Hz to carry a human voice. This bandwidth of 3000 Hz has been found adequate for human conversations. Frequencies lower than 300 and higher than 3300 are not carried well by voice graded lines (this is why the sound of delicate musical instruments is distorted on telephones). If a cable (carrier line) can carry between 30,000 to 42,000 Hz, then it can roughly support the following four voice channels (voice graded lines):

1. Channel 1: 30,000 to 33,000 Hz
2. Channel 2: 33,000 to 36,000 Hz

3. Channel 3: 36,000 to 39,000 Hz
4. Channel 4: 39,000 to 42,000 Hz.

At this point we should differentiate between data and carrier signals. A data signal represents the data and a carrier signal represents the signals of a medium (e.g., a telephone line) on which the data is carried. For the example just discussed, the data signals represent the voice and the carrier signals are in the range of 30,000 to 42,000 Hz. Note that the same data signal at various carrier frequencies represents the same information (e.g., data signals at channel 1 and 4 are the same). This is illustrated in Fig. 2.5b. This principle of dividing up the bandwidth of a carrier into data signal bandwidths, called frequency division multiplexing (FDM), can be used for a rough estimate of the minimum number of users of a cable. For example, if a cable has a BW of 2 MHz then it can support *approximately* 666 voice channels (telephone lines) by using the following simple formula:

No. of users on a carrier = carrier bandwidth/data bandwidth

Then with a carrier bandwidth of 2 MHz and data bandwidth of 3000 Hz, we obtain 666 users. Some modifications to this formula are needed to allow for "guard bands" (some room left between consecutive users) and for other multiplexing techniques (e.g., the time division multiplexing used in digital communications) which are more efficient than FDM. However, this gives us a gross estimate which may be useful for rough paper and pencil analysis.

We should note that in many cases, data and signals are used as synonyms because a signal is just a representation of data. The distinction is usually necessary for detailed communication engineering design, which is beyond the scope of this book.

2.2.2.2 Digital to Analog Conversion: Modems and Interfacing Devices

A modem (modulator/demodulator) is a hardware device which converts digital data to analog signals and vice versa. A modem is also called data circuit equipment (DCE) or "dataset" in communication systems because it interfaces between voice and data communication systems. Common modulation and demodulation techniques used in modems are as follows (Fig. 2.6):

- Amplitude modulation (AM), where the 0 and 1 bits are represented by the height of an amplitude. For example, 5 volts may be used to represent bit 0 and 10 volts may be used to represent bit 1.
- Frequency modulation (FM), where the 0 and 1 bits are represented by two different frequencies, say 1000 cycles per second and 2000 cycles per second, respectively.
- Phase shift modulation (PSM), where a certain phase (e.g., 90) is used to represent bit 0 and a change to bit 1 is indicated whenever the phase of the signal changes.

If one signal level carries more than one data bit, as shown in Fig. 2.6, then the modulation is called multilevel modulation. This technique is used in modems to

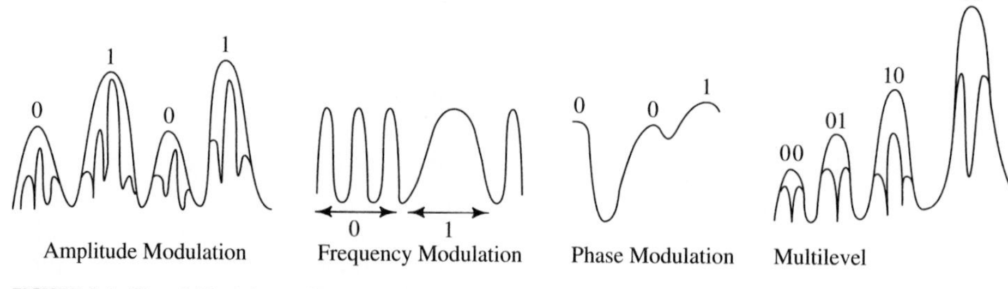

FIGURE 2.6 Signal Modulation/Demodulation

increase communication speed. For example, many modems have a switch which can be used to increase the data rate from 2400 bps (bits per second) to 4800 bps. This switch essentially starts sending two bits per signal instead of one, thus doubling the bits per second.

Many special modems are commercially available, including the following:

- Frequency shift key (FSK) and phase shift key (PSK) modems, which operate on full duplex by using one frequency to send and another to receive
- Limited distance modems, which provide higher speed at smaller distances (a few miles)
- Line drivers ("modem eliminators"), which connect devices for 2 to 4 miles without modulation/demodulation
- Acoustic couplers, which are low cost and low data rate (300 bps) modems
- Smart modems, which can execute program-controlled commands such as dial numbers and answer phones.

The choice of modems depends on the distance between device (50 feet, 2–4 miles, 10 miles, >10 miles), speed requirements, and cost. Many new modems are being developed for high-speed applications (see Defler, 1992 for a state-of-the-market survey).

An old but still very popular interface standard between modems and terminals (called data terminating equipment, DTE) is the EIA RS232-C standard. This standard, commonly referred to as the RS232 standard, was developed when computing equipment started using the telephone lines for data transmission. There was a natural need to develop a standard so that the digital computer devices could be connected to the telephone lines through modems. RS232 is officially limited to 20 Kbps for a maximum of 50 feet between the devices. In practice, many installations have used RS232 interfaces at 400 feet and higher distances. RS232-C interface standard is used heavily in the United States to connect many type of devices (printers, terminals, modems, etc.). It uses 25 pins, out of which a few (6 to 12) are used heavily. Figure 2.7 shows the most frequently used pins of RS232.

In most computing devices, RS232 is implemented in a microprocessor chip, known as UART (Universal Asynchronous Receiver Transmitter), which can be programmed to send/receive data. For example, IBM PCs contain a UART, which is actually an 8250 microprocessor chip. This chip provides transmit and receive registers

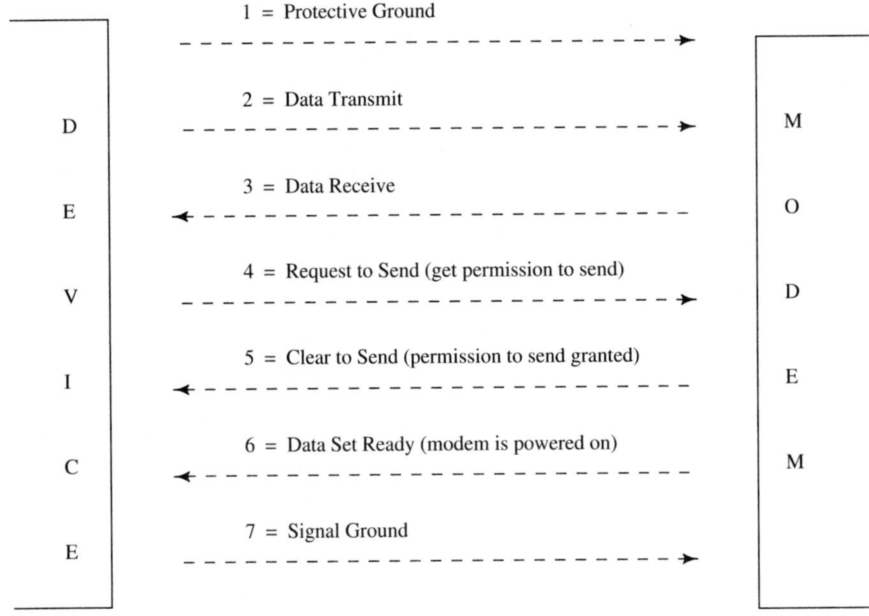

FIGURE 2.7 RS232-C Main Pins

for data transmission. In addition, it provides control registers for choosing line and modem options (e.g., data rate, stop bits) and status registers to see if anything has been received. The IBM Personal Computer Technical Reference Manual (PN-636453) describes the programming details about how these registers can be accessed. Programs can be written in BASIC, C, Pascal, and 8080 assembler to drive the RS232 interfaces. For example, many terminal emulation programs such as Kermit program the 8250 chip to send/receive data on serial communication lines.

In addition to the RS232 interface, many other interface standards have been developed. An example is the EIA RS449, which supports 2 Mbps at a 200-foot distance. It uses 37 pins and is compatible with the International Standards Organization (ISO) standards. RS449 is also a federal government requirement for many equipments and is favored by some network architectures, such as the Manufacturing Automation Protocol (MAP). Many adapters between RS232 and RS449 have been developed and are commercially available.

2.2.3 Digital Communication Networks

2.2.3.1 Analog Versus Digital Communications

Conceptually, a communication network is analog or digital depending on

- Data received/generated by the transmission facility
- Techniques used to handle attenuation over long distances.

Analog communication networks receive/generate analog data and use amplifiers to handle attenuation (see Fig. 2.8a). The analog data is either generated directly by a source (e.g., a human) or is converted to analog by modems. The main problem with analog communication networks, as shown in Fig. 2.8a, is that the amplifiers do not know the content of the inputs; they amplify whatever is received, including the noise.

In a digital communication network, the data received/generated by the transmission facility is digital, and repeaters are used in the transmission facility over long distances to recover the patterns of 1's and 0's (see Fig. 2.8b). The digital data may originate from a digital device such as a computer or it may be digitized before being fed into the transmission facility. Repeaters assume that the input is digital; thus when the signal is attenuated, the repeaters regenerate the original bit patterns (see Fig. 2.8b). Thus they filter the noise. However, repeaters cannot be used if the data is analog.

The communications industry is evolving toward the use of digital communication networks. These networks carry digital images of computer bits, voice, video, facsimile, graphics, and many other type of data. Digital communication networks are more attractive for several reasons:

- Digits are more rugged and free of noise because it is easier to detect 1's and 0's even in distorted messages. For example, if amplitudes of 10 volts and 5 volts are used to indicate 1's and 0's, respectively, then a receiver can detect a 1 if the amplitude is greater than 5 and a 0 for 5 volts or less. The analog data, once distorted, cannot be recovered.
- Repeaters along a transmission path can detect a digital signal and retransmit a clean (noise-free) signal. These repeaters prevent accumulation of noise along the transmission path. In contrast, if a distorted analog signal is amplified, then the distortion is also amplified.

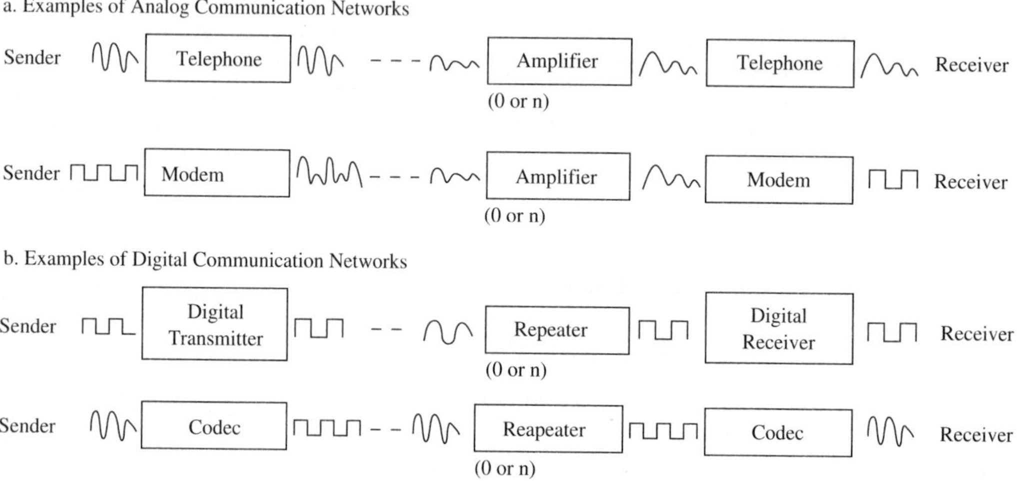

FIGURE 2.8 Digital versus Analog Communications

- Digital communication is especially suitable for computer networks because data bits can be directly fed into a communication medium without any modulation/demodulation (this is the idea behind the baseband local area networks, which we will discuss later).
- A single medium (e.g., a cable) can multiplex voice, data and video because they all appear as bits. This allows an organization to develop one *backbone* network to support all telephone lines, televisions and computers.
- Digital communications are becoming more economical largely due to the availability of chips which can digitize the analog signals efficiently. The theories of digital communications have been around for a number of years but were not economically feasible. It is expected that the costs of digital communications will continue to decrease due to the advances in very large system integration (VLSI).
- Digital communications are more secure than analog communications because digital data streams can be scrambled (encrypted) by using sophisticated computer techniques. The encrypted bits can be deciphered (decrypted) only by equally sophisticated decryption devices/algorithms. The encryption/decryption on analog data (such as human voice) is not sophisticated. This is why "secure" telephone conversations first convert voice to digits before encryption.
- Newer technologies such as optic fibers benefit from digital transmission and advances in voice digitization are reducing the bandwidth requirements for voice signals. The combined effect is that digital communications is the favored area of investigation and advancement.

Digital communications have been used by common carriers (telephone companies) for many years between telephone branch offices. *Integrated Services Digital Network (ISDN)* extends the digitization of the network into the customer premises (houses, offices). ISDN uses a "wall to wall" digital communication network to provide the users a universal access to a wide range of communication services. ISDN represents the means to integrate computing and communication technologies into a single framework. We will discuss ISDN in Section 2.6.

2.2.3.2 Digitizing Techniques and Codecs

Figure 2.9 shows a typical digital network with analog/digital (A/D) converters and interfaces. Digital data can be directly fed into a communication medium without any modulation/demodulation. However, the voice and video signals are analog and need to be digitized through A/D converters known as codecs (coders-encoders). The A/D technique commonly used is pulse code modulation (PCM). The basic principle of digitizing an analog signal is that the signal is sampled at twice the signal bandwidth to faithfully represent the signal. This is based on the following Nyquist formula:

$$\text{No. of digital samples per second} = 2 \times \text{bandwidth of analog signal}$$

To digitize voice, 8000 samples are taken in a second because the maximum bandwidth of human voice is 4000 Hz (the human voice is roughly filtered at 3000 Hz,

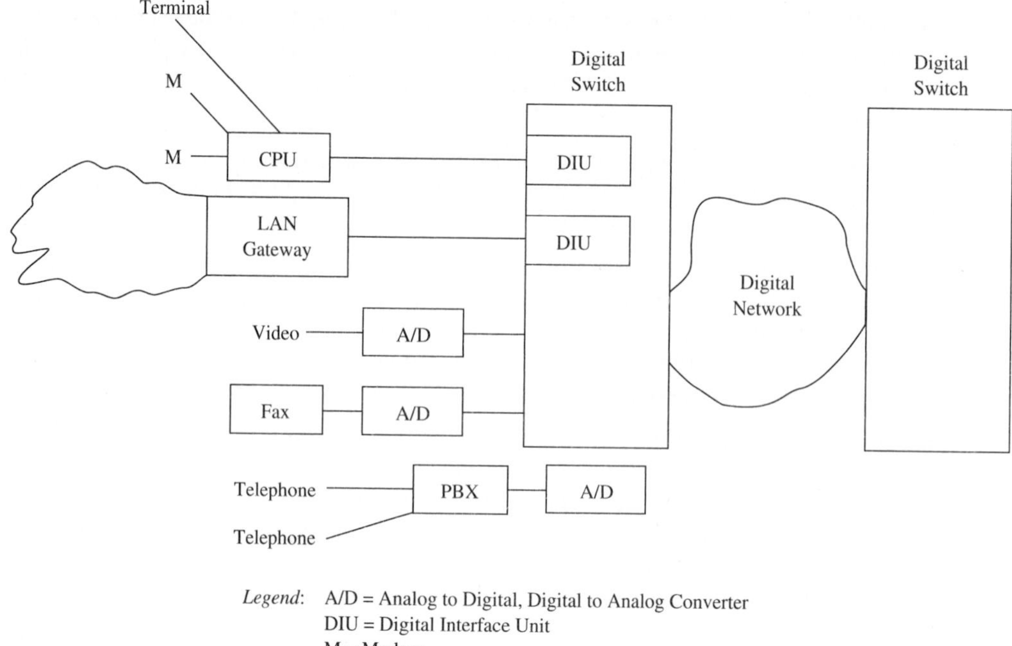

FIGURE 2.9 A Typical Digital Network

but this sampling rate improves the range). The pulse code modulation (PCM) digitizing technique consists of the following steps:

- *Sampling*: The analog signal is digitized at 8000 per second.
- *Quantizing*: Each sampled signal amplitude is converted to a level. PCM allows 128 levels of signal amplitude.
- *Encoding*: the amplitude is represented by bits. One byte (8 bits) is used to encode 128 levels (7 bits to represent 128 levels and 1 bit for supervisory and control use).

Thus one voice channel is converted to 64,000 bits per second (8000 × 8 data bits = 64,000 bps of data). This is the main reason why most digital transmission facilities provide 64 Kbps channels (each 64-Kbps channel can be used to carry one human telephone conversation). A 64-Kbps channel is termed a DS-0 channel.

Let us illustrate PCM by using another example in which one minute of voice signal needs to be stored after digitizing. First, there will be a need for 60 × 8000 = 480,000 samples. Since each sample occupies 8 bits (1 byte), the total storage required for one minute of digitized voice is 480,000 bytes. This illustrates that digitizing voice has important performance considerations—PCM would generate 8000 × 8 bits (i.e., 8000 bytes of data for only one second of human voice). Thus transmission of long conversations over communication lines poses large storage requirements especially if the voice needs to be stored at intermediate nodes. Many variants of PCM are being developed to address these problems <Black 1987, Chapter 7, Verma 1990, Chapter 1>.

In analog systems, the commonly used multiplexing scheme is FDM (frequency division multiplexing). In digital systems, the commonly used multiplexing scheme is TDM (time division multiplexing). In TDM systems, bits or small clumps of bits from different sources are interleaved on the same communication medium. *Framing* is used to identify which bits belong to which source so that the signals can be separated at the receiving side. Many variants of TDM have been developed over the years. Digital switches such as the PBXs (private branch exchanges) perform TDM so that one line can be shared by many digital users. In some cases, computing devices perform time division multiplexing so that one cable can be shared by many devices.

2.2.3.3 T Carriers (T1, T2, T3, T4 Lines)

Currently, the U.S. common carriers (telephone companies) provide the digital services (DS-1 to DS-4) through a family of *T Carriers*, which are offered as T1, T2, T3, and T4 carriers (see Table 2.1). The T carriers have been developed as standards for digital communications by the predivestiture Bell System.

The T1 carrier was developed by Bell Labs in the mid-1960s to operate over twisted pair cables and has been available to the general public since 1980. The T1 system supports 24 voice graded PCM channels. The total capacity of a T1 carrier is 1.544 Mbps. T1 carrier is used frequently to interconnect local area networks (LANs) of an enterprise, where each LAN may serve an office or a building of the enterprise. A subscriber can send data to remote sites by using *fractional* T1 facilities, which allow use of data rates starting at 56 Kbps up to 1.544 Mbps, in 56-Kbps increments. For example, two remote sites can exchange information at data rates of 56 Kbps, 128 Kbps, 184 Kbps, . . .1.544 Mbps.

The T2 carrier supports 96 channels with a total capacity of 6.3 Mbps. The T3 system supports 672 voice channels with a total capacity of 44.7 Mbps. The T4M system is the largest digital carrier, with 4032 voice channels with a total capacity of 274 Mbps. The T4M carrier can handle a considerable amount of traffic.

The digital carriers in other countries do not match the T1–T4 digital carriers used in the United States. Table 2.2 shows the European and the Japanese digital carriers. It can be seen that the European and the Japanese have a wider range than the U.S. carriers.

A new hierarchy of digital services, known as Synchronous Optical Networks (SONET), has been proposed by Bellcore (Bell Communications Research). SONET is a fiber-optic-based standard which provides a hierarchy of services ranging from

TABLE 2.1 U.S. Digital T-Carrier Services (Introduced by the Bell System)

Service Type	*Carrier Type*	*Million Bits per Second (Mbps)*	*No. of Voice Channels*
DS-1	T1	1.544	24
DS-1c	T1C	3.152	48
DS-2	T2	6.312	96
DS-3	T3	44.736	672
DS-4	T4M	274.176	4032

TABLE 2.2 Overseas Digital Carrier Services

Europe		*Japan*	
Carrier	*Speed (Mbps)*	*Carrier*	*Speed (Mbps)*
1	2.048	1	1.544
2	8.448	2	6.312
3	34.304	3	32.064
4	139.254	4	97.728
5	585.148	5	397.200

51.84 Mbps to 2488 Mbps—much higher speeds than the existing T-carrier technology. We will discuss SONET in Section 2.7.3.

The principles and theoretical foundations of digital communications have been discussed widely in the literature. An extensive discussion of T carriers, digital interfaces, digital interface units, digital synchronization and multiplexing for digital systems can be found in Powers <1990>. A readable overview of digital communications can be found in Black <1987, Chapter 7>. Verma <1990, Chapter 1> provides a good theoretical foundation of digital communications. Bartree <1986> features many chapters on various aspects of digital communications.

2.2.4 Communication Media Characteristics

Communication media are used in networks to transmit data over short or long distances. Selection and design of communication media play an important role in the cost, reliability and performance of networks. Communication media with high bandwidths and signal/noise ratios are desirable as evidenced by the following fundamental formula, derived by Claude Shannon in 1948:

$$\text{Maximum data rate (bps)} = \text{carrier BW} \times \log_2 (1 + \text{signal/noise})$$

Thus increasing the bandwidth and/or the signal to noise ratio can improve the data rate. Consider, for example, a voice-graded line with signal to noise ratio of 1000 (a common line characteristic):

$$\text{BW} = 3000 \text{ Hz for a voice graded telephone line}$$
$$\log_2 (1 + 1000) = 10 \text{ (approximately)}$$
$$\text{maximum data rate} = 3000 \times 10 = 30{,}000 \text{ bps}$$

To improve the maximum data rate, the bandwidth and/or the signal to noise ratio needs to be improved. High bandwidth media are also desirable because they can support several users. For example, several telephone users can be supported on one high bandwidth cable. Different communication media with different bandwidths, signal/noise ratios, reliability and cost are currently being used in various networks. Examples of the commonly used media are open wire pairs, twisted pair cables, coaxial cables, fiber optic systems, and wireless media.

Open Wire Pairs. This is the oldest, and at present almost obsolete, communication medium. Open wire pairs are low cost bare copper wires which were installed in the early part of this century for telephones and telegraphs. Some of these wires can be still found in some rural areas. Wire pairs are being replaced at present because they are susceptible to damage by weather and suffer from attenuation (signal loss) and crosstalk (interference) problems.

Twisted Pair Cables. These are used extensively in telephone circuits in buildings and trunks. Several wires are insulated and enclosed in a cable. A twisted pair cable may include up to 3000 wire pairs with a bandwidth up to 250 KHz. These cables do have better performance than open wires, but the signal/noise ratio is low due to crosstalk noise. Twisted pair cables are good for short-distance communications.

Coaxial Cables. These cables have been around since the early 1940s and are used extensively in local area networks, long distance toll trunks, urban areas, and cable TV. The technology consists of a single central conductor, surrounded by a circular insulation layer, and a conductive shield. Coaxial cables have high bandwidth (up to 400 MHz) with much higher-quality data transmission than the twisted pair cables. For example, a coaxial cable can support over 10,000 voice circuits by using the frequency division multiplexing technique mentioned previously. With different multiplexing techniques, coaxial cables can deliver high data speeds (above 10 Mbps) and support many data, voice, and video channels. This technology is limited due to signal loss at high frequencies.

Optical Fiber. This communication medium is showing more promise and potential for very high data transmission applications. The optical fiber uses light rays instead of electronic pulses for message transmission. A fiber optic cable is very thin, usually resembling a human hair, which uses special *cladding* so that the light rays cannot escape the cable and thus travel down the cable in a reflective path. The light source used in fiber optic is usually a laser or a light emitting diode (LED). Fiber optics show very high frequency ranges (higher than 20,000 MHz). Because of this high bandwidth, a single fiber optic cable can support over 30,000 telephone lines and can transmit data over 400 Mbps (remember the cable carrying all these telephone lines resembles a single human hair strand). Due to their very light weight and high bandwidths, fiber optic use is growing dramatically. Other reasons for the popularity of fiber optics are their resilience to fire and gaseous combustion (light waves do not generate electrical sparks), very low signal loss and error rates, high security characteristics due to the difficulties in tapping fiber optic cables, and decreasing costs of fiber optic devices. It should be noted that, at the time of this writing, a fiber optic connector is much more expensive than a copper cable tap. Thus the largest application of fiber optic cable is in enterprise "backbone networks," which interconnect many networks (see Fig. 2.10).

Wireless Media. Communication through satellites is the foundation of global wireless communications and global networks, in which users communicate with each other over long distances without a physical wire between them. A satellite is essentially a radio relay in the sky which receives signals from transmitting stations on earth and relays these signals back to the receiving stations on the earth (see Fig.

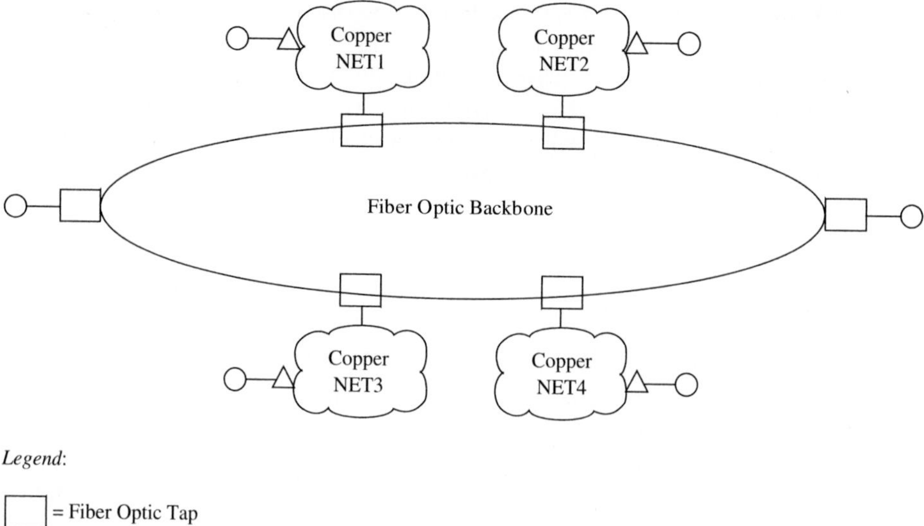

FIGURE 2.10 A Typical Fiber Optic Network

2.11). The satellites are placed in the earth orbit at 22,300 miles, called the Clark Belt after the famous science-fiction writer who first envisioned satellites in 1945. Once placed in the Clark Belt, the satellite rotates at the same speed as the earth's rotations so the satellite does not appear to move (called geosynchronization). Thus the sending and receiving dishes can stay pointed to the satellite without any readjustments. Satellites can provide high communications capacity and can support several thousand voice channels. However, each satellite message encounters a 0.25-second delay because of the distance a message has to travel between a sender and a receiver. In a satellite communication system, the transmission cost is independent of the distance between the sender and receiver (two stations 100 miles apart or 1000 miles apart still have to travel 22,300 miles to and from the satellite). Because of this, satellite

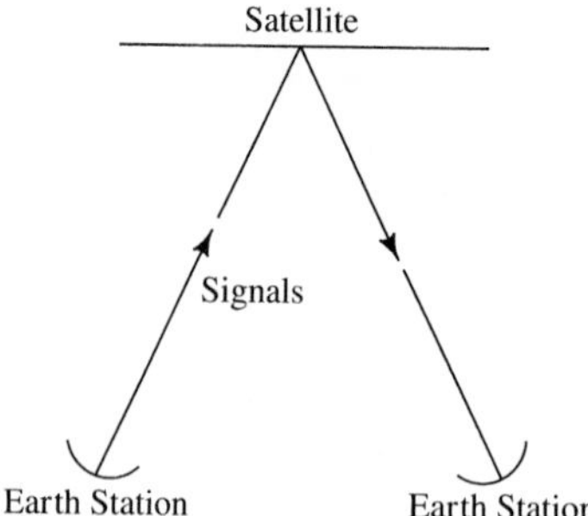

FIGURE 2.11 Satellite Transmissions

communication systems are used to broadcast (i.e., send a message to several receivers simultaneously). Use of satellites, especially the broadcast services, presents serious security problems which require extensive encryption/decryption, such as scrambling and well-protected keys. In addition to satellite systems, cellular telephones and residential cordless telephones (wireless systems) have been introduced in the mid-1980s. In cellular systems, the location of a sender/receiver is unknown prior to start of communication and can change during the conversation (see Section 2.7.8).

2.2.5 Network Layout and Topologies

Network topology is concerned with how to interconnect N devices together by using some type of communication medium. The following network topologies are common (see Fig. 2.12).

The fully connected network, shown in Fig. 2.12a, connects every device to other devices. For N devices, the number of connections are $N(N-1)/2$. So, to fully connect 10 devices, 45 cables will be needed. This option gives very high reliability of the network because if one cable fails, the message can be routed through another cable. However, it is too expensive for most practical cases and is used rarely.

The tree topology, depicted in Fig. 2.12b, connects the devices to a hub, which passes the messages from one device to the other. As we will see, tree topologies are very common in wide area networks because they are easy to monitor and diagnose/correct. For example, several terminals may be connected to a terminal server, or a terminal controller, which in turn is connected to a computer. Despite their popularity, tree topologies have two main weaknesses. First, if the hub fails, then the subnet managed by the hub fails. Second, the number of devices supported depends on the number of communication slots in the hub. For example, if the hub has only eight slots, then another hub will need to be purchased for the ninth device.

A ring connects the devices to form a loop, as illustrated in Fig. 2.12c. In earlier ring systems, each device on the ring served as a relay in which the message was received from one slot and sent out on the other. In these cases, if a device

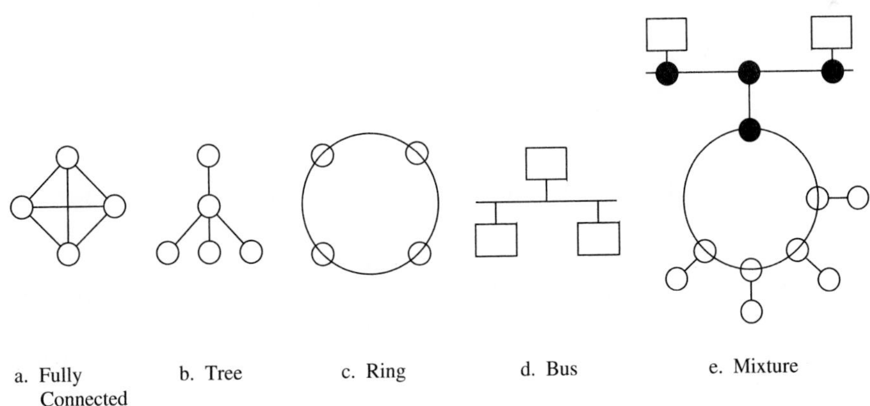

FIGURE 2.12 Example Topologies

a. Asynchronous Communications

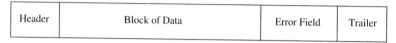

Start Bit	Character Bits	Stop Bit	Start Bit	Character Bits	Stop Bit	Start Bit	Character Bits	Stop Bit

b. Synchronous Communications

Header	Block of Data	Error Field	Trailer

FIGURE 2.13 Synchronous and Asynchronous Communications

failed, then the whole network failed. In modern rings, devices are attached to the ring cable so that if a device fails, the ring continues to work. The main advantage of a ring is that the number of devices connected on the network is not limited by the number of slots in any device (each device may use at the most two slots to be connected to the ring).[2] We will see that rings are used commonly in local area networks.

The bus topology, shown in Fig. 2.12d, connects the devices to a cable which is terminated at both ends. All devices on the bus can "listen" to the messages being passed on the bus and insert/retrieve messages whenever needed. The bus topologies are commonly used in local area networks. Perhaps the best example of the bus topology is the Ethernet local area networks, which will be discussed later. In addition, many factory networks, such as the Manufacturing Automation Protocol (MAP), also use bus topologies.

In addition to these basic network topologies, many mixtures can exist in large networks. For example, a backbone network may be a fiber optic ring to which many devices and local area networks are connected in a tree format, treating the backbone as a hub (see Fig. 2.12e). In small networks with high data rates, it is possible to think of devices to be fully connected logically even if the physical topology is a tree, bus, or a ring. This makes it easier to model a network. The choice of a network topology is a difficult problem which depends on many factors such as the physical location of the work activities, the type of devices that need to be connected, cost considerations, response time requirements, availability requirements, and vendor preferences. See Bertsekas <1992> and Ellis <1986> for a review of the approaches.

2.2.6 Asynchronous Versus Synchronous Transmission and Full/Half Duplex

The information transferred over a communication medium can be asynchronous or synchronous. In asynchronous transmission, also called start-stop transmission, data is transferred one character at a time, at an undeterministic or random time. For the start and end of a character to be recognized by the receiver, each character is

[2]Many ring-oriented LANs are actually wired as trees.

surrounded by a start and a stop bit; hence the name start-stop (see Fig. 2.13a). Asynchronous communications were introduced in the old telegraphic days when the start and stop bits physically started and stopped the paper tape mechanical processes on the receiver side. Asynchronous communications are still used very frequently in terminal communications. The sending and receiving logic needed for asynchronous communications is very simple and can be implemented economically in simple devices. The main difficulty with the asynchronous communications is that if a start bit is not recognized, then the whole character may be misread. Due to this, asynchronous communications are not used at high speeds because the chances of losing data bits are greater at higher speeds.

In synchronous data transmission, data is transmitted in blocks of many characters. Header and trailer characters are attached to each block so that the receiver can recognize the start or stop of a block (see Fig. 2.13b). Common examples of synchronous transmission are the transmission of each terminal screen as a single block and file transfers which send and receive many file records as blocks of data. Synchronous communications can operate at much higher speeds than asynchronous because the whole block can be transmitted by using one send command. The logic of generating the block headers and trailer fields is more complicated. In addition, sophisticated error-checking fields are generated and verified. The formats of the headers, trailers, and error-checking fields depend on the synchronization scheme being employed. Some systems, for example, include the start-stop bits in the data block, in addition to the block headers, trailers and error-checking fields. We will review the common synchronous transmission schemes in the next chapter.

The information can flow over a communication medium in one of the following modes:

- *Simplex*: One-way communications, always. This mode is rarely used today.
- *Half duplex*: Two-way communication, one at a time. This mode is used very commonly in many instances.
- *Full duplex*: Two-way communications, simultaneously. This is the fastest mode of information transmission.

It should be noted that to provide a full duplex path between two end-devices, all intermediate devices and media on the communication path must operate in full duplex mode.

2.2.7 Data Encryption and Compression Techniques

Data encryption has been used for a number of years in military applications to mask the military messages so that the hostile interveners could not understand the messages. Due to the increase of sensitive information handled by computer systems (e.g., financial data, confidential records), data encryption/decryption has become a major area of active work. When the data is transmitted over communication channels, it is possible for someone to tap a channel and gain unauthorized access. Thus, data encryption in communication systems is of vital importance. The objectives of data encryption are

- Privacy
- Authentication
- Data integrity.

In the simplest case, data is transformed by a key into an encrypted message. The encrypted message is then transmitted and decrypted on the other side by using the same key. Encryption/decryption can be performed by hardware and/or software. Modern computing systems have the ability to implement very sophisticated encryption/decryption techniques. The same encryption can be used on all data in a system, or encryption keys can be more "personalized." For example, instead of using the same encryption/decryption key on all data from all stations in a network, each station or user can use its own encryption/decryption key. A user can have his or her own encryption card which is inserted into a workstation before the user logs on. This card encrypts the data before sending it across the network. The encrypted data can be read only by those users or programs with access to the same encryption key.

A discussion of the encryption/decryption algorithms is beyond the scope of this book. A good overview of these algorithms can be found in Tannenbaum <1988, pp. 494–97>.

Data compression techniques are used to reduce the size of data that needs to be sent across communication channels. For example, instead of sending 200 consecutive blanks across a network, a data compression technique can send one blank character with a multiplier of 200. Data compression techniques can significantly reduce the transmission time. For example, I used a data compression routine three years ago which reduced the size of data to be sent from 95 million bytes to 7 million bytes, thus cutting the transmission time by 90 percent. This raised interesting tradeoffs between increasing link speed/cost versus the compression/decompression processing delays and costs. The common data compression techniques are as follows:

- *Data string encoding*. Commonly used data strings can be encoded for data transmission. For example, customer names can be represented by customer IDs for data transmission.
- *Word encoding*. Some words occur more often than others in natural languages. For example, *the* occurs more frequently in English than many other words. Such words can be encoded by using bit combinations for data transmission.
- *Frequency encoding*. Some words, or bit strings, are used repeatedly. For example, blank characters appear consecutively in many data files. A blank character followed by a frequency count can be used easily in such systems.

For a detailed discussion of data compression algorithms, see Tannenbaum <1988, pp. 490–94>.

2.3 Wide Area Networks

Wide area networks (WANs) are the oldest form of communication networks. WANs use the telecommunication facilities of common carriers (telephone companies) to exchange data between computing devices. We briefly review the telecommunication networks (networks owned by the telephone companies) before describing the WAN components, switching systems, and WAN design issues.

2.3.1 Telecommunications Overview

Since the first telephone patent by Alexander Graham Bell in 1876, more than 600 million telephones have been installed throughout the world <Datapro 1987>. This growth in the telecommunications industry, expected to continue at 6 percent annually, has led to large telecommunications networks with a variety of terminating equipments (e.g., telephones, computer devices), transmission facilities (communication lines), and switches. The telecommunication networks are designed to minimize the cost of end-to-end connections. For example, to fully connect 100 phones directly with each other, we would need about 5000 lines.[3] Naturally, the number of direct lines between 600 million telephones would be more than a normal human being would like to imagine.

Figure 2.14 shows a typical telecommunications network design. Most of this network is owned by the common carriers (telephone companies). On the customer premise (an office, a house), the user interacts with telephone equipment and computing devices which are connected to the local central office through a subscriber loop. A customer premise may also include other equipment such as local area networks and a private branch exchange (PBX). A PBX, also called a computerized branch exchange (CBX), routes the customer premise calls internally without going to the subscriber loop. The PBX provide the telephone extensions in office buildings (if you call an extension within your office, the PBX in your building routes the call to another phone in the building). A PBX/CBX may be used for all voice and data communications within an office.

The subscriber loop, also known as the local loop, consists of the wires, poles, conduits and other equipment that connects the customer premise equipment to the telephone company's central office. Before deregulation, the telephone companies had a monopoly on the local loop. At present, customers can use cable TV or microwave radio to bypass the local loop.

The local central office, often called an end-office, is the point where a local loop terminates. In a metropolitan area, many local central offices are located based on the population densities. A switch at the end-office routes the call to another end-office either by directly connecting to the end-office (if within the same area code) or through the interexchange switch. The telephone companies divide their service areas into exchanges, where an exchange roughly refers to a city or part of a city. The interexchange switches route calls between exchanges over trunks. These trunks are

[3]This is obtained by using the $N(N - 1)/2$ formula, for $N = 100$.

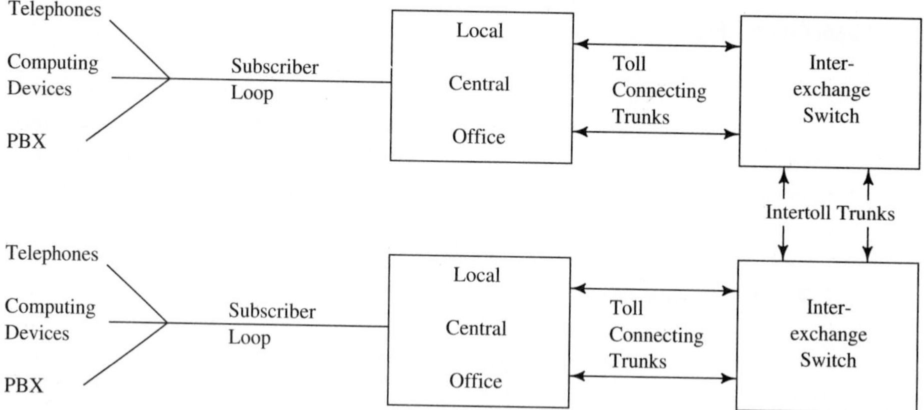

FIGURE 2.14 A Telecommunications Network

called toll trunks because they connect outside the free calling areas. The toll trunks are fast transmission facilities, at present almost all digital.

Many books and articles describe the telecommunications networks in more detail. James Martin's book, "Telecommunications and the Computer," first published in 1969 and now in its 3rd edition <Martin 1990>, is an excellent introduction to this area. The four volumes of Encyclopedia of Telecommunications by Froehlich and Kent <Froehlich 1990–1991>, the telecommunications handbook by Green <Green 1986>, the Datapro Report <Datapro 1987>, and survey papers such as <Falconer 1986> give a good state-of-the-market overview. Hawley <1991> gives a historical perspective on the U.S. telephone loop. The *IEEE Communications Magazine*, March 1991 issue is devoted to the telephone subscriber loop and should be consulted for engineering aspects of the telecommunication systems.

2.3.2 WAN Components

Figure 2.15 shows typical wide area network configurations. A conventional wide area network in which a mainframe is connected to many devices over a WAN is shown in Fig. 2.15a. The configuration shown in Fig. 2.15b shows a more contemporary view of WANs where many terminals, computers, and local area networks are connected through a packet switching system. We will concentrate on Fig. 2.15a to illustrate the various WAN components. The packet switching configuration is explained in the next section. Many of the existing WANs use the T1 carrier lines described earlier. As we will see in our discussion of high-speed (broadband) networks, the data rate of evolving WANs easily exceeds 100 Mbps.

A *front-end processor* (FEP) is a computer which controls the wide area network. The purpose of the FEP is to relieve the mainframe from handling the interrupts generated by the network devices. Without an FEP, each line is connected directly to the mainframe and the mainframe has to take the CPU cycles away from the applications to manage the network. Most of the available FEPs can connect between 200 to 500 communication lines and have processing power and main storage

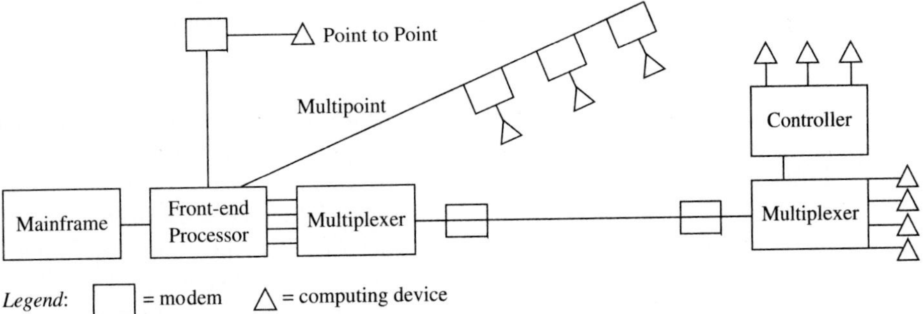

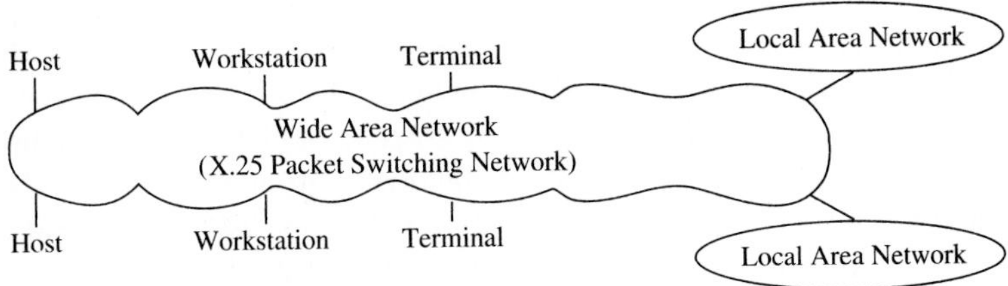

FIGURE 2.15 Typical Wide Area Network Configurations

to minimize the attention needed by the mainframe for network control. Some FEPs are special purpose communication processors (e.g., the IBM 372x FEPs) while others are general purpose computers (e.g., an HP3000) which are programmed for communications control.

The computing devices such as terminals (dumb, smart, and/or programmable), printers, sensors, laptop/desktop computers, minicomputers, and mainframes are the end-points in a WAN and are interconnected through telecommunication lines.

- These lines may be switched (dial up) or leased (permanently connected) between the end-points. The advantage of the dial-up lines is that a user can call from any location. However, the switched lines are voice graded telephone lines which are not good for reliable and fast data communications. (Modern modems are overcoming these limitations <Drefler 1992>.) A user may choose from different switched line rates such as WATS and 800 numbers. The leased lines guarantee a user the access between two end-points and can operate at T1 and higher speeds. However, these lines are expensive, especially when the end-points are communicating only occasionally.
- The lines may be point-to-point or multipoint. In a point-to-point system, one line connects two end-points. In a multipoint system, many devices share the same line. This is illustrated in Fig. 2.15a. The multipoint lines save modems and lines but are harder to debug in case of errors.

- The lines may use half duplex or full duplex transmission modes. To take advantage of full duplex lines, the software on the two end-points must operate in full duplex mode.

In the simplest case, a computing device may use a line (leased or switched) to communicate with a remotely located computer through modems, as shown in Fig. 2.15a. In many cases, dumb terminals are connected to a *controller* (also called a terminal server) where the terminal intelligence (e.g., cursor movement, highlighting) is embedded in the controller. Controllers basically connect several similar terminals together, as shown in Fig. 2.15a. An example of a terminal controller is the IBM 3274 controller which connects the IBM 3270 terminals, or IBM PCs which emulate the 3270.

Multiplexors are used so that one high capacity line can be shared by many slower devices. A multiplexor takes the input from several devices and sends it on the same line. On the other side, another multiplexor performs the reverse operation, as shown in Fig. 2.15a. For example, consider 10 stations in Chicago that need to communicate with a mainframe in New York. Instead of purchasing 10 long-distance lines, a designer can select a channel at 56,000 bps between Chicago and New York and use a multiplexor on both ends. The number of devices supported by a multiplexor depend on the type of multiplexing technique being used. The following simple formula can be used for rough estimates:

$$s_1 + s_2 + s_3 + \ldots s_n =< S/k$$

where S is the data rate in bits per second of the shared line, $s_1, s_2, \ldots s_n$ are the data rates of the devices being multiplexed, and k is a constant dependent on the multiplexing technique. For frequency division multiplexing (FDM), $k = 1$ because the bandwidth of the shared line is subdivided into the bandwidths needed by the devices. Modern multiplexers use statistical multiplexing techniques to allow many more devices (sometime four times more, yielding $k = 4$) to share the same line. A large number of T1 multiplexors are commercially available to connect analog and digital devices to T1 line. Details about multiplexors and multiplexing techniques can be found elsewhere <Black 1987, Stallings 1991>.

2.3.3 Switching Systems (Circuit and Packet Switching)

A switch determines a path between a source and a sink. As stated in Section 2.3.1, a telecommunication network uses switches to route traffic between various local and interexchange offices. Most computer users do not need to know how their messages are being switched and routed in large WANs. However, the concepts are of value from a communications network principles point of view. We illustrate the main switching techniques by using the simplified network shown in Fig. 2.16.

Circuit switching is the oldest switching method in which same path is used during a session. Circuit switching systems are used in telephone networks at

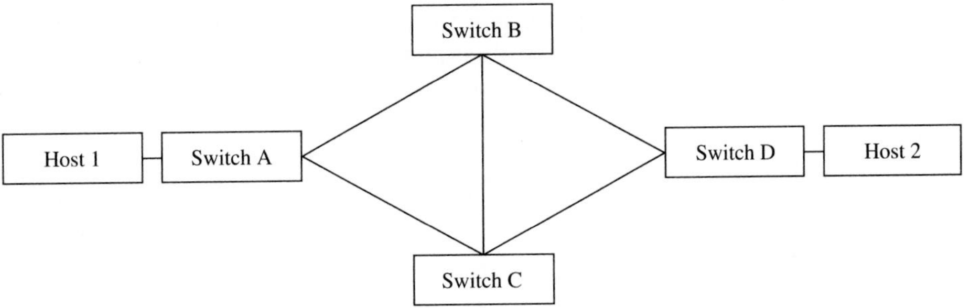

FIGURE 2.16 Example of a Switching System

various switching centers. The path between two customer premises is established at the "call setup" time. For example, the path between the two computers in Fig. 2.16 may be A-B-D. Once this path has been established, all data and voice messages travel this path. If a problem is encountered during a session, then the user must disconnect and then reestablish the session. This seems to work well for telephone conversations but causes problems in data transmission. Consequently, circuit switching is not a favored choice for most business data communications applications.

Message switching systems are used in some data communication applications. In these systems, a path is selected for each message. For example, three messages between the two computers in Fig. 2.16 may be routed on paths A-B-D, A-C-D, and A-B-C-D. The message switch operates as a "store and forward" system in which a message is stored at each switch and then forwarded to a path based on traffic congestion and availability of the path. Message switches can handle priority messages so that a higher-priority message can be sent before lower-priority messages. The programs at each switch review the message queues and forward the messages with higher priority.

Packet switching systems are currently the most popular systems for wide area data communications. In these systems, a message is broken into "packets," which are sent out to the network. The packet switches select the path for each packet and then assemble the packets into the original message at the receiving end.

The principle of packet switching can be illustrated by using a military example. If a caravan of 20 trucks has to pass through a city, it is better to break this big caravan into smaller "packets" of trucks (say 4 per packet) and then let each packet find its way to the destination. This technique can reduce total transmission time. For example, if a message is broken into five packets and the five packets are transmitted simultaneously, then theoretically the message can be transmitted in one fifth of the time needed to transmit the complete message. However, we need to keep the following things in mind:

- Enough paths must be available for the packets to travel in parallel. For example, in the network shown in Fig. 2.16, only four paths (A-B-D, A-C-D, A-B-C-D,

A-C-B-D) exist between the two computers. It would not be beneficial to break up a message into 10 packets when only four paths are available.

- The processing required to break up the message into packets and then to reassemble them on the other side adds overhead and delays.
- Additional logic and intelligence is required to detect out of sequence packets and lost packets.

Design of a packet switching system involves many problems of academic interest: optimal route selection for the packets (this is similar to the bus routing problems in operations research), optimal packet size selection, and development of protocols for proper sequencing control. A discussion of these topics is beyond the scope of this book. The interested reader is referred to Tannenbaum <1988> and Stallings <1991> for more details.

At present, many packet data networks (PDNs), also called "value added networks," are commercially available for subscribers to use. Many of these networks provide alternate paths for redundancy and not necessarily for traffic optimization. These networks use X.25, a standard discussed in the next chapter, which defines the formats and message exchange rules between switches. Examples of such networks are GTE's Telenet, Tymshare's Tymnet, and Hewlett-Packard's HPNet. Figure 2.17 shows how a subscriber can use such a network. Basically, the user devices are connected to the PDN through packet assembly/disassembly devices (PADs) which build the packets on one side and then assemble them into a message. The procedure to use a PDN is as follows:

- User dials a PDN access port.
- User goes through a logon procedure to access the network.
- A destination computer is specified.
- The data is sent through the PDN.

Packet switching networks are becoming more economical with evolving technologies. In practice, packet switches are expected to be the main delivery

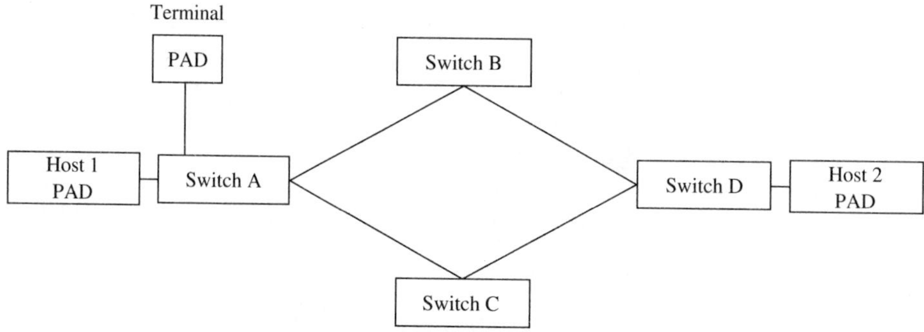

FIGURE 2.17 Example of a Packet Switching Network

mechanisms for wide area networks of the future. In particular, digitized data, voice, and images need to use one path independent of data type and packet switching seems to be the prime candidates <Mayo 1985>. The notion of breaking up human voice into packets which are sent on parallel paths and eventually reassembled on the receiver telephone may be difficult to digest but it indicates the power of digital communications. In these cases, we need to consider the impact of network delays on human voice and the effect of storing digitized voice (we had seen that one minute of digitized human voice can take 480 Kbytes, incompressed). We will consider the fast packet switches being developed for future networks in Section 2.7.

2.3.4 WAN Design Issues

Design of a WAN involves a large number of choices and tradeoffs. Let us consider a simple example to highlight the main decisions. Let us assume that a personal computer (PC) needs to access a database located on a mainframe. We have the following potential scenarios:

- If the PC is within 400 feet of the mainframe, then an RS232C interface which works within 50 to 400 feet at 20 Kbps data rate can be used to directly attach the PC to the mainframe.
- If the PC is within 10 miles of the mainframe, then we can use a limited distance modem over a leased line because these modems are relatively inexpensive.
- After 10 miles, but within the same area code, we can use a dial-up line or a leased line (point-to-point or multipoint).
- For different area codes, dial up or leased lines involve long-distance connection and can be expensive. A user may choose to purchase a multiplexor, which can allow many PCs in the same office to share one long distance line. The user may also choose a packet switching system to transmit data.
- The line speed needed to satisfy the response time requirement depends on the number of queries being generated by the PC and the speed/cost tradeoffs.
- If a large number of PCs need to connect to the mainframe, then the choices are to select a suitable multiplexor, location of the multiplexor, how many devices are local, how many are remote, etc. In addition, the PC may be connected to a local area network which is connected to a WAN.

In general, large WAN design problems are too complex to be solved through exact optimization techniques. For a detailed discussion of this topic, the interested reader is referred to the books *Transmission Performance of Evolving Telecommunications Networks*, by Gruber and Williams, Artech House Books, 1992 and *LAN/MAN Optimization Techniques*, by Van Norman, Artech House Books, 1992. *Designing Data Networks* <Ellis 1986> also has useful design calculations. Many sophisticated WAN network design tools are commercially available. For a state of the market review, see Van Norman <1990>.

2.4 Local Area Networks

2.4.1. Overview

Simply stated, a local area network (LAN) is a network of data communication devices within a small area (typically less than 10 kilometers). The main characteristics of local area networks, also called local networks, are as follows:

- *Private ownership*. The LAN equipment, including the communication media, are privately owned. A legal restriction in the United States does not allow individuals to string cables over public property (underground cables are allowed). All above-ground communication facilities are provided by the common carriers (AT&T, MCI, Regional Telephone Companies, cable TV companies). Thus if you want to communicate between two houses located across a road, you must purchase the common carrier facilities (i.e., you do not privately own the communication medium). This leads to an interesting way to look at a LAN: a LAN is independent of the common carriers. If you happen to own a city, then your LAN may cover the entire city. For the rest of us, our LANs may not go beyond a room.
- *High data rates*. The data rates of LANs are much higher than the common wide area networks. For example, most wide area networks use data rates ranging from 1200 bps (bits per second) to 1.54 Mbps, while most local area networks use data rates between 1 Mbps to 100 Mbps.
- *Low error rates*. The error rates in LANs are much lower than the typical wide area networks. This is mainly because of the short distance and the use of simple communication devices in LANs.
- *Broadcast services*. LANs typically broadcast the messages to receivers, in contrast to WANs, which usually select a receiver before sending a message. Broadcasts, if misused and disregarded, can cause many administrative problems.

Figure 2.18 shows a typical LAN in which many devices are connected together through communication media such as twisted pair cables, coaxial cables, or fiber optic cables. The devices on the LAN may be personal computers, workstations, terminals, printers, and/or sensors. These devices are interconnected by using the bus, ring, or tree topologies. A LAN "server" is a computer on the LAN which allows the users to

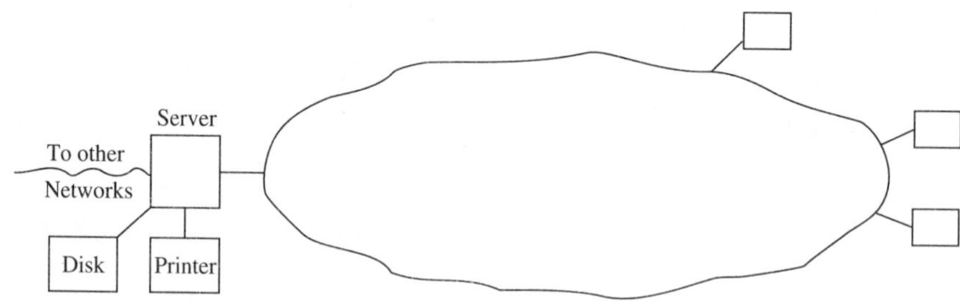

FIGURE 2.18 A Typical Local Area Network

share common resources. A server may be a personal computer, a workstation, a specialized computer, or a minicomputer. Common examples of LAN servers are as follows:

- *Printer sharing*. The computers and terminals on a LAN need to share one high-quality (Laserjet) printer because it is expensive to purchase a printer for each computer. A LAN provides access to a common printer (say, LPT2) which can be used by any LAN device.
- *Disk sharing*. Many LANs are configured so that one computer (LAN server) has a large disk on which many packages are installed. Many small computers with little or no disk storage (diskless workstations) access the server to retrieve the needed software. The LAN server provides another drive (say drive Z:) which can be accessed by any computer on the LAN.
- *File/database servers*. One file/database may be shared by several LAN users. The file/database server coordinates the data access for integrity control. For example, the server may lock the data resource at the file level (if one user is updating the file, then no one can access the file) or at a record level (deny access to the record being updated).

In many cases, a single server on a LAN provides the print, disk, and file/database services (e.g., the Novell Netware Server). It is also possible to assign the servers to many computers on a LAN.

In the last decade, a large number of LANs have emerged due to the replacement of terminals with microcomputers and office automation and word processing applications. In the early 1980s, more than 50 vendors were marketing LANs on different devices, using different communication media, protocols, and topologies. The IEEE 802 Committee on LANs was formed in 1980 to develop standards for LANs. The main mission of this Committee is similar to the mission of the International Standards Organization (ISO) Committee on Open System Interconnection (we will discuss ISO in the next chapter). The IEEE 802 Committee has been working closely with the ISO Committee and has endorsed the seven-layer ISO Reference Model, which we will discuss in the next chapter.

The IEEE 802 Committee has developed standards for communications (e.g., baseband and broadband), discussed in Section 2.4.2. In addition, techniques for message transmission and recognition have been approved (e.g., token passing and CSMA/CD). These techniques, called data link control techniques, will be discussed in Section 2.4.3. Other standards have been proposed by the IEEE 802 Committee by subdividing the lowest two layers of the ISO model into four sublayers. We will review these standards in Section 2.4.4.

When a LAN package is purchased, it may need cables; adapter cards, which connect the cables to the devices; LAN server software, which is used for sharing the resources (printers, disks, files); and station software, which is installed at each computer attached to the LAN. A LAN package may contain additional software such as NetBIOS, which is a high level software interface to send/receive data to/from the LAN adapter cards. We will review some of the available LANs in Section 2.4.5 to gain some practical insights into LAN operations. Section 2.4.6 reviews the LAN selection and design considerations.

2.4.2 Baseband and Broadband LANs

Baseband LANs use digital signals to transfer data between LAN devices. A baseband LAN uses digital signals by "pressing" the data to the communication medium so that the data itself becomes signals. This is a restricted use of the word *baseband* because in general communication systems *baseband* refers to the transmission of original analog or digital signals, without any modulation. Due to their digital nature, the baseband LANs are not suitable for voice and video. Baseband LANs use a relatively inexpensive 50-ohm thin coaxial cable. The thicker 75-ohm cable used in the cable TV systems is not needed for baseband systems. The entire bandwidth of the LAN cable is used for transmission of data. The baseband systems are simple, reliable and inexpensive because there is no need for any modulation/demodulation devices. However, baseband systems are limited to about 1 kilometer. Many commercially available LANs use baseband. Some of the best known examples are the Ethernet LANs and the IBM token ring LAN.

Broadband LANs modulate data before transmission. This is also a restricted use of the term *broadband* because in general communication systems, the term *broadband* refers to a channel with bandwidth larger than 4 KHz (voice line bandwidth). Due to the modulation/demodulation needed, broadband LANs need modems, sometime referred to as radio frequency (R/F) modulators. Each signal is assigned a frequency range and different channels are assigned through frequency division multiplexing. The off-the-shelf cable TV 75 ohm coaxial cables are used commonly in broadband LANs. Broadband LANs can operate on more than 10 kilometer distance range and can support several channels. They can also support multiple subnets and protocols on the same cable. For example, a coaxial cable with a bandwidth of approximately 400 MHz can be subdivided as follows (this is based on the design suggested by Harris and Sweeney <1983>):

- 10–25 MHz for low-speed data transmission. This can support several 56 Kbps and 9600 bps channels.
- 55–75 MHz for voice. This can support up to 5000 voice lines at 4 KHz per line.
- 175–210 MHz for high-speed data. This can easily support a 10-Mbps Ethernet channel.
- 210–240 MHz for video. This could support several video channels because each video requires 6 MHz.

Are broadband LANs better than baseband LANs? It depends. It can be seen that broadband LANs do have more applications, can support many subnets on one cable as shown in the example, and can cover longer distances. However, broadband LANs are more complex, require careful allocation of channels, and require periodic maintenance and tuning by communication engineers. Broadband LANs are also more expensive because they require more expensive cable and they require modems.

On the other hand, baseband LANs are inexpensive and reliable. Because baseband LANs can utilize the entire bandwidth of a cable, very fast transmissions between devices can be achieved by using baseband (up to 275 Mbps on fiber optic baseband LANs have been reported). However, baseband LANs are not suitable for voice and video applications and can be used only on short distances.

Obviously, both systems have their advantages and disadvantages. Baseband LANs work very well in small networks where there is no need for voice and video applications. Broadband systems serve well as backbones (highways) on which many channels (lanes) are supported. These channels may be used by small LANs (city streets) to connect to the backbone. The complexity of the broadband systems has been reduced by introducing *carrierband* systems, which are broadband systems restricted to a single channel (no FDM necessary). Carrierband systems can be used to satisfy the high distance requirements without the need for FDM equipment.

A good example of a LAN which uses broadband, carrierband and baseband is the Manufacturing Automation Protocol (MAP). Figure 2.19 shows a typical MAP LAN in which the MAP backbone is a 10-Mbps broadband cable which is spread across the factory floor. Many carrierband LANs, each at 5 Mbps, are connected to the backbone. Each carrierband LAN serves a factory "cell" (a collection of machines which perform a similar task such as painting). The MAP backbone can also be connected to a baseband Ethernet LAN, which serves an engineering department. The broadband, carrierband and baseband networks are interconnected through bridges and gateways, which we will discuss in the next chapter.

2.4.3 Link Control Protocols for LANs (Ethernet and Token Passing)

Link control protocols are used to describe the format and the rules used in exchanging messages between devices. For two devices to exchange messages, they must resolve the following issues:

- What is the address of the source and the destination device?
- When can the source send the data?

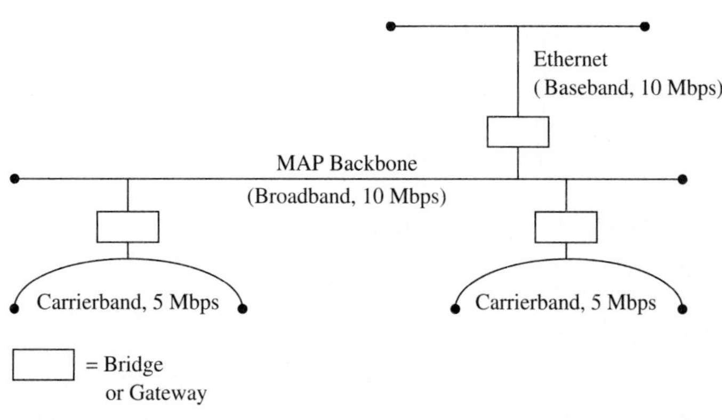

FIGURE 2.19 A MAP LAN

- How does the destination know that a message is waiting to be processed?
- What happens if a message is not transmitted properly due to an error?
- How can the receiver distinguish between the message being sent and the address of the sender? (These are all bit strings.)

A link control protocol is essentially an agreement between a sender and a receiver on these issues. Many link control protocols have been implemented for LANs. Some of these protocols are variants of the wide area network protocols, while the others have been developed primarily for LANs. We will describe three protocols (CSMA/CD, token ring, and token bus), which are used heavily in LANs. These protocols have also been adopted by the IEEE 802 LAN Standardization Committee.

2.4.3.1 CSMA/CD Protocol (IEEE 802.3 Standard)

CSMA/CD (Carrier Sense Multiple Access/Collision Detect) is very close to the heavily used Ethernet protocol. For most practical purposes, IEEE 802.3 and Ethernet are the same. We will review Ethernet in detail later. CSMA/CD is suited for bus topologies. This protocol is based on the University of Hawaii's Aloha system, in which all secondary stations transmit at "will" to the master (destination). If a collision occurs, then the stations wait for a random time and then retransmit. In the CSMA/CD system, the following steps take place (see Fig. 2.20a):

1. The sender first "listens" for another transmission on the line. The sender may listen for a frequency which determines if the line is being used (this is similar to using a telephone—if you pick up the phone and hear the dial tone, the line is not busy).
2. If the sender detects that the line is not busy, then the sender transmits the message.
3. If two stations send data at the same time, then a collision occurs. Each sender listens to the line while it sends a message to detect if a collision has occurred.
4. If a collision is detected, then the sender waits for a while and then retransmits.

2.4.3.2 Token Ring Protocol (IEEE 802.5 Standard)

This protocol is used in the IBM Token Ring LAN. A token is a packet that moves around a ring to which the LAN devices are attached. The token is used to send and receive messages. The following steps take place in this protocol (Fig. 2.20b):

1. A token moves around in the ring in one direction. At one time, only one token is present in the ring. (We will see that in FDDI, a token ring standard for fiber LANs, more than one token is allowed).
2. An empty token is detected by a station ready to send.
3. The sender puts the message on the token, marks the token "busy" by turning on some flag bits, puts the destination and source addresses on the token, and sends the token back into circulation.

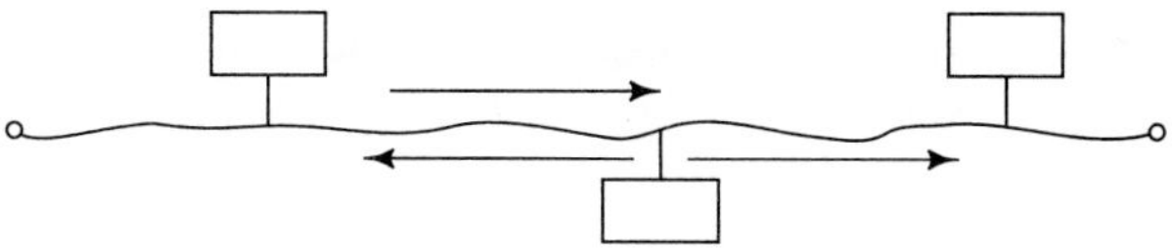

a. CSMA/CD

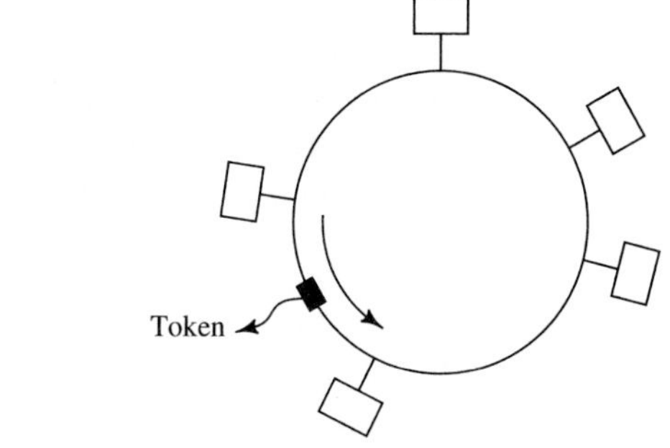

b. Token Ring

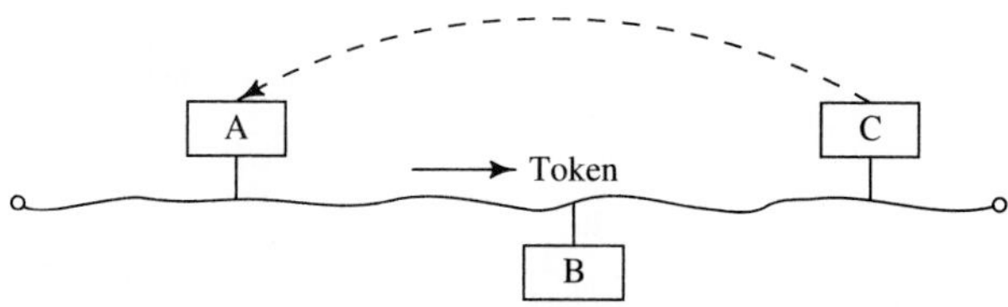

FIGURE 2.20 LAN Topologies and Protocols

4. The token passes every station and is checked at every station for a match between the station address and the token destination address.
5. If this is the destination, then the station receives the message, puts an "ACK" (positive acknowledgment) or "NAK" (negative acknowledgment if message was garbled) on the message, and sends the token out to the network.
6. The sender gets the "ACK" or "NAK" and frees up the token.

2.4.3.3 Token Bus Protocol (IEEE 802.4 Standard)

The Token Bus protocol is conceptually similar to the Token Ring protocol, with the difference that it operates on a bus instead of a ring. A station on the bus knows the address of the next station; the last station on the bus points to the first station. Thus the stations on a token bus form a logical ring. The token in this protocol is actually "the right to transmit," which is passed from station to station in descending numerical addresses. When the token bus is initialized, the station with the highest address gets the token (i.e., it can transmit). After it has transmitted, then the token is passed to the next lower address station. Now this station can transmit. There is no chance of a collision because at a given point only one station, the one with the token, can transmit. The token is passed from station to station by inserting the address of the receiver station in the token header. In reality, the Token Bus protocol is quite complex and is described in more than 200 pages of the IEEE 802.4 document.

2.4.3.4 Comparison of LAN Protocols

The frame formats of the three protocols are shown in Fig. 2.21. CSMA/CD is used very heavily in the engineering, manufacturing, and office environments. It has simple algorithm and provides good access at low workloads. CSMA/CD and Ethernet station interface cards are widely available for almost all computer systems at costs

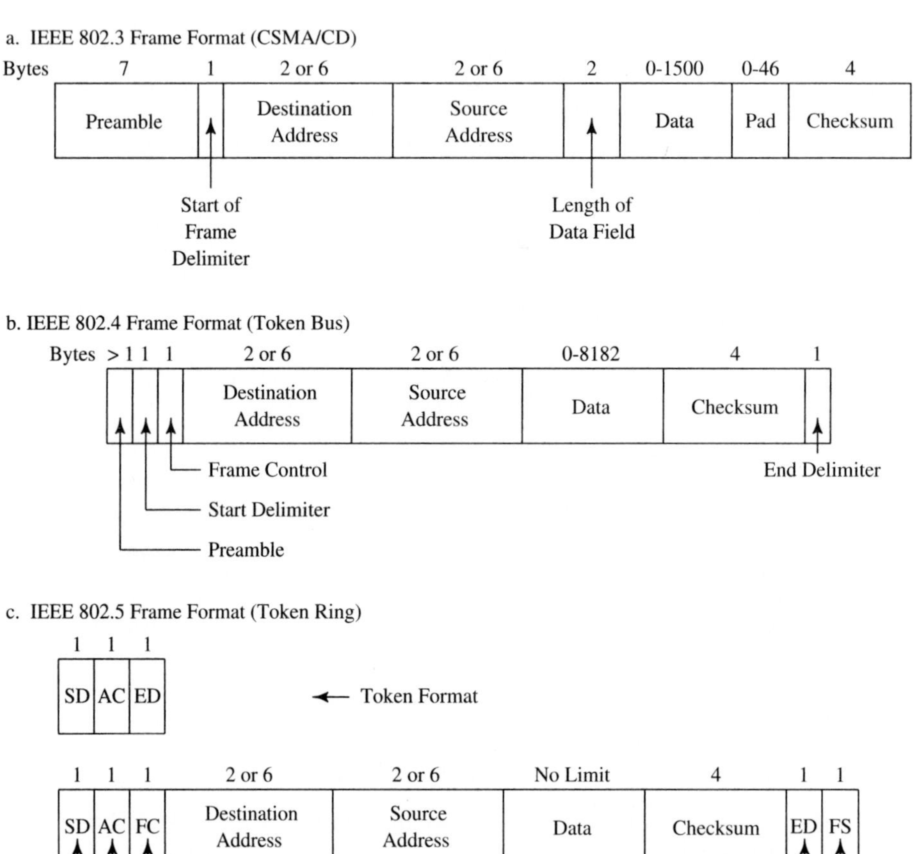

FIGURE 2.21 LAN Protocol Frames

less than $500. However, CSMA/CD is nondeterministic (i.e., the performance can degrade seriously due to collisions). The probability of collisions increases as the traffic on the network increases—a burst of sufficient activity can make the network unavailable for a while. This appears to be the main reason why CSMA/CD was not chosen for factory LANs; CSMA/CD can potentially bring the factory to a halt. Another weakness of CSMA/CD is that it requires a minimum message length (368 bits, as shown in Fig. 2.21) which restricts small messages.

The Token Ring is one of the oldest LAN protocol (it dates back to 1969). It also works well under heavy workloads but is inefficient for lightly loaded systems because in lightly loaded systems, the workstations have to wait for the token to arrive. It is not as complex as the Token Bus and is used widely in business environments, perhaps due to IBM's Token Ring LAN.

Token Bus has excellent throughput performance. Studies have shown that the throughput of the Token Bus increases as the data rates increase and levels off but does not decline with more traffic <Stallings 1992>. Token Bus is deterministic (i.e., the upper bound on performance can be determined because each station can only have the token for a deterministic time). In addition, Token Bus can also guarantee certain bandwidths which may be necessary for voice, digital video, and telemetry. The main disadvantage of Token Bus is its complexity and the overhead involved in lightly loaded systems. Token bus is used in many large manufacturing MAP environments. The books by Stallings on LANs <Stallings 1992, Stallings 1987> give a detailed analysis and evaluation of the LAN protocols.

2.4.4 LAN Standards

The IEEE 802 Committee was formed in 1980 to develop the standards for local area networks. The business pressure for the LAN standards is the need for low-cost LAN interfaces because the cost to connect equipment to a LAN must be much less than the cost of the equipment alone. The LAN interface chip manufacturers are not willing to commit resources unless there is a high-volume market. The Committee is currently organized into the following subcommittees:

- 802.1: High-Level Interface
- 802.2: Logical Link Control
- 802.3: CSMA/CD Networks
- 802.4: Token Bus Networks
- 802.5: Token Ring Networks
- 802.6: Metropolitan Area Networks
- 802.7: Broadband Technical Advisory Group
- 802.8: Fiber Optic Technical Advisory Group
- 802.9: Integrated Data and Voice Networks.

Each subcommittee is responsible for developing standards in its designated area, and the published standards are associated with the subcommittee title. For example, the

IEEE 802.4 standard for Token Bus was developed by the subcommittee 802.4. We have reviewed some of the standards already (802.3, 802.4 and 802.5). Let us now put these standards into a framework. Figure 2.22 shows protocol layered views of a WAN and a LAN. The bottom two layers are common to all networks because these two layers are responsible for physical transmission media (physical layer) and the message transmission and reception (data link layer). The application layer represents the user applications and is also common to all networks. The main difference is that LAN applications can interface directly with the network at layer 2. (Some LANs do bypass the intermediate layers.) Due to the importance of layer 2, it has been divided into two sublayers: Medium Access Control (MAC) layer and Logical Link Control (LLC).

The MAC layer controls the I/O to the physical layer entities. On transmission, this layer assembles the data into a frame with address and error-detection fields. On reception, it disassembles the arriving frame and performs address recognition and error detection. This layer also manages the communication over a physical medium such as copper and fiber optics cables. For example, the token is built, transmitted, and received/checked in this layer. The LAN protocols 802.3 (CSMA/CD), 802.4 (Token Bus), and 802.5 (Token Ring) have been developed for this layer. We have reviewed these protocols previously. More details about these standards can be found in Stallings <1987>.

The Logical Link Control layer is responsible for the transfer and formatting of data needed by applications. It basically makes sure that a frame received by the MAC layer is passed to the appropriate application in a station. LLC provides one or more service access points (SAPs) for the applications to interface directly with the LAN. For example, consider a LAN workstation which has three windows (programs) interacting with three different computers on the LAN. The three programs may be assigned three SAPs (say 1, 2, 3) in the workstation so that a message at SAP 1 is passed to program 1, the message at SAP 2 is sent to program 2, etc. This layer provides some of the functions, albeit at a simplified level, of the higher layers (e.g., network) not present in LANs. The IEEE 802.2 specifies the LLC

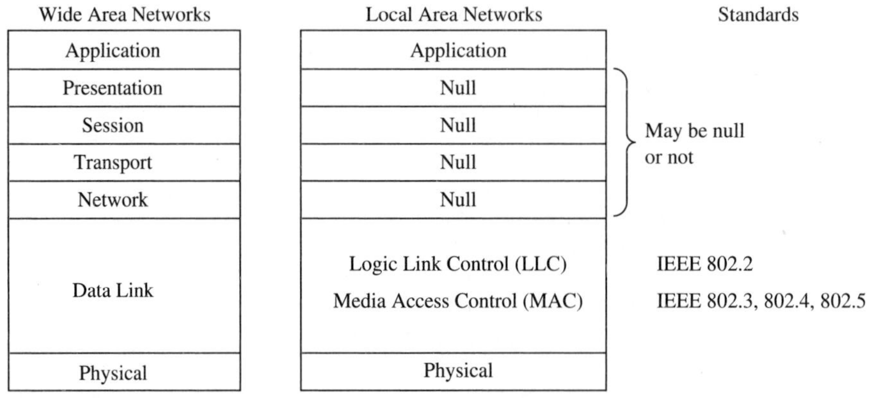

FIGURE 2.22 Protocol Stacks for Wide and Local Area Network Standards

standard with details about SAP formats, etc. Engineering details about LLC can be found in Stallings <1987>.

Figure 2.22 also shows the standards developed in these layers. Figure 2.23 shows the standard "profiles." For example, it shows that the standards for CSMA/CD are IEEE 802.2, IEEE 802.3 for baseband/broadband and twisted pair media. The highlights of the standards are as follows:

- The data link layer is subdivided into layers.
- Two topologies (ring and bus) have been adopted.
- Broadband as well as baseband are supported.
- CSMA/CD is recommended for bus (IEEE 802.3).
- Token passing for bus (IEEE 802.4) and ring (IEEE 802.5) have been adopted.
- FDDI (Fiber Distributed Data Interface) is chosen as a standard for 100 Mbps fiber LANs and MANs.
- Different transmission media (coax, twisted pair, fiber optic) have been adopted.
- 16-bit address for local access and 48-bit address for international access are supported. (48-bit addresses are used almost universally.)

The IEEE 802 committee is working with the ISO committee to assure that these standards will be used internationally. In addition, new standards will be developed for emerging LAN technologies. Gibson <1990> gives details about the IEEE 802 standardization activities.

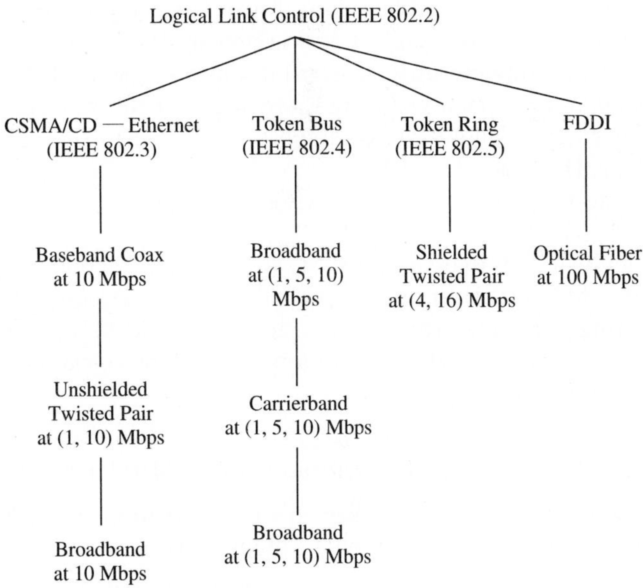

FIGURE 2.23 IEEE LAN Standards Hierarchy

2.4.5 Examples of LANs

Many LANs have been installed in organizations and many more LANs have been announced by the vendors. Examples of the main LANs are discussed by link protocol categories.

2.4.5.1 RS232 (Zero Slot) LANs

The RS232 LANs are inexpensive and slow local area networks which are adequate for small business environments. These LANs use RS232 ports so that there is no need for adapter cards. Most RS232 LANs are limited to 19.2 Kbps and eight devices. An example of such a LAN is EASYLAN, which can be used to connect IBM PCs in a star topology to a hub which works as a LAN server. The PCs can share the disk of the server and can also share a printer. The software cost is about $100 per PC so that $300 can get you started on a three-workstation "starter LAN." There is no need for adapter cards or cables, although RS232 cables are supplied by the vendor. The user installs the LAN software and workstation software on the PC. There is no need for disk formatting, etc.

2.4.5.2 IBM's Token Ring LAN

IBM officially announced it's Token Ring LAN in October, 1985. This LAN uses baseband and token ring link protocol. The initial Token Ring supported 4 Mbps data rate. A newer version operates at data rates of 16 Mbps. The main devices on the Token Ring LAN are IBM PCs, PS2s and printers. These devices are usually connected through shielded twisted pair (nontelephone) wires. The devices are connected to the ring by using a star topology (see Fig. 2.24). Token Ring provides Application Program Interface (API) for applications to be developed on top of the LAN. In addition, the Token Ring chipset and interface specifications are published so that vendors and users can develop interfaces to this LAN. The Token Ring software includes a print and disk server. LAN to LAN bridges are available to connect Token Ring LANs together to form a bigger LAN. In addition, a Host gateway allows the computers connected to the LAN to interact directly with the Host (see Fig. 2.24).

The Token Ring components are as follows:

- A multistation access unit (MAU), which is the actual ring on which the tokens travel. MAU is about one foot in width and allows eight devices to be attached to the ring. One MAU can be connected to other MAUs to form a larger network. It is common to find all MAUs of a building to be stacked in one location (e.g., the telephone closet).
- Drop cables, which connect the LAN devices to the MAU. These cables are strung in a building from the device location to the MAU location in a star topology.
- Network adapter cards, which are installed in each LAN device. These cards actually insert the messages on the token and remove/decipher the token messages.
- A Local Area Network Program, which is used to assign names, send/receive messages and share resources. This software is installed on the LAN server, and it

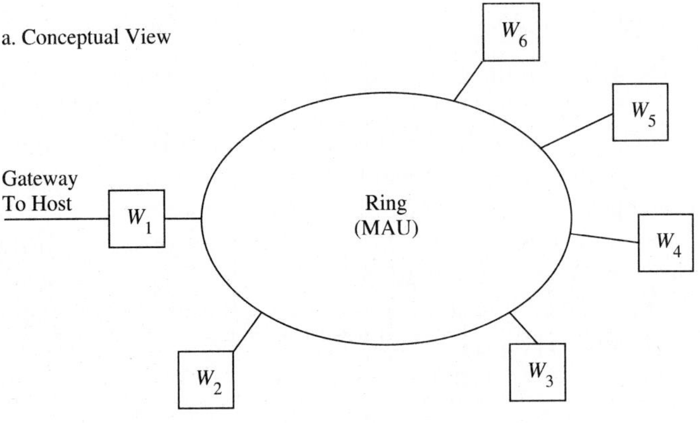

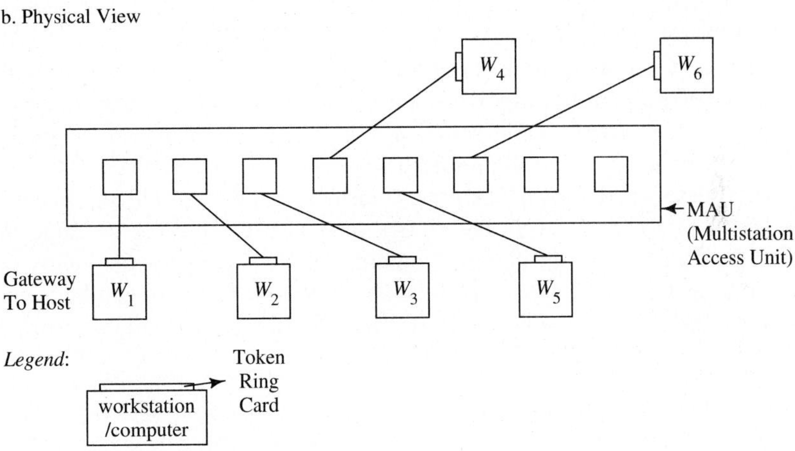

FIGURE 2.24 IBM's Token Ring LAN

supports several network status and administration commands such as NET USE (who is using the network).

- Workstation Software, which is installed on the computers in the network. This software connects the computers to the server and directs the calls referring to the network resources to the LAN server.
- Additional software, which supports application program interfaces to the Token Ring. An example is the NetBIOS software, which allows programs to interface directly with the Token Ring adapter cards. Another example is a file and/or database server software, which can be installed on the LAN server.

In a typical IBM Token Ring LAN, a server is a an IBM PS2 which is attached to a laser printer and houses many files that are shared by the workstations connected to the LAN. Details of the IBM Token Ring LAN can be found in Townsend <1987>.

2.4.5.3 Ethernet LANs

Ethernet LANs are by far the most frequently used in the industry today. The Ethernet standard was developed by Xerox in 1972. It has been adopted, collaborated and supported by DEC, Intel, and many other enterprises. Ethernet is similar to CSMA/CD, with minor differences in formats, framing, and terminology. It operates at 10 Mbps on bus topologies and is predominantly baseband oriented. An Ethernet local area network can be located in one building or can span a cluster of buildings. A very large number of Ethernet adapter cards are available for a variety of devices for under $500. In fact, Ethernet cards can be found for most computer systems at present. Due to the widespread availability of Ethernet cards, many LAN software packages run on top of Ethernet. Examples are Novell, Banyan, 3Com and Lifenet. In addition, Ethernet is used as the foundation for some network architectures such as Digital's DECNET. Ethernet interfaces to other networks are also available. Figure 2.25 shows a typical Ethernet LAN.

Novell's Netware is a commonly used LAN operating system on many Ethernet LANs. (Netware also works on token ring LANs.) Netware uses a dedicated CPU (e.g., a Motorola processor) or a PS2 as a server. Netware was initially designed for about 30 users for high-performance (recent versions of Netware go well beyond 100 users). It provides a file server which knows when files are opened, closed, and read/written and coordinates multiple access to files. Netware allocates and manages disk sectors and allows locking at transaction and record levels. In case of file locking conflicts, a user can wait for unlock or deal with an error message. A user can also ignore locking by an "ignore" command. Netware provides many interconnection options with other LANs. Details about Novell Netware can be found in the books <Ramos 1992, Christiansen 1991> and the literature available from Novell, Inc. At

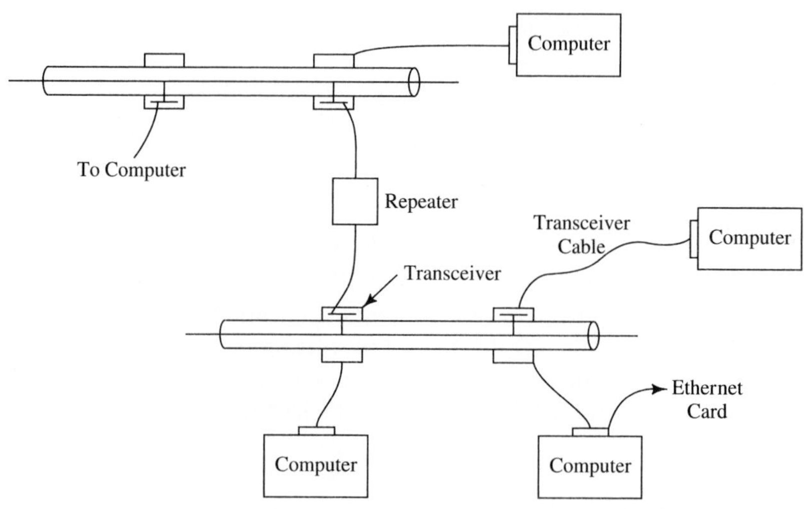

FIGURE 2.25 An Ethernet Operation

present, Novell provides many interconnectivity options to mainframes (see Schlack <1992>).

Let us review the Ethernet specifications in a little more detail (if this description makes you drowsy, skip it).

The Ethernet specification includes a Physical layer and a Data Link layer. The primary characteristics of the Physical layer include a data rate of 10 million bits per second, a maximum station (node) separation of 2.8 kilometers, a maximum of 1024 nodes or stations on a single Ethernet LAN, and support of a bus topology. The characteristics of the Data Link layer include multiaccess network control, in which access to the channel is fairly distributed to all nodes, and regulation of channel access through the Carrier Sense Multiple Access with Collision Detect (CSMA/CD) technique.

The functions of the Ethernet Data Link include data encapsulation/decapsulation and link management. Data Encapsulation/Decapsulation comprises framing, addressing, and error detection. Framing defines the format of message packets (the different fields of information within packets) that are broadcast over the local area network. Addressing handles source and destination addresses, and error detection detects physical channel transmission errors. Link Management comprises channel allocation and channel access. Channel allocation is responsible for efficient channel utilization, which is determined by the definition of packet size. Channel access is controlled by the CSMA/CD technique, part of which is carried out in each of the two layers. The Data Link layer responds to the channel or carrier sensing of the Physical layer by deferring transmission in the case of traffic, transmitting in the absence of traffic, and backing off and resending in the case of a collision.

The Ethernet Data Link layer provides a best-effort delivery service. It does not provide an error-control facility to recover from transmission errors. The data encapsulation function of the Data Link layer comprises the construction and processing of frames. The frame format reflects the data encapsulation functions of framing, addressing, and error detection:

- *Framing*: No explicit framing information is contained in the format since the necessary framing cues are present in the interface to the Physical layer.
- *Addressing*: There are two address fields to identify the source and destination nodes of the frame. Both address fields contain 48 bits.
- *Error detection*: A Frame Check Sequence field is used to check the accuracy of the information contained in each transmitted packet.

2.4.6 Issues in LAN Selection and Design

Selection and design of a LAN involves several factors:

- Type of applications and type of resources that need to be shared (printer, disk, file/database sharing)
- Response time and speed requirements

- Budgetary constraints
- Type of existing equipment that needs to be connected (IBM PCs, Macintoshes, robots, manufacturing devices, Apollos/Suns)
- The number of stations that need to be attached
- The training and knowledge of the staff and the user base
- Software packages and functions needed
- Workload characteristics (number of users and number of transactions per user)
- Cost of LAN expansion (new cable, additional stations)
- Maximum limitations of the available LANs (maximum length of cable, maximum workstations, and maximum users and sessions)
- Security, back-up/recovery features
- Documentation and support provided by the vendor
- Vendor "staying" power
- Transmission media preferences (twisted pair, coaxial cable, cable TV, microwave and/or wireless, fiber optics)
- Topology considerations (bus, tree, ring).

In practice, before a LAN is selected, several other competing technologies such as controllers, PBXs, and minicomputers need to be evaluated. Let us review some of the options through an example. Consider an office which has six personal computers (PCs) for word processing and for handling a simple order processing system. There is a need for a high-quality printer and some file storage for order processing. The following options are available to the user:

- *Sneaker Net*: In this case, the PCs are not connected through any cable. The data is shared by trading diskettes by hand or by mail. This option is attractive for occasional (once or twice a week) access across PCs. However, in order to share a common printer, the file to be printed will need to be copied to a diskette and then used at the "printer station." This solution does not fit typical distributed computing needs very well.
- *Controllers and PBXs*: In this case, the PCs are connected to a controller with a printer, which allows the PCs to share the printer (e.g., an IBM 3274 controller). Other examples are simple RS232 patch boxes and data PBX. For an RS232 patch box, all PCs connect to a patch box where short jumper cables are used to interconnect the PCs. Many software packages can be used to communicate between PCs. This option is very inexpensive but is slow (9600 bps) and clumsy. A better option may be a data or digital PBX which essentially automates the patch box. However, this option is used very rarely.
- *Local Area Networks (LANs)*: PCs on a LAN have a permanent physical connection (cable) which is shared by using a scheme such as CSMA, token ring, FDDI, etc. We can choose a variety of LANs depending on the performance requirements

and budgetary constraints. The following list shows the performance and cost features of the various LAN options:[4]

Link Protocol	*Data Rate*	*Cost Per Station*
Asynchronous (RS232)	9.6 Kbps	$100 per station
CSMA/CD (Ethernet)	10 Mbps	$300 to $500 per station
Token Ring	4 or 16 Mbps	$700 to $1000 per station
Token Bus	5 or 10 Mbps	$3000 to $5000 per station (These are MAP costs)
FDDI	100 Mbps	$2000 to $8000 per station

A LAN server can be used to store commonly accessed data. In addition, a printer can be attached to the LAN server for print sharing. In our example, we can use a LAN to share a printer and do some local order processing. To use the LAN, the LAN hardware/software will need to be installed. The LAN software may include the server software to be installed at the server and the workstation software to be installed at each PC. In addition, NetBIOS for application program interface (API) to the network adapter card, additional operating system routines needed for LANs, and any application software (programs + databases) may be needed. The complexity of installing, maintaining and managing a LAN largely depends on the capabilities of the server, which may be configured as a print server, a disk server, file server and/or a database server. All server functions can be installed at one station or can be distributed to many stations. A server function may occupy between 150 to 300 Kbytes of the station's main memory. Choice of a LAN configuration needs to be carefully examined for management as well as maintenance considerations.

The interested reader is referred to Behm <1988>, Ben-Artzi <1990>, Chernick <1987>, Halsall <1990>, Joseph <1988> for LAN management considerations. We will consider this issue in Chapter 4.

- *Minicomputer systems*: In this case, the requirements for local processing are large enough so that a LAN server is replaced with a minicomputer or even a mainframe. Minicomputers use multiprogramming operating systems with sophisticated resource sharing schemes which allow many users (usually around 100) to share printers, files, and databases. Minicomputers also provide the facilities for running complete application systems. For example, if the office in our example was a department store which needed to keep local price and inventory information about products, then a minicomputer may be needed for local order processing and inventory control systems.

In short, the issue of LAN selection and design involves several major decisions: (1) Should a LAN be used instead of a controller/PBX or minicomputer? (2) Which LAN should be selected? and (3) How should a given LAN be configured, maintained and managed? In LAN selection, performance evaluation of LANs is an important

[4]These costs are given for illustrative purposes only.

TABLE 2.3 Additional Sources of Information for LANs

Books on LANs

1. Stallings, W., *Local and Metropolitan Area Networks*, 4th ed., Macmillan, 1992.
2. Martin, J., *Local Area Networks: Architectures and Implementations*, Prentice Hall, 1989.
3. Hutchinson, D., *Local Area Network Architectures*, Addison-Wesley, 1988.
4. Rhodes, P., *LAN Operations*, Addison-Wesley, 1991.
5. Hancock, B., *Designing and Implementing Ethernet Networks*, QED Information Sciences, 1988.
6. Townsend, C., *Networking with the IBM Token-Ring*, TAB Books, 1987.
7. Reiss, L., *Introduction to Local Area Networks with Microcomputer Experiments*, Prentice Hall, 1987.

Magazines and Trade Journals

1. *LAN Technology*
2. *LAN Magazine*
3. *Byte Magazine*
4. *PC Magazine*
5. *PC World*
6. *PC Week*
7. *Data Communications*

area. Methods for performance evaluation include analytical modeling, simulation, benchmarking, vendor supplied analysis, analysis published in journals, and past experience/knowledge. We will discuss this topic in a later chapter.

We have reviewed the LAN technology briefly. Many books, articles and magazines are available for additional information. A partial list of additional sources is given in Table 2.3.

2.5 Metropolitan Area Networks

2.5.1 Overview

The metropolitan area networks (MANs) extend the scope of local area networks beyond the customer premises to cover a geographical area (e.g., a city or a county). A common definition (there are many slightly varying definitions) is that a MAN is a large LAN under the control of one authority and using a shared transmission medium. A MAN typically covers 50 km diameter and operates at speeds above 50 Mbps. Due to its size and speed, a MAN can be used as a backbone which transports messages between various LANs and PBXs. Three approaches are being developed for MANs:

- The FDDI standard, discussed in Section 2.5.2, is popular for MANs because it operates at 100 Mbps over 100 km. However, FDDI is aimed at the data communications users; voice communications is of little concern in this standard.
- The DQDB standard, discussed in Section 2.5.3, has been adopted by the IEEE 802.6 Committee as the primary MAN standard. This standard offers up to 155 Mbps data rates.

- The SMDS (Switched Multimegabit Data Service) is being developed by the telephone companies as a MAN as well as WAN offering. Initially targeted at the low-cost T1 (1.54 Mbps) and T3 (45 Mbps) transmission services, SMDS will provide access to a very high-speed and reliable public packet switching network. Due to the importance of SMDS to MAN as well as WAN communications, we will review SMDS briefly in Section 2.5.3 and discuss it in more detail in Section 2.7.

Many MANs are being deployed to interconnect several LANs. In addition, a wide area backbone may interconnect many MANs together to form a wide area network. The WAN backbone may be a T1/T3 network or may rely on newer technologies such as ISDN, B-ISDN, SMDS, and SONET, to be discussed later. It is desirable to operate the WAN backbone at 100 Mbps or higher to interconnect the MANs and LANs, which are also operating at these speeds. This provides "wall to wall" 100 Mbps and higher networks for many of the future applications (see Section 2.7).

2.5.2 Fiber Optic MANs/LANs and FDDI

The LANs discussed in Section 2.4 were developed in the 1980s and are copper LANs. Although copper LANs work adequately for many applications, they do not satisfy the high bandwidth and security requirements of metropolitan area networks. Fiber has high bandwidth, is thin and lightweight, is not affected by electromagnetic interference from heavy machinery, and has excellent security due to difficulties in wiretapping. Due to these reasons, fiber optic is becoming increasingly popular for metropolitan area networks. Engineering details about fiber optics can be found in the following books:

- *Technician's Guide to Fiber Optics* <Sterling 1987>
- *Fiber Optic Communications Design Handbook* <Hoss 1990>
- *Optical Fiber Communications* <CSELT 1981>.

FDDI (Fiber Distributed Data Interface) is the best known standard for fiber optic local and metropolitan area networks. FDDI uses token rings to operate at 100 Mbps over distances up to 200 Km with 500 to 1000 stations connected. FDDI is also designed for very low error rate (at most one error in 2500 million bits transmitted). An FDDI network can be used as a MAN or a LAN. Although an FDDI LAN can be used as any other LAN, the high bandwidth capabilities of FDDI make it a prime candidate for a backbone to which many other copper LANs are connected. Figure 2.26 shows a typical FDDI backbone to which token ring, Ethernet, and token bus copper LANs are connected through gateways. As we will see in the next chapter, gateways are used to interconnect different networks. The backbone can be used within an enterprise or in a metropolitan area. A successor to FDDI is FDDI-II, which has been modified for voice or ISDN traffic, in addition to the ordinary traffic. Commonly, both FDDIs are just referred to as FDDI.

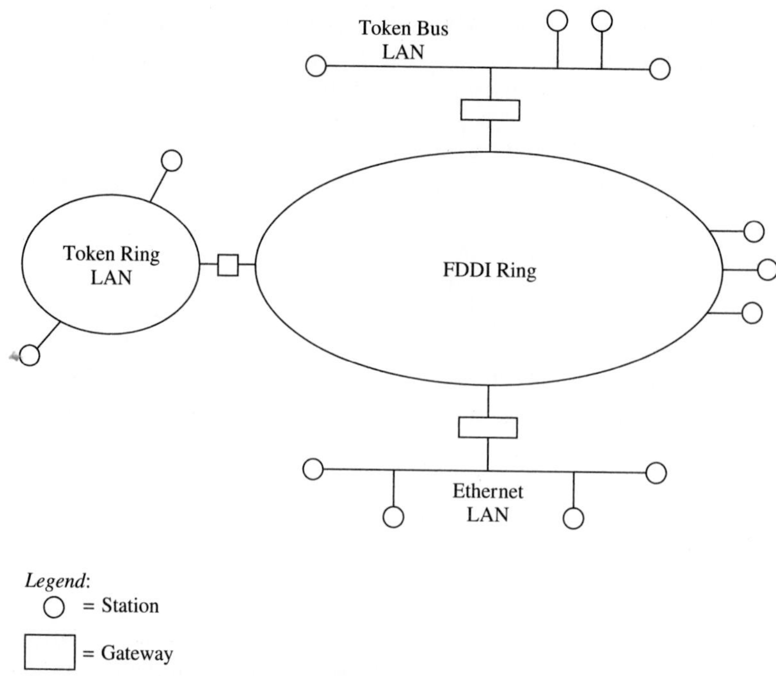

FIGURE 2.26 An FDDI LAN as a Backbone

FDDI uses LED instead of lasers as light sources primarily due to their lower costs and safety to eyesight (laser beams when viewed directly can be disastrous to human eyes). The FDDI cabling consists of two fiber rings, one transmitting clockwise and the other counterclockwise (Fig. 2.27a). If one ring breaks, the other can be used as a backup. If both break, say due to fire and sabotage, the two broken ends can be joined together to form a single loop (Fig. 2.27b). FDDI defines two classes of stations, A and B. Class A stations are more expensive and are connected to both rings so that if one fails, it can transmit by using the second ring. Class B stations are cheaper and are connected to only one ring. An installation can choose any number of class A and class B stations, depending on the budgetary and fault tolerance requirements.

The protocols used by FDDI are very closely related to the IEEE 802.5 Token Ring protocol. The station captures the token before it can transmit in a manner similar to IEEE 802.5. The main difference between the IEEE 802.5 and FDDI is that in FDDI, a station can generate another token after it has transmitted its frame on the first token. Due to this, multiple tokens can be floating around in an FDDI ring. The FDDI frames are slightly different from the token ring frames due to voice digitizing PCM and ISDN data allowed in FDDI. The protocol requires each station to keep track of the time elapsed between tokens received by a station through a timer. A priority algorithm is used to pace the traffic so that high-priority messages can be transmitted when traffic is high (the interarrival time between tokens is higher than usual).

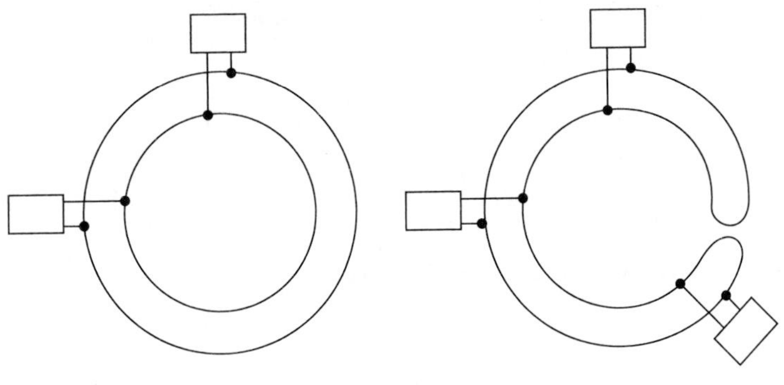

a. Fiber Ring Cables
b. Fiber Ring After Failure

FIGURE 2.27 Fiber Optic LAN Configurations

FDDI-II has been developed to enhance the capabilities of FDDI. For example, it adds circuit switching and can be extended to 620 Mbps. FDDI-II can be used as a backbone to PBXs and can be optionally configured as FDDI-I. In addition to FDDI, many other fiber optic networks have been developed in the last five years. Examples are Fibernet II, which is an Ethernet compatible fiber LAN; S/NET, which is a star topology fiber LAN; FASTNET, which is a bus oriented fiber LAN/MAN; and DATAKIT, which is an integrated LAN/MAN/WAN. Details about these networks can be found in Tannenbaum <1988> and Stallings <1992>.

2.5.3 DQDB and SMDS MANs

DQDB (Distributed Queue Dual Bus) is an IEEE 802.6 approved MAN standard. It first started at T_1 to T_3 speeds (1.54 Mbps to 45 Mbps), can currently go up to 155 Mbps, and is expected to go at higher speeds in the future. DQDB is designed to operate on fiber media and can go beyond 50 kilometers. The DQDB architecture, shown in Fig. 2.28, consists of two one-way busses (hence the name dual bus) which are used to carry user messages. The top bus carries messages "upstream" and the bottom bus carries message "downstream." Let us assume that the users U_1, U_2 and U_3 are placed left to right on this network. Then a user U_2 goes through the following steps in order to send a message to U_3:

- Use the downstream bus to find an empty packet (i.e., go to U_1 for an empty packet).
- Use the upstream bus to send the data to U_3 in the empty packet just obtained.

If U_2 wants to send data to U_1, then it uses the downstream bus to transfer data. This simple technique provides full duplex, highly reliable communications which can use packet switching techniques. It is expected that DQDB will eventually support FDDI. DQDB directly competes with FDDI for private MANs being provided by many vendors. DQDB is superior to FDDI because it can operate at higher speeds and can support voice communications. Thus it is comparable to FDDI-II. See <Bisdikian 1992> for a performance analysis of DQDB networks.

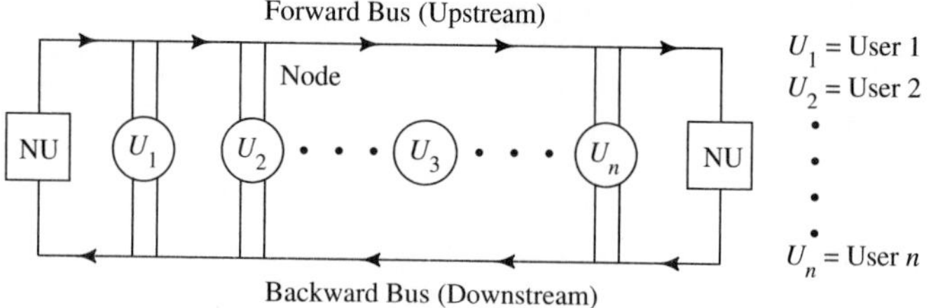

FIGURE 2.28 Distributed Queue Dual Bus (DQDB)

A competitor to DQDB is the emerging Switched Multimegabit Data Service (SMDS) being offered by the telephone companies. Developed at Bellcore, SMDS is intended to provide a public MAN at high speeds. The main strength of SMDS over FDDI and DQDB MANs is that it is intended to provide a 24 hour a day, 7 days a week public service similar to the telephone service. SMDS promises low delay (20 millisecond for 95 percent of the packets at 45 Mbps), extremely low error rate (about 5 undetected errors in 10 trillion), high packet delivery rate (about 1 packet loss for every 1000 delivered), and expected speeds in the range of 500 Mbps and above. In addition, SMDS is expected to provide WAN services. We will examine SMDS in more detail in Section 2.7. See Stallings <1992>, Chapter 6, for DQDB details.

2.6 ISDN and Broadband ISDN

2.6.1 Integrated Services Digital Network (ISDN)

2.6.1.1 ISDN Overview

According to The Consultative Committee for International Telegraph and Telephone (CCITT), ISDN is defined as follows <Knight 1987>:

> A network, evolved from the telephone network, that provides end-to-end digital connectivity to support a wide range of services, including voice and non-voice services, to which users have access by a limited set of standard multipurpose user-network interfaces.

Figure 2.29 illustrates the generic ISDN concept. ISDN combines digital lines with standard interfaces to provide integrated services in voice, data, graphics, text and video over the same physical lines. It attempts to provide a set of international standards and interfaces to allow computers, telephones and terminals to communicate freely with each other without any vendor imposed limitations. The interfaces are digital and operate at two levels: user-to-network and network-to-network.

The services provided by ISDN come in two flavors: basic, which builds on the existing two wire loops, and primary, which is built on the T1 carrier digital technology. The *basic services* are intended for home users or very small businesses. These services provide two 64-Kbps channels (called the B channels) and one 16-Kbps channel

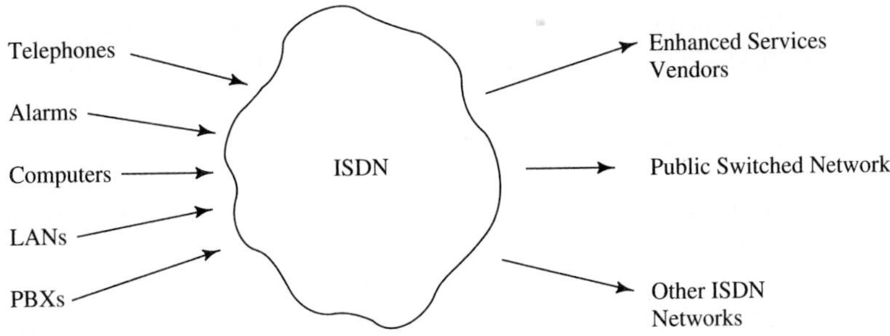

FIGURE 2.29 The User View of ISDN

(called the D channel). These "2B + D services" are supported on the same wire pair that provides voice-grade telephone service. The B channels can be used for telephone, voice and video and the D channel can be used for low-bandwidth applications such as alarms. We will give technical details of B and D channels later. The *primary services* are intended for larger businesses because they provide as many as 23 B and one D channel. These B channels at 64 Kbps can support many business applications. The primary services are also referred to as the 23B + D services. The primary services can deliver a data rate of 1.54 Mbps, the same as T1 service.

ISDN has the support of many key telecommunications organizations like AT&T, Regional Bell Operating Companies, Bellcore, Northern Telecomm, Siemens, ITT and NEC. In addition to the telecommunications companies, many computer companies (e.g., IBM), manufacturing companies (e.g., GM), and electronic mail and office automation companies are developing interfaces to ISDN. Many LANs are also beginning to use ISDN cards to connect to ISDN switches. At present, ISDN is commercially available in the United States, France, Germany, and Great Britain.

2.6.1.2 ISDN Applications

The main features of ISDN for an end user are as follows:

1. The users can have ubiquitous access to voice, data, and images through a single network. The key point is that these interfaces are based on international agreements.
2. Smaller ISDNs may be used as building blocks for larger ISDNs. Conceptually, an international organization can have its own local ISDNs as part of a nationwide ISDN that, in turn, is part of a larger international ISDN.
3. The emphasis in ISDN is on *S*, the services. A potential future scenario is that every office, and perhaps home, will have a connector to which a user will connect his or her telephone, television and computer, thus allowing computers to directly read/write from telephones, terminals and other devices located anywhere in the world.
4. Telephones will be able to send/receive data packets. Since the data packets do not have to go to the same destination as the voice call, this allows several

facilities. For example, a busy phone can deliver a message to the caller, and one can find out who is calling or waiting on line before even answering the phone.

5. ISDN services will also provide telemetry such as remote meter reading, alarm sensing, and energy management.

Several applications of ISDN have been reported in the literature. Here are some examples:[5]

- Interactive telephone directories, in which the telephone users have a small terminal which can be used to retrieve telephone numbers, business hours, etc. This experiment, conducted in France, eliminated the need for telephone directories and yellow pages.
- A hospital medical information system, in which the patient ID is used to retrieve his or her medical history, physician's name and other needed information.
- Police 911 information systems, in which the caller phone number is used as a key to search a city map database. This allows the 911 operator to instantly display the location of the caller without having to ask any questions. This is especially useful when the caller is a child or someone under great physical danger.
- A real estate search program, which intermixes text, voice, pictures and moving videos to help a customer look for a house. The user first specifies a range of costs and names of areas to be searched. The system produces a list of houses that satisfy these conditions. The user then selects a house from the list. A picture of the house and textual description of the house is displayed. If interested, the user may elect to "visit" the house. This invokes a video window which walks the user through the house. The user can stop, skip forward, or backspace the video through commands.

2.6.1.3 ISDN Architecture

Figure 2.30 shows the architecture of ISDN. The user terminal equipment (TE1) is connected to the ubiquitous ISDN network termination device (NT1) through a CCITT-defined reference point *T*. The ISDN switches may correspond to existing telecommunications central offices with special ISDN services or may be privately owned switches.

An NT2 may be optionally introduced between TE1 and NT1. The major application of NT2 is a digital PBX (Private Branch Exchange) where several TE1s, say in an office, are connected to an NT2 which, in turn, is connected to NT1 (see Fig. 2.31). This arrangement would allow TE1s to communicate with TE2 (non-ISDN devices), computers on a local area network in the office, or access remote TE1s. This facility is similar to the current PBX, where a user can call any extension or dial 9 for the outside world. The interface between TE1 and NT2 is defined as *S* interface, which is electrically and physically identical to the *T* interface. In short, the following types of devices are used on the customer premises:

[5]Many of these applications can be implemented on digital networks without ISDN. However, ISDN interfaces make these applications available to a wider range of users.

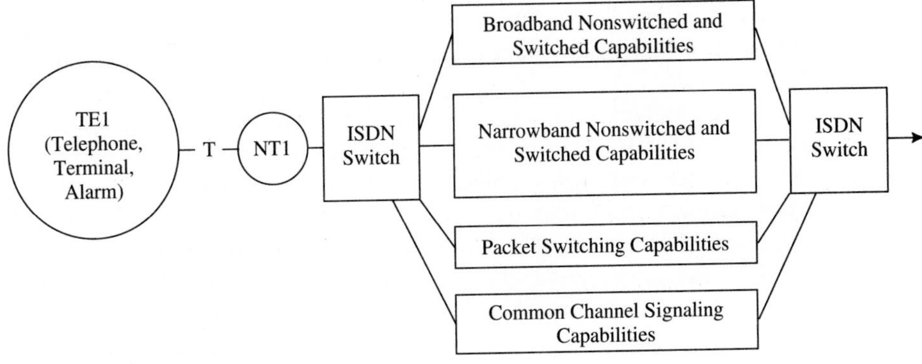

FIGURE 2.30 ISDN Facilities

- NT1: Network boundary
- NT2: Customer PBX
- TE1: ISDN terminal (telephone, TV, computer, alarm, etc.)
- TE2: Non-ISDN terminal
- TA: Terminal adapter to connect a non-ISDN terminal to ISDN.

ISDN uses a digital communication network. Bit streams crossing the *T* reference point (to the user and from the user) contain signaling bits (called D bits) and content or "bearer" bits (called B bits). Recall that the *T* interface connects a user to a switch. The B and D bits are multiplexed (sent simultaneously) over a given bit stream that may be moving toward the user or toward the network.

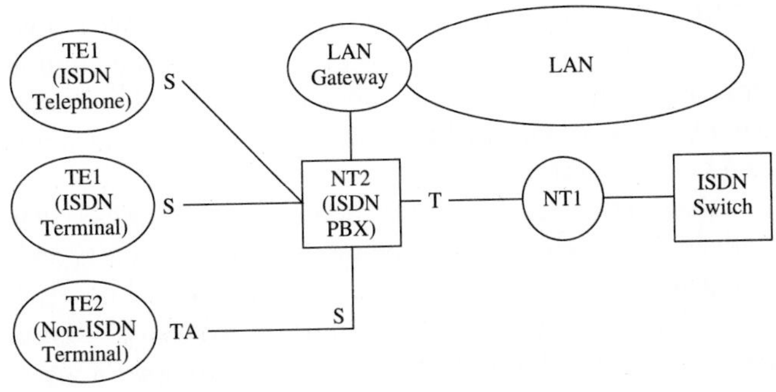

FIGURE 2.31 PBX in ISDN

The D channel is used for all control signals like placing of calls and disconnects. It can be also used for low-bandwidth applications such as alarms and for signaling to other terminals.

The B channels contain the actual user and application bits for the duration of a connection. The B bits cross the *T/S* interfaces in 8-bit (byte) chunks. In some cases, all 8 bits are devoted to one application task; in other cases, the first 4 bits may be used for task 1, bits 5 and 6 may be used for task 2, bit 7 for task 3, and bit 8 for task 4. Assuming a 64-Kbps (64,000 bits per second) B channel, this would allow task 1 to be a 32-Kbps transmission of speech, 16-Kbps transmission of data communication, etc. Thus on a single B channel, one voice and several data communication sessions are serviced.

CCITT is attempting to keep the number of interface structures at an absolute minimum. Two main interfaces have been defined so far: the basic access and the primary access.

The basic access interface is defined at the *S/T* level. It defines how a TE1 (user terminal) will interface with NT1/NT2 (network termination). An example of this interface is the interface between telephone set and the telephone switch. The formula for this interface is as follows:

$$n\mathrm{B} + \mathrm{D}$$

where n = 0, 1 or 2, B = 64 Kbps, and D = 16 Kbps. The most common basic interface proposed is the 2B + D which is anticipated for most metropolitan areas in the next few years. The 2B + D interface is supposed to operate on the existing local loop using single copper wires.

The primary access interface is defined between the ISDN switches and is expected to operate at a much higher transmission speed. The most common primary access interface is the 23B + D interface, where D and B channels operate at 64 Kbps. The primary access interface operates on fiber optics and other high bandwidth media. Details of ISDN interfaces and architectures can be found in Verma <1990>.

At present, ISDN applications are limited. For example, most of the primary accesses (23B + D) discussed earlier have been implemented between major switching centers. Very few basic accesses (2B + D) have been implemented so far. The first priority for 2B + D will be business areas which will allow businesses to connect to ISDN switches. It is commonly believed that all homes will not have 2B + D access until the end of this century.

About half of the telephone network in North America is digital with the current T-Carrier technology, which allows digital communications at 56 Kbps. Some experts estimate that full ISDN service will not be available for nearly 10 years due to the technical problems of signaling, framing and "ones density" <Stallings 1991>. It would be advantageous to use the current T-carrier technology, sometimes referred to as IDN (Integrated Data Networks) without the *S* of Services, before full ISDN is available.

To summarize, the differences between ISDN and current technologies are <Verma 1990>:

1. The transport of information in ISDN is independent of the type of service. At present, data communications facilities are different from voice communications. This service independent transport will allow new and existing services to evolve based on user needs without having to design communication facilities.
2. Currently, voice and facsimile communications require separate connectors, and separate billing procedures and addresses. ISDN will allow one connector, one billing, and planning source for all the services.
3. ISDN will allow users to monitor and control network resources.

The main promise of ISDN is that it can facilitate telephones, computers and terminals to communicate with each other based on established and well-defined interfaces. This will play a key role in the design and development of information systems of the future which will use voice, data and video devices for innovative applications. The main limitation of ISDN is that it does not provide transmission speeds greater than the available T carriers (i.e., 1.54 Mbps). Many observers say that ISDN is too little too late. The next generation of ISDN, Broadband ISDN (BISDN), will overcome this limitation by providing 150 Mbps and higher data rates. BISDN, discussed in the next section, will operate over fiber optic links which extend to the customer premises. Due to the expense and effort involved in wiring the customer premises with fiber, BISDN is not expected to appear until the next century.

Many books have been published which contain extensive coverage of ISDN. Examples are the books by Stallings <1989, 1991> and by Kessler <1990>. Another book, edited by Pramode Verma, *ISDN Systems*, <Verma 1990>, has many authoritative papers on the architectures, technologies and applications of ISDN. A complete chapter on ISDN is included in the book by Bartree <1986>. In addition, many technical papers and trade journal articles cover various aspects of ISDN. The interested reader can find numerous sources of extensive information. For example, many issues of the IEEE Communications in the last five years have explained various aspects of ISDN (see, for example, the August 1992 issue). A North Holland journal, *Computer Networks and ISDN*, has published many technical papers on this subject. The business and application aspects have been reviewed repeatedly in the *Business Communications Review*. *The IEEE Network*, September 1989, is a special issue on ISDN applications. Many ISDN applications are announced in trade newspapers like *Computerworld*, *Network News*, and *Communications News*.

2.6.2 Broadband ISDN

Broadband ISDN (BISDN) is intended for end-to-end digital communications using high-speed fiber optics all the way to the subscriber. Instead of the conventional ISDN which offers 64 Kbps and 1.5 Mbps lines, BISDN offers data rates from 1.5 Mbps to more than 155 Mbps for WANs. A major application for BISDN is multimedia applications for domestic and common office use. These applications require very high data rates and integration of computers, telephone, and television technologies.

BISDN is expected to offer the individual high speed services of several evolving transmission technologies as options so that the users can choose from many broadband services. Examples of the two such transmission technologies are SONET and SMDS, which are discussed in Section 2.7.3. Figure 2.32 shows a conceptual view of BISDN. Notice that BISDN is expected to provide customer access to the broadband telecommunication services of the future in a manner similar to the ISDN access to current telecommunication services.

Due to the difficulties and costs involved in replacing the current subscriber loops with fiber optics, BISDN is not expected to be available for a decade. Most of the fundamental research on BISDN was conducted in the last decade. The earliest BISDN experiments investigated wideband capabilities using circuit switching. Early experiments in Germany, France and the United States provided a large number of different data rates to the user based on the service requirement. Experiments in packet switching led to the concept of fixed length information "cells" (packets) over the communication channels. This approach, commonly known as the *Asynchronous Transfer Mode (ATM)*, makes processing more predictable in the telephone switches. Several early BISDN experiments have been reported. An example is the 1989 trial in Germany (BERKOM) which focused on medical applications and included high-performance image transfer and realtime video connections. NTT in Japan and Bellcore, BellSouth and NYNEX in the United States are involved in many major projects. Bellcore is actively working on generic requirements for BISDN.

BISDN is expected to usher in a new era of communications in the twenty-first century with audio and visual communications of high quality and large variety available to home and business users. Although narrowband ISDN is not a prerequisite for BISDN, the latter is a natural technical successor to the former and shares many common features. A CCITT task force has prepared a list of potential broadband services for BISDN.

Due to the distant application of BISDN, many details about BISDN are not currently available. Generic requirements for BISDN are being developed at the time of this writing. These requirements are prompting early interactions between equipment vendors. Many sources for additional information are available. The ISDN book by Stallings <1992, 2nd edition> has an overview of BISDN. Handel <1989> describes the evolution of ISDN into BISDN and gives details of the BISDN standardization efforts. Architectural and technical overview of BISDN is given by Byrne <1989>. Additional details about BISDN can be found in Reingold <1992>, White <1991>, McQuillan <1990>, and Kahl <1987>.

FIGURE 2.32 Conceptual View of BISDN

2.7 High-Speed Networks: Trends in Networking

2.7.1 Overview and Taxonomy

The network technologies are advancing at a very rapid pace. The main evolutions in the last three decades, in rough chronological order, have been as follows:

1. Terminal-to-computer communications using asynchronous and synchronous devices over switched or leased lines
2. Public packet switching services using the X.25 standard
3. Use of local area networks and data PBXs on customer premises
4. Growth of digital networks and ISDN
5. Growth of high-speed broadband services which exceed 100 Mbps data rates
6. Trend toward intelligent networks
7. Increased availability of cellular, wireless and satellite networks
8. Developments of large and intelligent supernetworks which interconnect many LANs, MANs and WANs.

We have reviewed the first four aspects of network technologies in our discussion so far. The remainder of the network technologies, collectively known as high-speed networks, represent an area of vital growth in networks of today and tomorrow. These networks, shown conceptually in Fig. 2.33, combine high speed, intelligent

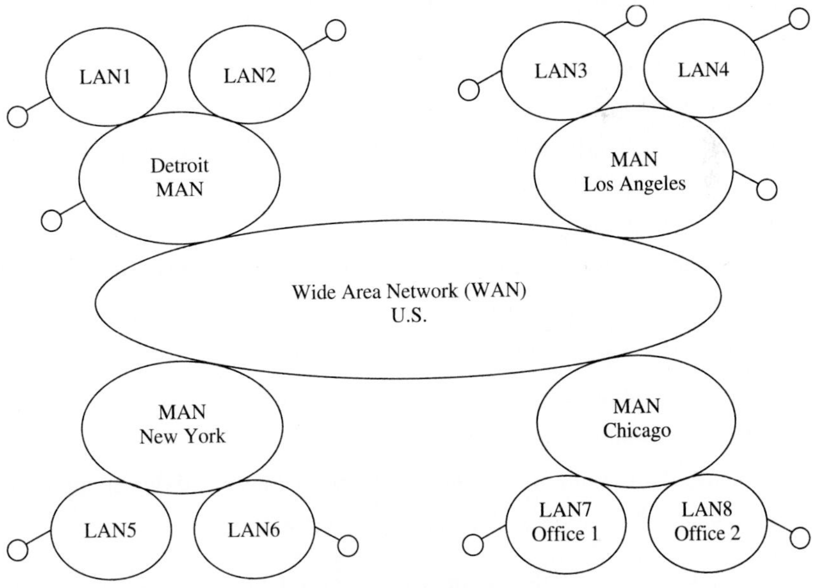

FIGURE 2.33 High Speed, Intelligent Supernetworks of the Future

LANs, MANs and WANs to support the expected future applications and provide exciting opportunities for the future. This section exposes the reader to the main issues and approaches in high-speed networks. The reader should keep in mind that most of the technologies in this section are rapidly moving from state of the art to state of the market and state of the practice. This technology will take full hold in the mid-1990s and will be widely used in the next century.

The high-speed networks discussed here are also called "broadband networks." This is somewhat confusing to many users because the term *broadband* is used differently in the communication industry. Conceptually, broadband services support communications which utilize a bandwidth larger than the voice graded 4 KHz bandwidth. However, broadband services in LANs indicate modulated signals (see Section 2.4.2). Broadband networks, for evolving technologies, refer to 100 Mbps or more data rates and are driven by the newer applications. (The 1 to 20 Mbps services are sometime referred to as the *wideband* services.) Due to this confusion, we will not emphasize the term *broadband* to refer to the high-speed (more than 100 Mbps) networks discussed in this section.

The demand for high-speed LAN-to-LAN interconnection is driving high-speed requirements (it is silly to connect high-speed 100 Mbps LANs through a 56-Kbps WAN). Multimedia applications also require more than 100 Mbps. Steady growth of applications in imaging, high-definition TV, client-server computing, and large distributed databases also require high-speed services. Another driver for these networks is the expected growth in data communications over voice communications. Currently data traffic in typical organizations is 30 percent, the rest is voice. This equation is expected to reverse with data traffic to comprise 70 percent of the network traffic in organizations. We discuss multimedia applications in Section 2.7.2 to illustrate how this application area can affect networks of the future.

The high-speed networks are characterized by

- Fiber optic transmission media
- Data rates at 100 Mbps or even in Gigabps over wide areas
- Ability to handle millions of packets per second as compared to thousands per second of today's networks
- Designed to handle data, voice and video
- Extremely low error rate of bits transmitted (10^{-14} as compared to 10^{-6})
- More error control at end-points than intermediate "hops"
- Network propagation delay is significant compared to transmission delay
- Low switching delays (2 to 5 milliseconds versus 50 to 100 millisecond)
- Intelligent and large in size
- Active development of standards before widespread deployment of products
- Concerted research and development efforts.

Unfortunately, these networks have added numerous new terms, jargon and vocabulary to an already terminology-rich field. Consider, for example, the following terms: SONET, SMDS, BISDN, ATM, frame relay, cell relay, SS7, supernetworks, etc. What do these terms mean and how are they interrelated? Figure 2.34 presents a taxonomy which may help to put some of these terms in perspective.

At the lowest level of high-speed networks are the fiber optic digital technologies. SONET (Synchronous Optical Network), discussed in Section 2.7.3, uses fiber optic to provide data rates which are much higher than the currently popular T1 and T3 lines. Growth in the use of fiber optics for local, wide and metropolitan area networks is unprecedented. The WAN data rates of more than 100 Mbps provided through SONET offer many interesting scenarios because at present, the transfer rate between a CPU and a local disk is at about 100 Mbps. Thus a user could potentially access a file on a local disk, on a LAN server in the same building, or on a computer in another city with roughly the same speed. This raises the question of remote versus local processing: What is remote and what is local? Due to this, many observers feel that the high-speed networks will eliminate the notion of distance in communications <McQuillan 1990>.

The next level of technologies shown in Fig. 2.34 is the intelligent networks, which have moved the intelligence from the network switches to databases. These networks and the associated standard, Signalling System 7 (SS7), are discussed in Section 2.7.4.

At the next level, the standardization efforts are laying the foundation for widespread deployment of high-speed technology over fiber networks. Examples of MAN standards, already discussed, are FDDI, DQDB and SMDS. In wide area networks, frame relay (variable sized packets) and cell relay (fixed-sized packets) are being used in the fast packet switching systems. Fast packet switching systems are discussed in Section 2.7.5.

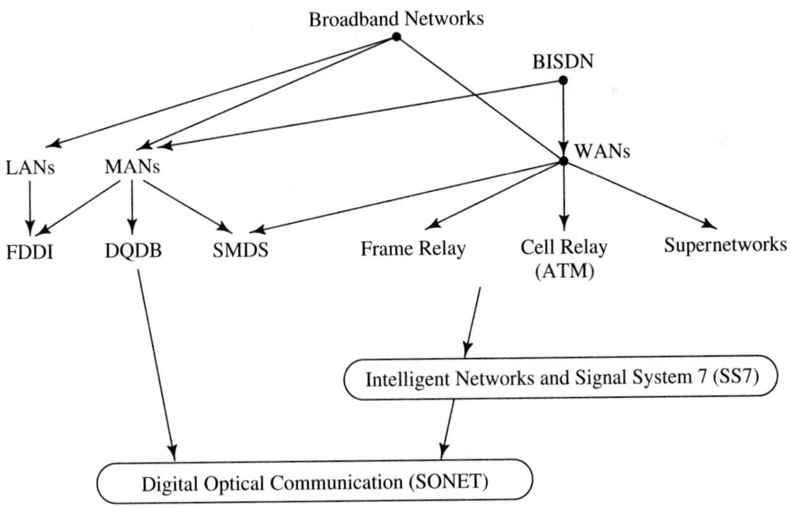

FIGURE 2.34 A Taxonomy of High-Speed (Broadband) Network Technologies

SMDS is being developed as a standard for broadband MANs as well as WANs. SMDS, discussed in Section 2.7.6, is expected to provide a public high-speed network which will satisfy the needs of a wide range of users. Broadband ISDN (BISDN) is expected to provide many of the technologies discussed so far to end users through a limited number of interfaces. This role of BISDN is discussed in Section 2.7.7. Cellular networks, wireless LANs, and satellite networks, although not normally included in high-speed networks, are discussed in Section 2.7.8 for completeness and their potential impact on future technologies.

Supernetworks are being developed which combine many high-speed LANs, MANs, and WANs. In addition, the research efforts of many government and industrial laboratories are directed toward development of high-speed services in the range of 1000 Mbps (1 Giga bps). An example is the National Research and Education Network (NREN), which has been proposed to operate at 3 Gbps. These networks are discussed in Section 2.7.9.

2.7.2 Multimedia Applications and Networks

Multimedia applications support data, voice, video and facsimile on the same physical links. The multimedia networks support several interesting applications in office automation and factory automation due to the tight integration of voice and data, such as <McQuillan 1991, Little 1991>:

- Innovative applications in document storage and retrieval systems which intermix voice, data, and images
- Multimedia electronic mail, which can allow the correspondents to exchange formatted text, pictures, animations, audio, and video
- Applications in teleconferencing, which establish a group rapport through a feeling of "presence" and body language. An example is remotely located workers participating in the development and modification of multimedia documents
- The voice annotation of text and graphics, and "videotex videos" with synchronized animation and music
- The multimedia mix, which includes digitally coded images and moving videos
- Audio and visual two-way communications on the broadcast and cable TV.

2.7.2.1 Examples of Multimedia Applications

Many multimedia applications are being reported in the literature. Here are some examples:

- The previously mentioned real estate search application in which a user searches for a house by using a combination of text, voice, pictures and video. A user first browses through descriptions and pictures of the houses on his or her workstation. A "visit" to the house can be requested which plays a movie about the house on a window of the workstation.

- The Digital News System, which was demonstrated in the EDUCOM 1990 conference in Atlanta <Hoffert 1991>. This system integrates interactive computing, newspapers, televisions and high-speed networks into one news package. This system combines the best aspects of newspapers (user control in browsing, selecting and reading) and television (dynamics and power of moving images and sound) and personal computers (interactive commands and displays). The users of this system could "drive" the news by directly going to the items of interest or browse through news items.
- The MediaView digital publication system, which was designed to take maximum advantage of the media-rich hardware and software capabilities of computer systems such as NEXT <Phillips 1991>. MediaView extends the what-you-see-is-what-you-get (WYSIWYG) word processing metaphor to multimedia components such as graphics, audio, video, and object and image-based animations. These components are subject to the select/cut/copy/paste paradigm just like text thus giving the user powerful editing capabilities. In addition, anything Mediaview displays on the screen can be printed on a printer or stored as a PostScript or TIFF file for processing by other applications.

2.7.2.2 Network Implications

The main implication of the multimedia applications is that they require very high bandwidth networks. For example, consider the following case presented by McQuillan <1990>. A color workstation screen requiring 1024 x 1024 bit resolution with 24 bits of color would require 24 million bits of data storage. For moving video, each frame (screen) needs to be transmitted several times per second. At 30 frames per second, 720 million bits would need to be transmitted per second. In other words, the communication channel would need 720 Mbps data rate. This is much higher than the FDDI and many other technologies of 100 Mbps. At present, cards are becoming available for workstations for 30:1 data compression. Even with 50:1 compression, this still requires 15 Mbps to support one multimedia application.

Let us compare this with an application which uses character strings (text data) for screen input/output. An all text screen may only contain 1024 characters, or 8 K bits. Even if a full screen needed to be sent 30 times per second (a relatively high frequency for text transmission), the channel data rate needed is about 240 Kbps.

It remains to be seen whether video communications emerge as a separate networking application or as an integrated component of data communications. In the latter case, a videoconference may appear as another window on a workstation.

An overview of the multimedia networks and services can be found in Verma <1990, Chapter 8>. McQuillan <1991>, and Little <1991> present a networking perspective of multimedia. *IEEE Communications Magazine*, May 1992, surveys activities in multimedia services, standards, and applications. Many detailed technical papers on multimedia communications can be found in the August 1992 issue of *Computer Communications.* The April and July 1991 issues of the *Communications of the ACM* have many articles on the standards, environments and applications of the multimedia systems. The May 1990 issue of *Computer Communications* is devoted to multimedia communications and has many papers on the transport services, network architectures, databases, and applications of multimedia applications. Shepherd and Salmony <Shepherd 1990> give details about how some of the network standards are being extended to handle multimedia networks.

2.7.3 SONET (Synchronous Optical Network)

Synchronous Optical Networks (SONET) is one of the basic high-speed transmission technologies of the future. SONET was proposed by Bellcore based on the requirements from the Bell Operating Companies (BOCs) to interconnect high-speed fiber networks. SONET is a fiber optic based standard which provides a hierarchy of services ranging from 51.84 Mbps to 2488 Mbps. Higher rates will be possibly included into SONET services as the technology for higher data rates becomes available. These services represented as OC-1 through OC-48 are hierarchies of line speeds that can carry data at much higher speeds than the existing T-carrier technology. Table 2.4 shows the SONET OC (optical carrier) level characteristics and the existing T-carrier services. Some SONET rates are being considered for immediate BISDN application: 155.52 Mbps, 622 Mbps, and 2.4 Gbps.

It can be seen that SONET can carry data almost 50 times faster than the popular T3 rates (OC-48 can carry up to 2488 Mbps). It also provides higher quality of signals and end-to-end network monitoring <Violino 1991>. SONET concentrates on multiplexing low-speed channels to high-speed fiber optic trunks. Basically a SONET frame, called a SONET payload, can represent 52 Mbps. Each byte in the payload represents a 64 Kbps channel (DS-0 speed). The SONET standard was proposed to ANSI in 1985 and to CCITT in 1986. The SONET hierarchy shown in Table 2.4 was approved by both bodies by 1988. In addition, the frame structures for SONET hierarchies were approved. Babcock <1990> gives a good overview of the SONET

TABLE 2.4 The SONET Hierarchy of Services

Level	*Line Data Rate (Mbps)*
OC-1	51.84
OC-3	155.52
OC-9	466.56
OC-12	622.08
OC-18	933.12
OC-24	1244.16
OC-36	1866.24
OC-48	2488.32

T-Carrier Services

Service Type	*Carrier Type*	*Million Bits per Second (Mbps)*	*No. of Voice Channels*
DS-1	T1	1.544	24
DS-1c	T1C	3.152	48
DS-2	T2	6.312	96
DS-3	T3	44.736	672
DS-4	T4M	274.176	4032

hierarchies and frame formats. SONET planning and engineering details can be found in Aprille <1990>, and Sandesara <1990>. The SONET standards are reviewed in Violino <1991>.

2.7.4 Intelligent Networks

Most existing telecommunication networks use switches which are preprogrammed for routing the traffic between end-points. Many advanced future network services depend on the concept of an intelligent network. Figure 2.35 shows a simplified view of an intelligent network architecture. In this service, the customer-dialed number is not the network address of the terminating line. Instead, this number is an index into a database that contains the address and the attributes of a selected carrier. The database contains large amount of information about the network and is not replicated at every switch (several switches share a few replicated copies). The database and the processing programs can provide the intelligence needed to determine the desired carrier based on user specified characteristics. An example of this service is the 800 service being provided by AT&T and several regional telephone companies. The subscriber 800 call is used to search a database which contains information about various 800 carriers. The carrier selection may be based on minimal cost, time of day, day of the week, end-point locations, etc.

The main idea of intelligent networks is to move the intelligence away from the switch and into a database. Thus each user call is handled as a transaction. A new signaling system, called Signalling System 7 (SS7), uses this smart database and dumb switch concept to provide the intelligent network features. SS7 is the foundation for many of the high speed services being developed.

The main advantage of the intelligent networks over the conventional switching systems is that intelligent networks can be easily customized because more "knowledge" is embedded in the database. In the older systems, the functionality was concentrated in the software programs and hardware of the switches. In addition,

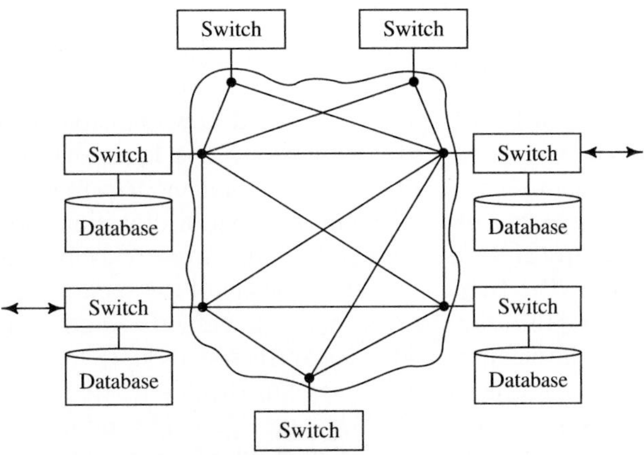

FIGURE 2.35 Simplified View of Intelligent Network

the same switch can be used by a wide range of users because the need to reprogram the switches is minimized. The intelligent network views the telecommunications infrastructure as an interactive distributed computing system in which each user call is handled as a work session (a transaction). Different applications (media, computer-based analysis tools) can be activated and deactivated during the course of a work session by using software and databases. This leads to many interesting potential applications. Details about intelligent networks can be found in Berman <1992>, Duran <1992>, and Browne <1986>. The February 1992 issue of *IEEE Communications Magazine* is devoted to the intelligent networks and contains many articles on the evolution, standards, operations, and management aspects of intelligent networks.

2.7.5 Fast Packet Switching Networks

Broadband LANs and MANs use token ring and Ethernet type techniques for message delivery and recognition. For example, FDDI uses token ring. The high-speed WANs use fast packet switching systems which move millions of packets per second over fiber networks. Fast packet switching systems are much more reliable than older packet switching systems. In addition, these networks have intelligent end-points which can deal with errors in transmission. These systems use the following techniques:

- Move the error processing and flow control from the network to the end-points. Frame relays, discussed later, support such technologies.
- Simplify the switch processing to route the message through the network. The Banyan Switch, discussed later, satisfies this requirement.
- Employ new multiplexing techniques to multiplex different traffic patterns into SONET frames. Asynchronous Transfer Mode (ATM) is such a technique.
- Use connectionless instead of connection-based services to eliminate the call-setup time.

2.7.5.1 Frame Relay

Frame relay can be viewed as a stripped down version of X.25 packet switching systems (see Appendix A for a review of X.25). It removes much of the X.25 tables and processing overhead, thus providing a giant step toward fast packet switching systems. Frame relay allows dynamic bandwidth allocation and provides error control and flow control at the network end-points. Frame relay uses variable-length packets, called frames. The frame sizes are typically of the same length generated by LANs (token ring and Ethernet LANs generate variable-length frames). An advantage is that frame relay is intended to give WAN speeds at T3 level (45 Mbps), which is not possible through other technologies. Due to this, frame relay is being thought of as being the next generation of X.25 systems. Many T1 vendors are providing frame-relay services. Examples of the frame relay standards are LAPD (link access procedure-D) I.122 and Q.931.

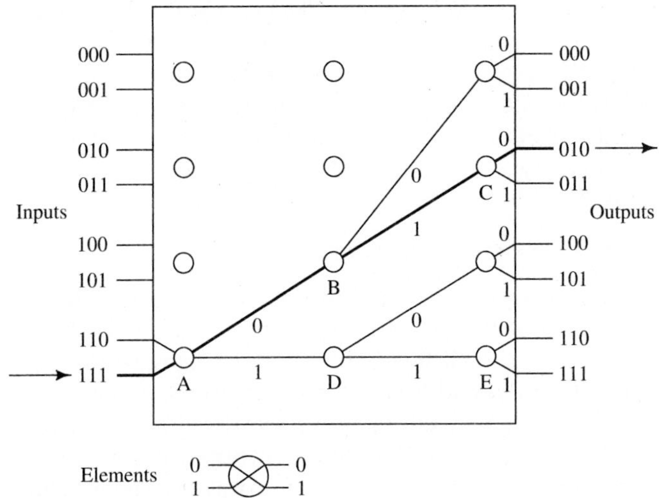

FIGURE 2.36 Banyan Switch

Frame relay assumes very reliable and fast fiber networks. The main limitation of frame relay services is its poor flow control (it drops packets) and no error control. It is not a good idea to run frame relay on noisy networks <Nolle 1992>.[6]

2.7.5.2 Fast Switches

Switches are used in large networks to route messages to their destination. A special type of switch, called Banyan switch, is used in high-speed networks to minimize switching delays. A Banyan switch is essentially a multistage switch in which there is exactly one path from any input to any output (Fig. 2.36). The address of a node (source or destination) is represented by an n-tuple with each component being 0 or 1 (for example, the nodes in Fig. 2.36 are represented by 000, 001, 111, etc.). Thus the switch attempts to connect, say, node 111 to 110. The switch consists of a number of elements where each element receives inputs on two "wires" (0 and 1) and routes them to outputs (0 and 1). A switching element is displayed in the inset in Fig. 2.36. Each stage of the switch operates on one bit of the address. The bold line in Fig. 2.36 illustrates the operation of this switch by showing how an input from node 111 is routed to node 010. The switching element A, D and E would be used if the input from 111 needed to be routed to 111.

2.7.5.3 Cell Relay and ATM (Asynchronous Transfer Mode)

Cell relay uses fixed-length packets and is used in the T1 multiplexers. The frame size in the cell relay systems is 48 bytes of data plus a five-byte header. Cell relays are expected to be used in BISDN and SMDS systems (see next section). ATM uses cell

[6]At the time of this writing, frame relay at 45 Mbps has been demonstrated in trade shows but not commercially available.

relay for multiplexing bursty traffic into SONET. Why is ATM needed? It is easy to multiplex constant traffic (synchronous) into SONET, but it is not easy to multiplex bursty traffic (asynchronous) into SONET. ATM multiplexes bursty traffic into SONET payload by representing each cell as one byte in the SONET payload. The main advantage of ATM over other multiplexing techniques is that it uses small, fixed-sized packets and simple protocols which are essential for fast packet switching. The *Computer Networks and ISDN Systems* journal, Vol. 24, No. 4, 1992, is a special issue on ATM.

2.7.5.4 Connectionless Services

In large networks with thousands of stations, "connectionless" communications may be used instead of the "leased line" connection-oriented service which requires a connection to be established before data exchange. In connectionless services, no connection is established between the end-points which saves considerable time in large networks. Instead, each party sends a "datagram," which contains the data being sent plus the destination address and the routing information. This datagram fights its way to the destination, finding alternate paths in case of failures and congestions in the network. Datagrams were used initially in LANs, where the message was "broadcasted" to all stations and picked up by the addressed station. The idea of using datagram services in large networks was introduced in the ARPANET project. It is being used increasingly in LANs and MANs. The main implication of the connectionless service is that the senders and receivers must do their own error checking to handle missing and out of sequence datagrams. We will treat this subject in the next chapter.

2.7.6 Switched Multimegabit Data Service (SMDS)

SMDS, introduced by Bellcore, is a public packet switched data service that provides LAN-like performance and features over wide or metropolitan area networks. SMDS currently allows several remotely located LANs to communicate with each other at 45 Mbps (T3 speeds). The objectives of SMDS are to

- Provide customers with the ability to interconnect LANs, computer systems, and workstations across a MAN and WAN.
- Provide a public (24 hour a day, 7 days a week) MAN/WAN solution at high speeds which may eventually support faster services than the private FDDI, DQDB, and frame relay networks. In addition, SMDS is expected to provide MAN as well as WAN services.
- Provide high throughput and low delay performance (20 millisecond for 95 percent of the packets at T3 speed).
- Support extremely low error rate (about 5 undetected errors in 10 trillion) and high packet delivery rate (about 1 packet loss for every 1000 delivered).
- Allow integration into existing communication architectures—that is, evolve the SMDS service as the underlying technologies (e.g., SONET) evolve without changing user access points.

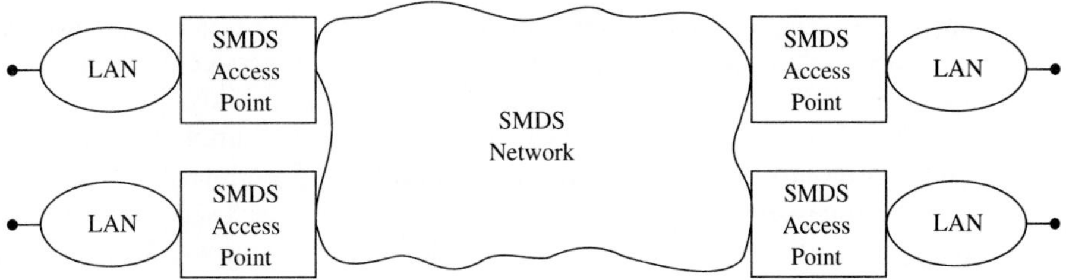

FIGURE 2.37 SMDS Network

Initial deployments of SMDS provide T1 and T3 speeds, with higher speeds expected in the future. It is expected that telephone companies will deploy SMDS in three phases as of 1992. Figure 2.37 shows a typical SMDS configuration. The users would access the SMDS public network through SMDS access points. Many equipment vendors, such as SUN Microsystems, are beginning to develop SMDS cards for SMDS access. Early SMDS applications were demonstrated at the Interop '90 show in San Jose, California. The SMDS connections were established between remote sites in St. Louis, Missouri, Atlanta, Georgia, Cedar Knolls, New Jersey, White Plains, New York, and San Jose, California. An application by a medical-imaging company showed how to transfer digitized X-rays and other medical pictures at high speeds between remotely located sites. Additional demonstrations included editing, file transfers and graphics over high-speed networks. Many more applications have been demonstrated in Interop '91 and Interop '92. For example, Bell Atlantic demonstrated an SMDS connection between Philadelphia and Washington, D.C. in the Interop '92 Conference. This demonstration showed file transfers and terminal emulation services via the SMDS services from a Novell Network.

SMDS is based on the IEEE 802.6 switching standard and currently uses T1/T3 speeds. SMDS appears to provide more attractive functionality than FDDI. For example, SMDS can be used over long distances, while FDDI is limited to customer-owned fiber (multimode fiber). In addition, SMDS can support limitless stations, while FDDI is restricted to 500 stations. Moreover, FDDI stations cannot be more than 2 km apart, while no such restriction exists for SMDS. FDDI may, however, be a better alternative in a campus environment where the above restrictions do not present a problem (FDDI operates at 100 Mbps while SMDS at present operates at 45 Mbps). SMDS may be best used to interconnect FDDI rings over wide areas. SMDS is also a better alternative to frame relay packet switching because SMDS is fully defined and uses fixed cell sizes. Frame relay gives many options which can lead to incompatibilities and uses variable length messages which leads to complex processing. More details about SMDS technology can be found from Bellcore and in articles by Dix <1990>, Piscitello <1990>, and Lang <1990>.

2.7.7 The Role of Broadband ISDN (BISDN)

BISDN is an all fiber optic ISDN operating at more than 100 Mbps slated for the early twenty-first century. BISDN, as explained earlier in this chapter, is expected to allow the subscriber (home, business) to access a variety of technologies from a single service access point. A typical application of BISDN would be to allow SMDS, fast packet switching systems, FDDI MANs or any other services as options to a BISDN user (Fig. 2.38). For example, if two remotely located LANs need to be connected, BISDN will give the user the choices between various technologies based on the speed and cost requirements. The LANs may need high-speed interconnections due to, say, image processing applications which require rapid exchange of large data files. In other cases, the two sites may be using videoconferencing, which requires integration of voice, data, and images at high speed.

Let us consider the use of Broadband ISDN (BISDN) in interconnecting FDDI MANs to form very fast wide area networks. Due to the 100 Mbps speed of FDDI MANs and the BISDN wide area networks which interconnect them, it is possible to envision end-to-end 100-Mbps networks. However, FDDI is primarily designed for data communications, while BISDN is expected to carry voice communications. Due to this, the FDDI and BISDN standards need to be harmonized. For details, refer to Verma <1990>.

2.7.8 Cellular Networks, Wireless LANs, and Satellite Networks

Cellular Networks. Cellular telephones and residential cordless telephones (wireless systems) were introduced in the mid-1980s. These relatively new technologies are enjoying widespread public approval with a rapidly increasing demand. To meet this demand, a second generation of technologies is emerging with digital speech transmission and the ability to integrate cordless systems into other networks. In the meantime, researchers are developing the third generation of technologies for the next century.

The unique features of the cellular and cordless networks are as follows:

- The senders and receivers of information are not physically connected to a network. Thus the location of a sender/receiver is unknown prior to start of communication and can change during the conversation.
- The communication channel between senders/receivers is often impaired by noise, interference and weather fluctuations.
- The bandwidths, and consequently data rates, of communication channels are restricted by government regulations. The government policies allow only a few frequency ranges for wireless communications.

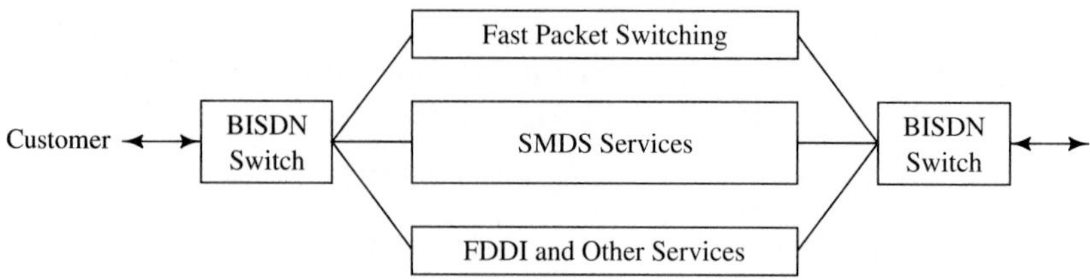

FIGURE 2.38 Broadband Networks and BISDN

The current wireless systems use many different, incompatible standards which rely on analog frequency modulation techniques. Each cordless telephone, for example, comes with its own base station and needs to be only compatible with that base station. The second generation wireless systems will use three major standards: one for North America, one for Western Europe, and a third for Japan. These systems will be designed as components of a larger network. Unfortunately, the three second generation standards are not compatible. The focus of the third generation systems is on a single network which will combine all first and second generation wireless services.

Many groups are at present working on the architectures, standards and the underlying technologies related to the cordless and cellular services. Examples of the groups are researchers at Bell Communications Research (Bellcore) and Rutgers University Wireless Information Network Laboratory (WINLAB). A technical overview of the trends and research in cellular and wireless services can be found in Goodman <1991>. The *Encyclopedia of Telecommunications*, Vol. 2, Froehlich <1991>, has four chapters devoted to the cellular technology, systems design, regulatory matters and subscriber products.

Wireless LANs. Wireless LANs are an area of interesting development. In such LANs, workstations in a building can communicate with each other without having to be connected to physical cables. This is a major benefit because LAN wiring can be the most expensive component of a LAN. At the time of this writing, wireless LANs have several limitations such as extremely short distances, lack of wireless adapter cards for PCs and workstations, limited connectivity to other LANs, and relatively low speeds. However, this technology is still in its infancy. In addition, the popularity of portable computers is expected to fuel the demand for wireless LANs. Wireless technology can also be used to interconnect LANs across buildings. Examples are the Motorola Altair Plus and Altair Vistapoint modules.

Currently available wireless LANs use one of three signal types to transmit data: infrared, spread spectrum, and narrowband microwave. Infrared signals behave like ordinary light (they cannot penetrate sold objects). Thus infrared wireless LANs are limited to data transmission to line of sight. Infrared technology is simple and well proven (it is used commonly in remote controls for VCRs and TVs). In addition, infrared signals are not regulated by the Federal Communications Commission (FCC). Spread spectrum is most widely used in wireless LANs. These LANs transmit in the industrial, scientific, and medical bands designated by the FCC. These bands are not licensed but are regulated by the FCC to prevent interference. This technology was developed for military and intelligence operations (the message is "spread" over a range of frequencies to make it jam-resistant). Wireless LANs based on narrowband microwave technology use the 18.82-to-18.87 GHz and 19.6-to-19.21 GHz frequency ranges. These frequency ranges are licensed by the FCC, which means that a vendor must be approved by the agency to use these frequency ranges. Many wireless LAN vendors consider this to be a restriction. For detailed tradeoffs between the different type of wireless LANs, the underlying technologies, potential applications, and the market trends (see Mathias <1992>, Axner <1992>, Arnum <1992>).

Satellite Networks. Satellite communication systems are also growing steadily. In general, the market for satellite systems can be subdivided into three segments:

1. High data rates (hundreds of megahertz) for the commercial broadcast markets and common carrier satellite communication systems
2. Intermediate data rates (9.6 Kbps to several Mbps) for government and corporate data networks
3. Low data rates (less than 9.6 Kbps) for point-of-sale terminals, credit-card verification, reservation systems, and others.

Many vendors are providing satellite services and/or using private satellites. Examples of the vendors are Motorola, IBM and Hewlett-Packard. It is expected that satellite communication systems will see more growth in the first category. The December, 1991 issue of *Telecommunications* has many articles on satellite systems.

2.7.9 Supernetworks and Gigabit Networks

Interconnection and integration of LANs, MANs and WANs into large networks, called supernetworks or networks of networks, is an area of considerable growth. In these systems, many LANs are interconnected through WANs to form large networks serving thousands of stations. The primary business pressure behind these networks is that a large number of LANs need to exchange information with each other. Supernetworks are used in one organization or can be established between many organizations for cooperative work. Perhaps the best-known example of a supernet is the Internet,[7] an outgrowth of ARPANET (Advanced Research Project Agency Network), which at present connects more than 60,000 computers located at different academic and research centers. Another example is the EDSNET, which serves all EDS and GM customers around the globe.

Figure 2.39 shows an example of a supernetwork. Many of the current and future supernetworks will continue to use X.25 based packet switching systems to interconnect copper and fiber LANs (see Barrett <1991> for an extensive review of the X.25 based supernetworks). The future supernetworks are expected to employ newer technologies such as BISDN, SONET, and SMDS, as shown in Fig. 2.39. The high-speed wide area network will connect many cities, where each city may be supported by one or more FDDI metropolitan area networks which serve as backbones to many copper LANs. Technical details and examples of using SMDS WANs to interconnect FDDI LANs/MANs are given by Clapp <1991>.

The U.S. government High Performance Computing Act of 1991 is expected to provide a Gigabit supernetwork for advanced research. This Act has approved the formation of a National Research and Education Network (NREN), which will operate at 3 Gbps. The spirit of NREN is the same as the ARPANET project. When fully developed, NREN will provide a powerful basis for experimenting with advanced technology which will become commercial in the next century. Many Gigabit

[7]The term *Internet* (note the capital *I*) is used to refer to the ARPANET originated supernetwork.

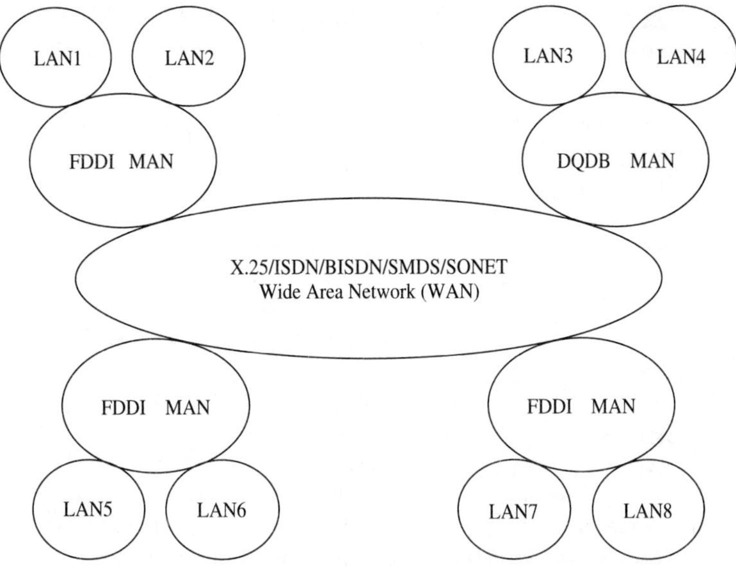

FIGURE 2.39 A Supernetwork Example

testbeds are operational at present. An example is the AURORA Gigabit network, established by Bellcore, which connects Philadelphia, Morristown, Yorktown Heights, and Cambridge <Biersack 1992>. Many other research activities at present are being directed at Gigabit networks (see the *IEEE Communications Magazine*, April 1992, and the *Computer Networks and ISDN Systems*, Vol. 24, No. 2, 1992, for many papers on this topic).

2.7.10 Summary of High Speed Networks

It can be seen from the preceding discussion that the networks are moving toward fiber optic multimedia systems, with interconnected LANs, MANs and WANs, operating at 100 Mbps or more. Figure 2.40, based on Kleinrock <1992>, shows the tradeoffs between the various competing technologies. It can be seen that for steady traffic patterns and relatively low speed requirements, T1 and T3 services are adequate. However, as we move into bursty traffic for high speeds, then SMDS and BISDN show a great deal of promise.

The following statements summarize current and future high-speed trends:

- New applications are expected to drive the demand for high-speed networks.
- ISDN and T1 networks are currently available.
- FDDI and T3 networks are beginning to be deployed.
- SMDS, DQDB and frame relay networks are imminent in 1992 and beyond.
- BISDN will become available toward the end of this century to provide a common access to the technologies mentioned before.

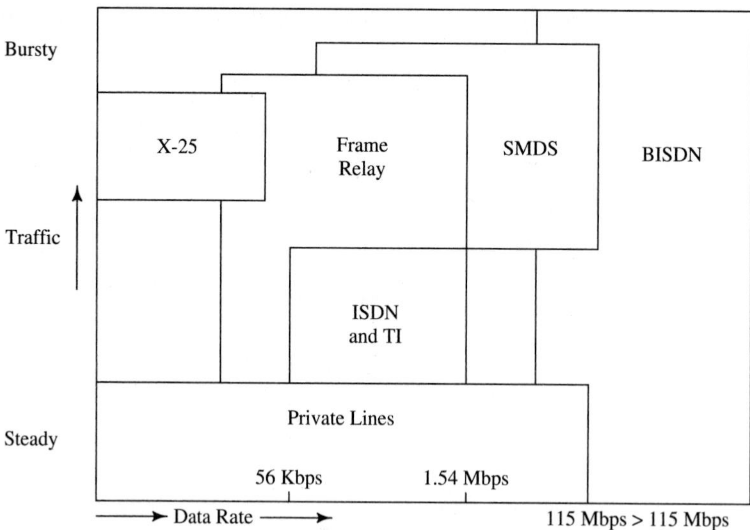

FIGURE 2.40 Broadband Technology Choices (Kleinrock, 1992)

- NREN will hopefully be as valuable to the networking in the next century as ARPANET has been in the 1970s and 1980s.

2.8 Network Performance Overview

Performance means different things to different people at different times. Some of the common usages of the term *performance* are as follows:

- *Response time performance*: Does this system provide adequate turnaround per user?
- *Throughput performance*: Does the system maximize number of services per unit time?
- *Economic performance*: Is this system worth the cost?
- *Availability performance*: Does this system satisfy the availability restrictions?

The focus of this section is on response time performance and availability performance.

2.8.1 Response Time Performance

Simply stated, response time of a transaction (a unit of work) is the elapsed time between transaction arrival and completion. A transaction is routed, processed and delayed for each service it needs. Examples of the services needed are CPU cycles, disk accesses, and communication transmissions. In the simplest case, the total response time RT of a transaction is given by the sum of all processing and queuing delays:

$$= \Sigma \text{ processing time} + \Sigma \text{ queuing time (busy + lockout)}$$

The methods used for response time estimation are analytical, simulations and/or benchmarks. Choice of a method depends on accuracy needed (absolute versus comparative), time and money allowed for the analysis, flexibility needed in the model and size of the problem (some tools are good for small networks only). We will introduce a simple analytical method which can be used for quick paper and pencil estimation of response times. A model is introduced which first ignores queuing, and adds it later.

Without queuing, RT, the response time of a transaction, is given by

$$\text{RT} = \sum_i N(i) \cdot S(i) \tag{2.1}$$

where $S(i)$ = time needed for completion of service i and $N(i)$ = number of times service i is needed. These two parameters can be easily measured. In these formulas, dot $(\cdot)$ is used to indicate multiplication. The example shown in Table 2.5 illustrates the usefulness of this simple formula. This formula can be used to calculate lower bounds (best case) of response time estimates.

Let us now add the impact of queuing on response time calculations. Queues are formed due to two reasons: The device providing the service may be busy, or it may be locked by another activity. The first condition is an indication of workload (too many services requested), and the second condition is a result of resources being reserved (e.g., a file being updated) by one activity. In this section, our primary focus is on queuing due to workload.

We need to introduce another parameter, $A(i)$, to handle queuing. $A(i)$ = arrival rate of requests for service i. For example, if a workstation sends 10 messages per second on the network, then $A(i) = 10$. The following formula shows utilization $U(i)$ of a server i:

$$U(i) = \text{server } i \text{ utilization} = A(i) \cdot S(i) \tag{2.2}$$

A rule of thumb used in queuing calculations is that $U(i)$ should be kept below 0.7 to avoid queuing. The theoretical foundation for this rule of thumb is the following well-known M/M/1 (Markovian arrival, Markovian service time, 1 server) formula <Kleinrock 1976>:

$$\text{Queue length at server } i = Q(i) = U(i)/[1 - U(i)] \tag{2.3}$$

Thus $Q(i)=1$, if $U(i) = 0.5$; $Q(i)$ reaches infinity if $U(i) = 1$. The basic assumptions of the M/M/1 queuing formula are as follows:

- Arrivals at the server are independent of each other.
- Service times are independent of each other.

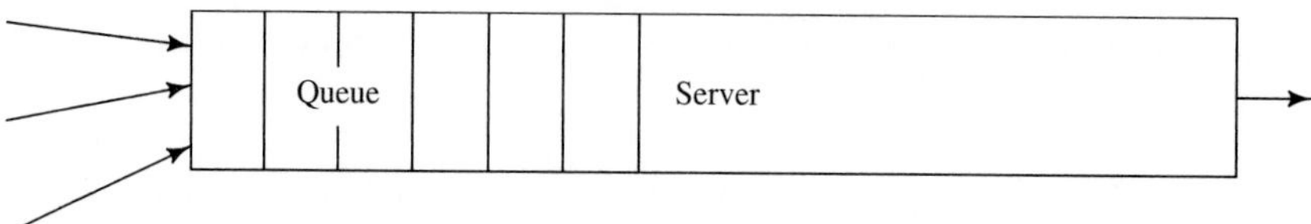

FIGURE 2.41 A Single Server Queuing System

It is not necessary for the users to know that these two assumptions are based on stochastic processes and queuing theory. For example, these arrival and service time patterns are called Poisson and Exponential distributions, respectively, in stochastic processes. Poisson arrival rates and Exponential server times are referred to as Markovian behavior in queuing systems.

The net effect of queuing is that the service time increases due to queuing. The service time $S(i)$ is replaced with $S'(i)$ (see Fig. 2.41):

$$S'(i) = \text{service time at server } i \text{ after queuing} = S(i) + S(i) \cdot Q(i) \tag{2.4}$$

The example shown in Table 2.6 illustrates the impact of server utilization on queue length and response time. This example essentially reworks the example shown in Table 2.5 by adding queuing calculations.

So far we have focused on queuing for a single server. In most practical situations, a queuing network is formed where output of one server becomes an input to another server (Fig. 2.42). Jackson's Theorem <Kleinrock 1976>, shows that the following very useful results apply as long as Poisson arrival and Exponential server assumptions hold at each server in the queuing network.

- Each server can be treated independently.
- Arrival rate at a server is the sum of all arrivals from all sources.

Jackson's theorem is used heavily because it applies to stochastic routing also—that is, if a message is routed to server i with probability $p(i)$. In fact, even when the Poisson

TABLE 2.5 A Simple Example of Response Time Estimation

PROBLEM: A program P reads a 12-byte customer account number from a terminal, searches a database for the account number (on the average 2 I/O are needed to locate a customer, one to read the index and the second to read the record). It then displays the customer information (120 bytes) on the terminal. P runs on a computer C which is connected to terminals through 1200 bps lines. If C can complete 10 I/O per second on the average, then what is the response time experienced by a user sitting on a terminal T. We can assume that each byte occupies 10 bits in the network (8 bit data, 2 start/stop bits).

SOLUTION: Three services are needed to complete this transaction:

$S(1)$ = transmit time (input to program) = 12 × 10/1200 = 0.1 sec
$S(2)$ = transmit time (output to program) = 120 × 10/1200 = 1 sec
$S(3)$ = time per I/O service = 1/10 = 0.1 sec

Total response time RT = $S(1) + S(2) + 2 \times S(3) = 0.1 + 1 + 2 \times 0.1 = 1.3$ sec

In this case, the bottleneck (the service where most time is consumed) is the communication line.

TABLE 2.6 Impact of Queuing

Consider the same customer file example in Table 2.5. We want to consider the impact of queuing on computer C. The following table shows the utilization, the average queue length, the average wait time, and the total service time at the I/O server (computer C). We assume initially that the requests for customer records arrive 1 per second on computer C. This gives us $A(3) = 2$ ($A(3)$ shows the number of I/O per second). This rate is adjusted to study the queuing. The service time $S(3)$ is 0.1 as computed in Table 2.5. We have dropped the index in this table for simplicity.

Arrival Rate A	*Service Time* S	*Utiliz.* $U = A{\cdot}S$	*Queue Length* $Q = U/1 - U$	*Wait Time* $= SQ$	*New (Total) Service Time* $S' = S + SQ$
1	0.1	0.1	0.11	0.011	0.111
5	0.1	0.5	1.0	0.1	0.2
8	0.1	0.8	4.0	0.4	0.5
9	0.1	0.9	9.0	0.9	1.0
10	0.1	1.0	????	????	????

It can be seen that the queue length increases exponentially with an increase in U (Q goes from 4.0 to 9.0 when U increases from 0.8 to 0.9). This is the basis for keeping U to be less than 0.7 in most systems.

Let us now recompute the total response time calculated in Table 2.5 after queuing. Assume that the requests for customers arrive at 4 per second. This yields $A(3) = 8$ for which the new service time per I/O is $S'(3) = 0.5$, as shown above. The new total response is given by:

Total response time RT $= S(1) + S(2) + 2 \times S'(3) = 0.1 + 1 + 2 \times 0.5 = 2.1$ sec

In other words, the response time has almost doubled (from 1.3 to 2.1 sec) due to queuing at the central computer.

arrival and Exponential service time assumptions are not satisfied, this formula is used because there is no other straightforward method for the analytical calculations of response times in queuing networks. Table 2.7 gives another example to illustrate queuing calculations in a network.

The main points about response time calculations are as follows:

- Response time can be roughly estimated in terms of easily observable parameters: A, N, and S.
- Utilization U is a good indicator of server congestion. U should be kept less than 70 percent to avoid excessive queuing.
- In a network of devices, the device with the largest U is the bottleneck.
- U can be reduced by decreasing the arrival rate A, decreasing the service time S, or both. For example, in the customer file example described in Tables 2.5 and 2.6, A can be reduced by putting the customer file at more than one computer and S can be reduced by purchasing a faster disk.

The following procedure may be utilized to estimate the performance of a network:

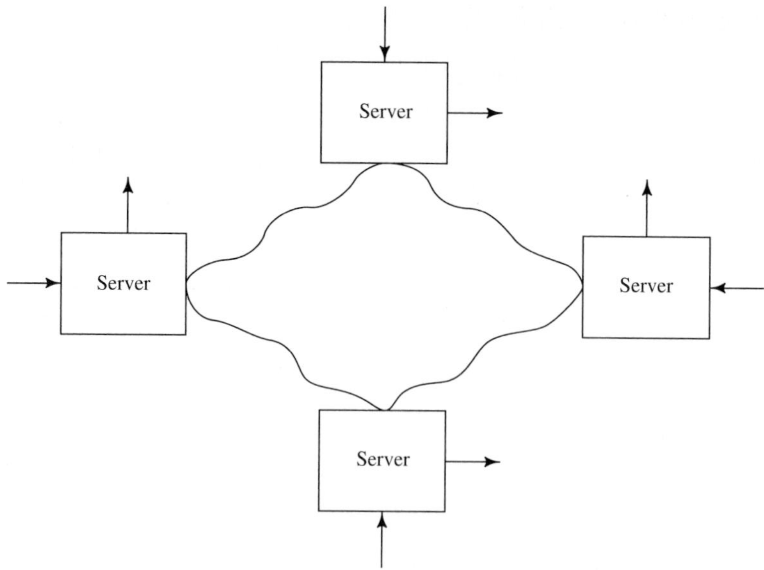

FIGURE 2.42 A Queuing Network Stystem

- Perform best-case analysis by ignoring queuing. In this case, only S and N are needed for computations (see equation 2.1). These calculations can be used as a starting point.
- Determine if performance constraints are satisfied. If not, then there is no need for queuing analysis because if a system does not satisfy the best-case calculations, then it will not satisfy conditions with workload.
- Study the effect of queuing and workload by estimating arrival rates A. The estimate A may be at peak time or average time. Estimate total time including queuing by using the equations 2.2 through 2.4.
- Try to reduce U to less than 0.7 for most devices in the network. In addition, determine the bottleneck device (devices with largest U). Try to reduce U by decreasing A and S.
- If detailed analysis of a configuration is needed, then you may need to simulate.

The examples shown in Tables 2.5, 2.6 and 2.7 illustrate this procedure.

This review of network response time calculations is intended for quick paper and pencil analysis and rules of thumb which can be useful for insights into performance tradeoffs. Extensive literature on network performance evaluation exists. The book by Bertsekas and Gallager, *Data Networks*, second edition, Prentice Hall, 1992, contains extensive discussion on performance analysis of digital networks of today and tomorrow (Arpanet, SNA, Decnet, Ethernet, FDDI, DQDB, ATM, etc.). *Transmission Performance of Evolving Telecommunications Networks*, by Gruber and Williams, Artech House Books, 1992, and *LAN/MAN Optimization Techniques*, by Van Norman, Artech House Books, 1992, contain good user-oriented discussion on

TABLE 2.7 Example of Performance Evaluation

Problem

A company has a corporate network which consists of five Ethernet LANs connected to a mainframe through 56-Kbps lines (see figure). Each LAN has about 20 workstations which generate one message per second; each message is 1000 bytes (10 bits per byte). Most workstations interact with each other on the LAN with only 10 percent of the messages being sent to the mainframe. The messages sent to mainframe access a corporate database which services 50 I/O per second. The organization is concerned about the growth of workstations on the LAN and the impact of these workstations on the mainframe. We can assume that additional workstations will do similar work (generate same traffic pattern).

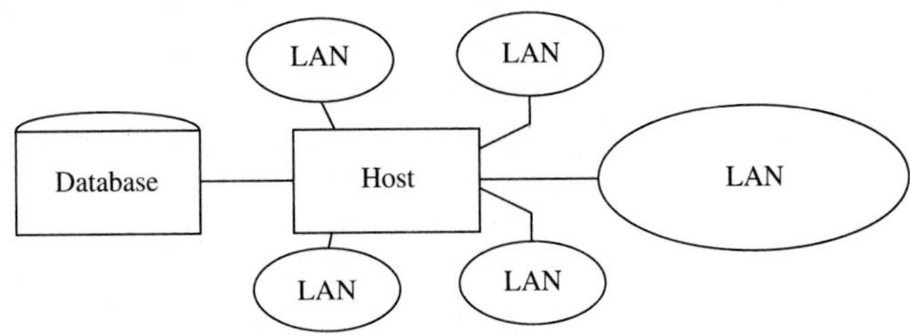

Solution

1. Congestion on LAN cable (calculated for each LAN):
   - Arrival rate A at LAN cable = 20 per sec (20 workstations per LAN)
   - Service time S at cable = average message length/data rate
     Average message length = 1000 bytes, data rate = 10 Mbps (Ethernet)
     $S = (1000 \times 10)/10{,}000{,}000 = .001$ sec
   - Utilization U of the server = $A \times S = 20 \times .001 = 0.02$
   - Since U is small, the ethernet LANs can easily handle the current workload. If the workstations increased to 100, then $A = 100$ per sec and $U = 100 \text{ x } .001 = 0.1$, which is less than the utilization guideline of 0.5 to 0.7.

2. Congestion on WAN Lines (calculated for each line)
   - Arrival rate A at WAN Line = 0.1×20 (10 percent of LAN traffic)
     $A = 2$ per sec
   - Service time S at WAN line = average message length/data rate
     Average message length = 1000 bytes, data rate = 56 Kbps
     $S = (1000 \times 10)/56{,}000 = 0.178$ sec
   - Utilization U of the server = $A \times S = 2 \times 178 = 0.356$
   - Since U is small, the WAN lines can handle the workload. However, if the workstations increase to 100, then $A = 10$ per sec and $U = 10 \times .178 = 1.78$, which is disastrous (U of 1 or greater can cause infinite queuing). In this case, a faster Line or subdivision of each LAN into smaller LANs with 50 workstations are alternatives.

3. Congestion on mainframe database:
   - Arrival rate A at database = $0.1 \times 20 \times 5$ (messages from 5 LANs)
     $A = 10$ per sec
   - Service time S at database = $1/50 = 0.02$ per sec
   - Utilization U of the server = $A \times S = 10 \times .02 = 0.2$
   - Since U is small, the database can handle the current workload. However, if the arrival rate A tripled due to more LANs or more workstations per LAN, the $U = 0.6$, which may cause problems. In this case, it may be better to divide the database into two copies (if the information is read only).

network performance analysis and optimization. An "oldie but goodie" book on theoretical foundations for queuing network calculations is by Kleinrock, *Queuing Systems*, Vol. 2, Wiley, 1976. Many papers on network performance can be found in the IEEE Network Special Issue on Modelling Computer Networks, July 1988.

2.8.2 Network Availability

Network transmission errors and component failures reduce the availability of a network to the user. Transmission errors can occur due to the distances between components, number of components and environmental factors (e.g., weather). The electronic causes can be white noise, impulses, crosstalk and attenuation. The components that can fail are lines, modems, communication controllers, switches, etc.

From a user point of view, availability reflects the percentage of time a system can be used by a user (human or program). Different measures of availability ai of component i have been suggested. Here are two:

$$ai = \text{availability of component } i$$
$$= \frac{\text{Mean time between failures}}{\text{Mean time between failure + Mean time for repair}}$$
$$= \frac{\text{Total "promised" time} - \text{outagetime}}{\text{Total "promised" time}}$$

Both formulas yield the same results. The choice is largely dependent on what statistics are kept in the organization.

The challenge is to determine system availability V in terms of the availabilities $a_1, a_2, a_3, \ldots$ an of the n components in the system. Given three components with availabilities a_1, a_2 and a_3, the system availability V can be determined by the following basic formulas (see Fig. 2.43):

$$V = a_1 \cdot a_2 \cdot a_3 \text{ if } a_1, a_2, a_3 \text{ are serial}$$
$$V = 1 - ((1 - a_1)(1 - a_2)(1 - a_3)) \text{ if } a_1, a_2, a_3 \text{ are parallel}$$

For a mixed network, the many parallel paths can be reduced into one path with equivalent availability. For example, consider the network shown in Fig. 2.43c. We can compute the availability as follows:

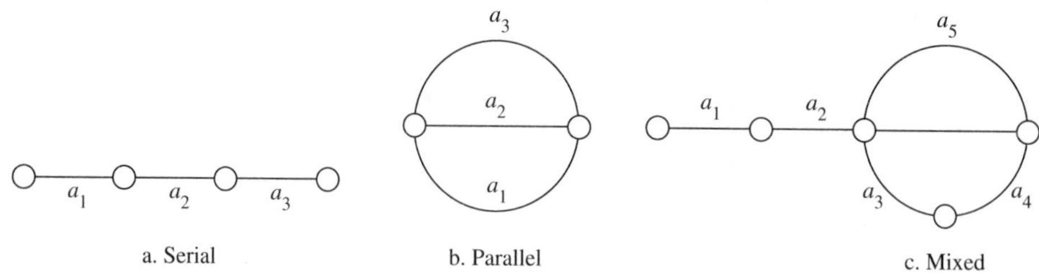

FIGURE 2.43 Network Availability

$$V = a_1 \cdot a_2 \cdot (1 - (1 - a_5)(1 - a_3 a_4))$$

or

$$V = a_1 \cdot a_2 \cdot a' \text{ where } a' = (1 - (1 - a_5)(1 - a_3 a_4))$$

In large networks where several users use portions of networks, it is possible to create user profiles where each profile describes the network components used. For example, the following profiles may exist for users H_1, H_2, H_3:

$$H_1 = (c_1, c_2, c_5, c_9, c_{25})$$
$$H_2 = (c_1, c_2, c_3, c_4, c_{20})$$
$$H_3 = (c_1, c_4, c_5, c_6, c_7, c_8, c_{20})$$

where $c_1, c_2, \ldots c_{25}$ are the network components. The availability for each user profile can now be calculated separately by using the formulas discussed earlier. These profiles can also be useful in estimating impact of a component failure. For example, failure in c_1 will impact H_1, H_2 and H_3, while failure in c_5 will impact only H_1.

The availability V of a system should be translated into business impact. For example, let us assume that the availability V of a large packet switching network for September 1990 is 0.97. This sounds good. However, let us translate this into potential business loss due to network "unavailability" of 0.03. Assuming that the network operates 24 hours a day and 7 days a week, then the network was unavailable for $0.03 \times 720 = 21.6$ hours. This is almost a day! Assuming that the network handles an average traffic of 5,000,000 packets a day, and the users pay 1 cent per packet to the network owner, this indicates a financial loss of almost $50,000 to the network owner. Even if the unavailability could not be measured in terms of dollars, the loss of one day of work activity is much clearer to the user than the availability of 0.97.

2.9 Management Summary and Trends

Communication networks needed for the physical transmission and recognition of data between interconnected devices are moving toward digital communication systems. These systems receive digital data which is regenerated over long distances by eliminating the noise. A hierarchy of digital services, known as the T carriers, are widely in use. Digital communications are increasingly being used for transmission of data, voice and video in communication systems. ISDN (integrated system digital network) is a major step in this direction. ISDN basically gives a user a single point to access a variety of services.

A wide variety of communication media (e.g., copper cables, fiber optics, satellites) are used for the actual transmission of analog/digital signals. The most interesting developments are in fiber optics and the cellular/cordless communication systems. Fiber optics show very high frequency ranges. A single fiber optic cable can support over 30,000 telephone lines and can transmit data over 400 million bits per second (a fiber cable carrying all these telephone lines resembles a single human hair strand). Other reasons for the popularity of fiber optics are their resilience to fire and gaseous combustion (light waves do not generate electrical sparks), very low signal loss and error rates, and high security characteristics. Cellular telephones and residential cordless telephones (wireless systems) are relatively new technologies but are enjoying widespread public approval because they fit our mobile life styles.

Network facilities are generally classified into three categories based on the geographical area covered:

- Local area networks (LANs), which do not use common carrier facilities over short distances with speeds up to 100 Mbps. LANs are commonly used to interconnect computers within the same building and organization.
- Metropolitan area networks (MANs) are essentially large LANs which cover an entire metropolitan area (a city, a suburb, etc.). The evolving metropolitan area networks can be used to interconnect LANs within a metropolitan area.
- Wide area networks (WANs), which use common carrier facilities over long distances commonly with speeds in the range of 1.5 Mbps. WANs are used to interconnect remotely located sites and equipment.

The major trends in network technologies and facilities are as follows:

- Evolution of very fast network technologies, which can send information at 100 million bits per second (Mbps) or higher at short as well as long distances. Examples of such technologies are high-speed networks such as SONET, SMDS, FDDI and BISDN. The major implication of this technology is the "disappearance" of distance. In other words, data access from a local file, a file located across the hall, or a file located across the continent have roughly the same speed. These developments also raise the question, If access speeds at local and remote sites are comparable, then why distribute (i.e., why put data at a local site) if it can be accessed as quickly from a central site? However, this argument assumes that the speed of local I/O will not increase to outweigh the communication speed gains, the latency delays over widely spread WANs will be insignificant, and the number of I/Os for future applications will be smaller. We will see this debate for a few years to come.
- Integration of voice, data, and video services into a single offering. These technologies basically use digital communication techniques to intermix data with other pieces of information. Examples of these technologies are ISDN and broadband ISDN. These technologies lend especially to interesting applications in image processing and multimedia systems which present text, sound, and moving videos to users.
- Development of standards at several levels by various bodies. For example, the IEEE 802 standards describe the interconnection and physical message exchange between devices and physical media. The telecommunications industry is developing standards for telecommunications service offerings. We will consider standards in more detail in the next chapter.

- Evolution of supernetworks in which a high-speed wide area network connects many cities, where each city may be supported by one or more metropolitan area networks which serve as backbones to many LANs.
- Integration of LANs, MANs, and WANs with the broadband ISDN services.

Further Studies. Many books on data communications cover different aspects of communication technologies discussed in this chapter. Many books have been mentioned in appropriate sections of this chapter. Overall, the books by W. Stallings <1987, 1989, 1991, 1992> and U. Black <1987> are especially good. The following major journals are recommended for continued state of the art information:

- *Computer Networks and ISDN Systems*
- *Computer Communications*
- *IEEE Network Magazine*
- *IEEE Communications Magazine*
- *IEEE Transactions on Communications*

For a state of the market and practice evolution, the following trade journals are recommended:

- *Data Communications*
- *Business Communications Review*
- *Communications News*
- *LAN Technology*
- *LAN Magazine*
- *Byte Magazine* (special issues on LANs and communications)
- *PC Magazine* (special issues on LANs and communications)

Problems and Exercises

1. What are the main differences between wide area, local area, and metropolitan area networks? Describe one example in each case.
2. What are the main differences between analog and digital communications? Why is digital communication preferred over analog communications? What techniques are used to convert analog signals to data?
3. What are the advantages of media with high bandwidth over media with low bandwidth? Name two media with high bandwidth.
4. What are the T-carrier lines and how can they be used to service wide area networks? Are T-carrier lines always digital?
5. What are the main advantages of ISDN over current systems? Give two examples of ISDN applications.

6. Someone has asked you to connect 10 terminals located in Chicago to a New York office. List the main decisions you need to make and the information you will need for making the decisions. What will you recommend without asking any questions (can you?)?
7. Compare and contrast the features of token ring, Ethernet, and FDDI LANs.
8. Roughly how many workstations can be supported on a token ring LAN (4 Mbps), on an Ethernet LAN, and an FDDI ring? Assume that each workstation generates a 1000-byte message per second (assume each byte is 10 bits on the network).
9. Which technology of all the emerging technologies will have the most impact on the communication technologies?
10. If you had to choose between frame relay, FDDI, and SMDS, what would you choose and why?
11. List 5 to 10 management implications of the topics discussed in this chapter.

CASE STUDY: Network Technologies at XYZCORP

XYZCORP is embarking on developing a network design for its existing applications and for its future multimedia applications. The management has divided the network design problem into three projects: WAN design for inventory and order processing at the stores, LAN design for the corporate office, and high-speed network investigation for future multimedia applications. You have been asked to participate in all three projects. Details of the projects are given next.

Project A: Wide Area Network Design

XYZCORP is installing a computerized checkout system to control inventory and to speed up the checkout process at each store. There are 40 stores in 4 states, 10 stores per state. The new checkout system has a standalone processor at each store which is connected to each checkout position. This processor maintains a database with this store's inventory, a separate database that records each day's transactions, and another database with prices of items sold at this store. Several point-of-sale (POS) terminals are connected to the processor.

At checkout, a point-of-sale terminal reads the code on an item and gets the price information from the store's price database. The POS terminal also posts each sale to the transaction database. The processor updates inventory every hour.

At the end of each day, the main computer facility in Chicago will read the transaction, inventory, and customer files and send a new price file.

Given the following information, determine the least expensive configuration (leased, direct dial) to allow the main computer to read/send files to the 40 stores each night (within seven hours—each store closes at midnight and opens at 7 A.M.). The cost information given here is only for illustrative purposes.

1. Each store keeps information about 2000 preferred customers. Each customer requires a record of 100 characters.
2. Each store handles 1000 transactions of 100 items each, and each item requires a record of 80 characters.
3. Each store carries 20,000 items, which are represented in the inventory database with a 100-character record and in the price database with a record of 40 characters.
4. Data are transmitted with 10 bits per character, in blocks of 500 characters. You can assume the following formula for transmission time:

   $$\begin{aligned}\text{Transmission time} &= \text{no. of bits transferred/line speed(bps)} \\ &\quad + \text{no. of blocks} \times \text{turnaround delay per block}\end{aligned}$$

   Turnaround delay per block (modem delay, propagation delay, reaction time, etc.) can be assumed as 0.1 sec.
5. In addition to the transmission time, the file read/write time at the mainframe and the stores should be considered. Each file record is read from the store, sent over the communication line, and written to the mainframe file. You should use the following formula to estimate the total time to transfer files:

   $$\begin{aligned}\text{Total file transfer time} &= \text{no. of reads} \times \text{time per read} \\ &\quad + \text{no. of writes} \times \text{time per write} \\ &\quad + \text{transmission time}\end{aligned}$$

   You can assume that 20 read/writes can be issued per second at the local stores and 50 reads/writes can be issued per second at the mainframe.
6. The leased line charge is $200 per month between area codes and $70 per month within an area code. You can assume that all stores within a state are in the same area code.
7. Direct dialing line cost is 20 cents for the first minute and 10 cents for each additional minute. It should be noted that dial-up lines are not preferred unless significant saving can be shown.
8. Modem purchase costs are as follows:

Speed	*Cost*
2400 bps	$ 100.00
4800 bps	$ 300.00
9600 bps	$ 500.00

9. T1 carrier provides 24 lines, each at a speed of 56 Kbps, at a monthly rate of $1200 per month. In addition, fractional T1 allows a user data rates starting at 56 Kbps up to 1.544 Mbps, in 56-Kbps increments. Each 56-Kbps increment can be assumed to cost $1200 per month.

10. Will you use a multiplexer? Where and how?
11. If all 40 stores sent the requests to the mainframe disk, what will be the queuing introduced at the mainframe disk? Specify the additional assumptions and develop a rough solution. What will you do to avoid this queuing?

You may assume that the 40 stores can simultaneously receive/send information from the mainframe. This implies that

1. At least 40 modems are available on mainframe side.
2. The mainframe operating system can run 40 jobs simultaneously.
3. The databases at the mainframe allow concurrent updates at record type level (record type level locking granularity).

Deliverables

1. A hardware and communication layout of the chain stores
2. The calculations to justify the results. You should show the calculations as a spreadsheet with rows to show the speeds and columns to show the line options (leased, DDS, MUX, etc.).
3. A list of additional assumptions, if any.

PROJECT B: Local Network Selection

The new corporate headquarters, a three floor 300 foot × 500 foot building, will house the data processing (first floor), administration and distribution (second floor), and marketing/corporate planning and management offices on the third floor. Each floor will have the office layout as shown in Fig. 2.44. Each person in the office wants a desktop computer. You are to recommend a layout of the workstations (terminals or microcomputers) for the three floors of the headquarter.

Each room on the first floor should have access to the main computer located on the first floor, as shown in Fig. 2.44. You can assume that each terminal/PC has an RS232 serial interface card. You can also assume that RS232 distance limit is 150 feet as a guideline for connecting local equipment. You can choose a LAN on the first floor or connect the workstations to the mainframe through terminal controllers or data PBXs.

A terminal controller TC1 (also called a terminal server) costs $2000 and can connect up to 20 terminals by using RS232 interfaces. The terminals can be connected to TC1 as local lines or over modems, limited distance or regular. A limited distance modem costs about $50. The output of a TC1 is also serial RS232; thus several TC1 can be connected to another TC1 to form a tree type topology. TC1 multiplexes terminals by using TDM (time division multiplexing), where the speed of the outgoing line cannot be less than the sum of input lines.

While designing the first-floor layout, you need to keep the following factors in mind:

Floor 1 Layout — Chicago Office

Note: Each regular office room is assumed to be 10 feet × 10 feet.
Each double office room is assumed to be 20 feet × 30 feet.

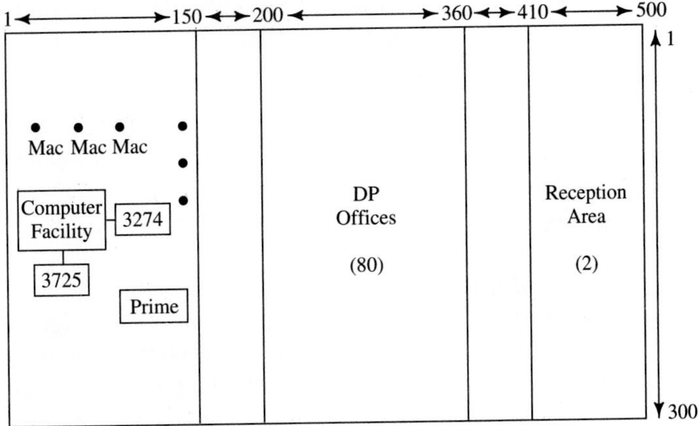

Floor 2 Layout — Chicago Office

Payroll AR/AP

(20)

Order Processing

(10)

Personnel

(5)

Floor 3 Layout — Chicago Office

Top Management Offices

(10)

Marketing Offices

(10)

Meeting Halls

Note: The number of workstations in each area are indicated in parentheses. The workstations are assumed to be equally distributed in each area.

FIGURE 2.44 Corporate Office Layout

1. Most work done on the first floor is word processing, accessing mainframe files, software development and technical support (planning, designing, installing and modifying the system hardware/software).
2. Each workstation can generate one message per second on the network and the message size can be assumed to be 1000 bytes (10,000 bits).
3. Most people in the DP department do not want a dumb terminal.
4. Some people in the DP department do not like IBM PCs and insist on MACs for "quality" word processing and graphics. Three MACs will be placed as indicated in Fig. 2.44.
5. The company has no experience and knowledge of any data PBXs.

On the second floor, the Administrative Department (payroll, AR/AP, order processing) is considering a LAN. This department has a budget of about $30,000 for this project and has currently bought three IBM PCs for order processing. This department wants to install a LAN with 10 PCs in their office and claims that entering orders on standalone PCs does not help them to access information from their mainframe computer. As a matter of fact, they have found that standalone PCs are not very useful besides word processing. They would like to

1. Allow the PCs to share a laser printer
2. Connect the PCs so that all PCs can share and exchange information stored in three Dbase3 databases
3. Somehow connect the PCs to the main computer (the mainframe we talked about in Project A) so that each PC can directly send/receive information from the mainframe in addition to other branch office PCs
4. Allow some growth so that in future between 20 and 30 PCs could be supported on the second floor
5. Show where else in the office LANs can be used.

The third floor at present has not specified any requirements. They need occasional access to the mainframe. They will be happy with anything and are very open to suggestions and recommendations.

Deliverables. You should produce a layout of the hardware, with estimated costs (cost calculations can be ignored in initial analysis). The building cabling cost can be estimated at $2 per foot. Your proposal should show all the hardware and software needed with the number of LANs, number of servers, etc. on all floors. You should also answer the following questions:

1. Will you choose one big LAN to span all three floors, or will you choose one LAN per floor? Justify your answer.
2. What is the tradeoff between IBM's Token Ring versus Ethernet in this case? What will you recommend at each floor?
3. Would a "zero-slot" LAN be of any value to this project?

4. A communication company is recommending a headquarter backbone coaxial cable with 400 MHz bandwidth to support the entire corporate office. Can this coaxial support 200 stations at 9600 bps, about 200 telephone lines and 3 LANs at 10 Mbps?
5. Would you recommend an FDDI LAN in this project?

PROJECT C: High-Speed Services for Future Applications

Management is interested in exploring the use of new and innovative applications in voice, data and images for office automation, factory floors and engineering CAD/CAM work. There is a particular interest in a paperless company. A task force has been established to identify the future applications for the next five years that may benefit the company. In addition, the task force is to identify a network strategy which shows how the emerging high-speed networks can be used for these applications. Your specific responsibilities are as follows:

- Make a list of about 10 innovative new applications that could be evaluated for business justification later. You should just list the names and write a few sentences about each applications.
- Outline an overall network layout of the company in the late 1990s. Your outline should show a company wide backbone with interconnected WANs, MANs and LANs.
- Specify where the evolving technologies such as ISDN, FDDI, SONET, SMDS and BISDN may be utilized in this network.

Hints About the Case Study

Project A: WAN Design. The reader should review the section on performance and especially the examples in Tables 2.5, 2.6 and 2.7 before proceeding with this project. The file transfer time per store should satisfy the following equation:

I/O time (store + mainframe) + transmission time < = 7 hours

1. *I/O time estimates at stores and mainframe*: Assume that each record written or read is an I/O. Calculate the total number of records, TR, in all the files (customer file, transaction file, inventory files, price file). Then the I/O time for one store = no. of records (Time per Host + Local I/O) = TR (0.02 + 0.05)
2. *Transmission time*: First calculate the total data TD in bits being sent across the network per store. This is simply the total file size (customer file, transaction file, inventory files, price file). This is several million characters.

   - No. of blocks sent = TD / 5000
   - Data transfer time for line speed SP = TD/SP

3. Calculate the minimum speed SP which satisfies the following equation:

$$TD/SP + (TD/5000)\ 3\ 0.1 + TR\ (0.07) < = 7 \text{ hours}$$

Solution of this equation for SP gives the minimum speed. For example, if SP = 22 Kbps, then use the lines with 56 Kbps. A T1 multiplexor in each state may be used to save the communication costs (review Section 2.3 for additional insights).

4. It may be desirable to decrease the file transfer time further. Here are some of the options: send only the data that has changed, block the files (i.e., read several records per I/O), use faster lines, etc.
5. The mainframe may get congested due to several stores sending data to it. The arrival rate A at the mainframe may exceed 40 per second. Use the simple formula given in Section 2.8 to find the expected queuing at the mainframe (the time per I/O at the mainframe is known). To reduce queuing, faster disks can be used or the host files can be spread across many disks (e.g., a disk at mainframe can be dedicated to receive all data from one store). This reduces the arrival rate at each disk.

Project B: LAN Design. The reader should thoroughly read Section 2.4 before solving this problem. Here are some general hints:

1. In most practical cases, one LAN per floor is chosen instead of one large LAN that is "snaked" through different floors. The LANs are connected through a backbone (the company on which this case study is based on also chose this).
2. Ethernet LANs are preferred in environments where many different devices (PCs, MACs, SUNs, HPs, etc.) are being connected (almost all devices support Ethernet cards). IBM Token Ring would work fine in this environment because many of the devices are IBM PCs.
3. A "zero-slot" LAN may be useful in a small office such as the personnel office.
4. The coaxial cable with 400 MHz bandwidth can easily support 200 stations at 9600 bps, about 200 telephone lines and 3 LANs at 10 Mbps. The simple FDM formula can be used for this purpose. For simplicity, it can be assumed that 9600 bps needs 9600 Hz bandwidth, etc.
5. The coaxial cable can easily serve as the backbone in the corporate office (there is enough of capacity for three LANs plus many other services). An FDDI LAN can also be used as the backbone to interconnect the LANs at each floor (this may be an overkill at present, but may be useful in the future).

Project C: Broadband Networks.

- The new applications for XYZCORP can include the examples listed in Section 2.7.2 for manufacturing, business, engineering and retail stores. The multimedia applications need special attention.
- The network layout of the company in the late 1990s should show a company wide backbone which interconnects each LAN at an office. This is a mapping of Fig. 2.39

to XYZCORP. The evolving technologies such as ISDN, FDDI, SONET, SMDS and BISDN described in Section 2.7 should be reviewed for their utilization in this network.

References

"*An ISDN Primer: Technology and Network Implications*," edited by Business Communications Review.

Aprille, T., "Introducing SONET into the Local Exchange Carrier Network," *IEEE Communications Magazine*, Aug. 1990, pp. 34–38.

Arnum, E., "Wireless Messaging —Will the Rubber Meet the Road?" *Business Communications Review*, July 1992, pp. 48–55.

Axner, D., "Can Microwave Expand Its Horizon?" *Business Communications Review*, July 1992, pp. 43–47.

Babcock, J., "SONET: A Practical Perspective," *Business Communications Review*, Sept. 1990, pp. 59–63.

Barret, J., and Wunderlich, E., "LAN Interconnection Using X.25 Network Services," *IEEE Network*, Sept. 1991, pp. 12–17.

Bartree, T., *Digital Communications*, Howard W. Sams, 1986.

Behm, J., et al., "The Enterprise Network Manager," *Enterprise Network Event Conf. Proc.*, Baltimore, Md., May 1988, pp. 6.27–6.37.

Ben-Artzi, A., Chandna, A., and Warrier, U., "Network Management of TCP/IP Networks: Present and Future," *IEEE Network Magazine*, July 1990, pp. 35–43.

Berman, R., and Brewster, J., "Perspectives on the AIN Architecture," *IEEE Communications Magazine*, Feb. 1992, pp. 27–33.

Bertsekas and Gallager, *Data Networks*, 2nd ed., Prentice Hall, 1992.

Biersack, E. W. et al., "Gigabit Networking Research at Bellcore," *IEEE Network*, Mar. 1992, pp. 42–49.

Bisdikioan, C., "A Performance Analysis of the IEEE 802.6 (DQDB) Subnetwork with the Bandwidth Balancing Mechanism," *Computer Networks and ISDN Systems*, Vol. 24, No. 5, 1992, pp. 367–386.

Black, U. D., *Data Communications, Networks and Distributed Processing*, 2nd ed., Reston Publishing Co., 1987.

Browne, T. E., "Network of the Future," *Proc. IEEE*, Vol. 74, No. 9, Sept. 1986.

Byrne, W., et al., "Broadband ISDN Technology and Architecture," *IEEE Network*, Jan. 1989, pp. 23–28.

Cheong, V., and Hirschheim, *Local Area Networks: Issues, Products and Development*, Addison-Wesley, 1983.

Chernick, M., Mills, K., Aronoff, R., and Strauch, J., "A Survey of OSI Network Management Standards Activities," Technical Report NMSIG87/16 ICST-SNA-87-01, National Bureau of Standards, 1987.

Christiansen, P., *Networking with Novell Netware*, Computer Science Press, 1991.

Clapp, G., "LAN Interconnection Across SMDS," *IEEE Network*, Sept. 1991, pp. 25–32.

CSELT Staff, *Optical Fiber Communications*, McGraw-Hill, 1981.

Datapro Research Corporation, "An Overview of World Telecommunications," Dec. 1987.

Dix, F., Kelly, M. and Klessing, R., "Access to a Public Switched Multi-Megabit Data Service Offering," *ACM SIGCOMM Computer Communication Review*, July 1990, pp. 46–61.

Drefler, F., "Maximum Modems: 14,400 bps and Rising," *PC Magazin*e, Mar. 17, 1992, pp. 285–339.

Duran, J., and Visser, J., "International Standards for Intelligent Networks," *IEEE Communications Magazine*, Feb. 1992, pp. 34–43.

Ellis, R., *Designing Data Networks*, Prentice Hall, 1986.

Falconer, W. E., and J. A. Hooke, "Telecommunications Services in the Next Decade," *Proc. of the IEEE*, Vol. 74, No. 9, 1986.

Farowich, S.A., "Communicating in the Technical Office," *IEEE Spectrum*, Apr., 1986.

Froehlich, F., and Kent, A., *Encyclopedia of Telecommunications*, Vols.1, 2, 3, 4, Marcel Dekkar, Inc., 1990–1991.

Gibson, R., "IEEE 802 Standards Efforts," *Computer Networks and ISDN Systems*, 19, 1990, pp. 95–104.

Goodman, D., "Trends in Cellular and Cordless Communications," *IEEE Communications Magazine*, June 1991, pp. 31–40.

Green, J. H., *The Dow Jones-Irwin Handbook of Telecommunications*, Dow Jones-Irwin, 1986.

Halsall, F., and Modiri, N., "An Implementation of an OSI Network Management System," *IEEE Network Magazine*, July 1990, pp. 44–53.

Hancock, B., *Designing and Implementing Ethernet Networks*, QED Information Sciences, 1988.

Handel, R, "Evolution of ISDN Towards Broadband ISDN," *IEEE Network*, Jan. 1989, pp. 7–13.

Harris and Sweeney, "Example of a Broadband Layout," *Datamation*, Mar., 1983.

Hawley, G., "Historical Perspectives on the U.S. Telephone Loop," *IEEE Communications,* Mar. 1991, pp. 24–30.

Hoffert, E., and Gretson, G., "The Digital News System at EDUCOM: A Convergence of Interactive Computing, Newspapers, Television and High-Speed Networks," *Comm. of the ACM,* Apr. 1991, pp. 113–116.

Horwitt, E., "ISDN Passes First Real-World Test," *Computerworld*, Vol. xx, No. 47, 1986.

Hoss, R., *Fiber Optic Communications Design Handbook*, Prentice Hall, 1990.

Jain, R., *The Art of Computer Systems Performance Analysis*, John Wiley, 1991.

Joeseph, C., and Muralidhar, K., "Network Management: A Manager's Perspective," *Enterprise Network Event Conf. Proc.*, Baltimore, Md., May 1988, pp. 5.163–5.174.

Kahl, P., "The Broadband ISDN, an Upward Compatible Evolution of the 64 Kbps ISDN," *Proc. IEEE Internat. Conf. on Communic. (ICC), Seattle*. June 1987, pp. 609–613.

Kaminski, M. A., Jr., "Protocols for Communicating in the Factory," *IEEE Spectrum*, Apr. 1986.

Kenedi, R., and C. L. Wong, "Architectures for Implementation," *IEEE Communications Magazine*, Vol. 24, No. 3, 1986.

Kessler, G., *ISDN*, McGraw-Hill, 1990.

Kleinrock, L., *Queuing Systems* —Vol. 2, John Wiley, 1976.

Kleinrock, L., "The Road to Broadband Networks," *Technology Transfer Institute Seminar*, Jan. 1992.

Knight, Fred, "CCITT's Director on the Evolution of ISDN," *Business Communications Review*, Jan.-Feb., 1987, pp.27–32.

Lang, L., and Watson, J., "Connecting Remote FDDI Installations with Single-Mode Fiber, Dedicated Lines, or SMDS," *ACM SIGCOMM Computer Communication Review*, July 1990, pp. 72–82.

Little, T., "Multimedia as a Network Technology," *Business Communications Review*, May 1991, pp. 65–70.

Martin, J., *Local Area Networks*, Prentice Hall, 1989.

Martin, J., *Telecommunications and the Computer*, 3rd edition, Prentice Hall, 1990.

Mathias, C.J., "Wireless LANs: The Next Wave," *Data Communications*, Mar. 21, 1992, pp. 83–87.

Mayo, John, "Computer Communications: Today and the Decade Ahead," Keynote Address, First Pacific Conference on Computer Communications, Seoul, Korea, Oct. 1985, pp. 2–8.

McNamara, J., *Technical Aspects of Data Communications*, Digital Press, 1977.

McQuillan, J., "Broadband Networks," *Data Communications*, June 1990, pp. 76–86.

McQuillan, J., "An Introduction to Multimedia Networking," *Business Communications Review*, Nov. 1991, pp. 74–79.

Nolle, T., "Getting Real about Frame Relay," *Business Communications Review*, May 1992, pp. 31–36.

Phillips, R., "MediaView: A General Multimedia Digital Publication System," *Comm. of the ACM*, July 1991, pp. 75–83.

Piscetello, D., and Kramer, M., "Internetworking Using SMDS in TCP/IP Environments," *ACM SIGCOMM Computer Communication Review*, July 1990, pp. 62–71.

Powers, J., and Stair, H., *Megabit Data Communications*, Prentice Hall, 1990.

Purtan, P., and Tate, P., "The ISDN Ingredient," *Datamation*, Jan. 1, 1987, pp. 78–82.

Ramos, E., Schroeder, A., and Simpson, L., *Data Communications and Networking Fundamentals Using Novell Netware*, MacMillan, 1992.

Reingold, L., and Lisowski, B., "Sprint's Evolution to Broadband ISDN," *IEEE Communications*, August 1992, pp. 28–31.

Reiss, L., *Introduction to Local Area Networks with Microcomputer Experiments*, Prentice Hall, 1987.

Ross, F., and Hamstra, R., "FDDI—A LAN Among MANs," *ACM SIGCOMM Computer Communication Review*, July 1990, pp. 16–31.

Rudin, H. , "Trends in Computer Communications," *IEEE Computer*, Vol. 19, No. 10, 1986.

Sandesara, N., Ritchie, G., and Engel-Smith, B., "Plans and Considerations for SONET Deployment," *IEEE Communications Magazine*, Aug. 1990, pp. 26–34.

Schlack, M., "Netware's Latest Mainframe Link," *Datamation*, Apr. 15, 1992, pp. 62–65.

Shepherd, D., and Salmony, M., "Extending OSI to support synchronization required by multimedia applications," *Computer Communications*, Sept. 1990, pp. 399–406.

Snelling, R.K., and K.W. Kaplan, "Services and Revenues Requirements," *IEEE Communications Magazine*, Vol. 24, No. 3, 1986.

Stallings, W., *Handbook of Computer Communications Standards, Vol. 2, Local Network Standards*, MacMillan, 1987.

Stallings, W., *ISDN: An Introduction*, 2nd ed., MacMillan, 1992.

Stallings, W., "Local and Metropolitan Area Networks," 4th Edition, MacMillan, 1992.

Stallings, W., *Networks and Data Communications*, 3rd ed., MacMillan, 1991.

Sterling, D., *Technician's Guide to Fiber Optics*, Delmar Publishers, Inc., 1987.

Tannenbaum, A., *Computing Networks*, 2nd ed., Prentice Hall, 1988.

Townsend, C., *Networking with the IBM Token-Ring*, TAB Books, 1987.

Van Norman, H., "WAN Design Tools: The New Generation," *Data Communications*, Oct. 1990, pp. 129–138.

Verma, P., *ISDN Systems*, Prentice Hall, 1990.

Violino, R., and Knight, F., "SONET Moves Down a Long and Winding Road," *Business Communications Review*, July 1991, pp.49–52.

White, P., "The Role of the Broadband Integrated Services Digital Network," *IEEE Communications*, Mar. 1991, pp. 116–121.

Wienski, R.M., "Evolution to ISDN within the Bell Operating Companies," *IEEE Communications Magazine*, Vol. 24, No. 3, 1986.

Chapter 3

Network Architectures and Network Interconnectivity

Problems and Exercises
Case Study: Network Architectures for XYZCORP

3.1 Introduction

The computer communications industry has experienced tremendous expansion in the 1970s and 1980s, largely the result of advances in network technologies and facilities, discussed in Chapter 2, and lower prices for both equipment and transmission media. Due to this expansion, many computer manufacturers, common carriers, software vendors and data communications equipment manufacturers are providing a plethora of communications-related hardware/software products. These products provide different functions at different levels with different price/performance ratios in networks. These networks can be small local area networks, large wide/metropolitan area networks, or supernetworks, described in Chapter 2.

The objective of this chapter is to answer two fundamental questions:

- How do all the hardware and software products fit together to form a functioning ("operable") network?
- How does one network interconnect with other networks?

These questions lead us to a discussion of network architecture standards and protocols. Simply stated, a *network architecture* describes the components, the functions performed and the interfaces/interactions between the components of a network. A single network architecture standard is desirable because the customers need to interconnect different systems, of different vintages, from different vendors. Section 3.2 gives an overview of network architectures.

The Open System Interconnection (OSI) Reference Model is currently the best known network architecture standard. This standard presents a functional view of the network, where each layer performs well-defined functions and provides known services to the next higer layer. This functional model provides a common vocabulary and a reference framework for comparing different vendor offerings. The principles and the layers of the OSI Reference Model are explained in Section 3.3. We review and highlight the OSI Reference Model as a framework for understanding and analyzing the state of the art as well as state-of-the-market literature in this field.

Network architectures have been an area of considerable activity in the last 20 years. Section 3.4 gives an overview of the main architectures and uses the OSI Model as a framework for comparing/contrasting network architectures such as Transmission Control Protocol/Internet Protocol (TCP/IP), IBM's System Network Architecture (SNA), Manufacturing Automation Protocol (MAP) and LAN network architectures. A brief overview of the evolving network architectures for high-speed (broadband) networks is also included. The tutorials at the end of this book give details about the following popular network architectures in different sectors of the computing industry:

- Appendix A: OSI Protocols
- Appendix B: TCP/IP
- Appendix C: IBM's SNA
- Appendix D: MAP and TOP

Section 3.5 concentrates on network interconnectivity and uses the OSI Model for classifying and defining various interconnectivity devices (e.g., routers, bridges, gateways, protocol converters). This section also illustrates different levels of interconnectivity (device interconnectivity, network interconnectivity and application interconnectivity) through simple examples. Practical implications of open networking and the role of OSI in open networking conclude this discussion.

The case study at the end of this chapter shows how the material discussed in this chapter can be used to develop an overall network layout and architecture for the XYZCORP. The projects discussed reflect the major architectural and interconnectivity activities needed.

3.2 Overview of Network Architecture Standards

3.2.1 Definitions and Background

The architecture of any system describes the components (what are the pieces of a system?), the functions of components (what do they do?) and the interfaces/interactions between the components of a system (how do they interoperate with each other?). The following definition of computer architecture by Fred Brooks, author of *The Mythical Man-Month*, distinguishes architecture from engineering:

> "Computer architecture, like other architectures is the art of determining the needs of the user of a structure and then designing to meet those needs as effectively as possible within economic and technological constraints. Architecture must include engineering considerations, so that the design will be economical and feasible; but the emphasis in architecture is upon the needs of the user, whereas in engineering the emphasis is upon the needs of the fabricator."

A *network architecture* defines the components, the functions and the interactions/interfaces (protocols/standards) between the components of a network. It encompasses hardware, software, standards, data link controls, topologies, and protocols. It defines the functions of, and the interfaces between, three type of components:

- Network hardware components such as cables, modems, communications controllers, adapter cards, etc.
- Communication software modules, which establish and monitor sessions between remotely located processes and allow for exchange of data and control messages
- Application programs (user processes) which use the networks.

These components may be very simple or quite complex depending on the size of the network and the nature of devices supported (mainframes, minicomputers, microcomputers, terminals). Network architectures provide a systematic approach to describe the various categories of networks and define exactly what components will be supported and how. A *protocol* is a set of precisely defined rules of behavior between two parties. As we will see, protocols in network architectures define the formats and the rules of interaction between peers. Protocols play a key role in integration and interconnectivity in distributed systems.

Figure 3.1 presents a simple network architecture model. In this figure, several computers are connected to the network. One or more user applications (e.g., order processing) may run on each computer. Application Support Services "connect" the applications to the network. Network Services provide exchange of messages between the computers.

The functions performed by the application and network services vary widely between the size and complexity of networks and the stations. In the 1970s, these services were viewed as layers where each layer performed a specific function. Different researchers, vendors and standardizing bodies have proposed different layers. For example IBM's SNA (System Network Architecture) uses 7 layers; Digital's DNA (Digital Network Architecture) uses 6 layers; Department of Defense's Suite, commonly referred to as the TCP/IP Suite, uses 4 layers; the OSI Reference Model uses 7 layers; and General Motors' MAP (Manufacturing Automation Protocol) and Boeing's TOP (Technical Office Protocol) also have 7 layers.

Even though the number of layers differs between vendors, in all cases the lower layers provide low-level (closer to the physical network) functions, while the high-level functions (application interfaces) are performed by the upper layers. For example, the

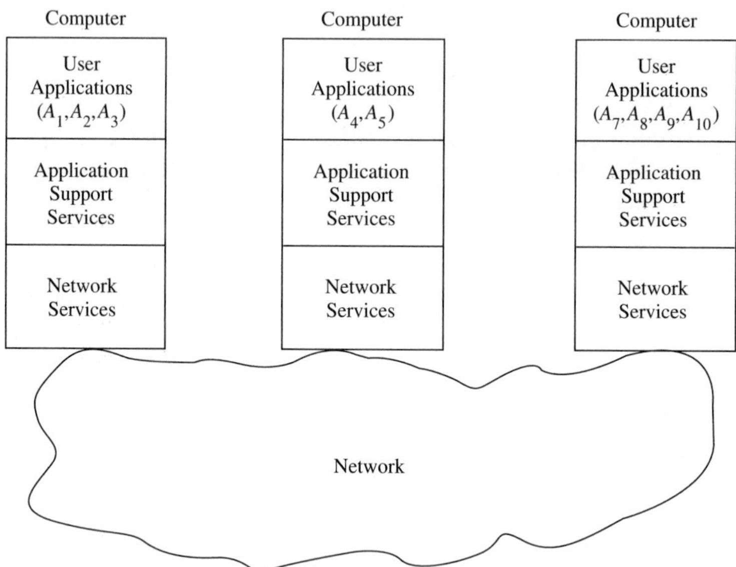

FIGURE 3.1 A Simple Network Architecture

first layer is physical link; the last is the application layer in most network architectures. In these layered systems, the data expands at source as it goes through different layers (additional pieces of information are added as headers in each layer) and shrinks at the sink (headers are removed successively). We will see this in Section 3.3.

3.2.2 Motivation for Network Architecture Standards

A *standard* is an agreed upon formal specification of a system, its services and/or the protocols used by the system services. International standards are very much like treaties between different parties—they specify high-level goals as well as detailed procedures. The need for a single network architecture standard has been felt by vendors as well as customers since the mid-seventies. This is because the customers need to interconnect systems from different vendors. It is also hoped that standards can drive toward lower product prices due to open competition and mass production. In addition, the growing number of different computer networks need to be connected. However, when communication is desired among heterogeneous computers and networks (different vendors, different models of same vendor), the software development effort can be a nightmare. Different vendors use different data formats, data exchange conventions, terms, and products. The following statements from the manager of General Motor's Manufacturing Automation Protocol (MAP) Program perhaps best describe the situation <Kaminski 1987>:

> Only 15 percent of the 40,000 programmable tools, instruments, controls and systems already installed at General Motors facilities are able to communicate with one another. When such communication does occur, it is costly, accounting for up to 50 percent of the total expense of automation because of the special wiring and the custom hardware and software interfaces needed.

Even within one vendor's product line, different models of a computer may communicate in unique ways. Thus some standards are needed to interconnect heterogeneous systems. A do-it-yourself special-purpose approach to communications software development is too costly to be acceptable. It is better for the computer vendors to adopt and implement a common set of conventions. For this to happen, a set of international/national standards must be introduced by appropriate organizations. Such standards encourage the vendors to implement the standards because the products would be less marketable without them. The customers can also require that the standards be implemented by any prospective vendor.

It is difficult to develop a single standard that can handle all possible computer communications. The problem of communication between applications on different computers must be decomposed into manageable parts. Hence a structure or architecture is needed to define the set of generic communication functions in any network. The International Standards Organization (ISO) established a subcommittee in 1977 to develop such an architecture. The result was the Open Systems Interconnection (OSI) Reference Model, which provides a framework for defining standards for linking heterogeneous computers. The OSI Model defines a set of generic functions as layers and provides a framework for connecting "open" systems for distributed applications processing. In this context, the term *open* denotes the ability of any two systems conforming to the Reference Model and the associated standards to connect. This Model is described in Section 3.3.

3.2.3 Network Standardization Bodies

Three types of organizations are currently involved in standards and architecture development: standards organizations, computer manufacturers and large organizations. All define rules of a network and how its components can interact. But there are major differences.

Examples of the standards organizations are as follows (see Table 3.1):

- International Organization for Standardization, commonly known as the International Standards Organization (ISO), published the description of a comprehensive architecture for computer networks. This model, referred to as the ISO Open Systems Interconnection (OSI) Reference Model, is described in Section 3.3.
- International Telegraph and Telephone Consultative Committee (CCITT) developed a complex and sophisticated architecture for computer networks (e.g., X.3, X.25, X.28, X.29 and X.75).
- Institute of Electrical and Electronics Institute (IEEE) committee on LANs (IEEE 802 committee) has developed several local area network standards.
- International Electrotechnical Commission (IEC) develops standards and products relating to electrical engineering.
- American National Standards Institute (ANSI) develops standards for software in the United States. Examples are ANSI Fortran, ANSI C, ANSI SQL, etc.

These standardizing bodies describe or recommend the use of particular standards. Implementation of the architectures and building of the machines described is handled by computer manufacturers or by common carriers or teleprocessing administrations. These bodies operate independently but, fortunately, cooperate with each other for coexistence and interoperability. For example, the ISO/IEC Joint Technical Committee 1 (JTC 1) is composed of ISO and IEC technical committees which are charged with standardization of information technology systems. ANSI is providing administrative support to JTC 1. The CCITT and ISO, in particular, have been working very closely with each other; although ISO is ahead on data networking standards.

The computer manufacturers have implemented many proprietary network architectures for their own equipment. Examples are IBM's SNA (Systems Network

TABLE 3.1 Major Network Standardization Bodies

- International Standards Organization (ISO)
- International Telegraph and Telephone Consultative Committee (CCITT)
- Institute of Electrical and Electronic Engineering (IEEE)
- International Electrotechnical Commission (IEC)
- American National Standards Institute (ANSI)

Architecture) and Digital Equipment Corporation's DECnet. These proprietary network architectures allow the computer manufacturers to introduce new technology to support their equipment. Many computer manufacturers provide gateway facilities to allow connections between computing systems that conform to different network architectures (e.g., an SNA to DECnet gateway).

Some large organizations and research establishments have developed their own network architectures. Some of these architectures have become de facto standards or have been adopted by the standardizing bodies. The best-known example is the DOD Protocol Suite, commonly referred to as the TCP/IP Protocol Suite, which was developed by the ARPANET project. In addition, General Motors' MAP (Manufacturing Automation Protocol) and Boeing's TOP (Technical Office Protocol) are well known. The common carriers such as AT&T, Bell Regional Companies, and Western Union may employ/extend architectures devised by standards organizations for linking teleprocessing equipment. We will compare and contrast many of these standards in Section 3.4.

3.3 The Open System Interconnection (OSI) Reference Model

3.3.1 Overview and Terminology

The Reference Model for Open Systems Interconnection (OSI), commonly referred to as the OSI Model, was proposed by the International Standards Organizations (ISO) Committee 97 in March, 1977. This Model, published as ISO Document 7498, consists of 7 layers shown in Fig. 3.2. The objective of the ISO subcommittee was to describe a hierarchical or layered set of generic functions that every network must fulfill. Such a generic definition makes it easier to develop interfaces between the growing number of different networks. The ISO subcommittee precisely defined the set of layers and the functions/services performed by each layer. According to the conceptual framework in Fig. 3.2a, the first four layers (Physical, Data Link, Network, and Transport) are lower-level layers which are responsible for the delivery of data between applications. These layers perform the following functions (additional information about these layers is given in the next section):

- The Physical Layer is concerned with transmission of bit streams over physical medium and deals with the mechanical, electrical, functional, and procedural characteristics to access the physical medium. For example, the physical interfaces such as RS232 and communication techniques (broadband, baseband) are handled by this layer.
- The Data Link Layer provides for the transfer of information across the physical link by sending blocks of data (frames) with necessary synchronization, error control, and flow control functions. For example, this layer handles the reception, recognition, and transmission of tokens and Ethernet messages.

a. OSI Model

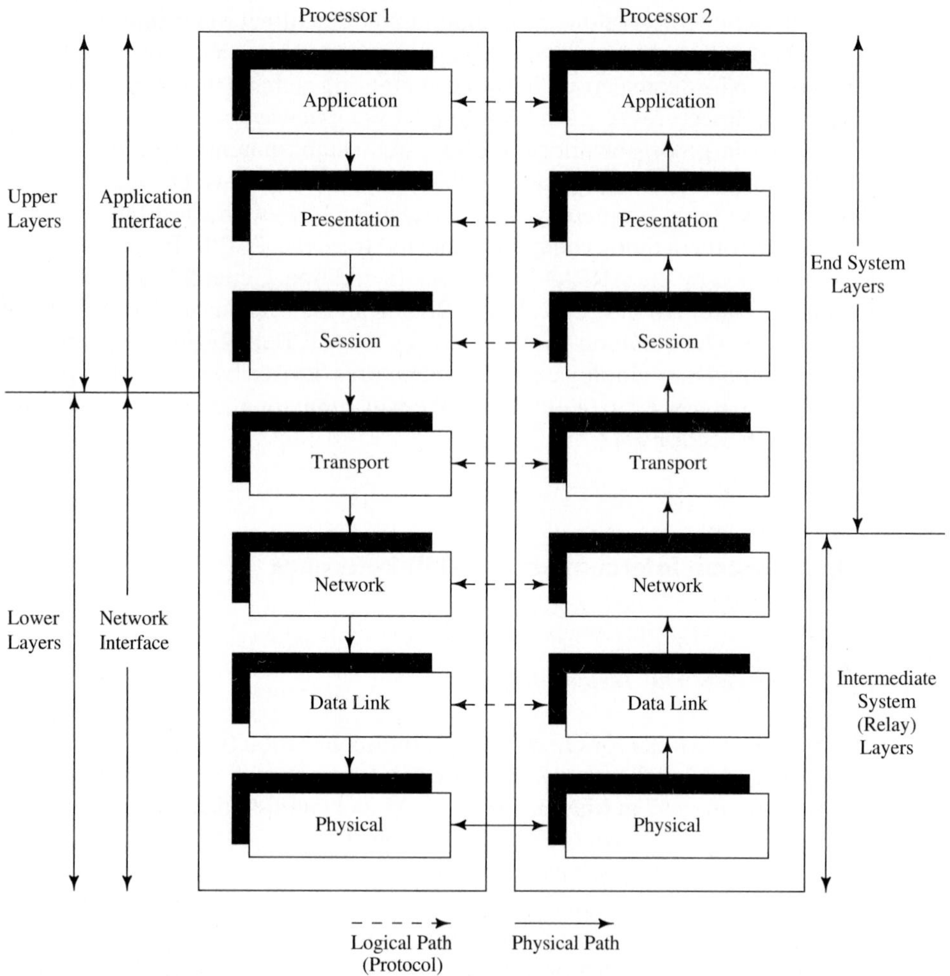

b. End Systems and Relay Systems

End System

7
6
5
4
3
2
1

Intermediate System

3
2
1

End System

7
6
5
4
3
2
1

FIGURE 3.2 OSI Model Layers

- The Network Layer provides upper layers with independence from the data transmission, switching and routing technologies needed when the end devices have to cross many networks. For example, the packet switching activities of breaking up and reassembling the messages are performed by this layer.
- The Transport Layer provides transparent transfer of data between end systems and is responsible for end-to-end error recovery and flow control. The Transport Layer only resides in end systems (see Fig. 3.2b). For example, in a large network with many interconnected LANs and WANs, the transport layer at the end systems will make sure that the messages exchanged between end systems of this network are not lost while fighting their way through various LANs and WANs. A message may be exchanged correctly between two stations of a LAN in a building but it may not be sent properly to a remote computer located in another city.

Whereas the lower four layers are responsible for transport of information between applications, the upper layers support applications (Fig. 3.2a). Specifically,

- The Session Layer controls the communication between applications by establishing, managing, and terminating connections (sessions) between cooperating applications. For example, this layer establishes the full versus half duplex interactions between applications.
- The Presentation Layer provides independence to the application processes from differences in data representation (syntax). The encryption/decryption for security purposes is usually performed in this layer.
- The Application Layer supports the application and user processes which need network services. Examples of the services provided by this layer are terminal emulation, file transfer, electronic mail, distributed database managers, etc.

Figure 3.2b illustrates the concept of end systems and intermediate systems in OSI. An *intermediate system* only performs functions related to the lowest three layers of the Reference Model (e.g., routing, flow control, and bit transmission). Functions of intermediate systems are implemented in *relay systems*. An example of a relay system is a router which connects many LANs together. An *end system* provides the functions above the Network Layer (Transport, Session, Presentation, Application), in addition to the lowest three layers. Examples of end systems are computers on which applications reside. End system is a synonym of *host*, a term commonly used to refer to computers where applications reside. We will discuss these systems in more detail in our discussion of network interconnectivity (Section 3.5). The physical aspects of communication networks discussed in Chapter 2 are concerned with layers 1 through 3 of the OSI Model.

Services, Protocols and Standards. The following terms are used frequently in OSI:

- *Service*: The functions performed by layer N for layer N+1.
- *Protocol*: The precise rules of information exchange between two peers.
- *Standard*: An agreed-upon formal specification of the protocols and/or the services.

Let us discuss these terms a little more. Each OSI layer performs a set of related functions. These functions are viewed as services by the next higher layer. For example, encryption/decryption is a service provided by Layer 6. Layer N hides unnecessary information from layer $N + 1$ (for example, layer 7 does not have to worry about encryption/decryption). In turn, layer N relies on layer $N - 1$ to perform more primitive functions and to conceal the details of those functions. The same set of layered functions must exist in two systems to communicate with each other.

A protocol specifies two things: the message format (e.g., bit pattern) and the rules to interpret and react to the messages. Protocols are the "visible" aspect of OSI because they are the basis for interconnection. Protocols can be tested and verified for conformance. Communication is achieved by having corresponding (peer) entities in the same layer in two different systems communicate via a protocol.[1]

Standards can specify high-level views as well as detailed procedures. The OSI standards specify the OSI Reference Model, the services to be provided by the different layers of the Model and the protocols for exchange of information between peers. At present more than 1000 OSI standards have been published <Folts 1990>. These standards define information such as the OSI Reference Model itself, the many services provided by the 7 layers of the Model (different services are defined for different industries and applications) and the detailed protocols between peers at different systems.

Entities. There are one or more entities in each layer of a system. An *entity* implements functions of that layer and the protocol for communicating with peer entities in other systems. Examples of an entity are a process implemented on a chip or a software subroutine. Each entity communicates with entities in the layers above and below it across an interface (a port) called a *service access point (SAP)*. An entity at layer N requests the services of layer $N - 1$ via invocation of primitives. An example of a primitive is a subroutine call.

Connection-based and Connectionless Communications. The OSI Model supports connectionless as well as connection-based communications. The basic idea of connection-based service, also called a reliable service, is that before any communication between two entities at layer N takes place, a connection between end systems at $N - 1$ must be established. Connection-based communications involves three phases: connection establishment, data transfer, and connection release. Due to the overhead of connection establishment and connection release, several systems use a "connectionless" service. The notion of connectionless service is almost oximoronic: How can you provide a service when you are not even connected? Basically, a connectionless service means that the communicating parties send and receive self-contained data packets without apriori connection (i.e., there is no separate connection establishment and connection release).

An analogy will explain the difference between connectionless versus connection-based services. Connection-based services are similar to the telephone communication while the connectionless services are similar to the postal system. If you use

[1]This strict separation does not hold for layers 1 and 2 because these layers are commonly implemented in one adapter card.

a telephone, then you first dial the number (connection establishment), talk (data transfer), and hang up (connection release). In this case, you establish a connection before data transfer. In contrast, you do not establish a connection before you send a message in a letter, and there is no assurance that the receiver has received the message. However, you can design your own protocol to make sure that the mail was delivered (e.g., put a note in your letter indicating that the receiver must call you immediately to claim one million dollars he has won in a lottery). Due to this analogy, the connection-based service is referred to as a virtual call and the connectionless service is referred to as a datagram service. Details on how these services are used in OSI are given in Appendix A.

3.3.2 OSI Layers

The OSI recommendation identifies seven functional layers, as shown in Fig. 3.3: Application, Presentation, Session, Transport, Network, Data Link, and Physical. We now highlight the main services of the seven layers and mention some examples of standards and protocols in each layer. It can be seen from Fig. 3.3 that the examples include CCITT standards (indicated by X.*nn*) and the ISO standards (indicated by ISO*nn*). Description and discussion of the ISO standards and protocols are provided in Appendix A.

Physical Layer (Layer 1): This layer defines the electrical connections between the transmission medium and the computer system. It specifies how many wires or pins will be used to carry the signals, which wires are used to carry specific signals, and the size and shape of the connectors or adaptors between the transmission medium and the physical link. It also describes the speed at which data will be transmitted, and whether data (represented by voltages on a line, radio signals, or light pulses) are allowed to flow in full or half duplex mode.

This layer covers the physical interface between devices and the rules by which bits are passed from one to another. The objective is to make sure that a bit 1 sent is recognized as 1 on the receiver. For example, the physical layer standards are used to define the device modem interfaces (voltage levels, pin numbers, usage, etc.). The Physical Layer has mechanical, electrical, functional and procedural characteristics. Examples of standards at this layer are the well-established DTE (data terminal equipment) to DCE (data circuit-terminating equipment) such as RS-232-C, RS-449/422/423, and X.21. In addition, the ISDN physical connection to the user equipment is defined here.

Data Link Layer (Layer 2): This layer is responsible for establishing and controlling the physical link (circuit) of communication between communicating parties (end and/or intermediate systems). This layer also resolves competing requests for a shared communications link (i.e, who can use the circuit, and when) and ensuring that all forms of data can be sent across the circuit (make sure that data bits are not misinterpreted as commands, and vice versa). OSI supports connection-based as well connectionless data link protocols.

Connection-based data link includes error detection and correction and definition of the beginning and ending of the data field. This provides the means to activate,

Layer 7—Application Layer

User-level formats and procedures, programs, operators, devices
Examples: Virtual Terminal, FTAM, X.400 e mail,
CMISE (Common Management Information Service Element),
EDI (Electronic Data Interchange),
ODA (Office Document Architecture),
X.409 (Message Handling Systems),
X.500 (Directory Services)
TP (Transaction Processing)

Layer 6—Presentation Layer

Management of entry, exchange, display, & control of data; interface transformation and application

Example: ISO 8822 (Connection-Oriented Presentation)

Layer 5—Session Layer

Session administration services, control of data exchange; delineating/synchronizing data operations

Examples: X.215 and X.225 (Session Service and Protocol Definition), accepted as ISO 8326 and 8327

Layer 4—Transport Layer

Transparent transfer of data between sessions; optimize use of available communications services

Examples: X.214 (Transport Service Definition) and X.224 (Transport Service Definition) equivalent to ISO8072 and ISO8073

Layer 3—Network Layer

Form and route packets across networks of networks

Examples: X.25, X.75, ISDN interfaces (I.450/I.451), subnetworks (ISO 8473)

Layer 2—Link Layer

Data flow initialization, control, termination, recovery

Examples: HDLC, IEEE 802.3, IEEE 802.4, IEEE 802.5, IEEE 802.6
FDDI frames, ISDN frames (1.441)

Layer 1—Physical Layer

Electrical/mechanical interfaces to communication media

Examples: RS232, RS449, X.21, ISDN interfaces (I.430, I.431), FDDI physical interface

FIGURE 3.3 OSI Reference Model: Functions and Services

maintain, and deactivate the link and transforms a raw communication circuit into an error free line for the next higher layer. Connectionless data link (e.g., LLC class 1) does not maintain a connection between the communicating parties and does not guarantee the order of the data units delivered.

Examples of standards at this layer are the LAN frame formats for CSMA/CD, token ring, token bus, and FDDI. The ISO standard HDLC (high-level data link control) for wide area networks includes the IBM's SDLC (synchronous data link control). The ISDN frame formats are also included in this layer (see Appendix A, Section A.3 for more details).

Network Layer (Layer 3): This layer is responsible for routing of packets or blocks of information across the physical network in a connection-based or a connectionless mode. The Network Layer knows about the physical connections and paths between the transport entities in a session. Thus it relieves the Transport Layer of the need to know anything about the underlying network technologies used to connect end systems. The connection-based network service is responsible for establishing, maintaining, and terminating connections across a physical network. It also collects billing and accounting information from message routing and network resource utilization.

This layer is responsible for breaking up a message into packets and routing the packets over packet switching networks. The lower layers (layers 1 and 2) actually transfer the packets over the direct links of a packet switched network. The Network Layer services provide a transition between the end system services (layer 4 and above are performed in computers) and the services that are performed in the intermediate systems (front end processors, switches and routers). The Network Layer protocols operate at end-system-to-end-system, end-system-to-intermediate-system, and intermediate-system-to-intermediate-system levels.

In the simplest case, the Network Layer manages a direct link between end systems. More common situations involve a packet switched wide area network. In this case, the Network Layer must provide the WAN with sufficient information to switch and route data between hosts (end systems). More complex situations involve "internetworks" (a network of physical networks) where the physical networks may be interconnected to each other directly or indirectly. Data transfer in such a case is usually accomplished through an Internet Protocol (IP) and is used by a Transport Layer protocol. IP is responsible for internetwork routing and delivery and sits on top of layer 3 or 2 at each network for intranetwork services. IP is sometimes referred to as "layer 3.5."

The best-known example of layer 3 is the X.25 Packet Layer Protocol (PLP), which is used in commercial packet switching systems. X.25 is implemented in the first three layers: Layer 1 uses X.21, layer 2 uses the X.25 Link Access Protocol (LAP and LAPB) and layer 3 uses the Packet Layer Protocol (PLP). X.25 supports a virtual call (connection-oriented) protocol in which a call is made and acknowledged before data can be transmitted. Datagram (connectionless) services are not supported in X.25. X.25 is explained in Appendix A at the end of this book. More details about X.25 can be found in the X.25 book by Deasington <1989>. Other common examples are the X.75 standard and the ISDN packet switching interfaces (I.450/I.451). More details about the Network Layer are given in Appendix A, Section A.3.

Transport Layer (Layer 4): This layer, residing in end systems, provides a transparent mechanism for the exchange of data between processes in end systems. Data exchanges at this level are end-to-end and not concerned with the details of the underlying communications facility. The Transport Layer supports connection-based as well as connectionless communications.

The connection-based Transport Layer provides for connection establishment, data transfer and connection release. This protocol may be used to optimize the use of network services and provide a requested quality of service to session entities. For example, the session entity might specify acceptable error rates, maximum delay, priority, and security. In effect, the Transport Layer serves as the user's liaison with the communications facility. Connection-based Transport Layer standards have been published as ISO documents ISO8072 and ISO8073. These standards were originally proposed as CCITT X.214 and X.224.

The connectionless Transport Layer does not provide for connection establishment and connection release, hence this protocol is much simpler and efficient. Since there is no connection establishment phase, it is not possible to negotiate a quality of service. In addition, this protocol requires higher-level layers to provide some error control for lost or out of sequence messages.

The complexity of a transport protocol depends on the type of service it can get from layer 3. If layer 3 is reliable with a virtual circuit capability, then layer 4 can be connectionless. If layer 3 is unreliable (connectionless), then the transport layer protocol may have to be connection based. ISO has defined five classes of connection-bassed transport protocol, each oriented toward a different underlying service. The most complex version is similar to the DOD's Transmission Control Protocol (TCP). More details about the Transport Layer are given in Appendix A, Section A.4.

Session Layer (Layer 5): This layer provides the mechanism for controlling the dialogue between applications. The Session Layer is responsible for establishing the connection between applications, enforcing the rules for carrying on the dialogue, and attempting to reestablish the connection in the event of a failure. At a minimum, the Session Layer provides a means for two application processes to establish and use a connection, called a session. In addition to session establishment and release, it may provide services such as normal and expedited data transfer, token management to exercise the right to use certain functions, dialogue control at full or half duplex, error recovery and control through synchronization/resynchronization points, and exception reporting for unanticipated situations.

The dialogue rules specify both the order in which the applications must communicate and the flow control information to avoid an overload. If an application is sending data to a printer with a limited buffer size, the agreed-upon dialogue may be to send a buffer-size block to the printer, wait for the printer to signal that its buffer has been emptied, and then send the next block of data. The Session Layer is responsible for controlling this flow and avoiding buffer overflow at the printer. Examples of the Session Layer standards and protocols are X.215 and X.225 (Session Service Protocol Definition), which have been accepted as ISO 8326 and 8327.

Presentation Layer (Layer 6): This layer accepts data from the Application Layer and provides generalized formatting of the data. Thus, if there are data preparation functions common to a number of applications, they can be provided by the Presentation services, instead of being embedded in each application. Examples of the Presentation functions are encryption, compression, terminal screen formatting, and conversion from one transmission code to another (such as EBCDIC to ASCII). The main focus of this layer is on the syntax of the data exchanged between application entities and on resolving the differences in format and data representation.

The CCITT X.409 specifies (Message Handling Systems) and ISO 8822 (Connection-Oriented Presentation) are examples of this layer. Many file conversion and code conversion protocols are supported by this layer. Another example is a virtual terminal protocol, which converts between specific terminal characteristics, and a generic or virtual model used by application programs.

Application Layer (Layer 7): This layer provides a means for application processes to access the OSI environment and contains mechanisms to support distributed applications. Examples of services at this layer are file transfer, terminal emulation and electronic mail. The Application Layer is functionally defined by the user. Data known to or generated by one application may be needed by another application or system user. The content and format of this information is dictated by the business problem being addressed. The application determines the data to be sent, the message or record layout for the data, and the function or activity codes that identify the data to the receiving application.

The Application Layer services depend on application type (business, engineering, office automation, network management, etc.). Due to the dramatic increase in the nature of distributed applications, a large number of application layer services have been defined. Examples of the services are virtual terminal, FTAM (file transfer access method), and X.400 (electronic mail). Examples of some of the recent application services are CMISE (Common Management Information Service Element) for network management, MMS (Manufacturing Message Specification) for manufacturing applications, DTP (Distributed Transaction Processing) for distributed business applications, EDI (electronic data interchange) for financial data exchange applications, and ODA (office document architecture) for office automation. We review some of these protocols in Appendix A.

3.3.3 Information Flow in the OSI Model: An Example

The objective of any data communications network is to exchange data between applications or between users. To do this, the information to be transferred must be formatted, packaged, routed, and delivered. The receiver must then unpackage and possibly reformat this information. These are essentially the functions performed by the seven layers. The information from the application layer in processor 1 moves down through the lower layers in its node until it reaches the physical layer, which physically transmits the data to the physical layer in processor 2. The data then work their way up through the layers in processor 2 until they reach the application layer of that processor. Each layer in the sending processor performs work for or acts on behalf of its peer layer in the receiving processor. Thus, presentation layers support

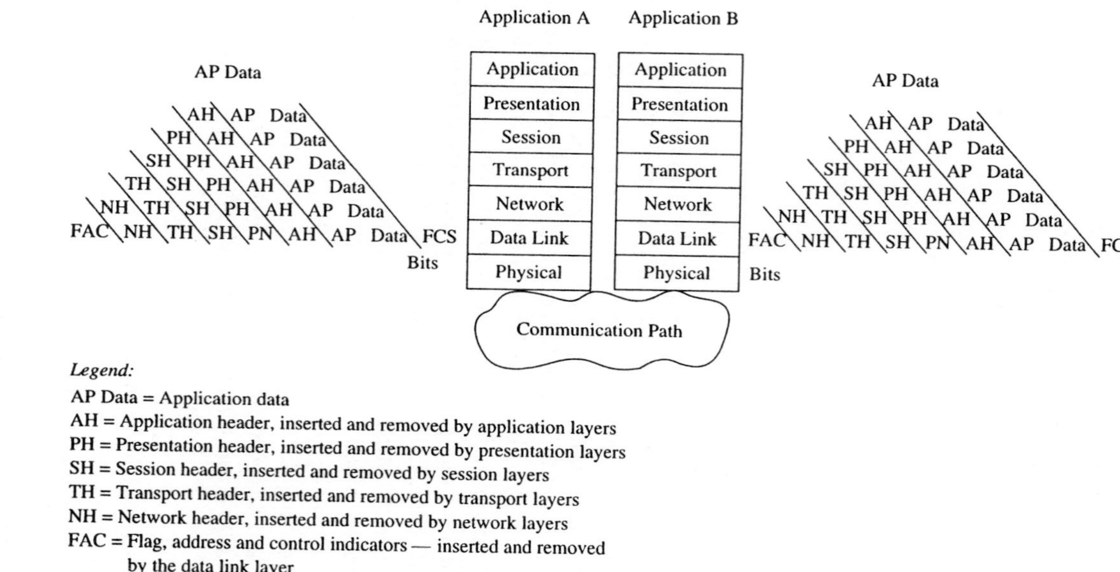

Legend:

AP Data = Application data

AH = Application header, inserted and removed by application layers

PH = Presentation header, inserted and removed by presentation layers

SH = Session header, inserted and removed by session layers

TH = Transport header, inserted and removed by transport layers

NH = Network header, inserted and removed by network layers

FAC = Flag, address and control indicators — inserted and removed by the data link layer

FCS = Frame check sequence field — inserted and removed by the data link layer

FIGURE 3.4 Information FLow in OSI

presentation layers, session layers support other session layers, etc. Between the different layers are interfaces through which the data pass.

Figure 3.4 illustrates the information flow in the OSI Model. Communication is between applications in the systems. If application A in computer C_1 wishes to send a message to application B in C_2, it invokes the application layer (layer 7). Layer 7 at C_1 establishes a peer relationship with layer 7 of C_2, using a layer 7 protocol. This protocol requires services from layer 6, so the two layer 6 entities use a protocol of their own. Similarly layers 5, 4, 3, 2 and 1 all have their own protocols. It should be emphasized that the actual bit transfer is only done at the physical layer, which actually passes the bits through a transmission medium. Above the physical layer, each protocol entity sends data down to the next lower layer in order to get the data across to its peer entity.

When application A has a message to send to application B, it transfers the message to an application entity in the application layer. A header is appended to the message that contains the required information for the peer layer 7 protocol. The original message, plus the header, is now passed as a unit to layer 6. Layer 6 treats the whole unit as data and appends its own header. This process continues down through layer 2, which builds a frame with both a header and a trailer. This frame is then passed by the physical layer onto the transmission medium. When the frame is received by the target system, the reverse process occurs. As the data proceeds to higher layers, each layer strips off the outermost header, acts on the information contained in the header, and passes the remainder up to the next layer. Some layers may fragment the data unit it receives from the next higher layer into several parts. For example, the network layer breaks the application messages into "packets" for packet switching systems. These data units must then be reassembled by the corresponding peer layer before being passed up.

Figure 3.5 illustrates the information flow and the message format in the OSI Model through an example. Suppose a process P_1 on computer C_1 issues the message: "Deposit 100 to account no. AC5." The user program finds out that process P_2 is authorized to handle account credits/debits. Note that the message is now appended with the sender and receiver information (P_1 and P_2). This data unit is transferred to lower layers, where the sender and receiver computers are identified (C_1 and C_2) and added to the message. The transport layer establishes a path between C_1 and C_2. Note that if P_1 and P_2 were on the same machine, then the transport layer services would not be needed (the session layer in C_1 can establish a session within C_1). The network layer, say, decomposes the message into two packets (1 and 2). The two packets are now converted into frames, which are routed to the network. Note that the network consists of many subnetworks, which are connected through intermediate systems C_3 and C_4. This network provides two alternate paths for messages (one through C_3, the other through C_4). Let us assume that packet 1 is routed through C_3, and packet 2 is routed through C_4. These two packets will be reassembled into a single message by the network layer at C_2. If, for example, C_4 crashes and packet 2 is lost, then the network and transport layers will assure that the lost packet is retransmitted. Note also that the headers are successively removed as the message moves up in the target system. The final message "Deposit 100 to AC5" is eventually received by the process P_2 at C_2.

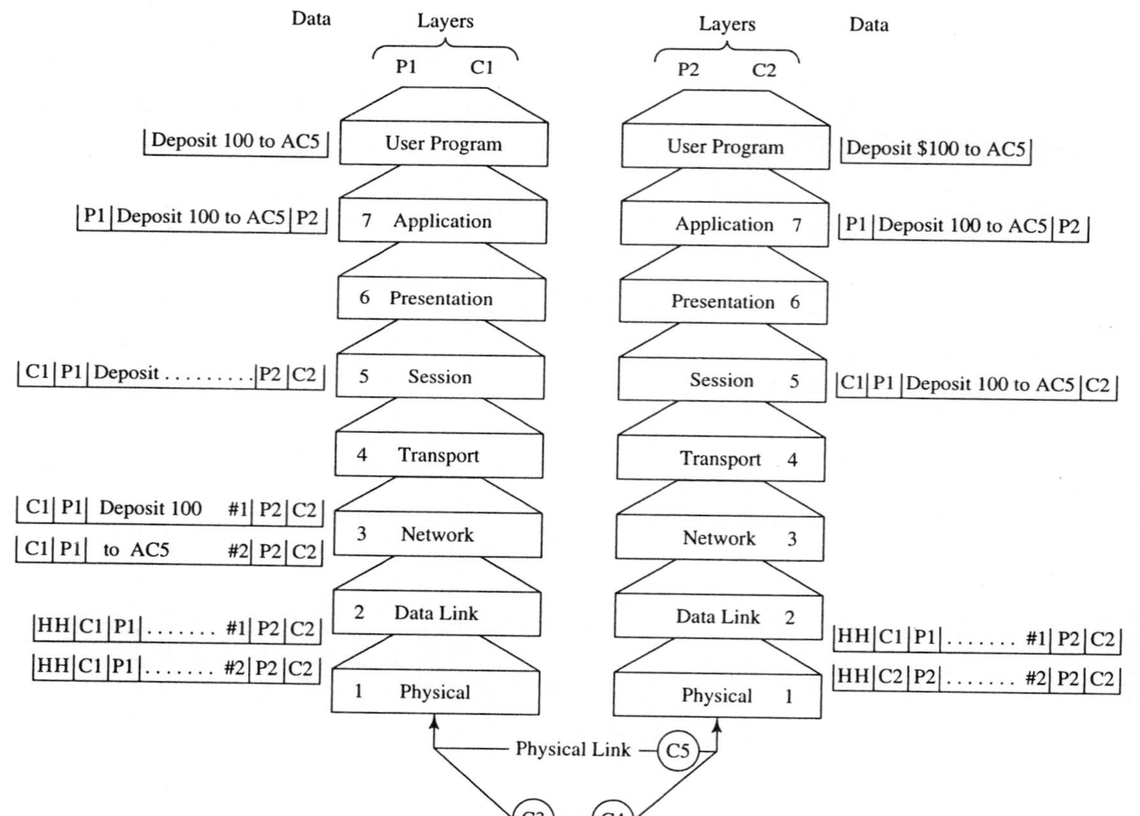

FIGURE 3.5 Example of Information Flow

3.3.4 Protocol Overview

As stated previously, a protocol is a set of precisely defined rules and conventions for behavior between two parties. For example, diplomatic protocols define the conventions and rules to be observed by diplomats. According to the OSI Model, a communication protocol is defined as rules of exchange between entities at same layers of the OSI Model. Thus the data link protocols define the rules of exchange between the layer 2 entities, the transport protocols define the rules of exchange between the layer 4 entities and the application protocols define the rules of exchange between the application layer entities of two systems. Higher-level protocols (e.g., business processing protocols) can also be defined by using this framework.

Protocols, especially at higher layers, guarantee correct exchange of information. A protocol consists of two basic elements:

- Format of message, which shows precisely how the data, the commands/flags, the sender/receiver identification, and the response will be sent and received (recognized) by the two entities
- Rules of message exchange, which specify what to do if a message is received incorrectly, not received, received out of sequence, or is distorted.

For example, the X.25 protocol defines the format of the packets exchanged and the rules to handle out-of-sequence packets. Similarly, X.400 protocol defines the format of the messages exchanged and the rules to handle out-of-sequence messages in electronic mail.

Protocols play an important role in integration and interconnectivity in distributed systems because they are "visible" and can be tested for conformance. Lower-level protocols are used to physically interconnect devices, while higher-level protocols are used to interconnect applications. For example, to connect two computers on a physical cable, the two computers must use the same link protocol (e.g., Ethernet, token ring, SDLC). Since most link-level protocols are built in adapter cards, the same type of adapter card must be used to connect two computers over a physical link. Obviously, the message sent by an Ethernet card will not be understood by an SDLC or token ring card. Protocol converters may be needed to convert one type of link protocol to other (many Ethernet to token ring protocol converters are commercially available). Similarly, the same application protocols are needed to connect higher-level applications. Since most higher-level protocols are embedded in software, software protocol converters or gateways may be needed to convert higher-level protocols.

Appendix A gives an overview of the OSI protocols. Examples of the protocols discussed are LAN protocols, SDLC, ISDN protocols and Application Layer protocols. More details about communications protocols can be found in Stallings <1991>, Tannenbaum <1988>, Schwartz <1987>, and Bertsekas <1987>. The IEEE Tutorial, *A Practical View of Computer Communications Protocols*, edited by McQuillen and Cerf, contains many good articles on communication protocols. In addition, several computer communication journals publish special issues on communication protocols. An example is the *Computer Networks and ISDN Systems*, Vo.l. 24, No. 3, 1992, Special Issue on Protocol Specification, Testing and Verification.

3.4 Examples and Analysis of Different Network Architectures

In the last 20 years, many network architectures have been developed for different sectors of the computing industry. The OSI Model can be used as a basis for describing and comparing the available network architectures. Here are some examples.

3.4.1 LAN Network Architectures

Some local area networks (LANs) use only layers 1, 2, and 7 of the OSI Model. Layer 1 of LANs may support broadband or baseband cables and layer 2 may use IEEE802.3, IEEE802.4 and IEEE802.5 protocols. The IEEE 802 Committee has divided layers 1 and 2 into sublayers (see Fig. 3.6). In some LANs, layers 3, 4, 5 and 6 are absent. Some functions of these layers are simplified and included in the Application, DataLink and Physical Layers of the LAN architecture. However, many LANs support all seven layers.

The Application layer of LANs usually includes LAN server software such as print servers, file servers, and user profile managers. In addition, this layer supports the workstation software which routes the workstation requests to the server. For example, the Novell Netware LAN server functions are performed in the application layer.

The Data Link Layer has been subdivided into two sublayers. The logical link control sublayer actually provides the simplified version of the services provided by layers 3 to 6 of the OSI Model. It provides the service access points so that applications at different LAN stations may be able to communicate with each other and controls the exchange of data. The IEEE 802.2 (now called 8022) specifies the services and the protocols provided by the logical link control (LLC) sublayer. The medium access control (MAC) sublayer interfaces with the physical media and provides some of the services of the Data Link Layer of the OSI Model.

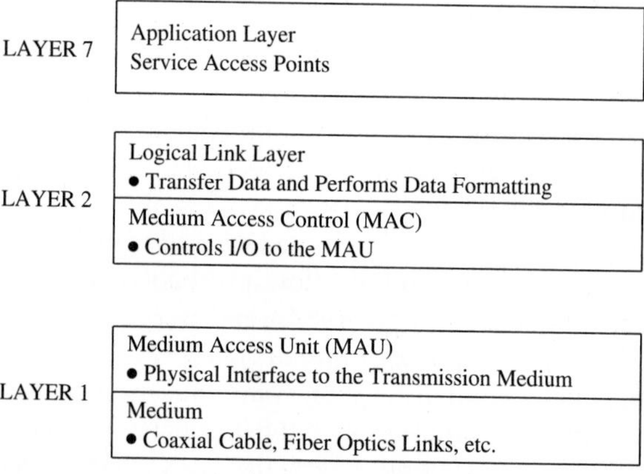

FIGURE 3.6 LAN Layers Defined by the IEEE802

The Physical Layer is also subdivided into two sublayers: The medium access unit sublayer provides physical interface to the transmission medium, and the medium sublayer consists of the transmission media such as coaxial cable, fiber optics links, etc.

Different LANs use different layer 3 to 6 protocols (in some LANs these layers are null). The following two are used most widely at present:

- NetBIOS
- IPX/SPX

NetBIOS (Network Basic Input Output System) is a Session Layer programming interface for IBM PC LANs. NetBIOS is a de facto standard for IBM PC LANS and is currently supported by all major LAN vendors. For example, NetBIOS stack can run in the Novell Netware LANs. Basically, NetBIOS provides a programming interface at the OSI Session Layer level for sending/receiving data in LAN environments. Technical details about NetBIOS can be found in the *IBM Technical Reference Manual*, SC30-3383-2, 1988.

Internetwork Packet Exchange (IPX) and Sequenced Packet Exchange (SPX) are used in the Novell Netware LANs. IPX/SPX stack is available on many other LANs for connectivity and interoperability. IPX, a datagram delivery service, operates at the OSI Network Layer level while SPX, a connection-based service, operates at the OSI Session Layer. Technical details about IPX/SPX can be found in the Novell Netware manuals and tutorials. The book *Data Communications and Networking Fundamentals Using Novell Netware* by Ramos, Schroeder, and Simpson (McMillan, 1992) gives additional details about Novell Netware LANs.

An area of active standards development is concerned with the wireless LANs. For example, wireless LANs at 2 Mbps are commercially available. A large installed base of wired (copper or fiber optic) LANs currently operates at 10 Mbps. The wireless LANs are also being aimed at this speed, at least, for an equivalent performance. A summary of the IEEE802 activities in wireless LANs is given by Hayes <1991>.

3.4.2 Transmission Control Program/Internetp Protocol (TCP/IP)

In the late 1960s and early 1970s, the Defense Advanced Research Projects Agency (DARPA) defined a set of network standards and protocols for interconnecting many computers in the ARPANET (Advanced Research Projects Agency Network). Initially referred to as the DOD (Department of Defense) or ARPANET Protocol Suite, these protocols were intended for military networks. For example, the following five original DOD protocols were issued as military standards:

- Internet Protocol (IP): MIL-STD-1777
- Transmission Control Protocol (TCP): MIL-STD-1778
- File Transfer Protocol (FTP): MIL-STD-1780

- Simplified Mail Transfer Protocol (SMTP): MIL-STD-1781
- Terminal emulator (TELNET): MIL-STD-1782

In the last 20 years, these protocols have dramatically grown in popularity and have become the de facto standards for large heterogeneous networks. Although many new protocols have been added to the DOD Suit, Transmission Control Protocol (TCP) and Internet Protocol (IP) are the best-known DOD protocols. At present, the entire DOD/ARPANET Protocol Suite is commonly referred to as the *TCP/IP Protocol Suite.* In this book, we will use TCP/IP Protocol Suite, or just TCP/IP Suite, to refer to the DOD/ARPANET Protocol Suite.

The TCP/IP Suite addresses the layer 3 and above issues (see Fig. 3.7). Internet Protocol (IP) is roughly at layer 3 and can reside on a very large number of physical networks such as Ethernets, token rings, FDDI, ISDN, and X.25 packet switching systems. Transmission Control Protocol (TCP) resides on top of IP and is responsible for reliable transport between end systems. TCP connects the application layer processes to IP and provides the functions that are roughly equivalent to layers 4, 5 and 6 of the OSI Model. The application layer of this network architecture provides a rich set of file transfer, terminal emulation, network file access, and electronic mail services. Examples of the popular application layer services in TCP/IP are as follows:

- Telnet (terminal emulator)
- FTP (File Transfer Protocol)
- NFS (Network File Services)
- SMTP (Simplified Mail Transfer Protocol)
- SNMP (Simplified Network Management Protocol).

The TCP/IP Protocol Suite consists of many protocols which have evolved over the last 20 years. The main power of TCP/IP is due to the following reasons:

- The TCP/IP Suite is available on almost all computing systems today, including microcomputers, minicomputers, and mainframes (it is estimated that there are more than 200 TCP/IP vendors at present). For example, TCP/IP can be used to transfer files between IBM, DEC, SUN, PRIME, Macintosh and several other machines. In addition, TCP/IP is closely associated with the Unix operating system

User Applications	
Telnet FTP SMTP X windows	TFTP NFS Ping RPC SNMP
Transmission Control Protocol (TCP)	User Datagram Protocol (UDP)
Internet Protocol (IP)	
Physical Network	

FIGURE 3.7 TCP/IP Protocol Suite

and most Unix vendors support TCP/IP. For example, the SUN Microsystems Unix and the Hewlett-Packard HP-UX systems include TCP/IP as part of the basic software package.

- The TCP/IP Suite is based on the experience gained in the ARPANET project, which resulted in the Internet supernetwork—one of the largest heterogeneous networks in the world with over 60,000 interconnected computers. ARPANET itself was discontinued in 1990, but it supported the evolution of different types and numbers of computers over a long time (ARPANET evolution is illustrated in the "ARPANET Maps: 1969–1990," *Computer Communications Reviews*, Oct. 1990, pp. 81–110).
- IP, the lowest protocol in this Suite, can reside on a very wide variety of physical networks such as Ethernets, FDDI-based fiber optic LANs, dial-up lines, X.25-based packet switching networks, or ISDN digital networks. The internet technology used by IP allows many computers to communicate across many networks.
- TCP, the layer above IP, supports a very wide variety of higher-level (application) protocols which allow users to emulate terminals, transfer files, and send/receive mail between different computers.
- The TCP/IP Suite provides a framework and the tools for *interoperability*, where interoperability refers to the ability of diverse computing systems to cooperate in solving computational problems.
- Simplified Network Management Protocol (SNMP), a recently developed TCP/IP-based network management protocol, has become widely accepted by vendors and users for network management in heterogeneous networks. Due to the growing importance of network management, SNMP has furthered the popularity of TCP/IP Suite as the glue between disparate networks and devices.

Due to these reasons, TCP/IP has become the main de facto standard for interconnecting heterogeneous computer systems. For example, according to an International Data Corp. report, more than 30,000 TCP/IP-based backbone networks were operational in April, 1990. Due to its popularity, the TCP/IP Protocol Suite continues to evolve. The Internet Activities Board (IAB) provides a framework and focus for most of the research and development of these protocols. IAB was originally organized by DARPA to promote R&D. At present, IAB has evolved into an autonomous organization consisting of many task forces with various charters. A series of technical reports, called Internet Request for Comments (RFC), describe the protocol proposals and standards. As we will see in this chapter, an RFC is a formal document which can become a standard. For example, almost all of the current TCP/IP protocols are specified as RFCs. TCP/IP is discussed in detail in Appendix B.

3.4.3 IBM's System Network Architecture (SNA)

System Network Architecture (SNA) was introduced by IBM in 1973 as a single network architecture for all computer communication products in IBM environments.

SNA is IBM's strategic solution and long-range direction for computer communication networks. At present, SNA is the heaviest used proprietary network architecture—more than 40,000 SNA networks are operational worldwide <Berson 1990, page 11>. Because of this, many vendors have developed interfaces between different network architectures and SNA.

SNA was originally released for centrally controlled, single mainframe, hierarchical networks. It has evolved over the last two decades with facilities for networking between mainframes, peer-to-peer communications, and extensive network management. For example, SNA has added support for large networks, dynamic routing, multiple mainframes, packet switching and LAN systems, voice/image processing, network management operations, peer-to-peer networking, distributed cooperative processing, and interconnectivity to other networks. Due to the strategic position of SNA, it is a key component of IBM's Systems Application Architecture (SAA), which is a framework for transportable applications across all IBM mainframes, minicomputers, and workstations.

SNA is arranged in 7 layers, although the 7 layers of SNA do not exactly correspond to the 7 layers of the OSI Model (see Fig. 3.8). Synchronous Data Link Control (SDLC) is used in the first two layers of IBM's wide area networks, and token ring protocol is used in IBM LANs. The Network Control Program (NCP) roughly performs the layer 4 functions and resides in a front end communications processor (e.g., IBM's 3725). Layers 5 and 6 of SNA are handled by the Virtual Telecommunications Access Method (VTAM), which resides in IBM mainframes. The main application layer protocol offered by IBM is the Advanced Program to Program Communications (APPC) protocol, which supports distributed cooperative processing for business applications. SNA and LU6.2/APPC are discussed in Appendix C. Due to the strong market presence of SNA, many "gateways" are available to connect SNA to X.25, TCP/IP, and other types of communication networks.

SNA Layers	*SNA Architectural Components*
Network Users	
End User and Network Services Layer Access Method	VTAM (Virtual Telecommunications Access Method)
Presentation Services Layer	
Data Flow Control Layer	
Transmission Control Layer	NCP (Network Control Program)
Path Control Layer	X.25, ISDN,
Data Link Control Layer	SDLC (Synchronous Data Link Control), & Token Ring
Physical Layer	

FIGURE 3.8 SNA Layers and Components

3.4.4 Manufacturing Automation Protocol (MAP) and Technical Office Protocol (TOP)

The Manufacturing Automation Protocol (MAP), developed by General Motors in the early 1980s, used the OSI Model as a general framework for defining the protocols needed for manufacturing plants. MAP uses a subset of the OSI standards. For example, MAP uses broadband facilities at layer 1 and the IEEE 802.4 (Token Bus) protocol at layer 2. The application layer protocols of MAP use the OSI standards such as FTAM. The major application layer offering is Manufacturing Message Specification (MMS), which has been developed especially for manufacturing applications. For example, MMS allows development of flexible manufacturing software and robot control systems. MAP and MMS are discussed in Appendix D.

The Technical Office Protocol (TOP) was developed by Boeing for office applications. TOP was developed in close cooperation with MAP and is also based on a subset of OSI. Figure 3.9 shows the MAP and TOP layered architectures. It can be seen that TOP uses baseband services at layer 1, IEEE 802.3 (Ethernet) at layer 2 and the X.400 (Message Handling System) at layer 7. Other than a few minor differences, the layer 3 through 6 protocols of TOP and MAP are essentially the same. TOP is also discussed in Appendix D.

3.4.5 Network Architectures for High-Speed (Broadband) Networks

New architectures are being developed for the evolving high-speed broadband networks. The main characteristics of these networks are as follows:

- The transmission rate is in the range of several Giga bits per second in fiber links. This is in contrast to the current few Million bits per second in coaxial cables.
- The error rate has fallen from 10^{-6} to 10^{-14}, a big reduction.
- Node processing delay becomes significant compared to data transmission delay.

ISO Layers	*MAP*	*TOP*
Application	ACSE, FTAM, NM/DS, MMS	ACSE, VT, FTAM, MHS
Presentation	ISO Presentation Service	ISO Presentation Service
Session	ISO Connection Oriented Service	ISO Connection Oriented Service
Transport	ISO Class 4 Transport	ISO Class 4 Transport
Network	X.25	X.25
Data Link	IEEE 802.2 LLC IEEE 802.4 Token Passing Bus	IEEE 802.2 LLC IEEE 802.3 CSMA/CS IEEE 802.4 Token Passing Bus
Physical	10 MBPS Broadband (802.4) 5 MBPS Carrierband	Broadband (802.4) Baseband (802.3)

FIGURE 3.9 MAP and TOP

- The rate at which messages are generated is lower than the message transmission rate in many application areas.

The multilayered architectures discussed earlier were developed in the last two decades for networks which suffered from the "SUE" (slow, unreliable, expensive) effect. These architectures perform too much error checking and incur considerable processing delays in several layers and consequently are not suitable for high-speed networks of the 1990s and beyond. Network architectures for high-speed networks are an area of considerable research activity. The main features of these architectures are simple algorithms, end-to-end protocols and regular topologies.

The algorithms are simplified to reduce node processing overhead. In addition, the frequency of executing these algorithms is minimized to further reduce processing overhead. Thus an attempt is made to use simple, albeit rough, calculations which may not give the "optimal" results because finding the optimum may take too long. This principle is used frequently in routing algorithms.

End-to-end protocols are used because more processing is done at the end-points and not in the intermediate "hops." In existing systems, for example, a message between Chicago and Los Angeles may go through 10 hops, with each hop performing some checking—the message is stored, checked and forwarded to the next hop. In the case of high-speed networks, all intermediate error checking is bypassed because the destinations can do all checking and the message can be retransmitted, if needed. The low error rate and high transmission speed more than compensate for retransmission activity.

Regular topologies are used throughout the network to simplify routing. Example of a regular topology is a hypercube network in which each node is located at a vertex of an n-dimensional hypercube (Fig. 3.10). The address of a node is represented by an n-tuple, with each component being 0 or 1 (for example, the nodes in Fig. 3.10 are represented by 000, 001, 111, etc.). In this network, the nodes with only one different component are directly connected (for example, 000 is directly connected to 001, 010 and 100). This allows a quick calculation of the number of hops between two nodes (for example, the number of hops between 000 to 111 is 3). This calculation simplifies the task of routing and eliminates the need for consulting routing tables.

The high-speed network architectures are refining the lower-layer protocols which are concerned with routing, medium access control, and flow control/conges-

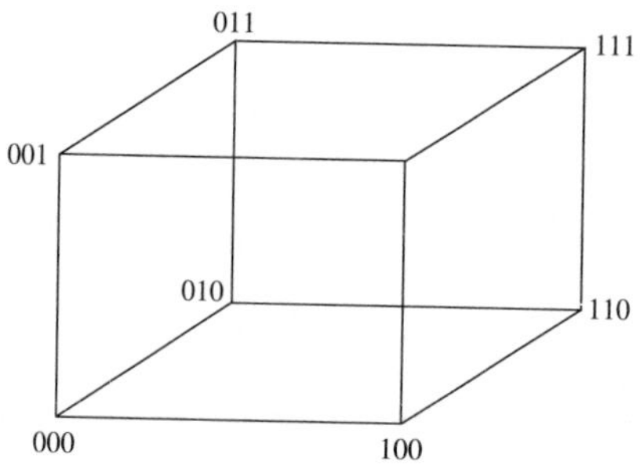

FIGURE 3.10 Hypercube: Example of a Regular Topology

tion control. The main emphasis is to streamline and minimize the processing at lower layers and leave the error checking and sequence control to higher layers. For example, the older X.25 packet switching systems perform too much error checking in the first three layers. This processing is an overkill in the high-speed and reliable fiber optic networks of the future. Many different protocols are being researched and developed at present for these evolving networks. Examples of the routing algorithms are the Open Shortest Path First (OSPF) and Intermediate System to Intermediate System (IS-IS) standards <Perlman 1991>. Another example is the Xpress Transfer Protocol which is being developed for fiber optics and very fast networks. An overview of XTP is given in Sanders <1990>. The *IEEE Communications Magazine*, October 1991 issue is devoted to the congestion control in high-speed networks. Doshi and Johri <Doshi 1992> provide a tutorial on communication protocols for high-speed packet networks. A thorough survey of high-speed local area networks and their performance can be found in AbeySundara <1991>.

In addition to the network architectures which are applicable to all high-speed networks, special network architectures are being developed for specific applications. For example, work is being done in the area of network architectures for multimedia applications (see, for example Dupuy <1992>, Sheppard <1992>, Shepherd <1990>, and Little <1991>). Many standards are also emerging for the evolving broadband network technologies. Examples are the IEEE 802.6 Distributed Queue Dual Bus (DQDB) standard and FDDI enhancements for metropolitan area networks, the SMDS standards for high-speed public MANs and WANs, the SONET standards for the fiber optic transmission facilities, the asynchronous transfer mode (ATM) protocol for fast multiplexing, and the Broadband ISDN (BISDN) standard for integrated access to very high-speed networks. We reviewed these standards briefly in the previous chapter. Another interesting area of research is dynamic network architectures where the number of layers visited by each message is not static. For example, O'Mally and Peterson <O'Mally 1992> describe the ideas behind a dynamic network architecture in which the number of layers visited by a message can be a variable.

Due to the evolving nature of these protocols, a detailed discussion is beyond the scope of this book. The interested reader should refer to the IEEE periodic publications such as the *IEEE Network*, *IEEE Communications Magazine*, and *Communication Protocol Conference Proceedings*. Other sources are the special conference proceedings and the workshops on broadband and high-speed networks. The Phoenix BISDN Workshop, March 19–21, 1991, in Phoenix, Arizona is an example.

3.4.6 Miscellaneous Network Architectures

In addition to the network architectures discussed so far, several other network architectures have been developed and continue to be used and enhanced. Examples of some of these network architectures are as follows:

- DECnet (also called DNA) was developed by the Digital Equipment Corporation (DEC) in the mid-1970s. Initially developed for peer-to-peer communications for 32 nodes in Phase I, DECnet has evolved into an extensive enterprise-wide network architecture which can support over several million nodes. At the lowest layers,

DECnet is heavily Ethernet oriented with offerings in broadband Ethernet, baseband Ethernet, thickwire Ethernet and thinwire Ethernet. DECnet supports an Open Systems Applications Kernel (OSAK) for distributed applications. At present, DECnet supports many of the OSI and TCP/IP protocols. DECnet Phase V, the latest offering, is fully compliant with the OSI Model with support for ISDN and network management. Details about DECnet can be found in Malmud <1991>, and DEC <1990>.

- Hewlett-Packard has developed HPNET and HPAdvancenet for Engineering , PRIME has PRIMENET; and Honeywell Bull has Distributed Computing Architecture. All these vendors are also moving toward TCP/IP and OSI.
- DOD has sponsored development of DDN (Defense Data Network) as frameworks for interconnecting many military systems.
- Many proprietary factory network architectures have been developed and continue to exist on many factory floors. For example, factory networks from Allen-Bradley support Data Highway and Data Highway Plus for factory floor devices. In 1989, Allen-Bradley and DEC announced a joint product, called the PYRAMID Integrator, which connects the factory floor networks (e.g., Data Highway) with DECnet. PYRAMID has become a competitor to MAP, especially in small manufacturing companies, because it allows interconnection of established networks on the factory floor to be connected to the engineering and corporate offices through DECnet interfaces to SNA. In addition, it is much cheaper than MAP.

3.4.7 Comparison of Network Architectures

Figure 3.11 shows how the functions provided by many available network architectures compare with OSI. The following observations can be made from this analysis:

Layer	*OSI Model*	*MAP*	*TOP*	*LAN*	*IBM SNA*	*DEC DNA Phase Y*	*ARPANET*
7	Application	MMS FTAM	X.400 FTAM	Server (Nos)	LU6.2, APPC	OSI	TELNET NFS
6	Presentation	ISO	ISO	NetBIOS, ↑	VTAM	Stack ↑	
5	Session	ISO	ISO	IPX/SPX,			
4	Transport	ISO TPU	ISO TPU	or	NCP		TCP
3	Network	X.25	X.25	Null ↓		↓	IP
2	Data Link Control	Token Bus (802.4)	Ethernet (802.3)	Token Ring, 802.6, 802.3, and 802.4	SDLC or X.25 or ISDN	802.3 ISDN	Many Options
1	Physical	Broadband	Baseband	Broadband or Baseband		Broadband or Baseband	

FIGURE 3.11 Comparative Architectures

- Many network architectures provide 7 layers. However, there is not a one-to-one mapping between the OSI Model and older network architectures such as SNA and ARPANET.
- The OSI layers define the relative issues addressed by most networks, even if the exact layer meanings may change. For example, layer 1 and 2 are always concerned with station attachment and layer 7 supports applications in the network.
- Vendors can provide layer 7 protocols and services without having to provide all of the lower layers. For example, MMS was originally developed for MAP but is now available on DECnet, Ethernet LANs, and Tandem TCP/IP networks. Similarly, APPC was originally developed on SNA but is now available on token ring LANs, DECnet, and SUN TCP/IP networks.
- The advancements in communication technology are hidden from higher layers. For example, most network architectures are planning to support fiber optics and ISDN services at the first two layers without having to modify the higher-level layers. However, this is not exactly true for the applications being designed for the emerging high-speed networks. In some cases, high-speed application requirements are being mapped to the lower-level capabilities (i.e., develop special applications for special lower-level capabilities).

The main observation is that most network architectures support layered views although there is no one-to-one mapping between layers of different network architectures. In addition, most vendors are currently supporting TCP/IP and are pledging to support OSI.

3.5 Network Interconnectivity (Internetworking)

3.5.1 Interconnectivity and Network Architectures

The OSI Model can be used to classify the interconnectivity issues at three levels:

- *Physical station interconnectivity*: This defines how the stations will be connected through physical cables and adapter cards. The layer 1 and 2 issues of voltage levels, analog versus digital interfaces and link control message formats and flow control are important for this type of interconnectivity.
- *Network interconnectivity*: This defines how a station S_1 connected to a network NET1 can communicate with a station S_2 connected to a network NET2. The layers 3 and 4 issues of routing and transport between end systems are important for this type of interconnectivity. Network interconnectivity is also called *internetworking*.
- *Application interconnectivity*: This defines how the data between an application A_1 on station S_1 is shared/exchanged by an application A_2 on station S_2. The higher-level

issues of using terminal emulation, file transfer, client-server interactions, and remote data access are important for this type of interconnectivity.

The following example will illustrate these levels of interconnectivity. Consider a room full of workstations that need to exchange information with each other and also need to access a database located on a remotely located mainframe.

The physical station interconnectivity requires the workstations to be interconnected with each other and also with the mainframe. For example, if all stations have Ethernet cards, then an Ethernet cable can physically interconnect the stations to form an Ethernet LAN. Every station on the Ethernet LAN will have an Ethernet address. The LAN server can then be connected to the mainframe over an X.25-based packet data network (PDN) using, say, T_1 lines. The mainframe will have an X.25 address which is in a different format than the Ethernet format.

The network interconnectivity will require messages to be exchanged and understood between the Ethernet LAN and the X.25 network. For example, the mainframe as well as the LAN stations should be able to recognize each other's addresses. This can be accomplished either by running the same layer 3 to 4 software on the LAN server and the mainframe (e.g., the ISO stack or the TCP/IP Suite). In case of TCP/IP, all computers will be assigned IP addresses so that they can communicate with each other (the Ethernet and X.25 addresses are one level below the IP addresses). For example, the mainframe may have an IP address of 128.22.32.01 while the workstations on the Ethernet may be assigned addresses between 128.22.30.01 to 128.22.30.20. It is also possible to use a gateway, discussed later, between the mainframe and the LAN server. We will discuss the network interconnectivity devices in the next section.

The application interconnectivity requires that, at least, files can be transferred between all workstations and the mainframe. Even though the stations between networks know each other's address, they have to agree on how to exchange data. For example, if one computer compresses a file before sending, the receiver has to know how to decompress the file. File transfers between the LAN workstations are supported by the LAN software. However, file transfer between the workstations and the mainframe requires the same file transfer packages to operate at the mainframe and the LAN. For example, Kermit or TCP/IP FTP can be used for file transfer. If the same packages are not available, then some conversion will be needed between the two file transfer packages. The issue of application interconnectivity in distributed computing is quite complex and can involve topics such as terminal emulation, file transfer, client-servers, distributed databases, electronic mail, etc. We will concentrate on application interconnectivity in Part III of this book.

Discussion of internetworking in this section is brief. For more information, the following books are recommended:

- Perlman, R., *Interconnections: Bridges and Routers*, McGraw-Hill, 1992.
- White, G., *Internetworking and Addressing,* McGraw-Hill, 1992.
- Stallings, W., *Networks and Data Communications*, 3rd edition, McMillan, 1991 (chapter on internetworking).

3.5.2 Network Interconnection Devices (Routers, Bridges, Gateways)

A communication network is a collection of equipment and physical media, viewed as one autonomous whole, that interconnects two or more end systems. In most real life situations, many networks are interconnected to form internetworks. Each constituent network of an internetwork is called a subnetwork. We will use the terms of subnetworks and internetworks when necessary—the internal configuration of a network (i.e., it is formed from many small networks) is irrelevant to the end user. The subnetworks are interconnected through intermediate systems (relays). The most frequently used relays, illustrated in Fig. 3.12a, are discussed here by using the OSI Model as a framework. This section will introduce you to these relays. The underlying techniques used in these devices are reviewed in Appendix A, Section A.5. For a detailed technical discussion of this topic, the book *Interconnections: Bridges and Routers*, by Perlman <1992> is recommended. More information can be found in Cypser <1991>, Nadler <1988>, Seiffert <1988>, and Stallings <1991>.

3.5.2.1 Repeaters

Repeaters are used to interconnect segments of an extended network with identical protocols and speeds at the physical layer. As discussed in Chapter 2, repeaters basically regenerate the digital signals and operate at layer 1. An example of repeaters are the DEREPs (DEC Repeaters) used to interconnect two DECnet subnetworks in two different buildings of a campus.

3.5.2.2 Bridges

A bridge connects two similar or dissimilar LANS to form a larger network at the data link layer. Bridges are simple devices which only operate at layer 1 and 2 of the OSI Model and do not deal with any higher-level issues such as network routing and session control. Bridges require that the networks have consistent addressing schemes and packet sizes. Since bridges also interconnect networks, they automatically include the repeater functions. For example, the DEC Ethernet LAN is limited to 2.8 kilometers. The DEC LAN Bridge 100 is used to interconnect small Ethernet LANs to make a "super" LAN which can be extended to 22 km and support up to 8000 stations. In this case, the bridge is providing repeater functions. Common examples of using bridges are as follows:

- Interconnections of LANs with different layer 1 technologies. Bridges are used frequently to connect broadband LANs to baseband LANs. For example, DEC supports many bridges to connect broadband Ethernet to baseband Ethernet and thinwire Ethernet to thickwire Ethernet. Similarly, in the MAP manufacturing environments, bridges are used to connect the 10-Mbps MAP broadband backbone with the 5-Mbps carrierband LANs (see Fig. 3.12b). A bridge between two LANs (LAN_1 and LAN_2) will basically read a message from LAN_1 stations, pass the messages destined for LAN_2 to LAN_2 in the needed layer 1 format, and pass the rest back to LAN_1.

a. Interconnectivity Devices (Layered View)

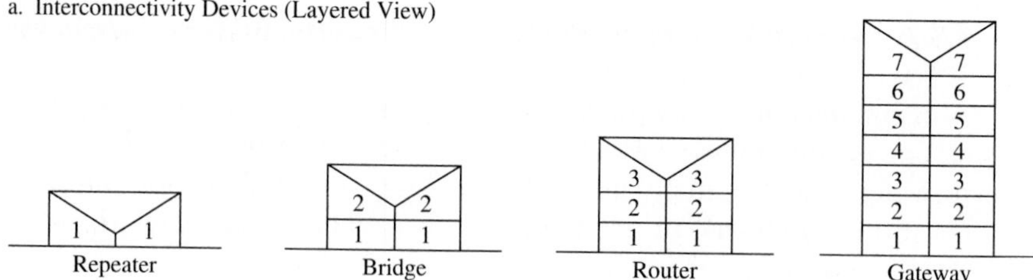

b. Bridges

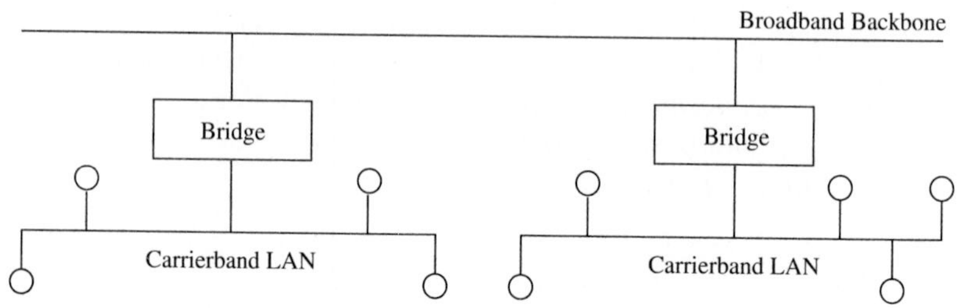

c. Routers

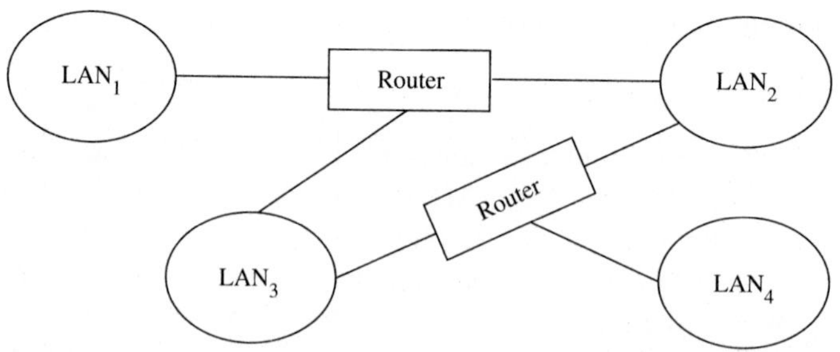

d. Gateways

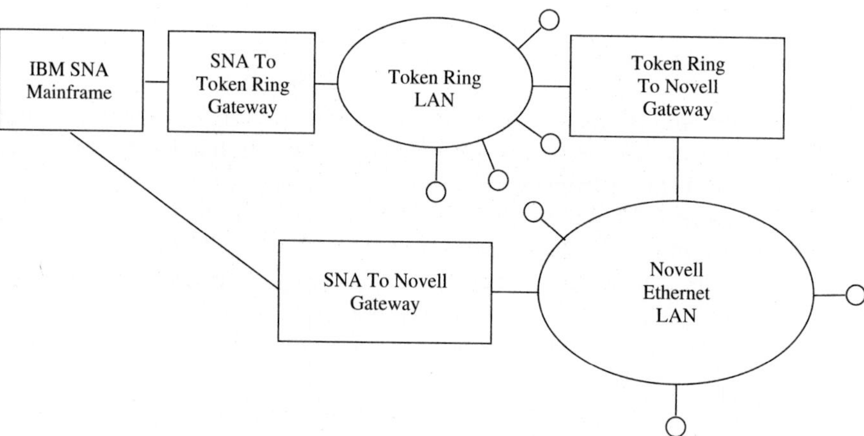

FIGURE 3.12 Network Interconnectivity Devices

- Bridges can be used to divide a large network into smaller subnets to control traffic. For example, consider an Ethernet LAN with 100 stations. Since all 100 stations chattering simultaneously can cause collisions, a bridge can be used to subdivide the network into two 50-station LANs. This division must be done carefully. Let us assume that S_1 and S_2 frequently exchange information. In this case, it is better to keep S_1 and S_2 on the same subnet; otherwise the bridge could become a bottleneck. The division of a network must subdivide the network in such a fashion so that the escape ratio of each subnet (percentage of messages leaving the subnet) is minimal. This can be achieved by grouping the devices that exchange information frequently in a subnet.

3.5.2.3 Routers

A router operates at layers 1, 2 and 3. It finds a path for a message and then sends the message on the selected path. A router may appear to be the same as a bridge but the main distinguishing feature of a router is that it knows alternate routes for a message and uses the alternate route to send a message if the primary route is not available (Fig. 3.12c). Consequently, a router must know the network topology (a layer 3 issue). A discussion of routing algorithms is beyond the scope of this book (something should be beyond the scope of this book!). Due to the routing algorithms, routers are more complex and more expensive than bridges. In telecommunication systems, routers are also called switches. Some bridges, called "brouters" (like "brunch"), include some routing facilities and compete with routers <Sevcik 1992>.

"Multiple protocol" routers are becoming available to allow different network protocols to use the same "wire," i.e., the backbone network. These routers, for example, allow one corporate backbone to be shared by different protocols such as TCP/IP, OSI, SNA, DECnet, Appletalk, Novell and Token Ring. The main advantage of these routers is that different wiring is not needed for different protocols. Many multiprotocol routers are becoming available from IBM, DEC, and other vendors, and are reviewed regularly in trade journals such as *Data Communications*. See Section A.5, Appendix A for more details about multiprotocol routers.

3.5.2.4 Gateways

In most large networks, protocols of some attached subnetworks need to be converted to protocols of other subnetworks for end-to-end communications. A gateway connects two dissimilar network architectures and is essentially a protocol converter. A gateway can convert protocols at any layer to achieve interoperability. In practice, many gateways translate an application layer protocol from one network architecture to a corresponding application layer protocol of another architecture (see Fig. 3.12d). A gateway may be a special purpose computer, a workstation with associated software (e.g., a PS2 with gateway software), or a software module which runs as a task in a mainframe. Here are some examples:

- Ethernet to token ring gateways convert layer 2 protocols. Another example of a layer 2 gateway is the IBM 3708, which converts serial to SDLC (an IBM layer 2 protocol).
- OSI to TCP/IP gateways allow OSI and TCP/IP subnetworks to interoperate by converting OSI Transport Layer Class 4 (TP4) to TCP (see Appendix A for more on this).
- Digital's SNA gateway allows DEC devices to communicate with IBM mainframes by converting the DEC application protocols to IBM 3270 protocol. This allows IBM mainframe applications to be accessed from DEC applications.
- LAN-Host gateways allow LAN users to access mainframe applications by converting LAN layer 7 protocols to mainframe layer 7 protocols. An example is the token ring to SNA gateway. Such gateways can be used in situations where several stations can do local processing, interact with other stations on a LAN, and logon to a mainframe and submit/receive jobs through the LAN-Host gateway.
- MAP gateways allow non-MAP stations to communicate with MAP stations by convertion to MAP protocols. Examples are the DECnet-MAP gateways, SNA-MAP gateways, etc. Such gateways can be used in situations where a LAN of several programmable controllers and robots needs to connect to a MAP backbone. These devices can communicate through MAP gateways. When a controller implements MAP, then the gateway can be replaced with the direct attachment.
- TCP/IP to SNA gateways allow TCP/IP and SNA applications to communicate with each other interactively. An example is the Sybase Open Net Gateway, which converts TCP/IP Socket calls to SNA LU6.2 for client-server applications between MVS hosts and TCP/IP Unix machines.
- OSI to OSI gateways may be needed to interconnect a connectionless OSI subnetwork to a connection-based OSI subnetwork.
- Electronic Mail gateways allow different electronic mail packages to exchange mail by converting one mail format to another. An example is the Softswitch Mail Gateway, which converts many mail protocols for mail exchange.

We should observe that the aforementioned terms are not always adhered to in the commercially available products. For example, some bridges are marketed as routers and many routers are marketed as gateways.

3.5.3 Interconnectivity Examples

Figure 3.13 shows how four stations C_1, C_2, C_3 and X_3 can be interconnected by using the interconnectivity devices discussed earlier. C_1 and C_2 are fully compatible (e.g., IBM PS2s) and can be connected directly through a cable or through routers if C_1 and C_2 belong to two different networks. C_2 and C_3 have different layer 1 and 2 facilities (e.g., C_2 may have an Ethernet card and C_3 a token ring card), so C_2 and C_3 are connected through a protocol converter. C_3 and X_3 have two different

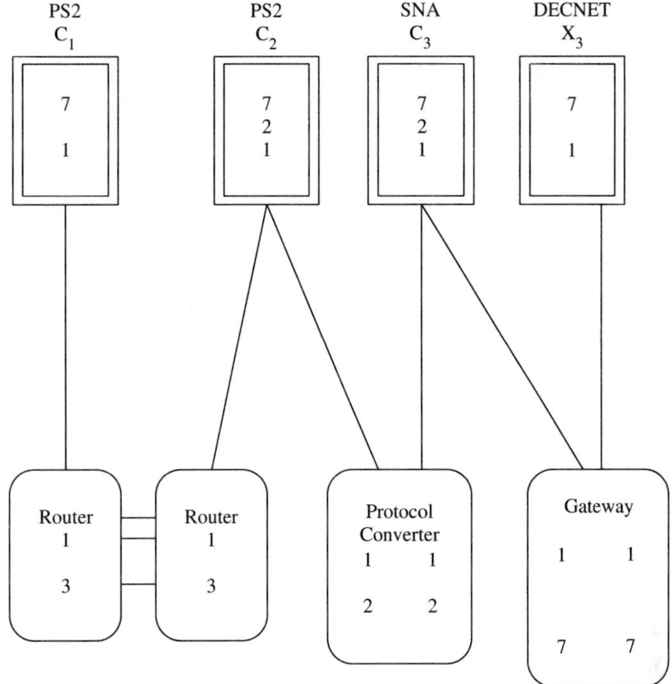

Note: A protocol converter is a gateway which operates at layer 1 and 2 (usually).

FIGURE 3.13 Routers, Converters, Gateways

network architectures (e.g., SNA and DECnet), so they are connected through a gateway.

Figure 3.14 shows how an SNA host can be connected to two LANS (a TCP/IP and an IBM token ring) and a few remote terminals (T_1, T_2, T_3). All devices with a token ring card are connected to the token ring cable. This LAN is connected to the SNA mainframe through a token ring/SNA gateway which converts the 3-layer token ring LAN architecture to the 7-layer SNA architecture. The TCP/IP to SNA gateway serves a similar purpose. Note that the workstation WS_1 is connected to WS_2 directly, perhaps through a dial-up modem.

Figure 3.15 shows a large network in which a backbone, perhaps a FDDI metropolitan area network, is connected to many subnets through routers and gateways. The backbone uses TCP/IP (i.e., TCP/IP is the native protocol stack). The TCP/IP subnets only use routers to exchange information amongst each other. However, an SNA subnet will need to use a TCP/IP to SNA gateway, in addition to a router, to communicate with a TCP/IP subnet. The routers are important in this network because they can recognize the destination and route the messages to the destination. Most of the routers in this configuration would support multiple protocols. The gateways would convert different protocols (e.g., MAP to TCP/IP, OSI to TCP/IP, SNA to TCP/IP). It may be possible to purchase one "box" which provides routing as well as gateway functions, or to install router/gateway software on a PS2 or SUN worksta-

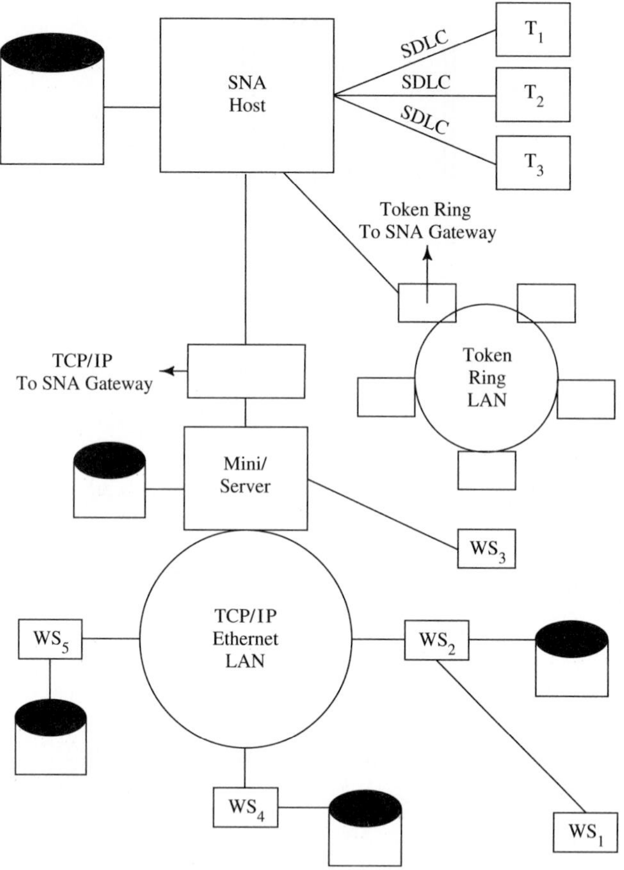

FIGURE 3.14 Network Interconnectivity

tion. The subnets may be located across a wide area network and may be connected to the backbone through T carriers at 1.54 Mbps or through the evolving high speed networks at 1 Gbps or higher.

These examples illustrate the device-to-network and the network-to-network interconnectivity scenarios. Application interconnectivity is handled by the higher-level layers at the end systems. Two applications at two different end systems, independent of the network interconnectivity option chosen, need to agree on the format and rules of message exchange. When this is not easily done, application gateways are introduced in the network. For example, two subnets may use different E-mail systems. However, to exchange mail from one subnet to another, a mail gateway may be needed with security features. Application interconnectivity is discussed in Part III of this book.

Before leaving this topic, we should note that the most efficient way to internetwork is to use a common Network Layer protocol throughout the network.

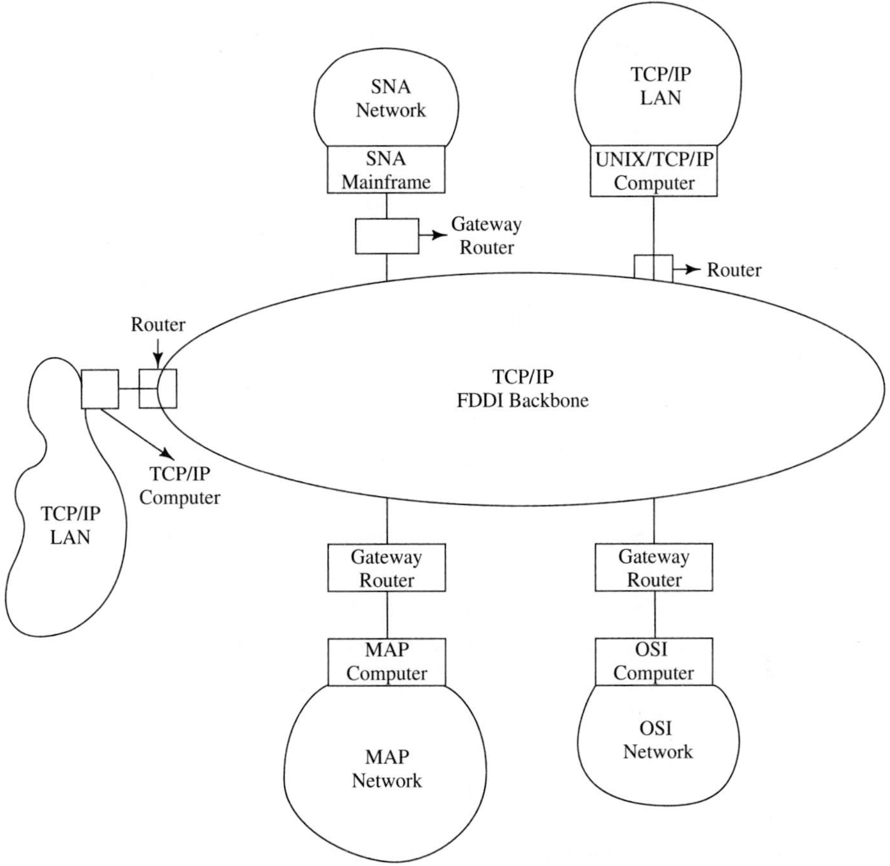

Notes: The backbone carries TCP/IP traffic. The TCP/IP LANS connected to this backbone only need routers (no translation needed). All other networks need some gateways in addition to routers.

FIGURE 3.15 Interconnecting Heterogeneous Network

Examples of these protocols are the TCP/IP Internet Protocol and the ISO connectionless layer 3 protocols.

3.5.4 Open Networking and the OSI Model

An open network is a vendor-independent network which conforms to international standards. "Openness" does not imply any implementation but refers to the mutual recognition and support of the applicable standards. The OSI Model is a framework for open networking. The term *Open Systems Interconnection* (OSI) qualifies standards for the exchange of information among systems that are "open" to one another because of their mutual use of the applicable standards. The main strengths of the OSI Model are as follows:

- The Model provides a framework for development of products from different vendors which can interoperate in a heterogeneous network.
- The Model provides a common vocabulary of terms and definitions which reduces the confusion among the vendors. For example, the Model clearly defines protocols and services. A protocol is defined as the rules between same level layers (e.g., link layer). A service exists between two adjacent layers of the Model. Due to this Model, the terms *data link protocol*, *transport protocol*, *session protocol*, and *application protocols* have universal meanings.
- The layering concept hides unnecessary information and reduces complexity. For example, layer N can use the facilities of $N - 1$ only and provide services to $N + 1$ only. This shields higher-level layers (closer to applications) from changes and details of lower-level layers (closer to data transmission technologies).
- The services of each layer are specified precisely so that a vendor can develop a product which may only offer one layer of services.
- The complexity of a system can be represented by the number of layers supported (e.g., a system supporting layers 1 and 2 is just an adapter card; a system supporting all 7 layers is a general purpose computer).
- It is not an implementation model. Each layer can be implemented as a separate unit, partially embedded in local operating systems or combined into one software package or a card.
- The OSI Model links the enterprise applications with communication technology advancements. The lower layers define station connectivity and are sensitive to advancements in the communication system technologies (transmission techniques, communication media), while the high-level layers define how the user and application processes interact with other remote processes and are sensitive to the enterprise activities.

However, the OSI Model has faced some criticism. A common criticism concerns the complexity of the Model for small and simple networks: Is it efficient to require every communication to undergo seven layers of processing, on the sender and receiver side, when the devices are within a few feet of each other? In response to this criticism, connectionless protocols at lower levels can be used to expedite processing. A Request For Comments (RFC1006) describes how the OSI upper layers (Session, Presentation, and Application) can operate on TCP/IP. This allows OSI services on TCP/IP networks.

Another potential problem with OSI is that the OSI documents describe many options which may be implemented differently. Thus difficulties in OSI product implementations exist. It is thus possible for two independent implementations of the same standard not to interoperate. For example, the X.25 implementations vary between different packet switching vendors.

Due to these difficulties, the standardization efforts are being subdivided into three areas:

Base standards: These define the procedures and the infrastructures from which different options can be chosen. The OSI standards discussed previously are examples of base standards.

Profiles: These define subsets and/or combinations of standards for specific functions (e.g., factory automation) and conformance tests for interoperability.

Registration mechanism: This provides the means to specify detailed parameters, if needed, with the base standards or Profiles.

The OSI standards are shifting focus to Profiles to promote interoperability and conformance. Each Profile document, released as ISP (International Standardized Profile), identifies the base standards to accomplish a function, lists the choice of permitted options, and suggests suitable values for parameters left unassigned in the base standards. Profiles do not contradict the base standards and modify the base standards only if it is deficient. Profiles may contain specific conformance requirements to promote uniformity in conformance tests. The ISO TR 10000 document describes a framework and taxonomy of International Standardized Profiles. Many ISPs have been developed and many more will be developed in the next few years. GOSIP (Government Open Systems Interconnection Profile) is an example of a Profile. Many governments are developing their own GOSIP to guide the development of networks in their countries (e.g., US GOSIP and UK GOSIP). GOSIP is not only a functional standard but also is used for procurement. For example, the US GOSIP specifies the base standards at different layers which are used as a basis for procuring government networks (see GOSIP <1988>, Shirey <1990>, Jain <1990, Chapter 9>).

The comparison of international versus proprietary/corporate standards is a thorny issue. Obviously, it is desirable to follow international standards due to vendor independence (the "open" systems) and potential widespread use. However, international standards take longer to develop (sometime due to vendor disagreements) and in many cases, do not translate into products. The proprietary standards are "closed" but are usually based on implemented systems. The cooperation and coexistence of proprietary and open standards is an area of major activity at present. We will discuss this topic in more detail in Chapter 9.

One school of thought is that OSI will become the backbone which will interconnect many other, perhaps proprietary and evolving networks (see Fig. 3.16a). As a backbone, OSI will take the role of an internetworking vehicle instead of a replacement tool. This implies, however, that many OSI to non-OSI gateways will be needed. At present, TCP/IP is becoming such an "internetworking" backbone due to the availability of vendor products and TCP/IP to non-TCP/IP gateways. Figure 3.16b shows how OSI upper layers can run on a TCP/IP network. A "convergence function," RFC1006, has been defined to allow OSI upper layers (5, 6, 7) to run on TCP/IP networks. This has the benefit that the rich set of functions supported by the OSI upper layers can be supported on the widely used TCP/IP networks. This is also a good transition strategy to move non-OSI applications to OSI without having to change the underlying physical network. The interested reader is referred to Appendix A, Section A.5, for a discussion of OSI interworking. Details about TCP/IP are given in Appendix B.

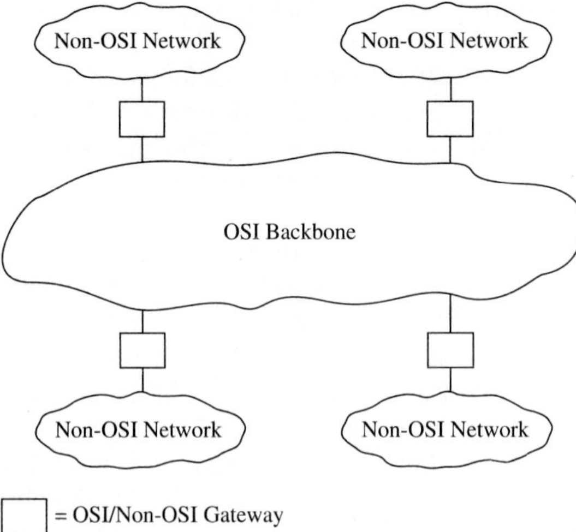

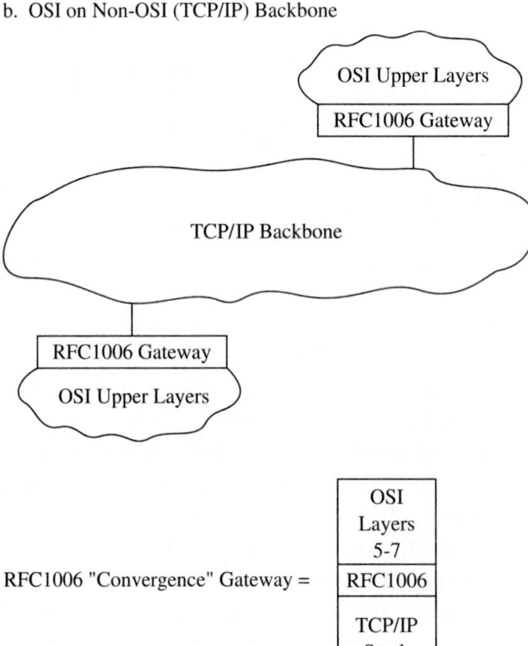

FIGURE 3.16 OSI in Non-OSI Environments

3.6 Management Summary and Trends

Network architecture standards are needed for compatibility of intervendor and intravendor network products and services. This is an important issue because the advances in network technologies and facilities have led to an explosion of network related hardware/software products from many computer manufacturers, common carriers, software vendors and data communications equipment manufacturers. These products provide similar functions differently. Standards are needed to assure that all the products fit together to form a functioning network. In addition, standards assure a large market and can drive for lower costs through competition and mass production.

The Open Systems Interconnection (OSI) Model has achieved nearly universal acceptance as the main network architecture standard. The OSI Model is the basis for the "open" systems movement, which emphasizes open environments in which different products from different vendors can be "glued" together to form functional systems. It provides not only a framework for developing standards but also defines a common vocabulary for discussing network design and open network architectures. Virtually all standards activities for communications are proceeding within the OSI Model. Many customers (for example the U.S. Government agencies) are demanding OSI compatibility and the industry is beginning to respond. For example, the Enterprise Network Event (ENE) held in May, 1988, in Baltimore displayed many vendor products and demonstrated an open OSI based network which connected many companies in the United States, Europe, and the Far East.

The OSI Model presents a layered view of the network, where each layer performs well-defined functions. This functional model divides the network activities into seven layers. The high-level layers of this model (Application, Presentation, and Session) are concerned with the issues related to the applications in different machines. The four lower layers (Transport Network, Data Link, and Physical) provide the transparent data exchange between computers.

According to the OSI Model, a communication protocol is defined as rules of exchange between entities at the same layers of the OSI Model. Communication protocols play an important role in integration and interconnection. The discussion of protocols and the OSI Model in this chapter lays a good foundation for comparing different network architectures, defining and classifying network products and discussing levels of interconnectivity. The lower-layer protocols define station connectivity and are sensitive to advancements in the communication system technologies (transmission techniques, communication media), while the high-level layers define how the user and application processes interface with the network and are sensitive to the enterprise activities. From this point of view, the OSI Model links the enterprise activities with communication technology advancements.

The OSI Model can be used as a framework for comparing/contrasting various network architectures (SNA, MAP, TCP/IP, DECnet, etc.) and for classifying and defining network interconnectivity products (e.g., routers, bridges, gateways, protocol converters). For example, to connect two devices on a physical link, the two must have the same link protocol (e.g., Ethernet, token ring, SDLC). Protocol converters may be needed to convert one type of link protocol to other (many Ethernet to token ring protocol converters are commercially available). Software protocol converters or gateways may be needed to convert higher-level protocols.

The following state-of-the-art trends in network architecture standards are worth noting:

- New network architecture standards are focusing on integrating newer technologies into existing networks. Examples are the standards being developed for cellular networks, multimedia networks, and broadband networks. The standardizing bodies are cooperating with each other in these standards.
- More work on network protocols is being done for newer and faster networks. The work is being done on protocol efficiency as well as reliability. An example is the Xpress Transfer Protocol, which is being developed for fiber optics and very fast networks. Another example is the work being done in the area of protocols for multimedia applications.
- The OSI standards are shifting focus toward interoperability of networks between functioning areas of organizations. An example is the development of OSI Profiles, which define subsets and/or combinations of standards for specific functions (e.g., factory automation) and conformance tests for interoperability. The ISO TR 10000 document describes a framework and taxonomy of international standardized profiles.

The state-of-the-market and state-of-the-practice trends appear to be as follows:

- The OSI Model will continue to provide a unifying framework between many network architectures and options available to the users. However, the actual replacement of existing networks with OSI networks remains to be seen. It will be important to see how the OSI Profiles play out.
- The standardization bodies and the vendors do not always agree on standards. The clout of vendors and standardization bodies will continue to be important in the acceptance of standards.
- It is becoming fashionable to use layered architectures in many disciplines. For example, AT&T's CIMA (Computer Integrated Manufacturing Architecture) uses a layered architecture to define the various functions in a computer integrated manufacturing (CIM) environment <Campbell 1988>.

Additional Readings: The interested reader can find additional information about network architectures and the OSI Model from the main references listed in Table 3.2. Network interconnectivity (internetworking) is an important topic and is discussed heavily in the literature. The books by Cypser <1991>, Perlman <1992>, and Stallings <1991> provide many details. The following journals and magazines are recommended for continued studies:

- *Internetworking: Research and Experience*
- *Computer Networks and ISDN Systems*

TABLE 3.2 Main Sources for Additional Information

1. Black, U., *OSI: A Model of Computer Communications Standards*, Prentice Hall, 1991.
2. Cameron, D., *OSI: An International Standard for Open Systems*, Computer Technology Research Corporation, Charleston, S.C., 1991.
3. MacKinnon, D., McCrum, W., and Sheppard, D., *An Introduction to Open Systems Interconnection*, Computer Science Press, 1990.
4. Jain, B., and Agrawala, A., *Open Systems Interconnection: Its Architecture and Protocols*, Elsevier, 1990.
5. Rose, M., *The Open Book: A Practical Perspective on OSI*, Prentice Hall, 1990.
6. Stallings, W., *Networks and Data Communications*, 3rd ed., Macmillan, 1991.
7. Henshell, J., and Shaw, H., *OSI Explained: End to End Communications Standards*, 2nd ed., Prentice Hall, 1991.
8. Seiffert, W. M., "Bridges and Routers," *IEEE Network Magazine*, vol. 2, pp. 57–64, Jan. 1988.
9. Stallings, W., *Handbook of Computer Communications Standards*, Macmillan, 1987, vol. 1 (ISO Model).
10. Tanenbaum, A., *Computing Networks*, 2nd ed., Prentice Hall, 1988.
11. Meijer, A., and Peeters, P., *Computer Network Architectures and Protocols*, Computer Science Press, 1983.
12. Proceedings of the IEEE, Special Issue on Open System Interconnection, Dec. 1983.

- *IEEE Network Magazine*
- *IEEE Communications Magazine*
- *Computer Communications*
- *Data Communications* (product highlights and regular column on internetworking)
- *Business Communications Review* (case studies and market analysis)

Problems and Exercises

1. What is a network architecture and what role does it play in computing networks?
2. What is needed for network architecture standards? List and discuss at least three network architecture standards.
3. Why was the OSI Model developed? What are the significant features of this Model?
4. Explain, through an example, the main features of the OSI layers.
5. What are protocols and why are they important in interconnectivity? Describe at least 10 different protocols at different layers. (You should review the material in Appendixes A, B, C, and D before answering this question.)
6. Choose one of the major network architectures and describe it in some detail. (You will need to read Appendixes A, B, C, or D to answer this question.)
7. What are the different levels of interconnectivity in networks? How do they help in practical situations. Describe at least two different examples which illustrate network interconnectivity.

8. How is interconnectivity related to interoperability, portability, and integration?
9. In your opinion, what role will OSI play in open networking? Will it replace the other N network architectures, will it become the internetworking vehicle or the $N + 1$st architecture?

CASE STUDY: Network Architectures for XYZCORP

The Information Systems Department at XYZCORP is in the process of developing an overall network layout and architecture for the corporation. The following projects reflect the major activities involved. Your consulting firm has been hired to lend help in these projects.

Project A: Network Architectures and Interconnectivity

The corporate office site houses an IBM mainframe under SNA and uses a token ring LAN within the office. The manufacturing plant site uses a large MAP LAN and the engineering office site uses a Unix TCP/IP LAN. The corporate center needs to be connected to the manufacturing plant and the engineering office to transfer files and provide corporate wide information sharing. Management wants to understand the various interconnectivty issues and approaches.

Deliverable: Prepare a management presentation which uses the OSI Model as a framework for discussing the various issues in corporate wide information exchange. The purpose of the presentation is management awareness. The presentation should be between 10 to 15 viewgraphs and should contain the following pieces of information:

- Identification of various levels of interconnectivity between the corporate office, manufacturing plant and engineering offices.
- A layout of how the three sites will be connected using appropriate interconnecting devices. Recall that the three sites are in different cities.
- Identification of what packages and products will be needed to exchange information between any two stations in the corporation (any station in corporate office should be able to access information from any station in the manufacturing or engineering sites).
- Analysis of what advantages/disadvantages the corporation will have in moving toward an open architecture.

Project B: Networking Laboratory

The Information Systems Group is considering a "Networking Lab" for investigation, evaluation and experimentation of network hardware and software with special interest in the ISO products. The Lab will initially consist of:

1. Two IBM PCs, with RS232 and token ring cards
2. Two MACs with Ethernet cards
3. One SUN workstation with Ethernet card

You have to design the Lab so that all these computers are interconnected and can transfer files between any two computers of the Lab. In addition, the Lab computers need to be connected to the IBM Mainframe for transferring files. You have to investigate the following issues:

1. How to Connect two PCs together
2. How to connect the MACs to the PCs
3. How to connect the SUN to the MACs and PCs
4. How to connect the Lab computers to the IBM mainframe
5. How to transfer files between two PCs, PCs and MACs, PCs and SUN, and IBM mainframe and SUN

Deliverables

1. Network Lab layout with hardware cables, adapter cards and PCs.
2. Specifications of the file transfer packages that will run on the host, the PCs, the MACs and the SUN. The specifications must show the main functions to be performed by the file transfer packages in terms of the ISO layers. The objective of the specifications is to purchase or develop proper file transfer packages.
3. Recommendation of OSI products, if any, may be useful.

Project C: Long-Range Network Plan: An Open Network

You are also to recommend a long-range network plan which shows how all sites (engineering facility, manufacturing operations, corporate offices, and stores) will be interconnected in the next five years. The company is interested in moving toward open networking as soon as possible and wants to understand the various options and tradeoffs between the options. You need to keep the following current scenario in mind:

- ISO and TCP/IP are the future direction
- The manufacturing facility uses MAP
- The corporate office uses SNA
- The engineering group will use VAX, Decnet and Ethernet (TCP/IP is a strong competiter in this group)
- The stores are connected to the corporate office through SNA

You are to show what specific interfaces you will need and how you will select these interfaces so that product requirements from the Chicago office can be downloaded to engineering computer for design and the design specifications can be downloaded to a manufacturing program, which in turn can be sent to area and cell controllers to drive the robots and other devices.

Your solution of this assignment should show an integrated approach so that all of the business processes can directly interface with the manufacturing processes to provide an "advanced automatic factory." In particular you should discuss the tradeoffs between the following scenarios:

1. All plants use OSI Model and products.
2. All plants use TCP/IP protocol Suite.
3. Mixture: Corporate office uses SNA, manufacturing office uses MAP, engineering office uses TCP/IP protocol Suite. Assume that TCP/IP is also installed on all plants and can be used as an internetworking backbone.
4. Same as 3, but use OSI as the internetworking backbone.

You should describe the advantages and disadvantages of proprietary versus open network architectures by using the following evaluating factors:

- Cost
- Performance
- Manageability
- Speed of implementation
- Vendor support
- Ease of problem diagnostics
- Future growth
- Any other factors

Project D: Training

The management at XYZCORP is concerned that their information systems staff is not very familiar with any of the issues involved in network architectures and protocols. Use the OSI Model to show which staff member (application developers, systems programmers, network planners, information systems managers, computer operators, end users, etc.) needs to know about what services (layers). You may use a scale of 0 to 5 (0 means needs no knowledge, 5 means needs thorough knowledge) to indicate the training needs.

Hints About the Case Study

Project A basically requires a review of the OSI Model and an understanding of the discussion on different network architectures and network interconnectivity (Sections 3.3 and 3.4). Project B can be solved by reviewing the interconnectivity examples discussed in Section 3.5. Project C requires a review of open networking (Section 3.5.4). However, the reader may benefit from the review of the material in Appendixes

A, B, C and D on the various network architectures. These appendixes also include the XYZCORP design of manufacturing, engineering and corporate networks for additional insights. Project D is a straightforward, but very useful, application of the OSI principles in staff training.

References

Abeysundara, B., and Kamal, A., "High Speed Local Area Networks and Their Performance: A Survey," *ACM Computing Survey,* June 1991, pp. 221–264.

Bertsekas, D., and Gallager, R., *Data Networks,* Prentice Hall, 1987.

Belisle, P., and Janson, H., "OSI—What Is next?" *Enterprise Conference Proc.*, June 1988, pp. 4-1–4-28.

Berson, A., *APPC: Introduction to LU6.2*, McGraw-Hill, 1990.

Black, U., *OSI: A Model of Computer Communications Standards*, Prentice Hall, 1991.

Black, U., *Data Communications, Networks and Distributed Processing*, 2nd ed., Reston, 1987.

Cameron, D., *OSI: An International Standard for Open Systems*, Computer Technology Research Corporation, Charleston, S.C., 1991.

Campbell, R., "An Architecture for Factory Control Automation," *AT&T Technical Journal*, 1988.

Chapin, A.L., "Connections and Connectionless Data Transmission," *Proc. of the IEEE*, Vol. 71, pp. 1365-1371, .

Comer, D., "Internetworking with TCP/IP," two volumes, Prentice Hall, 1991.

Conard, J.W., "Services and Protocols of the Data Link Layer," Proc. of the IEEE, Vol. 71, Dec. 1983, pp. 1378-1383.

Cypser, R.J., *Communications for Cooperative Systems*, Addison-Wesley, 1991.

Cypser, R.J, "Evolution of an Open Communication Architecture," *IBM Systems Journal*, Vol. 31, No. 2, 1992, pp. 161-188.

Deasington, R. J., *X.25 Explained: Protocols for Packet Switching Networks*, 2nd ed., Prentice Hall, 1989.

DEC Handbook, "Networks and Communications Buyer's Guide," Sept. 1990.

Doshi, B.T., and Johri, P.K., "Communication Protocols for High Speed Networks," *Computer Networks and ISDN Systems*, Vol. 24, No. 3, 1992, pp. 243-275.

Dupuy, S., et al., "Protocols for High Speed Multimedia Communications," *Computer Communications*, July/August 1992, pp. 349-358.

Folts, H.C., ed, "Compilation of Open System Standards," McGraw-Hill, edition IV, Vol. 1 to 6, 1990.

GOSIP: Government Open Systems Interconnection Profile, U.S. Department of Commerce, Federal Inf. Process. Standards Publication 146, August 15, 1988.

Hayes, V., "Standardization Efforts for Wirelss LANs," *IEEE Network*, Nov. 1991, pp. 19-20.

Henshell, J., and Shaw, H., *OSI Explained: End to End Communications Standards*, 2nd ed., Prentice Hall, 1991.

Jain, B., and Agrawala, A., *Open Systems Interconnection: Its Architecture and Protocols*, Elsevier, 1990.

Janson, P., Molva, R., and Zatti, S., "Architectural Directions for Opening IBM Networks: The Case of OSI," *IBM Systems Journal*, Vol. 31, No. 2, 1992, pp. 313-335.

Kaminski, M., "Manufacturing Automation Protocol (MAP)—OSI for Factory Communications," *87 International Symposium on Interoperable Information Systems: ISIS Conf. Proc.*, 1987.

Lane, M., *Data Communications Software Design*, Noyd Fraser Publishing, 1985.

Little, T., "Multimedia as a Network Technology," *Business Communications Review*, May 1991, pp. 65-70.

McClain, G., *The Open Systems Interconnection Handbook*, McGraw-Hill, 1992.

MacKinnon, D., McCrum, W., and Sheppard, D., *An Introduction to Open Systems Interconnection*, Computer Science Press, 1990.

Malmud, C., *Analyzing DECnet/OSI Phase V*, Van Nostrand Reinhold, 1991.

Meijer, A., and Peeters, P., *Computer Network Architectures and Protocols*, Computer Science Press, 1983.

Nadler, G., "Internetworking—Bridges, Routers, and Gateways," *Enterprise Conference Proc.*, June 1988, pp.1-1–1-12.

O'Malley, S., and Peterson, L., "A Dynamic Network Architecture," *ACM Transactions on Computer Systems*, Vol. 10, No. 2, May 1992, pp. 110-143.

Perlman, R., *Interconnections: Bridges and Routers,* McGraw-Hill, 1992.

Perlman, R., "A Comparison Between Two Routing Protocols: OSPF and IS-IS," *IEEE Network Magazine*, Sept. 1991, pp.18-24.

Proceedings of the IEEE, special issue on open system interconnection, Dec. 1983.

Purser, M., *Data Communications for Programmers*, Addison-Wesley, 1986.

Rose, M., *The Open Book: A Practical Perspective on OSI*, Prentice Hall, 1990.

Schwartz, M., *Telecommunications Networks: Protocols, Modelling and Analysis,* Addison-Wesley, 1987.

Sanders, R., and Weaver, A., "The Xpress Transfer Protocol (XTP)—A Tutorial," *ACM Computer Communication Review*, Oct. 1990, pp. 67-80.

Sevcik, P., "Making the Right Connections: Routers, B/Routers and INPs," *Business Communications Review*, May 1992, pp. 37-46.

Shepherd, D., and Salmony, M., "Extending OSI to Support Synchronization Required by Multimedia Applications," *Computer Communications,* Vol. 13, No. 7, Sept. 1990, pp. 399-406.

Shepherd, D., "Protocol Support for Distributed Multimedia Applications," *Computer Communications*, July/Aug. 1992, pp. 359-366.

Shirey, R., "Defense Data Network Security Administration," *Computer Communication Review*, Vol. 20, No. 2, Apr. 1990, pp. 66-71.

Seiffert, W.M., "Bridges and Routers," *IEEE Network Magazine*, Vol. 2, Jan. 1988, pp. 57-64.

Stallings, W., *Handbook of Computer Communications Standards*, Vol. 1 (*ISO Model*), Macmillan, 1987.

Stallings, W., *Handbook of Computer Communications Standards*, Vol. 2 (*LAN Standards*), Macmillan, 1987.

Stallings, W., *Handbook of Computer Communications Standards*, Vol. 3 (*DOD Protocol Suite*), Macmillan, 1987.

Stallings, W., *Networks and Data Communications,* 3d edition, McMillan, 1991.

Tanenbaum, A., *Computing Networks*, 2nd ed., Prentice Hall, 1988.

TOP 3.0 Specifications, Society of Manufacturing Engineers, 1988.

White, G., *Internetworking and Addressing*, McGraw-Hill, 1992.

Chapter 4

Network Management

4.1 Introduction

Simply stated, network management is concerned with the policies, procedures, and tools needed to manage networks. The basic idea is to manage networks in a manner similar to management of any other corporate resource such as capital and data. Network management is of crucial importance to distributed computing because decentralized/distributed applications that are accessed by many users across the network are increasing steadily. In addition, the increased use of workstations, LANs, and client-server distributed cooperating processing applications is highlighting the role of networks in organizations.

Distributed computing furthers the importance of networks because most organizations have been relying on interconnected networks to support critical centralized transaction systems which are accessed from many remote sites. As stated earlier, 25 to 80 percent of companies' cash flow is being processed through telecommunication networks. As the reliance of organizations on networks has increased, the size (number of users, number of lines, number of nodes) has also increased and so has the complexity (number of vendors, device types, networking options, voice/data communications, network architectures and protocols, etc.).

Due to the combined reasons of importance, size and complexity, most organizations have realized that it is essential to manage networks just like other corporate assets. Consequently, network management has become one of the most important topics in communication systems today, as evidenced by the active development, standardization, and research activities in the last five years. This is an area of strategic importance for most enterprises because the availability, performance, and user support of networks is critical to the survival of corporate information systems.[1]

The importance of network management is highlighted in the literature. For example, John Donovan <Donovan 1988>, in a *Harvard Business Review* article entitled "Beyond Chief Information Officer to Network Manager," emphasizes that the best way to manage computing is to manage the networks that connect them and leave the individual computing management to the users. In addition, the common carriers are beginning to offer network management capabilities as part of the telecommunications offerings. Consider, for example the following statements <Turner 1991>:

> "Throughout the balance of this decade, the carriers will continue to expand their network-based management building blocks in an effort to differentiate their transmission services in the marketplace. . . . For example, it will not be sufficient for a carrier to simply offer 800-type services. Instead, an 800 service will have a network-based element management system to automatically route calls to a backup calling center when the primary center is busy."

[1]Terry Peak, my colleague at Bellcore, postulates: "Any mechanized system will evolve faster than the administrative tools to manage it." This seems to be true for DCS in general, and network management in particular.

This chapter exposes the reader to the evolving area of network management. Our objective is to define the main concepts and the terminology associated with network management, and describe the pertinent standards, products, approaches and techniques. The reader of this chapter should be able to answer the following questions:

- What is network management and why is it so important to enterprises?
- What are the main standards and products in this area?
- What are the trends in this field and what are the open questions?
- How are computing technologies, especially expert systems, being employed to automate the network management operations?

Network management, even though very important, does not cover the critical issue of managing distributed applications (network management primarily addresses layer 1 to 4 issues). In Chapter 10, Section 10.5.1 we will discuss distributed applications management and outline relevant standards such as Open Software Foundation's Distributed Management Environment (OSF DME).

4.2 Concepts and Overview

4.2.1 Definitions

The term *network management* was formally first used by IBM in 1986 when IBM announced NetView. Since then many vendors, corporations and standardizing bodies have been introducing products and defining different aspects of network management. Although the network management systems vary slightly between different vendors and corporations, the following functions defined by the International Standards Organization (ISO) are commonly used to define the functional characteristics of network management <ISO 1987>:

- *Fault management*—detecting, diagnosing and recovering from network faults
- *Configuration management*—defining, changing, monitoring, and controlling network resources and data
- *Accounting*—recording usage of network resources and generating billing information
- *Performance analysis*—monitoring current and long-term performance of the network
- *Security*—ensuring only authorized access to network resources
- *Resource management/user directory*—supporting directories for managing network assets and user instructions

We will use these functions throughout this chapter as a framework for describing and evaluating various network management approaches and products.

Figure 4.1 shows conceptually how network management can be achieved in large networks. Fig. 4.1a shows a single level model in which a global (enterprise) manager directly communicates with the network devices. This model works well for small or homogeneous networks in which all devices communicate with the global manager by using the same protocol (for example, if all devices supported SNA or OSI or TCP/IP). Figure 4.1b shows a more realistic situation for large heterogeneous networks with devices from different vendors supporting different network architectures. In this case, the enterprise manager communicates with different domain managers where each domain manager supervises its own network. This is called "tiered" or hierarchical network management.

Standards are needed in network management to provide an enterprise wide approach. Standardizing efforts are proceeding in two general directions <Herman 1991>:

Management protocol interface: This is the interface between the devices being managed and the computers which are doing the management.

Application programming interface (API): This is the interface between applications (network management or other) and the network management software.

As we will see, standards in management protocols have been developed actively in the last five years. Best-known examples are the Common Management Information Protocol (CMIP) by ISO and the Simplified Network Management Protocol (SNMP) for TCP/IP-based networks. These protocols view a network in terms of managing systems and managed systems (Fig. 4.1c). A *manager* is a software module which resides in the managing systems. An *agent* is a software module which resides in each managed system to monitor the status of *managed objects*. For example, in a LAN of 20 computers, each computer may contain an agent which monitors the managed objects in each computer such as disks and printers. A host-based manager may communicate with the agents periodically to obtain the status of the network. The manager-agent dialog is the basis of the management protocol standards. These standards define three things:

- What is the format of the management information and what are the rules for information exchange?
- How is the information transported between the managers and the agents?
- What specific information will be exchanged (what an agent can provide and what a manager can request)?

The first two problems are typical in any protocol standard development (see Appendix A for a discussion of generic protocols). The third problem, although not necessarily unique, is quite complicated in network management. The collection of management information that a manager or an agent knows is called Management Information Base (MIB). A manager must know the MIB of its agents. We will discuss MIB in more detail in Section 4.4 and 4.5.

At present, attention is being paid to API standards for network management. This is mainly because APIs make it possible for users and third party vendors to

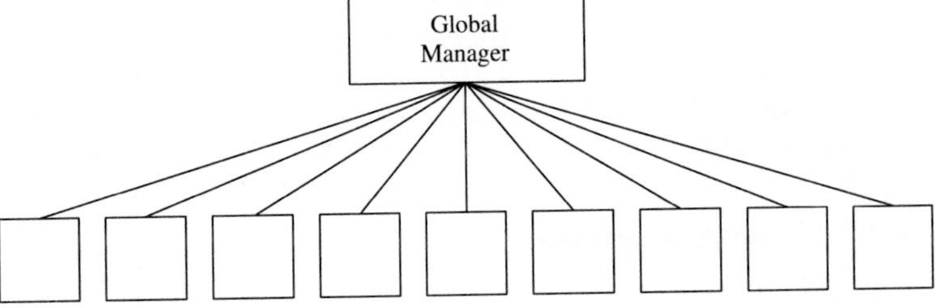

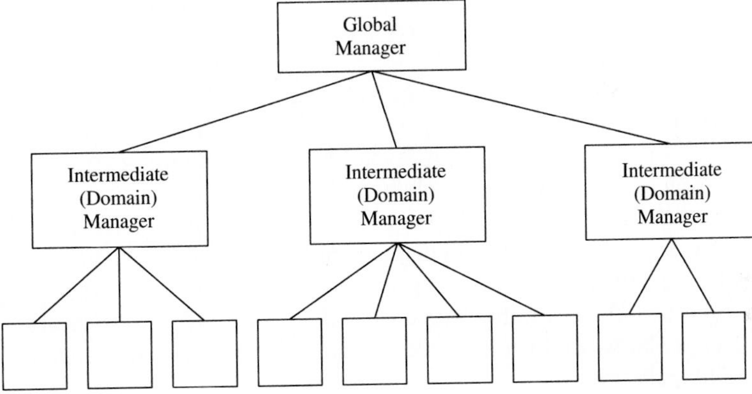

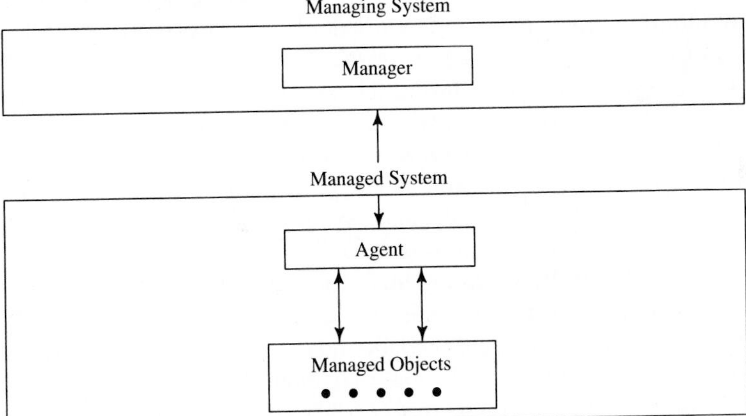

FIGURE 4.1 Conceptual Views of Network Management

develop applications which use network management information. IBM, for example, has provided API to NetView which, in turn, promotes software development around NetView. As more software is written, it becomes important to standardize the APIs so that this software can be ported to other environments. Open Software Foundation (OSF) has initiated an effort in this direction under its Distributed Management Environment (DME) request for technology. We will discuss DME in Chapter 10.

4.2.2 Historical Developments

Since the 1970s, some of the network management functions have been emphasized more than others and the tools have evolved from manual and standalone tools to sophisticated knowledge-based integrated systems. The methods and tools in network management have evolved in three stages.

Stage 1 (1970s): During this stage, the main focus was on fault management (e.g., terminals unable to logon, modem problems, communication line problems) for small (a few hundred devices) networks. The faults were managed through a "problem control desk" which received customer calls, recorded the problems and dispatched technicians to diagnose/correct the problems. The technicians used manual procedures, system display commands and ran diagnostics on equipment. Most diagnostic tools were primitive and stand-alone. An example of a more sophisticated tool in this stage is IBM's NCCF/NPDA (Network Center Control Facility/Network Problem Determination Aid), which was introduced to diagnose SNA networks.

Stage 2 (1980s): During this stage, most of the concepts, terminology and products for network management were developed for homogeneous (single vendor), medium sized (few thousand devices) networks. In most cases, the network management vendors integrated existing network diagnostics tools with network monitoring and control tools into network management systems (NMSs). The first NMS, NetView, was introduced by IBM during the spring of 1986. NetView basically integrated many of the network diagnostics and control tools developed in the 1970s and early 1980s into a single package (see Section 4.3). Many other NMSs have also been developed by network vendors for proprietary networks. Examples are DEC's EMA, AT&T's StarKeeper, and Avant-Garde's Netcommand. We will discuss some of these tools later in this chapter.

Stage 3 (1990s): NMS development is focusing on managing networks of networks (internetworks) for thousands of devices connected over thousands of lines, which may cross international boundaries. In most cases, the human network managers cannot see the device (they might have never seen it) being diagnosed and the type and manufacturer of a device is not known. Due to the complexity and size of networks being managed, this stage is witnessing developments in three areas: (1) the growth of network management standards, (2) the evolution of "enterprise management systems" which integrate individual network management systems for large heterogeneous environments, and (3) the increased utilization of expert systems and database technologies in network and enterprise management. The main network management standards being developed are

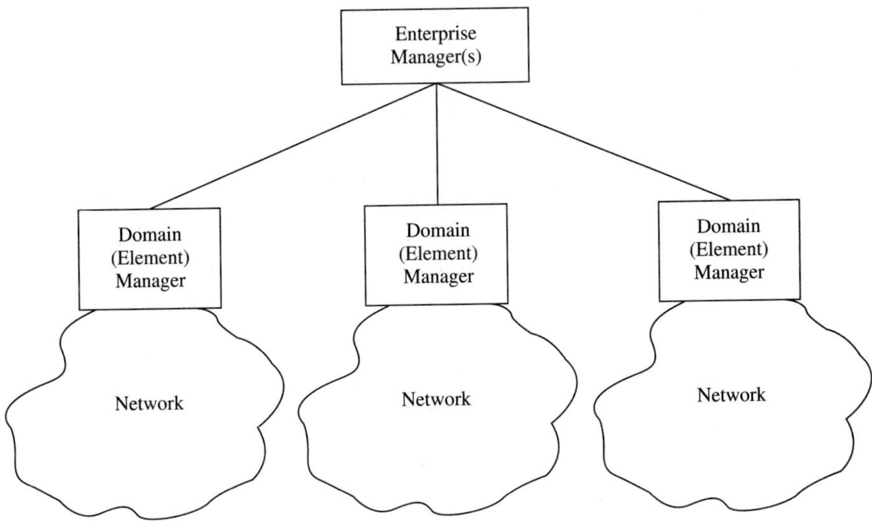

FIGURE 4.2 An Enterprise Management System

the Common Management Information Protocol (CMIP) by ISO/OSI and the Simplified Network Management Protocol (SNMP) for TCP/IP based networks (see Section 4.4 and 4.5).

The enterprise management systems coordinate various other network managers for managing large heterogeneous environments (see Fig. 4.2). As shown in Fig. 4.2, the individual network management systems (called domain or element managers) manage portions of the network and pass information to the enterprise manager. We will discuss enterprise management in Section 4.6. The next generation of network management tools are appearing as expert support systems (ESS) and decision support systems (DSS) to support the network planning, installation, maintenance and performance activities. These systems are exploiting the advances in AI, database technologies and software engineering for large and complex network management and enterprise management systems. Ideally, these systems would have a common user interface which invokes tools that access network configuration information for problem solving (see Section 4.7).

4.2.3 Organizational and Support Considerations

Although we will focus primarily on network management tools and technologies, the organizational structures and the administrative processes to utilize the tools properly are equally important. Many administrators tend to collect the tools without sorting out the procedural and organizational details needed to use the tools <Joseph 1990, Joseph 1988>. Ingredients of a successful network management system are as follows (see Fig. 4.3):

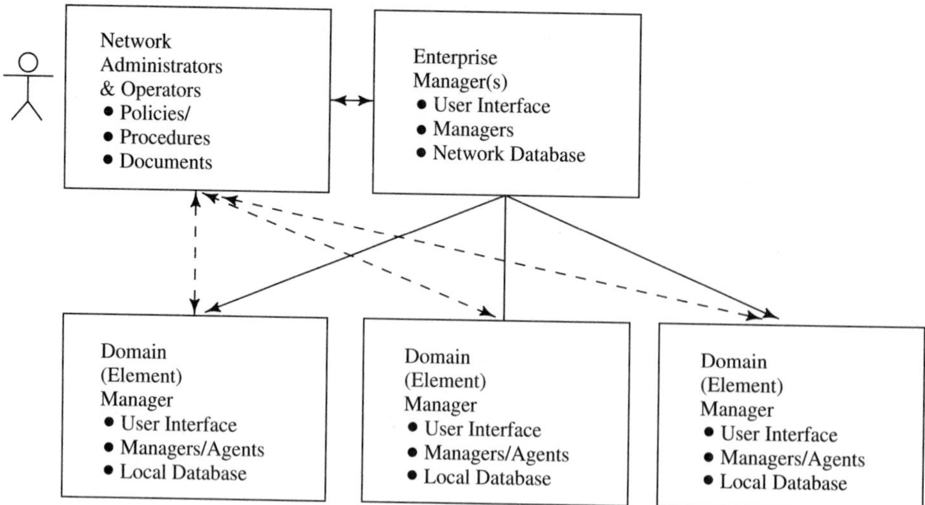

FIGURE 4.3 A Network Operations Center

- A Networks Operations Center (NOC) where the network experts monitor, diagnose and control the network.
- An integrated toolset which gives the NOC personnel timely information for decision making. The network management toolset behaves as a management information system and/or decision support system. It is desirable for the NOC personnel to access the toolset from a single workstation with a common user interface.
- Policies and procedures about how the NOC will handle normal as well as emergency situations and describe how the NOC personnel will work with the personnel assigned to computer hardware/software diagnostics. For example, if a user cannot access a network resource, who will they call first?

In addition to an NOC, the functions of network planning, administration and security must be recognized and delegated to proper organizational units. In some cases, these functions may be assigned to properly trained NOC personnel and/or tools. In other cases, these functions may be assigned as additional responsibilities to corporate planning and security groups. For large, multisite organizations it may be appropriate to conduct these functions through committees which oversee these areas.

Due to the complexity of the network management systems, several techniques are being employed to model and analyze network management applications. Object-oriented analysis (OOA) shows particular promise because network components (e.g., nodes, links, workstations, modems, multiplexors, communication controllers, etc.) can be viewed as objects. In addition, different types of devices can be represented as instances which inherit common properties from object classes <Olson 1990>. The object-oriented approach has been adopted by the ISO/OSI

Forum for specifying network management standards. We will discuss this issue in Section 4.7.

We should comment here about the trend toward open architectures for network management. The ISO/OSI network management standards allow users to develop their own applications for special purposes. In addition, the proprietary network management systems provide application program interfaces (APIs) for user programs. It is important for the organizations to understand the financial as well as legal aspects of developing user application programs. An interesting discussion of the legal pitfalls in network management can be found in Sapronov <1990>:

> "... integration of the network management product with other products on the network may violate intellectual property rights in the interfaced products or, equally troubling, may violate restrictions on the use of the interfaced products and thereby expose the user to substantial liabilities."

This article makes the interesting case that the open standards are not copyrighted; thus the interfaces built around open systems do not create any legal problems.

4.3 SNA Network Management: NetView

NetView is one of the first integrated network management systems.[2] Introduced in the spring of 1986, NetView is an IBM strategic product for managing diverse networks and systems. NetView runs on IBM mainframes under the MVS or VM operating system and provides a set of commands to review, monitor, diagnose and correct network resources. A new version of Netview, AIX Netview 6000, runs on RS6000 workstations and is intended for Unix-based TCP/IP networks. It initially consolidated previous IBM network management products such as NPDA (network problem determination aid) and NLDM (network line diagnostics manager) into a single package. Since its introduction, NetView capabilities have been extended greatly (see *IBM Systems Journal*, Vol. 31, No. 2, 1992, special issue on Network Management for Netview directions and evolution).

NetView can function as an enterprise wide manager. NetView is an integral part of IBM's System View, which goes beyond NetView's network management to applications management in distributed environments <Szabat 1992, Guruge 1991>. The initial release of NetView provided an operator interface to different network management functions from a single terminal. The user interface was extended later to provide consistent access to all tools. The second release of NetView, announced in the spring of 1987, extended the NetView functions to include management of operating system and major subsystems such as TSO and CICS. This release also automated some of the routine network operator tasks.

Release 3 of NetView, announced in the fall of 1988, introduced high-level language (C, PL1, REXX) support for NetView procedures, application program

[2]This section uses some of the IBM terms and components. The reader unfamiliar with IBM environments is advised to review Appendix C: SNA and LU6.2/APPC before proceeding.

interfaces, and exit routines. Later releases have added Graphical User Interface support, interfaces to mainframe relational databases (DB2), interfaces with open systems (SNMP and CMIS), and interfaces to mainframe change and configuration management systems <Cypser 1992, Stevenson 1992>. For example, the latest announcement in Netview family, Netview 6000, is targetted for TCP/IP network management <Chou 1992>. The architectural components of NetView are as follows (Fig. 4.4):

- The Command Facility, called the Network Control Command Facility (NCCF), allows the network operators/administrators to logon to NetView, issue commands/scripts, and receive responses.
- The Hardware Monitor collects diagnostic information from various network devices such as lines, controllers, terminals, and workstations. It gives alerts to the operator about the devices in trouble. This monitor, called the Network Problem Determination Aid (NPDA), was originally available as a standalone tool for SNA in the late 1970s.
- The Session Monitor collects the data about the SNA sessions (LU-LU, PU-PU, etc.) and displays this data for analysis. This monitor, called the Network Logical Domain Monitor (NLDM), was also available as a standalone tool for SNA in the late 1970s.
- The Status Monitor displays the conditions of SNA nodes, LUs, PUs, etc.
- The Browse, Help Desk and Help facilities allow the operator to view network logs, and they provide step-by-step procedures to solve problems and instructions on how to use NetView, respectively.

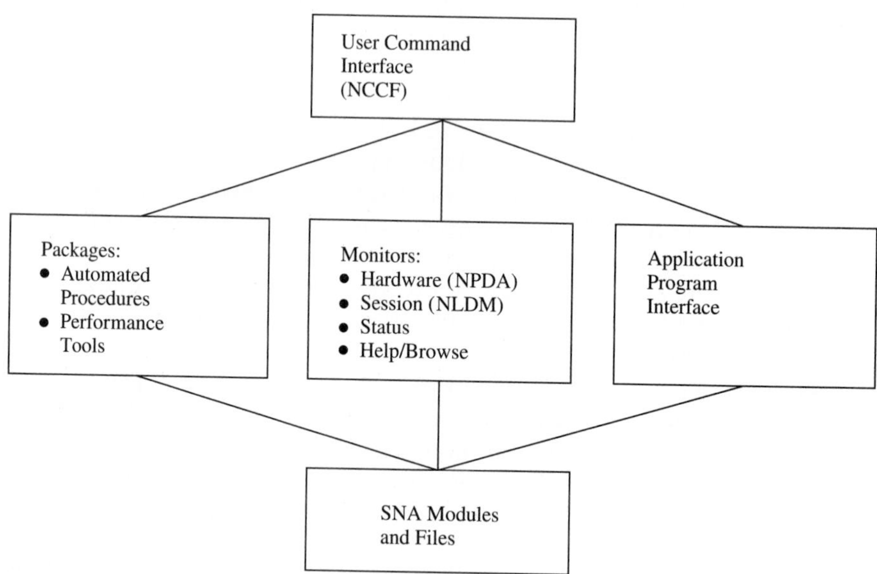

FIGURE 4.4 NetView Comoponents

TABLE 4.1 Typical NetView Commands

- NPDA—enter the interactive hardware monitor
- DISPLAY—display the status of an SNA resource
- ACT—activate SNA resources
- INACT—deactivate SNA resources
- BROWSE—access the network log
- HELP—access the NetView Help facility
- HELPDESK—enter the IBM provided online HelpDesk facility for expert help

These functions can be performed by multiple operators. An Application Program Interface (API) facility allows assembler, PL1 and REXX programs to be invoked from NetView. In addition, IBM provides many NetView add-ons. Examples of these packages are automated commands, a configuration and change manager for AS/400 and PS2, and a network performance monitor. Examples of some of the commands a network operator/administrator can issue are listed in Table 4.1.

NetView is based on IBM's Open Network Management, which is subpart of an Open Communications Architecture, a framework for managing large SNA networks. The interfaces and message formats of this Architecture have been published for other vendors and users to develop specialized applications. The Architecture defines three types of points (Fig. 4.5):

- *Focal points*: These points reside on the mainframe and provide the NetView functions.
- *Entry points*: These points represent the SNA devices which are managed by the focal points.

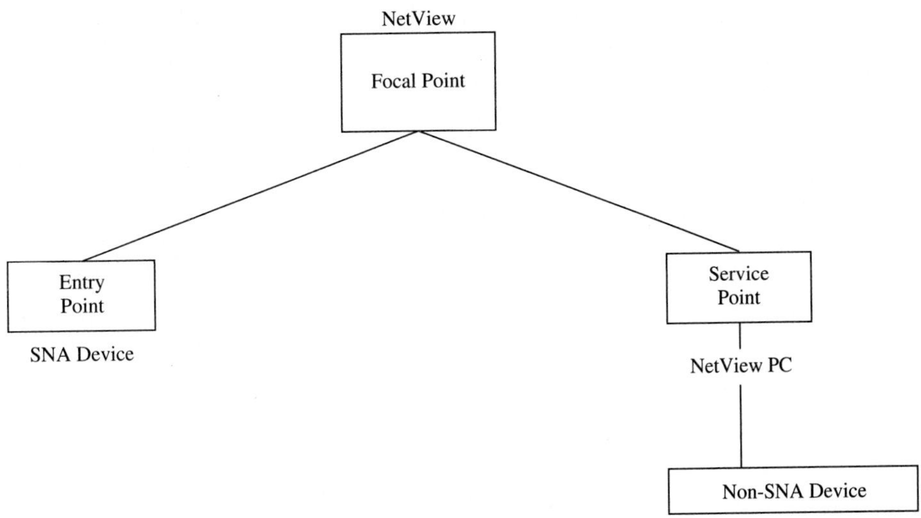

FIGURE 4.5 IBM's Open Management Architecture

- *Service points*: These points represent the non SNA devices (e.g., token ring, X.25 links) which are also managed by NetView. The support points are provided through NetView/PC. The original version of NetView/PC was written under MS DOS on PC; the current release is available under OS/2 on PS2.

The focal point can be a weakness in NetView because if the focal point fails, then NetView would also fail. Thus, secondary focal points are supported as redundant points, which can take over in case the primary focal point fails, and nested focal points, which provide distributed management support for portions of large networks.

The Open Management Architecture has been extended to include LAN management. Token Ring LANs are viewed as specialized subsystems in a network which are managed through a service point. Figure 4.6 shows the main components of NetView LAN Management. The NetView residing at the mainframe focal point can provide an overall monitoring of all LANs. The IBM LAN Manager provides a service point interface to the focal point by passing the information collected at the individual LAN workstations to the focal point. The distributed management servers reside on a single ring and are usually located on the bridges. These servers collect error statistics on the ring, the bridges, and the changes in the ring configurations and pass this information to the LAN Manager.

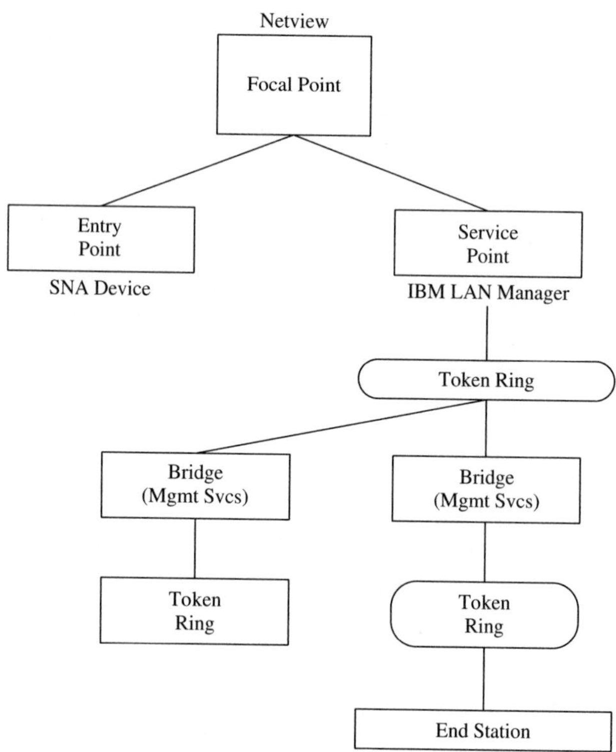

FIGURE 4.6 Netview LAN Management

TABLE 4.2 Main Netview IBM Manuals

- Network Program Products, General Information, GC30-3350
- Network Program Products, Planning, SC30-3351
- Netview Operation Primer, SC30-3363
- Netview Installation and Administration Guide, SC30-3476

The main strength of NetView is that it is a stable product which includes mainframe as well as local area network management facilities. However, Netview and IBM's Open Management Architecture are not industry standards for open network management in heterogeneous networks. Instead, the OSI network management standards, discussed later, have been adopted by the industry. IBM has announced OSI/Communication Subsystem (OSI/CS), which provides a full implementation of the OSI seven layers on IBM SNA networks. OSI/CS will support the OSI Common Management Information Protocol.

Most of the information on NetView is embedded in the IBM manuals shown in Table 4.2. *IBM Systems Journal*, Vol. 31, No. 2, 1992, is devoted to Network Management and is an excellent reference for Netview strategies and directions. The critical analysis by James Herman in *Business Communications Review* and Patricia Seybold's *Network Monitor* is especially valuable.

4.4 TCP/IP Management: Simple Network Management Protocol (SNMP)

The Internet Activities Board (IAB) met in early 1988 to determine a strategy about how to manage the growing TCP/IP networks.[3] The meeting recommended two parallel standards: the *Simple Network Management Protocol (SNMP)* as a short-range solution and the *Common Management Information Services and Protocol Over TCP/IP (CMOT)* as the eventual long-term solution. The TCP/IP community has focused primarily on specifying SNMP mainly because CMOT is essentially the same as the ISO standard CMIS (Common Management Information Services), but it runs on TCP/IP networks. As a first step, SNMP has extended an earlier network management called Simple Gateway Monitoring Program (SGMP), which was designed to monitor the TCP/IP routers (these were called gateways in TCP/IP networks). Another effort has been trying to determine how the SNMP network management protocol can be implemented on OSI (called CMIT). This section mainly discusses SNMP. We will discuss CMOT in the next section because CMOT is essentially the same as CMIS.

Figure 4.7 shows the SNMP architecture. Simply stated, SNMP views a network in terms of *managers*, which manage the network and *agents*, which represent the

[3]This section uses some of the TCP/IP terms. The uninitiated reader may review Appendix B: TCP/IP before proceeding.

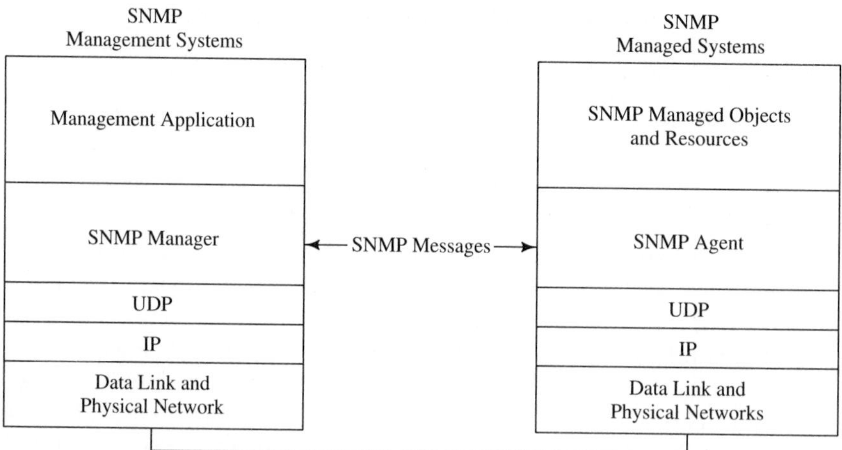

FIGURE 4.7 SNMP Architecture

resources being managed. The SNMP managers are designed primarily to provide the following two facilities from remote sites in large TCP/IP networks:

- Fault management
- Configuration management.

Note that many other OSI network management functions (e.g., security management) are not included in SNMP. However, SNMP protocols can define many types of data, thus they can be used to collect and view data outside the realm of SNMP "standard" functions. For example, limited performance monitoring is possible with SNMP by storing and viewing performance data at appropriate intervals. SNMP uses the less reliable UDP instead of the reliable TCP services. The network management applications using SNMP are provided with a set of simple primitives (Get, Set, Get-Next) which are specified in the ISO Abstract Syntax Notation One (ASN.1) language. In addition, a Trap message allows six types of events to be reported asynchronously. SNMP specifies a core of 100 objects, termed MIB-1, which comprise a management information base (MIB). MIB-1 only specifies fault management and configuration management objects. MIB-II has also become available and contains additional 185 objects. SNMP specifications consist of the SNMP protocol over a UDP/IP stack, MIB-1 and MIB-II, and the rules for the Structure of Management Information. The SNMP managers and agents can use the following commands and packet types for network management:

- GetRequest—used by the manager station to query agents on the status of objects
- GetNextRequest—a GetRequest that sequentially steps through the MIB
- SetRequest—manager directs a change in the value of a MIB object
- GetResponse—agent answers a GetRequest
- Trap—agent notifies the manager that a significant event has occurred.

Figure 4.8 shows a simple example of an SNMP conversation. If needed, statement 1 unlocks a resource (e.g., a device) for issuing queries (resources can be "locked" by administrators). After this, statement 2 shows a request by the manager to receive the status of the device unlocked. Statement 3 displays the response from the agent about the device status. The main features of SNMP are as follows:

- SNMP uses the UDP connectionless protocol. This means that there is no overhead involved in establishing the connections. The applications may need to employ some type of protocol to assure that messages sent from one side are received properly on the other side.
- SNMP applications are limited in several ways: The amount of information retrieved in one request is limited (cannot link several replies for one request), the MIB browsing is slow and tedious, no direct imperative commands (e.g., shut down a system) are supported, and SNMP traps are always unconfirmed. These limitations do not exist in CMIP/CMOT.
- SNMP devices are named via IP addresses and SNMP objects are represented using a subset of ASN.1.
- SNMP uses polling to communicate with the devices being managed. Thus the SNMP manager polls each device to retrieve diagnostics information. The polling method works well for small networks (about a hundred devices) but is very inefficient for large networks because a great deal of time is spent in polling. In contrast, event-based management is employed in some systems (e.g., CMOT) which respond to certain conditions. Event-based systems are harder to implement but are more efficient for large and complex networks.

What may appear as limitations of SNMP are in fact design philosophies which trade complexity for speed and reduced overhead. SNMP has been accepted very widely in the market, especially in LANs. At the end of 1992, more than 50 vendors were providing SNMP support on their devices. The number of SNMP vendors is expected to exceed 100 in a few years. It appears that most TCP/IP vendors are planning to package SNMP as part of the network software. This should be contrasted to less than 10 vendors who support CMOT. Due to its popularity, SNMP is also being supported on non-TCP/IP transport mechanisms. Although, the SNMP standard specifies how the network messages will be transported by using the UDP protocol

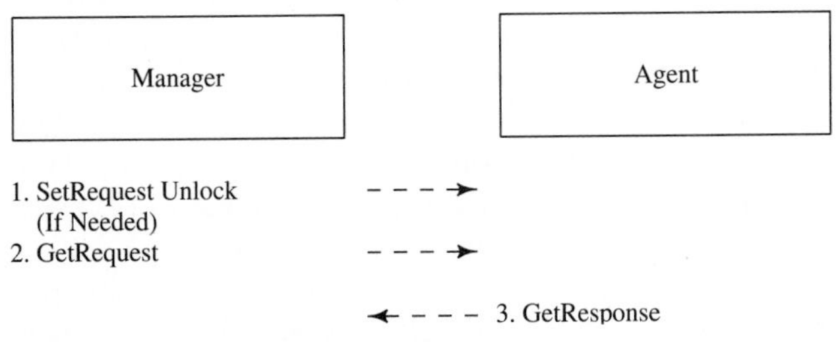

FIGURE 4.8 A Simple SNMP Example

over IP, SNMP has been implemented over Ethernet, LLC, Xerox Network Service (XNS), and Appletalk. In addition, SNMP is expected to be supported on top of the OSI 7-layer stack. SNMP is also being positioned to go beyond network resources to manage operating system resources for several systems (e.g., Berkeley Unix, DECnet, Ethernet, LANs). Sunnet Manager, a popular network manager in TCP/IP networks, and IBM's new Netview (Netview 6000) are based on SNMP. Due to its popularity, SNMP has emerged as the de facto network management standard for heterogeneous systems. The major reasons for the popularity of SNMP are:

- SNMP has provided vendors the opportunity to deliver open multivendor network management products. Before SNMP, no nonproprietary protocol for managing heterogeneous networks was available. CMOT and CMIS are still on the drawing boards and do not help the users who need immediate help.
- SNMP is relatively simple to implement and does not require large investment from a vendor. In addition, some SNMP development kits are commercially available.
- SNMP can be implemented with small amount of processing and memory resources. Thus SNMP functions can be added to many small systems (e.g., workstations) without a redesign.
- SNMP does not allow many options. Thus it is easy to show interoperability between different vendors without extensive conformance tests.

However, the following limitations of SNMP should be kept in mind:

- SNMP may not be suited for large networks because it uses polling to communicate with the managed devices.
- SNMP is slow in accessing large amounts of data.
- The UDP protocol employed by SNMP requires some application logic for message delivery and response.
- SNMP does not include manager-to-manager support for hierarchies of managers.
- SNMP employs limited authentication (security) services and a management information model which is cumbersome for large and complex systems.

Several groups are currently working on improving the SNMP specifications to address some of these limitations. Many extensions to SNMP are pending at present. It will be interesting to see how CMOT competes against the "improved" SNMP. In the future, the users will have several choices to manage heterogeneous networks: (1) Use SNMP as a network manager on top of TCP/IP throughout, (2) use CMOT as a CMIP network manager on top of TCP/IP throughout, (3) use CMIT as a SNMP network manager on top of OSI stack throughout, or (4) use SNMP/CMOT to pass information to a proprietary network manager (e.g., NetView). The choice will be largely dependent on the availability of robust and reliable products.

Open literature in TCP/IP network management is now becoming available. A book by Marshall Rose, *The Simple Book: An Introduction to Management of*

TCP/IP Based Internets <Rose 1990> gives a detailed coverage of SNMP and TCP/IP network management. The RFC 1098, April 1988, <Case 1988> is the original description of SNMP. A detailed comparison of SNMP and CMOT can be found in <Ben-Artzi 1990>. A state-of-the-market analysis of SNMP is given by Jander 1991 and Dolan 1991. A critical analysis of SNMP is given in "SNMP: The Simple (Strained?) Network Management Protocol," by Tim Lee-Thorp <Lee-Thorp 1991>.

4.5 OSI/ISO Network Management Standard: CMIS/CMIP

ISO has initiated its OSI network management standards effort by defining a network management model. The network management model extends the seven-layer OSI Model to include additional concepts and interfaces needed for exchange of network management data. This extension of the OSI Model, called the OSI Management Framework, defines a new service/protocol in the application layer (see Fig. 4.9). Three terms are used frequently in the OSI Management Framework:[4]

- *Common Management Information Service (CMIS)* defines the building blocks needed to carry out a network management function. Examples are the services (e.g., display device status, vary devices online/offline, etc.) needed to manage networks.
- *Common Management Information Service Elements (CMISE)* are the actual software routines which support the CMIS functions. For example, a CMISE may be the routine which collects the device status data.
- *Common Management Information Protocol (CMIP)* specifies the bit patterns of the messages used by CMISE/CMIS to exchange management information. For example, CMIP defines the format in which the device status information is transmitted and processed in the OSI Management Framework.

The OSI Management Framework uses the OSI layers to transfer the CMIP data between devices. A network device, called a manager, uses CMIP to send commands or request data from other devices, called agents. An agent can be a single device such as a workstation or a collection of network devices with common properties (e.g., modems).

To implement the OSI Management Framework on a particular open system, the management as well as the agent functions of CMIP will need to be implemented. Simply stated, the managers should be able to request device status data from agents and send commands such as device restart to agents by using the CMIP messages. The agents should be able to recognize the CMIP messages and respond to them accordingly. In addition, the agents should be able to send event messages to the manager as alerts. The OSI standards do not require a centralized management system. Thus the management functions can be implemented on more than one device. To support

[4]The reader should be warned that this framework is complex due to many terms and concepts.

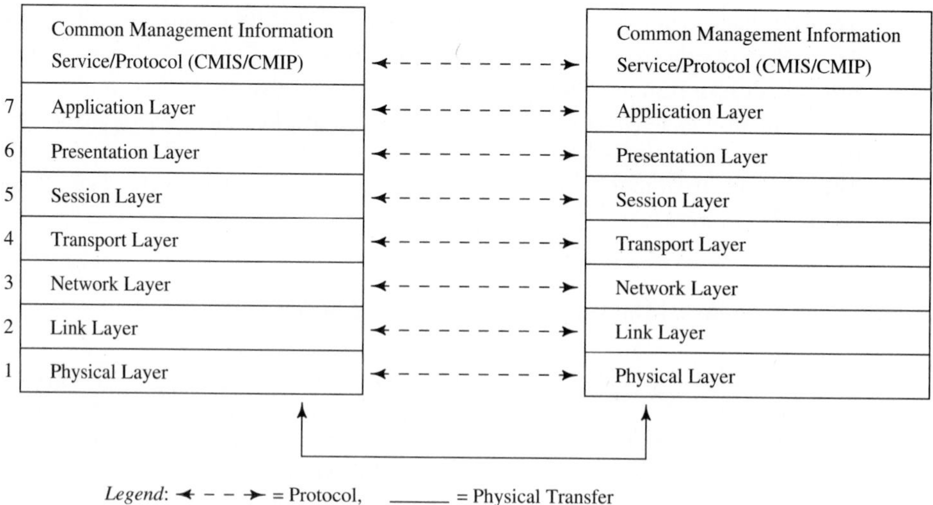

FIGURE 4.9 The OSI Management Framework

large multisite systems, the managed systems can be subdivided into several domains, each with its own domain manager.

The OSI network manager can invoke the following Application Association Service Elements (ASEs):[5]

- Fault Management ASE for detecting, diagnosing, and recovering from network faults
- Configuration and Name Management ASE for defining, changing, monitoring, and controlling network resources and data
- Accounting Management ASE for recording usage of network resources and generating billing information
- Performance Management ASE for monitoring current and long term performance of the network
- Security Management ASE for ensuring that only authorized access is made to network resources

This collection of ASEs to perform the various management services is referred to as the Management Services Association Service Elements (MSASE). In response to a network management query (e.g., to diagnose a device), an appropriate MSASE component (e.g., the Fault Management ASE) is invoked.

Figure 4.10 shows a simplified example of a CMISE session, described by Embry <1990>, about a device which encounters an error condition. Statement 1 creates a device object instance by using a CreateRequest command. The agent

[5]An ASE, defined in the OSI Model, is a collection of software routines which perform certain functions.

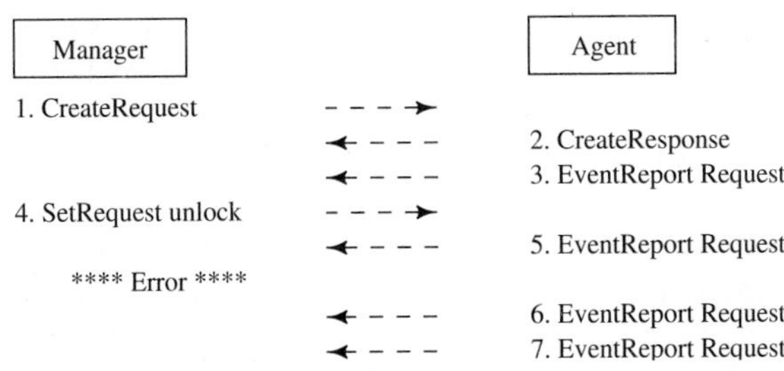

FIGURE 4.10 A CMIS Example

receives this command and creates an instance of the device. Statement 2 acknowledges the successful receipt of the CreateRequest (confirmation) command, and statement 3 indicates that an object instance was created successfully. Statement 4 "unlocks" the object instance just created and statement 5 shows the response to the unlock statement. Now the device is being used in the network. Let us assume that an error occurs on the device. The device agent sends two event reports: one to indicate that an error has occurred with appropriate error status information, and another to indicate that the device has been varied offline (logically disconnected). The manager receives these events and develops an appropriate course of action (not shown in Fig. 4.10).

The OSI standards use an object oriented approach to define the CMIP data and commands. Any managed resource (hardware or software) is modeled as an object. A managed resource can be a simple object (single device) or a compound object (a collection of devices or a network). To manage an OSI network, the network manager must be able to monitor the OSI resources (objects) in various subsystems to obtain real-time data on performance and congestion to diagnose problems and optimize network usage. In most cases, the data is kept as counters which can be retrieved by the network manager. The definition of a managed object includes

- Attributes that describe the object
- Operations that an object can execute
- Events the object can generate.

Object-oriented modeling allows objects to be defined at several levels. The most general level of definition is an *object class*, which defines the highest level of attributes, operations and events associated with an object. Lower level objects can inherit the properties (attributes, operations, and events) from a class object. For example, an object class called a server would include the attributes, operations and events associated with a server. Different types of servers (print server, file server, database server, etc.) can be defined as subclasses of the server class which inherit the properties from the server class.

Each server in the network is represented as instances of object subclass. For example, if a network contains three file servers, two print servers and one database server, then the network to be managed will consist of six object instances corresponding to the six actual servers. The attributes of server object instances may represent the server location, the operations may represent the functions performed (e.g., print file), and the events may represent the server error conditions (e.g., server hung).

The set of object instances in a network is referred to as a Management Information Base (MIB). The OSI standards define how each instance is identified so that it can be retrieved. The physical storage organization of the MIB is left to the implementers. The object instances are identified by using a tree structure where the root of the tree is the object class with various nodes referring to object subclasses. The OSI standard which describes this method of defining MIB is called the Structure of Management Information (SMI). In addition to the structure of MIB, the SMI defines a set of common attributes and objects needed for basic network management.

An implementation of an OSI Network Management System, described by Halsall and Modiri <Halsall 1990>, is shown in Fig. 4.11. This system consists of three SUN workstations connected on a TCP/IP Ethernet LAN. The first workstation is the manager and the next two workstations are the agents. The agents use the OSI file transfer package (FTAM) to exchange information between the agents. The manager contains a set of MSASE procedures for the five ASEs (fault management, performance management, accounting management, configuration management, and security management). These MSASE components use the services of CMISE which communicates with the agent procedures, called Local Management Application Entities (LMAE). The communications between the manager and the agents use the message formats specified by CMIP. This network management system was imple-

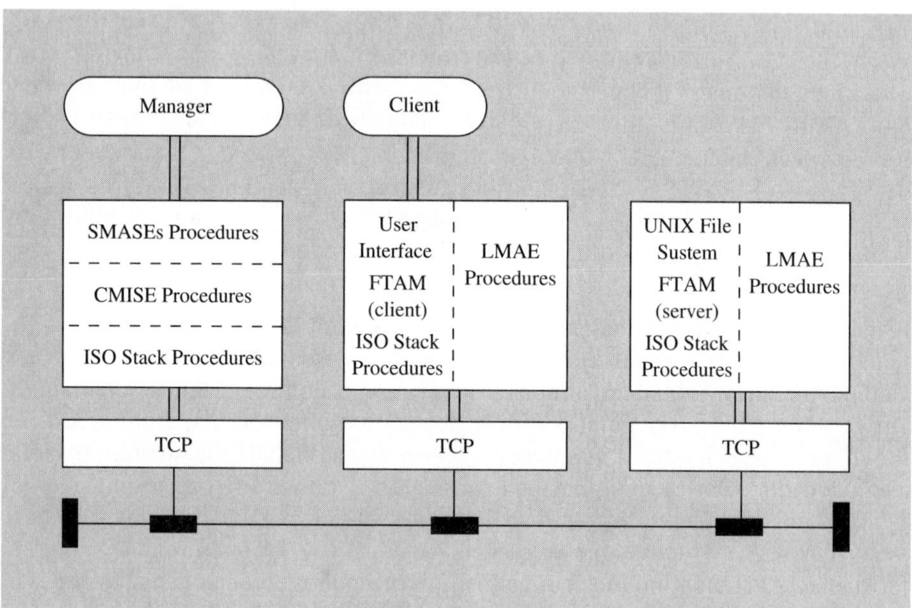

FIGURE 4.11 An Experimental OSI Network Management System (Source: Halsall 1990)

mented on the ISO upper-layer stack which runs on top of the TCP/IP lower-layer Protocol Suite in Unix environments.

To illustrate the use of this system, let us assume that the Performance Management (PM) MSASE is invoked. This ASE supports the following MSASE commands, which correspond to the CMISE service shown.

MSASE Service	MSASE Command	CMISE Service
PM	get	M-GET
	put	M-PUT

When the "PM.get" command is executed, it is mapped to the CMISE M-GET service primitive with the following parameters:

Object Class = PM
Object Instance = name of account
Result = returned result.

Execution of this request results in a response unit to be generated in the CMIP format and shipped back to the manager. This get command is used to retrieve the counter kept in each agent to indicate how many times the FTAM GET command has been executed. FTAM keeps counters in each agents about how many times the FTAM GET and PUT commands have been executed. The purpose of the PM.get command is to retrieve the FTAM get command counters from the agents. This information can be used by the network manager to know how many file transfers between the agents are taking place. More information about this implementation with description of the MSASE services, CMISE services, CMIPS, user screens, and operational details can be found in Halsall <1990>.

Several implementations and extensions of the OSI Network Management Model have been reported. Notably, the Hewlett Packard's OpenView Network Management Architecture (OpenView NMA) is largely based on the OSI Network Management Model (it uses the CMIS standard), with a few extensions. For example, it extends the manager component into two parts: the management application and a common user interface. This allows several applications to interact with a single user interface. In addition, the agent has been expanded to included interactions between the agent and the managed object (for example, an agent may be a workstation and a managed object may be a LAN). The Hewlett-Packard OpenView NMA supports a Network Management Server which comprises of: Presentation Services, Data Management Services, Communications Protocols, and the Distributed Communications Infrastructure. The communication protocols and infrastructure are based on the OSI protocol suite and CMIS/CMIP. Herman <1990> gives a good overview of the HP OpenView NMA.

Due to the active participation in industry, a nonprofit *OSI Network Management Forum* was created in 1988 to expedite interoperability of network management products and services. At present, the Forum has over 100 members from all over the world. The Forum is at present defining the message sets, objects, naming standards, and conformance tests for interoperability. The objectives of the Forum are as follows:

- Provide a framework for interoperability of systems that manage communications and networks.
- Allow implementers the freedom to satisfy their own performance and functional requirements.
- Provide a flexible and extensible architecture for management of a diverse array of networks from different vendors.
- Align the activities with the ISO and CCITT standards. If some issues have not been addressed by ISO/CCITT, then the Forum suggests a position and submits the position to the standardizing bodies for consideration. Once a position has been approved by ISO and CCITT, the Forum is committed to conform to it.

It is important to differentiate between the Forum and the work of the ISO/CCITT. These standardizing bodies are trying to define how OSI and telecommunications networks should be managed while the Forum is trying to define how these network management systems should interoperate. The focus of the Forum is on the interoperable interface—the point where the management systems meet to exchange management data. The Forum has introduced yet another term, Conformant Management Entity (CME), to refer to a network management system that supports the Forum's standards for exchanging management data across multiple networks. Details about the OSI Network Management Forum and CME can be found in Embry <1990>.

The main strengths of the OSI Network Management Model are that it uses the object-oriented approach, which is very powerful and extensible, and it is based on the OSI Model, which enjoys broad industry acceptance and support. In addition, the work of the OSI Network Management Forum will help in addressing the interoperability issues. The main weakness of this Framework is that it is complex due to too many terms and concepts. Another difficulty is that at present very few networks that are based on OSI are commercially available. Due to this, the investment in open systems management is difficult to make. Consequently, CMOT (CMIS on TCP/IP) is receiving more attention. Yet another weakness is that the OSI Network Management Forum does not provide a framework for user interface integration. This has been addressed by the HP OpenView NMA.

We have reviewed the main features of the OSI Network Management Standard and have introduced the reader to the main terms and components. Table 4.3 summarizes the main network management standards being developed by ISO and CCITT. Many documents from the OSI have been published to give details about this standard. The following are examples of some of the relevant documents:

- ISO/EC JTC1/SC21/WG4 N., "OSI Systems Management Overview," 1988
- ISO 7498 (Part 4)—OSI Management Framework
- ISO 9595 (Part 6)—CMIP/CMIS
- ISO 10040—Systems Management Overview
- ISO 10165 (Part 1, 2, 4)—Structure of Management Information
- ISO 10164 (Part 1 to Part 11)—System Management Functions

TABLE 4.3 OSI Network Management Standards

- 7498-4: OSI Basic Reference Model—Part 4: Management Framework
- 9595/6: Common Management Information Service/Protocol
- 10040: System Management Overview
- 100165: Structure of Management Information
  - Part 1: Management Information Model
  - Part 2: Definition of Management Information
  - Part 4: Guidance for the Definition of Managed Objects
- 100164: Systems Management Function
  - Part 1: Object Management Function
  - Part 2: State Management Function
  - Part 3: Attributes for Representing Relationships
  - Part 4: Alarm Reporting Function
  - Part 5: Event Reporting Management Function
  - Part 6: Log Control Function
  - Part 7: Security Alarm Reporting Function
  - Part 8: Security Audit Trail Function
  - Part 9: Objects and Attributes for Access Control
  - Part 10: Accounting Metering Function
  - Part 11: Workload Monitoring Function
  - Part 12: Test Management Function
  - Part 13: Summarization Report

4.6 Heterogeneous Network Management and Enterprise Management Systems

The OSI Network Management Model, the TCP/IP Protocol Suite Management and NetView were developed in the late 1980s. In addition to these systems, several proprietary network management systems were developed and deployed in the 1980s. In the 1990s, the emphasis has shifted to integrated management of heterogeneous networks which are interconnected to form an enterprise network. Enterprise networks serve the entire corporation and consist of many LANs and WANs, which are supported by different vendors with multiple protocols. We will first review two special cases of network management (LAN management and manufacturing network management) before discussing the enterprise network management issues and approaches.

4.6.1 LAN Network Management Systems

Network management for LANs has gained significance due to the growth of LANs in corporations. The special characteristics of LAN systems for network management are as follows:

- Between 50 to 100 workstations, with different capabilities, are supported.
- Many bridges and routers are used to connect the LANS to other LANs or WANs.
- Several (3 to 10) servers which provide print, file, and database services are commonly used in one LAN.

- Many different protocols and vendors are employed in LANs. Although at present most LANs are converging to Ethernet or token ring, it is common to see Ethernet, token ring and Appletalk-Localtalk LANs in the same organization (in some cases, in the same building or room).
- LAN messages are broadcast on the LAN backbone, which allows any station to receive information (traffic statistics, errors, etc.) about other stations. This allows any device to be used as a monitoring device.

LAN management has been an afterthought because most LANs were initially small and the importance of managing LANs was not universally recognized <Dolan 1991, Fresko-Weiss 1987>. Initially, most LAN management was conducted through dedicated measurement devices and analyzers for fault isolation and correction (e.g., the "sniffer"). In some cases, bridges and routers have been programmed to record network traffic statistics, albeit with some performance penalties. The problem of LAN network management became important when several LANs were interconnected to form large LANs. These LANs run TCP/IP, NetBIOS, Novell NetWare IPX/SPX, XNS, DECnet, and other network protocol stacks. An architecture is needed to manage LANs so that a LAN can be managed from remote sites. The following network management capabilities for LANs are needed:

- *Fault management*: The faults in the workstations, servers, bridges, routers, and cables need to be detected and corrected. These problems are complicated due to the multiplicity of devices and protocols.
- *Performance management*: The performance of interconnected LANs which operate at different speeds, connected through bridges and routers, cause serious performance bottlenecks due to congestion.
- *Security management*: The broadcast nature of LAN transmission (a tapped device can see everything going on in the network) creates a vulnerable situation.
- *Configuration management*: The LAN manager should know who is connected to the LAN and what software/hardware is being used at the workstations. This is important for configuration management as well as security purposes. The main challenge is to know the LAN configuration in the absence of a centralized network configurator in LANs.
- *Accounting management*: The billing for resources used has not been considered in LAN network management. It is difficult to know the resources utilized per server because LANs use datagram services (any workstation can send any message at any time).

Many LAN network management products are becoming available from LAN vendors such as Novell, 3Com, SUN, HP, IBM and DEC. These systems use management protocols such as SNMP, CMOT, and CMIP, over NetBIOS, IEEE 802.1 and Novell Netware IPX/SPX. It seems that the TCP/IP Simple Network Protocol (SNMP) has become the LAN management standard among many available LANs. Some LAN vendors such as SUN Microsystems are packaging SNMP agents on the

LAN servers (Sunnet manager is widely used). CMIP and CMIP over TCP/IP (CMOT) are available from only a few vendors.

4.6.2 Management of MAP Networks

The Manufacturing Automation Protocol (MAP) Task Force has specified network management specifications for manufacturing networks <MAP/TOP 1987>. The scope of MAP Network Management Model has been narrowed to allow quick implementation but is expandable for future considerations. The Model is intended only for MAP segments (collection of nodes which have full or Mini-MAP support) and ends at a non-MAP gateway. It is not intended for wide area networks. The architecture of MAP Network Management, based largely on the OSI Network Management Model, provides four basic application services:

- *Fault management*: Diagnose and correct failures in manufacturing devices and area/cell controllers.
- *Performance management*: Control and measurement of performance for realtime operations of manufacturing devices such as robots.
- *Configuration management*: Determine and control state of the system (e.g., what manufacturing devices are connected to what cell and area controllers).
- *Event processing*: Detect/report unscheduled events (e.g., interruption of an assembly line).

Each application service runs in an application processor which can reside at one node or be distributed among many nodes (see Fig. 4.12). Each application processor (e.g., the configuration management process) provides an operator workstation (human-machine interface) which provides human interface for network administrators and operators. The actual functions of the application process are performed by agents and managers in a manner similar to the OSI Network Management Model. Agents and managers may operate in each layer of the MAP node to collect needed data. The management information base (MIB) contains the information on manufacturing resources (Robots, numerical controllers, cell controller, etc.). The network management protocol defines the formats of the messages between agents and managers residing on the MAP LAN. More information about the MAP Network Management can be found in the MAP/TOP 3.0 Specifications and the paper by Joseph and Muralidhar <Joseph 1990>.

Many vendors in the manufacturing sector have announced support for MAP Network Management. A good example of a MAP Network Management implementation is the ENTERPRISE Network Manager, which managed a portion of the devices in the ENTERPRISE Networking Event 1988 <Behm 1988>. This Network Manager was developed to demonstrate the viability of network management for MAP/TOP networks. It supported a subset of the network management services defined in the MAP/TOP 3.0 specifications. The capabilities for human-machine interface, full MAP interfaces, and an expert system for configuration generation,

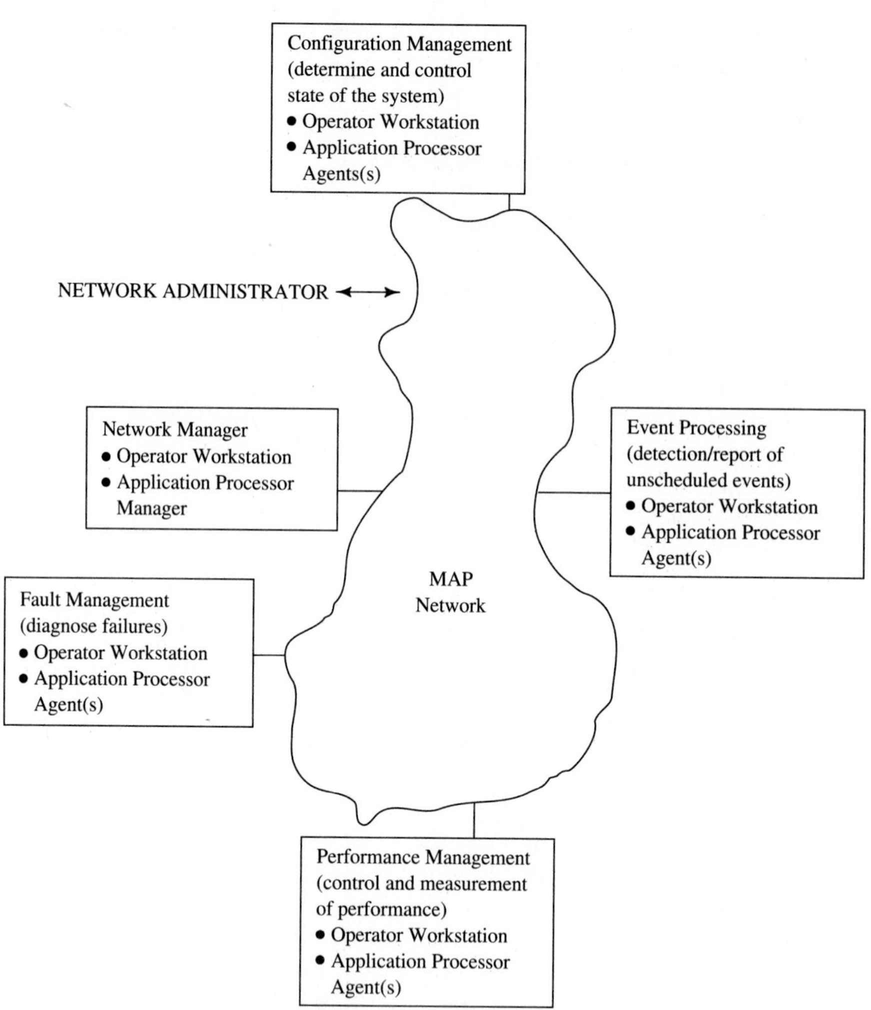

FIGURE 4.12 MAP Network Management Standard Conceptual View

called MAPCON, were provided. MAPCON is described elsewhere <Muralidhar 1987>.

4.6.3 Enterprise Network Management

Enterprise network management is concerned with integrated management of all backbone networks in an enterprise. The characteristics of these networks are as follows:

- Many LANs, MANs and WANs at different speeds are interconnected in a variety of ways.

- The networks consist of voice and data communications systems that may be tied into common carrier networks.
- Between 1000 to 5000 stations (microcomputers, minicomputers and mainframes) are connected to the enterprise networks. These stations may be from different vendors running different operating systems, database managers and transaction managers.
- Different network architectures are used in different parts of the organization. For example, corporate headquarters may use SNA, engineering offices may use TCP/IP, and manufacturing plants may use MAP. In addition, many LANs in different parts of the organization may exist.
- Many distributed applications which use distributed databases and/or client-server systems are being developed and deployed on enterprise networks. These applications create unique traffic patterns and error conditions which are difficult to manage.
- Different network management systems may be used in different parts of the organization. For example, IBM's NetView may be used to manage the SNA network, DEC's EMA may be used to manage DECnet, and SNMP may be used to manage the TCP/IP LANs and MANs.

Due to these special characteristics of enterprise networks, enterprise network management is viewed as a multilevel facility in which different domain (element) managers manage portions of the network and communicate with each other. One or more enterprise network managers may be needed to manage the domain managers. In addition, the enterprise network management may go beyond network management to the management of all resources (operating systems, application software, and databases) in an enterprise.

A conceptual view of enterprise network management is presented in Fig. 4.13. The enterprise network manager uses a client-server paradigm to communicate with the individual domain managers and may use CMIP as a communication management protocol between the enterprise manager and the domain managers. The functions of enterprise network management can be described by using the, by now familiar, network management functions:

- *Fault management*: The faults in the individual domains are detected and corrected by the domain managers, while the faults among the domain managers are resolved by the enterprise manager. Because each domain manager may use its own network management protocol, standards for diagnostic messages between different domains are needed (CMIP may be used here). A particular challenge is to diagnose the faults in distributed applications which cross many domains (e.g., an application which uses workstations, LAN servers, minicomputers, and mainframes from different domains).
- *Performance management*: The performance of interconnected domains which operate at different speeds, connected through communication controllers and switches, cause serious performance bottlenecks due to congestion. Performance

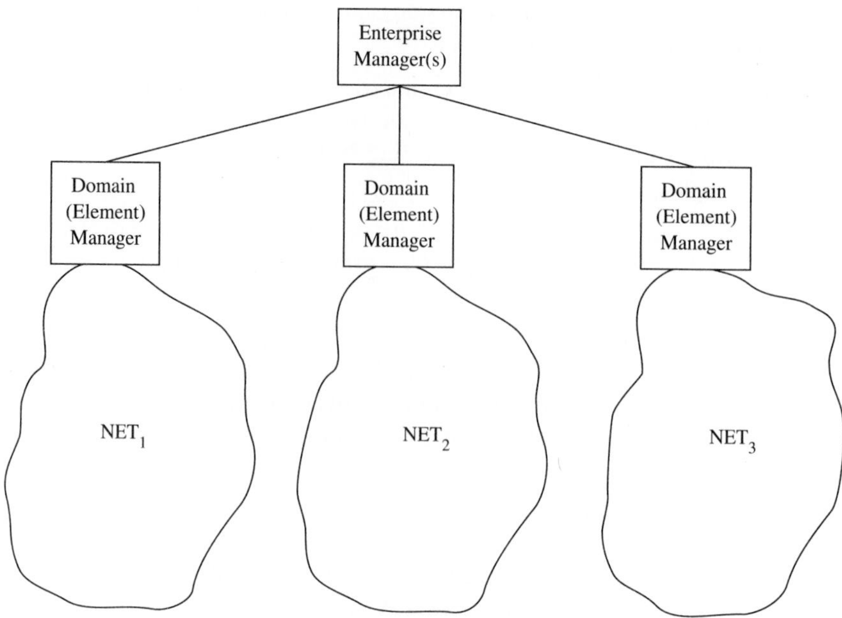

FIGURE 4.13 A Conceptual Model of Enterprise Network Manager

management in distributed applications which cross many domains is especially challenging. For example, an application causing relational database joins between different sites can generate bursts of transmission messages across many domains.

- *Security management*: The enterprise-wide security management is nontrivial because of the use of broadcasts and encryptions at various levels. It may be advisable to utilize a few authentication servers to assure enterprise-wide security. The authentication servers essentially "greet and clear" the users before allowing access to any resources.
- *Configuration management*: The enterprise manager should know who is connected to the enterprise network, where is it connected (who is the domain manager), and what configuration is being used in different domains.
- *Accounting management*: It is important to know how to bill for the enterprise network services. It is difficult to compute the bills because different algorithms may be used in different domains.

Obviously, enterprise network management will become increasingly important in this decade as larger and more complex networks continue to grow. Four different developments in this area are worth mentioning: DEC's Enterprise Management Architecture (EMA), AT&T's Accumaster Integrator, IBM's System View and HP's Open View.

EMA is specifically designed to integrate multivendor networks through an object-oriented data repository which specifies the hardware and software resources that the system must manage. EMA uses network protocol independent remote procedure calls (RPCs) for information exchange between different domain managers. This makes it possible to deploy different software modules on different platforms from different vendors.

The Accumaster Integrator is a Unix-based integrated system which uses a relational database management system for configuration data and a flexible user interface. Accumaster also uses the OSI network management standards (CMIP/CMIS) for management services and protocols.

IBM's System View goes beyond NetView's network management to applications management in distributed environments <Guruge 1991>. In particular, it attempts to minimize the effort needed to manage the large number of products that run on IBM mainframes, minicomputers and microcomputers. NetView is an integral part of System View. IBM's approach to enterprise network management is described in Szabat <1992> and Stevenson <1992>.

OpenView is based on the ISO network management standards and provides a common user interface to all network management tools. OpenView Window provides APIs (application program interfaces) for programmers to write backend applications on network management. This provides a basis for user interface integration. OpenView has adopted CMIP/CMIS as a strategic direction and supports SNMP as a short-range solution. Analysis and evaluation of these offerings can be found in trade journals such as the Patricia Seybolds *Network Monitor* (1989 through 1992 issues), and the *Networking Management* magazine.

4.7 Technology Applications in Network Management

Network management systems are large and complex systems which can benefit from application of a wide range of technologies. The following statements typify the challenges of developing network management systems (NMSs):

- The performance of an NMS should be good for different load conditions on networks of different sizes. In other words, an NMS should not cause any performance problems on the network it is managing.
- An NMS must be reliable and fault tolerant; a failure in the network must not cause the NMS to fail.
- An NMS should be flexible so that it can be modified easily to reflect the changes in the network.
- An NMS has realtime processing requirements (must be able to detect unscheduled events and respond to them quickly).
- An NMS is a distributed application in which the data as well as the programs exist at many sites.

Due to these challenges, NMS development should exploit the latest techniques in expert systems/artificial intelligence, software engineering, operations research and database technology. Most of the examples of applying these technologies to NMS at present are in the area of expert systems and AI <Slomon 1991, Cronk 1988>. Other technologies need more attention.

Figure 4.14 shows a conceptual model of a network management system which can be used as a framework for evaluating the techniques and tools needed for network management. The following functional modules support the NMS shown in Fig. 4.14:

- *User interface program (UIP)*: This module supports a variety of information storage and retrieval modes (commands, menus, query languages, graphics, and speech).
- *Configuration manager*: This module is used to define, change, monitor, and control network resources.
- *Diagnostic/fault manager*: This module will detect, diagnose and repair, if possible, network problems.
- *User resource manager*: This module is responsible for managing user directories and user profiles.
- *Planning manager*: This module supports planning at two levels: long-range planning through simulations and expert systems to determine the best configurations

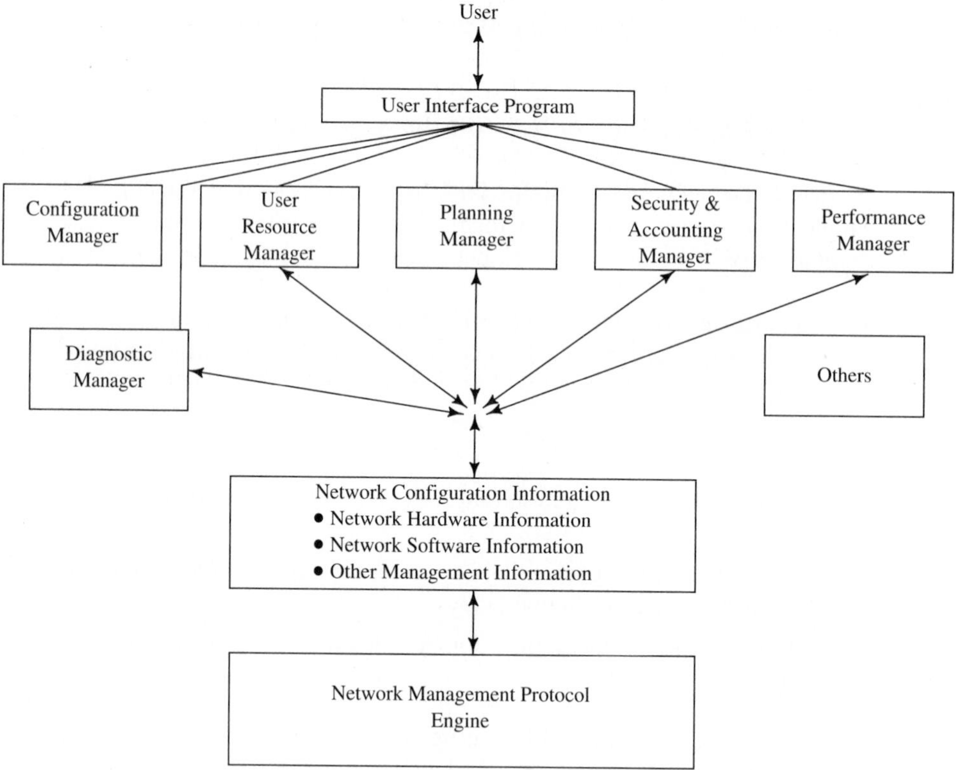

FIGURE 4.14 Conceptual Model of Network Mangement Systems

for future workload requirements, and contingency planning for short-term problems like equipment or subnet failures.

- *Performance manager*: This module closely works with the planning manager to provide statistics on network capacity utilization, average delays, congestion points, etc. This module will also provide advice on equipment maintenance by recording error statistics and suggesting courses of action to minimize the mean time between failure.
- *Security and accounting manager*: This module will ensure authorized access to the network and generate billing information.

The information needed by these modules may be stored in a network configuration database. A network management protocol engine is needed to transfer the information back and forth among network managers and agents. The techniques and tools discussed next can be employed and extended to support this model. A prototype based on this model is described by Umar <1992>.

4.7.1 Artificial Intelligence (AI) and Expert Systems

The AI techniques can be applied effectively in all of the NMS modules at two levels. First, the network management software itself can be made more intelligent by making appropriate decisions when enough information is available and asking for only minimal additional information. This is an important feature in network management because the network management system should not collect and retain a large amount of information and thus itself become a bottleneck in the system. Secondly, each module can be "knowledge based" so that the knowledge can be updated periodically. This is especially important for the diagnostics and planning modules. Over the last five years, many expert systems for network management have been developed and deployed (see Cronk <1988> for a discussion of about 20 expert systems for network management). Examples are as follows:

1. Expert systems for diagnostics and debugging which keep knowledge about debugging procedures as a set of rules. These rules may be invoked automatically when an event occurs or manually whenever certain problems and symptoms are detected. Expert systems is a natural application in fault management because diagnosing a network problem requires a great deal of expertise. It is also possible to translate a network diagnostics procedure into a rule based expert system where the rules represent the procedure to be used by the human expert. Figure 4.15 shows a conceptual model of a knowledge-based diagnostics system. The network configuration and the failure event data are processed by the diagnostic rules and corrective procedures. Most of the existing expert systems in this area are oriented toward LANs or WANs. Expert systems to diagnose problems in heterogeneous internets (networks of LANS, MANS and WANS from different vendor) need special attention. Some of the ideas from high-level symbolic debuggers, such as ALADIN, may be employed in this area.

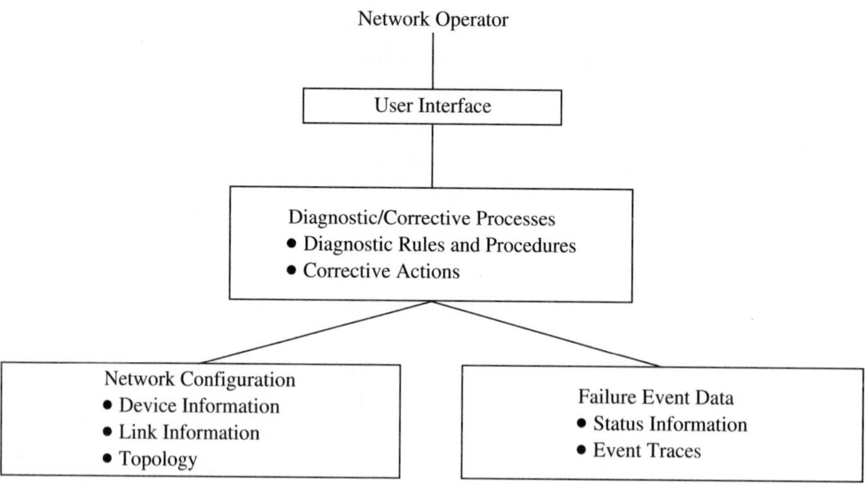

FIGURE 4.15 A Sample Network Diagnostics System

2. Intelligent monitoring tools which detect the deviation from normal behavior (e.g., average transmission delay) and trigger proper corrective procedures, which are represented as rules. An example is the Bell Northern Research DAD, which monitors data packet networks. An area that needs special attention is machine induction and learning. Machine induction can be used to process trouble reports/diagnostic data, find out patterns hidden in the data and generate rules for diagnostics. These rules are "learned" by the system and used in future problem solving <Bernstein 1989>.
3. Expert systems to help the managers in planning, configuring and purchasing the network devices. Most of the work in expert systems for network planning and configuration has focused on local area networks <Tanica 1986, Stollof 1986>. An example of such a system is ELAND, which configures local area networks based on a set of user requirements <Ceri 1990, Tanica 1986>. For example, ELAND generates a LAN design, the software, the computer systems and file allocations for a given application description. Figure 4.16 shows a conceptual model of a knowledge-based LAN configurator (CHOOSLAN) which configures a LAN based on the organizational and application requirements <Minders 1990>. The current work in expert systems for LANs needs to be explored for these possibilities. More expert systems for network planning need to be developed. Examples of the expert systems in network management are given in Cronk <1988>, Reddy <1986>, and Goyal <1986>. Slomon <1991> gives a state-of-the-market review of network management expert systems.

4.7.2 Database

The network configuration database is a critical component of NMS because it keeps all of the information needed for the different functional modules described earlier. The currently available database technology is based on relational calculus. Relational

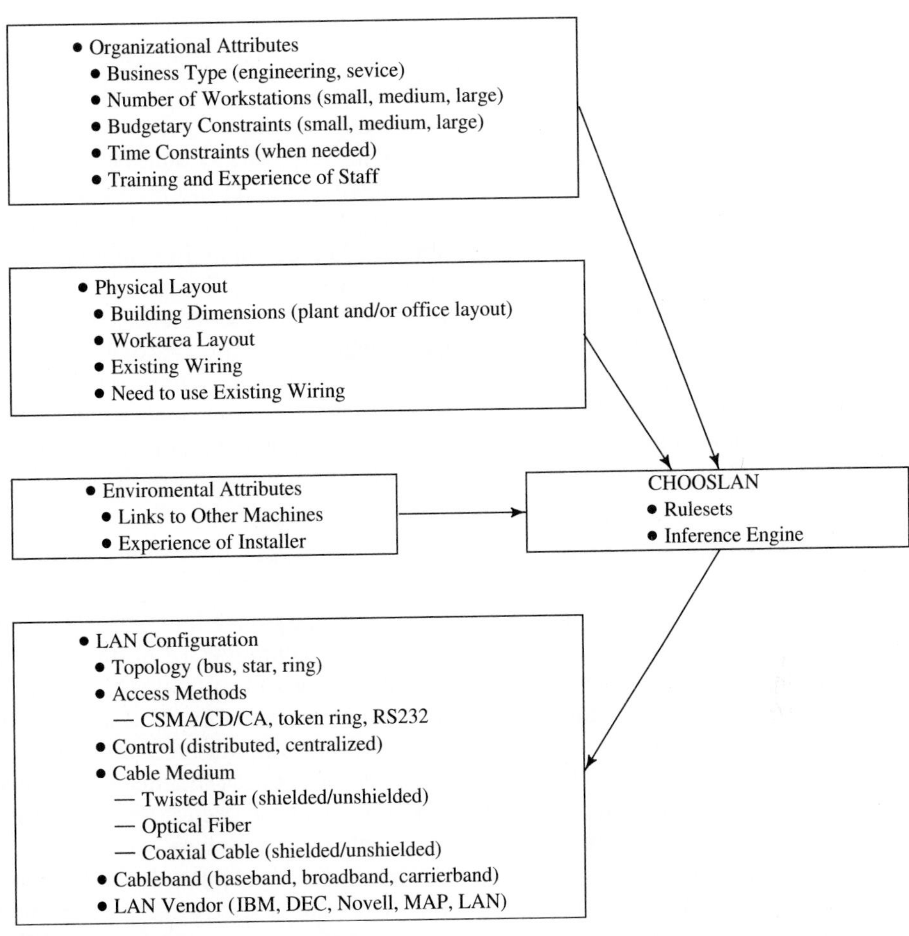

FIGURE 4.16 XYZCORP Network Layout

databases and SQL can be used for network configuration database <Umar 1992>. However, relational databases are not well suited for representing complex information needed in network management. The database management system (DBMS) with great promise for network management are the object-oriented databases which allow storage and retrieval of objects, where an object is a collection of data elements and operations that manipulate the data elements. (A review of the relational and object-oriented database technologies is given in Appendix E.) Examples of objects are a program variable, a device, a family of devices (e.g., multiplexors), a LAN or a large network. In each case, the object is represented by at least two properties: data structure and operations. For example, the following two objects can be defined:

```
1. Object Name    = workstation
 . Data Structure = workstation type, vendor name, cost,
                    operating system used, etc.
 . Operations     = boot, restart, login, use, logout, etc.
```

```
2. Object Name    = LAN
 . Data Structure = LAN type (e.g.,token ring), LAN vendor, etc.
 . Operations     = start, login, print service, file service, etc.
```

The object-oriented database model is more naturally suitable for representing complex relationships. These properties make the object-oriented approach attractive to network management. For example, the OSI Network Management Model uses an object-oriented approach to describe the Management Information Base (MIB). Although OSI does not specify how MIB can be physically stored, an object-oriented database management system is natural for MIB. Object-oriented database management systems (OODBMS), the DBMS which can store, retrieve and manipulate objects, have been an area of active research and exploration for the last five years. The use of OODBMS for actual network management applications is an area of considerable interest among the research and development communities. Some NMSs, such as the DEC EMA, use OODBMS for network configurations.

4.7.3 Software Engineering

Network management applications consist of large and complex software modules which can benefit from software engineering techniques of portable and reusable software, common user interfaces, and integration of tools/data.

The latest techniques in object-oriented programming and design can be used in network management to provide transportable and reusable software (see Appendix E for a review of object-oriented concepts). An area that needs special attention is finding and implementing machine-independent representation of machine-dependent objects in networks because in large heterogeneous networks it is important not to burden the network manager with unnecessary machine-dependent details. The class hierarchy of object-oriented approaches can be used effectively in this area and is the primary motivation for using an object-oriented approach in the OSI Network Management Model. Olson <Olson 1990> gives a detailed description of how object-oriented concepts can be used in network management.

Perhaps one of the most important issues in network management is a common user interface through which a user can access many tools residing anywhere in the network. This approach, called the user view integration, is the main feature of Hewlett-Packard Open View Network Management Architecture. As mentioned previously, the OSI Network Management Model does not specify a common user interface; this is considered a weakness of the Model. Emerging user interface standards such as X Window can be used to support the User Interface Program (see Fig. 4.14).

Another consideration is tool integration around the network configuration database. All tools and modules shown in Fig. 4.14 should use the common network configuration database. Specifically, the operations research predictive and performance models need to be integrated for performance evaluation and network bottleneck analysis. In the past, most performance evaluation tools and simulation models use their own data files which contain some of the network configuration data. This duplicates the effort and is unnecessary. In addition to the predictive models, the expert systems discussed earlier should also use the common database for knowledge processing <Umar 1992>.

Examples of application of software engineering, AI, and database techniques in network management is the NMS being developed for the Stanford University network and the ANM system, which combines a distributed database with an AI engine to automate network management <Feridan 1988>. An interesting example of NMS simulators to manage NMSs can be found in Kheradpir <1992>.

4.7.4 Network Technologies and Distributed Systems

The advancement of networking technologies and distributed systems itself can help in the development of NMS. Examples of interesting technologies are multimedia networks, distributed database management systems (DDBMS), and client-server systems.

Multimedia networks provide facilities for exchanging voice, video and data over communication facilities. These technologies can be extremely useful in supporting an advanced network operations center where the staff can solve problems in groups even if they are geographically distributed. This problem-solving approach, referred to as groupware, allows remotely located experts to see and hear each other while solving problems. Video and graphics can be especially useful in problem solving by allowing the experts to see the device components which may be remotely located.

The use of distributed databases for network management is attractive because the network database is inherently distributed. The current distributed database management systems (DDBMSs) are primarily relational and oriented toward business applications. Considerable work needs to be done in developing the next generation of DDBMSs for network management and in studying the problems of realtime and object-oriented distributed database management systems <Sha 1988, Spooner 1986, Abbot 1988, Cohen 1982>. We will discuss distributed databases in Chapter 6.

The client-server systems allow remotely located processes to communicate interactively with each other. The underlying model describes communications between service consumers (clients) and service providers (servers). Clients and servers are independent parallel processes, which may run on the same machine or on separate machines. This model fits very well within the network management framework. For example, the relationships and interactions between a manager and agents in the OSI Network Model use the client-server paradigm. In addition, the relationships between the enterprise manager and the element managers is also client-server oriented. Many client-server systems are becoming commercially available and the facilities for developing client-server systems (e.g., the remote procedure call facility) are becoming more powerful. We will discuss the client-server systems in detail in Chapter 5.

It should be noted that although these technologies will help solve some of the network management problems, they will introduce new problems for network management. Why? The reason is simple. The underlying network that needs to be managed will become more complex and intricate. If this sounds like Catch 22, it is.

4.7.5 Fault Tolerance

Fault tolerance means that no single point of failure will cause the entire system to fail. Fault tolerance in network management has two implications: A fault tolerant network reduces the burden of network management fault tolerant modules, and the network management software itself should be fault tolerant even if the network being managed is not fault tolerant. Although networks are becoming reliable and fault tolerant, we are far from being flawless. To design fault-tolerant network management systems, redundancy is usually incorporated in hardware, software and data. For example, redundant databases allow access when one site fails, and redundant communication channels allow different paths to the same device.

4.8 Management Summary and Trends

Network management is concerned with the policies, procedures and tools needed to manage networks in a manner similar to any other corporate resource (capital, data). This is an area of strategic importance for most corporations due to the growing importance, size and complexity of networks. The functions defined by ISO (fault management, configuration management, accounting, performance analysis, security and resource management) are commonly used to define the functional characteristics of network management. During the early stages (1970s) of network management, the main focus was on fault management for small networks. Network management systems (NMSs) were developed in 1980s as a collection of tools for homogeneous (single vendor), medium sized (few thousand devices) networks. Many NMSs in this stage basically integrated many of the network diagnostics and control tools developed in the 1970s and early 1980s into a single package. Examples of the NMSs developed in this stage are IBM's NetView and Avant-Garde's Netcommand. NMS development at present is focusing on managing networks of networks (internetworks) for thousands of devices over thousands of lines from multiple vendors which may cross international boundaries. The main emphasis at present is to automate the network management activities through expert systems.

An essential aspect of network management, sometimes overlooked, is the organizational structure and the administrative processes to utilize the NMS properly. Ingredients of a successful network management system are a Networks Operations Center (NOC), an integrated toolset which gives the NOC personnel timely information for decision making, and policies and procedures about how the NOC will handle normal as well as emergency situations. It is also important for the organizations to understand the financial aspects of developing user network application programs.

The following observations highlight the main trends in network management:

Growth in Open Architectures and Standards in Network Management. The trend toward open architectures and standards for network management will continue because these standards allow users to interconnect heterogeneous networks and to develop their own applications. The main network management standards being developed are the Common Management Information Service (CMIS) by ISO/OSI and the Simple Network Management Protocol (SNMP) for TCP/IP based networks. The current status of these two standards is as follows:

- TCP/IP SNMP has become a de facto standard for managing heterogeneous networks. This is primarily due to the simplicity of this management protocol. In addition, the availability of TCP/IP on almost all computer-communication systems makes SNMP development and deployment easier. For example, SNMP has been implemented over Ethernet, LLC, Xerox Network Service (XNS), and Appletalk. In addition, SNMP is expected to be supported on top of the OSI 7-layer stack.
- The full OSI network management standard (CMIP/CMIS) is widely accepted as a long range future standard, and major future products are adopting this standard.

Increased Emphasis on Enterprise Network Management. The major area of work at present and in the near future is enterprise network management which integrates individual network management systems for large heterogeneous environments. Enterprise network management consists of: (1) management of all networks (LANs, WANs, MANs) of an enterprise, (2) division of network management functions among domain (element) managers which manage portions of the network, and (3) management of application resources (data and programs) in addition to the network resources such as the links, modems, and communication controllers.

Increased Automation of Network Management Activities. Network management systems are large and complex applications which are increasingly relying on automation technologies such as AI/expert systems, object oriented databases, common user interfaces, client-server systems and fault tolerance. Due to the complexity and size of networks being managed, the next generation of tools are appearing as expert support systems (ESS) and decision support systems (DSS) to support the network planning, installation, maintenance and performance activities. These systems are exploiting the advances in AI, database technologies and software engineering for large and complex network management and enterprise management systems. Ideally, these systems would have a common user interface which invokes tools that access network configuration information for problem solving.

Recognition of Organization Design and Procedures. The focus of network management will shift from tools to organizational design and procedures for effective network management. For example, one or more network operations centers will be formed in organizations from which the network administrators will view, monitor, analyze, and control the enterprise network. These operations centers may be integrated with the existing Help Desks (Hotlines), where the users can call to seek help on any of the problems related to enterprise products and services.

Shift to Distributed Applications Management. It is being recognized in many cases that network management is only a portion of the bigger problem. For example, network management primarily concentrates on layers 1 to 4 issues. The higher-level issues of managing distributed applications are concerned with fault management, performance management, accounting, security and configuration management of application processes that are at different sites. This area is currently being worked into standards.

Additional Readings. Two recent books, *Network Management*, McGraw-Hill, 1992, by U. Black, and *Cost Efficient Network Management*, McGraw-Hill, 1992, by L. Ball, provide a good discussion of the subject matter. IBM Systems Journal, Vol. 31, No. 2, 1992, is devoted to Network Management and has many good articles. Many papers on network management are appearing in scientific as well as trade journals. Examples of the state-of-the-art sources are the *IEEE Network Magazine* special issues on network management (e.g., the March 1988 and July 1990 issues), the *Computer Communications* November 1990 special issue on network management, *IEEE Communications* and *IEEE Spectrum* magazines during the 1989–1992 period, and the ISO documents. The state of the market and practice is covered well in trade journals, such as the *Business Communications Review*, Patricia Seybold's *Network Monitor*, *Networking Management* (PennWell Publication), *Network Computing* (CMP Publication), *LAN Technology* (M&T Publication), and McGraw-Hill's *Data Communications Magazine.*

Problems and Exercises

1. Define network management and describe why it is important in distributed computing.
2. Suppose an organization is planning to develop a corporate-wide network management strategy and and toolset to support the strategy. The networks of the organization consist of a plethora of IBM SNA, TCP/IP, DECnet, Token Ring, Novell Netware, and Appletalk networks. Suggest the steps to be taken in developing the strategy. Also list the strategy which outlines the policies, procedures, organizational structures and tools needed.
3. Develop a table which compares and contrasts the main features of OSI CMIP, TCP/IP SNMP and IBM's NetView.
4. Suppose you are starting a company to develop network management tools in a heterogeneous environment. Which network management protocol will you choose and why? Which technology (AI, database, fault tolerance) will you invest in and why?

CASE STUDY: Network Management for XYZCORP

The network for XYZCORP has been designed and is shown in Fig. 4.17. The corporate management is interested in developing a network management strategy. As a first step, you have been asked to propose a network operations center (NOC) with appropriate tools and organizational procedures. Your proposal should contain the following pieces of information:

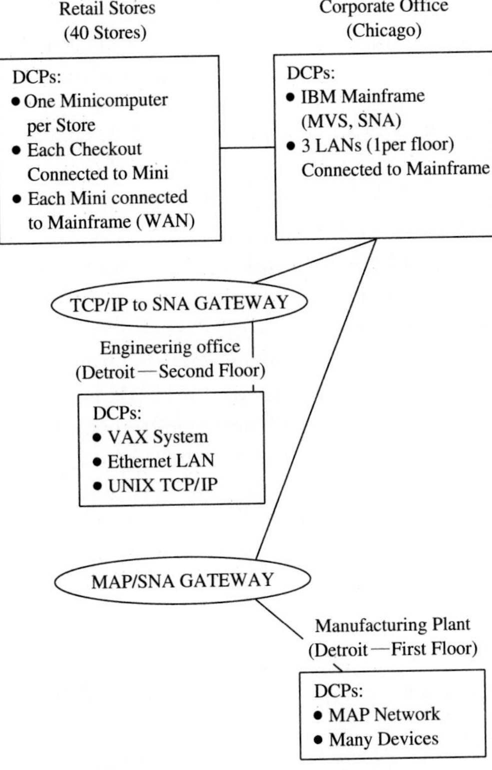

FIGURE 4.17 XYZCORP Network Layout

- A physical design of the NOC with all necessary equipment.
- A review of existing network management systems and a recommendation of what network management systems will be used where and how. The management is especially interested in knowing how NetView and SNMP will interoperate.
- A recommendation about how the MAP network and other LANs in the corporation can be managed?
- A long-range strategy which shows how some of the evolving systems (e.g., CMOT or CMIS) fit in the NOC. Can SNMP always be used for XYZCORP?
- How can the network management strategy be extended to include applications management?

Hints About the Case Study

The XYZCORP NOC can reside at the corporate office for a global network management approach. The NOC usually consists of many display units which monitor the status of the network. In the simplest case, one monitor can be assigned to Netview for SNA, one for SNMP and one for MAP. A network configuration database can provide the basis for interoperability between different network management tools. This can include the Netview, SNMP, MAP and LAN tools. The configuration shown in Fig. 4.14 presents a conceptual view which can be useful in this context. Ideally, the network configuration database should be object-oriented but a relational database can serve this purpose quite well mainly due to the availability of SQL interfaces from many tools. Comparison and evaluation of tradeoffs between CMIP and SNMP is left to the reader. Just one hint: SNMP appears to be more oriented toward network hardware management than application management. The OSI standards are much more powerful. For extension of network management to distributed applications management, the discussion in Chapter 10 (Section 10.5.1) should be consulted. The discussion of DME is especially important in this area. In the case of XYZCORP, network management would focus on managing the corporate backbone, the SNA and TCP/IP networks, and hardware devices. Distributed applications management would concentrate on managing the applications such as flexible manufacturing systems and distributed order-processing systems for XYZCORP.

References

Abbott, R., and Garcia-Molina, H., "Scheduling Real-Time Transactions," *SIGMOD Record*, Mar. 1988.

Ball, L., *Cost Efficient Network Management,* McGraw-Hill, 1992.

Behm, J., et al., "The Enterprise Network Manager," *Enterprise Network Event Conf. Proc.*, Baltimore, Md., May 1988, pp. 6.27-6.37.

Ben-Artzi, A., Chandna, A., and Warrier, U., "Network Management of TCP/IP Networks: Present and Future," *IEEE Network Magazine*, July 1990, pp. 35-43.

Black, U., *Network Management,* McGraw-Hill, 1992.

Brusil, P., and Stokesberry, D., "Toward a Unified Theory of Managing Large Networks," *IEEE Spectrum*, Apr. 1989, pp. 39-42.

Case, J., et al., "A Simple Network Management Protocol," *RFC 1098,* Apr. 1988.

Ceri, S., and Tanica, L., "Expert Design of Local Area Networks," *IEEE Expert*, Oct. 1990, pp. 23-33.

Chernick, M., Mills, K., Aronoff, R., and Strauch, J., "A Survey of OSI Network Management Standards Activities," Technical Report NMSIG87/16 ICST-SNA-87-01, National Bureau of Standards, 1987.

Chou, J. et al., "AIX Netview/6000," *IBM Systems Journal*, Vol. 31, No. 2, 1992, pp. 270-285.

Cohen, D., Holcomb, J.E., and Suryanarayana, M.B., "Distributed Database Management to Support Network Services," *IEEE Conference on Communications*, 1982.

Cronk, R., Callahan, P., and Bernstein, L., "Rule-Based Expert Systems for Network Management," *IEEE Network*, Sept. 1988, pp. 7-21.

Cypser, R., "Evolution of an Open Communications Architecture," *IBM Systems Journal*, Vol. 31, No. 2, 1992, pp. 161-188.

Dolan, T., "SNMP Streamlines Multi-Vendor Network Management," *LAN Technology*, Feb. 1991, pp. 29-38.

Donovan, J., "Beyond Chief Information Officer to Network Manager," *Harvard Business Review*, Sept.-Oct. 1988, pp. 134-140.

Embry, J., Manson, P., and Milhan, D., "An Open Network Management Architecture: OSI/NM Forum Architecture and Concepts," *IEEE Network Magazine*, July 1990, pp. 14-22.

Feridan, M., Leib, M., Nodine, M., and Wong, J., "ANM: Automated Network Management System," *IEEE Network*, Mar. 1988.

Fresko-Weiss, H., "Who Manages The Network," *Personal Computing*, Mar. 1987, pp. 107-114.

Goyal, S., and Worrest, R. W., "Expert Systems in Network Maintenance and Management," International Communications Conference'86, Toronto, June 1986, pp. 1225-1229.

Guruge, A., "IBM's System View: Adding Function to Form," *Data Communications*, Nov. 1991, pp. 99-112.

Halsall, F., and Modiri, N., "An Implementation of an OSI Network Management System," *IEEE Network Magazine*, July 1990, pp. 44-53.

Herman, J., *Multivendor Network Management*, Northeast Consulting Resources, Inc. Course, Sept. 1990.

Herman, J., "Network Management Directions," *Business Communications Review*, Feb. 1989, pp. 81-83.

Herman, J., "Network Management Directions," Regular column, *Business Communications Review*, 1988-1991.

Herman, J., "A New View of Open View," *Patricia Seybold's Network Monitor*, Mar. 1990.

Herman, J., "Network Management Directions," *Business Communications Review*, June 1991.

ISO, International Standards Organization, TC97/SC21/WG4, "Information Processing Systems—Open System Interconnection—Basic Reference Model Part 4," *OSI Management Framework*, DIS, ISO, Aug. 1987.

Jander, M., "Users Rate SNMP Multivendor Network Management Systems," *Data Communications*, Nov. 1991, pp. 113-120.

Joeseph, C., and Muralidhar, K., "Network Management: A Manager's Perspective," *Enterprise Network Event Conf. Proc.*, Baltimore, Md., May 1988, pp. 5.163-5-174.

Joeseph, C., and Muralidhar, K., "Integrated Network Management in an Enterprise Environment," *IEEE Network Magazine*, July 1990, pp. 7-13.

Kheradpir, S. et al., "Managing the Network Manager," *IEEE Communications Magazine*, July 1922, pp. 12-21.

Lee-Thorp, T., "SNMP: The Simple (Strained?) Network Management Protocol," *Business Communications Review*, Oct. 1991.

Minders, A., "CHOOSLAN: An Expert System for Choosing and Managing LANs," M.S. Thesis, University of South Africa, 1990.

MAP/TOP Users Group, "Manufacturing Automation Protocol Specification—Version 3.0," Implementation Release, MAP/TOP Users Group, July, 1987.

Muralidhar, K., and Irish, B., "MAPCON: An Expert System for Configuration of MAP Networks," Industrial Technology Institute Technical Report, Aug. 1987.

Olson, L., and Blackwell, A., "Understanding Network Management with OOA," *IEEE Network Magazine*, July 1990, pp. 23-28.

Rathnasabapathy, R., "Network Management: User Requirement Analaysis," Presentation at IFIP WG 6.6 meeting.

Reddy, Y., and Uppulari, S., "Intelligent Systems Technology in Network Operations Management," International Communications Conference—86, June 1986, Toronto, pp. 1220-1224.

Rose, M., *An Introduction to Management of TCP/IP Based Internets*, Prentice Hall, 1990.

Sapronov, W., Hunter, J., and Friend, W., "Legal Pitfalls in Integrated Network Management," *Business Communications Review*, Nov. 1990, pp. 46-50.

Sha, L. et al., "Concurrency Control for Distributed Real-Time Databases," *SIGMOD Record*, Mar. 1988.

Sloman, J., "Automating Network Management," *LAN Technology*, July 1991, pp. 32-44.

Smith, R., "Report on the 1984 Distributed Artificial Workshop," *The AI Magazine*, Fall 1985, pp. 234-243.

Spooner, D., "An Object Oriented Data Management System for Mechanical Cad," IEEE 1986 Conference on Graphics.

Stein, J., "Object-Oriented Programming and Databases," *Dr. Dobb's Journal*, March 1988.

Stevenson, J., "Management of Multivendor Networks," *IBM Systems Journal*, Vol. 31, No. 2, 1992, pp. 189-205.

Stollof, G., "LANPICK: An Expert System for Recommendation of Local Area Network Hardware and Software Products," M.S. Thesis, Department of Computer Information Science, The University of Pennsylvania, July 1986.

Szabat, M., and Meyer, G., "IBM Network Management Strategy," *IBM Systems Journal,* Vol. 31, No. 2, 1992, pp. 154-160.

Tanica, L., and Ceri, S., "ELAND: An Expert System for the Configuration of Local Area Network Applications," IEEE Conf. on Local Computer Networks, Oct. 86, Minneapolis, Minn., pp. 89-98.

Turner, M. J., "Network Management Services from AT&T and MCI," *Business Communications Review*, May 1991, pp. 55-60.

Umar, A., "An Open Database Architecture For Network Management," *Unix Systems Information Networking Group Conference Proc.*, Philadelphia, May, 1992.

PART THREE

Application Support Services

This portion of the book concentrates on application support services of the Distributed Computing Reference Model introduced in Chapter 1 (see the figure). The objective of application support services is to provide transparent access and management of resources across a network. The resources that the application systems need may be files, databases, printers, terminals, disks, CPUs, programs, directories, etc.

Chapter 5 gives an overview of application interconnectivity choices and separates it from network interconnectivity. It then concentrates on client-server (C-S) computing, which is the predominant method for interconnecting applications across networks at present.

Chapter 6 focuses on distributed database and transaction management systems which provide data location and transaction processing transparency. Other related topics, such as transaction management, database servers and LAN/WAN databases, are reviewed to present a complete range of topics in creating, defining, accessing, and managing data in network environments.

Discussion of the distributed operating systems and distributed computing platforms to transparently access and manage computer devices in a network is given in Chapter 7. The distributed operating systems make all I/O devices, memory units and processors in the network available to the user as if they belong to one centralized computer system.

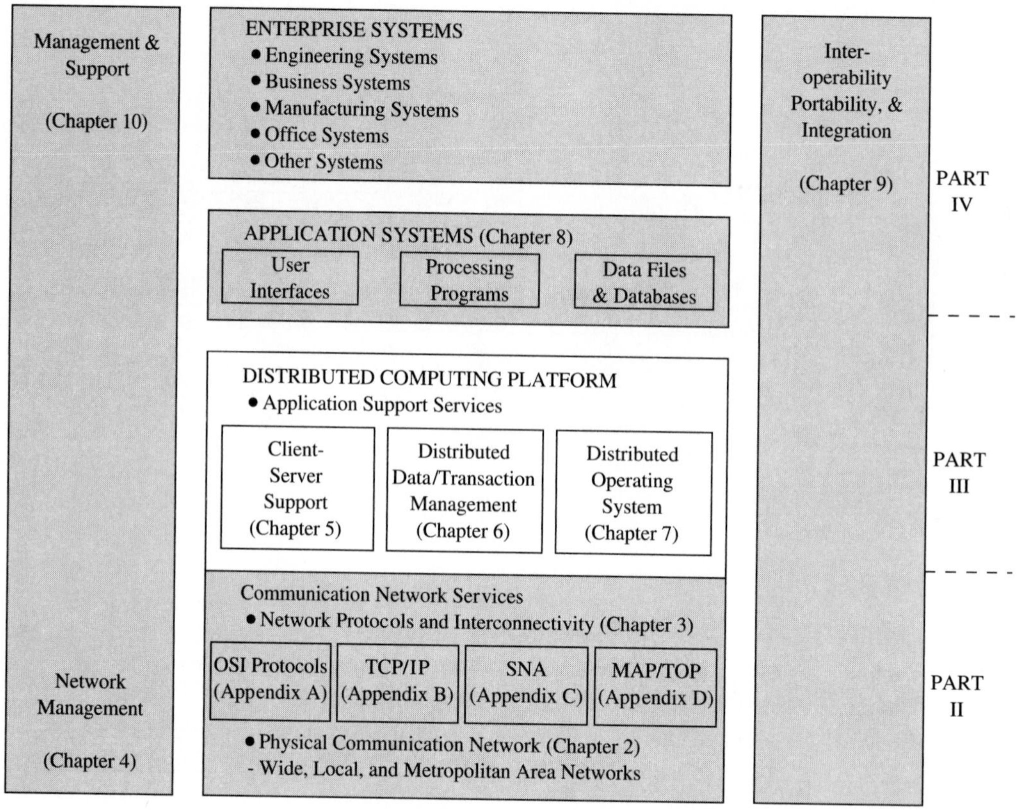

Management & Support

(Chapter 10)

ENTERPRISE SYSTEMS
- Engineering Systems
- Business Systems
- Manufacturing Systems
- Office Systems
- Other Systems

Inter-operability Portability, & Integration

(Chapter 9)

PART IV

APPLICATION SYSTEMS (Chapter 8)

User Interfaces | Processing Programs | Data Files & Databases

DISTRIBUTED COMPUTING PLATFORM
- Application Support Services

Client-Server Support (Chapter 5) | Distributed Data/Transaction Management (Chapter 6) | Distributed Operating System (Chapter 7)

PART III

Communication Network Services
- Network Protocols and Interconnectivity (Chapter 3)

OSI Protocols (Appendix A) | TCP/IP (Appendix B) | SNA (Appendix C) | MAP/TOP (Appendix D)

- Physical Communication Network (Chapter 2)
- Wide, Local, and Metropolitan Area Networks

Network Management

(Chapter 4)

PART II

Chapter 5

Client-Server Systems and Application Interconnectivity

5.1 Introduction

Interconnectivity in distributed computing involves three issues: station interconnectivity, network interconnectivity and application interconnectivity. Station and network interconnectivity, discussed in Chapter 3, are concerned with connecting computers to networks and networks to networks, respectively. These issues, handled by the lower layers of network architectures, enable data to be exchanged between remote computers. Application interconnectivity, the focus of this chapter, is concerned with how the applications at higher levels communicate with each other across a network. For example, suppose a bank teller in a Chicago bank needs to establish electronic fund transfer with a bank in New York. Then we have to consider the following issues:

- *Station interconnectivity*: How to connect the bank teller station (a PC or a terminal) to the Chicago bank network, say a bank LAN. For example, if the Chicago LAN is a Novell/Netware Ethernet LAN, then the bank teller station will have to be configured and connected through an Ethernet card and Novell software.
- *Network interconnectivity*: How can the Chicago bank LAN be connected to the New York bank. For example, if an X.25 packet switching WAN exists between New York and Chicago, then the appropriate routers will be needed to direct the traffic between Chicago and New York, and gateways will be needed to convert the Novell Ethernet protocols to X.25. We discussed these issues in Chapter 3.
- *Application interconnectivity*: How will the funds from Chicago accounts be transferred to New York accounts and vice versa. This involves issues of security, verification of request, audit trails, and handling of failures during fund transfer. This level of interconnectivity enables communications between the fund transfer applications in Chicago and New York.

Application support services, discussed in this chapter, are responsible for application interconnectivity. Figure 5.1 shows how application interconnectivity can be implemented. It shows that a use of higher-level services reduces application code. Section 5.2 reviews these application interconnectivity services and attempts to illustrate the wide range of available options. This section should be reviewed by the readers who need to develop an overall understanding of application interconnectivity.

The most popular application interconnectivity option at present is based on the client-server (C-S) model, in which a service consumer (client) requests a service provider (server) to perform a service. This model, described in detail in Sections 5.3 through 5.5, allows processes at different sites to exchange messages interactively (e.g., transfer funds, monitor the status of a robot, and query a database). Before C-S systems, processes at different sites communicated through terminal emulation or file transfer. For example, consider a workstation spreadsheet which needs data from three different databases at three different computers. The steps in the "old days" were as follows:

1. Logon to computer 1.
2. Extract needed information from the database.
3. Download the data to the workstation.
4. Repeat steps 1 through 3 for the other two computers.
5. Now (finally) run the spreadsheet on the workstation.

In a C-S system, the spreadsheet uses a client software package (e.g., a Lotus Data Lens) which accesses the three remote databases interactively during the execution of the spreadsheet. The aforementioned steps are bypassed. Section 5.3 discusses the concepts of the C-S systems and reviews the technical issues involved in developing and supporting C-S systems. Section 5.4 reviews the state of the art and state of the market C-S systems for distributed computing (e.g., SQL clients, terminal servers, window servers and X Window, file servers, and SQL database servers). The technical issues of C-S protocols, remote procedure calls, directory services, and development tools are discussed in Section 5.5. This section is intended primarily for developers of C-S software.

The discussion in this chapter is motivated by the following questions:

- What are the different application interconnectivity options in distributed computing, and what are the tradeoffs between these options?
- What are client-server systems, and what are their main features?
- Why and when should a client-server approach be used instead of other application interconnectivity approaches?
- What are the current applications of client-server systems? What are the future applications?
- What types of protocols and services are needed for the development of client-server systems?

5.2 Application Interconnectivity: Overview of Issues and Approaches

5.2.1 A Classification of Services

Distributed applications interconnect with each other through message exchange over a network. Figure 5.1 shows a classification of the application interconnectivity

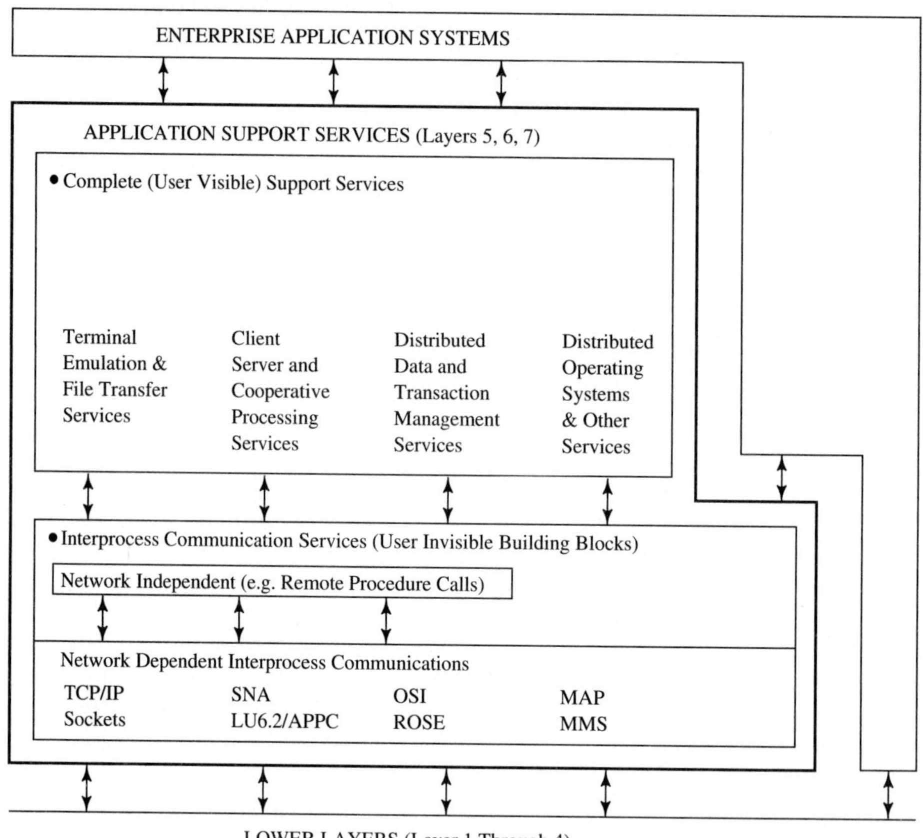

FIGURE 5.1 Application Interconnectivity Through Application Support Services

services, and Table 5.1 lists examples of the commonly known application interconnectivity services available in OSI, TCP/IP, SNA and MAP/TOP networks.

At the highest level in Fig. 5.1 are the enterprise applications systems (e.g., electronic fund transfer, order processing, inventory control, automated factories). Application interconnectivity is provided through application support services. These services are implemented in the higher layers (layers 5, 6, 7), although most of the activities are performed in the Application Layer (layer 7). It is advantageous to cast these services into the following two categories:

- *Complete (user visible) services.* These services can be directly used by the end users through commands without writing programs (however, application programs can be built on top of these services). Examples of these services are terminal emulation, file transfer, client-server support software (e.g., graphical query language tools which access remote databases), distributed data and transaction management (e.g., tools for accessing and manipulating distributed data), and miscellaneous services such as electronic mail.

TABLE 5.1 Common Application Interconnectivity Services

Note: These are broad categories for purpose of discussion. The services in each category are not exactly interchangeable.

High Level (Complete) Services

Terminal Emulation
- Telnet—TCP/IP
- Virtual Terminals—OSI
- 3270 Terminal Emulators—Ethernet/token ring LANs, SNA networks
- Kermit, ZModem, Procomm, CTRM, Crosstalk—Serial/dial-up networks

File Transfer
- File Transfer Protocol (FTP)—TCP/IP
- File Transfer Access Method (FTAM)—OSI
- 3270 Terminal Emulators—Ethernet/token ring LANs, SNA networks
- Kermit, ZModem, Procomm, CTRM, Crosstalk—Serial/dial-up networks

Client-Server Support Services
- File Servers (e.g. NFS)—TCP/IP, token ring, SNA, OSI
- Window Servers and X Window—TCP/IP, SNA
- Client Interfaces (e.g. Lotus Data Lens)—TCP/IP, SNA
- Database Servers (e.g. SQL Servers)—TCP/IP, SNA

Distributed Data and Transaction Management
- Remote Data Access (RDA)—OSI
- Distributed Transaction Processing (DTP)—OSI
- Proprietary Distributed Database Managers (Sybase, Oracle, Ingres, Informix)
- Proprietary Distributed Transaction Managers (NCR's TopEnd, Unix International's Tuxedo)

Miscellaneous Services
- Electronic Mail Services (X.400—OSI, SMTP-TCP/IP)
- Directory Services (e.g. X.500)—OSI and TCP/IP
- Distributed Applications Framework/Open Distributed Processing (OSI)
- Network Management Services (CMIS-OSI, SNMP-TCP/IP, Netview/SNA)
- Security Services (OSI, TCP/IP)
- Electronic Data Interchange (OSI, TCP/IP)
- Distributed Office Architecture (OSI)
- Job Transfer and Management (OSI)
- Distributed Operating Systems

Interprocess Communication Services (Building Blocks)

- Remote Procedure Call (RPC)—network independent service
- Berkeley Socket Application Programming Interface—TCP/IP
- Remote Operations Service (ROS)—OSI
- Manufacturing Message Specification (MMS)—MAP
- Advanced Program to Program Communications (APPC)—SNA

- *Interprocess communication (user invisible building block) services.* These services are commonly available to application developers. Examples of these services are remote procedure call (RPC) software, TCP/IP based Sockets, OSI based Remote Operations Service Elements (ROSE), OSI based Remote Data Access (RDA), SNA based Advanced Program to Program Communications and Logical Unit 6.2 (APPC/LU6.2), and MAP based Manufacturing Message Services (MMS). These services can be invoked only through application programs, usually through application programming interfaces (APIs).

Figure 5.1 shows that an application system can be built by using building blocks or higher-level services. The basic tradeoff is that higher-level services minimize software development effort while the building blocks allow more flexibility and efficiency. Here is the main point: use of higher-level services reduces application code. At present, more and more higher-level services are becoming available through off-the-shelf packages. From a management point of view, every attempt should be made to minimize the software development effort by exploiting the higher-level services before considering the building blocks. Just a caution: it is not easy to interconnect 3 applications which use 3 different levels of interconnectivity services (for example, one application uses sockets, the second uses RPC, and the third uses a distributed database manager). A brief overview of these two levels of services is presented next to illustrate the application interconnectivity tradeoffs. Chapter 8, Sections 8.5.4 and 8.6.2, show how these options can be used in developing distributed applications. It is expected, and hoped, that the future distributed computing platforms will provide many of these services as options available to the application developers, where the application developers will be able to choose the most appropriate service to satisfy the application needs. At present, we are far from it. We will visit this topic in Chapter 7, Section 7.6.

5.2.2 Complete (User Visible) Support Services

High-level services for application interconnectivity terminal emulators, file transfer, client-server (C-S) support software, and distributed data and transaction management systems (DDTMSs). Before the advent of C-S software and DTMS packages, many applications were connected by using terminal emulation and file transfer.

5.2.2.1 Terminal Emulation and File Transfer

Terminal emulation and file transfer have been used to interconnect applications, albeit poorly, since the late 1960s. Terminal emulation basically provides a remote access to a system. The user of a terminal emulator first starts the emulator and then uses it to logon to a remote machine. In the simplest case, a terminal emulator is a program which performs the following two functions:

- Read from the terminal keyboard and write to the communication channel.
- Read from the communication channel and write to the terminal display unit.

Terminal emulation can be used as the simplest method for interconnecting applications across heterogeneous networks. For example, an application can simulate the terminal keyboard/display features to send and receive messages to a remote application. The major disadvantage of terminal emulation is that the user must explicitly logon to each computer to access the needed resources. This is tolerable if the resources (e.g., files) are on one machine (i.e., a mainframe). However, this turns into a nightmare if the data is on 10 different machines with 10 different logons, 10 different passwords (passwords on different machines expire differently), many different command structures/utilities, and different data managers.

File transfer is commonly used to extract a portion of a file or a database and download it to a local site for offline processing. An application can invoke a file transfer package to download data from a remote site, operate on the data and then upload it if needed. These two methods, admittedly crude and old fashioned as compared to the interactive systems to be discussed later, are handy tools in a pinch. A few of the many commercial terminal emulation and file transfer packages are listed in Table 5.1.

In homogeneous networks (networks using the same network architecture throughout) terminal emulation and file transfer are accomplished through vendor-provided network software. For example, in IBM token ring LANs, the following instructions are used to transfer a file from a LAN server disk to a local device:

- > G: (set default device to G; G is a LAN disk)
- > copy f1 C: (copy file f1 from disk G to disk C).

In heterogeneous systems, Kermit is popular for quick and dirty serial transfer for terminal emulation and file transfer. Kermit is available on most computers at a very reasonable price (it is free!). The typical procedure for file transfer with Kermit is:

run Kermit on machine 1 (m1)
run Kermit on machine 2 (m2)
Issue: send from m1 f1 to m2 f2

For fast and reliable file transfer, TCP/IP-based facilities such as Telnet and FTP are used frequently. These facilities are available on mainframes, PCs, VAXs, MACs, SUNs, Hewlett Packards, and many other computers. TCP/IP is used widely in the Unix-Ethernet environments and is currently available on most networks on almost all computer systems. Telnet can be used to emulate a variety of computer systems as terminals and FTP can be used to transfer files between various computers. Telnet and FTP are described in Appendix B. The OSI virtual terminal and file transfer access methods (FTAM) can also be used for terminal emulation and file transfer.

It is important to note that the sender and receiver must use the same protocol. For example, consider a situation in which a file needs to be transferred between an MVS and a Unix environment. Fortunately, FTP is available on MVS as well as Unix environments because Unix and MVS support TCP/IP. Thus the user would use FTP. Without these, a "file transfer gateway" would be needed to translate between the file sender and receiver protocols.

File transfers suffer from the same limitations as terminal emulation. However, file transfers are still used frequently to extract needed data for local processing. This works well if the data change infrequently (e.g., monthly) and the file size is small. However, for large files which change frequently, this is not a good solution. For example, consider the situation in which 1000 customers want to run spreadsheets on corporate data located at mainframes. It becomes almost impossible to send the corporate data daily to the users.

5.2.2.2 Client-Server Computing and Distributed Cooperative Processing

Two models are very popular at present for application interconnectivity (other models are described in Section 5.2.3.1):

- The client-server (C-S) model, in which a service consumer (client) requests a service provider (server) to perform a service.
- The peer-to-peer model, in which either remotely located process can initiate an interaction.

The basic distinguishing feature of a C-S model is that a client initiates an interaction with a server by sending a message or by invoking an operation. In contrast, either process of a peer-to-peer model can initiate an interaction. A C-S model can be implemented over peer-to-peer protocols (the reverse is not necessarily true). Many distributed computing systems at present are based on the C-S model. This is why most of the discussion in this chapter is oriented toward C-S distributed computing (often known as client-server computing).

Distributed cooperative processing systems use peer-to-peer or C-S model for processes at different computers to interactively exchange information with each other (C-S computing is a subcategory of distributed cooperative processing). These systems provide a principal technology for application interconnectivity and far exceed the capabilities of terminal emulation and file transfer. The characteristics of distributed cooperative processing are <Gantz 1991>:

- The processes cooperate in realtime through message exchange and not through batch file transfers.
- Common user interfaces are provided for transparent access to resources located anywhere in the network.
- Data as well as processing can be distributed.
- Enterprise wide networks with interconnected WANs, LANs, and MANs provide network services.
- Multiple computer systems with different operating systems serve as computing platforms.

Figure 5.2 shows a distributed cooperative processing environment in which the cooperating processes are located throughout a network. In these environments, many computing systems may house print processes, file manager, terminal handlers, database managers, application processes, and user interface processes. Many processes may provide the same service or a service may be available from only one centralized process. These processes can invoke each other to solve a problem. For example, a print process may invoke a user interface to show that a job has completed printing and a user interface can later invoke a print process.

Although distributed cooperative processing can be configured in a wide variety of ways, Fig. 5.3 shows a typical configuration which uses the C-S model. According to this model, the clients reside at the workstations and the servers exist at the

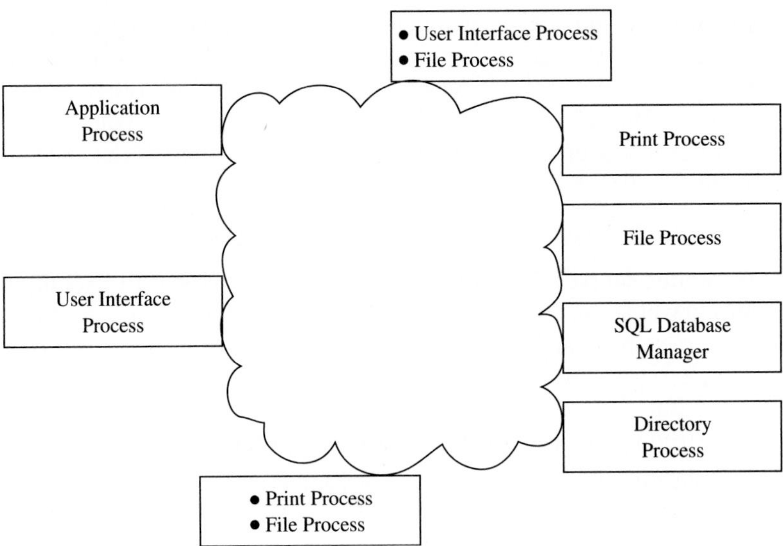

FIGURE 5.2 A Conceptual Distributed Cooperative Processing Model

department, region and enterprise levels. The clients are essentially user interface managers through which a user transparently accesses the various levels of servers. A departmental server can be a LAN server which provides local print, file and database services. A regional server may provide all common services that a region needs (e.g., a manufacturing plant). The enterprise server provides all corporate services of an

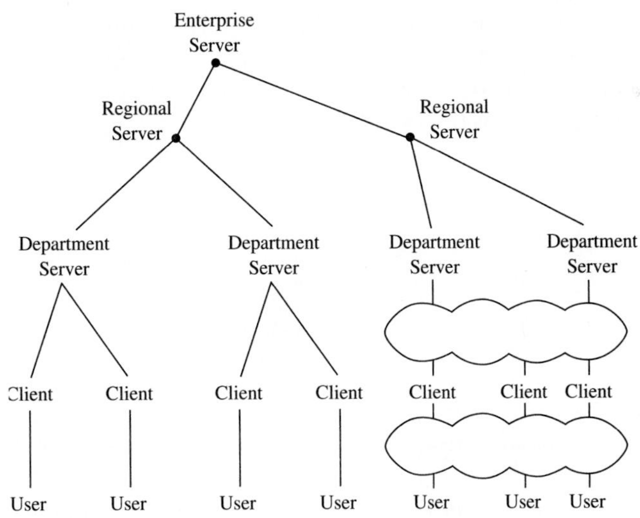

FIGURE 5.3 A Typical Client-Server Computing Model

organization. The major advantage of C-S computing is that a user can transparently invoke services which are distributed throughout the network. These resources are managed by C-S systems which cooperate with each other to support customer activities. This distributed processing model should be contrasted with the older centralized data processing model, shown in Fig. 5.4, in which all resources are limited to the central site.

5.2.2.3 Distributed Data and Transaction Management

Distributed cooperative processing (client-server or peer-to-peer models) is a general concept which can be implemented to support different configurations and situations. Here are some examples (Fig. 5.5):

- User interface processing is distributed, but the data and the application programs accessed by the user are at the same computer (Fig. 5.5a).
- Application programs are also distributed in addition to the user interfaces (Fig. 5.5b).
- Data are distributed in addition to the application programs and user interface processing (Fig. 5.5c).

The first situation, discussed frequently in this chapter, involves primarily the exchange mechanisms between the cooperating processes. The other two situations represent management of distributed data and programs, which introduces many complicating factors, discussed in the next chapter. Examples of the issues are: (1) how to present a common user view of data at different sites, (2) how to synchronize duplicate data, and (3) how to handle failures. These issues are handled by specialized software packages to be discussed in the next chapter.

A distributed database manager can reduce the application logic by allowing a user to access and manipulate data from several databases that are physically distributed to several computers. Basically, this package provides a transparent access to databases located anywhere in the network. For example, a user can access a customer database at a workstation, an inventory database at a PC and a financial database from a mainframe as if they resided on user's site.

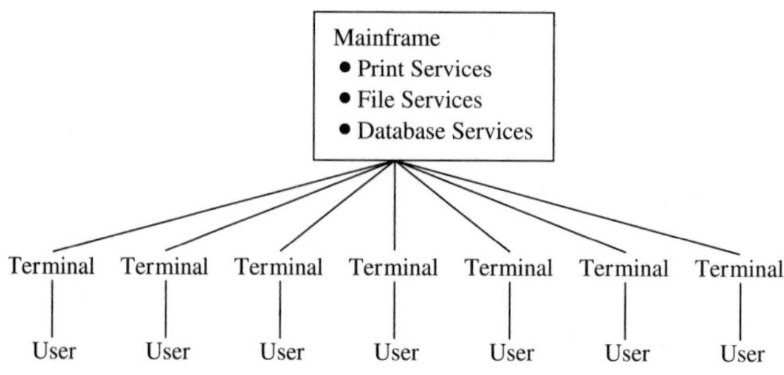

FIGURE 5.4 The Traditional Mainframe Model

a. Distributed User Interface Processing

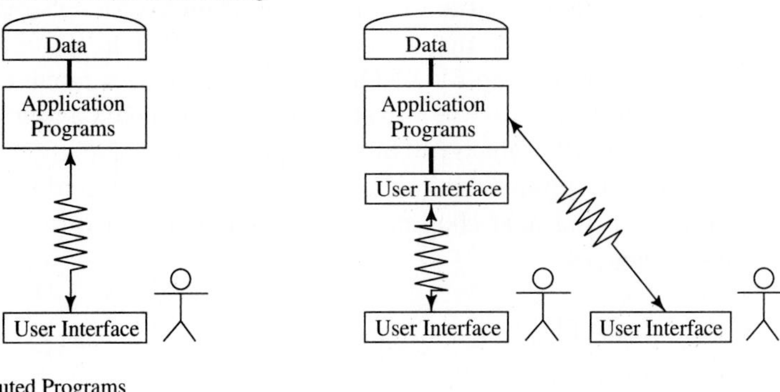

b. Distributed Programs

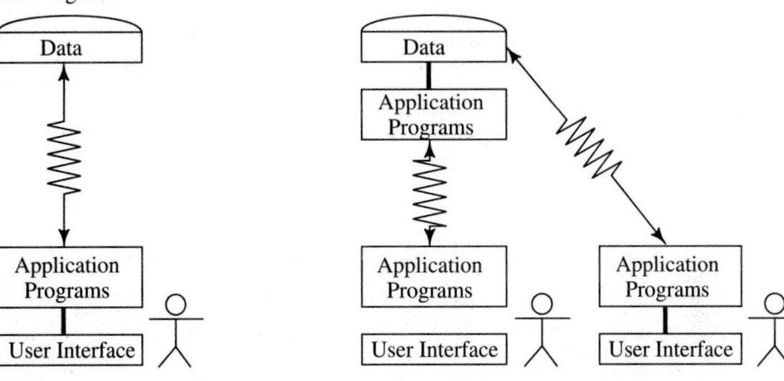

c. Distributed Data and Programs

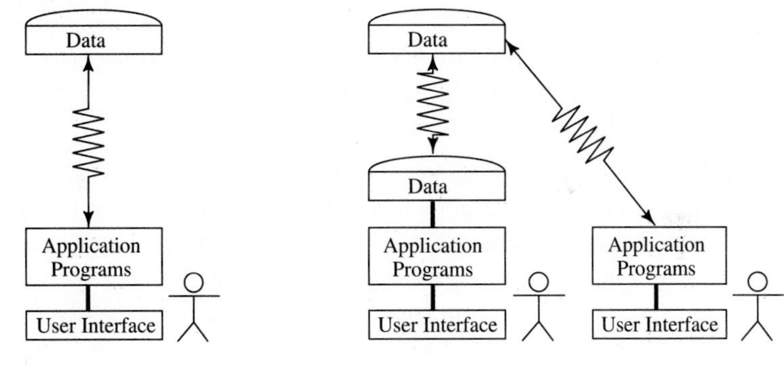

Legend:
-WWW- = is a remote (network) link
——— = is a local attachment

FIGURE 5.5 DistributedCooperative Processing Configurations

Distributed transaction managers coordinate the access to distributed data and to guarantee data consistency under system failures. These services may be embedded in distributed database managers or in independent distributed transaction managers such as TOP-END and TUXEDO. This, once again, is discussed in the next chapter.

In Chapter 6, we will introduce a distributed data and transaction management system (DDTMS) which will include management of all distributed data ("flat" files plus databases) and coordination between all distributed transactions. A DDTMS, described in the next chapter, is a collection of software modules which provides management of

- Distributed files
- Distributed databases
- Distributed transactions.

5.2.2.4 Miscellaneous Services

Table 5.1 lists many other services that can be used to interconnect applications. Here are some examples:

- *Electronic mail services*: These services are being used more frequently due to the popularity of electronic mail applications. Examples of the protocols to support these services are X.400 of the OSI and simplified mail transfer protocol (SMTP) of the TCP/IP Suite.
- *Network management services*: Many network management services and protocols have been developed to interconnect network management applications. Examples are the Common Management Information Protocol (CMIP) of OSI and the Simplified Network Management Protocol (SNMP) of the TCP/IP Suite. We have already discussed this topic in a previous chapter.
- *Electronic data interchange*: (EDI) This standard has been developed for business and financial applications (e.g., billing, purchase orders). Most applications of EDI have been intercompany (e.g., between material buyers and suppliers). Recent standards have been developed for the exchange of technical specifications, test results, service orders, bills, and financial data. EDI standards specify the syntax and semantics of business and financial documents but do not specify the method of transmission. Detailed information about EDI can be found in the Data Interchange Standards Association publications on EDI.
- *Distributed applications protocols*: Many protocols and standards have been introduced to support the development and operation of distributed applications. An example is the Distributed Applications Framework/Open Distributed Processing (DAF/ODP), which is an OSI framework and model for distributed applications. Other examples are Open Software Foundation's Distributed Computing Environment and Unix International's ATLAS. We will discuss these in Chapter 9.
- *Directory services protocols and security protocols*: These provide naming and security standards for distributed computing.

- *Distributed Office Architecture (DOA) and Format*: This is an OSI standard being developed for office automation.
- *Job transfer and management (JTM) protocols*: These protocols define the standards for office automation (e.g., document formats) and for batch remote job entry (RJE) to a remote computer and receive the results, respectively.

We have listed only a few of the application services and protocols being developed. Many other standards are being developed that will be of significance in the future. An example is the HyTime standard which is being developed to represent hypermedia (a combination of hypertext and multimedia) information. A review of HyTime can be found in the *IEEE Computer Magazine*, August 1991, pp. 81–84.

A major issue in providing application interconnectivity services is the integration of many of the services listed so far in the operating system kernel. These operating systems, called distributed operating systems (DISOS), are an area of active research. DISOS are constructed by using client-server and/or peer-to-peer models. We will discuss DISOS in Chapter 7.

5.2.3 Interprocess Communications (User Invisible Building Blocks)

The high-level services reviewed so far are built on top of basic building blocks, commonly referred to as interprocess communications (IPCs). These building blocks can be arranged in a variety of ways to support different paradigms and provide different type of services.

5.2.3.1 Paradigms for Interprocess Communications (IPCs)

Distributed programs communicate with each other through messages which travel over communication channels. The basic difference between parallel (concurrent) programs and distributed programs is that parallel programs can use shared memory to transfer information through global variables while the distributed programs cannot. Due to this reason only some of the algorithms and techniques developed for efficient parallel and concurrent programs are applicable to distributed programming <Andrews 1992>. This situation could change as the research in developing shared memory distributed computer systems makes progress (see Nitzberg <1991> for a survey of issues and approaches in shared memory for distributed computing).

Distributed programs (clients/servers or peers) can use different paradigms to exchange messages. (According to the Webster Dictionary, a paradigm is an example serving as a model. Thus the term paradigm and model are used interchangeably). Clients, servers and peers can use the following well known paradigms.

Request/response processing: According to this paradigm, one process makes a request and the other process responds to the request. The request can be simple (e.g., retrieve time of day) or complex (e.g., retrieve all customers from Chicago who have a good credit rating). Each request/response is treated as a separate unit of work, thus each request must carry enough information for a reply. This paradigm is currently used very heavily in C-S computing where a client issues a request and a server responds to it. This paradigm can also be used by peers where process 1 sends a request to process 2, process 2 sends the response back, and later sends an independent request to process 1.

Conversational processing: This paradigm allows remote programs to engage in a dialogue where each interaction is not a self-contained and independent unit of work. Instead, just like human conversations, the interactions depend on the context of the conversation (this implies that some context related information is kept and used during the conversation). An example of a conversation is calling a travel agent for an overseas trip: both parties ask many questions, think, search their knowledgebases, exchange information, and reach agreements (the agreement could be made because one of the parties is exhausted!). A business-oriented example of conversational processing, also called dialogue processing, is an executive information system in which a high-level view of budget is presented, which is later queried for more details on specific budget items. Conversational processing requires both parties to be alive during the conversation. In addition, the exchanges are usually synchronous (i.e. half duplex). This paradigm can be used by clients, servers or peers.

Queued message processing: In this paradigm, the receiver stores the incoming message in a queue and works on it when free. This model, used in many transaction processing systems (see Chapter 6), allows the senders to asynchronously send requests to the receiver (i.e., full duplex operation). Once a request is queued, the request is processed even if the sender is disconnected (intentionally or due to a failure). In queued message processing, arriving messages are first queued and then scheduled for execution. Once execution begins, the sender does not interact with the execution process. In contrast, the sender interacts with the executing message during conversational message processing. Queued message processing can be used for peer-to-peer or client-server paradigms.

These three paradigms are very popular and are supported by many suppliers. However, several other paradigms have been presented in the literature. Here are some examples (a detailed discussion of these, and other, paradigms with numerous examples for algorithm analysis can be found in Andrews <1991>):

One way data flow from one process to another. This can be used when response is not expected and is natural for batch programs which receive streams of input and produce streams of output. This technique minimizes control (handshaking) messages between distributed programs and is simplex (one way traffic). For example, this technique can be used in file transfers and invocation of remotely located text formatters (e.g., Unix Troff).

Broadcasting. In this paradigm, one program needs to send the same data to several other programs. Broadcasting is a commonly used technique in network technologies and is often implemented as a low-level primitive (e.g., in Ethernet). In order to implement broadcasting between application programs (e.g., to notify loss of a critical data file), the application programs have to choose and implement search criteria such as spanning trees.

Token passing between distributed programs. This technique, also borrowed from data link layer technologies, can be used between application programs to circulate messages.

Heartbeat and probe/echo processing. The processes send messages to neighbor processes and forward requests to successor processes, respectively. These algorithms are used in many cooperative processing situations where none of the servers have complete information. In these cases, the servers coordinate their work with each other by sending/receiving messages to neighbors and successors.

Replicated server processing. This is used when many servers at different sites perform same activities. For example, many name servers may be replicated in a network. The replicated servers can either choose one server to perform the task or split a task among many replicated servers for load balancing.

These paradigms can be implemented by using the protocols and services described in the next section. Which paradigm should be used when? The main consideration is minimization of the communication message traffic and reliability of the protocols. However, we need to keep the following factors in mind:

- *Application requirements*: Which paradigm best meets the application needs?
- *Time and money constraints*: How much time and money is allowed for this project?
- *Availability of IPC support software*: What is commercially available to satisfy application needs within the time and money constraints?

5.2.3.2 Services and Protocols for Interprocess Communications

The following interprocess communications services can be used to implement the paradigms discussed above:

- Network-independent services such as remote procedure calls (RPCs), remote data access, and X Protocols. RPCs are widely supported because they allow programmers to issue calls to processes which may be at a remote site. This enforces the desirable features of transparency where the two parties can be anywhere in the network. RPCs, discussed in Section 5.5.4, are used frequently to implement the request/reply paradigm (in fact, this paradigm is commonly referred to as the RPC paradigm). Remote Data Access (RDA) standards, discussed in Chapter 6, are being developed specifically for ad hoc query processing across computers. X protocols are used to support X Window.
- Network dependent protocols and services in which the remote messages are sent and received by using the commands of application layer or transport layer protocols of different network architectures. Examples are the TCP/IP based Sockets, OSI based Remote Operations Service Elements (ROSE), MAP based Manufacturing Message Services (MMS), SNA based Advanced Program to Program Communications (APPC), LAN based NetBIOS, and OSI based Message Handling Service (MHS). Many of these services, discussed in Section 5.5.3, are being implemented on different network architectures and computers. Although this introduces some platform independence, however, the developer still has to know

that he/she is interacting with a remote entity over *some* network. Most of these services are at layer 7 but some applications may use lower-layer protocols such as X.25 packets and Ethernet messages for performance purposes. In fact, if an application program interface (API) is available at any layer, applications can be built above that layer.

These services can be usually accessed by application programs through application program interfaces (APIs). An API is basically a set of software routines which can be called by application programs (APIs specify call parameters, return codes, etc.). For example, the Socket API allows a C program to issue calls such as CONNECT, READ, WRITE, etc.

Theoretically, a user can choose a paradigm which best suits the application needs and then implement the application by using any of the services discussed above. In practice, life is not so simple. For example, the response/request paradigm is implemented frequently by using RPCs in TCP/IP networks (available RPC packages are typically implemented by using TCP/IP Sockets), and conversational processing is widely supported on SNA networks by using APPC/LU6.2. The best choice may be to use a remote procedure call (RPC) facility and turn to other paradigms if RPC does not satisfy the problem requirements. As an example, a developer may decide that broadcasting is the best paradigm for an application. However, the available RPC services may not support the broadcast paradigm. In such a case, the developer has two choices:

- Implement broadcast messages by using a "low-level" application layer service such as TCP/IP Sockets, or
- Use the available RPC facility and "postpone" the development of broadcast messages.

Availability of off-the-shelf RPC facilities for application development creates interesting management versus technical tradeoffs. These issues are not commonly discussed in the academic/research literature. We will visit these issues again in Chapter 8, Section 8.6.2, when we discuss distributed applications development.

5.2.4 Standards in Application Interconnectivity: The OSI Application Layer

The OSI Application Layer structure provides a framework for standardizing the application interconnectivity options. Figure 5.6 describes the structure of the application layer. As stated previously, some of the application layer services are "complete services" (e.g., file transfer, electronic mail) while others are basic building blocks from which other complete services can be developed. Appendix A reviews these services.

The OSI basic stack consists of the ACSEs (Association Control Service Elements) plus the Presentation and Session Layer functions. This stack can be used to provide basic data transfer between any applications in the OSI Model. Many other services expand the OSI basic stack. For example, the OSI ROSE (Remote Operations Service Element) supports request/reply service for client-server applications,

7. Application Layer Complete (High-Level) Services & Protocols • Virtual Terminal (VT) • File Transfer Access Method (FTAM) • X.400 Electronic Mail • X.500 Directory Services • Remote Data Access (RDA) Basic Building Blocks • ACSE • Transaction Processing (TP) • CMISE • ROSE • Others
6. Presentation Layer 5. Session Layer 4. Transport Layer 3. Network Layer 2. Data Link Layer 1. Physical Layer

FIGURE 5.6 Structure of the OSI Application Layer

TP (Transaction Processing) supports distributed transaction processing, and CMISE is used fo network management. The complete services may use any of these basic building blocks.

These OSI-based standards in application interconnectivity are expected to be used in a diverse range of user applications. Since many of these standards are going through revisions and enhancements, it is best to refer to the latest ISO documents for details.

It is important to note, once again, that the sending and receiving applications must use the same protocols on both sides. To interconnect applications across heterogeneous networks, the user has two choices (see Fig. 5.7):

- Run the same application layer protocols on both sides. It is highly desirable to run the OSI application protocols on both sides. Many of the OSI application protocols are becoming available on non-OSI stacks to make this an attractive option. An example is the RFC1006 specification, which allows OSI upper layers to operate on TCP/IP.
- Use an application gateway to convert between the protocols. For example, an MVS LU6.2 application may interact with a Unix TCP/IP application through an LU6.2-to-TCP/IP gateway, and an X.400-based electronic mail package may communicate with an SMTP-based electronic mail package through an X.400-to-SMTP gateway.

a. Use Same Application Layer Protocols on Both Sides

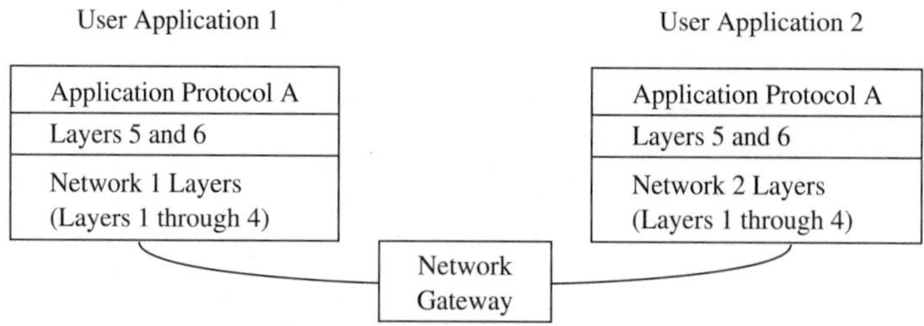

b. Use Different Application Layer Protocols on Both Sides

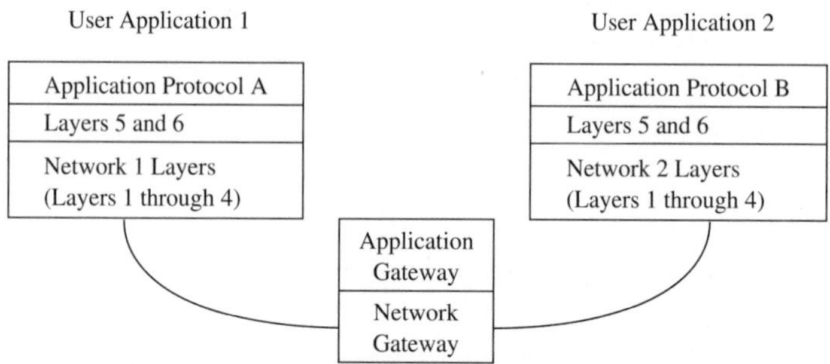

FIGURE 5.7 Application Interconnectivity across Differenct Networks

The first option is attractive and is becoming available for non-OSI protocols. Many vendors are providing layer 7 protocols and services which operate on different lower-layer protocols. For example, MMS (Manufacturing Message Specification) was originally developed for MAP but is now available on DECNET, Ethernet LANs and Tandem TCP/IP networks. Similarly, LU6.2/APPC was originally developed on SNA but is now available on token ring LANs, DECNET and SUN TCP/IP networks. It appears that the most popular application protocols will be available on all major network architectures. The implications of same layer 7 protocols on many networks are as follows:

- Specific application layer protocols can be used for specific application types independent of the network. For example, manufacturing applications residing on any network can use MMS for sending/receiving messages.
- Applications using the same application layer protocols can interoperate across networks. For example, an application residing on SNA can exchange messages with an application residing on TCP/IP by using ROSE or APPC.
- The advancements in lower layers are hidden from the application layer services. For example, most network architectures are planning to support fiber optics and ISDN services at the first two layers without having to modify the higher-level layers. (Unfortunately, this is not true in all cases. Some Gigabit network applications require specialized lower-layer services.)

5.3 Client-Server Computing Revisited

5.3.1 Definitions

We have informally introduced and discussed several terms such as client-server model, client-server computing, client-server applications, and client-server systems. Let us define these terms before proceeding with technical discussion of the components of C-S computing.

Client-server model is a concept for describing communications between service consumers (clients) and service providers (servers). Figure 5.8 presents a simple C-S model. As stated previously, the basic distinguishing feature of C-S model is that a client initiates an interaction with a server by sending a message or by invoking an operation. (In contrast, either process of a peer-to-peer model can initiate an interaction.) A server may become a client when it issues requests to another server. The client request and additional information is placed into a message that is sent to the server. The server's response is similarly another message that is sent back to the client. The clients and servers

- Are independent parallel processes
- May run on the same machine or on separate machines
- May run on dedicated machines (the term "server" is used commonly in LANS to refer to a machine which is dedicated to provide many LAN services)
- Can hide internal information
- Can be implemented over peer-to-peer protocols
- Allow enforcement of applications and structure rules at the server, thus reducing the need for "global rules"
- Require synchronized servers for duplicate data and failure management.

A *client-server system* is a system, hardware and/or software, which is based on the C-S model. Client-server systems are appearing in two main forms: client-server computing and client-server applications. We will use the term client-server system when it is not necessary to distinguish between implementations of the client-server model.

Client-server computing is an implementation of the C-S model to deliver computing services such as print services, mail services, file services, etc. In C-S computing, the clients and/or the servers may be specialized machines with specialized

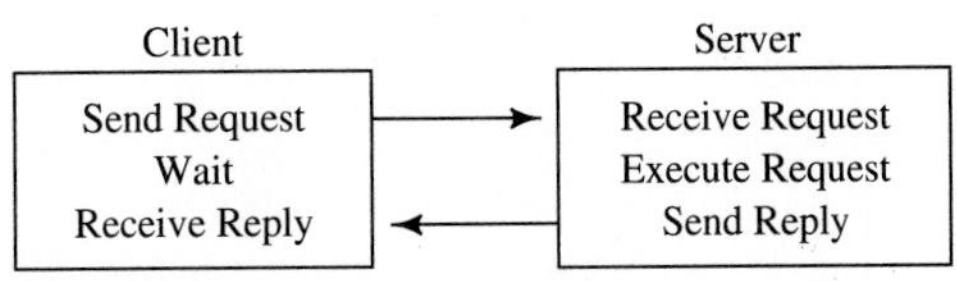

FIGURE 5.8 Client Server Model (Very High-Level View)

hardware/software capabilities, interconnected through a network. For example, in LANs, dedicated computers may be used as print servers, file servers, and database servers. In C-S computing, many servers may provide the same services or a service may be available from only one centralized server. A typical C-S computing environment is presented in Fig. 5.9. Examples of some of the commonly known clients and servers in C-S computing are discussed in Section 5.4.

Client-server applications are the applications which use the C-S model. For example, an order-processing application can be implemented by using the C-S model. In this case, application clients reside on workstation to perform initial checking and processing; the application servers are at the corporate mainframe to perform final approval and shipping. We will discuss client-server applications in Chapter 8.

Figure 5.10 shows a layered view of the main components of C-S computing: client processes, client interfaces, server processes, server schedulers and network interfaces. Let us review the functions performed in each component.

Client processes perform the application functions on the client side (see Fig. 5.10). Client processes can range from simple user interfaces and spreadsheets to complete application systems. A client process, commonly referred to as a client, has the following characteristics:

- It interacts with a user through a user interface. User interfaces are typically graphical user interfaces (GUIs) which allow users to issue queries and invoke services through icons. GUIs attempt to hide the location of the services by representing them through icons which a user can invoke through a pointing device (e.g., a mouse) without having to explicitly log on to different systems.
- It performs some application functions, if needed. Examples of the application functions include spreadsheets, report generation, and object manipulation.

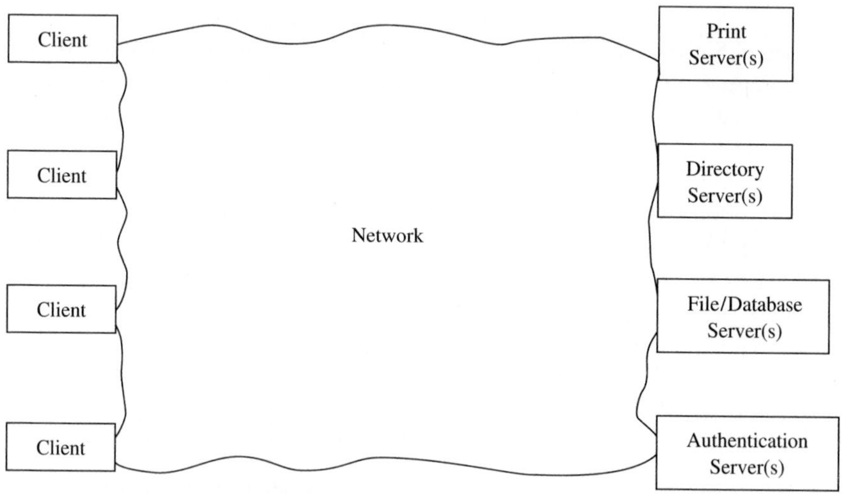

FIGURE 5.9 A Typical Client Computing System Server

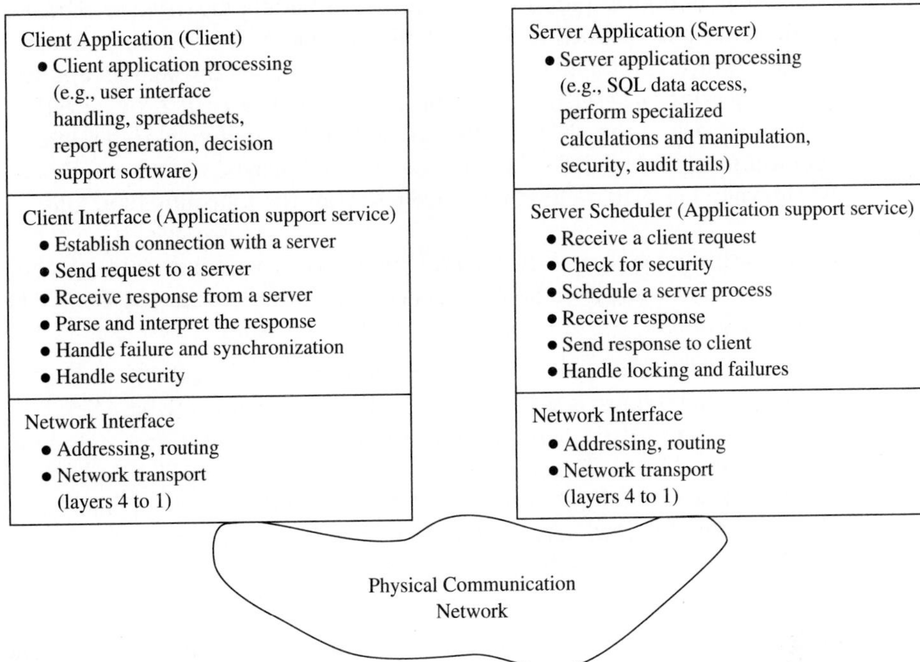

FIGURE 5.10 Client-Server Components

- It interacts with a client interface by forming queries and/or commands in a format understandable by the client interface. This interface is important because if a client interface changes, then the client application will have to change (different vendors provide different client interfaces). Ideally, this interface should be independent of networks, operating systems and platforms.
- It receives the responses from the client interface and displays them, if needed, on the user interface.

Server processes perform the application functions on the server side. A server process, commonly referred to as a server, has the following characteristics (Fig. 5.10):

- It provides a service to the client. Server processes can be very simple functions such as time of day (TOD), or sophisticated applications such as order processing, information retrieval or CAD/CAM services. Other examples of server processes are print services, database services, and mail services.
- Ideally, it hides internal information (e.g., the type of data being accessed) so that the clients do not have to know these details.
- It is invoked by the server scheduler (described later) and returns the results back to the scheduler.

Client interfaces play a crucial role by providing the interfaces between client applications and remote servers. Client interfaces are usually a set of software modules which can be invoked by the client processes through an application programming interface (API). For example, many SQL servers provide API/SQL software which a client process can use to send SQL statements to the SQL servers. In addition, most of the RPC software on a client side can be viewed as a client interface. As shown in Fig. 5.10, a client interface performs the following functions:

- Establish connection with a server by issuing commands through the network interface. For example, a Socket connect command is issued if a TCP/IP network is being used.
- Send request to a server by using a protocol understandable to the server. For example, the request is sent in a Sybase Server format if a Sybase Server is used on the other side. At present, different servers use different protocols. Standards in remote procedure calls and remote data access are expected to address this problem especially for database accesses. At present, different client interfaces may be needed for different servers. For example, Gupta Technologies offers different client interfaces for Sybase and Oracle servers to connect to the Gupta SQL Windows clients.
- Receive response from a server, and parse and interpret the response. Once again, the client interface must understand the format in which the server is sending the results.
- Handle failure and synchronization of activity if needed. For example, if the server disappears during communications, then the client interface software is responsible for detecting this failure and initiating proper actions.
- Handle security by passing the client ID and password to the server so that a user does not have to logon to different systems explicitly.

Server schedulers monitor the client requests and invoke appropriate server processes. As shown in Fig. 5.10, a server scheduler performs the following functions:

- It receives a client request from the network interface and parses the request. This interface can provide open services, which can receive requests from any clients that understand the server interface, or closed services which do not publicize the server interface specifications.
- It checks for security by authenticating the client. For example, server schedulers on MVS use Resource Access Control Facility (RACF) for verification.
- It schedules a server process to satisfy the client request. The service requested may be a single-step service in which the service is performed by the scheduler itself (e.g., a time of day service). Most requests require multistep, multithreaded, services in which the scheduler listens to the incoming messages, invokes a server process to handle the service, and goes back to monitoring.
- It receives response from a server process and sends the response back to the clients.

- It is responsible for handling locks and attempts to recover from failures in clients and/or other components.

The server schedulers can be quite complex depending on the type of services needed. Design of a multistep server scheduler is a complicated task which requires attention to scheduling, network protocols, error handling, performance and security. Typical multistep servers for mainframes range between $100,000 to $200,000. Open services need to include extensive security and reliability code because anyone can invoke them. In addition, server schedulers in large systems must be able to handle thousands of client requests. Workstation-based systems need to demonstrate the ability to handle thousands of requests typically found on mainframe systems. Server scheduling is also dependent on operating systems.

Network interfaces provide the basic addressing and transport mechanisms across a network. These interfaces communicate with the server schedulers and the client interfaces (Fig. 5.10). Typical network interfaces use TCP/IP, SNA, and LAN protocols such as NetBIOS and Novell Netware SPX/IPX. Many C-S systems at present are heavily based on LAN technology. This implies that they use "lightweight" (connectionless) protocols in which checking and sequencing are done by applications. They also assume a reliable network which may not be a good assumption for wide-area networks (WANs). The network interconnectivity issues we discussed in Chapter 3 are relevant to the network interfaces of client-server systems. For example, if a Unix TCP/IP client needs to access an MVS SNA server, then a TCP/IP to SNA gateway may be needed for network interface. This approach is used in the Sybase Client-Server systems.

It should be noted that the components discussed above are based on the functional model shown in Fig. 5.10. In practice, some client processes are bundled with client interfaces and some server schedulers include server processes. Literature on C-S computing is growing steadily. A technical review of C-S computing is given by Sinha <1992>. A conceptual framework for modeling distributed services from collections of servers is given by Nehmer <1992>. State-of-the-market and state-of-the-practice articles on client-server computing appear regularly in trade journals such as *Datamation*, *Database Programming and Design*, and *Data Communications*. The book by Inmon <1991> gives many details.

5.3.2 Pragmatic Overview of Technical Issues

Operating System Issues. Scheduling of server requests is dependent on operating systems. In some operating systems, such as Unix it is easy to schedule new requests by using forking and demons. However, in the MVS operating system, scheduling is done by transaction managers such as IMS and CICS, which are oriented toward a terminal-mainframe model. To build a server on MVS, considerable effort is needed to use IMS and/or CICS as server schedulers. In some cases, several instances of a server are installed on the same or different machines for performance or availability reasons. A server manager may be needed to create servers on demand and route requests to a duplicate server if one server fails. Server schedulers for MVS as well as

Unix environments are becoming commercially available. Examples are the INETD server scheduler for Unix and the IBM/370 Server Task Manager for MVS.

Interoperability Issues. Clients and servers must use the same or similar protocols and/or services in order to interoperate (work together). For example, if a server uses RPCs, then the clients must adhere to the specific RPC implementation used by the server. Unfortunately, different implementations of RPCs are available (e.g., SUN RPC, Netwise RPC, OSF RPC) which do not interoperate with each other. In another case, if TCP/IP Sockets are used by the clients and not by the server, then they will not interoperate. Basically, clients and servers must understand each other. This becomes a serious problem if clients and servers from different vendors are intermixed. Better standards are needed in this area. At present, client interfaces and server schedulers play a key role in interoperability as front ends to the client processes and server processes (see Fig. 5.10). For example, a client application can interoperate with different servers by using different client interfaces.

Failure Handling. Failure handling in C-S systems is nontrivial. A client and server can fail independently and then be restarted. For example, a server or the transport network may fail before the server had a chance to execute the request, or a server may crash after completing a request. For some services (e.g., read only), no harm is done if a service is requested several times whenever an error occurs. However, if the service performed updates, then some sequencing control is needed to assure that the same service is not executed more than once. Error handling becomes especially difficult when the server communicates with other servers to provide a service (e.g., a server responsible for managing distributed data may need to communicate with other sites where the copies of data exist). A variety of techniques, such as two-phase commit protocols, are used in such cases. See Chapter 6.

Security. Client-server systems introduce many security exposures. For example, it is the responsibility of the server schedulers and server processes to assure that unauthorized clients do not get access to servers. The clients and servers may use encryption routines and authentication protocols for information access. Here is one possible scenario:

- Client interface authenticates if the client can request the service.
- Client interface encrypts the data if needed.
- Server scheduler authenticates the client request.
- Server process decrypts the message, performs additional security checking and builds audit trails.

This is dramatically different from the traditional mainframe model, in which all users of the mainframe resources were under the control of a centralized security manager such as IBM's Resource Access Control Facility (RACF). The OSI standards for security are under development at present and are expected to address peer-to-peer security, which is more general than client-server.

Performance. The performance of a C-S system must be carefully evaluated. For example, the network delays as well as the node processing must be taken into account when designing distributed applications. For node processing, we need to examine the tradeoff of firing up a new server for every client request versus a single reentrant server, which is called repetitively. The main network performance consideration is minimization of the communication messages between clients and servers.

The network performance problems are aggravated due to several reasons. First, the network traffic patterns are not predictable, primarily due to the message traffic and remote joins between distributed databases. This presents challenges in estimating the bandwidth and the best/worst cases for a given network. Second, the network response time is hard to predict because a given message can be routed through several potential delay points. Third, the need for enterprise network management becomes more acute because all networks, LAN as well as WAN, provide transport services from clients to servers located anywhere in the network. In heterogeneous networks, the need for cooperation between network management applications will increase leading to an enterprise wide network management. In fact, an enterprise-wide network manager is itself a distributed cooperating processing application. Finally, the problems of scaling are not well understood. It is not clear, for example, how the current protocols and algorithms will perform on very large networks that may span many countries <Ozsu 1991>. We should keep in mind that the emerging high-speed broadband networks discussed in Chapter 2 will change many of the networking issues discussed at present.

Considerations in Building Client-Server Systems. At the highest level, developers of C-S applications have the following choices:

1. Buy off-the-shelf systems which provide all components (server scheduler, server process, network interface, client-process, and client interface).
2. Buy off-the-shelf open server scheduler, server processes, and network interface. Write your own clients and client interfaces.
3. Buy off-the-shelf server schedulers. Write your own server processes, clients, and client interfaces.
4. Write everything on your own.

The first choice is most desirable because suitable off-the-shelf systems can save a great deal of time and money. For example, Sybase, Ingres, Oracle, Gupta Technologies, Informix and Information Builders Inc. provide an extensive array of SQL servers, server schedulers, client processes (e.g., Lotus 1-2-3), client interfaces (e.g., API/SQL), and network interfaces (e.g., TCP/IP, SNA, Novell) on a variety of platforms (e.g., Unix, MVS, PC/PS2, Macs). However, this choice is not suitable for many applications which require specialized services. In those cases, the other choices should be evaluated.

In the simplest case, a client-server system needs only two instructions:

- Send a message.
- Receive a message.

However, as shown in Fig. 5.10, clients as well as servers need to establish/break a connection before sending and receiving messages. Additional states may be needed for locking and synchronization activities. In addition, the clients and servers can work as blocked (e.g., clients wait for server to respond) or unblocked (continue processing and be interrupted when the server is done). Client-server systems may support connection-based versus connectionless services with provisions for sophisticated error handling. They may also support procedures with deadlock detection and resolution, sequence checking, synchronization of resources with locking/unlocking for access control, rollback of changes due to failures and interrupts/shutdowns if needed. Additional functions shown in Fig. 5.10 indicate the level of effort needed to build C-S systems. We will discuss the issue of developing C-S systems in detail in Section 5.5.

5.3.3 Why Use Client-Server Computing

The main advantage of C-S computing is that processes at remote sites can cooperate interactively to solve problems. This has many advantages over the older terminal emulation and file transfer services. However, as indicated earlier, despite many C-S systems becoming commercially available, design and use of C-S systems introduces many scheduling, network protocol, error handling, and performance issues. The main question is, What are the considerations in migrating toward C-S computing?

Client-server computing allows desktop computers to be integrated with the intermediate and corporate computers. It is one of the best ways to fully utilize the growing processing power of desktop computers. (More than 100 million desktop computers are expected to exist in the United States in 1995, with total processor power to exceed 400 million MIPS by 1995 Gantz <1991>).

Client-server computing is also a key to gradual downsizing (i.e., migration of applications from mainframes to minicomputers and from minicomputers to microcomputers). For example, as a first step, the user interface processing can be downloaded to the microcomputers while continuing to obtain value from the mainframe services. Then the application programs and data may also be migrated, thus downsizing the entire application.

Will C-S computing succeed? While there is no guarantee, there are some positive indications. First, organizations are seriously trying to better utilize the desktop computers, and C-S computing is a good framework for using desktop computers for sophisticated user interfaces. Second, it is cheaper to develop applications on desktop computers than mainframes due to the cheaper MIPs at desktop computers (cost per MIP of a desktop computer in 1992 is less than $1000, while it is $200,000 per MIP for mainframes). Third, the push toward integrated environments (e.g., computer integrated manufacturing) lends easily to C-S model because existing applications on different platforms need to communicate with each other for integration. Fourth, many servers have become commercially available (e.g., the SQL servers Moad <1992>, White <1990>, Vinzant <1990>) to make it easier to develop C-S applications. Finally, improvements in database technologies (e.g., SQL queries) and C-S protocols (e.g., sockets, APPC, MMS and RPCs) have made it easier to develop homegrown C-S systems.

Although client-server computing shows many promises, it presents several challenges to management. Some of the challenges are as follows <Gantz 1991>:

- It is very difficult to determine network traffic patterns because some servers may need to coordinate in performing some of the functions.
- The software costs for C-S systems can be higher because a copy of client interface software is needed at each client site. For example, the costs of client interface software for thousands of workstations at $500 per workstation can add up.
- It is difficult to debug applications because a single application may be split across many computing systems. Client-server computing introduces many points of failures.
- The number of products, including network management modules, will increase dramatically.
- Large communication channel bandwidths will be needed to support realtime message exchange.
- The network will need to be managed rigorously to minimize the network failure and thus minimize the price of failing.
- The management and support issues are tough to deal with because many servers need to be developed and managed.
- Advances from several areas (e.g., object-oriented systems, database technologies, communication protocols, RISC-based computing) need to be monitored because these and other technologies influence C-S computing.

An area of special concern is the impact of C-S computing on networks. The network design and management problems are aggravated due to the reasons stated previously.

We should note that the C-S model is not suitable for applications where processes cooperate with each other as peers without any clients or servers. For example, it is interesting to think of a large computing network as a collection of intelligent cells which solve problems in a manner similar to the human nervous system. In human systems, who is client and who is server? Many of the OSI protocols support peer-to-peer interactions and could play an important role in the future of peer-to-peer distributed cooperative processing.

5.4 Examples of Clients and Servers in Client-Server Computing

In a C-S computing environment, a variety of servers, dispersed across a network, can be accessed from clients which may reside at different computers. In this section, we describe some of the servers that are commercially available. We start with simple servers and then describe more sophisticated servers.

5.4.1 Client Examples

Clients typically reside on desktop computers. However, a client may reside on a mainframe. For example, a client program on a mainframe may need to access a database server on a LAN. Here are some examples of clients, ranging from simple to more complicated:

- User interfaces and command processors, which allow a user to send commands to the server. An example is the command processor in LANs which allows users to send commands to print servers.
- An application programming interface (API), which allows programmers to develop client applications in C, Cobol, or other languages. An example is the TCP/IP Socket API which is currently available on PCs, Macs, Unix and MVS computers.
- Client tools which are preprogrammed to access remote servers. These tools do not require API level programming. Examples are the SQL query processors such as Clear Access, spreadsheets such as Lotus Data Lens, fourth generation languages such as PC/Focus, executive information systems such as Lightship, and graphical query generators such as ObjectView. These tools are installed on top of a client interface program which interfaces with the network software. For example, Lotus Data Lens is a client interface which converts the Lotus data access statements to SQL calls for database servers. Many tools are becoming available in this category. See Finkelstein <1992> and Zuck <1992> for a state-of-the-market review.
- Client applications, which access remote data when needed. For example, an order processing application on a workstation may behave as a client and access customer information from a remotely located database server. Some off-the-shelf client applications are beginning to appear in the market. See, for example, Ricciuti <1992> for a a review of human resource applications.
- Client application development tools, which allow development of client applications on workstations. For example, Oracle supports an application development environment which allows development of client applications for Oracle servers.

5.4.2 Terminal Servers

Terminal servers provide concentration services mostly for ASCII terminals. Many ASCII terminals are connected to a terminal server which is connected to a computer system (see Fig. 5.11). A terminal server takes requests from the terminals and passes them to a host. Although a terminal server represents the simplest aspects of a server, we are discussing this because at present more than half a million terminal servers are operational, serving more than 5 million clients (ports) in the marketplace <Hirsch 1990>.

The issue of developing terminal servers for heterogeneous distributed systems is important because in such systems many terminals (or workstations emulated as terminals) need to be connected to different computers supporting different communication protocols. Most of the current terminal servers support protocols such as DEC's Local Area Transport (LAT), Xerox Network Systems (XNS), TCP/IP, or OSI

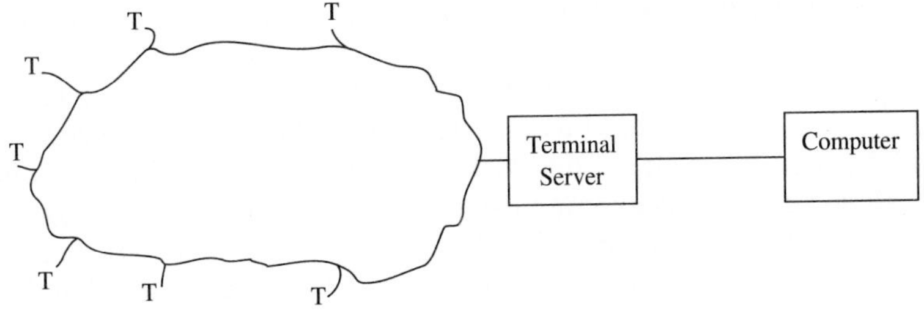

FIGURE 5.11 A Terminal Server

protocols. The main design criterion for terminal servers is performance—the server should pass the messages back and forth with minimal delay. This issue is especially critical for the systems in which large numbers of terminals, or workstations emulated as terminals, are connected to a mainframe. Other server design issues include flexibility, protocol interfaces, and security. A detailed discussion of the terminal server design issues with evaluation of various options is given in Nesset <1990>. An analysis of the state of the market in terminal servers can be found in Hirsch <1990>.

5.4.3 Window Servers and X Window

A window server manages a workstation screen and communicates with clients (applications) to perform screen operations. The need for window servers arises from the requirement to share workstation screens between local and remote applications. The workstation screens are increasingly using sophisticated high-resolution graphics for applications such as CAD and desktop publications. A window is an area of the workstation screen that behaves like a separate screen. This allows windows to support user communications with many applications from a single workstation. For example, five applications running on five different machines may keep five windows open on one workstation, one window per application. The user can interact with different applications by switching between windows by using a keyboard, a mouse, or other input devices.

A window server contains the logic for window operations such as graphical displays, pointing devices, menu selection, dragging of graphical objects to new positions, zooming and rubberband-like line drawings. This simplifies the user interface design of application programs. Basically, a window server is a more sophisticated terminal emulator in which the user interface is managed on the workstation itself and not on the host. The design of a window server is similar to other servers, such as file and printer servers. The clients of a window server are the application processes, which may be running anywhere in the system. Different types of client-server protocols are employed by different window servers. X Window uses remote procedure calls for client-server interactions. Other window servers, such as the SUN NeWS, use languages like PostScript. A window server must try to minimize the communications overhead. Most of the existing window servers minimize this traffic by collecting the messages and then releasing them together periodically. This technique works well for servers where no response is expected (e.g., enlarge screen, drag, color).

X Window is perhaps the best-known window server system and is currently a de facto standard for Unix based systems. This system was developed at MIT circa 1984 as a distributed, multitasking, device-independent and network transparent window server which communicates with interactive applications running on different types of computer systems. The device and network independence features distinguish the X Window system from other window systems, which are dependent on the computing systems and networks (e.g., the Apple Macintosh interface, Microsoft Windows, and Digital Research's GEM.).

Figure 5.12 shows the X Window conceptual model. As mentioned previously, an X client is an application and an X server is an X Window screen manager. The clients and servers communicate through a high-level protocol called X Protocol (or just X). The X Protocol provides the network transparency of X Window. X has been implemented on Unix interprocess communication (IPC), TCP/IP Protocol Suite, Ethernet, token ring, RS232, and many other data link protocols. Each workstation has its own window server which uses the hardware-dependent drivers for that workstation. An X server manages the screen, the keyboard, and a mouse with up to five buttons. The X Window system includes a library of graphics and windowing routines, Xlib, which are linked with X client applications as shown in Fig. 5.12. Although X Window has been primarily developed under Unix, it is not dependent on any operating system. Examples of other implementations of X Window are DEC's VAX/VMS and IBM's MVS.

A single X server may manage several windows on the same workstation or many X servers may run on the same multitasking workstation. In addition, a single

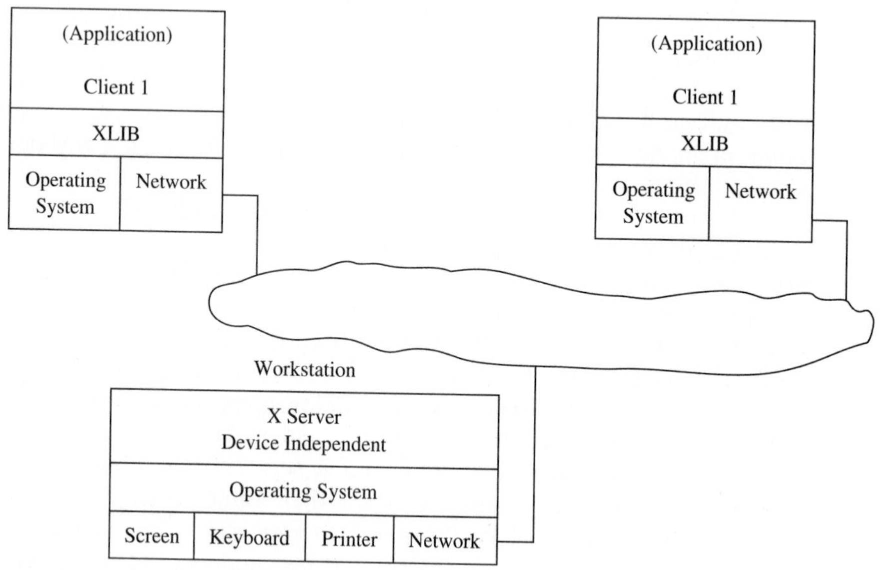

FIGURE 5.12 The X Windows System

X client application can open many windows on a remotely located workstation. This can allow sophisticated groupware systems in which a manager at one site can create windows at other sites for team problem solving. Since many windows can be opened on the same physical screen of a workstation, an intermediate program (window manager) is responsible for managing the workstation physical screen. The X servers issue requests to the window manager for allocating screen space. The communication between the X servers and the window manager is also in X. Conceptually, an X server consists of three layers (Fig. 5.12): a device-independent layer which communicates using the X protocol, an operating-system–dependent layer which communicates with the local operating system for task scheduling, and a device-dependent layer which consists of device drivers. When porting\X Window from one system to another, the operating system and device-dependent layers are modified.

We have highlighted the main features of the X Window servers. Detailed description of X Window programming is beyond the scope of this book. The interested reader is referred to many books on X Window <Scheife 1990, Johnson 1990>.

5.4.4 Distributed File Servers and NFS

Distributed file servers provide transparent access to files located anywhere in the network. The best-known file server is the SUN Network File Server (NFS), which presently is available on most computing platforms. Originally developed by SUN Microsystems, NFS has become a de facto standard for use in building distributed file systems. NFS is designed to be machine, operating systems, and transport protocol independent. It was initially available on Unix-based mini- and microcomputer systems. IBM has announced NFS support on its mainframes under MVS operating systems. This announcement has expanded the availability of NFS to all ranges of computing systems. NFS support on MVS has been expanded by IBM and some other vendors such as Fiberonics. This makes NFS the major mechanism for Unix to MVS interconnectivity.

NFS provides the ability for host computers and workstations running NFS to transparently share files across the entire network. For example, an IBM PC could transparetly access files resident on a MAC, Apollo, Sun or an MVS mainframe. In general, an NFS user at computer C can access a file F in the network without knowing the location of F. Here are the main steps (more details are given in Appendix B):

- Mount the directory of a remote computer (say n1) on your computer.
- Access the files in the remote directory transparently by referring to them or by issuing remote copy command (rcp f1 f2).

The user of NFS basically issues a MOUNT command to mount a remote directory from a remote host to the local host. The user can search the remote directories by using the LOOKUP command and can retrieve and delete remote files by using GET and REMOVE commands. The user can also display the attributes of remotely located files and access them as local files. An UNMOUNT makes the remotely located files unavailable to the local host.

But how can NFS be useful in client-server computing? Here are some examples:

- Two computers (say manufacturing controllers) can share a file (e.g., status information) through NFS. The status file may be located on one computer but the other computer can mount this file and read/update it as if it is a local file.
- A workstation compiler can be used to compile a source file that is located on another machine, say a host.
- Several distributed applications may use the same instructions and diagrams from a host. The host may keep the diagrams and instructions and the other applications may mount these files and access them.
- A central application may directly read the progress being made at various levels by different devices by mounting and accessing the appropriate device files.

Figure 5.13 shows the NFS server organization. The NFS client at C sends the file access commands to the NFS server. The server at host H receives requests from authorized clients at C to access the files at H as if they were local to C. The server at H must have the facilities to concurrently receive and process many client requests. The server at H also provides the facilities for file creation at H. The files at H appear as extensions to the local disk at C.

5.4.5 Database Servers

A database server receives database retrieval/update requests from an application (a client) and returns responses (data) to the client. This configuration, shown in Fig. 5.14, allows the database processing to be performed on different machines in a network. A database server is different from a file server. A file server allows multiple

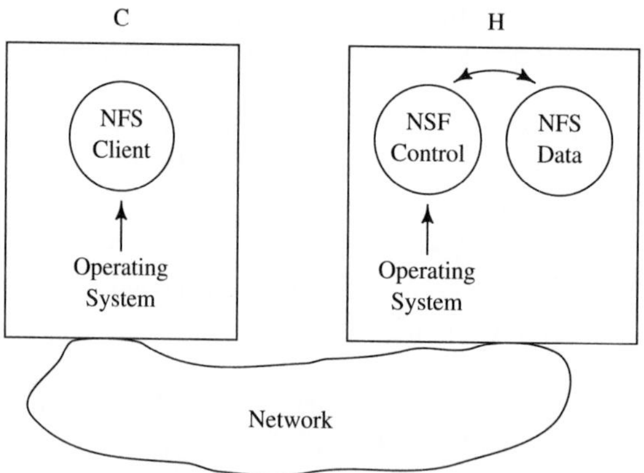

FIGURE 5.13 Network File Services

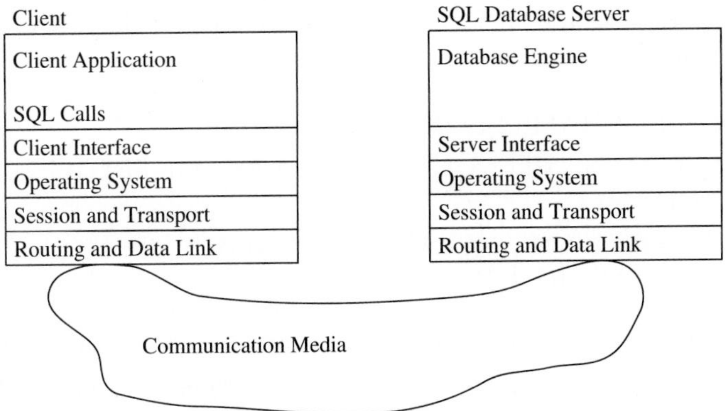

FIGURE 5.14 Typical SQL Database Server

users to simultaneously access flat files such as text files, object codes and sequential/indexed data files. A database server, on the other hand, allows multiple users simultaneously to retrieve databases which represent collections of related data. (The reader not familiar with database technologies should browse through the tutorial on database technologies and SQL in Appendix E.)

How is this different from distributed file servers such as NFS? First, NFS cannot be used for accessing databases, and second, NFS does not include any capabilities to manage duplicate data. Database servers are more complex than file servers because database servers are responsible for maintaining the integrity of a database under security and consistency constraints. They also support different views of data, provide record-level locking, and contain code for automatic logging, failure handling and data dictionary services. A database client-server system considerably reduces network traffic when compared to centralized database systems. This is because in a client-server system only the queries and results go across the network, not the screen formats and large data segments.

Although a database server can provide controlled access to almost any type of database, most present database servers are SQL based—they respond to SQL commands. A client builds an SQL query, which is sent across the network to an SQL database server, which processes the query and sends the response back to the client. Most of the SQL database servers, commonly referred to as SQL servers, have been developed since 1987. Initially developed for LANs, this technology is now moving to MVS mainframes <Snell 1992>. SQL is the standard query language for relational databases and is being used to access nonrelational databases. Appendix E gives a brief overview of SQL; more details about SQL can be found in Date <1990>. Although most SQL servers are designed around the standard bare-bone SQL, each vendor adds extensions to SQL to enhance performance. It is the responsibility of the user to choose extensions judiciously.

An SQL server maintains a dictionary which describes the format and relationships of data (data schema). Some servers provide dictionary facilities for valid data ranges and display formats (YYMMDD or YY/MM/DD). The client does not need to know the data types, lengths, etc. It just sends requests to retrieve the data by issuing an SQL query. For example, a client may issue the following SQL queries:

1. SELECT NAME FROM EMPLOYEE
2. SELECT NAME, ADDRESS, SALARY, AGE FROM EMPLOYEE WHERE AGE > 30
3. SELECT NAME, SALARY, AGE FROM EMPLOYEE WHERE AGE > 30 AND SALARY < 30K

The first SQL query lists names of all employees from an employee database; the second query lists names, addresses, salaries and ages of all employees older than 30; the third query is similar to the second query with an additional condition (salary < 30). Note that the client request does not specify where the employee database is located. This information is supplied by the client interface software (see Fig. 5.14). Each client machine loads the interface software that accepts the SQL calls from users or application programs and converts these calls into network messages that are sent to the server. This interface also receives, interprets, and converts the responses from the server.

Many SQL servers originated in LAN environments, and were installed on LAN server machines. For example, Novell Netware allows servers to be installed as network loadable modules (NLMs) on Netware servers. NLMs run as independent tasks under Netware core operating system. This has allowed several third-party vendors to develop SQL servers as Netware NLMs (see Glass <1992> for a discussion of Netware NLMs). At present, SQL servers run on PS2s, Unix workstations, minicomputers, and some mainframes. The communication protocols include token ring, Ethernet, TCP/IP sockets and APPC. Different vendors support SQL servers on different computing systems, which use different communication protocols with different performance and dictionary options. They also provide different levels of scalability (i.e., as an application grows, a user can migrate from a small server to a large server). Here are examples of some of the available SQL servers:

- Sybase SQL Servers
- Information Builder's EDA/SQL Servers
- IBM OS/2 Extended Edition Database Manager
- Oracle Server for OS/2
- Microsoft SQL Server
- Gupta Technologies' SQLBase Server
- Novell Netware SQL.

For a detailed discussion and analysis of these servers, the reader is referred to Moad <1992>, Ricciuti <1991>, Vinzant <1990>, and White <1990>.

Many database servers may cooperate with each other to manage distributed databases. These servers, called the distributed database servers, coordinate the client access to individual database servers, where each database server manages its own database. We will discuss this topic in more detail in Chapter 6.

5.4.6 CAD/CAM Servers

Dedicated CAD (computer aided design) machines can act as servers to clients located at many sites in the network. The clients may be X Window users or other programs at the plant hosts, area managers, cell controllers, or manufacturing devices. The CAD servers may provide the following services:

- Draw, scale, rotate and animate an object
- Build a solid model of an object
- Convert a feature-based design into geometrical data
- Test a design through simulation, stress analysis, heat analysis, and finite element modeling
- Retrieve existing designs based on similarity of features
- Send design information to other subsystems (product engineering, numerical part programming, robot programming, process planning, tool design, and material requirement planning system).

These services may appear as icons or as menu choices on user workstations located anywhere in the network. The CAD server may use graphic standards and may transfer data to other units by using the Interactive Graphic Exchange Service (IGES) standard.

The computer aided manufacturing (CAM) servers can provide the following services:

- Generate, edit and download numerical part programs based on the output received from CAD
- Prepare schedules, batches, and tool and fixture requirement files
- Serve as gateways between CAD, business systems and flexible manufacturing systems.

The most important role of CAD/CAM servers is that they can interact with each other plus other servers and clients in the network to provide a true integrated environment. In such an environment, the user performs a set of services without having to know the location and internal formats of data involved.

The CAD/CAM servers must support direct human clients as well as programs and machine clients.

5.4.7 Other Servers

Many other servers, in addition to the examples discussed so far, have been developed and discussed in the literature. Examples of some of these servers are as follows:

- Name servers, which translate a user specified name to a physical name of an object
- Directory servers, which replace the manual directories
- Process servers to create and terminate processes
- Time servers to retrieve and display time
- Gateway servers to convert messages and protocols between systems
- Application servers, which provide, for example, a bank checking service, to all clients.

5.5 How to Build and Utilize Client-Server Systems

5.5.1 Overview

Before building C-S software, it is important to ask if "zero-programming" solutions are available off-the-shelf. For example, many vendors at present support a variety of decision support, executive information system, 4GL, query language and form-building clients to access remotely located SQL servers <Finkelstein 1992, Zuck 1992>. If this does not satisfy your application needs, then you may have to build your own clients and servers, or develop software which interfaces with existing client-server support software.

Building C-S systems or interfacing with existing systems raises many questions (see Fig. 5.15):

- How simple or complex should the C-S model be? The complexity of the C-S model depends on whether the servers perform data updates or other functions which require synchronization.
- What functions are performed by the clients versus the servers?
- What application protocols are used by the clients and servers?
- What is the format of the parameters sent and received between clients and servers?
- How are the server processes scheduled and what algorithms are used in the server processes?
- How can the clients and servers uniquely identify the resources across large networks?
- What development tools and environments (programming languages, debugging aids and testers) can minimize the development effort?

A generic model is presented in Section 5.5.2, which can be simplified or extended for different situations.

The C-S processes use application protocols to send and receive information, as shown in Fig. 5.15. As stated earlier, these protocols are implemented in the application layer at two levels:

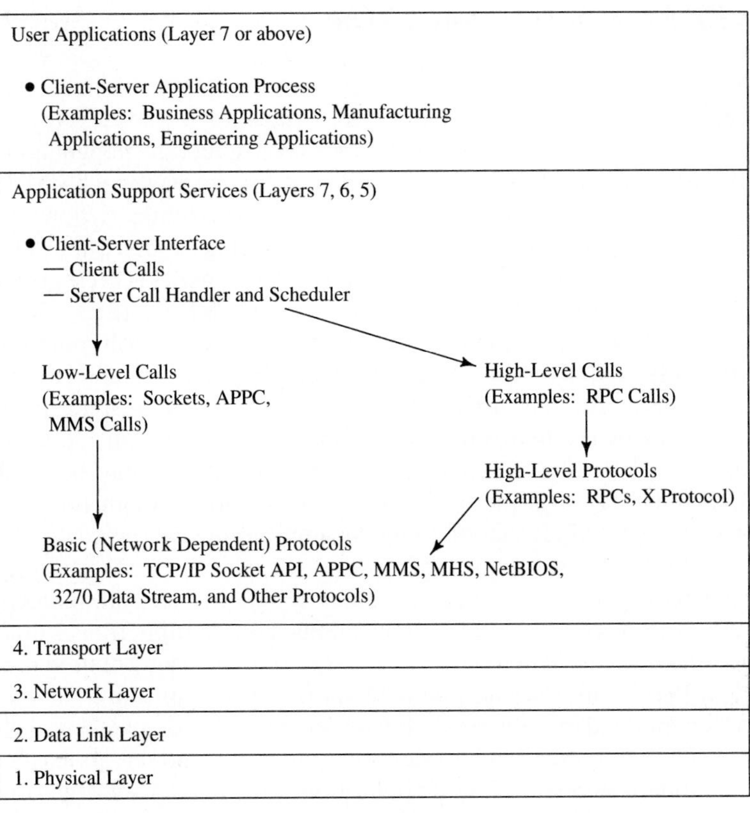

FIGURE 5.15 View of Client-Server Protocols and Services (Extended OSI Model)

- Basic (network-dependent) protocols, and services such as OSI-based Remote Operations Service Elements (ROSE), TCP/IP-based Sockets, SNA-based Advanced Program to Program Communications (APPC), MAP based Manufacturing Message Services (MMS), LAN-based NetBIOS, and OSI-based Message Handling Service (MHS). These services and protocols are discussed in Section 5.5.3.
- "High-level protocols" such as remote procedure calls (RPC). RPC is discussed in Section 5.5.4.

It is important to understand how the parameters are passed and results are returned in C-S systems. An OSI standard, ASN.1, can be used for this purpose (see Section 5.5.5).

Servers are responsible for scheduling the incoming requests. Scheduling of incoming requests, also called threading, depends on the type of operating system. The scheduled requests should invoke appropriate algorithms to minimize the communication messages between clients and servers. These issues are discussed in Section 5.5.6.

Clients can locate the servers through naming and directory services. In addition, specialized tools and environments are needed to minimize the effort in developing C-S systems. Sections 5.5.7 and 5.5.8 review these issues, respectively.

5.5.2 A Generic Client-Server Model

Figure 5.16 presents a generic client-server model which can be extended to handle peer-to-peer paradigm or reduced for simple applications. Many activities are performed in each state. The activities are represented by command primitives, which may be translated into the commands of specific software packages. This model allows for various states: the Initiation State, Begin Atomic Action State, Information Transfer State, Synchronization State, End Atomic Action State and the Termination State. A state transition diagram of the generic model is presented in Fig. 5.16a and the generic commands of this model are shown in Fig. 5.16b.

In the Initiation State the clients and servers establish communications, acquire resources needed for the service, agree on rules for information exchange, and initiate programs at different nodes (dynamically at run time or statically at compile time). This is the first state of a transaction and is required for all applications; the physical connection between the client and server machines may be established through lower-level layers of networks. A set of initiation commands (e.g., ESTABLISH ASSOCIATION) is supported by the application layer protocols.

In the Begin Atomic Action State, the clients and servers agree on locking the resources to maximize concurrent access to shared data by different transactions. This state is primarily needed for applications with multiple transactions which need to access same data. Two phase locking is a common protocol used in this state <Bernstein 1981>. This state may be optional for some applications and may be automatically generated by a distributed database manager for a higher-level application.

In the Information Transfer State, the clients and servers exchange information. This state is necessary for all application categories. A set of information exchange and status-checking commands is needed for communication between remotely located clients and servers.

In the Synchronization and End Atomic States the commit processing, deadlock resolution, and failure recovery in case of client-server failure and/or message loss are handled. Two phase commit is a commonly used protocol in this state <Bernstein 1981>. These states may not be needed for realtime and engineering applications and may be automatically generated by a distributed data and transaction manager for a higher-level application.

In the Termination State, the resources are freed, connections are terminated, and programs are halted. It is desirable to provide the ability to terminate remotely located processes through explicit terminate commands or due to other conditions that may prohibit a process from continuing. This state is needed for all applications. A set of termination commands is needed in this state.

Each activity in the model is presented by a request/response pair. In some cases, this pair may need to be extended for additional verification. For example, the following commands may be needed for a rigorously verified operation:

CLIENT	*SERVER*
1) COMMAND.Request	2) COMMAND.Indication
	3) COMMAND.Response
4) COMMAND.Confirm	5) COMMAND.Confirmed

a. The State Transition Diagram

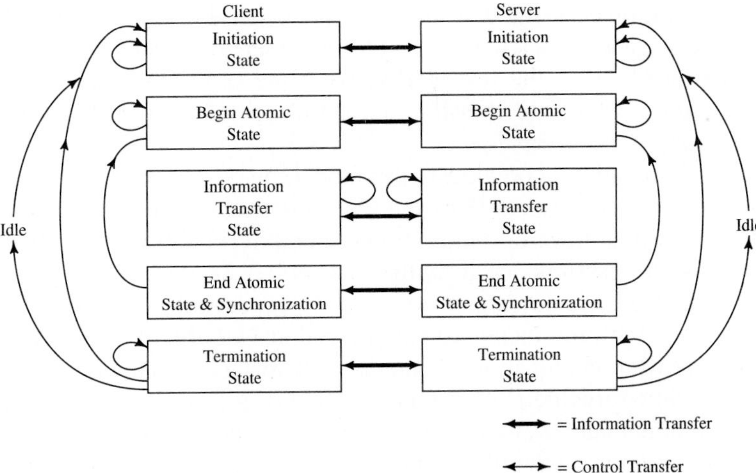

b. Generic Model Commands

	Client	Server
• Initiation State	1. ESTABLISH-ASSOCIATION.Request	• ESTABLISH-ASSOCIATION.Response
	2. ACQUIRE-RESOURCES.Request	• ACQUIRE-RESOURCES.Response
	3. INITIATE-PROGRAM.Request	• INITIATE-PROGRAM.Response
• Begin Atomic Action State	1. BEGIN-ATOMIC.Request	• BEGIN-ATOMIC.Response
	2. LOCK-RESOURCES.Request	• LOCK-RESOURCES.Response
• Information Transfer State	1. REQUEST-TO-SEND	• READY TO RECEIVE
	2. SEND-INFORMATION (normal) or SEND-IMMEDIATE	• RECEIVE-INFORMATION (normal) or RECEIVE-IMMEDIATE
	3. WAIT	• SEND ACKNOWLEDGEMENT
• Synchronization State	1. PREPARE-TO-COMMIT	• READY-TO-COMMIT
	2. COMMIT.Request or REFUSE TO COMMIT	• COMMIT.Response
	3. CANCEL/ROLLBACK ROLLED BACK	• CANCELLED/
• End atomic Action State	1. UNLOCK-RESOURCES. Request	• UNLOCK-RESOURCES. • Response
	2. END-ATOMIC.Request	• END-ATOMIC.Response
	1. TERMINATE-PROGRAM.Request	• TERMINATE-PROGRAM.Response
• Termination State	2. ABORT-PROGRAM.Request	• ABORT-PROGRAM.Response
	3. FREE-RESOURCES.Request	• FREE-RESOURCES.Response

FIGURE 5.16 A Generic Client-Server Model

(1) Request shows the command generated from the client, (2) Indication shows the operation performed by the server in response to the request, (3) Response shows the message sent back to the client from the server, (4) Confirm shows a message sent from the client to the server to verify if the server has successfully performed an operation, say a fund transfer, and (5) Confirmed is sent back from the server in response to a confirm.

As mentioned previously, this model can be customized for different categories of client-server systems. For example, a simple window client-server system consists of the Initiation, Information Transfer and Termination States. However, complex client-server systems such as the distributed database managers (DDBMs) must include the code for atomic transaction processing, synchronization, and failure-handling. With the increased commercial availability of DDBMs, the need to write synchronization and failure handling code in servers is restricted to the cases where the facilities provided by the DDBMs are not adequate or an appropriate DDBMs is not commercially available for a particular application area (e.g., distributed transaction processing on flat files and hierarchical, network, relational, and object-oriented databases).

5.5.3 Basic (Network-Dependent) Client-Server Protocols

5.5.3.1 Overview

Different basic client-server protocols are used in different industry segments. For example, the TCP/IP Socket application programming interface is used heavily in many engineering and scientific applications, Advanced Program to Program Communications (APPC) is becoming a de facto standard for distributed business applications, and Manufacturing Message Services (MMS) is the standard introduced in the Manufacturing Automation Protocol (MAP) for manufacturing applications. We illustrate these three protocols through an example and the generic client-server model introduced in Section 5.5.2. In addition to these three protocols, many other network-dependent protocols are used in C-S systems. Here is a quick synopsis of the protocols we will not discuss due to space shortage:

- ROS (Remote Operations) is the OSI Remote Operations standard which specifies request/reply protocols in an open environment. ROS utilizes ASN.1 to define the parameters being passed and the results of the remote operations. ROS also uses ASN.1 to indicate groups of operations into ASE for formal description. ROSE implements the OSI Remote Operations protocol standard. In the last few years, ROS has been enhanced to provide more object oriented specifications for user applications and to support connectionless transmissions. Although ROS/ROSE provide an excellent basic protocol standard for client-server systems in an open environment, industrial applications of this standard are rare. Details about ROS can be found in the ISO document ISO 9072.
- X.400 Message Handling System (MHS) is an open system standard for electronic mail. CCITT X.400 was initially recommended in 1984 and was later revised in 1988. X.400 specifies protocols between various functional entities of MHS, defines

addressing and routing functions, and outlines the support for the Electronic Data Interchange (EDI). X.400 is at present used heavily in corporate-wide e-mail systems (many of these systems use a C-S model between mail senders and receivers). Details about X.400 MHS can be found in the CCITT Recommendation X.400, "Message Handling Systems: Service and System Overview," Blue Book, Volume VII, 1988.

- NetBIOS (Network Basic Input Output System) was initially developed by Sytek, Inc. as a high-level (Session Layer) programming interface for IBM PC LANs. In the mid-1980s, NetBIOS became a de facto standard for IBM PC LANS and is currently supported by all major LAN vendors (Novell, Microsoft, Banyan). For example, NetBIOS stack can run in the Novell Netware LANs. Due to the popularity of NetBIOS, many LAN client-server systems use NetBIOS calls to exchange information between clients and servers. Basically, NetBIOS provides a programming interface at the OSI Session Layer level. Technical details about NetBIOS can be found in the IBM Technical Reference Manual, SC30-3383-2, 1988.
- Internetwork Packet Exchange (IPX) and Sequenced Packet Exchange (SPX) were introduced by Novell Corp. in their Netware LANs. Due to the popularity of Novell Netware LANs, the IPX/SPX stack is available on many other LANs for connectivity and interoperability. IPX, a datagram delivery service, operates at the OSI Network Layer level while SPX, a connection-based service, operates at the OSI Session Layer. Novell favors IPX as the communication protocol for C-S applications in Netware LANs <Sinha 1992>. Technical details about IPX/SPX can be found in the Novell Netware manuals and tutorials.

Three client-server protocols (TCP/IP Sockets, LU6.2, MMS) are analyzed through an example client-server application with the following steps:

- Data segment D at computer C3 is transferred to computer C2.
- Client CL at C1 establishes a connection with server SR on C2.
- Client CL sends requests to SR. SR processes these requests and sends responses back to CL.
- The connection between CL and SR is terminated.

This application represents common business, engineering and manufacturing situations. For example, in engineering applications, D could be a CAD file which is sent to C2 for analysis (e.g., stress analysis, drawing, simulation). We can assume that C2 is a specialized machine suitable for CAD work, while C1 is a general-purpose workstation. CL sends the analysis requests to SR and SR sends the results back to CL. In a business application, D could be an inventory file which is downloaded to C2 (which may be a store computer) from C3 (which may be a mainframe). The exchange of information between CL and SR may be the periodic update and synchronization of inventory data. In a manufacturing application, C3 may be a cell controller which downloads a program P as a data segment to robot C2. The client CL sends a request to C2 to activate program P, which actually is a status-monitoring program. CL then communicates with SR to retrieve the status information from P and send it back to CL.

This application can also be used to illustrate the differences between standalone and distributed processing. In a standalone (C1 = C2) environment, D would be a shared data entity between CL and SR, operating under a single operating system and a database manager which can take the responsibility of consistent/concurrent access and failure handling. When C1 and C2 are different, then CL and SR are under two different operating systems, perhaps using different database managers with different levels of hardware and software interfaces and many more points of failure. This increases the complexity of providing consistent/concurrent access and failure handling across networks.

5.5.3.2 TCP/IP Sockets

Many scientific/engineering C-S applications do not require extensive synchronization and failure-handling code. These applications are commonly developed on Unix by using TCP/IP for information exchange between the processes at different nodes. Berkeley Sockets, simply called sockets, are used frequently to develop Unix-TCP/IP client-server systems. Technically, the TCP/IP Socket services belong to layer 4 and 5 of the OSI Model and are application programming interfaces (APIs) which are used to exchange information among clients and servers. Sockets are described in Appendix B. Figure 5.17 shows a sample pseudo code for the example application where a data segment D has been transferred from C3 to C2 through the TCP File Transfer Protocol (FTP). CL sends retrieval requests to SR, which accesses D and sends responses to SR. This retrieval only application does not include extensive code for synchronization and failure handling. The basic TCP/IP Socket commands are also listed in Fig. 5.17 for convenience. A detailed description of Berkeley Sockets with numerous C examples is given in Chapter 5 of the book by Stevens, *Unix Network Programming* <Stevens 1990>.

5.5.3.3 APPC/LU6.2: Application Protocols for Business Applications

Many business applications require locking for concurrent access and commit processing for failure handling. Examples are financial transactions which must complete successfully or undo all changes made. Many proprietary and standard application layer protocols have been developed for business applications. LU6.2 is IBM's strategic protocol for interprogram communications for its SNA networks and has been used in IBM's Customer Information Control System (CICS) to access remote data. In most of the literature, APPC and LU6.2 are used interchangeably. In reality, LU6.2 is a protocol and APPC is an implementation of the LU6.2 protocol on different platforms such as APPC/MVS, APPC/PC, DEC/APPC, APPC/PC, and APPC/MAC. LU6.2 and APPC are described in Appendix C.

Figure 5.18 shows the APPC pseudo code for the example application and lists the basic APPC command verbs. The application programs use these verbs or application statements which activate these verbs. For example, an IMS or CICS program could issue calls with APPC verbs. Most of the code shown in Fig. 5.18 consists of basic instructions for connection and data send-receive. We have used the CONFIRM and CONFIRMED commands to illustrate how an application can ask for confirmation

TCP-Based Code

Server (SR)	*Client (CL)*
1. SOCKET	
2. BIND	
3. LISTEN	
4. ACCEPT	5. SOCKET
	6. CONNECT
	7. WRITE (to socket)
8. READ (from socket)	
• process request	
• Read local data (D)	
9. WRITE (to socket)	10. READ (from socket)
	11. CLOSE, EXIT

Berkeley Socket Command Summary (Basic Commands)

1. SOCKET—creates a socket and specifies socket type (TCP, UDP)
2. BIND—assigns a name to an unnamed socket (handle)
3. CONNECT—establishes a connection between local and remote server
4. LISTEN—server is willing to accept connections
5. ACCEPT—accept a connection and put it on queue
6. WRITE—send data on TCP socket
7. READ—read data from TCP socket
8. SENDTO—send data on UDP socket
9. RECVFROM—read data from UDP socket

Comments:

- Code does not use any locking or failure recovery.
- No synchronization and backout is provided.
  If systems fail, then restart.
  Data are sent as records to show sequencing control.

FIGURE 5.17 Pseudo Code of Program in Berkeley Sockets

of data received. These commands can be useful in committing changes in a transaction failure handling procedure.

5.5.3.4 MMS: Application Layer Protocols for Manufacturing

Manufacturing Message Specification (MMS) is the main Application Layer protocol for manufacturing applications. MAP and MMS are currently available on IBM PC under MS-DOS and will be available on DEC, HP, Tandem, Apollo, and several other computer systems. However, MMS is being developed for non-MAP networks also. For example, MMS has been implemented on RS232 (see Bryant <1988>). Thus MMS may become an Application Layer protocol which is available, like APPC, on many networks. We have described MMS in Appendix D. Fig. 5.19 shows a pseudo code of a manufacturing application where a cell controller downloads a program to a robot and then activates the program in the robot. The main MMS commands are also listed for illustration.

The main advantage of MMS for this example is that explicit commands are available for download/upload and program invocation at remote sites. In addition, MMS provides a large number of commands for status checking, error detection,

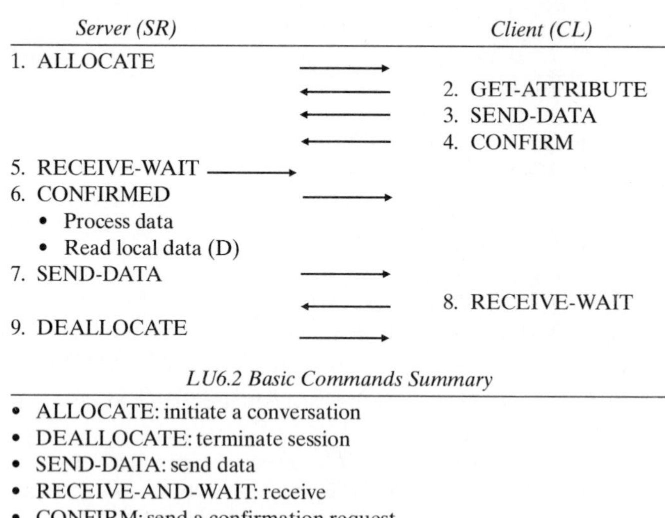

FIGURE 5.18 Example of APPC/LU6.2 Code

alarm detection and journaling, etc. Implementation of these commands using Unix IPC and APPC would be difficult and yield nontransportable code.

5.5.3.5 Summary and Comparison of Basic Client-Server Protocols

Table 5.2 summarizes the commands of the three basic protocols in terms of the Initiation, Atomic Actions, Information Transfer, Synchronization, and Termination states of the generic model. The following observations may be made:

1. TCP/IP Socket is a simpler protocol, while APPC as well as MMS are very extensive and complicated.
2. Sophisticated protocols such as APPC and MMS provide more command verbs than simpler protocols such as Sockets. It can be seen from Table 5.2 that MMS and APPC cover all states of the generic model while Sockets only cover four states. The major advantage of the sophisticated protocols is that they facilitate development of standardized applications. However, the disadvantage is that they are harder to learn, and it is harder to write simple applications due to the large number of choices and options.
3. There are several differences and similarities between APPC and MMS. Both are sophisticated protocols for distributed applications. Unlike MMS, LU6.2 does not use the object-oriented approach of object classes, object instances, and the like. However, it does support the many functions supported by MMS (e.g., remote program load). The main differences between APPC and MMS are that APPC supports extensive data security (e.g., encryption, several levels of passwords,

Cell Controller	Robot
1. INITIATE	2. INITIATE
3. STATUS	
4. INITIATEDOWNLOAD	
5. TERMINATEDOWNLOAD	
6. CREATEPROGRAMINVOCATION	
	7. START
8. SEND	9. RECEIVE
	10. STOP
11. ALARM	
12. JOURNAL	
13. CONCLUDE	

MMS Command Summary (main commands)

- INITIATE—Establish connection between two MMS users
- CONCLUDE—Terminate connection between two MMS users
- ABORT—Abruptly terminate connection
- CANCEL—Terminate a previous MMS service
- REJECT—Reject an unauthorized/invalid request
- READ—Read from a remote MMS user
- WRITE—Write to a remote MMS user
- STATUS—Check the condition of a server
- IDENTIFY—Obtain identifying information about a server (vendor name, model, revision)
- START—Start a program from the idle state
- STOP—Temporarily stop a program
- RESUME—Restart a program
- RESET—Put a program in the idle state
- INPUT/OUTPUT—Read/write from operator's console

/ SEMAPHORE COMMANDS—Create, delete, and verify semaphores
/ DOWNLOAD / UPLOAD COMMANDS—Download/upload programs and/or data files
/ EVENT COMMANDS—Define, delete, check, trigger, and notify events
/ ALARM COMMANDS—Extract, report, and reset alarm conditions
/ JOURNAL COMMANDS—Initialize, read, and write journal entries

Comments: The commands prefixed by an / indicate a group of commands.

FIGURE 5.19 Sample Program Pseudo Code in MMS

restricted access and privilege levels) and data integrity facilities (e.g., two-phase commit protocol). Similar facilities are not available in MMS.

4. The choice and use of application protocols is similar to the choice and use of compilers in many ways. First, different application areas need different protocols in a manner similar to different applications needing different compilers. Second, learning protocols is like learning programming languages; simple protocols like Sockets are easier to learn but may take longer to develop programs while more complicated protocols may take longer to learn but are easier for more complicated situations. Third, the choice of what protocol to use when is similar to choosing what programming language to use when.

TABLE 5.2 Summary of Basic Application Protocol Commands

	UNIX Sockets	*APPC*	*MMS*
Initiation State Commands	• SOCKET • BIND • LISTEN • ACCEPT	• ACTIVATE_DLC • ATTACH_LU • ATTACH_PU • TP_STARTED • ALLOCATE • CHANGE_LU • CNOS	• INITIATE • START • RESET
Begin Atomic Action State Commands	None	• ALLOCATE SYNC-LEVEL • SYNCPT	Assumed
Information Transfer Commands	• SENDTO/WRITE • RECVFROM/READ	• RECEIVE_AND_WAIT • RECEIVE_IMMEDIATE • SEND_DATA • SEND_ERROR • WAIT	• READ • WRITE % FILE COMMANDS • STATUS
Synchronization State Commands	None	• TEST • CONFIRM • CONFIRMED • GET_ATTRIBUTES • GET_TYPE • POST_ON_RECEIPT • PREPARE_TO_RECEIVE • REQUEST_TO_SEND • BACKOUT	% SEMAPHOR COMMANDS • CANCEL • REJECT % EVENT COMMANDS % ALARM COMMANDS
End Atomic Action State Commands	None	• SYNCPT • BACKOUT	• CANCEL • REJECT
Termination Commands	• UNIX EXIT	• DETACH_LU • DETACH_PU • TP_ENDED • DEALLOCATE • FLUSH	• CONCLUDE • ABORT • STOP • KILL
Miscellaneous Commands		• CONVERT • TRANSFER_MS_DATA	% JOURNAL COMMANDS % UPLOAD/ DOWNLOAD COMMANDS % OPERATOR CONSOLE COMMANDS

5. Tools are needed to simplify the task of building client-server systems and to hide the details of client-server systems development. Examples of the existing tools are RPCs, X Protocol for network independent protocols, and MMS-EASE for MMS, which simplifies MMS programming <MMS 1988>.

As stated previously, several other popular protocols, such as the OSI ROSE, X.400, and NetBIOS are not included in this analysis due to a shortage of space.

5.5.4 Remote Procedure Call (RPC)

A remote procedure call (RPC) facility allows a language level procedure call by the client to be turned into a language-level call at the server. In a remote procedure call, a local process invokes a remote process. RPCs have the main advantage that a programmer issues a call to a remote process in a manner that is very similar to the local calls. The RPC software hides all the network-related details from the client-server developers. For example, a single RPC call "open" may invoke many Socket commands such as SOCKET, BIND, LISTEN, CONNECT, and ACCEPT. As discussed in Section 5.1, RPCs are higher-level network-independent commands for client-server systems. The client call is referred to as *request* and the server results being returned are referred to as *responses*.

RPC is a type-checking mechanism in a manner similar to the local procedure call mechanism. RPC calls may be implemented in a compiler by using the same syntax as the local procedure calls. In many RPC facilities, the synchronization of the client and server are constrained because the client is blocked until the server has responded. In addition, binding between servers and clients is usually one-to-one to reflect the language procedure call primitives.

Many RPC systems are commercially available. Remote procedure calls (RPCs) are becoming widely available in Unix environments and some standards are beginning to emerge. Here are some examples:

- SUN RPC system
- Open Software Foundation's RPC
- Netwise RPC
- Novell Netware RPC
- Hewlett-Packard (Apollo) RPC
- IBM TCP/IP RPC
- OSI RPC.

Theoretically, RPCs can be built on top of any basic protocols and services such as LU6.2, Sockets or MMS. In practice, most of the available RPCs are built on top of Sockets.

Figure 5.20 shows the steps that take place in a remote procedure call. The client and server routines are in two separate processes, usually on two different systems. RPC software creates a dummy procedure with the same name as the server and places it in the client process. This dummy procedure, called a *stub*, takes the calling

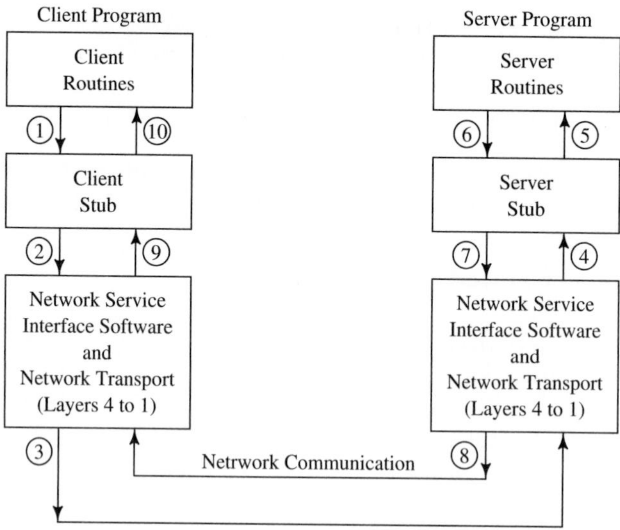

FIGURE 5.20 Remote Procedure Call (RPC) Facility

parameters and packages them into suitable network transmission messages. Another stub is generated for the server side to perform the reverse processing. The following steps are executed in order:

1. The client issues a call to a local procedure, called a client stub. The client stub appears to the caller as if it is a local procedure. This stub mainly translates the remote procedure call into appropriate network messages in the proper Network Interface Services format (Sockets, APPC, MMS, etc.). The stub also determines the actual network address of the server and "binds" to it (sometimes this is done by the runtime libraries).
2. The network messages are sent to the network transport mechanism of the network architecture of the client.
3. The messages are sent over the communication media by using layers 4 through 1 of the client system and are received by the network system of the server. If the network architecture of the client is different from the network architecture of the server, then a gateway may be needed (e.g., TCP/IP to SNA gateway).
4. The server network system contacts the server stub that a request has arrived for it.
5. The server stub gets the network message, translates it into a local procedure call format, and executes this call to the server.
6. The server processes the call and develops a response, which is sent to the server stub.
7. The server stub translates the response into one or more network messages, which are sent to the network system. The stub may cache many messages before an appropriate call to the server can be developed.

8. The server network system sends the response back to the client network system by using the layer 4 to 1 facilities. Once again, a gateway may be needed if the client and server network architectures are dissimilar.
9. The client network system sends the response messages to the client stub.
10. The client stub receives the response message, translates this message into call responses, and sends the responses back to the client. The stub may cache many messages before an appropriate response to the client can be developed.

It can be seen that many decisions are made in various steps of the remote procedure call. Examples of some of these decisions are stub generation, parameter passing, binding, server management, error handling, transport protocols, data representation, performance and security. These issues are briefly discussed next. For a detailed discussion of these issues, the reader is referred to Wilbur <1987> and Chapter 4 of the book on distributed systems by Coulouris and Dollimore <Coulouris 1988>. The book, *The Art of Distributed Applications: Programming Techniques for Remote Procedure Calls* by J. R. Corbin <Corbin 1991> gives many technical details.

Stub generation. Stubs can be generated automatically or by a programmer. For a programmer generated stub, the RPC system provides a set of functions which can be used to construct a stub. This mechanism is used by the SUN microsystem RPC. For automated stub generation, an interface definition language is provided, which is compiled by a stub generator to construct a client and server stubs.

Parameter passing. The passing of parameters between remote procedures creates special problems. For example, if the client passes parameters by value, then these values can be copied by the client stub into the network transmission messages. But if a parameter is passed by address, then it is difficult to pass because memory address on one system does not mean much on another system. For this reason, parameter by address in remote procedure calls is not always allowed.

Binding. Binding refers to establishing a contact between a client and a server. When a call to a server is received by the client stub, it tries to bind the client with an appropriate server on a remote site. Binding requires two major decisions:

- How to find an appropriate host for a service
- How to find the appropriate server on the chosen host.

This is a typical problem in networks. Where should the directory of hosts and servers be located? Some RPC systems use centralized directories to which the servers register when they are started. In other systems, each client system knows the address of the servers. For example, Open Software Foundation's Distributed Computing Environment (OSF-DCE) solves this problem by using a distributed DCE.

Server management. In some implementations of RPCs, several instances of a server are installed on the same or different machines for performance or availability reasons. In some implementations of RPC, there is a server manager which can create servers on demand and route requests to a duplicate server if one server fails. (This is more typical of transaction processing systems.)

Data representation. The data format of the client and server may be different especially when the client and server reside on different computing systems. Data translation may be done at the client or the server site. A common approach used in many RPCs is an intermediate data format which is used by all clients and server stubs in an RPC system. (This approach is used in the OSI RPC and the SUN RPC.)

Type consistency. It is important that the number and type of parameters sent by the client are consistent with the server parameters. This happens especially if the clients and servers are implemented in different programming languages supporting different data types. This issue is important in server design because a server must be able to handle corrupt requests.

Call execution and call semantics. In a distributed system, the client and server can fail independently and then be restarted. In such situations, it is not clear how many times a call to a server has been executed. For example, if a server or the transport network failed before the server had a chance to execute the request, then the call was not processed. However, if the server crashed after completing the request, then the request has been executed once. Some procedures do not harm anything if they are executed several times (e.g., time of day, reading a specific record from a file). The call semantics determine how often the remote service might be performed under fault conditions. The following semantics are possible.

- *Exactly once* means that the server procedure was executed once. This semantics requires extensive checking and is suitable for very reliable distributed systems.
- *At most once* means that the server procedure is performed once or not at all. The client as well as the server use sequenced protocol, in which a sequence number is attached to each request. This semantics is checked by the server process to make sure that the server process does not execute more than once.
- *At least once* means that the server process can be executed several times. This semantics allows the client to send the same request for a few times if the server does not respond. This semantics is suitable for read-only servers.

Transport protocols. Most RPC systems have been built on top of TCP/IP Protocol Suite. Either TCP or UDP is used to transmit the messages across the network. If an RPC system allows UDP as well as TCP protocol, then a parameter may be used in the RPC call for a choice. At present, other than TCP/IP, very few transport protocols are supported by the existing RPC systems. It is expected that RPC facilities will be available on other stacks such as OSI and SNA.

Error handling. Many error and exceptional situations can arise in remotely located client-server systems. For example, a server may crash or may go into a loop. In this case, the client may need to recover from the error by using timeouts or may need to stop the server. Similarly, a client may crash before getting response from the server. In this case, the server may hang around and may need to be stopped somehow. In addition, the transport network may fail while the requests and/or responses are being transmitted. Error handling becomes especially difficult when the server communicates with other servers to provide a service (e.g., a server responsible for managing distributed data may need to communicate with other sites where the copies of data exist). A variety of techniques, such as two phase commit, are used in such cases.

Performance and security. Implementation of RPCs introduces many performance and security concerns. For example, the network delays need to be taken into account when designing distributed applications. It has been reported that remote procedure calls incur two to three times more overhead than the local calls <Wilbur 1987>. Some performance studies have highlighted the performance impact of number of parameters and the parameter sizes <Birrell 1984>. This is especially serious when parameter data needs to be converted. A common technique in performance improvement is to use an object-oriented approach in which the server is called to perform operations instead of sending data structures back and forth. In addition, the impact of firing up a new server for every client request (perhaps through Unix forking) needs to be examined. It might be better to keep one reentrant server which is called repetitively every time a client needs the service. It is also important to verify the security of the client before sending the response to it. Multithreaded server environments help this. The Open Software Foundation supports a secure RPC to address the security issues.

Strengths and weaknesses of RPC. RPCs are well understood, are widely supported and can provide an easy transition from centralized to distributed programs. For example, a centralized program which consists of many procedures to perform specialized tasks can be distributed by simply replacing the procedure calls with the RPC calls to remotely located programs. However, RPC is not a panacea. In many cases, RPCs are awkward, especially because the parameter passing can be only through value and not by reference. The currently available RPCs do not support many paradigms such as queued message processing. Another limitation of RPCs is that they are not well-suited for adhoc query processing. For example, an adhoc SQL query can return many rows with many columns. It is very difficult to set RPC parameters between senders and receivers in this situation. For this reason, a separate data access standard, called Remote Data Access (RDA), is being developed by ISO (see Chapter 6). In a generalized client-server environment, RPC as well as RDA is needed.

Figure 5.21 shows a pseudo code for an RPC system. The system basically consists of six routines. RPC-EXPORT and RPC-LISTEN are used by the server when it starts up. RPC-EXPORT sends the server information (e.g., the socket number) to a directory so that clients can open connections with the server. The server then issues an RPC-LISTEN for any client to establish a session. RPC_OPEN establishes a session between the client and the server. This routine can be used to establish a connection-based or connectionless communication by using a parameter which can help the RPC software to generate appropriate Socket commands. RPC_SEND is used to send (in UDP or TCP format) and RPC_RECEIVE is used to receive data. RPC_CLOSE is used to terminate the session. These routines are compiled by the RPC software and included in the RPC-runtime libraries. The client and server issue the calls shown in Fig. 5.21. The client and server code is compiled to generate the client and server stubs. Note that the same routines can be used to build client-server systems on Sockets, APPC, and MMS by letting the RPC software to generate the appropriate network messages. It should be noted that most of the

RPC Routines:

- Routines RPC_EXPORT, RPC_LISTEN
- Routine RPC_CREATE
- Routine RPC_SEND
- Routine RPC_RECEIVE
- Routine RPC_CLOSE

Client Code	*Server Code*
1. call RPC_CREATE	0. call RPC_EXPORT, RPC_LISTEN
2. call RPC_SEND	3. call RPC_RECEIVE
5. call RPC_RECEIVE	4. call RPC_SEND
6. call RPC_CLOSE	

FIGURE 5.21 Pseudo Code Using RPC

current RPC software packages only generate Unix-based network messages (sockets, TLI, etc.).

5.5.5 Parameter Passing and ASN.1

The format of parameters passed between clients and servers depends on the type of server being used (some servers require a certain parameter format) and/or the RPC software being employed. A major problem in parameter passing is related to complex data structures (i.e., how to represent, encode, transmit and decode data structures between applications residing on different machines). To promote open exchange of information which may contain complex data structures, the OSI Abstract Syntax Notation (ASN.1) has been developed. ASN.1 is used as an interchange language in the OSI ROS, CMISE, MHS and X.500 standards. ASN.1 can be used to specify the format of protocol data units and to specify the services of Application Service Elements (ASEs). It is also being used in several newer areas. For example, HyTime is interchanged using ASN.1 (HyTime is a standard for representing hypermedia information).

ASN.1 consists of two components: a scheme to represent data structures, and an abstract syntax. Most of the coding, encoding, and conversion needed for ASN.1 is performed in the Presentation Layer of the OSI Model. (The coding/encoding can also be done by the Application Layer.)

A data structure defines the data types (e.g., character, integer), data lengths, and data layout. For example, the data structure in an electronic fund transfer application may contain the name, the address, the bank codes, the customer account number, and the amount to be transferred. The basic idea in ASN.1 is to define all the data structure types (i.e., data types) needed by each application and package them in a library. The data are sent by the application along with the ASN.1 data structure name. The receiving application receives the data and the identity of the data structure (usually in the first byte or bytes) and uses this definition to understand the received data structure and perform any conversion, if needed.

ASN.1 is specified in the Backus-Naur Form (BNF) grammar. Many compilers are currently available which convert ASN.1 notation to Pascal, C, and other languages. The following simple example illustrates this:

```
  ASN.1 Notation                          Pascal Code
Customer = SEQUENCE (                     type Customer = record
  name OCTET STRING, --30 characters       name : array¢ 1..301 of
                                                  character;
  age INTEGER                              age : integer;
  fulltime BOOLEAN                         fulltime: boolean;
```

The translation between ASN.1 syntax and a programming language for this simple example is obvious. However, ASN.1 has many unique features. For example, ASN.1 defines a special data type, ANY, which is essentially a union of all other data types. In addition, ASN.1 defines an OBJECT IDENTIFIER which consists of multiple words enclosed by braces. ASN.1 allows construction of additional data types from its basic data types and provides a macro definition facility.

The transfer syntax defines, for each value transmitted, four fields: the data type, the length of the data field, the data field itself, and the end-of-data indicator for variable-length data. This syntax allows an unambiguous definition of data structures being sent on the wire.

ASN.1 is described in the ISO standard document (ISO8824). This document has gone through many enhancements and revisions in the last several years. The serious reader should consult this document, at present published in four parts. An overview of ASN.1 is given in Tannenbaum <1988, Chapter 8>.

5.5.6 Server Design: Scheduling (Threads) and Algorithms

The server scheduler basically listens to the communication channel and invokes an appropriate process. The schedulers can be built by using operating system facilities, transaction managers or specialized application support environments. In Unix networks, for example, a demon process usually "listens" to a socket and then forks a server process. In IBM MVS, transaction managers such as IMS/DC and CICS usually schedule the server processes. In some literature, the scheduling of server requests is called *threads*.

Specialized scheduling facilities are becoming available in different environments for client-server systems. An example of the specialized application support environment for Unix is the INETD facility. INETD is essentially a Unix Demon which monitors the TCP/IP Sockets and invokes an appropriate server to handle a request. To be invoked by INETD, a server must be registered with INETD. An example of server register entries for a server SERV1, which is dedicated to socket number 2000 and which invokes a shell /usr/user1/servdum for user1, is as follows:

```
SERV1   2000         (in /etc/services file)
SERV1   ...    user1 /usr/user1/servdum (in /etc/inetd.conf file)
```

The server does not need to know anything about sockets—each read from STDIN is read from the socket and each write is sent to the socket. This eliminates the need for communication know-how for writing servers on Unix. Facilities like INETD are now becoming available on MVS through the Server Task Manager/370. In addition, an APPC scheduler has been introduced in MVS environments to schedule the APPC/LU6.2 requests and thus make the task of writing a scheduler easier.

The client-server interactions must be minimized for good performance. As stated in Section 5.2.3.1, the message interactions between distributed programs can follow paradigms such as request/response, queued message processing, and conversational processing. The choice of these methods depends on the type of application and the type of facilities available. For example, RPCs are not suitable for queued message processing. If queued message is required, then the programmers may have to be trained for non-RPC programming.

In addition to the message exchange, the server processes need to be efficient in terms of resource consumption. This depends on the algorithms used in the server processes. We have previously stated that the servers can be categorized as single- or multistep servers. In single-step servers, the scheduler itself performs the service. An example is the Date server in which a separate server process is not activated—the scheduler finds the date and returns it. In single-step servers, the server process is usually very small and must be very efficient. In a multistep server system, there are many choices, such as the following:

- Centralized server, which is invoked by many clients
- Schedule each process separately (i.e., no process sharing)
- Conversational server support
- Hierarchical servers for distributed databases (assume global knowledge)
- Replicated servers
- Sharing tasks between replicated processes.

In addition, the type of client-server application system can significantly complicate the task of development. The application may support connectionless or connection-based services with provisions for sophisticated error handling. It may support procedures with deadlock detection and resolution, sequence checking, synchronization of resources with locking/unlocking for access control, rollback of changes due to failures and interrupts/shutdowns if needed. Naturally, someone will have to provide this code, especially if the available products lack these capabilities.

We will visit some of these issues again in Chapter 8.

5.5.7 Naming and Dictionary Services

A client-server system needs to know the names and locations of the objects being managed. For example, a client needing access to a file should be able to access the file by its symbolic name without having to know its network address. A directory service provides a lookup service which translates an object name into a physical network address. For example, in the TCP/IP networks, the Domain Name Services are used to translate a Unix computer name such as BIRD to a physical network hardware address such as 18.32.1.22. In addition, naming and directory services can be used to enforce security by denying network addresses to unauthorized users. The

ANSI/OSI Directory Standard (X.500) is being developed for global naming and directory services. We will discuss naming/directory services in Chapter 7.

5.5.8 Client-Server Programming Languages and Tools

In addition to the aforementioned RPC facilities, special facilities have been introduced by many vendors to simplify the task of building client-server systems. Examples are Digital's DECmessageQ, Allen-Bradley's Network DTL (Data Table Library), Sybase's Data Base RPCs, Netwise's RPCs, and Hewlett-Packard's Integration Sockets. In addition, development of tools and environments for client-server systems is an area of considerable research. It is expected that the task of developing client-server systems will become easier in the next few years due to better development and diagnostic aids.

Most of the client-server systems are being developed by using traditional programming languages such as C, Pascal and ADA. Programmers code RPC calls or network dependent protocol verbs for message exchange. It appears that C is becoming a de facto programming language for client-server development. However, a large number of programming languages are being developed specifically for distributed software and client-server systems. These languages are being driven by the following requirements:

- The programs run on multiple processors and thus can maximize parallelism.
- The programs coordinate with each other through communication messages.
- The programs must be able to deal with partial failures.

An extensive survey of the programming languages for distributed systems is presented by Bal <1989>. This paper discusses 15 distributed programming languages and contains an extensive bibliography, which lists over 100 programming languages. We will discuss some of these languages in Chapter 8.

5.6 Management Summary and Trends

The client-server model is the most popular application interconnectivity option because it allows application processes at different sites to exchange messages interactively. This allows a user workstation to act as a client issuing service requests to print servers, file servers, database servers, etc., which may be located at many remote sites. Basically, a client-server system assumes that there are two communicating processes, one acts as a client and the other as a server. A given system may act as a server as well as a client. The clients and servers are independent parallel systems; may run on the same machine or on separate machines; may run on dedicated machines; can hide internal information; allow enforcement of applications and structure rules at the server, thus reducing the need for "global rules"; and require synchronized servers for duplicate data and failure management. Examples of some of the commonly known servers are as follows:

- LAN servers (e.g., print and file servers), which are used in LANs so that many users (clients) can share the same printers and files.
- Terminal servers (e.g., DEC terminal servers), which allow many terminals to share the same line
- Window servers (e.g., X Window), which manage user windows (screens) on a workstation
- Name servers, which show the location of a named object (e.g., file, program)
- Directory server, which may display the address, telephone numbers, etc, of a given person
- Authentication server, which checks to see if a particular user is authorized to access particular resources
- Database servers (e.g., SQL servers), which take a SQL query and return the desired information (note that the SQL server may in fact access an IMS database).
- Transaction servers (e.g., directory servers), which receive a transaction (e.g., update directory, search directory) and respond appropriately
- Application servers, where an application (e.g., credit checking) runs on, typically, a dedicated machine

Development of client-server software is not trivial and requires a great deal of training especially if low-level protocols are used. The need to develop client-server software should be evaluated carefully, and the growing number of commercially available servers should be considered seriously before considering in-house development. In many cases, it is better to develop clients which can access commercially available servers. Commercially available distributed data and transaction managers are also attractive alternatives because these packages automatically include code for consistent/concurrent data access and transaction failure handling in distributed networks, thus reducing the need for in-house software development. It is also better to use the high-level client-server protocols, if available, because they are transportable to many networks.

Development of C-S systems involves a variety of issues in security, performance, network independence, and failure management. An issue of particular importance to management is the interoperability of clients and servers supplied by different vendors. At present, many vendors use proprietary protocols between their clients and servers. This may lead to the situation where 10 client applications from 10 vendors may require 10 different servers to access the same database.

The following general trends in client-server systems are worth noting:

- The notion of client-server paradigm could be outdated due to the emergence of many new situations, in which processes cooperate with each other as peers without any clients or servers. The peer-to-peer OSI application layer protocols could play a significant role in this.
- The trend toward higher-level services and protocols which are independent of the underlying network architectures will continue. The RPC facilities will become

more sophisticated and may eliminate the need for network-dependent protocols. In addition, the notion of object-oriented message systems is becoming increasingly popular. In these systems, the clients and servers will be treated as objects which exchange messages. The format of the messages will be independent of the location of the objects.

- More off-the-shelf software will become available for "zero-programming" client-server computing. At present, many decision support applications which access remotely located SQL databases from spreadsheets are state of the market and practice. Other off-the-shelf client-server applications in manufacturing, finance and human resource management are also becoming available from database vendors. This trend will continue.

Problems and Exercises

1. What are the differences between application interconnectivity and network interconnectivity? Explain through an example.
2. Suppose financial information from a corporate mainframe is needed by the branch offices for spreadsheet analysis. List the options available and the tradeoffs.
3. Draw a conceptual diagram of client-server computing in an environment of your choice (e.g., business, finance, engineering, manufacturing).
4. We have reviewed several client-server systems. Describe a server that we have not described in this chapter.
5. Compare and contrast the basic protocols versus the RPC facility. Should the basic facility be used anywhere? Where and why?
6. Build a pseudo code for a simple echo client server system using sockets, APPC and RPC.
7. Develop a pseudo code for a Lotus 1-2-3 client which accesses an SQL server on a remote site. You may choose any of the protocols and facilities to develop the pseudo code.
8. List the factors you will use to evaluate off-the-shelf client-server systems.

CASE STUDY: Client-Server Systems for XYZCORP

The management at XYZCORP has embarked on an enterprise-wide interconnectivity project. The purpose of this project is to develop an overall information architecture in the company which will allow different applications at different sites to communicate with each other ("any data from any application anywhere in the company"). The management has been exposed to a lot of literature on client-server computing and is especially interested in interconnectivity through client-server systems. The company is at present struggling with developing a client-server approach to network operation center (NOC) for corporate network management (the case study at the end of Chapter 4). As a first step toward this architecture, the management is concentrating on the following application areas:

- *The Computerized Checkout/Inventory System*: This system, introduced in Chapter 2 case study, allows the XYZCORP stores to use corporate data (prices, inventory, etc.) through nightly file transfers. The file transfer solution described in Chapter 2 is not adequate because the data on the host changes many times a day. In addition, the company is planning to expand the number of stores and it is becoming too clumsy to transfer many files to hundreds of stores every night. It is desirable to use a client-server model which allows the store computers to interactively access the mainframe data.
- *Financial Information*: Financial and budgeting information at present is in an MVS DB2 database at the corporate mainframe. All stores and branch offices currently receive hardcopy reports once a month. In order to perform local spreadsheet analysis, the branch offices copy the data from hardcopy reports to their own computers (they have many data entry clerks who read the reports and type the report data into a spreadsheet template). These spreadsheets are then used for local analysis. This is very clumsy and expensive. A client-server model which allows spreadsheets at the user sites to interactively access the mainframe data seems to be natural for this application.
- *Electronic Mail*: The electronic mail system needs to be integrated with the aforementioned systems. For example, when an order is received, a message should be sent to the user on the user's E-mail system. This may involve client-server systems in which the mail senders and receivers interact with the financial and order processing client-server systems.
- *Electronic Data Interchange (EDI)*: The company is interested in using EDI to eliminate the paper work involved in order processing. Many of the hardware component suppliers for XYZCORP are currently using EDI to electronically send an order, receive the payment notice and then make payments through automated accounts payable.

This architecture should address the following issues:

- Levels of interconnectivity for each application area.
- A discussion of what application interconnectivity services are most appropriate for different applications.
- Definition of common user interfaces for different applications.
- Justification for client-server computing and identification of clients and servers for each application area.
- Identification of the cases where "basic" services and protocols such as Sockets and LU6.2 would be used instead of RPCs and complete services.
- Limitations of client-server computing for these applications which can be overcome by the peer-to-peer model.

Computerized Checkout/Inventory System: For this application, the station and network connectivity is handled by the SNA network which connects stores to the mainframe (Chapter 3 case study). Application interconnectivity has been mainly through terminal emulation and file transfer. The client-server model fits very well in this application because each store computer can act as a client and the mainframe can act as a server. A common user interface can provide end-user transparency so that the data is accessed from different sites without the explicit knowledge of the user.

Financial Information: The underlying network for this application is the same SNA network for stores. However, for the managers located in the manufacturing and engineering office, the TCP/IP network is used to provide station and network interconnectivity. It is natural to use a client-server model in this environment so that the user spreadsheets can act as clients to access remotely located data. (Many spreadsheet packages are providing remote data access facilities. Example is Lotus Data Lens.) The main challenge in this situation is to support clients on different platforms which access MVS data through SNA as well as TCP/IP networks. (Once again, products are becoming available in this area).

Electronic Mail and EDI: The underlying network for this application is the same as for the financial information (vendor networks can be assumed to be SNA and TCP/IP). Many products are becoming commercially available which translate mail formats between X.400, SMTP and IBM mail (Softswitch is an example of such a mail gateway). Most of these systems are also beginning to support EDI on top of the electronic mail (i.e., EDI runs as a higher-level application on E-mail).

Peer-to-Peer communication can be especially beneficial in highly interactive E-mail systems, flexible manufacturing systems and decision support systems which support group decisions. Many peer-to-peer applications are built by using lower-level protocols and services because RPCs restrict the applications to the client-server model.

References

Andrews, G. R., "Paradigms for Process Interaction in Distributed Programs," *ACM Computing Surveys*, Mar. 1991, pp. 49-90.

Andrews, G., and Schneider, F., "Concepts and Notations for Concurrent Programming," *ACM Computing Surveys*, Vol.15, No. 1, Mar. 1983, pp. 3-44.

Bal, H., Steiner, J., and Tannenbaum, A., "Programming Languages for Distributed Computing Systems," *ACM Computing Surveys*, Sept. 1989, pp. 261-322.

Barr, J., "Connectivity in the Factory," *Unix Review*, June 1987, pp. 33-42.

Bernstein and Goodman, "Concurrency Control in Distributed Systems," *ACM Computing Surveys*, June 1981.

Birrel, A. D., and Nelson, B. J., "Implementing Remote Procedure Call," *ACM Trans. on Computer Systems*, Vol. 2, pp. 39-59.

Bryant, S., "Implementation of Cell Control Using MMS," *MAP/TOP Interface*, Vol. 4, No. 4, Fall 1988.

Comeau Greg, "Networking with Unix," *BYTE*, Feb. 1989, pp. 265-267.

Corbin, J. R., *The Art of Distributed Applications: Programming Techniques for Remote Procedure Calls,* Springer-Verlag, 1991.

Coulouris, G., and Dollimore, J., *Distributed Systems: Concepts and Design*, Addison-Wesley, 1988.

Date, C., *An Introduction to Database Systems*, 5th ed., Addison-Wesley, 1990.

Davis, Ralph, "A Logical Choice," *BYTE*, Jan. 1989, pp. 309-315.

Finkelstein, R., "A Client for Your Server," *Database Programming and Design*, Mar. 1992, pp. 31-45.

Gantz, J., "Cooperative Processing and the Enterprise Network," *Networking Management*, Jan. 1991, pp. 25-40.

Glass, B., "Relying on Netware NLMs," *Infoworld*, Oct. 12, 1992, p. S80.

Griswold, Charles, "LU6.2: A View from the Database," *Database Programming and Design*, May 1988, pp. 34-39.

Hirsch, D., "Terminal Servers: Here to Stay," *Data Communications*, Apr. 1990, pp. 105-114.

Hurwicz, M., "Connectivity Pathways: APPC or NETBIOS," *PC Tech Journal*, Vol. 5, No. 11, Nov. 1987, pp. 156-170.

IBM (International Business Machines), "Advanced Program-to-Program Communication for the IBM Personal Computer, Programming Guide," Feb. 1986.

Inmon, W., "Developing Client/Server Applications," QED, 1991.

ISO/DP 9072/1 report, "Remote Operations Model—Notation and Service Definition," Geneva, Oct. 1986.

Johnson and Reichard, *Advanced XWindow Applications Programming*, MIT Press, 1990.

Kernighan, B. W., and R. Pike, *The Unix Programming Environment*, Prentice Hall, 1984.

Quarterman, J. S., Siberschatz, A., and Peterson J. L., "4.2BSD and 4.3BSD as Examples of the Unix System," *ACM Computing Surveys*, Vol. 17 No. 4, Dec. 1985, pp. 379-418.

Livingston, D., "Software Links Multivendor Networks," *Micro-Mini Systems*, Mar. 1988.

MMS Programmer's Guide, Concord Communications, Inc. 1988.

Moad, J., "Double Impact," *Datamation*, Aug. 1, 1992, pp. 28-33.

Naylor, A., and Volz, R., "Design of Integrated Manufacturing System Control Software," *IEEE Trans. on Systems, Man and Cybernetics*, Vol. SMC-17, No. 6, Nov./Dec. 1987.

Nehmer, J., and Mattern, F., "Framework for the Organization of Cooperative Services in Distributed Client-Server Systems," *Computer Communications*, Vol. 15, No. 4, May 1992, pp. 261-269.

Nesset, D., and Lee, G., "Terminal Services in Heterogeneous Distributed Systems," *Journ. of Computer Networks and ISDN Systems*, 19 (1990), pp. 105-128.

Nitzberg, B., and Lo, V., "Distributed Shared Memory: A Survey of Issues and Approaches," *IEEE Computer*, Aug. 1991, pp. 52-60.

Ozsu, M., and Valdurez, P., "Distributed Database Systems: Where are We Now?" *IEEE Computer*, Aug. 1991, pp. 68-78.

Pountain, D., "The X Window System," *BYTE*, Jan. 1989, pp. 353-360.

Ricciuti, M., "Universal Data Access," *Datamation*, Nov. 1, 1991.

Ricciuti, M., "Here Come The HR Client/Server Systems," *Datamation*, July 1, 1992.

Scheife, R., *X Protocol Reference Manual*, O'Reilly and Associates, 1990.

Sechrest, S., *An Introductory 4.3BSD Interprocess Communications Tutorial*, Computer Science Research Division, Department of Electrical Engineering and Computer Science, University of California, Berkeley, 1986.

Sinha, A., "Client-Server Computing: Current Technology Review," *Comm. of ACM*, July 1992, pp. 77-96.

Shatz, S. M., and J. P. Wang, "Introduction to Distributed Software Engineering," *IEEE Computer*, Oct. 1987.

Snell, N., "The New MVS: Tuned to Serve? " *Datamation*, July 15, 1992, pp. 76-77.

Stevens, W., *Unix Network Programming*, Prentice Hall, 1990.

Svobodova, L., "File Servers for Network-Based Distributed Systems," *ACM Computing Surveys*, Dec. 1984, pp. 353-398.

Tannenbaum, A., *Computer Networks*, 2nd ed., Prentice Hall, 1988.

Vinzant, D., "SQL Database Servers," *Data Communications*, Jan. 1990, pp. 72-86.

White, D., "SQL Database Servers: Networking Meets Data Management," *Data Communications*, Sept. 1990, pp. 31-39.

Wilbur, S., and Bacarisse, B., "Building Distributed Systems with Remote Procedure Calls," *Software Engineering Journal*, Sept. 1987, pp. 148-159.

Zuck, J., "Front-end Tools," *PC Magazine*, Sept. 1992, pp. 295-332.

Chapter 6

Distributed Data and Transaction Management

6.1 Introduction

A highly desirable goal of distributed computing is transparency: data location transparency (access and manipulation of remotely located data without knowing the location of the data in the network) and failure transparency (maintenance and recovery of consistent data after system crashes by managing transactions). Ideally, the data may be in text files, spreadsheets, CAD diagrams, relational tables, or object-oriented databases. Management of distributed data, in whatever form it exists, and the transactions which access the data are the focus of this chapter.

We introduce the concept of a distributed data and transaction management system (DDTMS): a collection of software modules, which manage all distributed data (files plus databases), and the associated transactions, which span many computers. Basically, a DDTMS includes the functionalities of a distributed database management system, a distributed file management system, and a distributed transaction management system. Design and implementation of DDTMS involve many challenges, such as the following:

- How to access data transparently in different formats and locations in a network
- How to update and manage duplicate data in a network
- How to maintain concurrency and consistency of data if the network and/or the data sites fail during transaction processing
- How to decompose a transaction to optimize response time in distributed systems and how to coordinate such a transaction.

A great deal of research literature has been published to address these challenges in the last 15 years. Although research continues, a major portion of the fundamental research in this area was conducted in the late 1970s and early 1980s.

Distributed data and transaction managers have moved from state of the art to state of the market in the mid-1980s and are commercially available at present from many vendors. State of the market practice examples, however, are sparse.

A large body of literature on theoretical aspects, implementation issues, prototypes, and commercially available products has accumulated over the years. For example, many papers have appeared on update synchronization algorithms, distributed query optimization, distributed deadlock detection, and failure management in partitioned networks where one part of a network cannot be accessed by other parts. It is difficult for a potential designer, manager, or end user to understand and digest this technical body of knowledge due to the formal content and differing terminologies. The main question is, Who needs to know what about distributed data and transaction management? The following views and viewers are presented to help in answering this question and to establish the organization of this chapter:

1. The external view is held by the end users and managers of a DDTMS environment. For this view, the DDTMS is transparent for the most part because the users only need to know the query formats and query responses which are supposed to be the same for a local or distributed system. The managers may need to know information about the general characteristics of DDTMS and advantages/disadvantages of DDTMS. The overview presented in Section 6.2 should be enough to satisfy the external viewers.
2. The intermediate view is for the application designers/programmers, database designers, and database administrators. For this view, the network hardware and software on which the DDTMS is implemented and the tradeoffs in centralization versus distribution of data are of primary interest. The discussion of distributed file management, distributed database management, and distributed transaction management in Sections 6.3 through 6.5 is intended for the intermediate view of this subject matter.
3. The internal view is needed by the DDTMS designers and systems programmers who have to design, install, configure, and modify DDTMS. Researchers in distributed data and transaction management also need this view. These viewers must have a good understanding of network hardware and software technology trends and must be familiar with state-of-the-art plus state-of-the-market approaches in concurrency control, query processing, and failure management in distributed systems. The material presented in Sections 6.6 through 6.10, coupled with the networking issues covered in Part II of this book, should serve as adequate introduction for these viewers. Additional details for internal viewers can be found in the following books:
   - Ozsu, M., and Valduriez, P., *Principles of Distributed Database Systems*, Prentice Hall, 1991
   - Elmagarmid, A., *Database Transaction Models for Advanced Applications*, Morgan Kaufmann Publishers, 1992
   - Bernstein, P. A., Hadzilacos, V., and Goodman, N., *Concurrency Control and Recovery in Database Systems*, Addison-Wesley, 1987

- Ceri, S., and Pellagitti, G., *Distributed Databases: Principles and Systems*, McGraw-Hill, 1984.

This chapter assumes that the reader has some understanding of database concepts. The reader not familiar with database concepts should review the tutorial in Appendix E before proceeding.

6.2 Distributed Data and Transaction Management Concepts

6.2.1 Review of Centralized System Concepts

Figure 6.1 shows a typical centralized computing environment with a *file management system* which manages flat files, a *database management system (DBMS)* which manages the access and manipulation of a database, and a *transaction management system (TMS)* which manages the interactions between the users and the DBMS. Let us briefly review these components.

A data file, also called a flat file, consists of a collection of records such as text statements, C program statements, or graphic data. Conceptually, a *database* is a collection of logical data items in which the granularity of a logical data item may be a file, a record, or an arbitrary collection of data fields. A database management system (DBMS) is a software package which manages the access and manipulation of a database by multiple users. Specifically, a DBMS (1) manages logical representations of data, (2) manages concurrent access to data by multiple users, and (3) enforces security and integrity controls of a database. The tutorial in Appendix E gives more details about database technologies and SQL, a common database access language. A *transaction* is a sequence of operations (data access and manipulation commands) which transform one consistent state of a system into a new consistent state. Transactions are atomic; they either happen in entirety or do not happen at all ("all or nothing"). For example, transferring money from one account to another account is a transaction. We will discuss transactions and transaction management in Section 6.5.

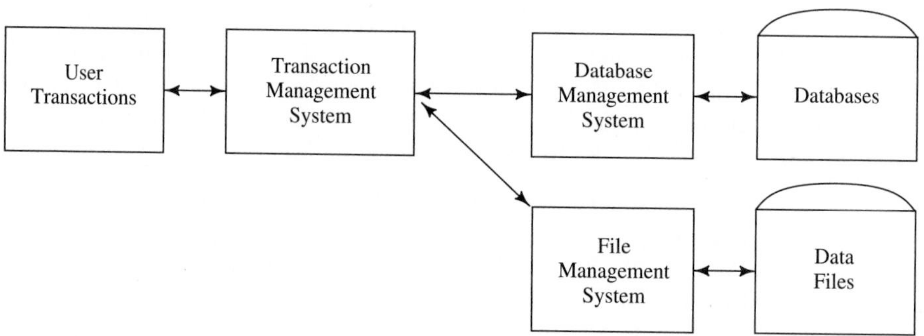

FIGURE 6.1 Conceptual View of a Computing Environment

6.2.2 Distributed Data and Transaction Management Overview

A *distributed data and transaction management system (DDTMS)* is responsible for managing all data (files plus databases) and the operations on the data in a distributed computing environment. A DDTMS is a collection of client-server modules which provides management of the following (see Fig. 6.2):

- Distributed files
- Distributed databases
- Distributed transactions.

The taxonomy in Fig. 6.2 shows the functions performed by the three components of a DDTMS: distributed file managers, distributed database managers, and distributed transaction managers. This view assumes that a DDTMS provides access and manipulation of all data, which may be in "flat" data files or in integrated databases in a network.

A *distributed file manager (DFM)* is responsible for providing transparent access, manipulation, and administration (e.g., security) of data files that are located at different computers in the network. The SUN Network File Services (NFS) system can be viewed as a DFM. Section 6.3 describes these services in more detail. A *distributed database manager (DDBM)* provides transparent access, manipulation, and administration of remotely located databases in a network. For example, an Ingres

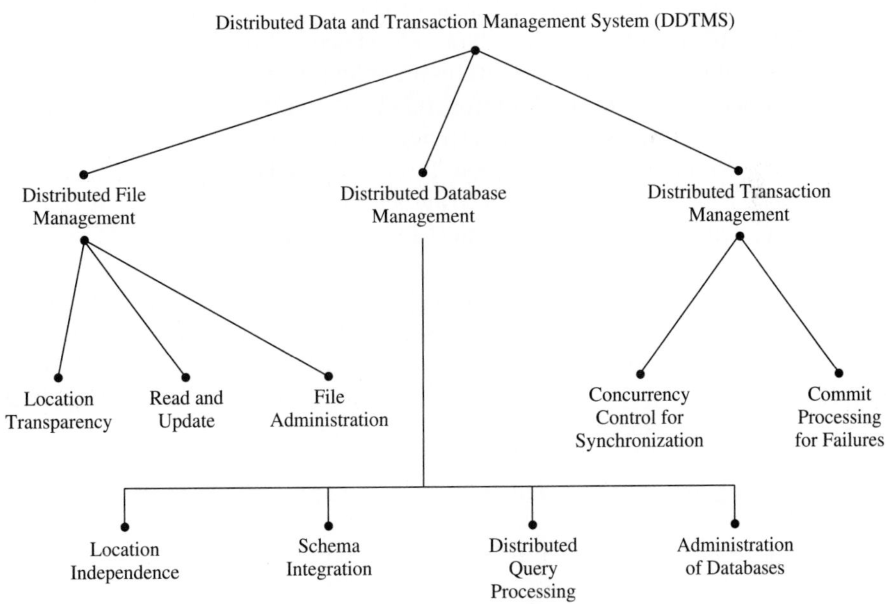

FIGURE 6.2 A Functional View of DistributedData and Transaction Management

DDBM allows a user to query relational databases located at many computers as if they were at one computer. We will describe DDBM in more detail in Section 6.4. A *distributed transaction manager (DTM)* coordinates the execution of a single transaction across multiple systems. DTM is responsible for assuring concurrency (i.e., simultaneous access) and commitment control (i.e., the transaction must be completed properly or entirely withdrawn in the event of a failure). Examples of DTM are AT&T Tuxedo, NCR Top-End, and Transarc Encina. Section 6.5 describes DTM services in more detail.

We should note that Fig. 6.2 presents a conceptual framework for studying and analyzing the access and manipulation of data in distributed computing. However, many commercially available products overlap the functionalities shown in Fig. 6.2. For example, many commercially available DDBMs include some of the DTM functionalities. In fact, many commercially available systems known as distributed database management systems provide most of the DDTMS functionalities.

Why separate the DFM, DDBM, and DTM when there is so much overlap? The reason is simple. At present, the products as well as standards are being developed in all these areas. The system architects have to determine how the existing DFM, DDBM, and DTM from different suppliers interoperate with each other. In the future, these differences may disappear and we will only have to consider an integrated DDTMS which provides all functionalities shown in Fig. 6.2.

Figure 6.3 shows the main modules of a DDTMS and depicts how these modules interact with the application system and the network services. This Reference Architecture will be explained in more detail in Section 6.6. Basically, the Reference Architecture views a DDTMS in terms of four functional modules: a User/Application Interface Manager (UIM), which parses the queries and determines the location of the data referenced in the queries; a Transaction Plan Generator (TPG), which generates an execution graph (plan) for the query, a Global Transaction Execution Monitor (GTEM), which supervises the execution and integrity control (global concurrency control and commit/recovery) of the query; and a Remote Communication Interface (RCI) for sending/receiving messages across a network. The Local Transaction Management System (LTMS) and the Local Data Management System (LDMS) modules perform the functions described in Section 6.2.1.

Although not shown in Fig. 6.3, the modules can be configured as clients and servers. The client modules can exist at locations where a user generates a query and the system plans and monitors its execution. The server modules exist where the data resides. This Reference Architecture does not imply that all computers must have both client as well as server modules of a DDTMS.

Let us explain this Reference Architecture through an example. Consider the following SQL query issued by a user or an application program at computer C1:

```
SELECT name, address FROM Employees;
```

Let us assume that the Employees table is located on computer C1. In this case, UIM will parse this query, determine that the data is at C1, and pass the query to the LDMS

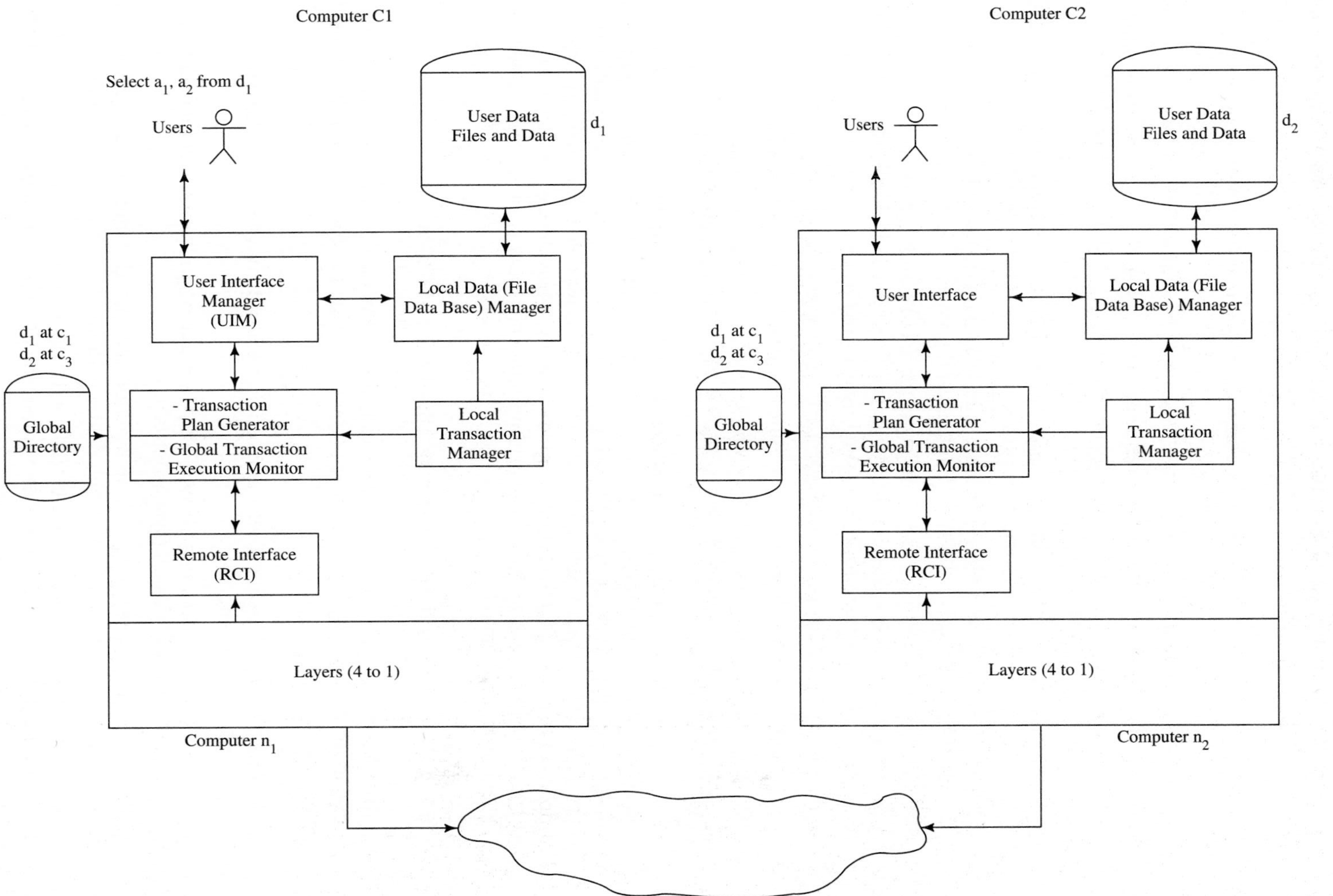

FIGURE 6.3 DDTHS Reference Architecture Overview

at C1. If the Employees table is at computer C2, then the following steps will take place:

1. UIM will determine, through a global directory, that the Employees table is on C2.
2. The TPG module will prepare the message to be sent to C2.
3. The GTEM module will issue requests for read locks on the Employee names and addresses at C2 (this step is bypassed if locking is not supported by the local transaction managers).
4. The RCI module will prepare and send the SELECT statement over to C2 by using whatever communication protocols are used between C1 and C2.
5. The RCI at C2 will receive the message and send it to the GTEM module at C2 (GTEM operates as a server scheduler in this case).
6. The GTEM will pass this request to the LTMS and LDMS at C2 for actual execution of the request. GTEM will receive the results of the SELECT statement and pass them to RCI for sending back to C1.
8. RCI will send the results of the SELECT statement back to C1.
9. The RCI at C1 will receive the results and pass them back to GTEM.
10. GTEM will free locks held, if any, and send the response back to the UIM module to display the results back to the user or application program.

Let us now consider a few variations. If the Employee table exists at more than one computer, then the plan generation must find the optimal site. Now, if the Employee table exists at more than one computer but it needs to be updated (say through an SQL Update statement), then the GTEM module would invoke a commit protocol (e.g., two-phase commit) to guarantee the consistency of the database.

We will review the various algorithms and techniques used in these modules in Sections 6.7 through 6.10.

6.2.3 Objectives and Advantages/Disadvantages of DDTMS

The primary objective of a DDTMS is transparency of data location and transaction execution. Specifically, a DDTMS attempts to provide the following levels of transparency:

1. *Location transparency*: Data items can be retrieved from any site without the user having to know the site.
2. *Replication transparency*: If one copy of a data item is updated, then all other copies are also updated (synchronized).
3. *Distribution transparency*: A transaction may be decomposed and routed to different sites to access distributed data without the knowledge of a user.
4. *Failure transparency*: If a site fails, a DDTMS will access the desired data from a different site, if possible, without the knowledge of a user. The DDTMS

will also assure that the transactions maintain database consistency in the face of failures.

Use of a DDTMS in an organization offers many advantages but at the same time introduces several unique technical as well as management challenges. For example, a DDTMS

1. Saves communication costs by providing data at the sites where it is most frequently accessed
2. Improves the reliability and availability of a system by providing alternate sites from which the information can be accessed
3. Increases the capacity of a system by increasing the number of sites where the data can be located
4. Improves the performance of a system by allowing local access to frequently used data
5. Allows users to exercise control over their own data while allowing others to share some of the data from other sites.

However, a DDTMS

1. Increases the complexity of the system and introduces several technical as well as management challenges, especially when geographical and organizational boundaries are crossed
2. Makes central control more difficult and raises several security issues because a data item stored at a remote site can always be accessed by the users at the remote site
3. Makes performance evaluation difficult because a process running at one node may affect the entire network
4. May deteriorate the overall performance of private wide area networks (WANs), which suffer from the SUE factor (slow, unreliable, expensive), as Gray pointed out <Gray 1987>.

Due to the advantages and disadvantages of a DDTMS, each application of DDTMS must be evaluated carefully.

6.3 Distributed File Management

A distributed file manager (DFM) allows transparent access and manipulation of remotely located files. This component of DDTMS supports open, read, write, and close of remotely located files from application programs and/or human users. It may provide access to a complete file or to a portion of a file across a network. Typically, DFM services include

- Selection and deselection of a remotely located file for access
- Creation and deletion of remote files
- Read and modification of remote file data and attributes (e.g., change a file's name)
- Control of the concurrency functions through locking/unlocking
- Security from unauthorized access.

Most of the distributed file managers are currently implemented as client-server systems in which each requester of a remote file service acts as a client which routes the file access commands to appropriate file servers in the network. File servers allow several users to share the same files, provide backup/recovery of shared files, allow users and the files to move around the network without retraining, and support diskless workstations.

Available distributed file managers support the above stated functionalities at varying degrees. Examples of the distributed file managers are the Open Software Foundation's Distributed File Server, IBM's Distributed Data Manager, the Andrews File System developed at Carnegie-Mellon, and SUN's NFS (Network File Services) system. An extensive discussion of file server issues can be found in <Svobodova 1984>.

6.4 Distributed Database Management

6.4.1 Overview

A distributed database manager is responsible for providing transparent and simultaneous access to several databases that are located on, perhaps, dissimilar computer systems. For example, three different databases (customer database, inventory database, and price database) located on three different computers are viewed by each user as if the databases were located at his or her site. Table 6.1 (page 315) lists 12 rules, and a basic zero rule, stated by Chris Date as the goals of a DDBM <Date 1987>. Implications of these rules are discussed by Krasowski <1991>. The specific functions provided by a DDBM which conform to these rules are as follows:

- *Schema integration*: A global schema is created which represents an enterprise-wide view of data and is the basis for providing transparent access to data located at different sites, perhaps in different formats. A *schema* shows a view of data. In a DDBM, the data may be viewed at different levels, leading to the following levels of schema (Fig. 6.4):
  - —The local internal schema represents the physical data organization at each machine.
  - —The local conceptual schema shows the data model at each site. This schema shows a logical view of data and is also referred to as the logical data model in database literature.

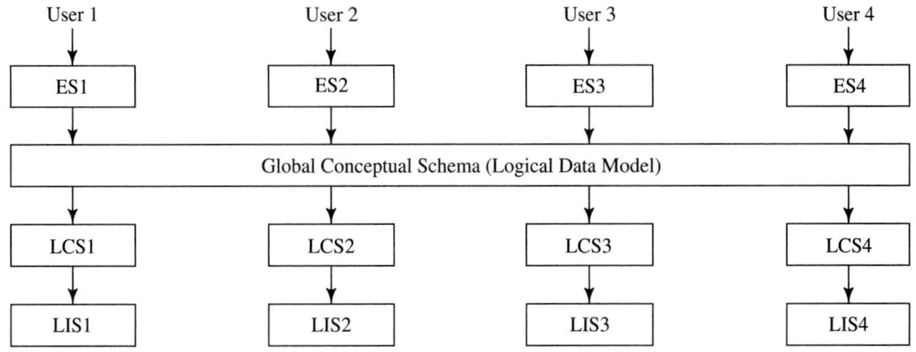

Legend: LIS = Local Internal Schema
LCS = Local Conceptual Schema (Local Logical Data Model)
ES = External Schema

FIGURE 6.4 Views (Schemas) in a Distributed Database

— The external schema shows the user view of the data.
— The global conceptual schema shows an enterprise-wide view of the data. This schema is also referred to as the corporate logical data model.

- *Location transparency and distributed query processing*: This provides transparency of data access and manipulation. The database queries do not have to indicate where the databases are located. The queries are decomposed and routed to appropriate locations. If more than one copy of data exists, then an appropriate copy is accessed. This allows the databases to be allocated at different sites and moved around if needed.
- *Concurrency control and failure handling*: These functions, usually implemented in a DTM, allow update synchronization of data for concurrent users and maintenance of data consistency under failures.
- *Administration*: Facilities are needed to enforce global security and provide audit trails.

The capabilities of a DDBM are illustrated in Fig. 6.5 where a parts database is located on a network of three computers—an IBM mainframe under MVS, a VAX system under VMS and an IBM PC under DOS. The three computers may use three different LDBMSs (local database management systems): IMS-DB, Ingres and Dbase3. A DDBM in this case would allow an end user, say at a dumb terminal, to

1. Create and store a new part anywhere in the network
2. Access a part number without knowing where the part number is physically located
3. Delete a part from one database without having to worry about duplicated parts in other databases

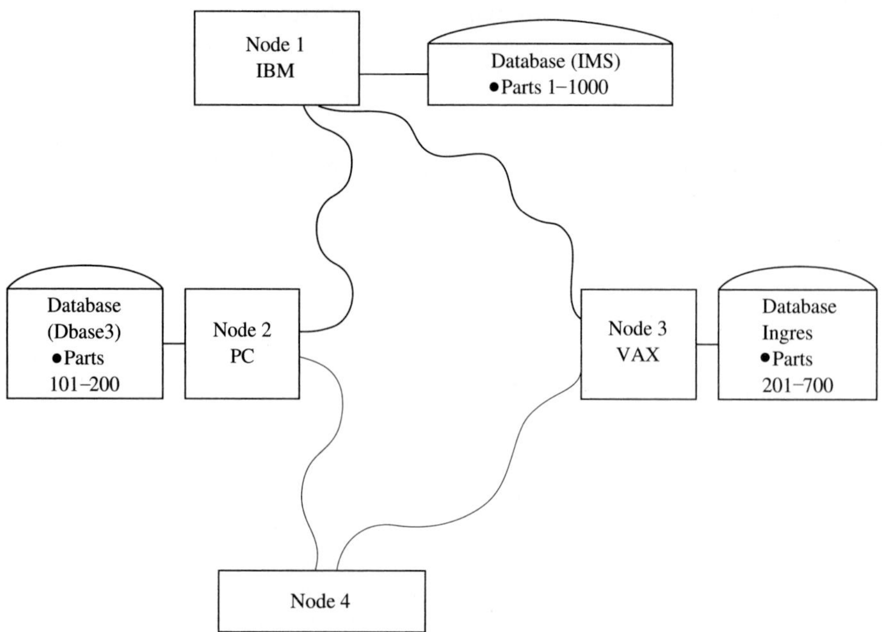

FIGURE 6.5 Example of a Distributed Database

4. Update a part description in one database without having to worry about how and when all the duplicated parts will be updated in other databases
5. Access a part from an alternate computer when, say, the nearest computer is not available.

Can a database server such as an SQL server be used as a DDBM? Obviously, the location transparency and distributed query processing can be provided by database servers. However, can a database server handle duplicate data and update synchronization? This can be accomplished if the database servers communicate with each other to synchronize the updates and handle network failures. So far, most of the database servers have been standalone. However, we will be hearing about distributed database servers in the future (see the discussion in Section 6.4.2). An area of considerable research activity, discussed in Section 6.4.3, is heterogeneous distributed databases. An ISO Standard in accessing and manipulating remotely located databases, called Remote Database Access (RDA), is described in Section 6.4.4. A complete architecture which shows how many of these functionalities are provided in a DDTMS is described in Section 6.6.

It is important to distinguish between a distributed database and a distributed database manager. A distributed database is a user database that is physically distributed to several computers, and a distributed database manager (DDBM) is a software package (or a collection of software modules) which manages distributed databases. An example of a distributed database is a customer database which may be partitioned and distributed to several regional customer sites for quick access. The same customer information may appear at more than one site (duplicated). An example of a DDBM would be an Oracle DDBM which gives an end user a single database view of the customer database.

6.4.2 Database Servers and Distributed Database Servers

Simply stated, a database server houses the database and controls user access to the database. The local user workstation behaves as a client. As stated in the previous chapter, a large number of vendors are developing SQL database servers which basically handle SQL calls from clients and respond with results.

Most of the database servers were originally developed for LANs (e.g., the Gupta SQL Server for IBM Token Ring LANs). Database servers in mainframe WAN environments are now available from database vendors such as Sybase, Oracle and Ingres. At present, vendor-provided terminal emulation is used heavily to access the WAN databases. IBM provides the intersystem coupling (ISC) and multiple system coupling (MSC) features for host-based databases such as IMS-DB.[1]

Basically, an MSC is a transaction router which routes a transaction to the site where it can access the data locally. An ISC environment allows a transaction at one site to communicate with a remote transaction. In this sense, the ISC environment is closer to a client-server model in which the client issues a call which is routed to a remote server. Details about ISC and MSC features can be found in the book by Date, *An Introduction to Database Systems*, Vol. 2 <Addison-Wesley, 1990>.

A distributed database server coordinates the client access to individual database servers, where each SQL database server manages its own database over a LAN or WAN. Consider an example where three databases D_1, D_2, and D_3 reside on three different computers under the control of three database servers (see Fig. 6.6). Let us assume that a client needs to access information from the three databases. The client can issue the following three queries:

- `SELECT a1, a2 FROM D1`
- `SELECT a3, a4 FROM D2`
- `SELECT a5, a6 FROM D3`

Each query will be sent to the appropriate server. After these queries have been executed, the client application may need to combine the responses for further analysis. Let us assume that the client application needs to join (combine) the attributes $a_1, a_2, \ldots, a_6$ from the three databases based on a given criteria. The client issues an SQL statement of the form (see Appendix E for SQL)

```
SELECT a1, a2,..., a6 FROM D1, D2, D3 where <condition>
```

In this case, who is responsible for the join—the client or the servers? If one of the three database servers is responsible for coordinating the join between databases residing under the control of several database servers, then this server becomes a

[1]IMS has two parts: IMS-DB is the database manager and IMS-DC is the transaction manager.

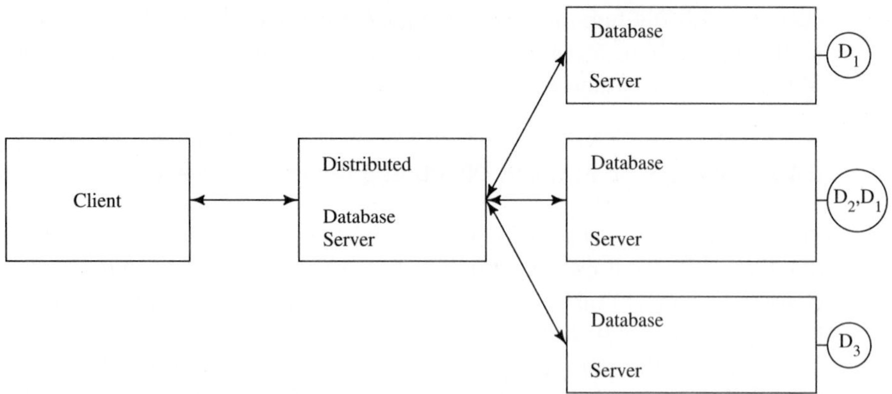

FIGURE 6.6 Distributed Database Server

distributed database server. The responsibilities of a distributed database server become more complex if some data is duplicated across servers.

The distributed database server must essentially address all of the aforementioned issues. It is possible to designate one server to be the distributed database server, which coordinates the interactions between several "local" database servers (see Fig. 6.6). In this case, a multilevel client-server system is used. The user application client issues the database calls which are received by the distributed database server. This server now acts as a client and issues requests to the standalone database servers. Practical aspects of distributed database servers can be found in Vinzant <1990>.

6.4.3 Heterogeneous and Federated Databases in Network Environments

Heterogeneous databases are of great practical significance because many real-life distributed databases are from different vendors, using different data models, and are accessed through a combination of LAN database servers and WAN database servers. For example, a common problem for a DDBM is to provide transparent access to the business, engineering, manufacturing and expert system databases that may be stored on Unix workstations, MVS mainframes, or PCs and that are interconnected through LANs, TCP/IP, and SNA networks. Database heterogeneity in a network can take several forms <Thomas 1990>:

- Databases may support heterogeneous data models (hierarchical, network, relational, or object oriented).
- Different query languages may be used in different databases (for example, different languages are used to access different object-oriented databases).
- Database management systems may be provided by different vendors.
- Computing platforms may be heterogeneous (microcomputer databases, minicomputer databases, and mainframe databases) operating under heterogeneous operating systems (Unix, MVS, OS/2).
- Networks may be heterogeneous (LANs, WANs, TCP/IP, SNA, DECNET, OSI).

Several terms are used to refer to heterogeneous database systems. For example, heterogeneous databases are also known as *multidatabase systems (MDBSs)*. An MDBS is an integrated distributed database system consisting of autonomous DBMS's which existed before integration <Soparkar 1991>. Yet another term used in this context is *federated databases system (FDBS)*. An FDBS is a collection of cooperating but autonomous component databases which are controlled and coordinated by a Federated Database Management System (FDBMS) <Sheth 1990>. A significant aspect of FDBMS is that the component databases may operate independently as heterogeneous systems but still participate in a federation. We will use the terms *heterogeneous*, *multidatabase*, and *federated database* synonymously, although some differences exist (see Litwin 1990 for discussion).

The basic feature that distinguishes these databases from the distributed databases discussed in Section 6.4.1 is the notion of transparency. It is almost impossible to provide complete transparency in heterogeneous databases because a complete global data schema is difficult to create. In fact, the lack of global data schema is the main distinguishing feature between heterogeneous and integrated distributed databases. Figure 6.7 shows three different levels of heterogeneity from a global schema point of view.

In the integrated distributed database approach shown in Fig. 6.7a, a single global schema is created which is used by all users and application programs. The local internal schema represents the physical data organization at each machine, the local conceptual schema shows the logical view of data at each site, and the external schema shows the user view of the data. As discussed in Section 6.4.1, the global conceptual schema shows an enterprise-wide view of the data. A global schema is created from the local schemas of the local databases. In practice, global conceptual schemas in large organizations are rarely achieved due to social and organizational factors.

In a heterogeneous distributed DBMS, a partial global schema may exist or it may not exist at all. Figure 6.7b shows the partial global schema (GCS) approach, in which only portions of the local conceptual schemas are used to build the GCS. The GCS may contain, for example, the most frequently accessed corporate data. The users can issue queries either through their own external schema or through the GCS. This approach is used in the "tightly coupled" federated databases <Sheth 1990>. The FDBMS may provide an integrated view of the data included in the GCS, where the user issues a query in a "global" query language against the partial GCS. An extensive discussion about the FDBMSs has been given by Sheth <1990>. Requirements and objectives of FDBMSs are discussed by <Kamel 1992>.

Figure 6.7c represents the approach in which no global conceptual schema exists. This approach is used in some multidatabase systems with very diverse schema (the loosely coupled FDBMS). One approach to accessing such database is a special multidatabase language, which allows users to define and manipulate autonomous databases. This language has special capabilities such as logical database names for queries, same definitions in different schema, etc. <Litwin 1990>. A DDBM may loosely couple the component DBMSs by providing a user interface which presents the various databases in a menu created directly from the local schemas (GCS is not used). The user may have to know the name, the local schema, and the query language of the individual databases.

a. Integrated Distributed Database Management

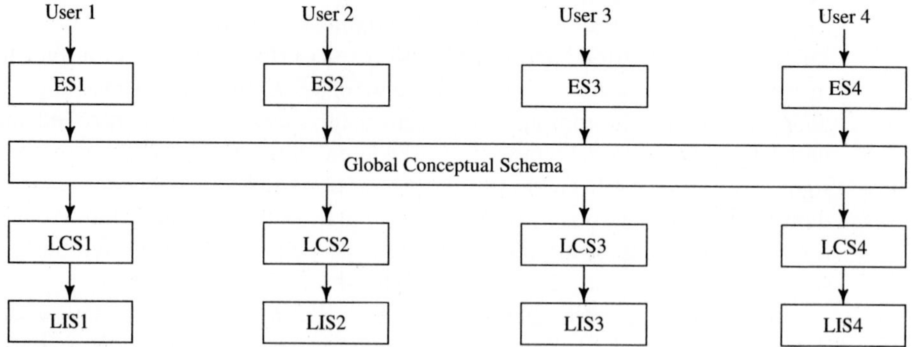

b. Heterogeneous DDBMS (Partial Global Schema)

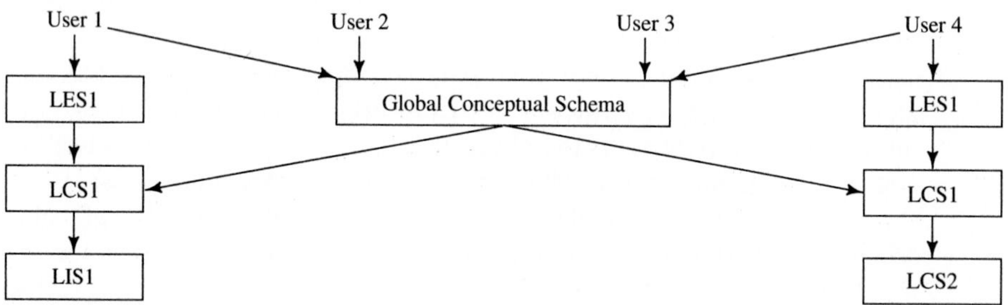

c. Heterogeneous DDBMS (No Global Schema)

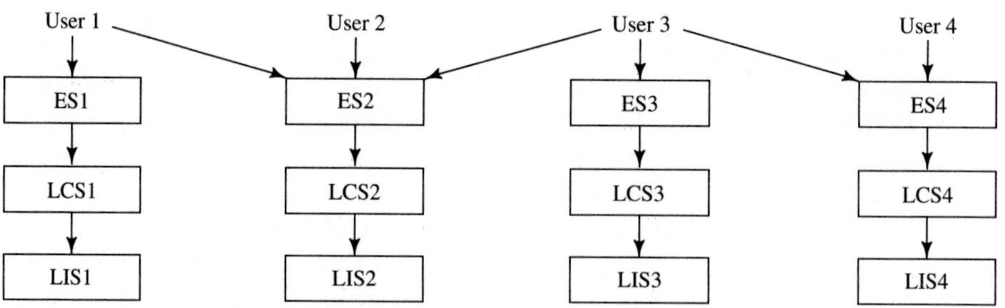

Legend: LIS = Local Internal Schema
LCS = Local Conceptual Schema
ES = External Schema

FIGURE 6.7 Different Models of Distributed Databases

Many heterogeneous DDBM products have been developed for use in production. Examples of some of these products are as follows:

- The Amoco Distributed Database System (ADDS), developed at Amoco, is used for uniform access to IMS, SQL/DS, DB2, RIM, INGRES and FOCUS.
- The DATAPLEX system, developed at General Motors Corporation, integrates IMS and SQL.
- The IMDAS system, was developed at the National Institute of Standards and Technology and the University of Florida, to allow data sharing in manufacturing environments.
- Ingres/Star from the Ingres Corporation, allows data access to Ingres as well as non-Ingres databases in a network.
- Mermaid, was developed at Systems Development Corporation to satisfy the Department of Defense requirement for accessing and integrating data stored in autonomous databases.

These products are reviewed in detail by Gomer Thomas <Thomas 1990>. Many survey and research papers describe the heterogeneous distributed databases. Perhaps the most detailed material can be found in *ACM Computing Surveys*, Special Issue on Heterogeneous Distributed Databases, September 1990; and *IEEE Computer*, Special Issue on Heterogeneous Distributed Databases, December 1991.

6.4.4 OSI Standard: Remote Database Access (RDA)

Remote Database Access (RDA) is an ISO Standard for accessing and manipulating remotely located databases. RDA provides capabilities for remotely

- Reading, inserting, updating, and deleting of database records
- Searching or listing data located in databases.

RDA supports a client-server model in which the application behaves as a client which issues requests to access remotely located databases. The database servers receive, parse, and execute the query (e.g., an SQL query) and send the results back to the client. Although the client and server can reside in the same machine, RDA was specifically defined to allow applications running in one vendor environment to access databases located in other vendor environments. It is important to note that the RDA standard is not intended to support distributed databases, thus update synchronization is not supported. In the client's view, the server is just a centralized database located at a remote site. The server may be implemented as a distributed database; but this is of no concern to the client. However, we will see in Section 6.5.2 that RDA does work in conjunction with ISO TP which allows synchronization.

The significance of RDA is that a user will be able to access RDA conformant remotely located databases from different vendors on different platforms. In this sense, RDA provides open access to databases located anywhere in the network.

The RDA standard is divided into two parts: a generic RDA standard, which specifies the aspects common to all data models, and a set of specialized standards for individual data models and languages. Currently, only an SQL Specialization has been standardized. Thus the standard can be used for relational systems or systems which provide a relational interface. ASN.1 is used to specify the format of RDA data units. The client-server communication is established through the ISO Association Control Service Element (ACSE). RDA may use the ISO Transaction Processing (TP) standard to manage transactions. The ISO TP standard is discussed in Section 6.5.3.

It should be noted that the RDA requirements are different from RPC requirements. Recall that RPCs are intended for program to program communications by passing a set of parameters. This model may not be suitable for remote data access because remotely accessed data cannot be strictly parameterized. For example, for ad hoc SQL queries, the database server may return many columns and many rows, depending on the type of query. RDA is more suitable for ad hoc queries than RPC.

6.5 Distributed Transaction Management

6.5.1 Review of Transaction Management Concepts

The concept of a *transaction* originates from the field of contract law <Gray 1981, Walpole 1987> in which each contract between two parties (a transaction) is carried out unless either party is willing to break the law. In computer science, a transaction is defined as a sequence of database *operations* (update and manipulation commands) that transform one consistent state of the system into a new consistent state <Eswaran 1976>. Examples of a transaction are electronic transfer of money from one account to another, a program with embedded SQL statements, single execution of a Cobol program, and an interactive query <Ozsu 1991 book, p. 259>. A transaction has four properties, known as the ACID properties:

- *Atomicity*: A transaction is treated as a single unit of operation; either all the transaction's actions are completed, or none of them are. This is also known as the "all-or-nothing property." If a transaction completes all of its actions successfully, then it is said to be *committed.*
- *Consistency*: A transaction maps one consistent (correct) state of the database to another. Informally, consistency is concerned with correctly reflecting the reality in the database. For example, if a company has 500 employees, then a database consistent with this reality should also show 500 employees. The notion of a consistent state is highly dependent on the semantics of the database. A set of constraints, called semantic integrity constraints, is used to verify database consistency.
- *Isolation*: A transaction cannot reveal its results to other concurrent transactions before commitment. Isolation assures that transactions do not access data that is being updated (temporarily inconsistent and incomplete during the execution of a transaction).

- *Durability*: Once completed successfully (committed), the results of a transaction are permanent and cannot be erased from the database. The DBMS ensures that the results of a transaction are not altered due to system failures (transactions endure failures).

Detailed discussion of the ACID properties for transactions can be found in Ozsu 1991, pp. 266–269. The implication of the ACID properties for transaction management are as follows:

- *Concurrency control*: This allows transactions to execute concurrently while achieving the same logical result as if they had executed serially. Concurrency control allows multiple transactions to read and update data simultaneously and includes transaction scheduling and management of the resources needed by transactions during execution. Transactions can be scheduled serially (single-threaded) to minimize conflicts or in parallel (multithreaded) to maximize concurrency.
- *Commit processing*: This allows commitment of transaction changes if it executes properly and removal of the changes if the transaction fails. The transactions usually "bracket" their operations by using "begin transaction" and "end transaction" statements. The transaction manager permanently enters the changes made by a transaction when it encounters the "end transaction" statement; otherwise, it removes the changes. Transaction managers also log the results of transactions on a separate medium so that the effects of transactions can be recovered even in the event of a crash which destroys the database.

In addition, a transaction management system (TMS) allows read/write operations from the user stations. Each station may be a terminal or a computer. Workstation read/write operations may involve the communication activities of establishing sessions, determining network routes, and assembling data link control messages. These operations can be described by using the layers 4 through 1 of the ISO/OSI Distributed Reference Model discussed in Part II of this book.

Transactions may be online updates or application programs written in a procedural language with embedded updates. A TMS may allow queued or conversational transaction processing. In queued transaction processing, such as found in IMS-DC, arriving transactions are first queued and then scheduled for execution. Once execution begins, the transaction does not interact with the user. In conversational transaction processing, such as found in CICS, the transactions interact with the outside world during execution.

In centralized systems, the TMS facilities have been traditionally integrated with the DBMS facilities, as shown in Fig. 6.8. This allows database queries from different transactions to access/update one or several data items. A transaction may be decomposed into subtransactions to optimize I/O and/or response time (see Jarke 1984 for a comprehensive discussion).

An example of commercially available TMS is CICS for MVS <Lim 1982, Nirmal 1992> or Tuxedo for Unix environments. It is not always possible to find separate TMSs in commercial products. In several cases, TMS facilities are embedded in communication managers, operating systems and/or database managers. An intro-

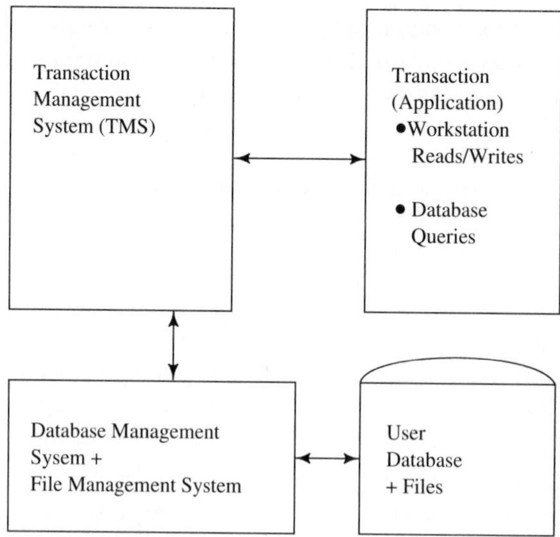

FIGURE 6.8 A Transaction Management System

duction to TMS facilities is given in the book by Ozsu <1991>, Chapter 10. For an extensive discussion of transaction management, see Elmagarmid <1992>, Leff <1991>, Walpole <1987>, Gray <1981>.

6.5.2 Distributed Transaction Management Concepts

A distributed transaction manager (DTM) allows multiple computers to coordinate the execution of a single transaction. This occurs when the data needed by a transaction resides at many computers. All the activities performed on different computers by a transaction must be completed properly or entirely withdrawn in the event of a failure in the network, application code, and/or computing hardware. Transactions in a DTM can be defined at two levels:

- Local transactions, which access only local data at one site
- Global transactions, which access data at several different sites.

A global transaction consists of several subtransactions and is treated as a single recoverable unit, called an atomic action. A global transaction must also pass the ACID (atomicity, consistency, isolation, and durability) test. Consequently, the main responsibilities of a DTM are as follows:

- Commit processing for failure handling and recovery.
- Update synchronization and concurrency control.

It is important for different sites to reach commit agreement while processing subtransactions of a global transaction. The most widely used solution to this problem is the two-phase commit (2PC) protocol, which coordinates the commit actions needed to run a distributed transaction. When a transaction issues a COMMIT request, then the commit action is performed in two phases: Prepare for commit and then commit. If a failure occurs in the prepare phase, then the transaction can be terminated without difficulty; otherwise all subtransactions are undone. Two-phase commit will be discussed in Section 6.9.2. Two-phase commit has been implemented in many systems and is included in the ISO Transaction Processing (TP) standard.

Many algorithms for update synchronization and concurrency control have been proposed and implemented in the last two decades. Most algorithms used in practice are variants of two-phase locking (2PL), which allows a transaction to lock the resources in the first phase and unlock in the second phase after performing reads/writes. Algorithms are also needed to resolve distributed deadlocks, which occur when transactions wait on each other. We will discuss 2PL and deadlock resolution algorithms in Section 6.9.1.

The activities performed on different systems can be coordinated by the DTM as queued or conversational transactions. In queued DTM, the transaction managers at different sites queue the incoming transactions and then execute them later, thus allowing for organizational boundaries and control between systems. In conversational DTM, the transaction managers interact with each other directly through the communication network.

Research in distributed transaction management is actively being pursued for heterogeneous databases <Pu 1991, Soparker 1991>. Commercially, three products provide DTM facilities: NCR's Top-End, AT & T's Tuxedo and Transarc's Encina.[2]

These products operate in Unix environments. It is expected that in the future more products will become available and products will operate across Unix and MVS environments. In addition, these products will conform to the ISO and X/open standards for distributed transaction management. We discuss these standards in the next section.

6.5.3 Open Standards for Distributed Transactions

Two open standards for distributed transactions are under active development:

- The X/Open Distributed Transaction Processing (DTP) Model
- The ISO Transaction Processing (TP) standard.

Figure 6.9 shows a simplified view of the relationships between these two standards. Conceptually, the OSI TP protocol is used between two distributed transaction managers (possibly from two different vendors) to communicate with each other in an open environment.[3]

The X/Open DTP defines two program interfaces: XA between the transaction manager and database systems, and AP-TM between application programs and the transaction manager.

[2]At present, these products provide commit coordination but not necessarily concurrency control.

[3]The actual OSI TP communication is between the communication managers which pass the information to transaction managers for interpretation and coordination.

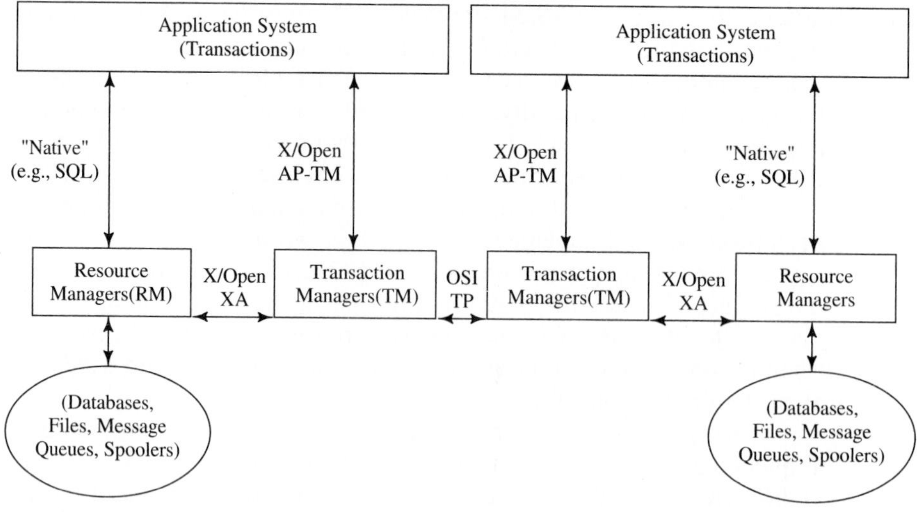

Note: This is a simplified view.

FIGURE 6.9 Open Standards for Distributed Transaction Management

OSI TP is a layer 7 application service element (ASE) designed to work with other layer 7 OSI ASEs such as:

- Commitment, Concurrency and Recovery (CCR), a two-phase commit protocol
- Association Control Service Element (ACSE), an association/release protocol
- User-ASE(s), a user-defined ASE which performs functions such as data transfer.

OSI-TP is a synchronization protocol between transaction managers (TMs). It does not provide data transfer and relies on the User-ASE(s) for data transfer. The protocol allows different levels of coordination between TMs; examples are "none" and "commitment." The coordination level "commitment" provides two-phase commit functionality through the CCR. The coordination level "none" bypasses this functionality and can be used as a starting point in distributed transaction management.

The X/Open DTP specifies the AP-TM and the XA interfaces. The resource managers (RMs) in DTP can manage files, databases, message queues, printer spools, etc. X/Open DTP does not define the interfaces between the application programs and RMs. These interfaces can be "native" depending on the type of RM. For example, SQL would be used between the application programs and a relational RM. The AP-TM interface defines how an application program issues statements such as "begin transaction" and "end transaction." The XA interface participates in the global two-phase commit protocol between TM and RM. With standardization of XA, multivendor DBMS products that support the XA interface can participate in global transaction coordination. At present, several TM vendors and relational DBMS vendors are in the process of implementing the XA interface.

6.6 A Reference Architecture for DDTMS

Figure 6.10 presents a Reference Architecture which synthesizes the distributed data and transaction management issues into a single framework. This architecture, briefly introduced in Section 6.2 through an example, satisfies the following four levels of transparency requirements discussed previously:

1. Location transparency
2. Replication transparency
3. Distribution transparency
4. Failure transparency.

In addition, the DDTMS may be expected to satisfy other requirements such as the 12 rules, listed in Table 6.1, to be satisfied by a DDBM <Date 1987>. This Reference Architecture is a synthesis of many architectures presented in the literature and can be customized to handle integrated as well as heterogeneous/federated/multi-database management systems and the evolving distributed transaction management standards such as X/Open DTP and OSI TP. Examples of the DDBM and DTM architectures presented can be found in <Ozsu 1991 book, Ozsu 1991, Sheth 1990, Cardenas 1987, Larson 1985, Decitre 1983, Gligor 1983, and Bernstein 1981 ACM>.

Figure 6.10 identifies the main functional modules of a DDTMS and shows how these modules interact with the Local Transaction Management system (LTMS) and Local Data Management Systems such as file and database managers. This architecture is presented at layers 5, 6, 7 of the ISO/OSI Distributed Reference Model. A Remote Communications Interface is introduced to provide the interface with remote sites across a network. A brief overview of the architecture is presented here and details are given in Sections 6.7 through 6.9.

User/application interface manager (UIM). This module translates the queries into a global form if necessary, determines the location of the data referenced in the queries, and passes control to LTMS if the transaction is local only or to the Transaction Plan Generator (TPG) if the transaction needs access to remotely located data. This module translates any schema (global to local) if needed. It is also responsible for gathering all user results generated during transaction execution and presenting the results to the user. Details of this module are given in Section 6.7.

Transaction plan generator (TPG). This module is responsible for generating an execution graph (plan) to optimize the performance of the arriving transaction. This may involve decomposing the transaction into subtransactions, which can run as local transactions on various nodes and translation of the global transaction into local transactions. Details of this module are given in Section 6.8.

Global transaction execution monitor (GTEM). This module receives the plan generated by TPG and is responsible for the initiation, execution, and integrity control (synchronization, reliability) of the transaction plan. Details of this module are given in Section 6.9.

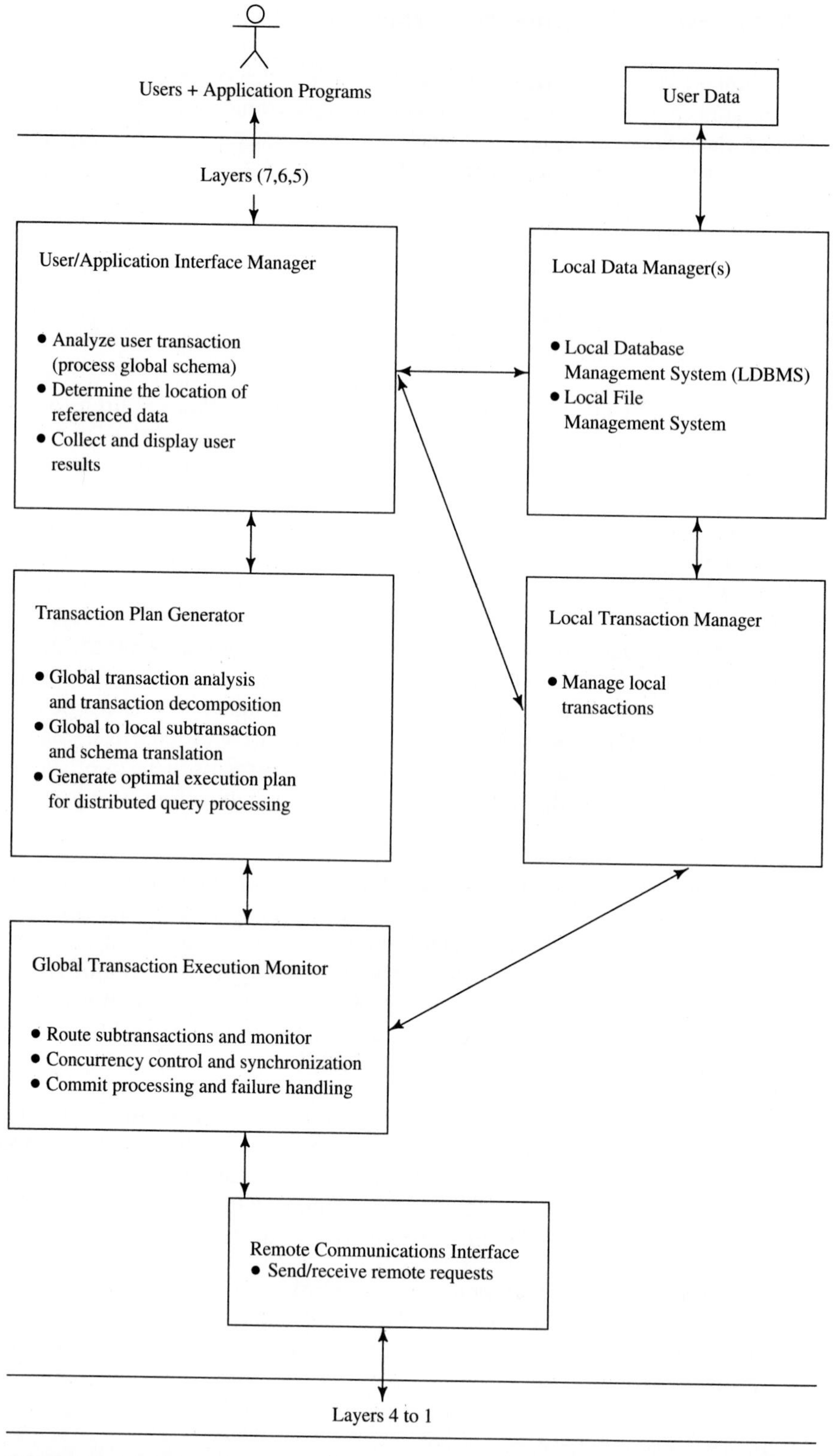

FIGURE 6.10 A DDTMS Reference Architecture

TABLE 6.1 The 12 Rules of Distributed Database Management

- Rule 0: The behavior of a DDBM should be the same as that of a Local DBMS.
- Rule 1: Each site in the network maintains its autonomy (i.e., the participation of a local DBMS in a DDBM must not require the local DBMS applications to be changed).
- Rule 2: There should be no reliance on central sites for the operation of DDBM.
- Rule 3: The DDBM should operate continuously and should not have any planned shutdown.
- Rule 4: The users of the DDBM should not know where the data is located.
- Rule 5: A DDBM should support fragmentation (breaking up of tables into subtables) for improved performance.
- Rule 6: More than one copy of a database should be supported and synchronized by the DDBM.
- Rule 7: Queries should be able to span many sites.
- Rule 8: Distributed transaction management (concurrency control and commit processing) should be supported by the DDBM.
- Rule 9: The DDBM should be able to operate under multiple hardware platforms.
- Rule 10: The DDBM should be able to operate under different operating systems.
- Rule 11: The DDBM should be able to operate under different network architectures and protocols.
- Rule 12: The DDBM should be able to operate on top of different (heterogeneous) local DBMSs.

Remote communications interface. This module prepares all of the messages that need to be sent to remote nodes in a particular format and receives the messages from the presentation layer and passes them to LTMS or GTEM sublayers. The protocols used in this sublayer may be the TCP/IP Sockets, ISO ROSE, remote procedure calls (RPC), Manufacturing Message System (MMS), APPC/LU6.2 protocols or the X.400 protocol proposed for electronic mail. These protocols were discussed in Chapter 6.

The Local Transaction Management System (LTMS) and the Local Data Management System modules perform the functions described in Section 6.2.

This architecture can be customized to represent tightly integrated or loosely coupled multidatabase systems. For example, in a tightly integrated DDTMS, more processing would be done in the user/application interface manager, transaction plan generator, and global transaction execution monitor. In a loosely coupled system, more processing would be done in the local modules (e.g., LDBMS and LTMS) than the global modules. In addition, this architecture shows how the transaction management modules interact with the database, the user interface modules, and the network interface services. For example, a commercially available distributed transaction manager would replace the TPG, GTEM, and, perhaps, the LTMS modules. This architecture also closely represents the X/Open DTP and the OSI TP standards model shown in Fig. 6.9.

6.7 User/Application Interface Management

User/application interface management performs the following functions:

1. Read and parse the user queries or application programming calls. These calls may be in X/Open AP-TM interface format or OSI RDA format.

2. Determine the location of the data referenced by this transaction. If all referenced data is local, then pass control to LTMS, else pass control to Transaction Plan Generator. This function involves reading of a global data directory, which shows what data items are located at what computers.
3. Collect and present results to the user.

The two major issues are the global schema definition and allocation of global directories, which store the global schema.

6.7.1 Global Schema Definition

A common global schema is needed to parse the query in global query format. The global schema shows all the data in the network and shows where the data is located. The problem of global schema design is straightforward if all the LDBMS are homogeneous but is nontrivial in a network with heterogeneous databases. At present most DDTMS are using SQL for schema definition and manipulation <Ozsu 1991 book, Rauch-Hinden 1987>. We have already discussed the schema design considerations for heterogeneous DDTMS. The interested reader is referred to <Sheth 1990, Litwin 1990, Cardenas 1987> for more details on this topic.

6.7.2 Global Directory Location

It is customary to show the <data, node assigned> pair in the global schema and store the global schema in a *global directory*. Due to the number of global directory accesses, it is crucial to allocate the global directory carefully. The directory allocation problem can be treated as a file allocation problem (FAP), where a file F is allocated to N nodes to minimize a given objective function. For example, Chu <Chu 1976, Chu 1984> has studied the directory allocation problem as a FAP. The following tradeoffs can be observed:

1. If the directory is at a central site, then the communication cost is high because every transaction will need to access the central site to locate data.
2. If the directory is at every site, then the update cost will increase due to duplicate directory updates.

It is common to replicate the global directory even if the data is not replicated. Another common approach in small networks is to store the directory at a central node with the following processing rules:

- Search the local directory at the arriving node.
- If not found, then search the directory at the central. site

Many other approaches for directory allocation are conceivable. For example, instead of one centralized directory, many "regional" directories may be established where each directory shows the location of data within a subnet (see Ozsu 1991 book, Bernstein 1987, and Goodman 1987 for details).

6.7.3 Discussion and Analysis

The design of user/application interface management is dependent on the requirements of supporting heterogeneous LDBMS and common global views. This issue is important at the transaction parsing and result generation steps.

The user transactions may use a uniform global query format such as SQL. They may also appear in different formats at different machines such as Dbase3 format on an IBM PC. The uniform global query format is preferable even though the user of an existing LDBMS may need to learn a new query language. At present, SQL is becoming a de facto standard for global query language.

The results of a transaction are collected and presented to the user at the termination of the transaction. A considerable result translation, join processing, and sorting may be needed if the transaction accesses data located in several heterogeneous databases.

6.8 Transaction Plan Generation (Distributed Query Processing)

6.8.1 Overview

Transaction plan generation constructs an execution plan to optimize response time and/or communications cost. Let us discuss a simple example to illustrate the processing of this module. Assume that a transaction T arrives at node n0 and accesses logical data items d1 and d2, where d1 is located on node n1 and d2 is located on node n2. T can be processed by using one of the following plans:

- T is executed at n0 and issues remote calls to n1 and n2.
- T is routed to n1, where it accesses d1 and issues remote calls to node n2. The results are coordinated at n1 and sent back to n0.
- T is routed to n2, where it accesses d2 and issues remote calls to node n1 The results are coordinated at n2 and sent back to n0.
- T is decomposed into t1 and t2, where t1 accesses d1 and t2 accesses d2; t1 is sent to n1 and t2 is sent to n2. The results are coordinated at n0.

The Transaction Plan Generator will determine and generate one of these transaction processing plans based on an optimality criterion. It can be seen that this problem becomes very complex for transactions which need to perform a series of operations, including joins, on many tables which are dispersed across a network (some tables may also be duplicated). The issues include which operations to perform first, how to do the joins, where to coordinate the results, and which copies of tables to include in the operations.

In general, the problem of determining optimal transaction processing plans is known in the literature as the "distributed query processing" problem <Ozsu 1991 book, Ozsu 1991, Bodarik 1992, Ceri 1984, Yu 1984, Hevner 1987>. This problem is the reverse of the optimal data allocation problem because in data allocation the data is allocated to nodes based on known queries, while in transaction processing the optimal plan is determined based on known data allocations. This is why some combined data allocation and query optimization algorithms have been proposed <Yu 1984, Hevner 1981>. In general, the problem of determining an optimal transaction plan is NP-hard (nonpolynomial hard), so in practice heuristic optimizations are used to derive a plan. The factors used in evaluating different plans typically include I/O and CPU capabilities of various nodes, the capabilities of the communication links, and the software available at different nodes (some nodes may not have the software to perform joins, sorts, etc.).

In short, the transaction plan generation is dependent on a large number of issues. We briefly review the following issues to expose the reader to the main concepts:

- Which method to use for accessing data from remote sites
- How to perform joins between tables located at different sites
- Which strategy to use to optimize response time and/or communications cost.

6.8.2 Methods for Accessing Remote Data

The two basic methods for accessing remote data are ad hoc remote access and remote procedure call (see Fig. 6.11).

Ad hoc remote access. This method provides a location-independent transparent access to data located anywhere in the network. As shown in Fig.6.11a, every data access request (e.g., SQL Select) is sent to the remote node through the Remote Communications Interface of the Reference Architecture. This method is very convenient but may cause excessive communication traffic. For example, 100 SQL calls result in 100 remote communication messages. This is commonly referred to as "dynamic SQL" because each SQL call is parsed and executed dynamically as it arrives. Most database servers support this paradigm.

Remote procedure call (RPC). This method allows the data at a remote site to be accessed by activating a remote procedure as shown in Fig. 6.11b. For example, instead of sending each SQL statement over the network, the client invokes a procedure which executes a set of predefined SQL statements (a procedure) on the server side. It can be seen from Fig. 6.11b that this can minimize the communication traffic. We discussed RPCs in a previous chapter. This is commonly referred to as "static SQL" because many SQL statements can be compiled and stored intro a procedure which can be called through an RPC. The main limitation of this method is that a program must exist at server to execute the request. The dynamic SQL paradigm does not require such a program and is thus suitable for ad hoc query processing.

a. Ad Hoc Data Access

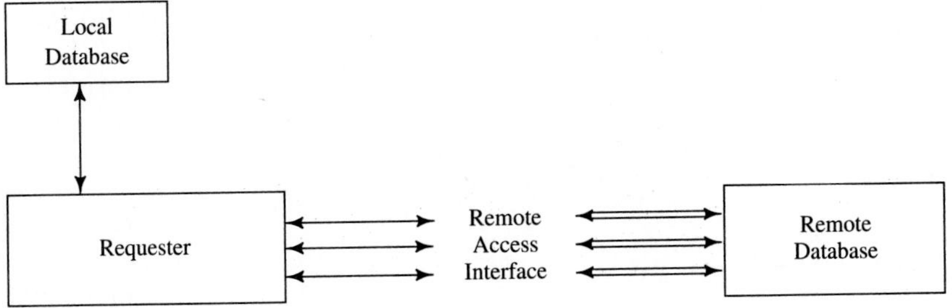

b. Remote Procedure Call(Requester/Server)

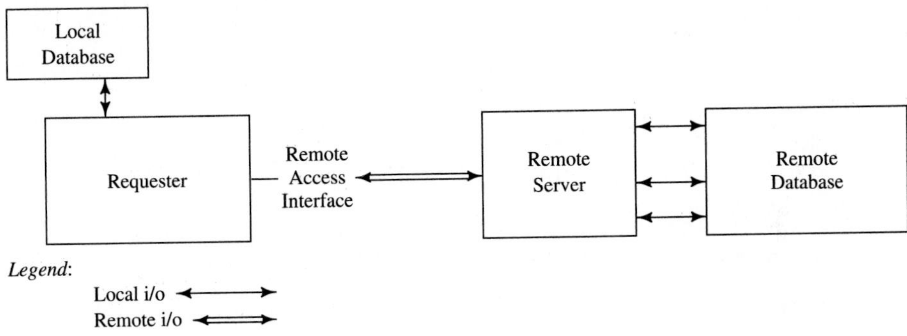

Legend:
Local i/o
Remote i/o

FIGURE 6.11 Remote Data Access Methods

6.8.3 Remote Joins and Semijoins

Since joins between remote sites can cause a considerable amount of communication traffic, a *semijoin* has been proposed to send only the necessary data <Bernstein 1981 JACM>. Figure 6.12 illustrates the semijoin operation. Simply stated, it consists of the following steps for joining R1 and R2 on attribute A:

1. Relation R1 is projected on attribute A, giving R1′.
2. R1′ is transmitted to R2 and joined with R2, giving R2′.
3. R2′ is transmitted to R1 and joined with R1, giving the final join.

Translation of a join into semijoin is an example of query decomposition.

6.8.4 Optimal Plan Generation

Determination of an optimal transaction processing plan is a difficult problem. Examples of existing methods are as follows:

Join Relation PAYROLL at node n1 with PERSONNEL at node n2 on Name

PERSONNEL (n1)		
NAME	*EDUC.*	*ADDRESS*
Sam	B.S.	Detroit
Joe	B.S.	NY
Pat	MBA	Toledo
Bob	B.S.	Detroit
Jack	M.S.	LA

PAYROLL (n2)		
NAME	*POSITION*	*SALARY*
Joe	Programmer	30k
Pat	Manager	40k

Steps in Semijoin:

1. Project PAYROLL on NAME at n2: gives PAYROLL′

NAME
Joe
Pat

2. Transmit PAYROLL′ to n1
3. Join PAYROLL′ with PERSONNEL at n1, gives PERSONNEL′

PERSONNEL′		
NAME	*EDUC.*	*ADDRESS*
Joe	B.S.	NY
Pat	MBA	Toledo

4. Send PERSONNEL′ to n2
5. Perform a join between PERSONNEL′ and PAYROLL at n2:gives the final answer

NAME	*EDUC.*	*ADDRESS*	*POSITION*	*SALARY*
Joe	B.S.	NY	Programmer	30K
Pat	MBA	Toledo	Manager	40K

FIGURE 6.12 Semijoin Operation

1. The "hill-climbing" algorithm developed for SDD-1. This algorithm uses semijoins to reduce the data transmitted and chooses a final node where all the relations are transmitted for final joins <Goodman 1979, Wong 1977>.
2. A family of algorithms to minimize either response time or total time for "simple queries," in which each relation contains only one common joining attribute, which is also the output of the query <Hevner 1979, Yao 1979>.
3. The decomposition method, in which a transaction is decomposed into subtransactions where each subtransaction accesses data at only one node. Then each subtransaction is routed to the remote site and the results are sent back to the destination node. This approach maximizes the concurrent operations of transactions. Decomposition strategies have been discussed extensively in the literature (see Yu 1984, Sacco 1981, Hevner 1987, and Chu 1984).
4. The evaluation algorithm introduced by Epstein 1978. This algorithm fragments one relation and replicates others so that each site containing a fragment and the replicated relations can process the join in parallel.

These algorithms differ in several assumptions: network topology, result site, cost function, and objective function. Detailed analysis of these algorithms can be found in Sacco <1981>. Recent trends in query optimization indicate heavy usage of artificial intelligence techniques to interpret statistical information about data distribution, make inferences, and employ pattern recognition <Epstein 1987>.

6.8.5 Discussion and Analysis

It is difficult to make general remarks about query optimization algorithms because each algorithm must be evaluated for a given application and network type. For example, Stone <Stone 1987> describes a case study in which an efficient serial algorithm performs better than a parallel query processing algorithm running on 64,000 processors. It is common to devise transaction processing algorithms which minimize communication cost and maximize use of CPU for slow networks, and minimize response time for fast networks.

It appears that duplicating data unnecessarily increases the complexity of query optimization and adds to the overhead. Although academic literature concentrates heavily on query decomposition and optimization techniques, several systems like Tandem Encompass and OSF DCE use remote procedure calls where data is managed by autonomous remote servers with minimum internode communications. A major supporter of remote procedure calls is Jim Gray <Gray 1987>, who claims that unnecessary data duplication is too expensive and the benefits in response time and availability are not worth the added overhead. This needs to be weighed in terms of the underlying network (WAN or LAN) and the effort needed to develop RPCs.

To summarize, transaction plan generation can be extremely complex if data is duplicated and dispersed at several sites. For most practical purposes, it may be best to assign data uniquely where it is most frequently used and utilize an efficient remote procedure call facility for remote users. The interested reader is referred to the literature in this area for additional information <Ozsu 1991 book, Ozsu 1991, Hevner 1987, Yu 1984, Ceri 1984, Sacco 1981, and Hevner 1979>.

6.9 Global Transaction Execution Monitoring

This monitor receives the plan generated by the Transaction Plan Generator and is responsible for monitoring the execution of the plan. It performs the following functions:

1. The transactions or subtransactions are initiated in the manner indicated by the plan.
2. The concurrency control and deadlock detection/resolution of the executing transactions are managed.
3. All failure and/or performance problems are monitored and handled.

4. All results collected from the transaction execution are sent to the User Interface Manager.

This module closely interacts with the Remote Communication Interface and LTMS. This module is at the core of distributed transaction management because the two main issues addressed by DTMS are the database concurrency control and reliability and error recovery. These two issues are discussed in Sections 6.9.1 and 6.9.2, respectively.

6.9.1 Database Concurrency Control

Concurrency control coordinates simultaneous access to shared data. The problem of concurrency control in centralized DBMSs is well understood, and one approach, called *two-phase locking*, has been accepted as a standard solution for a long time <Eswaran 1976>. However, concurrency control in distributed systems is an area of considerable activity with few accepted solutions. This is due to three main complicating factors. First, data may be duplicated in a DDTMS, consequently, the DDTMS is responsible for updating the duplicate data. Second, if some sites fail or if some communication links fail while an update is being executed, the DDTMS must make sure that the effects will be reflected on the failing node after recovery. Third, synchronization of transactions on multiple sites is very difficult because each site cannot obtain immediate information on the actions currently being carried out on other sites.

Due to these difficulties, over 50 concurrency control algorithms have been proposed in the past and still continue to appear (see, for example, Farrag 1987). Literature surveys have shown that most algorithms are variants of two-phase locking and time stamped algorithms <Bernstein 1987, Bernstein 1981 ACM>. However, several algorithms do not fall into any category. The three categories are briefly described and analyzed here. For a very detailed discussion of concurrency control algorithms, refer to Bernstein <1981 ACM>, Kohler <1981>, Bernstein <1987>, and Elmagarmid <1992>. More recent work has concentrated on concurrency control in complex database applications, which require long transactions, support interactive user control, and provide integrated access to large number of objects from large number of users <Barghouti 1991>. Discussion of these algorithms is beyond the scope of this book.

6.9.1.1 Two-Phase Locking Algorithms

Two-phase locking (2PL) uses read and write locks to prevent conflicts between concurrent operations. The 2PL algorithm consists of the following steps for a transaction T in an LDBMS which reads a data item x and writes a data item y:

- T obtains a readlock to data item x.
- T reads x.
- T obtains a writelock to data item y.
- T writes y.

- T releases the readlock on x.
- T releases the writelock on y.

The lock ownership is governed by two rules: (1) Different transactions cannot simultaneously own conflicting locks (read-write or write-write conflicting locks); and (2) once a transaction surrenders a lock, it may never obtain additional locks. This implies that each transaction goes through two distinct phases: a "growing" phase, when a transaction obtains locks; and a "shrinking" phase, when the transaction releases locks.

The 2PL algorithm can be implemented in DDTMS by using the following scheme:

- T obtains a readlock for x at node n, where it is going to be read.
- T obtains a writelock to all copies of data item y.
- T reads x.
- T writes y.
- T updates all duplicate copies of y.
- T releases the readlock on x.
- T releases the writelock on all copies of y.

Several variants of basic 2PL have been proposed:

1. *The Primary Copy 2PL*: A primary copy is designated for each data item x; read locks are granted by the primary node and the update locks are granted at each site where the data (primary or duplicated) is stored. This algorithm has been proposed by Stonebraker <Stonebraker 1979>.
2. *The Voting 2PL*: Read/write lock requests are sent to all nodes; if majority returns with lock granted, then lock is granted else transaction waits for locks. This algorithm is also referred to as the Thomas Voting algorithm <Thomas 1979>.
3. *Centralized 2PL*: The lock manager and lock tables are kept at a central node; if a transaction needs to access any x in the network, it must be granted lock from the central site. An extensive study of centralized 2PL locks has been conducted by Garcia-Molina <Garcia-Molina 1979>, who found that the performance of centralized locking schemes is better than expected. However, the single point of failure in the centralized 2PL is not desirable.

Several issues arise in the implementation of 2PL-based concurrency control algorithms:

1. What is the locking granularity—that is, the smallest database object that can be locked (database, file, record, field)?

2. What is the update synchronization interval (i.e., the time elapsed before updates on x are applied to all copies of x)? The updates may need to be applied at transaction run, hourly, or even daily, depending on the type of application.
3. Where should the lock tables be located?
4. Will a deadlock be caused due to locking? The following is an example of a deadlock with a cycle of length 3:

   - T1 must wait for T2 to release a lock.
   - T2 must wait for T3 to release a lock.
   - T3 must wait for T1 to release a lock.

   Deadlocks may occur more frequently in 2PL-based algorithms because all transactions obtain all locks in the growing phase and thus several transactions may wait on each other for locks. No accepted solution exists for this problem. One of the simplest techniques is to use "timeout," which forces a transaction to abort after it has waited for more than a timeout limit.

Detailed mathematical models and simulation results have been developed to determine which algorithm is best for what type of application with different granularities, synchronization intervals, and lock table locations <Garcia-Molina 1979>. Wolfson <Wolfson 1987> has given an extensive analysis of locking and commit protocols in DDTMS. Although it is difficult to make general observations, most of the available DDTMS use locking mechanisms which are variants of 2PL <Goodman 1987>.

6.9.1.2 Time Stamp Algorithms

Each transaction T is assigned a unique time stamp at the originating node. This time stamp is attached to each read and write request. In case of a conflict (i.e., two transactions trying to update the same data item x), the conflicting requests are serialized by time stamp. Read-write conflicts can also occur in time stamp algorithms. For example, if a transaction attempts to read a data item already written with a later time stamp, or vice versa (a transaction attempts to write a data item which has already been read by another transaction with a later time stamp), a read-write conflict occurs.

Although several time stamped concurrency control algorithms have been proposed <Bernstein 1981 ACM, Bernstein 1987, Ozsu 1991 book>, only a few have been actually implemented in commercial DDTMS. The major reason is that the conflicts are usually resolved by aborting one of the transactions. Time stamp algorithms may become inefficient due to too many aborts and restarts. This problem becomes even more serious if a universal clock is not available (transactions starting at "slow" sites keep aborting because they conflict with other transactions with recent time stamps).

6.9.1.3 Miscellaneous Concurrency Control Algorithms

Several algorithms have been proposed which combine the time stamped and 2PL algorithms, use unique approaches like Ellis Ring Algorithm <Ellis 1977>, or use certain pessimistic/optimistic assumptions about the nature of the system. An interesting example of a generalized concurrency control algorithm has been described by Farrag <1987>. This algorithm considers the 2PL and time stamped algorithms as special cases. Due to space limitations, only pessimistic/optimistic algorithms will be discussed here. The interested reader should refer to Bernstein <1987> and Ozsu <1991> book for others.

The pessimistic algorithm requires that a transaction secure all the necessary locks on data items before execution. If all the locks cannot be acquired, then the transaction will not start execution. This algorithm is essentially an extreme case of 2PL. Under 2PL, one can acquire locks gradually and release them gradually (general 2PL) or all at once at commit time ("strict 2PL"). In pessimistic algorithms, all locks are acquired at once (and possibly released at once). This algorithm can be represented by the following:

- T obtains a readlock to all data items x needed by T.
- T obtains writelock to all data items y needed by T.
- T starts execution.
- T reads x.
- T writes y.
- T writes all duplicate copies of y.
- T releases the readlocks on x.
- T releases the writelocks on y.

This algorithm is called pessimistic because it assumes that a large number of conflicts will be encountered by T, thus T should not be started without owning all locks.

An optimistic algorithm assumes that very few conflicts will occur and thus delays the validation step (determine if there are conflicts) until commit. Basically, a transaction presents its read set, write set, start time, and end time to the commit manager at commit time. The commit manager compares this information with similar information from other transactions which were active in the same time period to determine conflicts. If there is a conflict, then the transaction is aborted. Although optimistic algorithms can be implemented by using locks, the initial idea is based on time stamps. Here is one possible implementation:

- T starts execution.
- T reads x at initiating site.
- T writes y at initiating site.
- The new values of y are sent to all nodes with duplicate y.
- The new values are sent with a time stamp.
- If the new values are updated correctly with no conflicts, then the updates are made permanent;
- otherwise the update is discarded and applied again.

It can be seen that the optimistic algorithm will work well if there are very few conflicts. However, in case of several conflicts, there is no guarantee that a transaction will complete in finite time due to repeated restarts <Bernstein 1987>.

6.9.1.4 Discussion and Analysis

As mentioned previously, many database concurrency control algorithms have been published and continue to appear in computing journals (there may be between 60 to 100 algorithms by now). It is difficult to evaluate these algorithms because they use different terminologies, make different assumptions about the underlying DDTMS, are hard to understand, and are difficult to prove correct. Each author claims that his or her approach is the best. In addition, it is difficult to determine which of these algorithms has been implemented and which implementations are being used in commercial products instead of laboratory prototypes.

For a prospective DDTMS developer, the following approach is suggested:

1. Determine the real need for data duplication. The cost of concurrency control increases with more copies of data (too many locks/unlocks) and may outweigh the benefits.
2. Carefully examine the synchronization interval. Most concurrency control algorithms assume that data consistency needs to be maintained within a transaction. For data with long synchronization intervals, no concurrency control is needed (data can be synchronized daily, hourly, etc.).
3. For the DDTMS needing concurrency control, use a variant of 2PL, perhaps the primary copy 2PL because it is used most frequently.
4. The optimistic concurrency control algorithms seem to work very well when the transactions are short and the workload is light.
5. The time stamp algorithms work well for light workloads but degrade quickly with heavy workloads due to too many aborts and restarts.
6. Due to the enormous time investment, DDTMS designers should not undertake development of analytical or simulation models to measure the effect of concurrency control algorithms. In most cases, development of these models is a major task <Umar 1984, Garcia-Molina 1979>. If needed, consult the published analytical or simulation studies for more insights.

6.9.2 Two-Phase Commit for Failure Detection and Transaction Recovery

In an LDBMS, updates are made permanent when a transaction commits, and updates are rolled back if a transaction aborts. In DDTMS, a transaction may commit at one node and abort at another. For example, update completes at node n1 and fails at n2.

A transaction may terminate abnormally due to two reasons: "suicide," indicating that a transaction terminates due to an internal error like a program error, or "murder" indicating an external error like system crash <Gray 1979>. It is the responsibility of a DDTMS to remove all changes made by a failing transaction from all nodes so that the transaction can be reinitiated.

For atomic actions to be recoverable, the following two conditions must be met:

1. Updated objects are not released until the action is completed.
2. The initial states of all objects modified by the action can be reconstructed through the use of a log.

An extensive recovery system for distributed database management systems has been proposed by Gray <Gray 1979> and implemented in System R. This system consists of the following four protocols:

1. *Consistency locks*: This means that each transaction must be well formed and two-phase. A transaction is well formed if it locks an object before accessing it, does not lock an already locked item, and unlocks each locked item before termination. A transaction exhibits two-phase behavior if no objects are unlocked before all objects are locked. Transactions using 2PL are automatically well formed and two-phase.
2. *DO-UNDO-REDO log*: This is an incremental log of changes to the databases which records the before/after images of each update during the transaction processing (DO operation). This log also allows removal (UNDO) of a failed transaction's updates and reapplication (REDO) of the successful transaction's updates in the event of a database crash.
3. *Write-ahead log*: This protocol consists of writing an update to a log before applying it to the database.
4. *Two-phase commit*: This protocol coordinates the commit actions needed to run a transaction. When the transaction issues a COMMIT request, then a commit coordinator takes the following actions:

   Phase 1:

   1) Sends a PREPARE message to all cohorts (commit coordinators running on nodes participating in the execution of this transaction)
   2) Waits for a reply from all cohorts

   Phase 2: If all cohorts respond READY, then

   1) Writes COMMIT entry into the log
   2) Sends a COMMIT message to each cohort
   3) Waits for positive response from each cohort
   4) Writes a complete entry in log and terminates
      Else write abort message and terminate the transaction

   The two-phase commit has been implemented in several systems. Other approaches have been proposed and are being investigated. An extensive discussion of the reliability of distributed database management systems for no data replication, data replication, full replication, and network partitioning is given by Garcia-Molina 1987.

6.9.3 Combined Concurrency and Consistency Control Algorithms

In practice, the concurrency control techniques are combined with consistency control for failure handling and timeout for deadlock resolution into a single algorithm of distributed transaction management. For example, the algorithm shown in Table 6.2 combines the primary copy 2PL, two-phase commit, and timeout into a single concurrency and consistency control algorithm of a potential DDTMS. The algorithm is illustrated through a transaction which reads a data item x and writes (updates) two data items (y and z). The activities performed in reading x, writing y, writing z, and then doing the commit are stated in terms of locks, DO-UNDO-REDO logs, and timeouts.

6.10 DDTMS Configurations and Implementation Considerations

A DDTMS can be configured and implemented by using a variety of approaches in data allocations, directory definition and allocation, concurrency control algorithms, transaction processing strategies, and recovery management. The choice of appropri-

TABLE 6.2 A Combined Concurrency Control, Commit Processing, and Deadlock Algorithm

read x	1. obtain readlock from primary site of x 2. issue read x from any site
write y	1. obtain writelock from primary site of y 2. write y to a do-undo-redo log of primary site . write y to the primary site 3. write y to a do-undo-redo log of duplicate site . write y to the duplicate site (s)
write z	1. obtain writelock from primary site of z 2. write z to a do-undo-redo log of primary site . write z to the primary site 3. write z to a do-undo-redo log of duplicate site . write z to the duplicate site(s)
terminate (commit)	1. write commit message to the do-undo-redo log of primary site y 2. write commit message to the do-undo-redo log of duplicate site(s) of y 3. write commit message to the do-undo-redo log of primary site of z 4. write commit message to the do-undo-redo log of duplicate site(s) of z 5. if all commits are successful, then: —release all read locks for x —release all write locks for y —release all write locks for z —terminate transaction 6. if commits not successful (timeout), then —undo y at primary plus duplicate sites —undo z at primary plus duplicate sites —release all read locks for x —release all write locks for y —release all write locks for z —abort transaction

ate techniques and algorithms depends on the facilities to be supported by the DDTMS. Table 6.3 shows a simple framework to categorize the complexity of these decisions and to help the analysts evaluate appropriate products. The framework uses the following end user factors as the constrained variables:

- Homogeneous versus heterogeneous LDBMS
- Network control (central, distributed), where one node is designated to coordinate all DDTMS interactions
- Number of copies allowed in a network—that is, single, two copies (one at central site, one at local site), and more than two.

Based on these constrained variables, configurations 1 through 5 are defined in Table 6.3. For each configuration, the choices available in terms of database definition, directory allocation, concurrency control, transaction processing, and recovery management are listed. The configurations shown in Table 6.3 show the complexity range

TABLE 6.3 DDTMS Implementation Evaluation Model

Configuration 1: Homogeneous, centrally controlled, no data duplication data uniquely assigned (partitioned) to nodes

a. Database definition and translation: not difficult
b. Directory allocation: not difficult (use central site)
c. Database consistency/concurrency: relatively simple (no duplication)
d. Query optimization: simple (data at unique sites)
e. Failure handling: simple (no need to synchronize updates after failures)

Configuration 2: same as 1, copy can exist at host

a. Database definition and translation: not difficult
b. Directory allocation: not difficult (use central site)
c. Database consistency/concurrency: somewhat difficult (some duplication)
d. Query optimization: somewhat difficult (some duplication)
e. Failure handling: somewhat difficult

Configuration 3: same as 2, several copies can exist

a. Database definition and translation: not difficult
b. Directory allocation: somewhat difficult
c. Database consistency/concurrency: difficult (many choices)
d. Query optimization: difficult (many choices)
e. Failure handling: difficult (many choices)

Configuration 4: same as 3, not centrally controlled

a. Database definition and translation: not difficult
b. Directory allocation: difficult (many choices)
c. Database consistency/concurrency: difficult (many choices)
d. Query optimization: difficult (many choices)
e. Failure handling: difficult (many choices)

Configuration 5: same as 4, heterogeneous

a. Database definition and translation: difficult (many choices)
b. Directory allocation: difficult (many choices)
c. Database consistency/concurrency: difficult (many choices)
d. Query optimization: difficult (many choices)
e. Failure handling: difficult (many choices)

of a DDTMS. The simplest implementation of a DDTMS is for configuration 1 (homogeneous, centrally controlled, unique data allocation). It is most difficult for configuration 5, when the LDBMSs are heterogeneous, there is no central control, and the data can be replicated. This is why many products support configurations 1 and 2, and very few support configuration 5. Let us review this statement.

Several implementations support configuration 1 due to its simplicity. For example, most systems support relational DBMS, assume some level of centralized control, and allow limited or no data distribution. Remote procedure call (RPC) is supported by many systems, as discussed Chapter 5, to directly access the data where it resides. This approach allows a single application to access many databases (i.e., program P can access table T1 on node n1 and T2 on node n2). As shown in Table 6.3, this option is straightforward to implement due to the following reasons:

- Database definition and translation are not difficult because all LDBMSs are relational (SQL can be used everywhere).
- Directory allocation is not difficult because the central site can be used to house the global data directory.
- Database consistency/concurrency control is relatively simple because data is not duplicated and update synchronization is not needed.
- Query optimization is simple because data is at unique sites and the algorithms do not need to find the "nearest" data site for optimal results.
- Failure handling is simple because there is no need to synchronize updates after failures.

Configuration 2 is somewhat more difficult to implement because the database consistency/concurrency, query optimization, and failure handling must deal with limited data duplication. This configuration is supported by many vendor products. Configuration 3 becomes more difficult to implement because the number of options in database consistency/concurrency, query optimization, and failure handling increase due to many copies of data in the system. Configuration 4 becomes even harder to implement because the directory allocation is complicated due to many sites where the data can exist. Configuration 5 is the most difficult configuration to support because many choices and tradeoffs exist at all levels; consequently, it is not supported by vendor products.

Several products which provide many of the DDTMS facilities in the first few configurations have been announced for commercial use. Some of the commercially available DDTMS, listed alphabetically, are as follows:

- ADR/Dnet of Applied Data Research
- Cincom's Supra DDBM
- DB2 rel 2 of IBM
- Encompass of Tandem Computers
- Informix Star of Informix Software

- Ingres DDBM of Ingres Corp.
- Shard, Adaplex, and Model 204 of Computer Corporation of America
- SQL Server of Oracle, Inc.
- Sybase Database Server of Sybase, Inc.
- VAX Data Distributor of Digital Equipment Corp.

As mentioned previously, many of these products are marketed as distributed database management systems. Although most of these products support distributed databases, many products also allow access to data located in "flat" files. For example, the Sybase system can be used to access data that may be located in many different formats at different locations. Similarly, EDA/SQL provides over 40 data drivers for different files and databases.

It is beyond the scope of this book to discuss various DDTMS products. Some analysis can be found in Graham 1987, Rauch-Hinden 1987, Ricciuti 1991, Semich 1991, and McCord 1987. Some of the oldest implementations of DDTMS, (e.g., the Tandem Encompass, are described in detail by Gray <Gray 1987>. In addition to the commercially available DDTMS, several research and development DDTMS are being developed in different parts of the world. The book by Ozsu and Valduriez <Ozsu 1991> describes many such efforts.

6.11 Overview of Distributed Database Design

Once a DDTMS has been developed or purchased, then the users (application designers, database designers, administrators, application users) face the major decision of where to allocate the database. We briefly review the main concepts here and postpone detailed discussion to a later chapter.

The data allocation decision significantly affects the query processing, concurrency control, and reliability of a distributed database. A database D can be allocated to a network by using one of the following strategies:

1. D is allocated to a central node NC.
2. D is uniquely allocated to a node N, where it is most frequently accessed.
3. D is allocated to N and a duplicate copy of D is kept at the central node NC.
4. D is allocated to N and duplicate copies of D are kept at an arbitrary set of nodes N1, N2, N3, etc.
5. D is allocated to every node (replicated).
6. D is partitioned into D1, D2, D3 which are allocated by using strategies 1 through 5.

The cost/benefit of these allocations can be estimated in terms of storage cost, communication costs (cost to read, cost to update), response time and data availability. In addition, some of these allocations may not be feasible due to the software and/or hardware restrictions (for example, an Informix database cannot

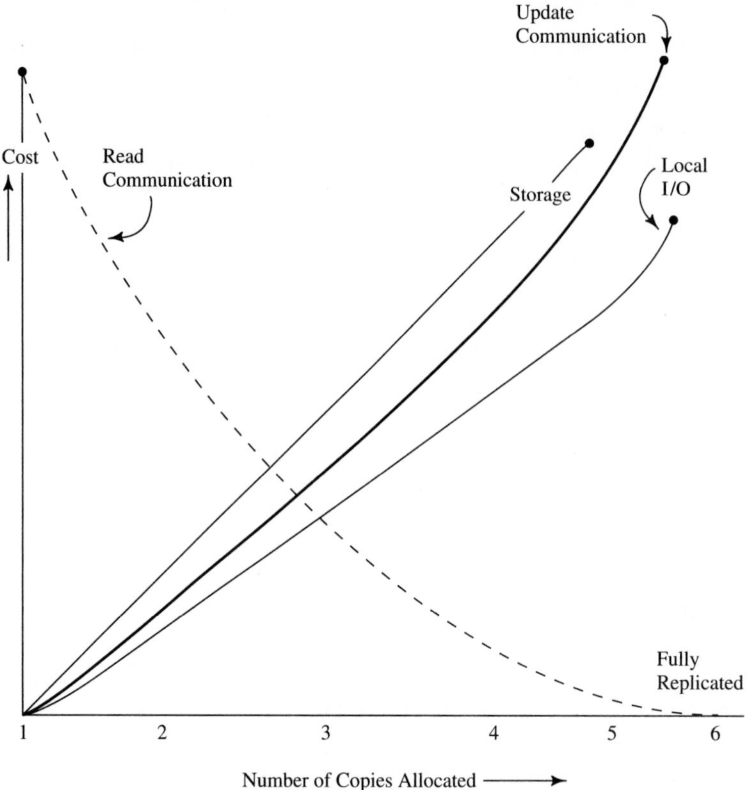

Notes:

- The cost does not necessarily indicate $ cost. It is a unit of resources needed which can be translated to $ costs.
- The number of copies indicates data duplication. In this example, six nodes are involved; hence six copies of a file mean fully replicated allocation.
- The local I/O means disk I/O at each node.
- The communication costs (read, update) indicate message traffic generated over the network. These costs include the locking/unlocking overhead.
- The storage cost indicates the amount of disk space occupied.

FIGURE 6.13 Data Allocation Tradeoffs

be allocated to IBM mainframes because Informix is not currently supported on MVS). Basically, duplicated data improves the availability and read performance but increases the storage and update synchronization costs (see Fig. 6.13). An optimal data allocation can be theoretically determined which minimizes the total cost (storage + communication + local I/O) subject to response time, availability, and hardware/software constraints. This problem, traditionally referred to as the

File Allocation Problem (FAP), in computing networks was first addressed by Wesley Chu in 1969 <Chu 1969>. Since then over 20 different file allocation algorithms have appeared in the literature <Bryand 1981, Bucci 1979, Buckles 1979, Casey 1972, Chandy 1976, Chang 1981, Chu 1969, Coffman 1980, Doty 1982, Eswaran 1974, Finckenscher 1984, Fisher 1980, Irani 1981, Khabbaz 1979, Kimbleton 1977, Koh 1985, Levin 1975, Mahmood 1976>. Earlier allocation problems were simple, while more recent methods are actual design methodologies which utilize the allocation techniques as one of the decisions <Umar 1984, Jain 1987, Ceri 1987>. A common FAP is formulated as follows:

- Given:
  Files f1, f2, f3,,,
  Nodes n1, n2, n3,,,,,
- Determine:
  ADN(f,n) = 1 if f is allocated to n, 0 otherwise
- To minimize:
  storage cost + communication cost + local processing cost
- Subject to:
  response time constraints
  availability constraints
  network topology
  security restrictions

Variants of this problem are cast into a mathematical programming problem and are solved by using nonlinear, integer, and/or dynamic programming methods.

Application of the existing FAP problems depends on the nature of the problem, the availability of information needed to reach an exact solution, and the need to determine optimal versus approximate solutions in real life. Based on my past experience in the distributed database allocations, it has been found that for several real-life situations, sophisticated FAP are needed rarely. In most cases, data allocation decisions can be made by exercising judgment and using real-life constraints of security and management. However, it is preferable to use simple analytical models to support the decisions and improve insights. A method which combines heuristics with formal models to allocate data in networks is described in Chapter 8, Section 8.5.3.

6.12 Management Summary and Trends

Distributed Data and Transaction Management Systems (DDTMSs) are concerned with

- Distributed data (files plus databases)
- Distributed transactions.

A DDTMS provides location transparency of read activity, store/update activity, transaction execution, and failures for files and databases in a network. Specifically, a DDTMS provides the following levels of transparency:

- *Retrieval transparency*: Data items can be retrieved from any site without the user having to know the site.
- *Update transparency*: If one copy of a data item is updated, then all other copies are also updated (synchronized).
- Transaction transparency: A transaction may be decomposed and routed to different sites to access distributed data without the knowledge of a user.
- *Failure transparency*: If a site fails, a DDTMS will access the desired data from a different site, if possible, without the knowledge of a user.

Design and implementation of DDTMS involves many challenges and choices. This chapter has attempted to clarify and categorize the main challenges and approaches. First, the components of DDTMS (distributed file managers, distributed database managers, and distributed transaction managers) are reviewed. Second, a reference architecture is shown which clusters the main issues into several modules. The architecture is used to explain the issues encountered and approaches available in database definition, concurrency control, query processing, and recovery/failure management. Third, the DDTMS configuration and implementation issues are summarized.

DDTMSs have moved from research to commercial products. However, the differences between the research results and commercial availability must be understood. Evaluation of commercial DDTMSs is difficult due to the discrepancies between promised versus available facilities. Due to the large amount of literature in this field, different viewers and views of DDTMS have been suggested to identify who needs to know what about DDTMS.

In general, the complexity of the DDTMS to be developed depends on the options supported (requirements to be satisfied). It is easier to develop DDTMS which support single-copy and homogeneous LDBMS approach. The difficulties encountered in implementing DDTMS must be carefully weighed against the advantages of DDTMS over centralized systems. For several applications, it may still be better to provide a centralized database or use a single-copy DDTMS after all of the costs for query processing, concurrency control, and failure management have been taken into account.

The following trends in DDTMS development are worth noting (see Ozsu <1991> book for additional information):

- SQL will continue as a standard for data access across all data sources such as files and databases, but
  - SQL conversion to nonrelational DBMS is not trivial.
  - All SQLs are not the same (e.g., ANSI SQL is a subset of DB2 SQL); most database vendors add "special" extensions to SQL.

- SQL Access Group, a consortium of database vendors, is trying to develop SQL standards.
- Relational database systems may not be adequate for engineering applications like CAD/CAM .

- More DDTMSs will attempt to include heterogeneous data located at heterogeneous computers, interconnected through heterogeneous networks.
- Standards in DDTMS will play an important role in the future. For example, the ISO Remote Database Access (RDA) standard for database access, and the ISO Transaction Processing (TP) and the X/Open Distributed Transaction Processing (DTP) standards are worth noting.

We have attempted to give an overview of an area in which the literature continues to grow. The following books are recommended for additional details:

- Ozsu, M. and Valduriez, P., *Principles of Distributed Database Systems*, Prentice Hall, 1991
- Elmagarmid, A., *Database Transaction Models for Advanced Applications*, Morgan Kaufmann Publishers, 1992
- Bernstein, P. A., Hadzilacos, V., and Goodman, N., *Concurrency Control and Recovery in Database Systems*, Addison Wesley, 1987.

The interested reader can find additional information in several journals and conference proceedings such as

- ACM Transactions on Database Systems
- ACM SIGMOD International Conferences
- IEEE International Conferences on Data Engineering
- International Conferences on Very Large Databases
- International Conference on Distributed Computing
- IEEE Transactions on Knowledge and Data Engineering
- Database Programming and Design.

Problems and Exercises

1. What are the differences between a DDTMS and a DDBM? Explain your answer through an example.
2. Describe a distributed file system other than NFS.
3. List the factors which can be used to evaluate different DDBM.
4. What are the advantages of using a client-server paradigm to deliver a DDBM?
5. What are the main issues and approaches in heterogeneous database systems?

6. What are the main functions provided by a DTM? How do these functions differ from a local transaction manager?
7. Define the following standards and describe their role in DDTMS:
   - ISO RDA
   - ISO TP
   - X/Open DTP
8. List the architectural components of the DDTMS architecture in which the following problems are addressed:
   - Concurrency control
   - Commit processing
   - Global schema generation
   - Deadlock detection
   - Distributed query processing
   - RPCs
9. If you had to build a DDTMS, what architectural blocks would you use and why?
10. List the tradeoffs involved in centralization versus distribution of a customer database. For example, what are the advantages of keeping the data at one site versus at multiple sites?

CASE STUDY: DDTMS for XYZCORP

The corporate-wide interconnectivity effort has raised many data and transaction management issues in XYZCORP. You have been asked to complete the following projects to clarify these issues. You should use the information about the company's operations, geographical distribution and the information architecture described in the previous chapters.

PROJECT A: XYZCORP Databases

You have to identify and list the major databases and the processing requirements for the databases for XYZCORP. You should identify at least three databases in business, three in engineering, and three in manufacturing systems. For each database, you should show at least five queries and transactions, in English, to retrieve and manipulate the information. In addition, show the complexity of data model and the programs (transaction or query) for each database.

PROJECT B: DDTMS Selection

It has been suggested that XYZCORP needs a company wide DDTMS. You have been asked to evaluate and select a DDTMS for XYZCORP. You may use the output of project A as an input to this assignment. The following steps are suggested:

1. List the names of the databases produced in project A which will benefit from a DDTMS. Why and why not?
2. List the advantages and disadvantages of a DDTMS specifically for XYZCORP.
3. List the requirements to be satisfied by the DDTMS. These requirements will serve as a basis for evaluating existing DDTMS and selecting an appropriate DDTMS. Your list should include the following:
   a. *Functional requirements*—the main things that a DDTMS should be able to provide, especially the requirements needed for XYZCORP.
   b. *Performance requirements*—the response time, availability, and integrity requirements
   c. *Management restrictions*—security facilities, time, and budgetary restrictions.
4. Prepare a list of candidate DDTMSs.
5. Offer a recommendation, which should indicate one of the following:
   a. Name of one DDTMS which satisfies the aforementioned requirements
   b. Name of one or more DDTMS which satisfies the most important of the aforementioned requirements, with a list of additional facilities that need to be developed
   c. No existing DDTMS is suitable, with a justification. Should XYZCORP develop a roll-your-own (RYO) DDTMS?

Your answer should include an evaluation model which lists the factors being used for DDTMS evaluation (e.g., read transparency, performance) and ranking of the candidates.

PROJECT C: Database Allocation

Decide where you would allocate the databases listed in project A. Specifically

- Which databases will be allocated to the corporate site, the stores, the manufacturing plant and the engineering plant.
- Which databases will you duplicate and why?
- What capabilities of a DDTMS are needed to serve the databases allocated to the different nodes.

Hints About the Case Study

Project A: You should review Appendix E before attempting this project. Table 6.4 is a good way to get started on this project. Many database names may be extracted from the applications (e.g., computerized checkout/inventory control, financial planning, EDI) listed in the case study of Chapter 5. An example of an entry in Table A is the customer database which has a simple data model (not very complex relationships). A query against this database may be "list all customers who have bought products this year" and a transaction against this database may be "increase the credit limit of each customer by $500."

TABLE 6.4

Database Name	*Database Type (HN,R,O)*	*Data Complexity (L,M,H)*	*Program Complexity (L,M,H)*	*Database Transactions (at least 5)*

Legend: HN (hierarchical or network), R (relational), O (object oriented)

Project B: Basically, any of the databases can benefit from a DDTMS if (1) the data can exist at more than one site and (2) if data is updated frequently from multiple sites. For example, customer databases and inventory databases can exist at many sites, are updated frequently, and thus need to be synchronized. A DDTMS would be needed for these databases. The functional requirements to be satisfied by a DDTMS may include the 12 rules shown in Table 6.1 (see Section 6.4.1 for discussion). It is important to review each rule and assign a weight (importance) appropriate for XYZCORP. For example, rules 9, 10, 11, and 12 are of critical importance to XYZCORP because different operating systems (MVS, Unix, DOS), different computers (mainframes, minicomputers, desktops), different networks (TCP/IP, SNA), and different databases (hierarchical, relational, object oriented) are used in this company.

Project C: This problem can be solved by using heuristics. For example, manufacturing databases can be allocated to manufacturing sites, store information may be kept at stores, etc. The discussion in Section 6.11 should help. A DDTMS would provide the location transparency so that data located anywhere can be accessed by any site.

References

Note: Many of these references are "older" because a great deal of fundamental work in distributed databases was done in the late 1970s and early 1980s.

Barghouti, N.S. and Kaiser, G.E., "Concurrency Control in Advanced Database Applications," *ACM Computing Surveys*, Sept. 1991. pp. 269-318.

Bernstein, P.A. and Goodman, N., "Concurrency Control in Distributed Database Systems," *ACM Computing Surveys*, Vol. 13, No. 2, June 1981, pp. 185-222.

Bernstein, P.A. and Chiu, D.W., "Using Semi-Joins to Solve Relational Queries," *JACM,* Jan. 1981.

Bernstein, P.A., Hadzilacos, V., and Goodman, N., *Concurrency Control and Recovery in Database Systems*, Addison-Wesley, 1987

Bodarik, P., et al., "Deciding to Correct Distributed Query Processing," *IEEE Trans. on Knowledge and Data Engineering*, June 1992, pp. 253-265.

Bryand, R.M., and Agre, J.R., "A Queuing Network Approach to the Module Allocation Problem in Distributed Systems," ACM Conf. on Measurement and Modelling of Computer Systems, Sept. 1981, pp. 181-190.

Bucci, G., Streeter, D.N., "A Methodology for the Design of Distributed Information Systems," *CACM,* Vol. 22, No.4, Apr. 1979, pp. 233-245.

Buckles, B.P. and Harding, D.M., "Partitioning and Allocation of Logical Resources in a Distributed Computing Environment," General Research Corporation Report, Huntsville, Alabama, 1979.

Cardenas, A.F., "Heterogeneous Distributed Database Management: the HD-DBMS," *Proceedings of the IEEE*, May 1987, pp. 588-600.

Casey, R.G.," Allocation of Copies of a File in an Information Network," *SJCC 1972*, AFIPS Press, Vol. 40, 1972

Ceri, S., and Pelagatti, G., *Distributed Databases: Principles and Systems*, McGraw-Hill, 1984.

Ceri, S., Pernici, B., and Wiederhold, G., "Distributed Database Design Methodologies," *Proceedings of the IEEE*, May, 1987, pp. 533-546.

Chandy, D.M. and Hewes, J.E. "File Allocation in Distributed Systems," *Proc. of the Intl. Symp on Computer Performance Modelling, Measurement and Evaluation*, Mar. 1976, pp. 10-13.

Chang, S.K. and Liu, A.C., "A Database File Allocation Problem," *COMPSAC*, 1981, pp. 18-22.

Chu, W.W., "Optimal file allocation in a multiple computer system," *IEEE Trans. on Computers*, Oct. 1969, pp. 885-889.

Chu, W.W., "Performance of File Directory Systems for Data Bases in Star and Distributed Networks," *1976 NCC*, Vol. 45, 1976.

Chu, W.W., "Distributed Data Bases," *Handbook of Software Engineering*, Edited by C.R. Vick and C.V. Ramamoorthy, Van Nostrand Reinhold, 1984.

Ceri, S., and G. Pellagitti, *Distributed Databases: Principles and Systems*, McGraw-Hill, 1984.

Ceri, S., Pernici, B., Wiederhold, "Distributed Database Design Methodolgies," *Proceedings of the IEEE*, May 1987, pp. 533-546.

Coffman, E.G., Gelenbe, E, et al., "Optimization of the Number of Copies in Distributed Databases," *Proc. of the 7th IFIP Symposium on Computer Performance Modelling*, Measurement and Evaluation, May 1980, pp. 257-263.

Cohen, D., Holcomb, J.E., and Suryanarayana, M.B., "Distributed Database Management to Support Network Services," IEEE Conference on Communications, 1982.

Date, C.J., *An Introduction to Database Systems,* 5th ed., Vols. 1 and 2, Addison-Wesley, 1990

Date, C.J., "Twelve Rules for a Distributed Database," *InfoDB*, Vol. 2, Nos. 2 and 3, Summer/Fall 1987.

Date, C.J., *A Guide to DB2*, Addison-Wesley, 1984.

Decitre, P., "A Model for Describing Distributed Database Management System Architecture," 16th Annual IEEE Electronics and Aerospace Systems Conference, Sept. 1983.

Doty, K.W., McEntyre, P.L., and O'Reilly, J.G., "Task Allocation in a Distributed Computer System," *Proc. of IEEE INFOCOM*, 1982, pp. 33-38.

Ellis, C.A., "A Robust Algorithm for Updating Duplicate Databases," *Proc. of 2nd Berkeley Workshop on Distributed Databases and Computer Networks*, ACM/IEEE, May 1977.

Elmagarmid, A., *Database Transaction Models for Advanced Applications*, Morgan Kaufmann Publishers, 1992.

Epstein, R., Stonebraker, M., Wong, E., "Distributed Query Processing in a Relational Database System," *ACM SIGMOD*, Austin, TX, 1978

Epstein, R., "Query Optimization: A Game of Time and Statistics," *Unix Review*, May 1987, pp. 28-29.

Eswaran, K.P., Gray, J.N., et al., "Notions of Consistency and Predicate Locks in a Database System," *CACM*, Vol. 19, No. 11, Nov.1976.

Eswaran, K.P., "Allocation of Records to Files and Files to Computer Networks," *IFIP*, 1974, pp. 304-307.

Farrag, A.A., and Ozsu, M.T., "Towards a General Concurrency Control Algorithm for Database Systems," *IEEE Trans. on Software Engineering*, Vol. SE-13, No. 10, Oct. 1987, pp. 1073-1078.

Finckenscher, G., *Automatic Distribution of Programs in MASCOT and ADA Environments*, Royal Signal and Radar Establishment, London, 1984.

Fisher, P., Hollist, P., and Slonim, J., "A Design Methodology for Distributed Databases," *Proc. IEEE Conf. on Distributed Computing*, Sept. 1980, pp. 199-202.

Fisher, M.L. and Hochbaum, D., "Database Location in Computer Networks," *ACM Journal*, V.27, N.4, Oct. 1980.

Garcia-Molina, H., "Performance of Update Synchronization Algorithms for Replicated Data in a Distributed Database," Ph.D. Dissertation, Stanford University, June 1979.

Garcia-Molina, H., Abbot, R.K., "Reliable Distributed Database Management," *Proceedings of the IEEE*, Vol. 75, No. 5, May 1987, pp. 601-620.

Gligor, V.D., and Fong, E., "Distributed Database Management Systems: An Architectural Perspective," *Journal of Telecommunication Networks*, Vol. 22, No. 3, pp. 247-270, Fall 1983.

Graham, G., "Real-World Distributed Databases," *Unix Review*, May 1987.

Gray, J., *Notes on Database Operating Systems, in Operating Systems: An Advanced Course*, Springer-Verlag, N.Y. 1979, pp. 393-481.

Gray, J., "The Transaction Concept: Virtues and Limitations," *Proceedings of Conference on Very Large Databases,* Sept. 1981, pp. 144-154.

Gray, J., "Transparency in Its Place," *Unix Review*, May 1987.

Gray, J.N., and Anderson, M., "Distributed Computer Systems: Four Cases," *Proc. of the IEEE*, May 1987, pp. 719-729.

Goodman, N., et al., "Query Processing in SDD-1: A System for Distributed Databases," *CCA*, Technical Report, CCA-79-06, 1979.

Goodman, N., "Interview with Phil Bernstein," *Unix Review*, May 1987.

Gylys, V.B. and Edwards, J.A, "Optimal Partitioning of Workload for Distributed Systems," *COMPCON*, Fall 1976.

Hebalkar, P.G., "Logical Design Considerations for Distributed Database Systems," *IEEE COMPSOC*, Nov. 1977, pp. 562-580.

Heinselman, R.C. "System Design Selection for Distributed Databases," *Proc. IEEE Conf. on Distributed Computing*, Sept. 1980, pp. 203-210.

Hevner, A.R., and Yao, S.B., "Query Processing in Distributed Database Systems," *IEEE Transactions on Software Engineering*, Vol. SE-5, No. 3, May 1979.

Hevner, A.R., "A Survey of Data Allocation and Retrieval Methods for Distributed Systems," School of Business and Management Working Paper #81-036, Univ. of Maryland, Oct. 1981.

Hevner, A.R., and Yao, S.B., "Querying Distributed Databases on Local Area Networks," *Proc. of the IEEE*, May 1987, pp. 563-572.

IDMS System Overview, Westwood, Mass., Cullinane Database Systems, 1981.

Irani, K.B. and Khabbaz, N.G., "A Combined Communication Network Design and File Allocation for Distributed Databases," 2nd Intl. Conf. on Distributed Systems, Paris, Apr. 1981.

Jain, H.K., "A Comprehensive Model for the Design of Distributed Computer Systems," *IEEE Trans. on Software Engineering*, Vol. SE-13, No. 10, Oct. 1987, pp. 1092-1105.

Jarke, M. and Koch, J., "Query Optimization in Database Systems," *ACM Computing Surveys*, June 1984, pp. 111-152.

Kamel, M. N. and Kamel, N. N., "The Federated Database Management Systems," *Computer Communications,* Vol. 15, No. 4, May 1992, pp. 270-278.

Kapp, D., and Leben, J., *IMS Programming Techniques,* Van Nostrand-Reinhold Company, 1978.

Khabbaz, G.N, "A Combined Network Design and File Allocation in Distributed Computer Networks," Ph.D dissertation proposal, Univ. of Michigan, 1979.

Kimbleton, S.R., "A Fast Approach to Network Data Assignment," *Proc. of 2nd Berkeley Workshop on Distributed Data Management and Computing Networks*, May 1977, pp. 245-255

Koh, K. and Eom, Y.I., "A File Allocation Scheme for Minimizing the Storage Cost in Distributed Computing Systems," First Pacific Computer Communication Symposium, Seoul, Korea, Oct. 1985, pp. 310-317.

Kohler, W. H., "A Survey of Techniques for Synchronization and Recovery in Decentralized Computer Systems," *ACM Computing Surveys*, Vol. 13, No. 2, June 1981, pp. 149-184.

Krasowski, M., "Integrating Distributed Databases into the Information Architecture," *Journal of Information Systems Management*, Spring, 1991, pp. 38-46.

Kroenke, D., "Database Processing," *SRA*, 1977.

Larson, B., *The Database Experts' Guide to DB2*, McGraw-Hill, 1988.

Larson, J. A., "A Flexible Reference Architecture for Distributed Database Management," *Proc. of ACM 13th Annual Computer Science Conference*, Mar. 1985, New Orleans, pp. 58-72.

Larson, B., "A Retrospective of R*: A Distributed Database Management System," *Proc. of the IEEE*, May 1987, pp. 668-673.

Lef, A. and Pu, C., "A Classification of Transaction Processing Systems," *IEEE Computer,* June 1991, pp. 63-76.

Levin, K.D and Morgan, L.H. " Optimizing Distributed Data Bases—A Framework for Research," *Proc. NCC*, Vol. 44, 1975, pp. 473-478

Lim, P.A., *CICS/VS Command Level with ANS Cobol Examples*, Van Nostrand Reinhold, 1982.

Litwin, W., Mark, L., and Roussopoulos, N., "Interoperability of Multiple Autonomous Databases," *ACM Computing Surveys*, Sept. 1990, pp. 267-293

Lu, P.M. and Yau, S.B., "A Methodology for Representing the Formal Specifications of Distributed Computer System Software Design," *Proc. IEEE Conf. on Distributed Computing Systems*, Oct. 1979, pp. 31-42.

Mahmood, S. and Riordan, J., "Optimal Allocation of Resources in Distributed Information Networks," *ACM Trans. on Database Systems,* Vol. 1, No. 1, Mar. 1976, pp. 66-78.

Mariani, M.P. and Palmer, D.F. (eds.), "Tutorial: Distributed System Design," EHO 151-1, IEEE Computer Society, 1979.

Mariani, M.P. and Palmer, D.F., "Software Development for Distributed Computing Systems," *Handbook of Software Engineering*, edited by C.V. Ramamoorthy and C.R. Vick, Van Nostrand, 1984, pp. 656-674.

Martin, D., *Advanced Database Techniques,* MIT Press, 1986.

McCord, R. and Hanner, M., "Connecting Islands of Information," *Unix Review*, May 1987.

Nirmal, B., "CICS Application and System Programming," QED, 1992.

Ozsu, M. and Valduriez, P., *Principles of Distributed Database Systems*, Prentice Hall, 1991.

Ozsu, M. and Valduriez, P., "Distributed Database Systems: Where Are We Now?" *IEEE Computer,* Aug. 1991, pp. 68-78.

Pu, C., Leff, A., and Chen, S., "Heterogeneous and Autonomous Transaction Processing," *IEEE Computer*, Dec. 1991, pp. 64-72.

Rauch-Hinden, W., "True Distributed DBMSes Presage Big Dividends," *Mini-Micro Systems*, May and June, 1987.

Ricciuti, M., "Universal Database Access," Datamation, Nov. 1, 1991.

Rothnie, J.B. and Goodman, N. "A Survey of Research and Development in Distributed Data Base Management," 3rd Conference on Very Large Data Bases, Tokyo, Oct. 1977, pp. 48-60.

Sacco, G.V. and Yao, S.B., "Query Optimization in Distributed Databases," Working Paper MS/S #81-029, College of Business Administration, University of Maryland, 1981.

Semich, J. and McMullen, J., "Sybase's Big Blue Connection," *Datamation*, Apr. 1, 1991.

Shatz, S.M., and Jia-Ping Wang, "Introduction to Distributed-Software Engineering," *IEEE Computer*, Oct., 1987, pp. 23-32.

Sheth, A.P., and Larson, J.A., "Federated Database Systems for Managing Distributed, Heterogeneous, and Autonomous Databases," *ACM Computing Surveys*, Sept. 1990, pp. 183-236.

Soparkar, N., Korth, H., and Silberschatz, A., "Failure-Resilient Transaction Management in Multi-Databases," *IEEE Computer*, Dec. 1991, pp. 28-37.

Stone, H., "Parallel Querying of Large Databases: A Case Study," *IEEE Computer*, Oct. 1987, pp. 11-21.

Stonebraker, M., "Concurrency Control and Consistency of Multiple Copies of Data in Distributed Ingres," *IEEE Trans. on Software Engineering*, SE-5, 3, May 1979, pp. 188-199.

Svobodova, L., "File Servers for Network-Based Distributed Systems," *ACM Computing Surveys*, Dec. 1984, pp. 353-398.

Tannenbaum, A.S, and van Renesse, R. "Distributed Operating Systems," *Computing Surveys*, Dec. 1985, pp. 419-470.

Tannenbaum, A.S., *Computer Networks*, Prentice Hall, 1981.

Teorey, T.J and Fry, J.P., *Design of Database Structures*, Prentice Hall, 1982.

Thomas, R.H., "A Majority Consensus Approach to Concurrency Control for Multiple Copy Databases," *ACM Trans. on Database Systems*, June 1979, pp. 180-209.

Thomas, G., et al., "Heterogeneous Distributed Database Systems for Production Use," *ACM Computing Surveys*, Sept. 1990, pp. 237-266.

Ullman, J., *Principles of Database Systems*, John Wiley, 1982.

Ullman, J., *Principles of Database and Knowledge-Base Systems*, Computer Science Press, 1988.

Umar, A., "The Allocation of Data and Programs in Distributed Data Processing Environments," Ph.D. Dissertation, University of Michigan, 984. Also published as Computing Research Laboratory report CRL-TR-22-84, University of Michigan, Ann Arbor, Mich.

Umar, A. and Teorey, T.J., "A Generalized Approach to Program and Data Allocation in Distributed Systems," First Pacific Computer Communication Symposium, Seoul, Korea, Oct. 1985, pp. 462-472.

Vasta, J., *Understanding Database Management Systems*, Wardsworth, 1985.

Vinzant, D., "SQL Database Servers," *Data Communications*, Jan. 1990, pp. 72-88.

Wilbur, S., and Bacarisse, "Building Distributed Systems with Remote Procedure Call," *Software Engineering Journal,* Sept. 1987, pp. 148-159.

Walpole, J. et al., "Transaction Mechanisms for Distributed Programming Environments," *Software Engineering Journal*, Sept. 1987, pp. 169-171.

Wolfe, P.E., "Computer Aided Design Report," Vol. 7, No. 4, Apr. 1987.

Wolfson, O., "The Overhead of Locking (and Commit) Protocols in Distributed Databases," *ACM Trans. on Database Systems*, Vol. 12, No. 3, Sept. 1987, pp. 453-471.

Wong, E., "Retrieving Dispersed Data from SDD-1: A System for Distributed Databases," Berkeley Workshop on Distributed Data Management and Computing Networks, 1977.

Woodside, C.M. and Tripathi, S.K., "Optimal Allocation of File Servers in a Local Area Network Environment," *IEEE Trans. on Software Engineering*, Aug. 1986, Vol. SE-12, No. 8, pp. 844-848.

Yao, S.B., "Optimization of Query Evaluation Algorithms," *ACM Trans. on Database Systems,* Vol. 4, No. 2, June 1979, pp. 133-155

Yu, C., and C. Chang, "Distributed Query Processing," *ACM Computing Surveys*, Vol. 16, No. 4, Dec. 1984, pp. 399-433.

Chapter 7

Distributed Operating Systems and Distributed Computing Platforms

Problems and Exercises
Case Study: Distributed Operating Systems and Platforms for CIMXYZ

7.1 Introduction

Distributed operating systems provide complete transparency to the end users so that the users view the network of interconnected computers as one computer system. A distributed operating system (DISOS) goes a step beyond the distributed data and transaction management systems (DDTMSs) which provide data location and transaction processing transparency. For example, consider a large distributed computing environment in which 50 print servers are spread across the network. At present users ask for specific print servers for printing; thus some servers are very busy while the others wait for work. A DISOS would automatically find an idle server in the network and thus balance the print workload. A DISOS makes all I/O devices, memory units and processors in the entire network available to the user as if they belong to one centralized computer system. In essence, distributed operating systems extend the scope of centralized operating systems to distributed computing (centralized operating systems balance the workload between various services on one machine).

The following questions motivate the discussion in this chapter:

- What are distributed operating systems and how do they differ from centralized operating systems?
- What are the design issues and approaches in DISOSs?
- What are distributed computing platforms (DCPs) and how do they support different levels of transparencies by integrating DISOSs, DDTMSs, and network architectures into a single framework?

Sections 7.2 and 7.3 review the main concepts of the centralized and distributed operating systems, respectively. The main design objectives of a DISOS (user interfaces, authentication, naming, scheduling, monitoring, etc.) are discussed in Section 7.4 and a few examples of DISOS are presented in Section 7.5.

A distributed computing platform (DCP) combines distributed operating systems, distributed database managers, distributed transaction managers, and network facilities to support different applications. From an application systems point of view, the term *distributed computing platform* is appropriate because it emphasizes the support role of distributed resource managers and networks.

The main objective of these platforms is to provide different levels of transparency to the users, application developers, designers, and managers. We define the following levels of transparency to be provided by a DCP:

- End user transparency
- Developer transparency

- Designer transparency
- Manager transparency.

Section 7.6 discusses these transparency issue and gives an overview of some DCP standards under development.

The reader should note that most of the material on distributed operating systems in this chapter is currently state of the art and not state of the market/practice. The following two books give more details about this topic:

- Tannenbaum, A., *Modern Operating Systems*, Prentice Hall, 1992
- Nutt, G., *Centralized and Distributed Operating Systems*, Prentice Hall, 1992.

7.2 Overview of Centralized Operating Systems

An operating system is a program, or a collection of programs, which allocates computer resources (memory, CPU, I/O devices, files, etc.) to processes (user commands, jobs, database managers, other operating systems). An operating system also gives the users a command language to invoke the operating system facilities and to access the computing resources. This command language, also called control language in some systems, is used to access editors, compilers, utilities, and other operating system resources. Typical functions performed by an operating system are as follows:

- Receive, parse, and interpret the user commands.
- Authenticate the user request for proper authority.
- Allocate the resources needed to execute the user commands if the user is allowed to access the resources.
- Schedule the user request as a process.
- Monitor the processes in the system.
- Free the resources held by the processes at termination.
- Display results of the user session with information about resource utilization, etc.

Figure 7.1 shows a functional model of operating systems. The user command manager parses and executes the user commands. The memory manager allocates the main memory and the hardware registers to various processes. Most memory managers include the capabilities to manage virtual memory and translate between virtual to real memory. The CPU (central processing unit) manager allocates the CPU to the processes. A variety of CPU scheduling schemes (time slicing, interrupt driven) have been employed in the operating systems. The file managers manage the data resources in the system. This normally includes catalogs, file sharing, etc. The I/O (input/output) managers steward all the local and remote I/O activities. The network communication facilities may be included in some operating systems as I/O facilities.

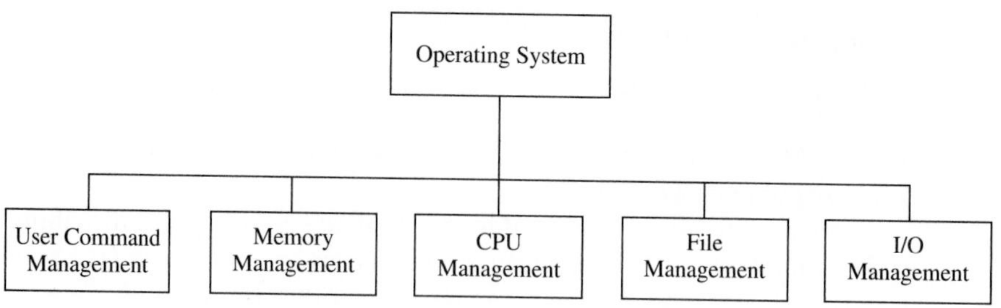

FIGURE 7.1 A Functional View of Operating Systems

A very broad range of operating systems have been developed in the last 25 years for multiple users. Some operating systems are built for specialized single-user systems, while others manage large mainframes. These operating systems can be categorized according to the following characteristics:

- *Number of users supported.* The operating systems intended for a single user (e.g., the MS/DOS for personal computers) are very simple because no resource allocation problems exist. As the number of users increases, the demands on allocation, scheduling and security/protection increases dramatically. An example of an operating system that handles a large number of users is the IBM MVS operating system for mainframes.
- *Degree of multiprogramming/multiprocessing.* A multiprogramming system can run several programs simultaneously, while a multiprocessing system traditionally can manage many processors simultaneously. Most microcomputers, minicomputers, and mainframes support multiprogramming as well as multiprocessing.
- *Batch versus interactive processing.* In a batch system, a user submits a job and then lets the system spool, schedule, run, and complete the job later. In an interactive system, the user interacts with the system while his or her job is being executed. An example of a batch application is a payroll program which prints checks, and an example of an interactive application is the airline reservation system. Some operating systems favor batch processing (e.g., mainframe operating systems), while others are oriented toward interactive processing (e.g., the workstation operating systems).

Many operating systems have been developed over the last thirty years. Examples of state of the market operating systems are DOS, OS/2, CP/M, Unix, VMS, and MVS. Perhaps the best-known operating system is Unix, which was developed at Bell Laboratories for software development. Unix is written in the C programming language and is currently available on personal computers, workstations, minicomputers, and mainframes. Unix is especially dominant in the mid-range computer hardware platforms. In fact, Unix is considered a de facto standard for open operating systems in the mid-range computing.

Many textbooks have been written on operating system principles, Unix, MVS, DOS, etc., and the interested reader should consult these books for additional information. The following is a sampling of these books:

- Coffman, E., and Denning, P., *Operating System Theory,* Prentice Hall, 1973
- Davis, W., *Operating Systems: A Systematic View*, 2nd ed., Addison-Wesley, 1983
- Turner, R. W., *Operating Systems: Design and Implementation*, Macmillan, 1986
- Tannenbaum, A., *Modern Operating Systems,* Prentice Hall, 1992
- Nutt, G., *Centralized and Distributed Operating Systems,* Prentice Hall, 1992.

7.3 Principles of Distributed Operating Systems

A *distributed operating system* handles its users very much like an ordinary centralized operating system but runs on multiple, interconnected computers <Tannenbaum 1985>. A distributed operating system (DISOS) provides complete transparency to the end-users so that the users view the network of interconnected computers as one computer system. Mullender et al. <Mullender 1990> describe the users of distributed operating systems as follows:

> "Users will not know which processor their jobs are using (or even how many), where there files are stored (or how many replicated copies are maintained to provide high availability), or how processes and machines are communicating."

In a vein similar to the centralized operating systems, a distributed operating system performs the following functions:

- Receive, parse, and interpret the user command from any computer.
- Authenticate the user request for proper authority. To handle security across multiple computers, global security tables need to be created, maintained, and accessed.
- Allocate the resources needed to execute the user commands if the user is allowed to access the resources. This provides the major source of transparency because the resources (files, programs, directories, I/O devices, memory units, CPU cycles) may be at any machine. Global information about all resources in the network needs to be created, maintained, and accessed for global resource allocation.
- Schedule the user request as a process or as a series of coordinated processes. The scheduling may involve dynamic resource allocation across multiple computer systems and determining the most appropriate resources across multiple computers for process execution.
- Monitor the processes in the system. This may involve fault tolerance on processes running on multiple computers.
- Free all the resources held by the processes at termination. This may involve resources across multiple computer systems which may need to be freed if portion of a process fails on one of the computers.

- Display results of the user session with information about resource utilization, etc. The results may need to be routed to sites which are different than the originating request.

It is not easy to build such systems across multiple heterogeneous operating systems. The challenges are many because a distributed operating system, in essence, extends the scope of a centralized operating system in a manner similar to a distributed database manager extending the scope of a centralized database manager. Figure 7.2 shows a functional model of distributed operating systems in terms of global and local functional components. The local components are part of the traditional local operating systems, while the global components are responsible for transparency between the local components. For example, the global user command manager would provide a unified user interface even if the local user command managers of various local operating systems are not the same. In fact, the X Window system, developed as part of the Athena distributed operating system, is a global user command processor which provides a uniform user interface for all users in the system.

We dealt with the challenges of providing data transparency in Chapter 6. In the case of a distributed operating system, *all* user activities are transparent to the end user. According to Tannenbaum <Tannenbaum 1985>,

> As a rule of thumb, if you can tell which computer you are using, you are not using a distributed (operating) system. The users of a true distributed (operating)

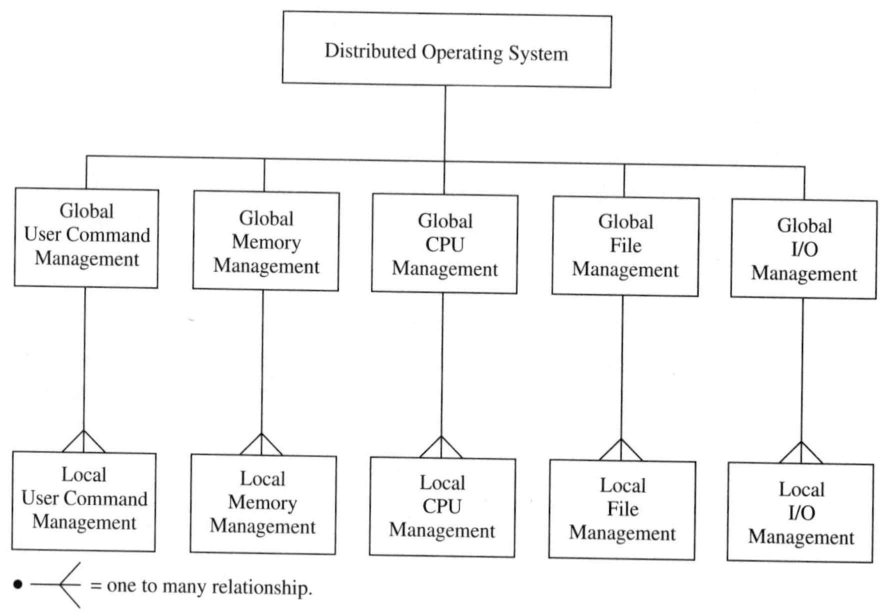

FIGURE 7.2 A Functional Viewof Distributed Operating Systems

system should not know (or care) on which machine (or machines) their programs are running, where there files are stored, and so on.

Most of the existing networks do not provide distributed operating system facilities. For example, in ARPANET, the user logs on to one computer system and always knows the computer he or she is using. In SNA environments, the user also knows computers (mainframes, token ring servers, etc.) on which the requests are being processed. The network operating systems used in LANs also do not provide any of the global and dynamic resource allocations used by a DISOS (users work on their own machines, files are transferred through explicit commands, etc.).

7.4 Design Issues in Distributed Operating Systems

Most of the existing operating systems have some networking capabilities added to the operating system services. Distributed operating systems are designed to be distributed among many machines. The major issues to be addressed in the design of a DISOS are as follows:

- Communication of processes between different computers
- Naming services for objects across multiple computers
- Global resource management (allocation, scheduling, deallocation)
- Scalability of services from a few workstations to thousands of workstations
- Compatibility at the binary code, execution, and protocol levels
- Fault management in distributed environments
- Security and protection across computers.

We discuss these issues in more detail here and show how some of the issues are related to similar discussions on distributed database management, distributed transaction management, and client-server systems.

7.4.1 Interprocess Communications

The distributed operating systems must have reliable and efficient mechanisms to communicate between remotely located processes. The traditional terminal emulation and file transfer mechanisms are obviously not adequate. The client-server and peer-to-peer paradigms introduced in Chapter 5 are best suited for DISOS implementation. In most cases, interprocess communication building blocks are better suited than complete services. As discussed in Chapter 5, the interprocess communications exist at two levels:

- Basic protocols, which are provided by the network facilities of the computer systems being served. Examples of these protocols are TCP/IP Sockets, APPC/LU6.2, and Manufacturing Message Specifications (MMS). As mentioned previously, these protocols are provided by different network architectures (TCP/IP Protocol Suite, SNA, MAP, etc.).

- Higher-level protocols, the remote procedure calls (RPCs), which are built on top of the basic protocols to provide an easy-to-use programming interface for remote process interactions. An RPC program issues a call to a remote procedure in a manner similar to local procedure call. RPCs are intended to be network architecture independent.

The choice of native protocols versus RPCs in a DISOS depends on the portability versus efficiency requirements. We discussed these services and protocols in Chapter 5. The native calls are more efficient but may not be portable across systems. However, TCP/IP Sockets are becoming available on most computing systems due to the popularity of TCP/IP.

7.4.2 Naming Conventions and Services

All operating systems must know the names of the objects (files, programs, directories, devices) they are managing. A distributed operating system must know the names of all the objects in the network and must be able to protect these objects from unauthorized access and manipulation. Some names are binary strings, while others are ASCII or EBCDIC user-friendly characters. In most distributed systems, name servers are used to translate the user-friendly names into the physical hardware identifiers. For example, in the TCP/IP networks, the Domain Name Services are used to translate a Unix computer name such as BLUE to a physical network hardware address such as 15.35.0.19. Name services involve the following steps:

- Find an appropriate name server. This is accomplished through global directories.
- The names of the objects to be used globally are registered in a name table. Each registered name has an external component, which is known to the users, and an internal component, which is used by the distributed operating systems to locate the objects physically.
- A process needing a service or a set of objects consults the name table to determine where the needed objects and services are located. The name server may translate the external object name into an internal physical address.

It is possible to have two-level name servers: one global name server and many local name servers. The global name server is consulted to determine the computer on which the object is located. The local name server at each computer shows the particular device within a computer (e.g., a disk) on which the object is located. This is in essence similar to the distributed (global) data directory discussed previously, in which the global directory points to a local database directory for exact data location and format. In large networks it is possible to have the following three levels of name services:

- A universal name server, which shows what objects are located in what subnets (network domains). The total network is assumed to be partitioned into several subnets (domains). For example, each LAN can be a subnet.
- A subnet name server, one per subnet, which shows the computer within the subnet where the resource is located.
- A local name server, one per computer, which shows where, within the computer system, the resource is located.

The main problem with this paradigm is that the universal name service can become a performance and availability bottleneck. To circumvent this problem, duplicate copies of universal names can be maintained, and/or naming conventions, similar to the telephone number systems, can be employed to identify subnets without an explicit table lookup. For example, the telephone area code indicates a region without an explicit table lookup. For distributed operating systems in small networks, such as LANs, it is possible to use a broadcast naming service in which the request for an object is broadcasted to the entire network. Each computer checks its local name table to find a match. If a match is found, it responds with a physical address; otherwise it ignores the request. The ANSI/OSI Directory Standard (X.500) is being developed for global naming and directory services.

7.4.3 Resource Management

Management of resources that are spread across many computers is difficult because a DISOS may not have current status information about what processes are active, what devices are being used, who is waiting on whom, what resources are locked, which processors are underutilized, etc. Status information of this nature is always available to the centralized operating systems because a centralized operating system can monitor all resources within a computer system. The problem of managing distributed resources without having current global status information is an area of active academic research and is the main impediment to the commercial availability of DISOSs. The following issues are of special interest:

- How can the workload be distributed among different servers which perform similar services?
- Which processors can be allocated for what tasks?
- How can the interdependent tasks be allocated to different processors?
- How can the workload be balanced between various hardware devices in the network?

For allocating processors, perhaps the best known scheme is to use the manager/worker concept from organizational design. The worker processors actually perform the work assigned to them, and the manager processors monitor their progress. Keeping in mind the organizational design guideline of between 5 to 10 workers per manager, a manager keeps track of 5 to 10 worker processors. This model fits very well within a LAN environment, where the LAN server can work as a manager and the stations on the LAN are the workers. For large networks, the managers report to higher authorities and so on, once again keeping the span of control to about 10. A committee may be assigned to oversee the entire "organization" so that committee members can step in to lend a helping hand if one or more managers are sick (overworked, crashed). Details about this scheme can be found in Tannenbaum <1985> and Wittie <1980>.

The task of scheduling processes on different processors is straightforward if the processes do not depend on each other and if the processors do not allow any multiprogramming. In such cases, each process is allocated to a processor from start to end. However, it is very difficult to schedule interdependent processes on many processors, where each processor can run many tasks simultaneously. This happens frequently in long-running transactions which consist of many interdependent processes. In such cases, it is important to avoid the situations where the interdependent processes are on different machines in different time slots, because this can cause excessive delays. Many schemes have been published for process scheduling based on the knowledge of the interprocess communication patterns and the number of processors. It has been suggested that all interdependent processes should be allocated to different machines in the same time slot. This potentially allows maximum parallelism with minimum delays because all interacting processes are scheduled at the same time on different processors. Some other researchers follow almost the opposite approach—they allocate all related processes to the same processor to minimize the interprocess communication. The issues of distributed process allocation are similar to the ones we have discussed in distributed optimal query processing (Chapter 6).

The objective of workload balancing is to assure that the processing activity handled by all processors is roughly the same. This can eliminate and/or reduce performance bottlenecks. This involves, at the minimum, information about queue lengths at different processors so that the less busy processors can be assigned work. Some systems, such as the IBM JES (Job Entry Subsystem) version 3, use these queues for job routing between machines.

During the execution of processes in distributed operating systems, deadlocks may occur. These deadlocks need to be detected and resolved. The problem of deadlock detection and resolution in distributed systems is in principle similar to the centralized problem. However, this problem is complicated due to the lack of status information across machines. Many articles have been published in this area. However, very few have been implemented. The most commonly used deadlock detection and resolution mechanism is timeout, in which a timer is used to detect if two processes have been waiting too long. At timeout (expiration of a prescribed time interval), one of the processes is "killed" to free up the deadlock.

7.4.4 Scalability

Many designs work well with a few computers but are not useful (scalable) as the number of computers grows. Distributed operating systems must be designed with scalability in mind because the network devices can grow dramatically without any control. In general, if a resource utilization grows linearly with the number of computers, it is not useful for large systems. For example, broadcast messages work well with a few computers but do not work well when thousands of computers are involved. Due to the scalability considerations, it is not possible to replicate directories and to allow each workstation to have a totally different configuration. Large systems tend to use regional locations for directories and standardize workstation configurations to handle the scalability problems.

7.4.5 Compatibility

In distributed systems, compatibility can be at the binary code, execution, and protocol levels. In binary code compatibility, all processors execute the same machine instruction set. In this case, an object (machine) code generated at one computer can be transmitted to and executed at another computer. Examples of the binary code compatible machines are Digital's VAX machines, SUN workstations, and IBM 370 series systems. In execution-level compatibility, the same source code can be compiled and executed on two different systems even if the two systems are not compatible at the binary code level. The protocol-level compatibility exists if different systems observe the same protocol. For example, the X Window protocol, commonly referred to as X, is a common protocol used in Athena DISOS between all systems even if the systems are not binary code and execution-level compatible. It is desirable to provide protocol-level compatibility in a DISOS because in most cases the different computers are usually not binary code and/or execution level compatible. Protocol-level compatibility allows common protocols for basic system services such as naming, file services, and authentication. This serves as a foundation for interoperability of diverse operating systems.

7.4.6 Fault Management

A hardware and/or software fault may reduce the availability (usability) of a system. A fault tolerant system continues to operate even after some hardware/software components have failed and are not available to the user. Fault tolerant systems attempt to keep the system availability high, albeit at lower performance, in the face of component failures. The key advantage of distributed systems is that they can be more fault tolerant than the centralized systems. This is due to two reasons: redundancy and atomic transactions.

Redundancy of data, processors, and I/O devices is a well-established technique for fault tolerance in distributed computing. Due to the availability of multiple computer systems, many copies of data can be kept and the same process can be executed on different processors. The issue of duplicate data was addressed in our discussion of distributed databases in Chapter 6. Duplicate processes are usually created by running a "shadow" process on machine B while the original process is running on machine A. Thus any changes made by the original process are also sent to the shadow so that the two processes are properly synchronized. If the main process fails, the shadow takes over and continues to run as if nothing happened. This technique is used in many state-of-the-market products, such as the Tandem Corporation's Fault Tolerant Computing systems. The main problem with redundant processes is that they can cause performance problems, especially if the message exchange rate of the redundant process is very high. This is an area where scalability is very desirable.

The issue of fault tolerance through atomic transactions has been discussed in Chapter 6. Basically, a transaction is atomic if it represents a single unit of work—either all the activities are carried out or none occur. For example, consider the example of a transaction which transfers $200 from account A to account B. This is an atomic transaction. The $200 must be either transferred to account B at the end or no transfer should take place. The atomicity of a transaction is maintained by introducing a COMMIT command. All the changes introduced by a transaction are committed when it terminates normally. Otherwise the changes are rolled back (undone). We discussed the two-phase commit process in Chapter 6.

It is possible to think of a global workflow manager in distributed operating systems. This workflow manager would coordinate the interactions between different transaction managers at different computers and would handle any failures (messages can and do get lost in distributed systems). The workflow manager would provide the combined functionalities of resource management (Section 7.4.3) and fault management.

7.4.7 Distributed Shared Memory Services

Distributed computer systems do not share main memory. This limitation creates many problems in developing distributed programs. For example, distributed programs cannot use global variables and can thus only communicate through messages. Some systems have implemented a shared memory abstraction on top of message passing distributed programs. The shared memory abstraction gives these systems the illusion of globally shared memory and allows programs to use the shared memory paradigm by using global variables.

A distributed shared memory system (DSM) provides a virtual address space shared among computers interconnected over a network. These systems allow remotely located programs to share memory and thus exchange information through global variables. Commercial availability of DSM would significantly change the way distributed applications are developed. For example, instead of relying on RPCs to exchange information between clients and servers, global variables could be used.

Research in DSM has been active since the early 1980s. DSM systems have been implemented using three basic approaches:

- Hardware techniques, which extend traditional virtual memory facilities on one machine to multiple machines across a network
- Operating system and library routines, which make memory accesses across a network location independent
- Compiler implementations, in which shared accesses are automatically converted to synchronization primitives among computers.

Designers of DSM systems make a wide range of choices. First, an appropriate structure (layout of shared data in virtual memory) and granularity (size of the unit of sharing: byte, word, page) must be decided. Second, the semantics for parallel memory update to maintain data consistency in shared memory must be understood. Third, the number of computers that can share distributed memory (scalability) needs to be chosen. Finally, the level of heterogeneity in processor memories (representation of integers and floating point numbers in memory) needs to be decided for DSM; it is difficult to build a DSM system between processors with very heterogeneous memory organizations. Different choices have been made and implemented in the DSMs developed at many universities and research establishments. Nitzberg <Nitzberg 1991> gives an integrated overview of the major issues, approaches, and examples in this area.

7.4.8 Distributed Services

In a distributed operating system it is easier for user-defined servers to provide the functions commonly provided by the operating systems. This decomposition of operating system services makes the operating system kernel design easy. Examples of the servers are as follows:

- File servers which allow users to locate, access, and manipulate files across networks
- Print servers to print any files in the network
- Process servers to create and terminate processes
- Terminal servers to control terminal operations
- Time servers to retrieve and display time
- Gateway servers to convert messages and protocols between systems.

This discussion is directly related to the client-server systems that we discussed extensively in Chapter 5. Basically, a client-server paradigm is a natural way to provide distributed services in distributed operating systems. These services, as stated previously, reduce the size of the distributed operating system kernel. Figure 7.3 shows an example of a hypothetical server-based operating system.

Many DISOS functions are based on combining the DDTMS, client-server systems, communication protocols, and distributed transaction processing functions into a single framework. The most unique features of DISOSs are global user interfaces and global processor allocation.

7.5 Examples of Distributed Operating Systems

7.5.1 Overview

At present, most of the distributed operating systems are state of the art and not state of the market/practice. One of the earliest DISOS was the Cambridge system <Need-

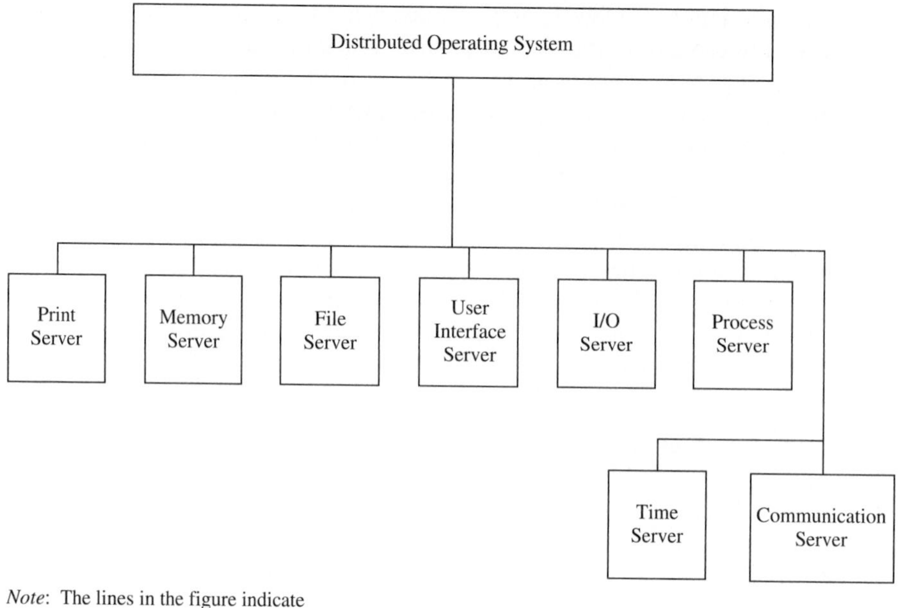

Note: The lines in the figure indicate connections.

FIGURE 7.3 A Server-Based Distributed Operating System

ham 1982>. Later systems were Locus <Walker 1983>, Amoeba <Mullender 1990, Tannenbaum 1990>, Athena <Champine 1990>, and Mach <Black 1990, Rashid 1986>. Here is a partial list of a few distributed operating systems, discussed alphabetically:

- Amoeba <Mullender 1990, Tannenbaum 1990> is being developed at the Free University, Amsterdam, to run on local as well as extended network environments. Amoeba has been developed on a wide area network through several countries in western Europe. Amoeba is described in more detail in Section 7.5.2.
- Andrew <Satyanarayanan 1990, Morris 1988> has been developed at the Carnegie Mellon University to support research computing. The objectives of Andrew are to support about 1000 workstations in a Unix and Ethernet environment, with plans to support 10,000 workstations. A distributed file system called the Andrew File System, developed as part of the Andrew project, is being used in many experimental file system projects.
- Project Athena <Champine 1990> was developed at the Massachussets Institute of Technology to support 24-hour campus-wide workstation-based computing. Athena, unlike Amoeba, is restricted to one campus. The objectives of Athena and Andrew are very similar. Athena has produced two very popular systems: X Window and Kerberos. We will describe Athena in Section 7.5.3.
- Locus <Walker 1983> is one of the earliest distributed operating systems, developed at the University of California, Los Angeles. Locus supports transparent access to

data through a network-wide file system. Locus supports resource replication for fault tolerance and degrades gracefully with failures in the network.

- Mach <Black 1990, Rashid 1986> supports transparent access to remote files between loosely and tightly coupled computers. Mach provides large address spaces for large programs and supports huge information transfers. We will describe Mach in Section 7.5.4.
- V <Cheriton 1988> is a testbed for research in distributed systems. The architecture of V consists of four logical components: a distributed Unix kernel, service modules, runtime support libraries, and additional user commands. V manages the workstations (clients) and the servers (back-end processors) transparently to give the user an impression of one large centralized system.
- Galaxy <Sinha 1991> is a distributed operating system being developed to investigate the limitations of current systems. Galaxy is intended for high performance on local and wide area networks. To achieve this, all broadcast messages and global locking is eliminated, the kernel is developed from scratch, multiple levels of interprocess communications are used, and an object-oriented model is used throughout.

In addition to these systems, several other experimental DISOSs have been reported in the literature. Examples of such systems are Dash, HCS, Grapevine, and Eden. For a description of these systems, the reader is referred to the surveys by Tannenbaum <Tannenbaum 1985>, Couloris <Couloris 1988>, and Champine <Champine 1990>. In the following sections, we review three systems: Amoeba, Athena, and Mach.

7.5.2 The Amoeba Distributed Operating System

Amoeba has been under development since 1980 at the Free University and the Center for Mathematics and Computer Science in Amsterdam. Amoeba appears to users as a centralized system, but it has the speed, fault tolerance, security, and flexibility needed for the future application systems. The architects of Amoeba claim that Amoeba is one of the fastest DISOS on its class of hardware <Mullender 1990>.

Amoeba uses an object-oriented approach. An object is a piece of data on which users can perform well-defined operations independent of the location of the object and the user. Operations on objects are implemented using remote procedure calls. Objects are managed by a diverse range of servers. Amoeba partially eliminates the need for a separate transaction management system by embedding the replication and atomicity in the file servers. Amoeba also provides a bridge for the Unix operating system users through a library of Unix system calls which are emulated on the Amoeba system.

Figure 7.4 shows the four architectural components of the Amoeba system: the pool of processors, the specialized servers, the workstations, and the gateways. The processor pool is a collection of computers with memory and network interface cards. For each task, a set of processors is allocated to the processes of the task. These processes are executed in parallel, and the processors are allocated dynamically to

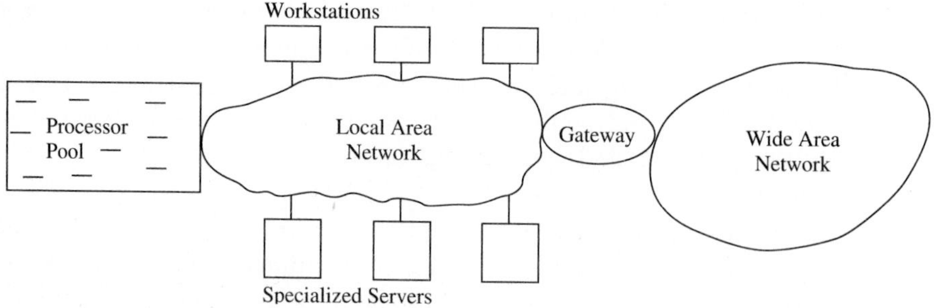

FIGURE 7.4 Amoeba Architecture

satisfy the processing needs of the user community. The workstations usually run user interfaces (windowing, mouse interrupts, colors, etc.) and handle user commands. The specialized servers provide a set of dedicated services such as file and print services. The gateways connect multiple remotely located Amoeba systems so that the users can view the entire system as a single centralized system. For example, many Amoeba systems located in different parts of Europe have been tied together through wide area networks and gateways.

The objects in Amoeba are both represented and protected by a *capability*. The capability of an object represents (1) the service port, which identifies the service that manages the object; (2) the object number, which uniquely identifies the object; (3) the rights field, which determines the operations that are permitted on the object; and (4) the check fields for cryptographic protection. The cryptographic information allows the capabilities to be managed by remotely located user processes. The Amoeba directory server maintains the mapping between the ASCII path names and the capabilities. The main facilities of Amoeba are as follows (for more information, the reader is referred to Mullender <1990> and Tannenbaum <1990>):

- The communication system uses a client-server paradigm in which the clients perform operations on objects through remote procedure calls. The server processes perform the requested operations and sends the responses back to the clients. To optimize performance and fault tolerance, many server processes may jointly manage several similar objects. Objects can be organized in class hierarchies, where the operations from higher levels can be inherited by lower-level objects. A class corresponds to each object.
- The Amoeba Interface Language (AIL) compiler generates the code needed to interface the remote procedure calls with the underlying Amoeba Network Transport mechanisms. The messages generated and handled by AIL contain headers (sender/receiver addresses, operations to be performed, the capability information, etc.) and the data.
- The servers for a service are located by first checking if the server port is known. If not, the Amoeba kernel broadcasts a "locate packet" to see if any other kernels can help to locate an appropriate server.

- The service port number is a 48-bit unique address. Amoeba assumes that if a user (client) knows the address of a service port, then it must be authorized to use this service. This appears to be the main security mechanism in Amoeba because space is sparsely populated.
- Amoeba directories are replicated at several sites for fault tolerance. The directory information can be encrypted for security.
- Amoeba processes can have multiple threads of control. Processes can be split over many computers. These processes, consisting of segmented virtual address spaces, can be remotely created, destroyed, checkpointed, restarted, migrated, and debugged.

7.5.3 Project Athena

Project Athena was established in 1983 at the Massachussets Institute of Technology to improve the quality of education through high-quality, campus-wide, workstation-based computing. This project has been sponsored primarily by IBM and Digital Equipment Corporation. The focus of Athena has been to provide a single human interface to all computing facilities located in the network. The Athena system at present consists of more than 1000 workstations, in 40 clusters of 10 to 120 workstations each, for use by students 24 hours a day. More than 150 servers (print servers, file servers, etc.) are accessed by the 1000 workstations. Some of the clusters serve specialized needs such as electronic classrooms and instruction development, while others serve general student population in student housing areas and in common work areas. The workstations supported by Athena are the Digital VAXstations, the IBM RT/PCs, and full-motion color videos. Athena also uses a client-server paradigm. The objects in the system are referenced by their name and located by their address or by their path.

The following main requirements were established for Athena <Champine 1990>:

1. Any user should be able to use any workstation.
2. The system must scale to support 10,000 workstations or more.
3. The system must be available 24 hours a day.
4. System services should be secure even if the workstations are not.
5. The system must support a variety of hardware platforms from different vendors.
6. All system applications must run on all workstations.

The Athena model consists of three components: workstations, servers, and the network (see Fig. 7.5). The designers of Athena provided a set of servers which were spread all across the network. These servers collectively provide the services that are normally provided by a centralized Unix-type time sharing system. The network as well as the service locations are transparent to the users. All services are available based on a single password which is entered by the users at the login time. In essence, any operating system can be used in Athena workstations and/or servers. It is only

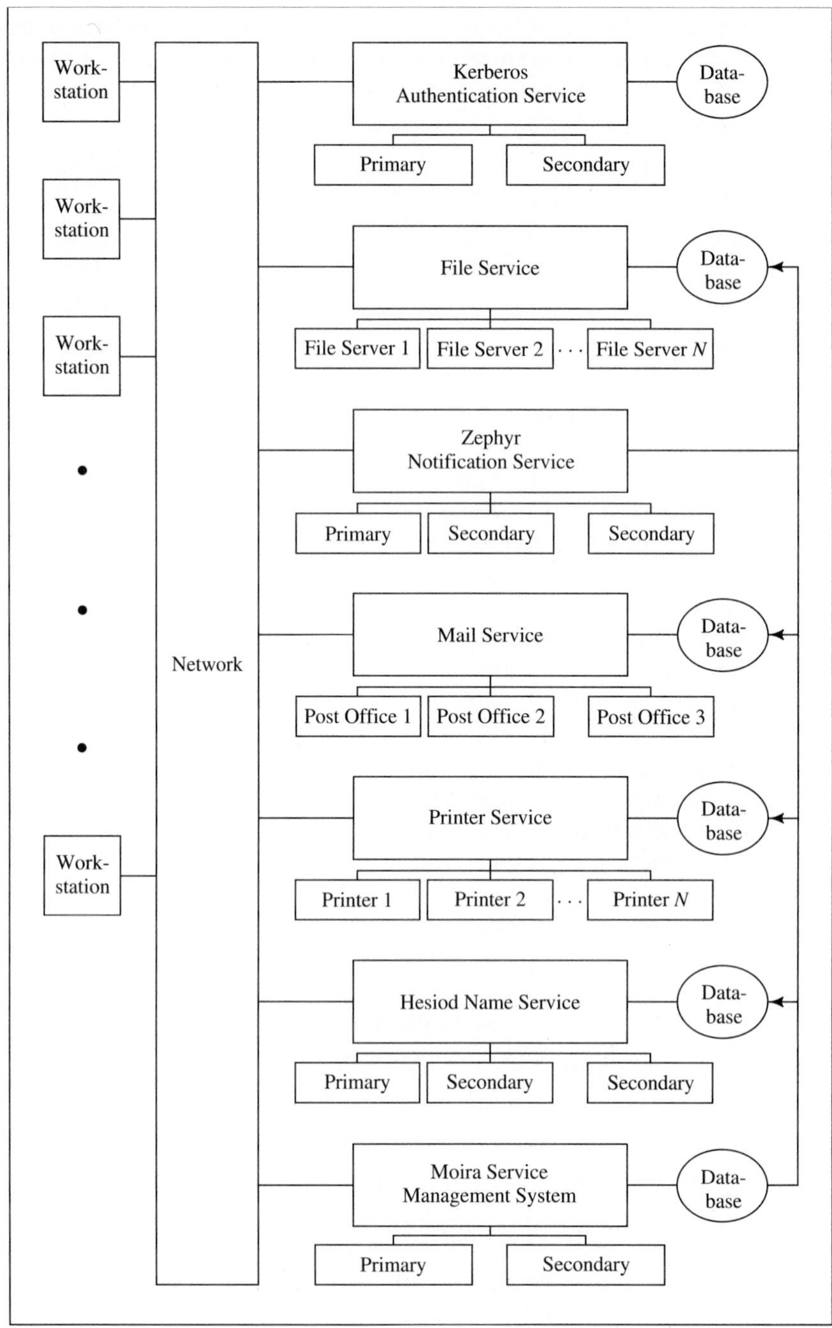

FIGURE 7.5 The Athena Model

required that the needed services (name services, authentication services, file access, and print services) be provided when an Athena command is received.

The scalability requirements in Athena are satisfied at the network, file storage, and labor levels. The network uses a fiber optic backbone and routers/gateways to subdivide the network into subnets. Many files are centralized to minimize disk utilization, and a few workstation configurations were used to minimize the labor costs (Ethernet interfaces, mouse, 1 MIP processor, 1 million pixel monochrome displays, and at least 4 megabytes of main memory). In addition, all communication protocols use the Berkeley Unix sockets over TCP/IP to minimize training and development costs. The use of Unix system provides a basis for interoperability and coherence. The X Windows system is used for all user interfaces. This windowing system, developed at MIT, provides a network-transparent, device-independent, vendor-neutral windowing environment. The network reliability is achieved by limiting the backbone interconnection to the routers only. This minimizes the exposure of the backbone to unfriendly elements (students!).

The security implementers assumed that the workstations were unsecure (anyone could walk up to a terminal and try out the system). An authentication system, called Kerberos, was developed to achieve system security from unsecure workstations. The Kerberos server is a third-party authentication server that validates the users of system services. Kerberos develops a unique session key for each client-server instance at the login time. This key is sent to the server for each server request. The server may elect to (1) ignore the key, (2) use the key when a client-server session is established, (3) use the key in every client-server interaction, and (4) use the key to encrypt the data.

To minimize the labor costs, a centralized support and management approach was used. The experience on the Athena project has shown the virtues of centralized management and support for distributed systems in terms of the quality of service and reduced costs. For more details about the Athena Project, the reader should refer to Champine 1990.

7.5.4 The Mach Distributed Operating System

Mach was developed in 1986 in Carnegie Mellon University (CMU), where it continues to be enhanced. It received widespread industrial recognition when it was chosen by Steve Jobs as the operating system for the Next workstation. Mach was originally developed on a DEC VAX machine. At present, it is available on many machines, including IBM PCs and SUN workstations. The objective of Mach is to be a multiprocessor system, where the processors could be tightly coupled around a shared memory unit or loosely coupled across a network. The capability of Mach to run on loosely coupled processors is of particular interest to us. Mach can operate on different types of processors with different types of memories that are linked together across a network.

Mach is similar to Unix, at least externally, because it is intended to be compatible with Berkeley 4.3 Unix. However, there are many differences. For example, Mach is designed to be extendible without significantly extending the kernel. In other words, the programs spend more time in user mode instead of the operating system kernel mode. Limiting the kernel size is important because the Unix kernel has been growing steadily as more functions are added to Unix. In addition, since different vendors have added different functions, users do not have a uniform way of accessing Unix resources. Another difference is that Mach is much more device independent than Unix, especially in memory management. The main distinguishing feature is the copy-on-write, which allows same data to be read by several processes. A copy is made only if data is to be modified. This feature eliminates the need for copying data and thus improves the system performance.

Mach has integrated the SUN NFS support with the CMU Andrew File System, added an external pager facility for virtual memory support, included a server for supporting distributed shared memory, and provided a network-wide transparent library mechanism. In addition, Mach supports TCP/IP protocol. Mach uses the virtual memory system for large address spaces for large programs and supports huge information transfers. These capabilities allow Mach to be used as a distributed operating system.

Mach uses four basic abstractions: task, thread, port, and message. A task is the address space and access rights of a program. A thread is the basic unit of CPU utilization and essentially represents a program counter. A task can have multiple threads, where each thread runs on a processor. A message is a collection of data objects used to communicate between threads. A port is an address for sending/receiving messages between threads. For example, thread t1 can write to a port p1, and thread t2 can read from p1. Detailed description of concurrency and parallelism in the Mach operating system can be found in Black <1990>.

Mach is funded heavily by the Defense Advanced Research Agency (DARPA) and many hardware manufacturers. There are many speculations about how Mach will compete with the Unix System V Release Version 5 (see, for example Fischer <1989>).

7.6 Distributed Computing Platforms

In the last few chapters, we described the distributed database management systems, distributed transaction management systems, client-server systems, and distributed operating systems. The reader might have noticed that there is some overlap between the functions of these systems and the level of transparency supported. We now turn our attention to the distributed computing platforms (DCPs), which combine the distributed operating systems, distributed data and transaction managers, and client-server support software with the underlying network services to support different applications. In general, a DCP must provide the following application support and network services (Fig. 7.6):

- Remote procedure call services
- Distributed file/database services, including remote data access
- Distributed transaction management services
- Global naming and directory services

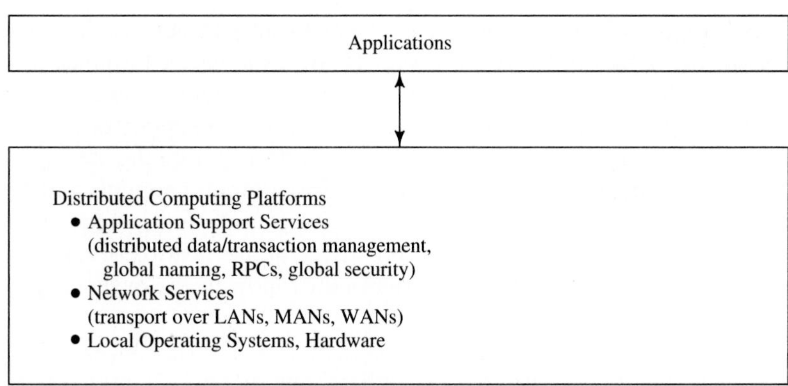

FIGURE 7.6 A Conceptual View of Distributed Computing Platform

- Global authentication and security services
- Local operating system facilities for scheduling and managing individual tasks
- Network support services such as session establishment, routing of messages, error handling, and network/device connectivity.

Future DCPs may combine and integrate these services into seamless services which are invoked by applications across a network. In other words, it may not be possible for us to tell what services are being provided by which component. The entire DCP may appear as a tightly integrated package which provides a range of networking, database, transaction management, RPC, naming, directory, security, and other services needed by the distributed applications. As we will see in Chapter 9, Open Software Foundation's Distributed Computing Environment (DCE) and Unix International's ATLAS are attempting to provide such a DCP.

The main objective of DCP, independent of the method used, is to provide different levels of transparency to the users, application developers, designers, and managers. A simple DCP with Network File Services (NFS) provides only file transparency, while DISOS and DDTMS increase this transparency to databases and computers. Section 7.6.1 discusses the transparency issue in distributed computing platforms. Section 7.6.2 presents a general distributed computing platform model, and Section 7.6.3 gives an overview of some DCP standards under development.

7.6.1 Transparency in Distributed Computing Platforms

The objective of any DCP is to provide transparency at the following levels:

- End user transparency
- Developer transparency
- Designer/architect transparency
- Manager transparency.

Figure 7.7 shows how these levels of transparency are delivered. The columns show the typical DCP technologies (network services, terminal emulation and file servers, distributed data and transaction management systems, and distributed operating systems) and the rows show the transparencies supported by these technologies.

The end-user transparency shows how transparent the user operations are from the underlying networks, operating systems, computer systems, and database/transaction managers. Ideally, a 100 percent user transparent system should operate as a single system in which the user is not aware of the location of activities. The end-user transparency can be defined in terms of the following major functional transparencies (see Fig. 7.7):

- *Network hardware transparency*. This shows that the end user does not have to know the physical network hardware media (e.g., cable, fiber link, satellite) and network topologies (ring, star, bus) being used by him or her. This level of transparency is provided by layer 1 to 4 of network architectures.
- *Network services transparency*. This is concerned with providing the same file transfer, terminal emulation, and electronic mail on different networks. Examples are the TCP/IP File Transfer Protocol (FTP) and Simplified Mail Transfer Protocol (SMTP), available on any system which uses TCP/IP. This level of transparency is commonly provided by terminal emulation, file transfer, and mail services.
- *User location transparency*. This shows that the end user can perform the same operations at any site in the network. This includes user interface and user commands. This type of transparency is provided by the network architectures and distributed operating systems. For example, the Athena system provides user location transparency.
- *Data location transparency*. This allows access, storage, and manipulation of data at any site by using the same commands. This type of transparency is provided by the distributed database managers and some file transfer and access servers. Examples are the SUN NFS system and the Informix Star distributed database manager.
- *Transaction execution transparency*. This indicates that a user does not know how and where his or her transaction will execute. For example, a transaction which needs to access data from three different computers may be decomposed into three different subtransactions and executed in parallel without the knowledge of the user. This type of transparency is provided by the distributed transaction managers, such as NCR's Top End.
- *Processor transparency*. This shows that the user does not know on what processor his or her commands are executed. This type of transparency is provided by the distributed operating systems. Examples are the Athena and Amoeba systems.
- *I/O device transparency*. This means that user can use any I/O device, such as a printer, in the network without having to know the location of the printer. This type of transparency is also provided by the distributed operating systems. Most distributed operating systems, including the LAN operating systems, provide location transparent printing through print servers.

	Network Services (Layers 1 to 4)	Terminal Emulation & File Servers	Distributed Database and Transaction Management	Distributed Operating System
User Transparency				
Network hardware transparency	x			
Network services transparency		x		
User location (command) transparency	x			x
Data location transparency		x	x	
Transaction execution transparency			x	
Processor transparency				x
I/O device transparency				x
Fault transparency	x	x	x	x
Developer Transparency				
User interface transparency				x
Program code transparency	x			
Data Access transparency		x	x	
Designer/Architect Transparency				
Interconnectivity transparency	x	x	x	x
Performance transparency	x	x	x	x
Availability transparency	x	x	x	x
Management Transparency				
Security transparency	x	x	x	x
Accounting transparency	x	x	x	x

Note: An x indicates that this type of technology supports the shown transparency level.

FIGURE 7.7 Transparency Support in Distributed Computing

- *Fault transparency*. This means that any faults in the network components, computing components, I/O devices, or any other components are hidden from the user. This type of transparency is provided cooperatively by the network architectures (network managers may route your message through an alternate path), distributed database managers (provide access to alternative databases), distributed transaction managers (use alternate sites for processing), and distributed operating systems (providing alternative processors).

In addition to the end user transparency, the application developers can be shielded from the details of different systems while developing applications. In other words, the application systems developed should be portable to different computing platforms interconnected through different networks. The developer transparency (application portability) can be discussed at three levels (see Fig. 7.7):

- *User interface transparency*. The same user interface should be portable to different platforms. The de facto standards in this area are the X Window and Microsoft Windows systems. This level of transparency should be ideally provided by the distributed operating systems.
- *Program code transparency*. The same program code should be portable to different platforms. The emerging programming code in this area is C programming. The remote program communications are not standardized at present. The de facto remote procedure call standards are SUN RPCs and OSF-DCE RPC. This level of transparency should be ideally provided by the network architecture layer 7 services.
- *Data transparency*. The database design and access should be portable across all network stations. The main standard for database access is SQL. For example, the OSI Remote Data Access (RDA) standard uses SQL. This level of transparency is provided by the distributed database managers which utilize SQL as the global query language.

Even if the developed applications are portable across a network, the application systems designers/architects will have to decide at what location the various application systems components should reside and how should they interconnect with each other. The design and architecture decisions of interconnection between application components can be made transparent by adopting standards. For example, if open standards for distributed data and RPC are chosen, then the designers do not have to worry about interconnection as the underlying platforms change. The choice of sites depends on performance and availability considerations. As the distributed computing technologies become more intelligent, the application system components will be moved *automatically* to appropriate locations for improvements in performance and availability. Under this scenario, the application components will be initially allocated somewhere in the system. As the application system is used, the statistics about its use are collected and the system is automatically moved around based on the usage patterns. As shown in Fig. 7.7, these intelligent facilities can be provided by a combination of network architectures,

DDTMSs, and DISOSs. At present, most of these facilities are not state of the market.

The management transparency means that the management of distributed computing becomes as simple as the management of centralized systems. For example, the security and accounting should be automatic in networks so that different procedures and software would not be needed. Software packages such as Kerberos provide these facilities. A great deal of work is still needed in this area.

7.6.2 A General Distributed Computing Platform Model

Figure 7.8 shows the general distributed computing platform (DCP) model, which we have used so far as a Reference Model. This Model can provide the levels of transparency discussed earlier. This DCP combines the services of local/distributed operating systems, local/distributed database management, local/distributed transaction management, and local/network communication services into a single framework.

According to this Model, the users access the applications through the communications services interfaces. The communication services consist of local communi-

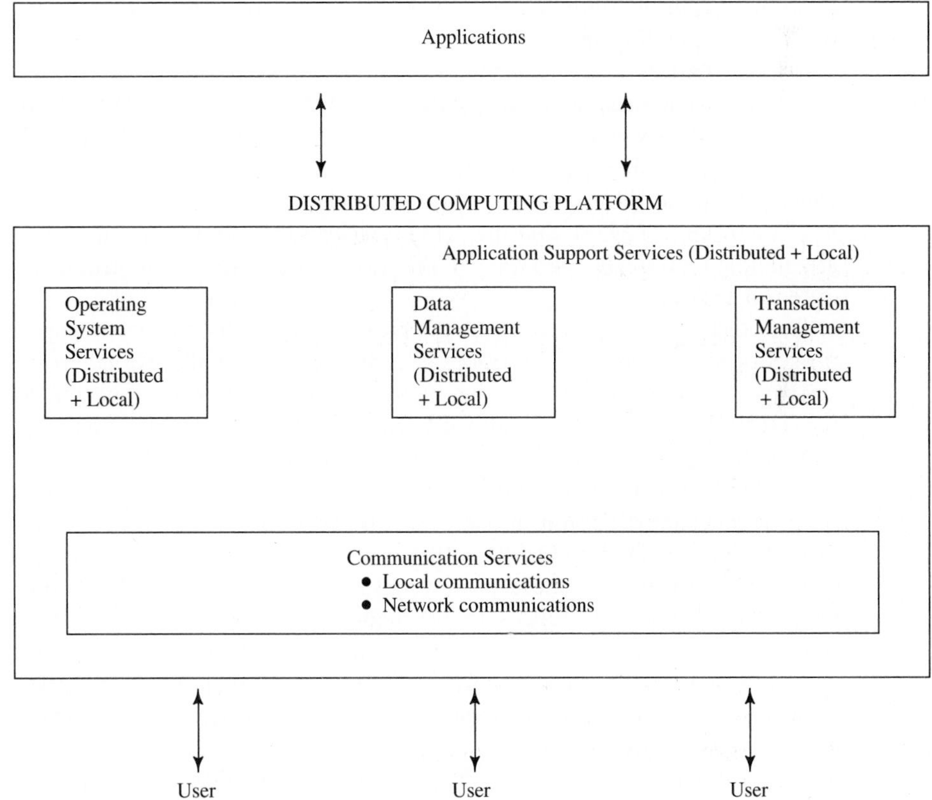

FIGURE 7.8 A Model of Distributed Computing Platforms

cations (e.g., Unix pipes) and network services (e.g., TCP/IP). The application systems may need to access local or remote data, support user interfaces at one or many sites, and may need to access many other resources. As shown in Fig. 7.8, the application systems may access these resources through the services provided by the operating systems, data managers, and transaction managers.

A local data manager enables the access and manipulation of data (files plus databases). As explained in Chapter 6, a distributed data manager (DDM) extends the scope of a local data manager by viewing the data stored in the entire network as one large data source. Distributed data managers provide the transparency of data location, data models, and database security and authority control. For example, if a user issues an SQL query, then the DDM will parse the query, find out the location of the target data, and manage the access/manipulation of data across computers. If the data to be accessed is at two different computers in two different formats, then the DDM will translate the query into the correct format and route it to the data sites.

A local transaction management system is responsible for initiating, monitoring, and terminating transactions in a computing system. A distributed transaction management system (DTMS) extends the scope of a local transaction management system by viewing related transactions in a network as one transaction. The distributed transaction management systems are responsible for initiating, monitoring, and terminating transactions across computing systems. In addition, a DTMS is responsible for serializing the transactions across computer systems in order to maintain data integrity. Each transaction is a unit of consistency. Thus, if a transaction is terminated (aborted) due to an error, then its effect must be rolled out. This becomes a difficult issue if one transaction was decomposed into subtransactions which execute at different sites. In these cases, failure of a site or network must be handled by the DTMS so that the data integrity is maintained and all subtransactions are handled properly. Variants of the two-phase commit algorithm are used in different DTMS.

A distributed operating system (DISOS), as discussed earlier, can handle the processor allocation, user interfaces, security, and device allocation across computer systems. In a distributed computing platform, the DISOS will cooperate closely with the DDTMS and DTMS and will complement/augment the facilities of these systems. It is possible for a DISOS to use a client-server paradigm to interface with the DDTMS and DTMS to provide distributed services. It is possible that some of these services may be built directly into the DISOS kernel, thus reducing the sizes of DDTMS and DTMS. On the other hand, the size of the distributed operating system kernel can be reduced by letting the DDTMS and DTMS servers do more processing. The exact choices to be made depend on the implementers of the distributed computing platform. At present, since DISOSs are not commercially available, many DISOS functions are being built in DDTMS, client-server systems, network access interfaces, distributed transaction processing, and even in some application systems.

It is obvious that some DCPs will be less powerful than the others, depending on the availability of the distributed resource managers such as DISOS and DDTMS. In a basic DCP, the only global facilities available are the network services and basic file transfer and terminal emulation. A complete DCP, on the other hand, will contain DISOS and DDTMS facilities, if available.

Let us illustrate the DCP through an example. Without the facilities of a complete DCP, the users can exchange files only but cannot perform any other operations. All resource allocation and security access is handled on a per-computer basis. For example, if a user on computer A wants to access a printer on computer B, then the user performs the following steps:

- Logon to computer B.
- Move the file from computer A to B after getting authority to move files.
- Issue the print command.
- Logoff from B.

This situation is not suitable for a large number of computers. In a complete DCP, all computers are considered part of one logical system. All system and security functions are performed at the system level and not at the computer level. To perform the aforementioned function, the user issues the following command:

- Print file F on printer P

7.6.3 Overview of Distributed Computing Platform Standards

In the last decade, several standards for the components of distributed computing platforms have been introduced by vendors, large corporations, and standardization bodies. The objective of these standards is to provide "open systems" in which different products from different sources can coexist. These standards fall into the following categories, according to the DCP model shown in Fig. 7.8:

- Standards in network services.
- Standards in local resource management.
- Standards in application support services.

Let us briefly review these standards.

Examples of the network service standards are as follows (see Appendix A for more details):

- Layer 1 and 2 standards for LANs, WANs, and MANs. These standards specify the communication media used (coaxial cables, twisted pair, optical fiber), transmission techniques employed (broadband, baseband, carrierband), transmission data rates allowed for each standard, and data link protocols such as token ring, Ethernet, FDDI, SDLC, etc.
- Layer 1 to 3 standards, which specify network interconnectivity in connection-oriented and connectionless modes. Examples are the X.25 packet switching standard and the ISDN standard.

- Transport layer standards for connection-based and connectionless services. Transmission Control Protocol (TCP), part of the DOD Protocol Suite which was developed for the ARPANET project, is one of the best-known layer 4 protocols, and runs on top of IP (Internet Protocol), a layer 3 protocol in the DOD Suite.

The main local resource management standard is the Unix operating system. However, many versions of Unix exist. Posix, a Unix-compatible operating system standard, is gaining importance as a vendor independent Unix operating system. Originally, Posix was a project of the IEEE Computer Society to define external specifications for Unix. In the last few years, the IEEE's Posix work has been endorsed and adopted by ANSI (American National Standards Institute) and NIST (National Institute for Standards and Technology).

The application support services standards appear as the application layer services and protocols of the OSI Model. Here are some examples:

- Terminal emulators such as the TCP/IP TELNET and the ISO VT standards
- File transfer standards such as the OSI FTAM (File Transfer Access Method) and the TCP/IP FTP (File Transfer Protocol)
- Distributed applications standards such as Distributed Applications Framework/Open Distributed Processing (DAF/ODP), Remote Data Access (RDA), Distributed Transaction Processing (DTP), Remote Operations Service (ROS), Manufacturing Message Standard (MMS), Network File Services (NFS), Remote Procedure Call (RPC), and Advanced Program to Program Communications (APPC). We reviewed most of these protocols in Chapters 5 and 6.
- Miscellaneous application protocols such as directory services protocols (e.g., X.500), OSI Security, Distributed Office Applications (DOA), Job Transfer and Management (JTM), Connectionless Upper Layers (CUL), and Application Programming Interfaces (API).

In addition, as we will see in Chapter 9, many individual DCP standards are being combined with the application architectures to form distributed computing architectures (DCP architecture + application architecture = distributed computing architecture). An example of such an architecture is the Open Software Foundation's Distributed Computing Environment (OSF/DCE). Many vendors (DEC, IBM, HP) are participating in OSF to determine how to balance proprietary versus open systems. OSF DCE is especially concentrating on interconnecting multiple products from multiple vendors. For example, part of applications may reside at mainframes, at Unix minicomputers or OS/2 microcomputers. The main focus of OSF is on distributed cooperative processing and on standards to help connections at many levels.

In essence, these architectures address the interoperability, portability, and integration issues of distributed applications on distributed computer systems. Due to the key role of distributed applications in these architectures, we will discuss this topic in more detail in Chapter 9.

7.7 Management Summary and Trends

Distributed operating systems (DISOSs) provide complete transparency to the end users so that the users view the network of interconnected computers as one computer system. These systems make all I/O devices, memory units, and processors in the network available to the user as if they belong to one centralized computer system. Most of the existing operating systems have some networking capabilities added to the operating system services. Distributed operating systems are designed specifically to be distributed among many machines. The major issues to be addressed in the design of a DISOS are as follows:

- Communication of processes between different computers
- Naming services for objects across multiple computers
- Global resource management (allocation, scheduling, deallocation)
- Scalability of services, from a few workstations to thousands of workstations
- Compatibility at the binary code, execution, and protocol levels
- Fault management in distributed environments
- Security and protection across computers

Many DISOSs have been developed in the last 10 years in universities and research laboratories. Here are some examples:

- Amoeba is being developed at the Free University, Amsterdam.
- Andrew has been developed at Carnegie Mellon University to support research computing.
- Athena was developed at the Massachussets Institute of Technology to support 24-hour, campus-wide, workstation-based computing.
- Locus is one of the earliest distributed operating system, developed at the University of California, Los Angeles.
- Mach is also being developed at Carnegie Mellon to support transparent access to remote files between loosely and tightly coupled computers.
- V is being developed as a testbed for research in distributed systems.

In addition to these systems, several other experimental DISOSs have been reported in the literature. Examples of such systems are Dash, HCS, Grapevine, and Eden.

A distributed computing platform (DCP) combines distributed operating systems, distributed database managers, distributed transaction managers, client-server support software, and network facilities to support different applications. The main objective of these platforms is to provide the following levels of transparency:

- End user transparency
- Developer transparency
- Designer transparency
- Manager transparency.

Several industrial and standardizing bodies are developing variants of distributed computing environments. Most of the work in DISOSs and DCPs is state of the art, with strong prospects for state of the market/practice.

The following trends appear to be obvious:

- The differences between distributed database managers, distributed transaction managers, client-server support software, and distributed operating systems will disappear with time. Instead, the application systems will invoke the resource management services needed (e.g., access data, send messages, receive messages, interact with the users); and these managers will cooperate with each other to provide these services transparently.
- The distributed computing platforms will integrate the underlying network services and the distributed resource managers to provide a "seamless environment" for application systems. All DCP components will cooperate with each other to provide transparent services.
- The personal computers, minicomputers, and mainframes will be components of DCPs of the future. At present, most DCPs are being developed around Unix environments, leaving the mainframes and PCs out of the picture.

Problems and Exercises

1. What are distributed operating systems and why should anyone interested in distributed computing know anything about these systems?
2. What are the main differences between a local and a distributed operating system? Explain your answer through examples.
3. List the main issues and approaches in distributed operating systems.
4. List the various aspects of distributed operating systems and discuss which aspects are of most fundamental importance to distributed computing.
5. Describe in detail a distributed operating system that has not been discussed in this chapter.
6. List the main services provided by a DCP. Show which services are provided by which components of a DCP.
7. We have discussed the capabilities of a DCP in providing end user, developer, designer, and management transparencies. Can you extend Fig. 7.7 to include any other levels of transparencies?
8. Give some examples of DCP that you are aware of.

CASE STUDY: Distributed Operating Systems and Platforms for XYZCORP

For a long range vision, you have been asked to review the literature on distributed operating systems and outline the advantages of using DISOSs in XYZCORP. An issue of immediate interest to XYZCORP is the proliferation of servers in the corporation. It is desirable to provide automatic server selection (i.e., choose any appropriate server) as a first step. In the long range, it is important to know how long XYZCORP will have to wait for a DISOS which will integrate the corporate MVS with the Unix and PC DOS operating systems. Specifically, you are to show the advantages of using a DISOS in:

- The corporate office
- The engineering office
- The manufacturing office.

The company is also interested in providing transparency and interoperability of all applications. Which standards will you choose at the following levels and why:

- Standards in network services
- Standards in local resource management
- Standards in distributed resource management

Hints About the Case Study

The short range goal of automating server selection can be met with off-the-shelf products or by developing customized procedures on top of existing software. A DISOS which integrates MVS, Unix, and PC-DOS and provides the facilities discussed in this chapter is perhaps an end-of-the-century state-of-the-market target. Although a DISOS is the "ultimate" in transparency and can be useful at any site in XYZCORP, it is perhaps most urgently needed in the manufacturing plants (too many devices talking to each other in real time). The standards for the second part of this project (DCP selection) are reviewed in Section 7.6.3. More details about these standards and open systems are given in Chapter 9.

References

Anderson, D., et al., "The Dash Project: Issues in the Design of Very Large Distributed System," Technical Report 87/338, Computer Science Division, Univ. of California, Berkeley, Jan. 1987.

Black, D., "Scheduling Support for Concurrency and Parallelism in the Mach Operating System," *IEEE Computer*, May 1990, pp. 35-43.

Champine, G., Geer, D., and Ruh, W., "Project Athena as a Distributed Computing System," *IEEE Computer,* Sept., 1990, pp. 40-51.

Cheriton, D., "The V Distributed System," *Comm. of the ACM*, May 1988, pp. 314-333.

Coulouris, J. and Dollimore, J., *Distributed Systems*, Addison-Wesley, 1988.

Fidge, C., "Logical Time in Distributed Computing Systems," *IEEE Computer,* Aug. 1991, pp. 28-33.

Fischer, S., "Mach, The New Unix," *UnixWorld*, Mar. 1989, pp. 64-70.

Morris, J., "Make or Take Decisions in Andrew," *Usenix Conf. Proc.*, Sunset Beach, Cal., Winter 1988, pp. 1-8.

Mullender, S., et al., "Amoeba: A Distributed Operating System for the 1990s," *IEEE Computer*, May 1990, pp. 44-53.

Needham, R.M. and Herbert, A.J., *The Cambridge Distributed Computing System*, Addison-Wesley, 1982.

Nitzberg, B. and Lo, V., "Distributed Shared Memory: A Survey of Issues and Approaches," *IEEE Computer*, Aug. 1991, pp. 52-60.

Nutt, G., *Centralized and Distributed Operating Systems,* Prentice Hall, 1992.

Rashid, R., et al., "Macg: A New Kernel Foundation for Unix Development," Usenix Conference, Sunset Beach, Cal., Summer 1986, pp. 93-112.

Satyanarayanan, M., "Scalable, Secure, and Highly Available Distributed File Access," *IEEE Computer*, May 1990, pp. 9-22.

Sinha, P., et al., "The Galaxy Distributed Operating System," *IEEE Computer*, Aug. 1991, pp. 34-41.

Tannenbaum, A., *Modern Operating Systems*, Prentice Hall, 1992.

Tannenbaum, A., et al., "Experience with the Amoeba Distributed Operating System," *CACM*, Dec. 1990, pp. 46-53.

Tannenbaum, A., "Distributed Operating Systems," *ACM Computing Surveys*, Dec. 1985, pp. 419-470.

Walker, B., et al., "The Locus Distributed Operating System," *Proc. 9th ACM Symposium on Operating System Principles*, Oct. 1983, pp. 49-70.

Wittie, L. and Van Tilberg, A.M., "MICROS: a Distributed Operating System for MICRONET, a Reconfigurable Network Computer," *IEEE Trans. on Computers*, Dec. 1980, pp. 1133-1144.

PART FOUR

Distributed Applications, Open Systems, and Management

This portion of the book concentrates on the highest layers of the Distributed Computing Reference Model (DCRM) introduced in Chapter 1 (see the figure). Our purpose is to conclude this book by showing how the platform issues of networks and application support services discussed in Parts II and III are interrelated with distributed application design and management.

In Chapter 9, we will introduce the principles of distributed applications and discuss the software engineering aspects of such applications. Our purpose is to illustrate how the various technologies, techniques, and standards covered so far can be used in developing distributed applications.

The next two chapters discuss the issues which are important at all levels of the DCRM. Chapter 9 describes the standards and architectures being introduced to address the interoperability, portability and integration issues. Chapter 10 describes the planning, staffing, organizing, and monitoring/controlling of distributed computing.

A discussion of major trends in distributed computing concludes this book. The reader of these chapters should be able to understand the interrelationships between the lower level issues of networks and the higher level concerns of application development and management.

Management & Support

(Chapter 10)

ENTERPRISE SYSTEMS
- Engineering Systems
- Business Systems
- Manufacturing Systems
- Office Systems
- Other Systems

Inter-operability Portability, & Integration

(Chapter 9)

PART IV

APPLICATION SYSTEMS (Chapter 8)

User Interfaces

Processing Programs

Data Files & Databases

DISTRIBUTED COMPUTING PLATFORM
- Application Support Services

Client-Server Support (Chapter 5)

Distributed Data/Transaction Management (Chapter 6)

Distributed Operating System (Chapter 7)

PART III

Communication Network Services
- Network Protocols and Interconnectivity (Chapter 3)

OSI Protocols (Appendix A)

TCP/IP (Appendix B)

SNA (Appendix C)

MAP/TOP (Appendix D)

- Physical Communication Network (Chapter 2)
  - Wide, Local, and Metropolitan Area Networks

Network Management

(Chapter 4)

PART II

Chapter 8

Distributed Applications and Application Downsizing/Rightsizing

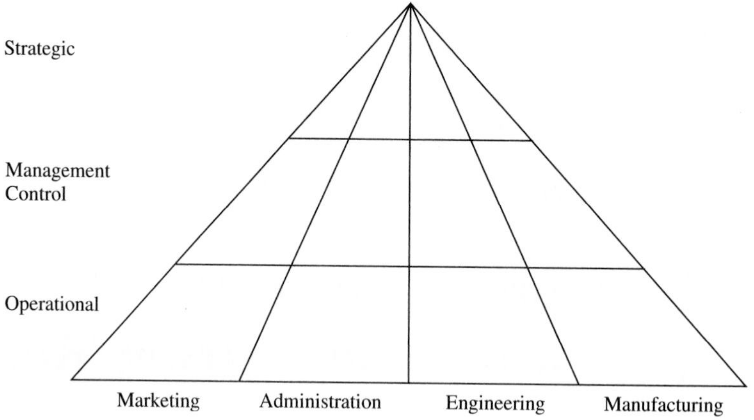

FIGURE 8.1 Enterprise Sytems

8.1 Introduction

Application systems directly support the enterprise activities and are the real reasons why most of the networks and computers exist.[1]

Examples of application systems are order processing systems, inventory control systems, airline reservation systems, etc. Application systems can be strategic applications to support the top management corporate activities, management control applications which support the middle management activities of budgeting and control, and operational applications which support the day to day activities of an organization. These applications may be designed as transaction processing, decision support, expert systems and/or executive support systems. Figure 8.1 and Table 8.1 show different classifications of application systems. The application systems at each level in Fig. 8.1 are further classified into functional areas such as marketing, manufacturing, engineering and administration. Table 8.1 lists examples of different types of application systems, at different levels of an organization, employing different types of techniques.

The main focus of this chapter is on *distributed application systems (DASs)* which span several computers. Thus any application which uses the client-server model is a DAS. Many downsized/rightsized applications are also DASs. "Downsizing" of applications has become a major issue in computing at present. Many reports are being published and conferences are being held on this topic (see, for example, the Yankee Group Report, "Downsizing Manufacturing Applications through Client-Server Systems," Dec. 1991, the "Downsizing/Rightsizing Conference," presented by the Boston University Corporate Education Center, April 27-May 1, 1992, Los Angeles, Computerworld Executive Reports on Downsizing/Rightsizing, August, 1992, and the Boston Group Report, MIS Week, Sept. 11, 1989). Downsizing refers to migrating applications from large computers (e.g., mainframes) to smaller and cheaper computers (e.g., minicomputers and desktops). To downsize an application, the designers may

[1]The terms *application* and *application system* are used interchangeably in this chapter.

TABLE 8.1 Examples of Application Systems

	LEVEL			CAPABILITY		
	Operational	*Mgt Control*	*Strategic*	*TPS*	*DSS*	*ES*
Marketing and Administration						
Accounts Payable	x			x	x	
Accounts Receivable	x			x		
Finance		x			x	x
General Accounting	x			x	x	
Marketing		x			x	x
Payroll	x			x		
Personnel	x			x	x	x
Planning			x		x	
Purchasing	x			x		
Sales		x		x	x	x
Engineering						
Intelligent CAD		x		x	x	x
Maintenance Manager	x			x	x	
Network Manager		x				x
Design Testing and Validation		x		x	x	
Information Flow Interface	x			x		
Manufacturing						
Facility Control		x		x		x
Inventory Control		x			x	
Material Handling	x			x		x
Area Control		x		x		
Cell Control	x			x		x
Workstation Control	x			x		
Equipment Control	x			x		

Legend:
TPS—Transaction Processing System
DSS—Decision Support System
ES—Expert System and/or Executive Support System

choose to migrate the entire application to one workstation (if it fits), or split the data, the user interfaces and the application logic among different computers by using a client-server model. We are primarily interested in the latter aspect of application downsizing. Rightsizing involves migration of applications to "right" platforms, i.e., keep large databases at mainframes and move the user interface processing to the workstations. Upsizing refers to connecting many independent workstation applications and moving some of the data and processing to mainframes so that the independent applications can be used as a whole. See Wohl <1992> for a business oriented discussion of these topics.

This chapter describes a methodology for distributing (splitting and moving) applications between different computers (mainframes, minicomputers, desktops, laptops, etc.). Organizations may need to make these application distribution decisions due to downsizing/rightsizing pressures or due to other reasons (only 3 out of 75 Fortune 1,000 companies interviewed by Forrester Research were not interested in downsizing <Radding 1992>). We will interchange the terms distribution, downsizing and rightsizing for convenience because they all lead to the same results: applications are split and moved around a network. The motivating question for this chapter is: which applications can be distributed/downsized/rightsized and how?

Section 8.2 gives an overview of distributed application system concepts, presents examples of distributed application systems, shows different models of distributed applications and outlines advantages/disadvantages of downsizing/rightsizing of applications. This section provides the necessary definitions and background information for this chapter.

How can the distributed application systems be developed and how can the applications be downsized/rightsized? What types of decisions and issues are unique to these topics and what type of tools and techniques can be employed to address these issues? Section 8.3 introduces the principles of distributed application engineering and establishes a framework to answer these questions. This framework can be used to develop new distributed applications and to downsize/rightsize existing applications (what to distribute and how?). The balance of this chapter describes the major phases (requirements, architecture, and implementation/testing) of distributed application engineering.

Section 8.4 gives an overview of requirements definition and analysis for distributed applications. Although most of the requirement definitions are not specific to DAS, requirements for interoperability, portability, and integration are important for DAS.

Architecture of distributed applications, discussed in Section 8.5, introduces the major activities that are unique to DAS. A distributed application architecture methodology, described in this section, identifies three major activities: partitioning (how to divide the application into components), allocation (where to put the data, the programs and the user interfaces), and interconnection (how to interconnect several applications and their components by using the application interconnectivity choices described in Chapter 5). The discussion in this section is the key to application distribution, downsizing and rightsizing.

After architectural choices, an application is designed in detail, implemented, and tested (Section 8.6). The following issues are addressed in this phase.

- Evaluate and select the distributed programming paradigms (the number and type of servers, client-server protocols to be used, options for distributed data and transaction management)
- Select the appropriate support environment (e.g., tools and vendor products to be used in development)
- Conduct a detailed local physical design at each computer (database design, program design) and choose implementation techniques (e.g., programming languages)

- Implementation and testing of programs, databases, and interconnections through languages and support environments.

The problem of software engineering at distributed sites and CASE (computer aided software engineering) is discussed in Section 8.7. This section attempts to answer the question: what is the state of the art and state of the market/practice in CASE tools for distributed software engineering?

The case study at the end of this chapter illustrates how applications can be downsized; and how the methodology introduced in Section 8.3 and explained in Sections 8.4, 8.5 and 8.6 can be used to distribute applications.

The reader of this chapter should understand the unique features of distributed applications and adopt a methodology to develop new distributed applications and downsize/rightsize existing applications. Sections 8.2 and 8.3 are intended for general overview, and Sections 8.4 through 8.7 are intended for application developers and designers.

8.2 Overview of Distributed Application Systems

8.2.1 Concepts and Definitions

Application system components. An application system logically consists of three components:

- Application datasets $D = (d_1, d_2, \ldots)$, which contain the information needed by the enterprise activities. Examples of this information are customer information, payroll information, design data, product information, and corporate plans. This data may be physically stored in flat files, relational databases, object-oriented databases, or under any other database management systems. More and more applications are beginning to store enterprise "knowledge" in the form of rules in databases. In addition, realtime databases may be stored in main memory for fast access.
- Application programs $P = (p_1, p_2 \ldots)$ to manipulate the application data. The programs may perform business operations (e.g., bookkeeping, credit checking), engineering/scientific functions (solid modeling, simulations, animations, drawings), manufacturing operations (e.g., robotics), and/or expert systems inferences.
- User interface programs $U = (u_1, u_2 \ldots)$ to process the user access to the application data and programs. The user interfaces may be simple text command/response systems, pull-down menus, graphical user interfaces, speech recognition systems and video systems with a pointing device (mouse). With the expected growth of multimedia applications, the user interfaces may include sophisticated combinations of voice, text, and video on the same screen.

Distributed application system (DAS). In a distributed application system (DAS), the programs P, the datasets D and the user interfaces U may reside at more than one computer of a distributed computer system. In a typical DAS, the user interfaces are allocated to user workstations and the programs and data may be dispersed to many sites in the network.

Network applications. These applications use networks to enhance the value of the applications. A network application may be a DAS (e.g., data at several sites), may consist of a collection of standalone applications which utilize the network to interact with each other, or may be a centralized application which is accessed from a network. We will not discuss network applications separately because these applications can be treated as a special case of distributed applications.

Object-oriented view of distributed computing. An object-oriented view of distributed computing simplifies analysis. A distributed computing environment can be viewed as a collection of objects in which each object is an identifiable entity in the system. For example, each file, printer, spreadsheet, program, user, communication line, workstation and device can be viewed as an object. Each object provides a service. The service is defined by an interface, which consists of a set of operations. For a user of the object, the interface shows the type of input and the results generated. A requester of the object service is called a client; the object providing the service is called a server. This model conforms to the typical OMG (Object Management Group) Model. Appendix E gives a quick overview of object-oriented concepts. For a detailed discussion of object-oriented software construction, refer to the book by Meyer <1988>.

Parallel versus distributed programs. Parallel (concurrent) programs can share main memory and utilize global variables. Distributed programs reside on different machines, so they must interact through message exchange only. Thus only portions of the theories developed for parallel programming apply to distributed programs.

Distributed computing platforms (DCP) versus distributed application systems. A distributed computing platform (DCP) provides all the resources needed by distributed applications. A DCP, as discussed in the previous chapter, consists of networks, computing hardware, and application support services such as distributed database managers, file servers, RPC facilities, and name directories, etc. One or more application systems (distributed or not) reside on each DCP and utilize the services provided by the DCP (see Fig. 8.2). A typical corporate DCP consists of a mainframe, many minicomputers that operate as file/database servers on LANs, and several workstations connected to LANs, or directly to the mainframe.

This distinction between DAS and DCP is significant because DCPs are becoming commercially available through vendors and most of the future application systems will be developed on these platforms. For example, almost all of the application systems for computer integrated manufacturing (CIM) will be developed on platforms consisting of manufacturing, business, and engineering networks. Traditionally, the distributed computing platforms that support distributed application systems have been called *distributed processing systems*.

An application system in distributed computing does not necessarily have to be distributed. On a given DCP, some applications may be distributed while others may be centralized. In addition, all components of an application system do not have to be distributed. Some DASs may have centralized data and programs but distribute user

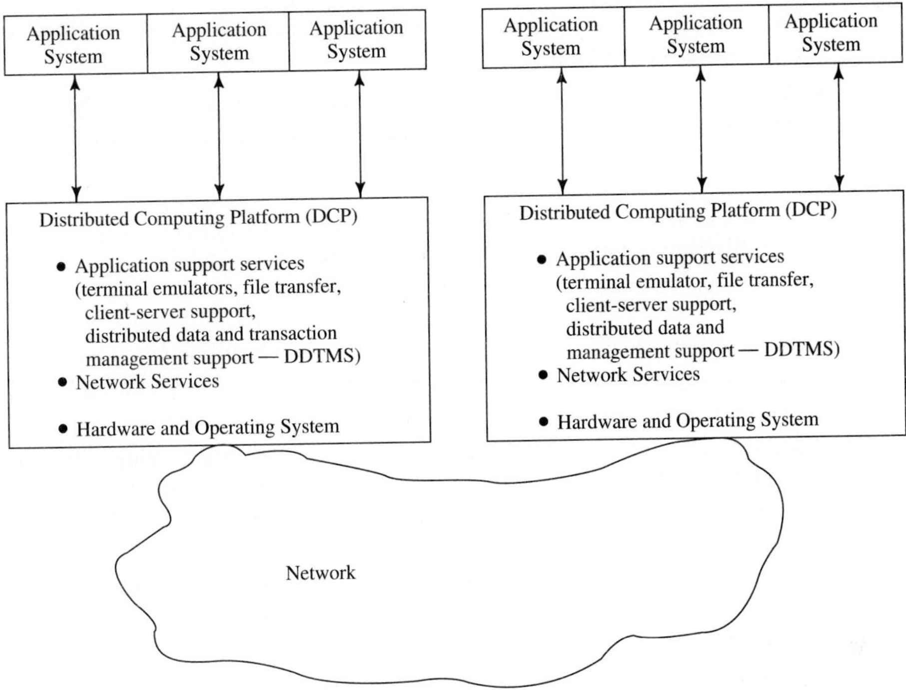

FIGURE 8.2 Distributed Application Systems versus Distributed Computing Platforms

interface processing. Other DASs may have centralized programs but distributed data. A distributed application system may or may not have distributed databases. In addition, the programs as well as the user interfaces may be distributed.

We should clarify that in some cases it is not possible to distinguish between application and system software. For example, in realtime embedded control systems, many of the application functions are coded in I/O routines and operating system schedulers for improved performance. In these cases, it is difficult to separate platforms from the applications. We will treat these systems as special cases, wherever possible. Our focus is on the situations in which several applications reside on the same computing platform (e.g., business, engineering, and manufacturing applications sharing the same corporate computers).

8.2.2 Examples of Distributed Application Systems

Common examples of DAS are as follows:

- An order processing system, in which the prices and inventory files are kept at the local stores for initial order processing. The final credit checking and invoice printing is done at a central site.
- A financial information retrieval system, in which the user interface resides on workstations and the information to be retrieved is at other sites. The workstation

user interface programs issue calls to appropriate back-end systems by using a client-server paradigm.

- A manufacturing control system in which the processes, the data and the user interfaces are distributed to cell controllers, program logic controllers, robots, and shop floor monitoring devices.

In addition to these "legacy" applications which are being distributed, several newer distributed application systems are emerging.[2]

Examples of such applications are as follows:

- Management decision support applications which utilize many modeling, analysis and evaluation tools residing on workstations which access remotely located information from many sites.
- Multimedia applications which combine data, voice and moving videos on the same workstation. In most cases, the text, the pictures and the moving video/voice appear on different windows of the same workstation. The information being displayed can be extracted from sources located anywhere in the network. The regular commentaries by John McQuillan on multimedia networks and applications in the Data Communications magazine and the Business Communications Review should be reviewed for a state of the market and state of the practice review.
- Image processing applications which require sending, processing and editing of images such as X-rays for the medical industry, photographs used in claims processing for the insurance industry, proofs and advertisements in the publication industry, and visualization of system dynamics in the aerospace industry.
- Video conferencing systems and groupware systems which allow remotely located workers to hold meetings, work on joint projects, collaborate on solving problems, and review and critique each other's work. Through text, video, and voice, these systems attempt to create an atmosphere in which remotely located workers interact with each other as if they were located at one site. See Johnson <1991> for a state of the market review of videoconferencing.
- Realtime applications in manufacturing and aerospace industries, among others, which require exchange of information between geographically distributed processors.
- Future collaborative computing applications which go beyond the computer conferencing and groupware software to solve problems cooperatively. These systems may include high definition TV and "artificial life" animations. See the December 1991, Communications of the ACM Special Issue on Collaborative Computing for a discussion of this topic. Technical details about collaborative computing can be found in the October 1992 issue of *Computer Communications*.

These newer applications are characterized by a high volume of data that needs to be transmitted interactively across networks. Many applications require 100 million bits

[2]The legacy, I guess, is that these applications are being passed on from old days to the new era.

per second (Mbps) data transfer rates with sessions that can last for several hours. These characteristics impose demands on the networks, computing hardware and the application software. Table 8.2 shows, for example, how many "applications" can be supported on a 150 Mbps channel.

8.2.3 Models of Distributed Applications

Figure 8.3 shows a few models of distributed applications. The simplest, and perhaps the most popular at present, is the distributed user interface model shown in Fig. 8.3a. In this model, the user interface is either completely or partially assigned to the end-user sites, usually a desktop computer. This model, used in many presentation intensive applications (e.g., XWindow), has the benefit that the user interface processing is parcelled out to the end-user sites. Figure 8.3b represents the distributed application program model in which the application programs, in addition to the user interfaces, are fully or partially assigned to the end-user sites. This model, used in many management decision support applications (spreadsheets, projections, simulations, etc.) further reduces the workload of the data sources. This model is especially appealing for the situations in which a small amount of data is accessed and a great deal of processing time is used in analyzing and presenting the data. Figure 8.3c represents the case where data, application programs as well as user interfaces are distributed to many sites. This model has many advantages but it presents challenges of distributed data and transaction management described in Chapter 6.

In essence, these three models represent the continuum between completely centralized (all data, application programs and user interfaces at one computer) and completely decentralized applications (no common data, application programs and user interfaces). As we will discuss later, these models provide the basis for a transition strategy from centralized to distributed applications in which the user interfaces are distributed first, followed by distribution of application programs and data.

In a given distributed computing environment, some applications may be centralized, some may be decentralized and others may be distributed in some form. Figure 8.4 shows an example of such an environment.

TABLE 8.2 Typical Applications on a 150-Mbps Channel

- 3,000,000 typists at 50 words/minute
- 30,000 FAX terminals
- 16,000 High-speed asynch terminals (9600 BPS)
- 2400 High-quality voice channels
- 100 High-quality stereo audio channels
- 100 Video teleconferences
- 15 High-speed local area networks (Ethernets)
- 6 High-resolution color images/second
- 3 Studio quality TV channels
- 1 High-definition TV channel

Note: These calculations are based on rough estimates.

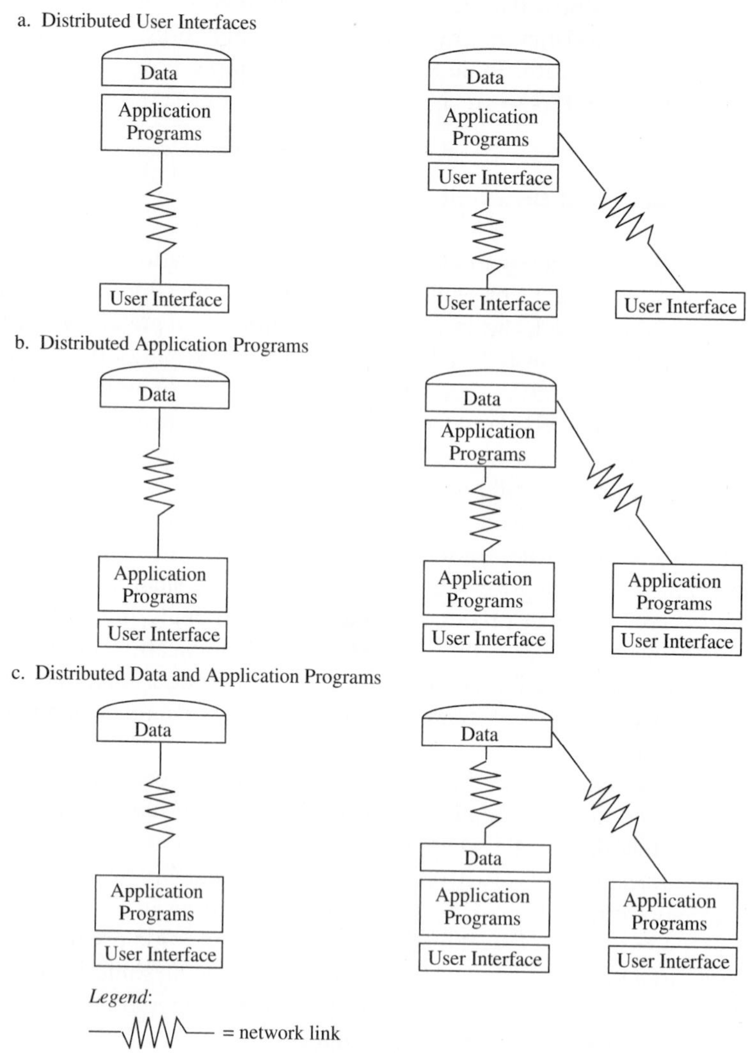

FIGURE 8.3 Distributed Application Models

Figure 8.5 shows a typical distributed computing platform on which several application systems reside. The DCP consists of a mainframe-host (H), a minicomputer M that operates as a file/database server on a local area network (LAN1), and several workstations connected to LAN1 or directly to H. The information exchanged between various computer systems is through terminal emulation, file transfer packages or client-server software. A DDBMS is installed on H and M to allow a user at WS2 to access and manipulate data transparently from H or M and the workstations employ a client which accesses print, file and database servers located in the network. At present, no distributed operating system is installed in this DCP.

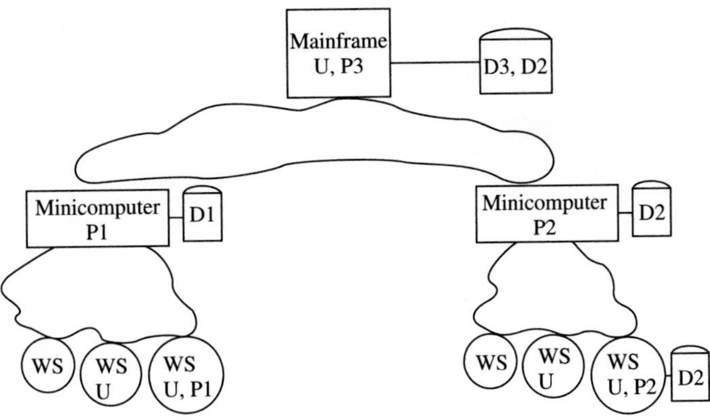

Comments:

- Two workstations are used as "dumb" terminals.
- The user interfaces reside at many workstations to access the programs P1, P2 and databases D1, D2 at the minicomputers.
- P1 also resides at one workstation.
- One workstation has U, P2, and D2.
- The database D2 is primarily read only and is assigned to several computers.
- Some of the programs and databases are at minicomputers for departmental (regional) application services.
- Some programs and databases are at the mainframe for corporate services.

FIGURE 8.4 A Typical Distributed Application System

Some application systems are centralized, some are decentralized and others are distributed on this DCP. For example, a payroll application system is centralized so that all the payroll data, the programs and the user interface processing reside at the host. A material requirement planning (MRP) system is distributed between the host and LAN1 so that portions of MRP data may be at the host and other at M. All word processing and CAD/CAM systems operate as standalone (decentralized) systems in LAN2. A common user interface may provide an integrated view of the applications even though the individual application components reside at different computers.

8.2.4 Why Distribute Applications and Why Downsize/Rightsize?

In general, a DAS provides many benefits to users by allowing the various activities to be dispersed across a network to maximize flexibility and availability. Given a DCP, users can configure their applications by using mixtures of mainframes, microcomputers, and minicomputers to meet different requirements and to respond to competitive pressures quickly. Other advantages of application system distribution are (this discussion is a rehash of advantages/disadvantages of distributed computing in Chapter 1):

- *Strategic factors*. Customers, suppliers, and companies do not exist at one site. Thus distributed applications, which tie these entities together can improve services and provide competitive edge.

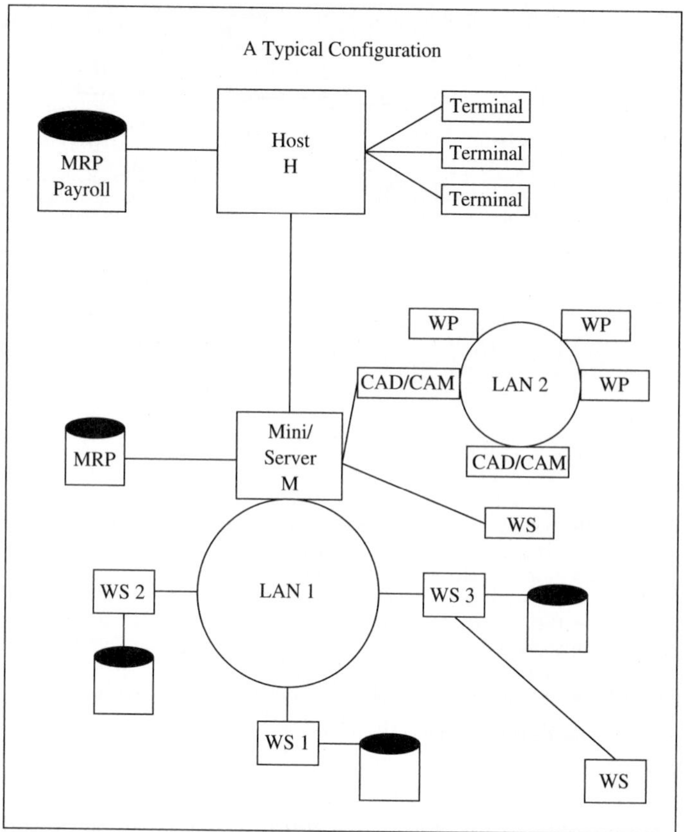

FIGURE 8.5 A Typical Configuration

- *Flexibility and configurability*. Distributed applications can improve performance and reliability through redundant data and processing. For example, distributed applications distribute workload among computing platforms.
- *Equipment costs*. The average cost per MIP (million instructions per second) on a mainframe is almost 100 times more than on a workstation. Distributed applications allow more economic use of computer equipment.
- *Development costs*. The cost and time to develop software on desktops may be lower due to the availability of interactive packages in several areas. For example, many packages for spreadsheets, graphics, fourth-generation languages and executive information systems make it very easy to develop business applications on desktop computers. However, this is not true in the development of large transaction processing applications.
- *User know-how and control*. The users of computing services are becoming increasingly computer literate and want to control their own applications. Distributed applications put data and processing close to the user.

- *User interfaces.* The desktops are well suited for sophisticated graphical user interfaces (GUI) with speech and multimedia capabilities.
- *Exploitation of special hardware.* Desktop computer software can use the hardware features of the these platforms. For example, specialized graphic devices can be used for CAD applications. In addition, each computer can be used as a dedicated server to satisfy requests from clients.

However, distributed applications present many technical and management dilemmas:

- *Increase in complexity.* Distributed application systems introduce complex issues and interdependencies which are not well understood. For example, one misbehaving application at one site may affect many applications residing at remote sites. In addition, many points of failures are introduced which make application recovery difficult.
- *Interoperability, integration, and portability issues.* Distributed applications raise these serious issues. These issues require many standards which require agreements between vendors and international/national organizations. We will discuss this topic in the next chapter.
- *Difficulties in large application design.* Breaking applications into pieces, where each piece can reside on a separate computer is non-trivial. In addition, as we have seen in Chapter 5, many application interconnectivity options need to be carefully evaluated.
- *Concerns for security and integrity control.* Interactions between data and programs on multiple computers introduce security and integrity control issues which are not easy to address. It has been found, for example, that backup and recovery of data across a network is not easy.
- *Software license costs.* Distributed applications may require many software licenses at many computers, thus potentially increasing the software costs. In contrast, centralized applications can use one software license for many users. However, software license costs are usually based on the potential number of users.
- *Lack of support and management infrastructure.* At present, many of the management and support issues have not been addressed (see Chapter 10).
- *Too many options and confusion.* It takes a long time for the developers to understand all options and make the best decisions. Developers need more training to develop efficient distributed applications. It is also difficult to differentiate between state-of-the-art, state-of-the-market and state-of-the-practice issues (we have tried to do this where possible).

Let us turn our attention from general advantages/disadvantages to specific issues related to downsizing. This topic is relatively new and sound studies of losses/gains in downsizing are scarce in the current literature. Most of the drive toward downsizing is based on cost savings (i.e., use less expensive hardware and minimize staff overhead). As indicated above, only 4 percent of Fortune 1,000 companies were not interested in downsizing. However, the numerous cases quoted in "Dirty Downsizing" by Radding <1992>, indicate the following:

- Some applications do not downsize well. Examples are the applications with large databases which are shared by thousands of users; the applications which are closely tied to other mainframe applications; the applications which require strong central security and control; and the applications which require around-the-clock availability.
- Expected cost savings (24 to 30 percent) have not been fully realized due to the need for staff retraining and hiring of consultants.
- Many people-related issues complicate the downsizing effort: traditional users may resist, new staff with new skills may be needed, and it may be difficult to align downsizing with corporate goals (too much diversity).
- Administrative problems are tricky: backup on many PCs across Ethernet LANs may take over 10 hours, coordination between multiple vendors causes headaches, and isolation of failure on multiple machines is difficult.

The continued growth of the underlying technologies in computing networks and application support services, discussed so far in Part II and III of this book, will help solve some of these problems. On the other hand, these technologies expose us to new problems, choices, issues and interfaces. This chapter will attempt to cast these tradeoffs into a methodology. The growth of "open" standards in distributed applications and systems architectures will help mitigate the complexity and confusion. We will discuss these standards in Chapter 9. The management and support issues, discussed in Chapter 10, need special attention. Good literature on application downsizing is sparse at the time of this writing; however, some articles on state of the practice are beginning to appear in the trade journals (see, for example, Edelstein <1992>, Wahl <1992>, Wreden <1992>, Radding <1992>).

8.3 Distributed Application Engineering: How to Downsize/Rightsize

8.3.1 Overview of Distributed Application Engineering

Ideally, there should be no difference between developing distributed versus centralized applications. However, at present and in the foreseeable future, many differences exist. *Distributed application engineering* is concerned with building, testing, deploying and maintaining distributed applications. Application engineering is synonymous to software engineering, although application engineering includes database design, user interface design, integration of off-the-shelf packages with in-house software, etc. Techniques for developing conventional centralized application systems are well known and have been covered in many textbooks in the last decade (see, for example, the textbooks by Meyer <1988>, Pankaj <1991>, Pressman <1987>, and Ramamoorthy <1984>). These techniques have evolved through several stages in the last

20 years (see Lewis <1990>). Although some attention has been paid to distributed software engineering (see, for example, Yau <1992>, Shatz <1988>, Shatz <1987>, Marianni <1984>, Patrick <1980>, Urban <1985>), more work is needed in this area. Available books are too narrow in scope; for example, the book by Corbin <1991> shows how to write distributed applications by using the SUN RPC, and the book by Coulouris <1989> does not address software engineering.

The distributed application engineering problem can be viewed in the following basic forms:

1. Develop a new distributed application, given a distributed computing platform (DCP).
3. Distribute (downsize) an existing centralized application on a DCP.
4. Develop distributed applications plus DCPs, given user requirements.
5. Develop a DCP, given a set of distributed applications.

The discussion in this chapter concentrates on the first three problems. The first two problems are very common at present. The third problem occurs most frequently in "mission oriented" embedded realtime systems and can be treated as a generalization of the first problem. For example, based on an initial application understanding, a platform can be chosen which is refined, modified and extended as more details about the application become available. Many real life problems are variants of the first three problems (i.e., application system needs to be defined, but some platform decisions are constrained while others are not). The fourth problem is not really a distributed application system problem. Instead it is a platform design problem, i.e., how to design a network, how to design the RPC software, how to design a distributed operating system, etc. We have reviewed these issues in Part II and III of this book. Due to our focus on applications in this chapter, we will assume that most of the platform issues have been decided and are input to this stage.

The distributed application engineering problems present several unique challenges:

- Distributed application systems tend to be larger and more complex than conventional centralized or standalone application systems.
- Distributed applications introduce many more decisions and choices (e.g., communication between systems, performance versus availability tradeoffs, failure handling, deadlock detection, etc.).
- The tools needed to make distributed application development transparent are not readily available.
- The underlying DCPs can exist in various forms and shapes (wide area networks, local area networks, metropolitan area networks), with numerous interfaces (bit level, data level, information level) and can provide a wide variety of information sharing facilities, such as terminal emulation, file transfer packages, file servers, distributed database managers, client-server software, and distributed operating systems.

- The tradeoffs in DAS development are numerous with serious side effects.
- A DAS should satisfy several additional requirements such as the transparency of location for application components, flexibility of adding and deleting computers where the software will run, recoverability from failures, and handling of unscheduled events at different computers.

Figure 8.6 shows a methodology for distributed application engineering. This methodology, based on the life cycle model, can be extended to incorporate the prototyping ("spiral") model in which the system is first developed as a prototype and then incrementally enhanced into a full system. This methodology can be used to answer the following questions: What are the activities that are unique to DAS

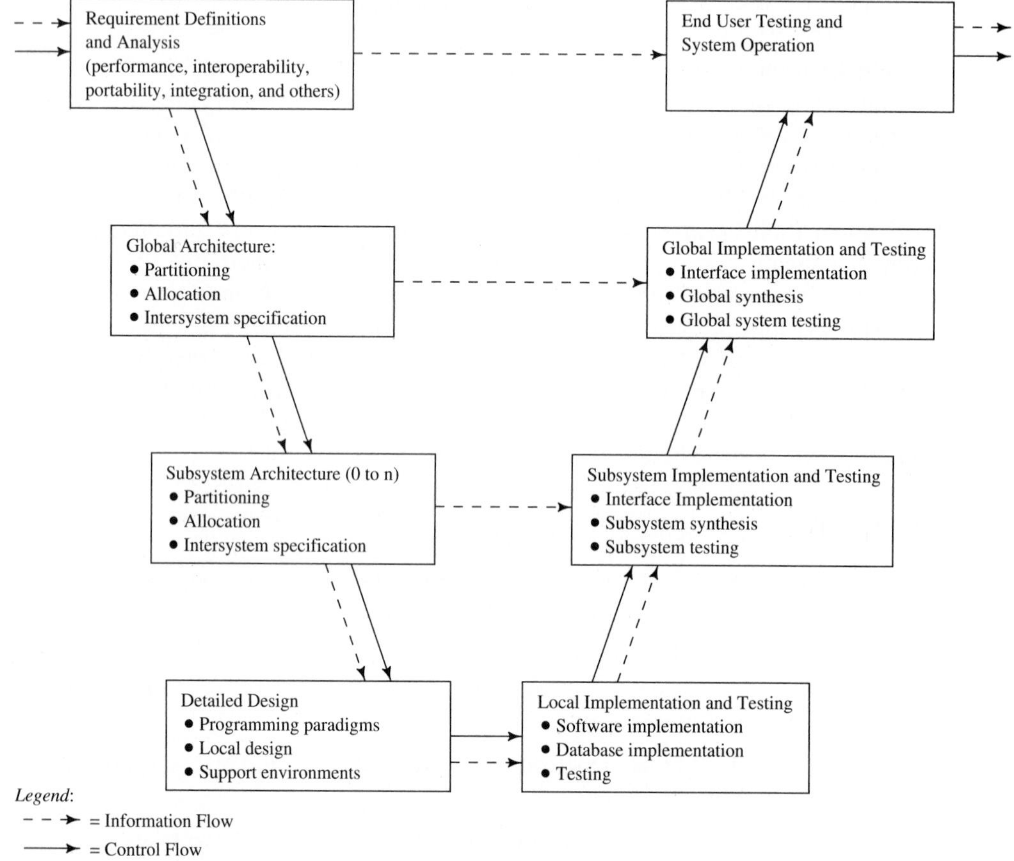

FIGURE 8.6 Distributed Application Engineering Methodology

development? What pieces of additional information are needed in the new activities? How can the large number of DAS issues be isolated and interfaced with non-DAS issues? and How do the evolving DCP technologies affect the DAS development?

Requirement definition and analysis is usually the first phase in developing any system. In this phase, the purpose of the proposed application system is defined, a business case is prepared, and a platform-independent application system model is specified which would satisfy the user requirements. This phase is independent of the type of platforms being used and is thus generally the same for centralized and/or distributed applications. Section 8.4 reviews these activities.

A series of architectural choices are made after requirement definitions. As shown in Fig. 8.6, the architectural choices are made at global (corporate) level, a subsystem (subnet) level, and at the local computer level. The number of levels depends on the size of the DCP. For example, in a LAN, only two levels of decisions are needed. In a corporate network, three levels of decisions need to be made. More levels of decisions may be needed in large supernetworks. The activity of "architecting" distributed applications concentrates on the global problems of identifying the major components of an application system, subdividing and grouping of these components into objects (partitioning), allocating these objects to computers (allocation), and then interconnecting/integrating these objects into a single functioning system. The decisions to purchase the products to be used in later phases are also made here. This task highlights the difference between the distributed and centralized applications, and is discussed in Section 8.5. As discussed in the next section, the downsizing/rightsizing decisions are also made in this task.

In the implementation and testing phase, the detailed designs of the local database, programs, user interfaces, and interprocess-communication are developed, and the designs are implemented into code which is tested and installed. In a manner similar to the architectural phase, this phase consists of many levels depending on the size of the DCP. As shown in Fig. 8.6, these tasks receive the architectural choices made in the architecture phase. The issues of particular importance for distributed applications are the distributed programming paradigms and application support needed for these applications. These topics are discussed in Section 8.6. After implementation, development may be continued in the maintenance activity; in particular the local as well as global programs and databases may be modified and extended.

8.3.2 A Downsizing/Rightsizing Strategy

The distributed system life cycle, combined with the distributed application models (Section 8.2.3), and the advantages/disadvantages of application downsizing/rightsizing (Section 8.2.4) provides a foundation for the following downsizing/rightsizing strategy:

1. Start with an analysis of centralized applications and identify the reasons why the applications need to be distributed. This analysis should be done in the requirements phase. The discussion in Section 8.2.4 should help this analysis. As stated in Section 8.2.4, the following applications are not good candidates: the applications with large databases which are shared by thousands of users; the applica-

tions which are closely tied to other mainframe applications; the applications which require strong central security and control; and the applications which require around-the-clock availability. Here is the key point: Do not undertake this effort without understanding the various tradeoffs (the saying: "if it is not broke, do not fix it" should be kept in mind).

2. Identify the applications which can be moved entirely to smaller machines without splitting. The reader should translate the factors in Section 8.2.4 into a checklist. This checklist will help identify such applications.
3. For the applications which should be split, distribute the user interfaces to the user sites as a first step. This provides end user transparency and offloads some of the central site workload. This also incurs minimal development costs and introduces the management to distributed applications with minimal risk. Use the steps in the architecture methodology (Section 8.5) to make this transition.
4. Gradually move the programs to the user sites on an as-needed basis. This further reduces the central site workload. It also introduces the issues of software licenses and program conversions from mainframes to smaller machines.
5. Later, move the data also to the user sites. Once again, the evaluation strategy described in Section 8.5 can be used in this transition. For example, the complexity introduced due to the management of distributed data and transaction management should be evaluated in this transition.

This strategy assumes availability of a DCP which supports client-server computing. The main advantage of this approach is that an organization can evaluate costs and benefits in a controlled manner. This will also allow an organization to gradually understand the implications of downsizing applications. The discussion in this chapter highlights the technical aspects of downsizing. The management implications are discussed in Chapter 10.

8.4 Requirement Definition and Analysis

Requirement definition and analysis involves two major type of activities: (1) specification which includes the preparation, modification and maintenance of the requirement documentation, and (2) examination which includes the review, evaluation and approval of the document. Table 8.3 shows typical information specified during requirement definition. The requirements are defined in terms of the functions performed, organizational/strategic objectives, and the restrictions of performance, policies, budgets, and operational behavior. Although most of this information can be specified for centralized as well as distributed applications, the following categories are of fundamental importance in DAS:

- *Organizational and strategic pressures*: Organizations may undertake the downsizing/rightsizing efforts for reasons such as cost reductions, overhead reduction,

TABLE 8.3 Common Requirement Definitions

- Functional requirements
  User commands (inputs) and responses (outputs)
  Tasks performed by the system
- Performance requirements
  Timing requirements (concurrency, internal events, and state transitions)
  Reliability and availability restrictions
  Intelligence requirements (inference, learning)
- Operational requirements
  Interconnectivity and integration needed
  Portability between computing platforms
  Interoperability and interfaces with other (existing/proposed) systems
- Policy restrictions
  Standards to be followed
  Application control restrictions (centralized/decentralized)
  Data access and manipulation restrictions (journaling, backup/recovery)
  Data allocation restrictions (site restrictions, synchronization interval)
  Program allocation restrictions (site restrictions)
- Budgetary restrictions (time allowed, money allowed)

improved flexibility of services and other business pressures. These factors should be noted clearly because they drive the entire application engineering effort.

- *Performance requirements*: Detailed timing requirements must be specified for most distributed applications, especially for embedded computer systems <White 1987>. The reliability and availability restrictions of an application significantly affect the allocation of application components to computers (e.g., high availability encourages duplicated data). The "intelligence" requirements for reasoning (inferencing) and learning should be specified clearly so that implementations at different computers adhere to these principles.

- *Operational requirements*: A user should specify the interconnectivity, integration, portability and interoperability requirements. For example, a user may specify that an application should be accessible from many computers and should interoperate in an open vendor-transparent environment. These issues arise because diverse applications in business, engineering and manufacturing written in different software and database formats residing on heterogeneous computing devices need to be interconnected and integrated through different communication media by using a variety of communication software packages. We will discuss these issues in more detail in the next chapter.

- *Policy restrictions*: It is important to specify the standards to be followed in user interface design, naming conventions and coding/documentation practices. In addition, any restrictions on data access and manipulation, data allocation, and program allocations should be clearly specified. For example, some data may need to be kept at central sites for security reasons and some programs should run on specialized processors.

It is common to create an application model by decomposing an application into subparts. Parnas <1972> gave one of the earliest discussions of this topic. Since then many papers have been written on this topic (see Paulson <1992> for a recent approach). Decomposition can be based on the following strategies:[3]

- *Functional decomposition.* This is one of the oldest techniques and was used heavily in the structured design methodologies in the 1970s. Basically, an application system is subdivided into subparts where each subpart performs a unique function. For example, an order processing application can be decomposed into initial processing, order verification, shipment processing, invoicing, etc.
- *Object-oriented decomposition.* In this case, the system is decomposed based on the objects in the system. For example, in an order processing system the main objects are customers and finished products. The order processing application can be decomposed in terms of customer-oriented processing and product-oriented processing. This approach allows packaging of data and relevant operations on data and thus may simplify the system modeling task <Schneiderwind 1989>.

Independent of the method used, the result of decomposition can be viewed and documented in terms of objects. Numerous approaches have been suggested for documentation and examination of specifications. Approaches vary from listing the "ills" of the document such as the noise, silence, overspecification, contradictions, and ambiguity to knowledge-based tools which help in the analysis activity by critiquing and evaluating the document <Meyer 1989>. Overviews of requirements analysis can be found in Pankaj <1991>, Pressman <1987>, Yeh <1984>, Zave <1984>. Reubenstein <1991> describes a Requirements Apprentice which automates many of the requirements analysis activities. Issues specific to distributed systems such as timing, parallelism and deadlocks, are discussed by Papelis <1992>, Chen <1983>. Once the requirements have been documented, they are circulated to and analyzed by the end users, the managers, the developers, marketing representatives, etc.

The application requirements shown in Table 8.3 can be specified through a specification language or a GUI with icons. In addition to the requirement definition, a specification facility may describe several other pieces of information generated during the life cycle. For example, Table 8.4 summarizes the information needed and generated in various phases that may need to be specified in a computer aided software engineering (CASE) environment (see Section 8.7). Consequently, a specification facility should possess the following desirable properties <Greenspan 1982>: (1) be "wide spectrum" so that it can support at least the requirement definition, functional specification and design activities; (2) have as few constructs as possible, yet be powerful enough to describe the real life situations in sufficient detail; (3) allow for incremental gathering and recording of information through levels of specifications; and (4) provide for smooth transitions from one activity to the next.

[3]In some methodologies, decomposition is described in "logical design" instead of requirement analysis.

TABLE 8-4 Life Cycle Spectifications

Life Cycle Phases	*Application System Knowledge Specified*	*Distributed Computing Platform Knowledge Specification*
Requirement Definition and Analysis Phase	• Application objective • Application transactions • Tasks (processes) • inputs/outputs • Datasets • Transaction arrival rate • Constraints • Dynamic behavior	• No. of workstations • Interconnections of workstations
Global and Subystem Architecture Phase	• Program objects • Data objects • Allocations	Hardware Subsystem • No. of computers • No. of links • Network topology • computer capacities • Link capacities Software Subsystem • DDTMS characteristics • client-server services (RPCs, directories, etc.) • Other services
Detailed Design	• Program design • Database design • Interprocess communication	• Computer characteristics • Network hardware characteristics • Network application protocols –RPC –APPC –OSI ROSE –MMS –Unix sockets • Others

8.5 Distributed Application Architecture

8.5.1 A Distributed Application Architecture Methodology

A distributed application architecture specifies

- The functional components of an application being developed (processes P, data entities D, user interfaces U)

- The allocation of the application system components (D, P, U) to the computers (computers) of the distributed computing platform (DCP)
- The application interconnectivity choices (client-server systems, distributed database managers, terminal emulators, file transfer packages, etc.) to exchange information between the application system components
- The distributed computing platform (DCP) which will support the distributed application (hardware components, operating systems, database systems, programming languages, network interconnections and network architectures).

In case of downsizing, the preceding information will show how the downsized application will be split across mainframes, minicomputers and desktop computers.

Figure 8.7 shows a simple example of a distributed application architecture problem. The inputs to this problem, shown in Fig. 8.7a, are an application system consisting of a common user interface U, three processes (P_1, P_2, P_3) and two logical databases (D_1, D_2) which need to be developed on a network consisting of a mainframe M, a minicomputer m and three workstations (w_1, w_2, w_3). Solutions to the distributed application architecture problem generate numerous potential scenarios. Assuming that the user interface U is assigned to all workstations (w_1, w_2, w_3), let us review the three scenarios shown in Fig. 8.7b (all these scenarios represent some level of downsizing):

1. Database D_1 and process P_1 are replicated at all workstations, everything else is at the mainframe. An example of such a DAS is a distributed order processing system in which the orders are processed initially at the arriving sites. D_1 is the read only customer information ("skeleton file") and P_1 is the processing program. The initial orders are later routed to a central location for administrative processing (P_2 and P_3 may be the customer verification and inventory control programs and D_2 may be the master database). The application interconnectivity between the mainframe and workstation programs may be through terminal emulation, file transfer, or client-server messages.
2. The databases D_1 and D_2 are allocated to mainframe M, minicomputer m and a few of the workstations, but the programs P_1, P_2 and P_3 are restricted to the mainframe. An example of such a DAS is a central network management system which performs all network management functions (represented, say, by P_1, P_2, P_3) at the central site. The network manager periodically retrieves/updates the network directories (D_1, D_2) located at remote sites. A DDBMS may be useful with realtime message exchange as client-servers or peer-to-peer cooperative processors.
3. A single copy of data D_1 and D_2 is allocated to the mainframe and is accessed by P_1, P_2, P_3 running anywhere in the network. An example of such a DAS is a manufacturing control system in which the manufacturing devices access and update the common status information D_1 located at the central controller. The application interconnectivity mechanism is realtime message exchange between P_1, P_2 and P_3 and the server of database D_1.

a. The Problem: Map an Application System to a Network:

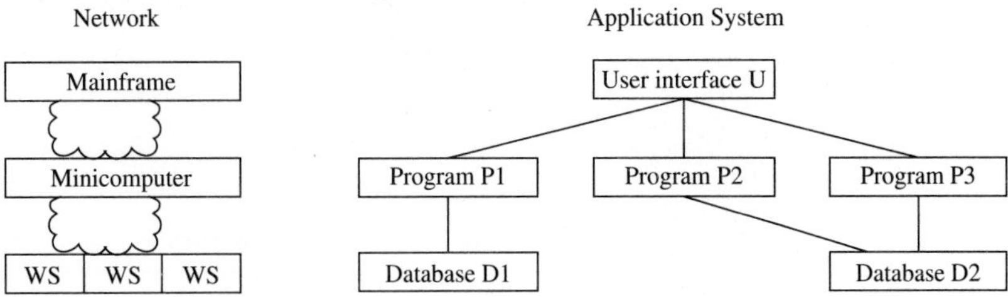

b. Potential Solution Scenarios (User interface is assigned to all workstations)

1. Database D1 and program P1 are at the WS, everything else is at the Host.

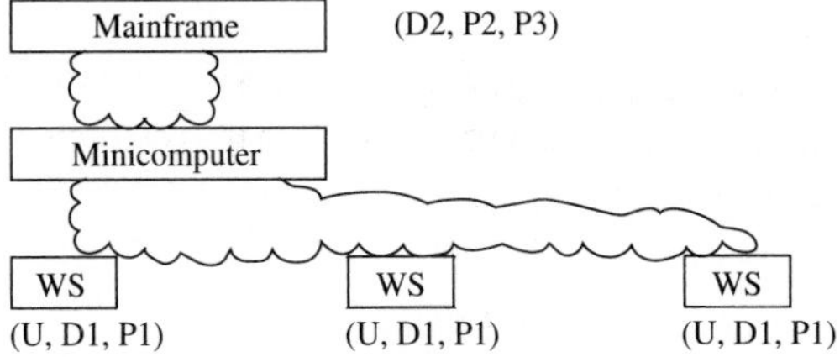

2. Databases D1 and D2 are distributed to several sites; programs P1, P2 and P3 are at the mainframe.

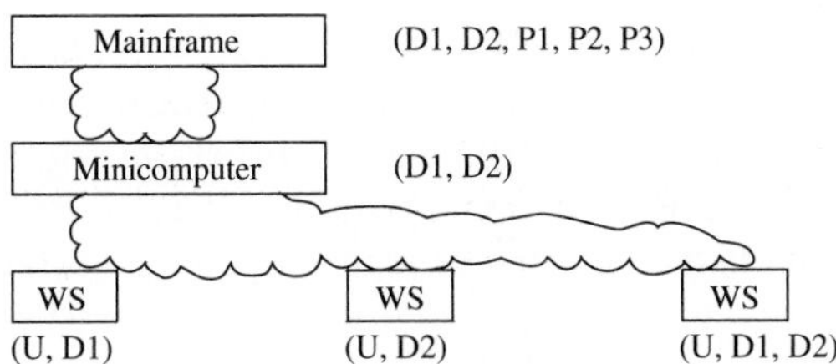

3. A single copy of data (D1 and D2) at the mainframe is accessed by programs running at several sites.

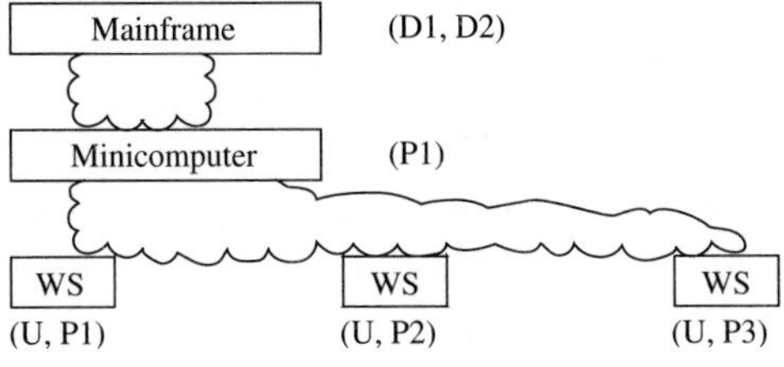

FIGURE 8.7 Example of Distributed Application Architecture

Figure 8.8 shows a generalized distributed application architecture problem. It is a complex problem which involves many rapidly advancing disciplines such as distributed software engineering <Shatz 1987>, distributed database design <Teorey 1989>, program and database fragmentation and allocation problems <Jain 1987,

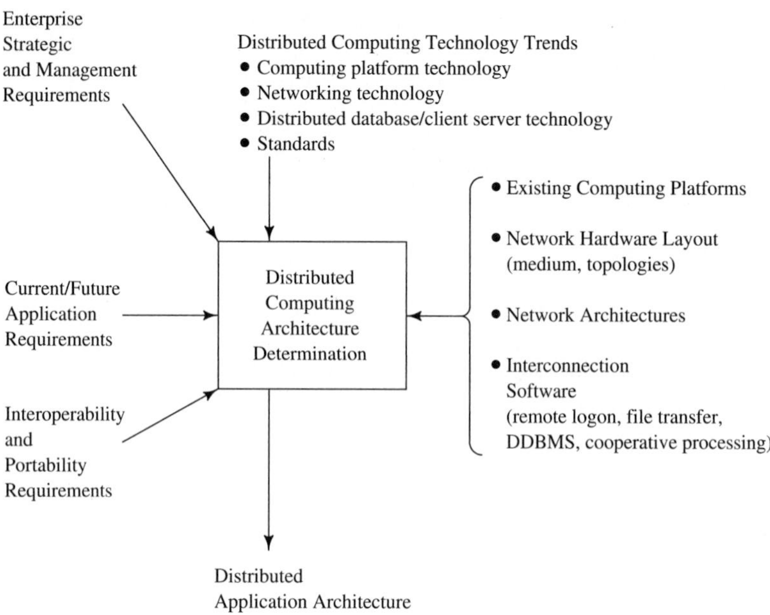

FIGURE 8.8 Distributed Application Architecture Problem

Umar 1985>, interconnectivity and integration issues <Nutt 1992, Moad 1990>, and the evolving standards in network and data architectures. Theoretically some of the architecture problems can be cast into mathematical programming problems and solved by using a combination of optimization algorithms and heuristics. In practice, however, a methodology is needed which combines the mathematical techniques with heuristics and rules of thumb. Figure 8.9 shows such a methodology. The methodology consists of three major steps:

- Decompose an application system into subparts and group/partition the subparts into objects (see Section 8.5.2). For example, the application data can be decomposed into several data units, and the application logic can be decomposed into several programs where some of these programs can act as clients while the others can be servers, etc. This step, discussed in Section 8.5.2, also addresses which components of a system should be purchased and which should be developed.
- Allocate the objects to various computers in the network. This includes the factors to be considered in downsizing/rightsizing. The factors may include security, response time, administrative support, availability, business pressures, etc. The main decision is to determine the best sites for allocation of data, processes and user interface handling. The performance can be improved by locating data at the sites where it is most frequently used and the availability can be improved by replicating programs and data to more than one site. However, this increases the complexity and security exposure of the application systems. This step is discussed in detail in Section 8.5.3.

- Decide what interconnectivity options will be used to connect the various application system objects. Interconnectivity with existing as well as future applications is analyzed. In addition, the tradeoffs between using terminal emulation, file transfer, distributed database managers, cooperative processing, or distributed operating systems are evaluated. This step is explained in Section 8.5.4.

As shown in Fig. 8.9, these steps may need to be performed iteratively before an acceptable architecture is reached. The decisions made in these steps accept a large number of inputs such as application system requirements (functional, performance, interconnectivity, etc.), the underlying distributed computing platforms (network architecture and design, computer systems, resource managers available), and the application architecture standards. The output produced by these steps shows an application architecture which consists of an application model, mapped to a model of the DCP.

8.5.2 Decomposition/Partitioning of an Application

Application decomposition, introduced in requirement analysis phase, is an important aspect of application architecture. Decomposition, wherever it is conducted, leads to a large number of objects. Partitioning groups these objects to minimize the number of objects to be allocated to the computers of DCP. For example, a simple application may be decomposed into 100 objects (files, programs) which may need to be allocated to 500 computers (mainframes, minis and workstations). This requires 100×2^{500} allocations. Evaluation of all these allocations is too large for even supercomputers.

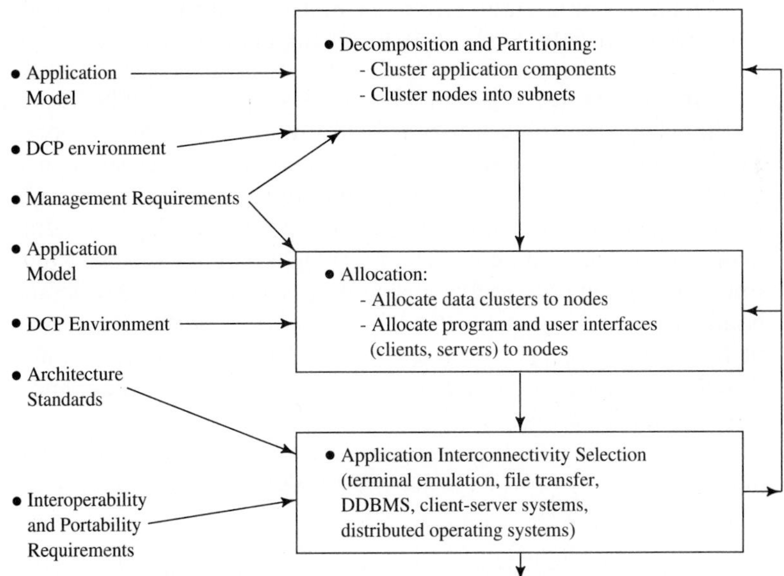

FIGURE 8.9 Distributed Application Architecture Methodolgy

1. Identify location-specific processes (objects) and assign them to the identified computers.
2. Separate all purchase processes from build processes (objects).
3. Cluster the build processes (objects) to minimize some objective.
4. Combine computers to reduce the problem (e.g., use a subnet instead of computer as an allocation unit).

FIGURE 8.10 A Partitioning Procedure

In general, allocation of k objects to n computers requires $k \times 2^n$ allocations. Note that an object can be allocated to multiple computers. Partitioning attempts to reduce k as well as n by using the procedure shown in Fig. 8.10.

Some application components are location specific—they must exist at a given specific location. For example, some sensitive information must be kept at the corporate office, manufacturing device status information needs to be kept on the plant floor, etc. The first step of partitioning attempts to identify the location-specific application components so that they can be eliminated from the allocation step. A component can be location specific due to

1. User requirements for some operations and data to be performed at certain sites
2. Security and management restrictions which require some components to be restricted to certain sites such as corporate office
3. Similarity and natural affinity of certain processes to certain sites (e.g., most manufacturing operations are performed at the plant floor)
4. Architecture matching the functionality (e.g., workstations for user interfaces and minicomputers for database servers)
5. Financial considerations (e.g., an animation must be performed on the machines which have software licenses for the animation packages).

In the next step of partitioning, a first-cut decision of buy/develop can be made on the decomposed objects to pragmatically reduce the choices. For example, a readily available business software package may automatically cluster many objects together and also may determine where these objects will reside. Current application systems often require a combination of purchased and developed modules which can be allocated to many computers. The advantages of purchasing software are the cost and time savings and presumably a wide user base. In-house development, on the other hand, is appealing due to its flexibility, in-house expertise reliance and better control of future direction. The decision usually depends on time and money available to develop the application system, a general trust of outsiders and numerous other organizational factors.[4]

It should be noted that in some applications, such as manufacturing control and defense systems, most of the software is developed in-house because off-the-shelf

[4]Many organizations choose to develop in-house software because it is harder to obtain budgetary approval for purchasing than to keep the current staff busy. In addition, many vendor products do not perform as advertised.

software for such applications is not available. The general trend toward open systems, discussed in the next chapter, is expected to make it easier to buy than develop by letting the users "package" applications purchased from different suppliers <Nutt 1992, Sections 1.2 and 1.3).

This author agrees with the widely held view that it is better to buy than to build. There is only one caution, especially for client-server applications: it is not a good idea to buy 20 application software packages which require 20 different servers and 20 different interconnectivity support packages to access the same corporate data. It is better to acquire one server which can support multiple clients from multiple suppliers (this may require some software development).

In the clustering step, similar objects are grouped together to form clusters. A cluster is essentially a collection of objects (or processes) which cannot be subdivided among computers. For example, a purchased product can be considered as a cluster because most purchased products cannot be subdivided into independent modules. This situation is changing somewhat due to open systems.

Two practical problems complicate clustering: measuring the effectiveness of the clusters and choosing the best clustering criteria <Shatz 1987>. In practice, clustering can be based on grouping of the purchased products (programs that are part of a purchased package are automatically clustered together), minimizing intercomputer communications, maximizing parallelism, and minimizing run-time processing and storage requirements. Some of these objectives can conflict with each other. For example, intercomputer communications can be minimized by grouping many processes into a single cluster which is allocated to one computer. However, this does not exploit parallelism. On the other extreme, each process could be allocated to a separate computer thus maximizing parallelism but generating too much communication traffic. In addition, precedence relationships between processes create special clustering conditions. For example, if process p_1 must precede p_2, then p_1 and p_2 should be clustered because p_1 and p_2 cannot run in parallel. Instead of trial and error, clustering can utilize formal techniques such as the following:

- Standard statistical clustering procedures <Everret 1974> which consist of choosing and computing an appropriate similarity or dissimilarity (distance) function and then utilizing hierarchical and mathematical programming techniques to minimize the distance function. For example, a distance function could indicate the amount of common data between processes. Buckles and Hardin <Buckles 1979> give several analytical examples of distance functions and describe a clustering procedure.
- Fuzzy logic, mode-seeking or clumping techniques for "fusing" similar objects. These techniques have been used in artificial intelligence and group technology in manufacturing <Negoita 1985>.

In most practical cases, clustering should be a quick procedure for minimizing number of objects. If a large mathematical programming algorithm is needed for clustering, then it is better to include clustering as a step in the allocation activity discussed later. This approach is used by Mariani and Palmer <Mariani 1979, Mariani 1984>.

In the last step of this methodology, the network is partitioned into subnets to minimize the number of allocation sites in the network. For example, consider a medium sized corporate network consisting of 1000 computers (mainframes, mini-computers, workstations and personal computers). Allocation of one object to this network would require 2^{1000} allocations. A simple observation can significantly reduce the size of this problem: The corporate network may be organized as 10 subnets where each subnet, say, consists of 100 computers. For example, the corporation may have 10 branch offices, each supporting a LAN. In this case, the files can be initially allocated to the 10 LANs and then the best place within each LAN can be found as a separate problem. In many cases, each LAN may have a designated server where some files should reside.

Example of Partitioning. Let us consider a situation in which 70 logical data files (d_1, d_2, d_{70}) need to be allocated to a 300-computer network.[5]

The following steps have been used to partition this problem:

- $d_1, \ldots, d_{40}$ were location specific due to security or other situations. For example, d_1-d_7 were restricted to one computer due to security restrictions, d_8-d_{11} must be allocated to a central site for management control and the other files were location specific because of the application area (factory floor, payroll, etc.). These files were allocated to the desired computers and eliminated from further allocations.
- $d_{41}, d_{42}, \ldots, d_{45}$ were part of a purchased CAD/CAM package. These were clustered into one cluster c_1.
- The remaining 25 files ($d_{46}, \ldots, d_{70}$) were clustered into 8 clusters to minimize intercomputer communication (the calculations were done by using a paper and pencil method).
- The 300 computer network was reduced into a 4 site network because the overall network consists of 4 subnets.
- The size of the problem is reduced to allocating 9 clusters to 4 sites.

8.5.3 Distributed Resource Allocation (Allocation of Data and Programs)

8.5.3.1 Overview

Distributed resource allocation assigns the objects produced in the partitioning step to the computers of a DCP. Examples of the objects are programs, databases, user interface processors, clients, and servers. We assume here that objects are assigned in the architecture phase statically (i.e., the assigned data and programs are not moved around dynamically during application execution). The dynamic resource allocation will perhaps be available through the distributed operating systems of the future. At that point, this whole step may need to be eliminated.

[5]This example is roughly based on an actual consulting assignment of this author

The following basic strategies can be used for allocating an object O:

- *Centralization*: O is uniquely assigned to a central computer n' or to a computer n where it is most frequently accessed. For example, a database server may be centralized because it manages sensitive data.
- *Duplication*: O is allocated to n and at least one more copy of O is kept at an arbitrary set of computers n_1, n_2, n_3, etc. For example, many copies of a name server, directory server, and authentication server may exist in the network.
- *Replication*: O is allocated to every computer in the network. For example, a user interface processor (client) may be replicated at every site.

The cost/benefit of these strategies can be estimated in terms of storage cost, development cost, communication traffic generated, response time, and availability. Fig. 8.11 briefly illustrates the tradeoff by showing the data duplication on x axis and costs on y axis. (This graph is repeated from Chapter 6.) It can be seen from Fig. 8.11 that:

1. The storage cost increases as the number of copies increases.
2. The communication traffic (cost) is shown in terms of read and update communication costs. The read communication cost decreases as the number of copies increases because most data can be found at local computers thus eliminating need for communication calls. The update communication cost increases with the number of copies because duplicated data will need to be updated.
3. The local I/O processing at each computer increases with data duplication. The increase is due to the locking/unlocking and logging activities to synchronize duplicate data and to prepare for failure handling (see Chapter 6 for more details).
4. The availability of data increases with the number of copies in the system.

An optimal allocation can be theoretically determined which minimizes the total cost (storage + communication + local I/O) subject to some response time and availability constraints. This problem, traditionally referred to as the File Allocation Problem (FAP), was first addressed by Wesley Chu in 1969 <Chu 1969>. Since then over 20 different file allocation algorithms have appeared in the literature <Buckles 1979, Casey 1972, Chandy 1976, Chang 1981, Chu 1969, Coffman 1980, Doty 1982, Eswaran 1974, Finckenscher 1984, Fisher 1980, Irani 1981, Koh 1985, Levin 1975, Mahmood 1976>. Earlier allocation problems used simple objective functions (e.g., minimize communication cost) and few constraints (e.g., file storage constraints). Later methods are design methodologies which utilize complex objective functions and constraints <Brahmadathan 1992, Ceri 1987, Jain 1987, Umar 1984>. A common allocation problem can be formulated as follows:

- Given:

  Objects O1, O2, . . .
  Computers $n_1, n_2, n_3, \ldots$

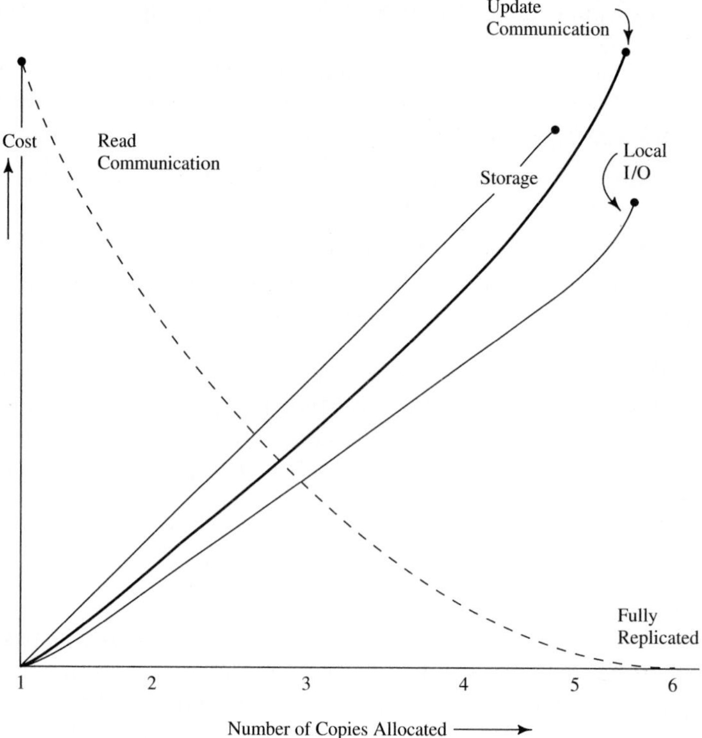

Notes:

- The cost does not necessarily indicate $ cost.
  It is a unit of resources needed which can be translated to $ costs.
- The number of copies indicates data duplication.
  In this example, 6 nodes are involved; hence 6 copies of a file mean fully replicated allocation.
- The local I/O means disk I/O at each node.
- The communication costs (read, update) indicate message traffic generated over the network.
  These costs include the locking/unlocking overhead.
- The storage costs indicates the amount of disk space occupied.

FIGURE 8.11 Data Allocation Tradeoffs

- Determine:

  AN(O,*n*) = 1 if O is allocated to *n*, 0 otherwise
- To minimize:

  storage cost + communication cost + local processing cost
- Subject to:

  response time constraints
  availability constraints

DCP configuration (network design and topology, application support services utilized)
management restrictions (security, time, money)

Variants of this problem have been cast into a mathematical programming problem and are solved by using nonlinear, integer and/or dynamic programming methods by the aforementioned researchers. However, many of the available techniques are academic and cannot be used in practical situations due to several reasons. First, the number of options in real life situations is very large. Second, the interrelationships between DCP configurations and assignment tradeoffs are not adequately represented in these algorithms. Third, many of the management and security restrictions are not included. Fourth, it is very difficult to translate real life large scale problems to mathematical programming and then solve them rigorously. Consequently, many simplifying assumptions are needed which limit the scope of the problem. Finally, most of the available research does not take into account the impact of emerging high-speed and reliable WANs, LANs and MANs operating at over 100 million bits per second. For example, most of the available work assumes slow and unreliable wide area networks of the 1970s.

An allocation procedure is suggested in Fig. 8.12 for a pragmatic solution of the distributed resource allocation problem. In the first step, a qualitative decision table helps the user to make major high-level decisions. In the next step, a simple analytical model aids in basic computations for gaining insights. In the final step, a detailed optimization algorithm can be employed, if needed. This hierarchical approach allows the analyst to gradually use more sophisticated tools for more complicated problems. This procedure can be used at the core of a knowledge-based decision support system for distributed resource allocations. The steps of this procedure are explained next.

8.5.3.2 High-Level Rightsizing/Downsizing Decisions

The primary purpose of high level rightsizing/downsizing is to reduce the size of the allocation problem by focusing on the tradeoffs between distribution choices. The following procedure can be used for evaluating these tradeoffs (see Table 8.5):

1. Verify and refine the results of the partitioning steps before proceeding. In fact, some researchers include the entire partitioning process in this step <Ozsu 1991>.
2. Define the application configuration choices available and planned in terms of distribution of data, programs and user interfaces. These are defined as columns in Table 8.5. Configuration 1 represents a centralized application system, configuration 2 shows a distributed user interface configuration, and configurations 3, 4, and 5 represent the more "downsized" configurations.
3. Define application and business requirements in terms of data sharing, pressures to downsize, flexibility and growth requirements, sizes of databases, connectivity requirements with other applications, security and control needs, performance constraints, availability constraints, budgetary constraints (cost, time), backup

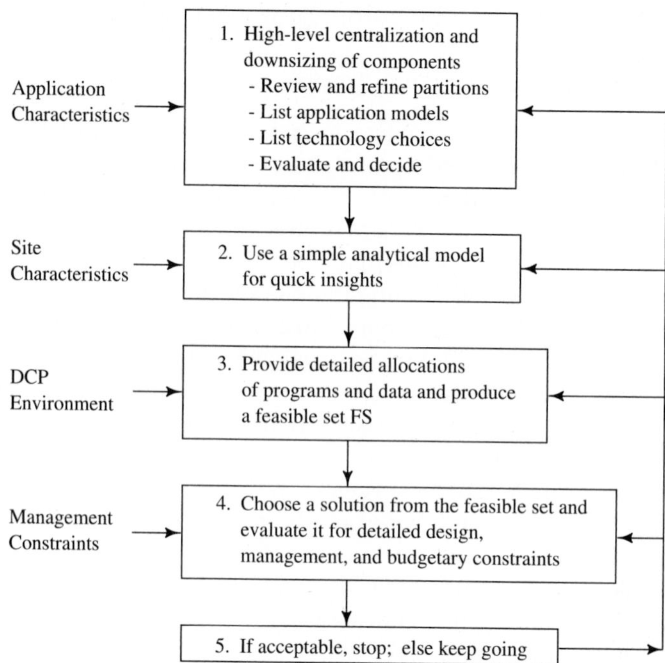

Application
Characteristics
1. High-level centralization and downsizing of components
- Review and refine partitions
- List application models
- List technology choices
- Evaluate and decide
Site
Characteristics
2. Use a simple analytical model for quick insights
DCP
Environment
3. Provide detailed allocations of programs and data and produce a feasible set FS
Management
Constraints
4. Choose a solution from the feasible set and evaluate it for detailed design, management, and budgetary constraints
5. If acceptable, stop; else keep going

FIGURE 8.12 A Distributed Resource Allocation Procedure

and recovery needs, user independence needs and user/staff training level. These needs, shown as rows in Table 8.5, should be specified during requirement definition.

4. Evaluate the possible configurations against the stated requirements for the specific application(s) by using some criteria as shown in Table 8.5. We will explain the entries in this table shortly. However, it should be emphasized that the purpose of Table 8.5 is to suggest a framework for evaluating the rightsizing/downsizing decisions. The actual requirements and the values assigned will depend on the particular application being distributed. Let us now briefly review the entries in Table 8.5:
   - Downsizing pressures are best satisfied by configurations 4 and 5 because all application components are distributed.
   - Flexibility and growth are also better satisfied by distributing data as well as programs.
   - Data sharing among thousands of users does become more difficult as data is more decentralized.
   - Applications which are tightly connected to other mainframe applications are harder to downsize.
   - Large databases are better handled at centralized mainframes.
   - Control and security needs, at present, are better satisfied by centralized systems, because distributed data introduces many security issues.

TABLE 8.5 Application Downsizing/Centralization Decision Table

	Application Configurations				
Enterp. & Appl. Needs	*Data-C Process-C User int. C (Conf.1)*	*Data-C Process-C User int. D (Conf.2)*	*Data-C Process-C User-D (Conf.3)*	*Data-D,U Process-D User-D (Conf.4)*	*Data-D,R Process-D User-D (Conf.5)*
Downsizing pressures	−3	+1	+2	+3	+3
Flexibility & growth	−1	+1	+2	+2	+2
Data sharing needs	+1	+1	+1	−1	−2
Interconnectivity needs	+1	+1	0	−1	−1
Large database needs	+2	+3	+3	−1	−2
Control & security needs	+3	0	−1	−2	−2
Availability needs	−1	−1	−1	1	+3
Performance requirements	−1	+1	+1	+1	+2
User training reqmts.	+3	−1	−2	−3	−3
User independence needs	−2	−1	−1	+3	+3
Development costs	+1	−1	−1	−1	−1
Maintenance & operation costs	+1	−1	−1	−2	−2
Backup and recovery ease	+3	+3	+1	−1	−2
Management & support considerations	+1	−1	−2	−3	−3

Legend: C = centralized, D = distributed, U = unique (only one copy), R = replicated

Evaluation factors (−3 to +3) indicate how well the configurations satisfy the requirements:
−3 = does not satisfy at all
+3 = very well satisfied
0 = no impact

- Availability needs are better satisfied by configuration 5 because it allows data duplication.
- Performance may improve with downsized applications because these configurations reduce the central site congestion.
- More training is needed to operate and manage distributed applications.
- User independence is better served by using configurations 4 and 5. Note that downloading of user interfaces does not help user independence (the data is still not under user control).
- Development costs may decrease by downsizing because end user computing may help.
- Maintenance and operation costs may increase due to multiple licenses and the need for expensive DDTMS.
- Backup and recovery procedures are easier with centralized applications.
- Management and support is harder in distributed applications due to a lack of standards.

Table 8.5 in essence attempts to automate the advantages/disadvantages discussed in Section 8.2.4. How does this Table help? It shows the tradeoffs between various choices. The decision can now be based on maximizing the benefits for the major critical requirements and understanding the impact (the negatives) of other requirements. For example, if pressures for downsizing are high, then configurations 4 and 5 should be adopted with an understanding of the risks/costs indicated by the negatives in Table 8.5.

8.5.3.3 Analytical Evaluation of Allocation Strategies

The high-level analysis does not show exactly what application system components should be allocated where. The following three allocation decisions need to be made:

- Where to allocate the user interfaces
- Where to allocate the application programs
- Where to allocate the data.

User interfaces can be allocated to any computer which has the necessary client-interface software to connect to the data servers. The main consideration is the license cost and software development costs for the user interface modules. The application programs can also be allocated for similar reasons. A special consideration for program allocation to a particular computer is the availability of specialized software needed (e.g., fourth generation languages, simulation software, etc.) on the user computer.

Data allocation is a different story. The allocations can be based on several factors such as amount of storage, read communications (cost, time), update communication (cost, time), local I/O at each computer, and response time. For example, unique allocation (assign one data object to one computer) yields a small amount of storage, high read communications traffic, small update communication and small local I/O at each computer. Duplicate allocation (more than one copy) yields a large amount of storage, small read communications traffic, high update communication and local I/O at each computer.

The simple analytical model shown in Table 8.6 can be used for this purpose. The model can compute the storage occupied, communication traffic and local processing traffic in terms of data allocations. These dependent variables can be used to compute rough estimates of response time and availability. This model can be easily translated to a C, Fortran or Pascal routine. It is also possible to extend this model into a distributed database design aid which can either predict the response time for given data distributions and/or determine near optimal allocations to minimize certain objective functions (see <Umar 1984, Umar 1985> for details).

8.5.3.4 Detailed Resource Allocation Procedure

If the simple paper and pencil computations are not enough, then a detailed optimal allocation algorithm may be needed. Figure 8.13 shows a simplified version of a data allocation algorithm. Many data allocation algorithms use an n-cube for an n-computer network in which each vertex of the cube shows an allocation A. Allocation is represented as 1 and no allocation is represented as 0 on the vertices of the cube (see Fig. 8.13). For example, the vertex 001 shows that a file (a server or a task) is allocated to computer 3 and not to computers 1 and 2. Thus as we move from vertex 000 to 111,

TABLE 8.6 Simple Analytical Model to Estimate Storage, Communication, and Local I/O

- ALLOCATE A DATASET d TO n computerS:
- CALCULATE STORAGE, READ/UPDATE COMMUNICATION, LOCAL I/O
- CALCULATE TIME, COST, ETC.

1. STORAGE OCCUPIED BY d - STORE (d) = $\sum_i$ FSIZE (d) . A(d, i)

   WHERE FSIZE(d): SIZE OF d IN BYTES
   STOR(d) = TOTAL STORAGE OCCUPIED BY d IN NETWORK
   A(d, i) = 1 IF d IS ALLOCATED TO computer i, 0 OTHERWISE
2. NO. OF UPDATES U(i, j, d) = UP(i,d) . A(d, j)   0 IF i=j
   WHERE U(i,j,d) : NO. OF UPDATES ISSUED BETWEEN i AND j FOR d
   UP(i, j) = NO. OF UPDATES ISSUED FROM i TO DATASET d
3. NO. OF RETRIEVALS R(i, j′, d) = RD(i,d) . A(d, j′)
   j′ IS THE CLOSEST computer, R(i, j′ , d) = 0 IF i=j′
   WHERE R(i, j, d) : NO. OF READS ISSUED BETWEEN i AND j FOR d
   RD(i, d) = NO. OF READS ISSUED FROM i TO DATASET d
4. NO. OF LOCAL I/O AT j = LIO(j, d) = $\sum_i$ U((i, j, d) + ,$\sum_i$ R(i, j, d)
5. CAN CALCULATE OTHER PARAMETERS:
   - TOTAL STORAGE COST = $\sum_d$ STORE(d)
   - RESPONSE TIME (WITHOUT QUEUING) at computer j

     $= \sum_i \sum_d$ R(i, j, d) . SPEED(i, j) + $\sum_i \sum_d$ U(i, j, d) .SPEED(i, j)

     $+ \sum_i \sum_d$ LIO (j, d) . IOSPEED(j)

EXAMPLE: ALLOCATE d TO 3 computerS: FSIZE = 100K
   .A = 1 0 1 , UP = 10 15 0 , RD = 10 15 20
   1. STORAGE = 100 × 1 + 100 × 0 + 100 × 1 = 200k
   2. UPDATES = U(i, j, d) =

	1	2	3
1	0	0	0
2	15	0	15
3	0	0	0

   3. READS = R(i, j, d) =

	1	2	3
1	0	0	0
2	10	0	0
3	0	0	0

more copies of files exist. In addition, as shown in Fig. 8.13, the cost (sum of storage, communication and local traffic) usually first drops and then increases rapidly with more copies of data. We can search down the cube until the cost starts to increase, and then ignore all the lower vertices. This very useful result, first indicated by <Chu 1969>, is included in the allocation algorithm listed in Fig. 8.13. More sophisticated versions of this algorithm can be found in <Jain 1987, Umar 1985>.

Application of the optimal allocation procedures depends on the nature of the problem, the availability of information needed to reach an exact solution and the need to determine optimal versus approximate solutions in real life. We have found that for several real life situations, sophisticated algorithms are needed rarely. In most cases, several data allocation decisions can be made by exercising judgment and using real life technology, application, and management constraints.

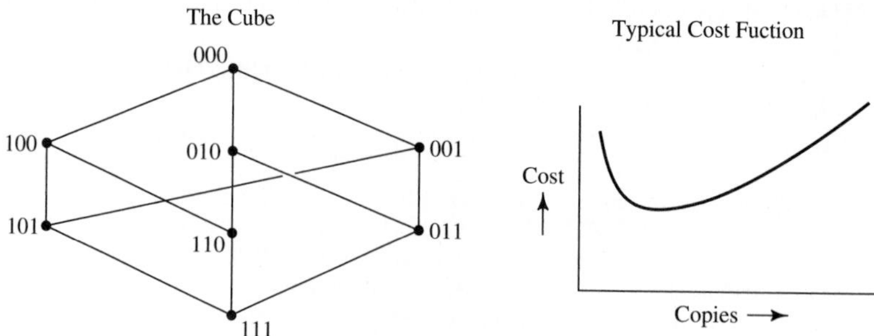

Legend:

- Vertex (100) means that the file is allocated to node 1 only.
- Vertex (101) means that the file is allocated to nodes 1 and 3 only.

A Simple Optimal Allocation Algorithm to Minimize Cost C:

1. Pick an allocation A with single object allocation (e.g., 001, 010, 100). Set C* = infinity.
2. Calculate the constraints for A.
3. If constraints violated, then reject this allocation, pick the next allocation A on the same level of the vertex and go to step 8.
4. Store A in a feasible set FS.
5. Calculate the cost function C for A.
6. Set A* = A, where A* is the optimal allocation and set C* = C where C* is the minimum cost.
7. Pick another A by adding one more copy on the cube (e.g., 101, 110, 011).
8. Calculate the constraints for A.
9. If constraints violated, then reject this allocation, pick the next allocation on the same level of the vertex, and go to step 8. If no more allocations left, then stop.
10. Store A in the feasible set FS.
11. Calculate the cost function C for A.
12. Compare C with C*. If C < C*, then set A* = A and C*= C. If not, then ignore all allocations with additional copies.
13. Pick another A if available and go to step 8. Otherwise stop.

FIGURE 8.13 A Simple Optimal Allocation Algorithm

It should be emphasized that availability of a distributed computing system does not mean that each application must be distributed. For several applications, it may still be better to provide a centralized database or use single copies of data after all of the costs for query processing, concurrency control, and failure management have been taken into account.

8.5.4 Application Interconnectivity Evaluation and Selection

After allocation of the application system components, we have to determine how the allocated applications interconnect with each other, and with existing and planned applications. From an architecture point of view, application interconnectivity can be achieved through the following services:

- Terminal emulation and file transfer
- Client-server query systems (these systems query data and processes located in the network by using the client-server paradigm)
- Distributed data and transaction management systems (DDTMS)
- Distributed operating systems

Table 8.7 shows a decision table to aid in choosing among these choices. It shows the various technology choices as columns and the conditions as rows. Distributed operating systems are not included because these systems will not be state of the practice for some time. The conditions listed are: level of transparency needed (data location may need to be transparent because the data moves around), number of systems on which the data exists (most data is on the mainframe), the cost of the link (long distance and international link costs are expensive), the duration of the session needed (one or two short queries versus all day interactions), the format of the target data (flat files, databases, etc.), data access mode (read versus update ratio) and size of the data stores (small files versus large databases). Other choices that can be included in this table are application requirements (e.g., interactive versus batch transfer), performance restrictions (sophisticated systems introduce delays) and the need to minimize application logic (use of sophisticated services minimizes program logic).

A clear choice can be made if the conditions listed in a column are satisfied. For example, terminal emulation is the best choice if transparency is not needed, number of systems to be connected is few, the link cost is low, the session duration is short, target data is in any format, target data size is large, and data access involves heavy updates. Table 8.7 leads us to the following conclusions:

- Terminal emulation can be used to access large centralized databases which are updated by many users. The disadvantage is that it requires explicit logon on to each system and requires knowledge of target system commands.

TABLE 8.7 A Decision Table for Application Interconnectivity Choices

Choices ...> Conditions	*Terminal Emulation*	*File Transfer*	*Client-Server Query System*	*DDDTMS*
• Transparency needed	none	none	data/process retrieval transparency	distribution and failure transparency
• No. of systems involved	few	few	large	large
• Link cost (e.g., long distance)	low	high	high	medium
• Session duration	short	long	long	long
• Target data format	any	flat files	any (theoretically)	relational (mostly)
• Target data size	large	small	large	large
• Data access needs	heavy update	heavy read	heavy read	medium updates

- File transfer is suitable for small read-only flat files which may require long interactions over expensive links. For example, CAD drawings and instructions are usually downloaded to shop-floor devices by using file transfer packages because this information is retrieved frequently from shop floors. As another example, customer information in Chicago which is retrieved frequently by stores in Detroit, New York and Atlanta all day could be transferred to the stores daily for local access. File transfer is not suitable for data that is updated frequently because the updates will need to be synchronized.
- Client-server query systems (CSQSs) provide transparent retrieval of data located anywhere in the network. These systems typically provide SQL access to data which may be in relational or non-relational format. These systems can access remote databases and/or remote processes through RPCs. Many clients and servers from many vendors are becoming available in this category (see Chapter 5).
- DDTMSs provide location transparency for duplicated data and distributed transactions. These systems are much more complex than CSQSs because they attempt to synchronize duplicate data and handle the failures of distributed transactions (see Chapter 6).

Let us illustrate how these options can be used in a medium sized manufacturing corporation shown in Fig. 8.14. In this company, a plant host supervises the operations of several area minicomputers which supervise the activities being performed in different areas of the corporation. Examples of the areas are manufacturing, engineering and business. A WAN connects many remote sites, say regional marketing offices, to the plant host. In a large, multi-plant corporation, the plant hosts may be connected to the corporate computer.

Terminal emulation and file transfer can be used by the remote site terminals and workstations to access the plant host. Some data files from the host may be transferred to remote sites and/or the area minicomputers for local processing and reports (e.g., spreadsheet analysis). This creates many copies of data which must

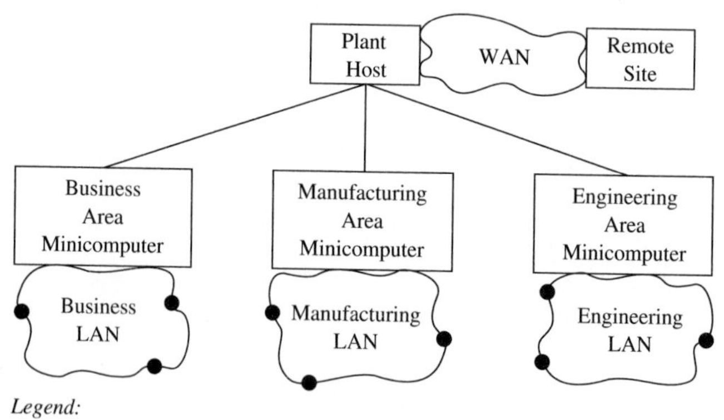

FIGURE 8.14 Example of Application Interconnectivity

restricted to read only or synchronized periodically. The data files may also be exchanged between area minicomputers. For example, the engineering minicomputer may download the manufacturing instructions to the manufacturing minicomputer for a product. These instructions may be sent to the machines for specific operations (drilling, painting, assembling, etc.). If only portions of a large file are needed at another site, then an extract program to select and send portions of files is needed. In addition, if data is changed frequently, then file transfers are too clumsy.

Client-server query systems (CSQSs) allow users to issue calls as clients to servers located anywhere in the network. The servers receive the message, and respond to the client through another message. Consider for example, the following typical situations:

- A client user interface can be installed at various regional sites which can present information from the plant host and servers from manufacturing, engineering, and business areas. These services are presented to the user as icons on the user interface.
- An spreadsheet program at a remote site asks for data from servers located somewhere in the network. The data is supplied to the spreadsheet client on an as-needed basis. This eliminates the need for file transfer.
- An engineer requests information about a product through a client program on his/her workstation. The information is retrieved from plant host and various minicomputers.
- The area and plant computers monitor the various stages of processing, providing status information to the inventory system, if needed. They also coordinate external devices such as bar code readers and label printers by using a client-server model.
- The entire system can be automated by using a client-server model. When a component arrives for processing at a robot, the robot sends an "initiation event" to the manufacturing minicomputer (a server). This server identifies the component, say by a barcode number, retrieves appropriate instructions to manufacture the component, and sends these instructions back to the robot. Later, the processing is initiated at the robot. Other events are sent by the robot to the area manager whenever major decisions have to be made and additional instructions are needed.

Obviously, CSQSs are superior to terminal emulation and file transfer. However, the performance, security, and failure handling in client-server systems need to be evaluated carefully (see Chapter 5, Section 5.3.2).

Distributed data and transaction management systems (DDTMS) should be considered when different data sources are accessed and updated from different transactions. The commonly accessed data can be partitioned and placed at multiple sites under a DDTMS so that any user can read/update data by using the DDTMS. In multiple plant organizations, the hosts may be networked to support a distributed database so that all data from all sites can be monitored. Frequently retrieved data may be duplicated. Most of the available DDTMS technology requires that data be in a relational format. For example, if some data is in a flat file or graphics file, then a DDTMS will not help. However, DDTMSs handle data synchronization automatically and the user query (e.g., an SQL call) is automatically converted to an appropriate remote call in an appropriate protocol by the DDTMS.

8.6 Detailed Design, Implementation, and Testing of Distributed Applications

8.6.1 Overview

After completion of an architecture, the design, implementation and testing activities are conducted (see Fig. 8.15).

Evaluation and selection of programming paradigms concentrates on the detailed mechanisms to be employed in application interconnectivity technologies chosen in the architecture phase. These choices are discussed in Section 8.6.2. After programming paradigms, a detailed local physical design is completed at each site (Section 8.6.3). Specialized languages and application support environments, discussed in Section 8.6.4, are being developed and proposed for implementing distributed programs. The following choices are made in this step:

Detailed Design

1. Evaluate and select the distributed programming paradigms
   - the number and type of servers
   - client-server protocols (RPCs, low level)
   - options for distributed database and transaction management
2. Conduct a detailed local physical design at each computer (database design, program design) and choose implementation techniques (e.g., programming languages)
3. Select distributed programming languages and application support environment

↓

Implementation and Testing

1. Program implementation
2. Define and populate the databases
3. Implementation of interconnections through languages and support environments
4. Testing: static and dynamic testing

FIGURE 8.15 Detailed Design, Implementation, and Testing Overview

- The language to be used for programming
- The database query language
- The user interface programming language.

These decisions are heavily influenced by the systems and application architectures discussed earlier and the standards being followed. Although many standards are still evolving, the following options seem to be adopted by most standards:

- C for programming language
- SQL for database access
- XWindow for user interface programming

The testing activities, reviewed in Section 8.6.5, concentrate on testing and debugging of distributed software. This section concludes the distributed software engineering life cycle.

8.6.2 Distributed Programming Paradigms

Distributed programs communicate with each other through messages which travel over communication channels. In message-passing programs, processes share logical channels which provide a communication path between remotely located processes. For example, a socket is a channel between TCP/IP programs, a session is a channel for LU6.2 programs and an application service point (ASP) is a channel between OSI programs. Two basic primitives are used in channels: send and receive. Additional primitives (e.g., open, bind, connect, close) may be used in different application support environments. In addition, channels can support asynchronous (nonblocking) and synchronous (blocking) communications and can be shared among many processes or operate as dedicated paths. This also depends on the application support environments of the machines on which the distributed programs reside.

Distributed programs may cooperate with each other as peers, as clients-servers or as distributed transactions with distributed data. These programs may even retrieve, update and store information by using terminal emulation and file transfer. We will not discuss terminal emulation or file transfer based distributed programs because these techniques are older, are not very flexible, and do not provide any end user transparency. Our focus is on distributed cooperative processing applications which use the CSQS or DDTMS interconnectivity options.

8.6.2.1 Development of Client-Server (C-S) Query Applications

Client-server query applications require three major decisions: (1) choice of a paradigm, (2) development of client programs, and (3) development of servers.

A C-S query application may use one of the following paradigms:

- Request/replies between clients and servers.
- Conversations between clients and servers.

- Queued messages between clients and servers.
- One way data flow from clients to servers.
- Broadcasts between a client and servers.
- Token passing between clients and servers.

We discussed these paradigms in Chapter 5, Section 5.2.3.1 (the reader should review this material before proceeding). A detailed discussion of these paradigms with numerous examples for algorithm analysis can be found in Andrews <1991>. Other thoughts are given by Gray <1986>.

The main consideration in C-S query applications is minimization of the communication message traffic. The request/reply model is the simplest and is widely used in the available RPC packages (this paradigm is commonly referred to as the RPC paradigm). This paradigm is used heavily by SQL clients which issue ad hoc queries and by clients to retrieve names from directory servers. Conversational processing is useful when state information needs to be saved during a session. For example, in a "drill-down" application, a manager first gets a high-level view of the budget and then drills down for more details to see why some items are over budget. Queued messages may be sent by clients to a server for later processing. One way data flow may be used by clients to initiate report processing at servers (some reports may take a long time to print and the clients do not need to wait for the response). Other paradigms, although attractive in several cases, are not used frequently. The best approach is to use a paradigm which is supported by available RPC and RDA (remote data access) facilities and turn to other paradigms if these facilities do not satisfy the problem requirements. Application Layer protocols of TCP/IP, OSI and SNA may be used to implement other paradigms.

Development of clients usually requires issuing API calls to a client interface package. Clients can be simple user interfaces or may include sophisticated program logic. Clients are responsible for building one or more queries, handling user interfaces, sending and receiving messages to the servers in a predefined format (in case of SQL queries, the clients must be able to parse the returned rows and columns), performing analysis on the results, and interfaces with communication networks and local operating systems. Development of clients can be considerably aided by available tools. Developers have the choice to buy an off the shelf client which works with a server (if available) or develop everything from scratch. More clients in different application areas (e.g., human resources, finance, manufacturing) are becoming available.

Development of servers is much harder than clients. Only a few servers are single-step servers in which the server scheduler itself performs the service (e.g., a time of day service). Single-step servers are relatively easy to develop. Most servers are multiple-step servers, i.e., they invoke a separate process for each in-coming request. These servers can be centralized (e.g., a single authentication server), hierarchical (e.g., distributed database servers which coordinate operations between many database servers), or replicated (e.g., replicated name and directory servers). We have discussed these topics in Chapter 5. How many servers should be allocated in a network? An algorithm, which extends the procedures discussed in Section 8.5.3, to determine optimal allocation of file servers in a local area network environment is given by Woodside <1986>.

An area of considerable industrial work addresses the non-trivial task of developing schedulers for servers. A server scheduler basically listens to the channel and invokes an appropriate process. (In some literature the scheduling of server requests is called "threading.") Typical server scheduler activities are as follows:

1. Receive the client requests.
2. Check for security.
3. Schedule a server process to handle the request.
4. Receive the response from the server process.
5. Send response back to the client.
6. Handle failures in server processes (timeouts, etc.).
7. Coordinate distributed updates.
8. Coordinate security and authentication with the server process (server scheduler as well as the server process may do their own authentication and journaling).

These functions can be built in the operating system, transaction managers or specialized application support environments. In Unix networks, for example, a daemon process usually "listens" to a socket and then forks a server process. An example of the specialized application support environment for Unix is the INETD facility. INETD is essentially a Unix Daemon which monitors the TCP/IP Sockets and invokes an appropriate server to handle a request. To be invoked by INETD, a server must be registered with INETD. In MVS, transaction managers such as IMS/DC and CICS schedule the server processes. An example of a specialized application support environment for scheduling in MVS is the Server Task Manager/370 <IBM 1991>. This facility is provided on MVS through the MVS TCP/IP network. The server can be used for SUN RPC and/or TCP/IP Sockets. An API allows server processes to be written in different languages. Functions of the Server Task Manager include: server directory, on a host, for locating a server; ability to create and terminate servers, based on the client demand; load balancing by allowing replicated servers; a "dialog" server for long term, exclusive conversational processing; and a server profile for defining server types and characteristics (e.g., dialog server, maximum servers allowed in this type).

Let us consider some practical considerations. In practice, designers/implementers of a distributed application system have the following choices:

- Purchase off-the-shelf applications which use the client-server model. For example, Ricciuti <1992> reviews many off-the-shelf client-server based application packages in human resource management.
- Purchase off-the-shelf open servers and build clients and other programs to invoke these servers. An open server has well defined interfaces and can be called from any client. An example of an open server is the Sybase Open Server.

- Custom build clients, servers and server schedulers. Server schedulers such as INETD and IBM's Server Task Manager/370 can be used to develop servers. The developers should choose portable/interoperable standards for interprocess communication while developing distributed programs.

8.6.2.2 Development of Distributed Data and Transaction Management Applications

Development of distributed transaction and data processing applications is quite complex. Here are some of the decisions that need to be made:

- What are the tradeoffs between centralized data with distributed transactions, distributed data with centralized transactions, and distributed data with distributed transactions?
- Which one of the paradigms (request/response, conversational, queued messages, etc.) should be used?
- How will the distributed transactions be developed to maintain data consistency after failures?

The tradeoffs between centralization and distribution of data and transactions have been discussed previously (Section 8.5.3). In general, centralized data with distributed transactions offers many advantages and makes failure handling easier. Distributed data which is updated by transactions in a network creates serious problems in update synchronization and failure handling. The choice of paradigms is similar to the C-S query applications. However, queued message processing offers many benefits for distributed transactions. This is because once a message is queued by the receiver, then the message is processed even if the sender fails or the communication channel fails.

Let us focus on the development of distributed transactions which require sophisticated error handling, deadlock detection and resolution, sequence checking, synchronization of resources with locking/unlocking for access control, rollback of changes due to failures and interrupts/shutdowns if needed. Assume that an available product provides only half of these services, and those also in a less than optimal manner. The designer then has the choice to build the entire system his or her way or purchase and extend the available products. It is natural to fully utilize available products instead of homegrown code. If the use of a distributed data and transaction management system (DDTMS) is chosen in the architecture phase, then the following features of a DDTMS need to be evaluated (we discussed these topics in Chapter 6):

- Database integrity and security
- Transparency of data and transaction execution location
- Serializability and concurrency of transactions
- Failure handling (atomicity)

Let us assume that a suitable DDTMS can be found (this is becoming easier with time). What type of decisions do the developers need to make after product selection? Here are two:

- Synchronization interval selection
- Global schema design

A synchronization interval defines the time interval in which copies of duplicate data must be synchronized. A transaction level synchronization states that the data must be synchronized within the execution of a transaction, i.e., a transaction is not complete unless all data copies are synchronized. Almost all of the update synchronization algorithms in distributed databases assume transaction level synchronization. In many real life situations, an hourly or daily synchronization is adequate. For example, airline reservation systems synchronize duplicated data periodically, banks synchronize accounts information periodically and price information is synchronized every night in many businesses. In practice, the choice of synchronization interval is a business decision which takes into account the potential loss of business due to out of synch data versus the cost of running expensive synchronization algorithms. Most of the existing DDTMSs allow different synchronization intervals.

The issue of global schema is important in heterogeneous DDTMSs. In a homogeneous DDTMS, individual external schema can be easily integrated. However, in a heterogeneous DDTMS, as discussed in Chapter 6, many choices exist. First, a single global schema may be created which is used by all users and application programs. Second, a partial global conceptual schema (GCS) may be created in which only portions of the local conceptual schemas are used to build the GCS. The GCS may contain, for example, the most frequently accessed corporate data. The users can issue queries either through their own external schema or through the GCS. Finally, no global conceptual schema may be created. This approach is used in some multi-database systems with very diverse data models. One approach to accessing such database is a special multi-database language which allows users to define and manipulate autonomous databases.

8.6.3 Local Software and Database Design

A detailed local physical design is completed at each site. This consists of the traditional program design (e.g., module structure, coupling and cohesion), and database design (e.g., normalization, physical database design) techniques. We will not repeat these techniques because they have been discussed extensively in the literature (see, for example, the books by Pressman <1987> and Teorey <1982>). However, many traditional software design principles can be extended and utilized in distributed programs. For example, the following principles have been used by Norman Schneiderwind in designing the US Navy's Stock Point Logistics Integrated Communications Environment <Schneiderwind 1989>:

- Use objects as a means of representing entities in distributed systems. This approach simplifies the modeling of allocation and system behavior without differentiating between data and functions.
- Use generalized modules (servers) for common application processing. For example, use a terminal server to imbed the code which might have otherwise been in application modules (e.g., conversion of screens and keyboard data).
- Make the modules as independent as possible by maximizing cohesion and minimizing coupling. This indirectly reduces the message traffic in the network.
- The objects should respond the same way to the same stimuli. All exception handling conditions should be restricted to one object so that this code is not spread over many object instances.
- Confine the knowledge of state information (e.g., status and progress of a transaction) to a single module to hide design decisions and control information.
- Make object access independent of location and dependent on service type only. This makes the design more portable.
- Minimize control message (i.e., handshaking) communication by using asynchronous message recognition system whenever appropriate. The RPC synchronous send-receive pair is not efficient in many cases (e.g., broadcast).

8.6.4 Distributed Programming Languages and Support Environments

Ideally, distributed programming should be the same as conventional centralized programming. However, the following special facilities are needed to support distributed programming:

- Ability to initiate several programs at different computers. The programs may be created dynamically during the execution of the software or may be created statically at compile time and then invoked later.
- Ability to provide communication between remotely located programs. The communications may be needed to transfer data, issue commands, check status, resolve deadlocks, etc. It is desirable to provide asynchronous communication between remote programs so that the execution of a program is not suspended while waiting for responses from another program. This may be accomplished through "native" communication protocols such as TCP/IP Sockets, LU6.2 and/or manufacturing message specification (MMS), or a suitable remote procedure call (RPC) software package.
- Ability to terminate remotely located programs. The programs of a distributed application system may be terminated when the main program is terminated, through explicit terminate commands or due to other conditions that may prohibit a program from continuing. For example, a CSP language program may terminate when none of the events it is waiting for can occur. Another condition for program termination may be a deadlock resolution by forcing a "timeout" which occurs when a program p1 has to wait for an event beyond a certain specified time limit.

- Provision to access and manipulate remotely located data. The data may be stored in flat files or databases under the control of hierarchical, network, relational or object-oriented DBMS.
- Facility for the servers to handle many concurrent and asynchronous requests simultaneously from many clients. The servers may need the facility to invoke (fork) new processes to handle the complex client requests. For example, if a server has to just supply time of day, this can be done by the server. However, if the server needs to query a database, it is better to create a separate process which queries the database.
- Facility for the clients to locate a server (which server to invoke), send the request to a server, receive response from a server, and parse and interpret the response.
- Ability to handle security (authentication and journaling) and handle failure (timeouts, distributed updates, two-phase commit) at the distributed sites (clients as well as servers).
- Ability to monitor and improve the runtime performance of the distributed programs. This should allow measurement of communication traffic, program wait states, deadlocks, etc.

One or more of these facilities may be provided by

1. Specialized distributed application support environments such as RPC packages, off-the-shelf open servers, server schedulers, and distributed data and transaction management systems
2. Special programming languages with proper support libraries and distributed operating systems.

Many specialized support environments (RPCs, RDAs, open servers and server schedulers) are being developed by vendors and researchers to support distributed programming. For example, special facilities have been introduced by the Open Software Foundation and Unix International for distributed programs. In addition, many vendors are trying to simplify the task of building client-server systems. Specifically, SUN's RPCs, Digital's DECmessageQ, Sybase's Data Base RPCS, and Hewlett-Packard's Integration Sockets are intended for this purpose. In addition, many distributed and transaction management systems are providing support for distributed programs.

How can these environments be compared, evaluated and selected? Table 8.8 suggests a list of factors which include client-server support, distributed database support, distributed transaction support, and operational/ management factors. It is becoming possible to find vendor environments which support all of these areas to some extent. Examples of such environments are the Enterprise Data Access/SQL (EDA/SQL) from Information Builders, Inc., Oracle Distributed Software Toolset, Gupta Technologies' SQL Windows, Sybase Open Interconnectivity, and Open Software Foundation's DCE. (We suggest that the reader complete Table 8.8 after reviewing some of these products). Of particular interest is the Open Software Foundation's Distributed Computing Environment (DCE) which provides application inter-

TABLE 8.8 Evaluation and Selection of Application Interconnectivity Technologies

	Product 1	*Product 2*	*Product 3*
Client-Server Support			
• RPC Facilities			
• Client support (e.g., Lotus)			
• Server scheduling			
• Server support (e.g., SQL servers)			
• Application programming interface			
Distributed Database Support			
• Data models supported			
• Read transparency			
• Update transparency			
• Duplicate data support			
Distributed Transaction Support			
• Failure handling			
• Concurrency control			
Other Support			
• Bulk data transfer capabilities			
• Encryption/decryption			
• Data compression/decompression			
Operation Support			
• Platforms supported (UNIX, PC, MVS)			
• Network interconnectivity			
(TCP/IP, LU6.2, LANs)			
• Security (authentication) support			
• Journaling and logging			
• Performance information			
• Printer and other devices supported			
• Isolation of users from each other			
Mangement Considerations			
• Cost			
• Conformance to open standards			
• Ease of use			
• Licensing (bulk versus single site)			
• Vendor staying power			
• Product documentation			
• Technical support from vendor			

connectivity in heterogeneous environments. DCE offering is composed of a set of services which are organized into two categories: Fundamental Services and Data-Sharing Services. Fundamental Services include software development tools such as RPCs, naming (directory) services, security services, time services, and threads services. Data-Sharing Services provide end user support such as distributed file system, diskless support and MS-DOS file and printer support services. These services are built on the Fundamental Services and are integrated into the operating system for use. These services are portable to many computers because they are written in C. Version 1 has been deployed on some computers (for example the Hewlett-Packard 700 Series) and new features are being developed. OSF supports ISO standards, Internet Standards and is a member of X/Open. The main advantage of OSF-DCE is that it is based on available open standards. DCE is discussed in Chapter 9.

A distributed program can be written in any third generation language such as C, Pascal, ADA or Cobol. However, several specialized programming languages like DPL, MML and LYNX <Silberschatz 1980, Ericson 1982, Castelli 1986, Scott 1987> are being developed specifically for distributed programming. The choice of programming language depends on the type of platforms being used and the type of capabilities needed. For example, software on Unix Networks is often written in C. Some specialized languages are used for specific distributed application systems. For example, Ladder and Zone logic is used heavily in writing manufacturing control software for programmable controllers.

An extensive survey of the programming languages for distributed systems is presented by Bal <1989>. This paper discusses 15 distributed programming languages and contains an extensive bibliography which lists over 100 programming languages. These languages are being developed to maximize parallelism, provide coordination through communication messages, and deal with partial failures.

Distributed object-based programming systems is an area of considerable academic research for distributed application support environments. Simply stated, an object-based programming language supports objects as a language feature but does not support the concept of inheritance. (The languages that support inheritance are referred to as object-oriented.) Thus languages such as C++ and Smalltalk are object-oriented, whereas ADA and Modula-2 are object-based <Chin 1991>. A distributed object-based programming system (DOBPS) is an amalgamation of object-based programming languages with distributed operating systems. This is due to the decreasing distinction between an operating system and the programming languages it supports. A DOBPS typically provides

- A distributed operating system, which allows a collection of computers (possibly heterogeneous) to be viewed as a single entity. A distributed operating system, as discussed in a previous chapter, provides a wide range of location transparency, fault tolerance, workload migration, recovery and integrity services, and resource management (memory management, processor management, disk management) across loosely coupled heterogeneous computers.
- Object-based programming languages, which allow object creation (structure definition and relationship definition), object management (performance, security,

reliability, synchronization), and object interaction management (object location, message passing, failure handling).

It can be seen that a combination of these two facilities can provide an extensive and efficient support environment for distributed programming. Most of the work in DOBPS is state of the art and not state of the market/practice yet. Chin and Chanson <Chin 1991> give an extensive survey of the work in this interesting area with numerous examples about how DOBPS are being developed in distributed operating systems such as Amoeba, Argus, CHORUS, Clouds, Eden, Emerald, and TABS/Camelot.

8.6.5 Implementation and Testing

Implementation activities are heavily dependent on the application support environments selected during detailed design. For example, in an environment such as EDA/SQL, code may need to be written only for a few special purpose clients. These clients would issue API/SQL calls to access remotely located data sources. In other cases, clients, servers, server schedulers as well as client interfaces need to be developed. Other than the implementation of code needed for remote message exchange, distributed programs can be implemented by using the well known structured and object-oriented programming techniques.

After implementation, the distributed application system is tested by using dynamic and/or static testing methods. In a dynamic testing environment, the system is tested by executing (running) the various programs. Static testing, on the other hand, relies on analysis and debugging of a system without having to run it.

Dynamic testing and debugging is more reliable but is very expensive in distributed systems. For example, it is difficult to create many error conditions in large distributed software systems due to a large number of potential global conditions. Another problem in dynamic testing is reproducing the error conditions. A great deal of work is needed in developing automated testers for distributed software.

Static testing mainly examines the control flow of programs and is not as accurate as dynamic testing. The main advantage of static testing is that expensive distributed testbeds are not needed. Moreover, this testing can be done while the system is not completely developed yet because static testing does not require a platform. However, it is not possible to determine all system faults through static testing.

It seems that some combination of static and dynamic testing is desirable for distributed software engineering. This issue has been discussed by Shatz <1988, Section 5>. Early thoughts on integration testing for distributed systems can be found in Chow <1980>.

After testing and installation, development may be continued in the maintenance activity. In particular, local as well as global programs and databases may be modified and new client-server protocols may be introduced. The main issue is configuration management for local as well as global changes to the application system. Considerable work is needed in this area. An example of a configuration manager for distributed applications is the Apollo Domain DSEE (Distributed Software Engineering Environment), now marketed by Hewlett-Packard.

8.7 Application Engineering at Distributed Sites: CASE Tools

The application engineering process itself can be distributed due to the following reasons:

- Different phases of one application may be conducted at different sites. For example, planning may be done at the corporate office, requirements may be developed at the user sites and software may be developed by an independent software house.
- Components of an application may be developed at different sites and then synthesized at another site. For example, different subsystems of a large application may be developed at different sites.
- Concurrent coauthoring, development and testing of applications at different sites. For example, requirements may be developed concurrently at different sites.
- A mixture of the foregoing.

Consider a problem in which an application with components A, B and C is assigned to different development companies U, V, W, X, Y, and Z. The system is supposed to be delivered to a government agency, H. Let us assume that company U is responsible for the overall project management and company Z integrates and performs the final acceptance tests of the application. We can also assume that many of these companies are competitors, so serious security and configuration management issues are introduced.

It is difficult to address problems of this nature without computer-aided software engineering (CASE) for distributed applications. The basic principles of CASE are as follows:

- Use the computer as a tool for automating the systems development process.
- Capture the system information in a database (repository) early in the system life cycle and then refine, expand and modify it as the system proceeds through different phases of system life cycle.
- Integrate the CASE tools so that the transitions between system life cycles are smooth.
- Use the database to support all life cycle activities and provide information for automated code generation, analysis, testing, and project management.

Most of the existing CASE tools and environments are centralized and produce standalone application systems. See Cronzier <1989> and Norman <1992> for analysis and trends of these tools; and refer to Communications of the ACM, April 1992, and IEEE Software May, 1992, for many state of the art articles on CASE. A CASE environment for distributed applications should have the following characteristics:

- It should help in the development of centralized as well as distributed applications. This implies that tools unique for distributed software engineering (resource allocation algorithms, distributed programming languages, RPC support, distributed application support environments, distributed database design aids, debugging and testing aids for distributed programs, etc.) must be included in the CASE toolset.
- It should be able to run on a collection of loosely coupled computer systems. This implies that the CASE database may be distributed to many sites. In addition, the CASE tools may operate at mainframes, minicomputers and workstations; thus allowing development of software at, say, a workstation and deployment at the mainframe.
- Collaborative computing, groupware systems, security, project management and configuration management tools should be included to allow different groups from different companies to work together on an application.

CASE environments which satisfy these requirements need considerable research. It is essential to view the process of software development at different sites itself as a distributed application system in which the database consists of the requirements, architectures and source code, and the programs are the software development tools such as the compilers, debuggers, design aids, requirements analyzers, etc. Figure 8.16 shows this conceptual framework. It includes a specification language for the description of requirements at various levels of detail; completeness and consistency analysis of the specifications; analytical and simulation tools for predictive analysis; allocation algorithms for application program and data assignments to computers of the network; distributed software support tools (RPC facilities, programming languages); project and configuration management support; and reasoning and inference capabilities. Other tools (knowledge-based planning aids, system decomposition aids, testers, compilers and application support environments, and execution monitoring tools) can also be included. The tools are integrated around a logical database where the specifications and documentations are stored and from where the analysis, modeling, management, inference and implementation tools extract the needed information. The database as well as the various tools may be distributed across a network. The physical location of the tools and database is transparent to the developers by using a DDBMS to manage the CASE database and by employing servers (e.g., a design server) which are accessed by clients at various development sites.

Research in the development of such environments is sparse. Many individual tools have been developed since the mid 1980s, but these tools have not been integrated into software engineering environments (see, for example, Alford <1985>, Bhatia <1986>, Bruno <1986>, Estrin <1986>, Greif <1992>, Soneka <1986>, Vefsno <1985>, Yau <1983>). A Software Engineering Environment for Distributed Systems (SEEDS) was developed at the University of Michigan as a research vehicle to investigate the feasibility of CASE environments for distributed systems <Umar

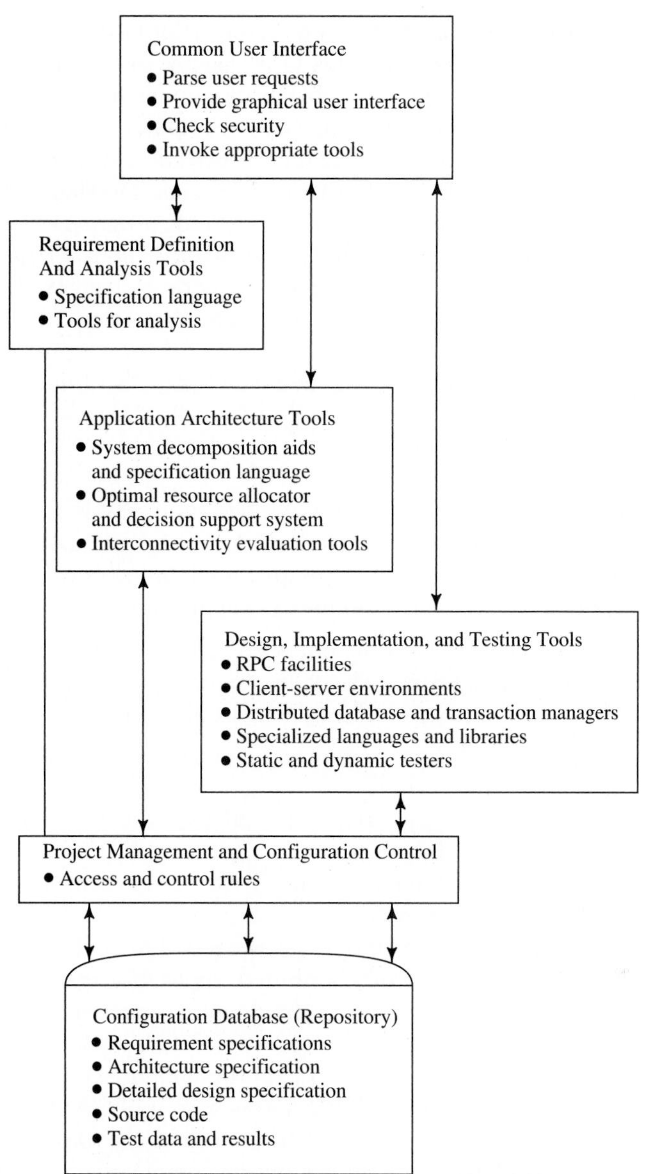

FIGURE 8.16 A Software EngineeringEnvironment for Distributed Software

1987>. The Generalized Specification Language (GSL) of SEEDS supports three different views (a user's view, an application designer's view, and a network designer's view) which are based on synthesis and extension of models of distributed systems <Chen 1983, Gallimore 1982, Hooper 1985, Hooper 1985b, Agrawal 1985, Avrun 1986, Wang 1986, White 1987>. The specifications defined in GSL are stored in a database and can be checked for completeness and consistency by using rules of systems analysis and design <Masiero 1986> and converting GSL specifications to Prolog code <Zhang 1987>. An allocator reads GSL specifications and produces near optimal allocations of program and data objects by minimizing the total cost of running an application system (communication cost + computer processing cost + storage cost) subject to the transaction response time, transaction availability and software development constraints <Umar 1984, Umar 1985>. A knowledge-based simulation tool generates a GPSS simulation program and Prolog programs which analyze the results of the simulation and recommend appropriate actions <Umar and Chase 1987>. Details about SEEDS can be found elsewhere <Umar 1987>. Environments like SEEDS can be developed as an extension of existing CASE environments like AD/Cycle <Mercurio 1990>.

Meta, a toolset for managing the execution of distributed applications after they are operational, has been developed at Cornell University <Marzullo 1991>. The Meta system includes facilities for

- Initializing the application in an orderly fashion. This is accomplished by declaring the application's structure to Meta through a Lomita data model, mapping application components to process groups, and defining sensors (e.g., CPU utilization, application throughput) to monitor the application behavior.
- Expressing policy rules for the intended behavior of the application under normal and abnormal conditions. The rules, expressed as typical "when condition do action" format specify the various courses of action for different conditions.
- Monitoring the performance and realtime behavior of the application.

Meta operates in Unix environments and uses the Isis distributed programming toolkit <Birman 1990>. Isis, also developed at Cornell, provides primitives for reliable programming and algorithms/tools for distributed synchronization, logging and recovery, and resilient recovery.

More research and development is needed to cover the development as well as execution management of distributed applications. Advances in collaborative computing and video conferencing should allow application developers at different sites to work with each other for software development. It will be interesting to see the role of distributed object-based programming systems in CASE toolsets for distributed applications. In addition, the inclusion of CASE toolsets for distributed applications in open system architectures such as the OSF Distributed Computing Environment will have some impact on the commercial availability of this technology. We will discuss OSF-DCE and other open systems architectures in the next chapter.

8.8 Management Summary and Trends

In a distributed application system (DAS), the programs, the datasets and/or the user interfaces may reside at more than one computer of a distributed computer system. The client-server paradigm is becoming increasingly popular in realizing distributed application systems in which the workstations serve as clients which access needed information from the "back-end" processors located anywhere in the network. In addition, most of the downsized and rightsized applications are DASs.

Development of distributed application systems, called distributed application engineering, involves numerous choices and options which are dependent on the type of networks and type of applications being used. We have presented a methodology for development of distributed application systems and for application downsizing/rightsizing. A great deal of attention in the literature has been paid to the development of networking technologies and not to the development of DAS. For example, many papers on distributed systems focus on the networking and resource management problems. However, as more and more networking technologies become commercially available, the focus is shifting to application systems development for a given DCS.

We have presented an approach which shows the following:

- How can the requirements of a distributed application be specified?
- How to develop the distributed application architecture which shows what components of the application are allocated where and how do they communicate with each other?
- How to decide which applications are right for distribution/ rightsizing/downsizing?
- What tools and techniques are needed to implement and test distributed software?

A CASE environment can be developed which extends the conventional tools to include the tools needed for developing distributed systems. More work is needed in this area.

It is expected that software engineering in distributed systems will eventually become transparent to the developer. In the meantime, the following trends are worth noting:

- Object-oriented technologies will be utilized more and more in distributed software engineering.
- RPCs will make software development in distributed environments similar to conventional software development.
- Automated tools for distributed software will be developed and integrated into existing CASE toolsets.
- The life cycle activities will be extended to include distributed systems activities.

Problems and Excercises

1. Describe a distributed application system of your choice in detail. What are the advantages and disadvantages of this application?

2. Point out the major differences between conventional and distributed software engineering.
3. Your company has asked you to propose a requirement definition standard for specifying distributed applications. Provide an outline of the standard.
4. Consider the application system shown in Fig. 8.7. Develop the architecture of this system by using the steps of the distributed application methodology described in Section 8.5. For each step, list the major decisions, the techniques/tools employed and the final choices made by you.
5. Expand and improve Table 8.5 to make it general for any downsizing decision evaluation.
6. For the application architecture determined in question 5, work through the detailed design, implementation and testing steps. For each step, list the major decisions, the techniques/tools employed and the final choices made by you. In particular describe the programming paradigms and distributed programming languages which interest you the most.
7. Complete Table 8.8 to evaluate some of the application interconnectivity products.
8. Discuss how the methodologies, tools and techniques outlined in this chapter would change for real time embedded control systems and for newer applications such as multimedia applications.
9. Consider the problem of application development by companies U, V, W, X, Y, and Z (described in Section 8.7). List the management steps you will take to complete this project (assume that the CASE tools which you can utilize are the current state of the market).

CASE STUDY: Distributed Applications For XYZCORP

A strategic application system plan has been completed for XYZCORP. The plan has produced a list of applications which support the business processes (payroll, accounts receivable / accounts payable, order processing, marketing information systems, and computerized checkout system), engineering processes (CAD, CAE, computer-aided process planning) and manufacturing processes (material requirement planning, production scheduling and flexible manufacturing systems). Fig. 8.1 has shown these applications. These applications will reside on the XYZCORP distributed computing platform (DCP) shown in Fig. 8.17. Two projects have been initiated to develop a rightsize/downsize strategy and to develop an overall application architecture for XYZCORP.

PROJECT A. Application Rightsizing/Downsizing Strategy

It is your responsibility to develop an application rightsizing/downsizing strategy for the applications shown in Fig. 8.1. Your deliverables are:

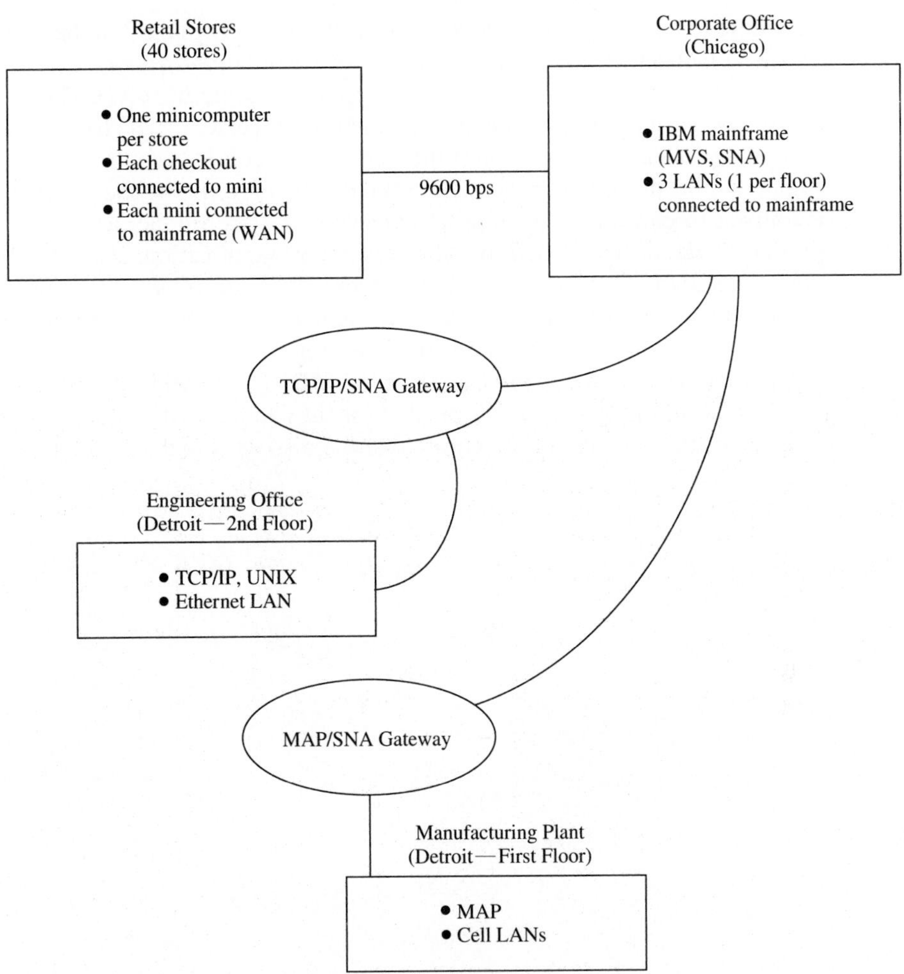

FIGURE 8.17 Distributed Computing Platform for XYZCORP

- A checklist of factors to be considered for application rightsizing/downsizing.
- A decision table which can help in making the rightsizing/downsizing decisions.
- Recommendation of the applications which should be downsized, why and how?

PROJECT B: Distributed Application Architecture for an Integrated Manufacturing Control System

XYZCORP is interested in integrating and automating the order processing, CAD/CAM and the "manufacturing" processes of the company products (radios, TVs, VCRs, calculators, IBM PC clones). This system, referred to as the IMCS (Integrated Manufacturing Control System), will receive a customer order and assemble and pack a product for shipping within half an hour of order reception. You have been asked to design IMCS by using the methodology discussed in this chapter.

Figure 8.18 shows a simplified conceptual diagram of IMCS. The first stage in this system is an order processing system which processes orders for a product. If the specified product is in stock and the customer credit is acceptable, the product is shipped to the customer from the finished product inventory. The product inventory is adjusted to show products shipped. For an out of stock product, a CAD/CAE system produces the design based on the customer specification. The design is then downloaded to a Computer Aided Process Planning (CAPP) system where the manufacturing program is automatically created which shows how the product will be assembled. The CAPP system uses the information about available assembly equipment to generate the process plans. An MRP (Material Requirement Planning) system determines the materials needed for the product. MRP systems use sophisticated algorithms to take into account quantity discounts, vendor preferences, various

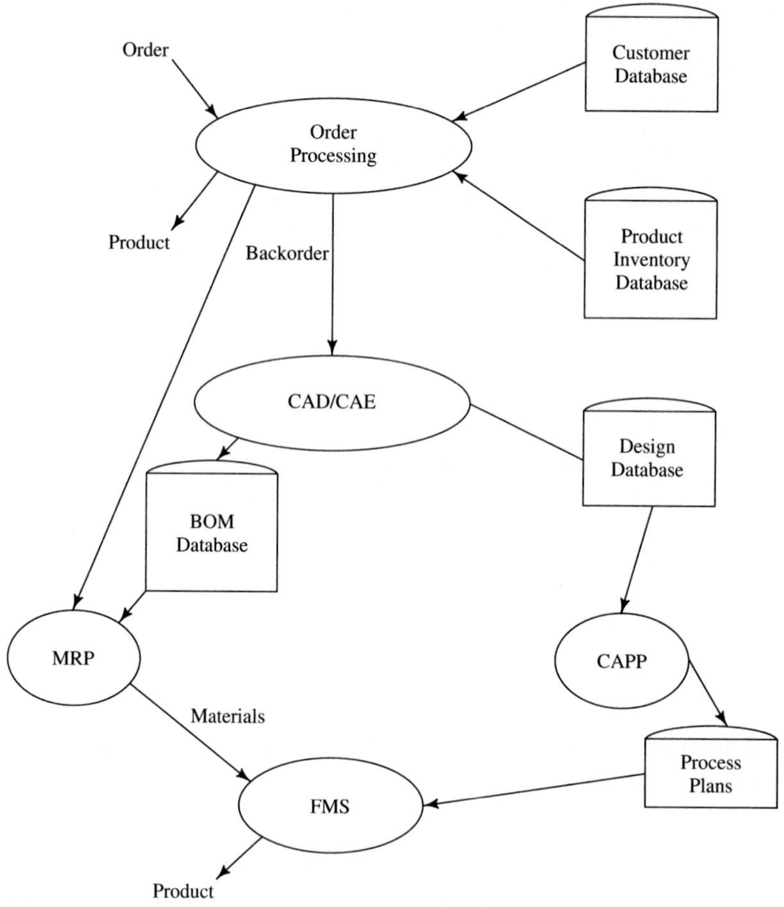

FIGURE 8.18 Integrated Manufacturing Control System (IMCS)

capacity constraints and factory status. The manufacturing program is downloaded to a flexible manufacturing system (FMS) which consists of an area controller, two cells and several manufacturing devices. FMS also receives a production schedule (how many products to manufacture) and needed raw materials. Because FMS is a realtime system, it must conform to the constraints of realtime control on factory floors.

The deliverables are as follows:

- Allocation of the IMCS components to various sites of the XYZCORP distributed computing platform (DCP) shown in Fig. 8.17.
- Indication of which processes will need to span more than one computer and why.
- Specification of the interconnection methods being used in this architecture. Specifically, show which one of these methods will be used to exchange the information between the manufacturing, business, and engineering processes of the IMCS:
  - Client-server query systems
  - Terminal emulation/file transfer
  - Distributed file servers such as NFS
  - Distributed data and transaction managers
- Which programming paradigms and programming languages you will use in this system.
- Which standards will be used to make the implementation choices in programming languages, user interfaces, database access, etc.

In addition, you have been asked to develop a methodology for embedded real time systems and multimedia applications for XYZCORP.

Hints About The Case Study

Project A: The discussion in Section 8.2.4 introduces many factors which can be used to develop a checklist. Examples are strategic factors, flexibility and configurability, equipment costs, development costs, etc. The decision table shown in Table 8.5 can be used to make the rightsizing/downsizing decisions. This Table may need to be extended and modified. In order to identify the applications which should be downsized, you may want to complete Table 8.5 for each application. For example, while completing this Table for order processing, you will need to understand the database size, data sharing needs and other factors shown in Table 8.5. This exercise, although tedious, can lead to many insights and is highly recommended.

Project B: The steps of the methodology introduced in Section 8.3 and explained in Sections 8.4, 8.5 and 8.6 can be used to design IMCS. For example, the information about IMCS discussed above is a good starting point to specify the requirements stated in Section 8.4. Most of the effort is spent on application architecture discussed in Section 8.5. In the partitioning step (Section 8.5.2), the data and programs of order processing, CAPP, CAD/CAE and FMS are clustered. For example, the CAD/CAE and CAPP applications can be clustered together because these two applications are closely interacting. The allocation step (Section 8.5.3) could show, for example, that the order processing system should be allocated to stores, the CAD/CAE and CAPP systems should be assigned to the engineering plant and FMS should be assigned to the manufacturing site. Application interconnectivity (Section 8.5.4) could show that client-server support with some file transfer would be needed to provide the level of interaction needed between the IMCS applications (the decision table shown in Table 8.7 should help). For example, order processing could interact with CAD/CAE in real time. The discussion in Section 8.6 should help to identify the programming aspects of IMCS. Table 8.8 could be used to evaluate and choose a proper support environment for IMCS. We can safely assume that IMCS is not available off-the-shelf. The programming choices should be SQL, C, RPCs and OSI RDAs (if available).

References

Note: Many of the references are older because they refer to the work in distributed applications in the last two decades.

Agrawal, V.K., Patnaik, L.M., and Goel, P., "Towards Formal Specification of a Distributed Computing System," *International Journal of Computer and Information Sciences*, Vol. 14, No. 5, 1985, pp. 277-307.

Alford, M.W. "SREM at the Age of Eight: The Distributed Computing Design System," *Computer*, Apr. 1985, pp. 36-46.

Andrews, G.R., "Paradigms for Process Interaction in Distributed Programs," *ACM Computing Surveys*, Mar. 1991, pp. 49-90.

Andrews, G.R., *Concurrent Programming: Principles and Practice*, Benjamin/Cummings Publishing Co., 1992.

Avrunin, G.S., Dillon, L.K., Wilden, J.C., and Riddle, W.E., "Constrained Expressions: Adding Analysis Capabilities to Design Methods for Concurrent Software Systems," *IEEE Trans. on Software Engineering*, Feb. 1986, pp. 278-292.

Bal, H., Steiner, J. and Tannenbaum, A., "Programming Languages for Distributed Computing Systems," *ACM Computing Surveys*, Sept. 1989, pp. 261-322.

Bhatia, S. and Ally, A., "Performance Advisor: An Analysis Tool for Computer Communication Systems," IEEE International Communications Conference '86, Toronto, June 1986, pp. 206-211.

Birman, K.P., et al., *Isis—A Distributed Programming Environment: User's Guide and Reference Manual, Version 2.1*, Dept. of Computer Science, Cornell University, N.Y., Sept. 1990.

Brahmadathan, K. and Ramarao, K., "On the Design of Replicated Databases," *Information Sciences*, Vol. 65, Nos. 1 and 2, 1992, pp. 173-200.

Bruno, G. and Balsamo, A., "Petri Net-Based Object-Oriented Modelling of Distributed Systems," *OOPSLA '86 Proc.*, Sept. 1986, pp. 284-293.

Buckles, B.P. and Harding, D.M., "Partitioning and Allocation of Logical Resources in a Distributed Computing Environment," General Research Corporation Report, Huntsville, Alabama, 1979.

Castelli, G. and Simone, "An Experimental Distributed Programming Language: Design and Implementation," IEEE Phoenix Conf. on Computers and Communications, March 1986, pp. 406-411.

Casey, R.G., "Allocation of Copies of a File in an Information Network," *SJCC 1972*, AFIPS Press, Vol. 40, 1972.

Chandy, D.M. and Hewes, J.E. "File Allocation in Distributed Systems," *Proc. of the Intl. Symp. on Computer Performance Modelling, Measurement and Evaluation*, Mar. 1976, pp. 10-13.

Chang, S.K. and Liu, A.C., "A Database File Allocation Problem," *COMPSAC*, 1981, pp. 18-22.

Chen, B. and Yeh, R., "Formal Specification and Verification of Distributed Systems," *IEEE Trans. on Software Engineering*, Nov. 1983, pp. 710-722.

Chin, R. and Chanson, S., "Distributed Object-Based Programming Systems," *ACM Computing Surveys*, Mar. 1991, pp. 91-124.

Chow, T.S. "Integration Testing of Distributed Software," *Proc. IEEE Conf. on Distributed Computing*, Sept. 1980, pp. 706-711.

Chu, W.W., "Optimal File Allocation in a Multiple Computer System," *IEEE Tran. on Computers*, Oct. 1969, pp. 885-889.

Coffman, E.G., Gelenbe, E., et al., "Optimization of the Number of Copies in Distributed Databases," *Proc. of the 7th IFIP Symposium on Computer Performance Modelling, Measurement and Evaluation*, May 1980, pp. 257-263.

Corbin, J. R., *The Art of Distributed Applications: Programming Techniques for Remote Procedure Calls*, Springer-Verlag, 1991.

Coulouris, G. and Dollimore, J., *Distributed Systems: Concepts and Design*, Addison-Wesley, 1989.

Crozier, M., et al., "Critical Analysis of Tools for Computer-Aided Software Engineering," *Information and Software Technology*, Vol. 31, No. 9, Nov. 1989, pp. 486-496.

Decker, W.F. and Miller, S. P., "A Practical Tool for Verification of Communications Software: A Formal Methodology for Generating Test Metrics," IEEE Phoenix Conf. on Computers and Communications, Mar. 1986, pp. 470-477.

Doty, K.W., McEntyre, P.L. and O'Reilly, J.G., "Task Allocation in a Distributed Computer System," *Proc. of IEEE INFOCOM*, 1982, pp. 33-38.

Edelstein, H., "Lions, Tigers, and Downsizing," *Database Programming and Design*, Mar. 1992, pp. 39-45.

Ericson, L.W. "DPL-82: A Language for Distributed Processing," *Proc. IEEE 3rd Intl. Conf. on Distributed Computing*, Oct. 1982, pp. 526-531.

Estrin, G., Fenchel, R.S., Razouk, R.R., and Vernon, M.K., "SARA (Systems Architecture Apprentice): Modeling, Analysis, and Simulation Support for Design of Concurrent Systems," IEEE Trans. on Software Engineering, Feb. 1986, pp. 293-311.

Eswaran, K.P., "Allocation of Records to Files and Files to Computer Networks," *IFIP*, 1974, pp. 304-307.

Everret, B., *Cluster Analysis*, Heinemann Educ. Books Ltd., London, 1974.

Feldman, J.A., "High Level Programming for Distributed Computing," *CACM* 22, 6, June 1979, pp. 353-368.

Finckenscher, G. *Automatic Distribution of Programs in MASCOT and ADA Environments*, Royal Signal and Radar Establishment, London, 1984.

Fisher, M.L. and Hochbaum, D., "Database Location in Computer Networks," *ACM Journal*, Vol. 27, No. 4, Oct. 1980.

Fedchak, E. , "An Introduction to Software Engineering Environments," *Compsac*, 1986, pp. 456-463.

Frost, V.S., and K.S. Shanumgan, "Hybrid Approaches to Network Simulation," IEEE International Communications Conference '86, Toronto, June 1986, pp. 228-234.

Gallimore, R.M. and Coleman, D. *Specifying Distributed Programs*, Lecture Notes in Computer Science, No. 134, Program Specification, Edited by J. Stauntstrup, Springer-Verlag, 1982.

Gray, J., "An Approach to Decentralized Computer Systems," *IEEE Trans. on Software Engineering*, June 1986, pp. 684-692.

Greenspan, S.J., Mylopoulos, J., and Borgida, A., "Principles of Requirements and Design Languages: The Taxis Project," International Symposium on Current Issues of Requirements Engineering Environments, edited by Y. Ohno, OHMSHA Ltd., 1982, pp. 107-113.

Greif, I., et al., "A Case Study of CES: A Distributed Collaborative Editing System Implemented in Argus," *IEEE Trans. on Software Engineering*, Sept. 1992, pp. 827-839.

Hooper, J. W., "BPL: A Set-Based Language for Distributed System Prototyping," *International Journal of Computer and Information Sciences*, Vol. 14, No. 2, 1985, pp. 83-105.

Hooper, J.W., Ellis, J.T., and Johnson, T.A., "Distributed Software Prototyping with ADS," IEEE/ACM 8th International Conference on Software Engineering, London, England, Aug. 1985, pp. 216-223.

"IBM Server Task Manager/370, Server Writer's Guide," Manual No. SC23-0595-00, IBM Corporation, 1991. *IEEE Guidelines for the Documentation of Software in Industrial Computer Systems*, Institution of Electrical Engineers, London, 1985.

IEEE Guide to Software Requirements Specifications, ANSI/IEEE 830-1984, IEEE, Inc., 1984.

IEEE Trans. on Software Engineering, special issue on Distributed Systems, Jan. 1987.

Kleinrock, L., "Distributed Systems," Communications of the *ACM*, Nov. 1985, Vol. 18, No. 11, pp. 1200-1213.

Irani, K.B. and Khabbaz, N.G., "A Combined Communication Network Design and File Allocation for Distributed Databases," 2nd Intl. Conf. on Distributed Systems, Paris, Apr. 1981.

Jain, H., "A Comprehensive Model for the Design of Distributed Computer Systems," *IEEE Transactions on Software Engineering*, Oct. 1987, pp. 1092-1104.

Katz, R., Scachi, W., and Subrahmanyam, P., "Environments for VLSI and Software Engineering," *The Journal of Systems and Software*, 4, 1984, pp. 13-26.

Koh, K. and Eom, Y.I "A File Allocation Scheme for Minimizing the Storage Cost in Distributed Computing Systems," First Pacific Computer Communication Symposium, Seoul, Korea, Oct. 1985, pp. 310-317.

Larson, R.E., et al., "Distributed Control: Tutorial," IEEE Catalog No. EHO 199-O, Oct. 1982.

Levin, K.D. and Morgan, K. H., "Optimizing Distributed Databases—A Framework for Research," *Proc. NCC*, 1975, Vol. 44, pp. 473-478.

Lewis, T. G. and Oman, P. W., "The Challenge of Software Development," *IEEE Software*, Nov. 1990, pp. 9-14.

Mahmood, S. and Riordan, J.S., "Optimal Allocation of Resources in Distributed Information Networks," *ACM Transaction on Database Systems*," Vol. 1, No. 1, Mar. 1976, pp. 66-78.

Mariani, M.P. and Palmer, D.F. (eds.), "Tutorial: Distributed System Design," EHO 151-1, IEEE Computer Society, 1979.

Mariani, M.P. and Palmer, D.F., "Software Development for Distributed Computing Systems," *Handbook of Software Engineering*, edited by C.V. Ramamoorthy and C.R. Vick, Van Nostrand, 1984, pp. 656-674.

Martin, R. "The Standards Test for Portability," *Datamation,* May 15, 1989.

Marzullo, K., et al., "Tools for Distributed Application Development," *IEEE Computer*, Aug. 1991, pp. 42-51.

Masiero, P.C., "An Implementation of Structured System Development Methodology Using the System Encyclopedia Manager," PRISE TR0026, The University of Michigan, Ann Arbor, Mich., 1986.

Meyer, Bertrand, *Object-Oriented Software Construction*, Prentice Hall, 1988.

Meyer, B., "On Formalism in Specifications," *IEEE Software*, Jan. 1989.

Moad, J., "Contracting with Integrators," *Datamation*, May 15, 1989.

Moad, J., "The New Agenda for Open Systems," *Datamation*, April 1, 1990.

Mercurio, V., et al., "AD/Cycle Strategy and Architecture," *IBM Systems Journal,* Vol. 20, No. 2, 1990, pp. 170-188.

Negoita, C., *Expert Systems and Fuzzy Sets*, Benjamin-Cummings, 1985.

Nitzberg, B. and Lo, V., "Distributed Shared Memory: A Survey of Issues and Approaches," *IEEE Computer*, Aug. 1991, pp. 52-60.

Norman, R. and Forte, G., "Automating the Software Development Process: CASE in the '90s," *Comm. of ACM*, Vol. 35, No. 4, Apr. 1992.

Nutt, G., *Open Systems,* Prentice Hall, 1992.

Ozsu, M. and Valduriez, P., "Distributed Database Systems: Where Are We Now?" *IEEE Computer,* Aug. 1991, pp. 68-78.

Page-Jones, M., *The Practical Guide to Structured Systems Design*, Yourdon Press, 1980.

Pankaj, J., *An Integrated Approach to Software Engineering*, Springer-Verlag, 1991.

Papelis, Y.E., and Casavant, T.L., "Specification and Analysis of Parallel/Distributed Software and Systems by Petri Nets with Transition Enabling," *IEEE Trans. on Software Engineering*, Mar. 1992, pp. 252-261.

Patrick, R.L., *Application Design Handbook for Distributed Systems*, CBI Publishing Co., 1980.

Parnas, D.L., "On the Criteria Used for Decomposing Systems into Modules," *Comm. of the ACM*, Dec. 1972, pp. 1053-1059.

Paulson, D. and Wand, Y., "An Automated Approach to Information System Decomposition," *IEEE Trans. on Software Engineering*, Mar. 1992, pp. 174-189.

Pressman, R., *Software Engineering—A Practitioner's Approach*, 2nd ed., McGraw Hill, 1987.

Radding, A., "Dirty Downsizing," *Computerworld*, Aug. 10, 1992, pp. 65-68.

Ramamoorthy, C.V. and Vick, C.R., *Handbook of Software Engineering*, Van Nostrand, 1984.

Ramamoorthy, C.V., Garg, V. and Prakash, A., "Programming in the Large," *IEEE Trans. on Software Engineering*, Vol. SE-12, No. 7, July 1986, pp. 769-783.

Ricciuti, M., "Universal Data Access!" *Datamation*, Nov. 1, 1991.

Ricciuti, M., "Here Come The HR Client/Server Systems," *Datamation*, July 1, 1992.

Rubenstein, H. and Waters, R., "The Requirements Apprentice: Automated Assistance for Requirement Acquisition," *IEEE Trans. on Software Engineering*, Mar. 1991, pp. 226-240.

Scott, M. L., "Language Support for Loosely Coupled Distributed Programs," *IEEE Trans. on Software Engineering*, Vol. SE-13, No. 1, Jan. 1987, pp. 88-103.

Silberschaatz, A. "A Survey Note on Programming Languages for Distributed Computing," *Proc. IEEE Conf. on Distributed Computing*, Sept. 1980, pp. 719-722.

Shatz, S.M. and Wang, J., "Introduction to Distributed Software Engineering," *IEEE Software*, Oct. 1987.

Shatz, S.M. and Wang, J., "Tutorial: Distributed Software Engineering," IEEE Computer Society, No. 856, 1988.

Schneiderwind, N., "Distributed System Software Design Paradigm with Application to Computer Networks," *IEEE Trans. on Software Engineering*, April 1989, pp. 402-412.

Teorey, T.J. and Umar, A., "Distributed Database Design Strategies," *Database Design and Programming*, Apr. 1989.

Teorey, T.J and Fry, J.P., *Design of Database Structures,* Prentice Hall, 1982.

Umar, A., "The Allocation of Data and Programs in Distributed Data Processing Environments," Ph.D. Dissertation, Univ. of Michigan, Ann Arbor, Mich., 1984.

Umar, A. and Teorey, T.J., "A Generalized Approach to Program and Data Allocation in Distributed Systems," First Pacific Computer Communication Symposium, Seoul, Korea, Oct. 1985, pp. 462-472.

Umar, A. and Teichroew, D., "Computer Aided Software Engineering for Distributed Systems," Proc. of IEEE Region 10 Conference on Computer Communications, Seoul, Korea, Aug. 1987.

Umar, A., Chase, T., and Teichroew, D., "A Knowledge-Based Simulator for Distributed Systems," CASE Conference, Ann Arbor Mich., May 17-19, 1987, Ann Arbor, Mich.

Ural, H., "Logic Specifications for Communication Systems," IEEE Phoenix Conf. on Computers and Communications, Mar. 1986, pp. 121-128.

Urban, J. and Bobbie, P., "A Software Engineering Methodology for Distributed Software Development," First Pacific Computer Communication Symposium, Seoul, Korea, Oct. 1985, pp. 100-110.

Vefsno, E. A., "DASOM—A Software Engineering Tool for Communications Applications Increasing Productivity and Software Quality," IEEE/ACM 8th International Conference on Software Engineering, London, Aug. 1985, pp. 26-33.

Wang, Yu, "A Distributed Specification Model and Its Prototyping," *IEEE COMPSAC* '86, pp. 130-137, 1986.

White, S., "A Pragmatic Formal Method for Specifications and Analysis of Embedded Computer Systems," Ph.D. Dissertation, Polytechnic Institute of New York, May 1987.

Witty, R.W., "Software Engineering," 6th Annual Lecture of the C&CD of IEEE, Dec. 1984.

Wohl, Amy, "Is Downsizing Right for You?" *Beyond Computing*, IBM Publication, Aug./Sept. 1992, pp. 10-11.

Woodside, C.M and Tripathi, S.K., "Optimal Allocation of File Servers in a Local Area Network Environment," *IEEE Trans. on Software Engineering*, Aug. 1986, Vol. SE-12, No. 8, pp. 844-848.

Wreden, N., "The Ups and Downs of Downsizing," *Beyond Computing*, IBM Publication, Aug./Sept. 1992, pp. 12-15.

Yau, S.S. and Caglayan, "Distributed Software System Design Representation Using Modified Petri Nets," *IEEE Trans. on Software Engineering*, Vol. SE-9, No. 6, Nov. 1983, pp. 733-745.

Yau, S. S., Jia, X., and Bae, D. H., "Software Design for Distributed Computer Systems," *Computer Communications*, Vol. 15, No. 4, May 1992, pp. 213-224.

Yeh, R., Zave, P., Conn, A., and Cole, G., "Software Requirements: New Directions and Perspectives," *Handbook of Software Engineering*, Van Nostrand, 1984.

Zave, P. "The Operational Versus the Conventional Approach to Software Development," *Communications of ACM*, Feb. 1984, pp. 104-118.

Zhang, X., Umar, A., and Teichroew, D., "Semantic Analysis of Software Specifications," published in the *Eighth Annual Conference on Computer Aided Software Engineering*, Ann Arbor, Mich., May 1987.

Chapter 9

Open Systems: Interoperability, Portability, and Integration Standards

Problems and Exercises
Case Study: Open Systems for XYZCORP

9.1 Introduction

Simply stated, an open system is a vendor transparent environment in which the users can intermix hardware, software and networks of different vintages from different vendors. Several standards and frameworks have been, and are continuously being, introduced to facilitate open systems. At present, open systems are of vital importance to information systems managers, users, and vendors due to several reasons, such as the following:

- The cost and time spent in application development and application conversion must be minimized. Open systems allow applications to easily migrate (port) between computers. This protects the investment in applications. In addition, open systems can offer several software components which can be "packaged" together to build applications. This reduces the cost of developing applications. In essence, open system standards allow the users to decouple the applications from the underlying computing systems and the networks so that changes in computers and networks do not necessitate modifications of the application systems.
- Users want the freedom to mix and match the most competitive products (in terms of price, performance, or service) from a myriad of sources. Open systems provide this freedom. In essence, the users are moving from a single vendor environment (1970s) to a vendor-neutral environment.
- Open systems are based on open standards and are not copyrighted. Hence development of interfaces with these systems does not expose the user to expensive intellectual property lawsuits <Sapronov 1990>.
- Small vendors want to build pieces of an environment which is controlled by another vendor. In addition, the large vendors want to extend their offerings by selectively including products from smaller vendors. This is possible through open system standards.
- The complexity of designing distributed applications which span several computers must be minimized by eliminating unnecessary choices. The applications which span several computers are attractive because they allow the users to configure applications based on the response time and availability constraints. However, these applications, as described in the previous chapter, are quite difficult to design. Open system compliant applications can run on many computers and networks. Thus the decision of choosing a computer and a network *prior* to application development is eliminated.
- The cost of interconnecting existing and future systems should be minimized. The open systems standards explicitly and clearly specify the interfaces between systems to reduce this cost.

- The user access to a system should be consistent across all environments to minimize end user retraining. Open systems for user interfaces provide a framework for achieving this.
- Support of management concerns and security/integrity control must be embedded in the systems in a uniform manner. The management and security standards in open systems address this.

For these reasons, several standardizing bodies are contributing to the "open movement." Table 9.1 lists the names of the main participants. These bodies specify standards and frameworks and facilitate introduction of products which conform to the frameworks and standards. Distributed computing is a cornerstone of open systems. Most open systems standards assume distributed computing <Rashid 1989, Rose 1990, Runyan 1989>.

This chapter discusses open systems standards and frameworks and describes a few examples to illustrate the various issues and approaches. It is also our objective to synthesize many of the services described so far into an open system architecture. Section 9.2 defines open systems and explains the issues of interoperability, portability and integration in open systems. Section 9.3 describes open architectures which consolidate network architectures, application support architectures and application architectures. Sections 9.4 through 9.7 describe examples of selected standards, vendor offerings, consortium efforts, and corporate attempts at open systems. Open architectures raise several questions: What impact do these architectures have on distributed application design, what can the organizations do while open standards are evolving, and how can the applications be developed to take advantage of open standards and architectures? An example of how one organization, Bell Communications Research, is dealing with these questions is presented in Section 9.8.

The reader of this chapter should be able to answer the following questions:

- What are open systems and why are they important?
- What roles do interoperability, portability, and integration play in open systems?
- What are the major standards and architectures that have been proposed and are currently available?

TABLE 9.1 Key Players in the Open Systems Movement

- ANSI—American National Standards Institute
- CCITT—International Telegraph and Telephone Consultative Committee
- COS—Corporation for Open Systems
- IEEE—Institute of Electrical and Electronic Engineering
- IEC—International Electrotechnical Commission
- ISO—International Standards Organization
- NIST—National Institute for Standards and Technology, formerly NBS
- OSF—Open Software Foundation: Formed by the Berkeley UNIX vendors
- Unix International Inc.—Formed by AT&T UNIX vendors
- X/Open Consortium—formed by hardware vendors

- Who are the major players in the open systems movement, what are they doing, and how are they cooperating with each other, if at all?
- What do the acronyms like OSI ODP/DAF, X/OPEN CAE, IBM's SAA, Digital's NAS, OSF's DCE, and UI-ATLAS mean? What do they have to do with open systems?
- What is the impact of open systems standards and architectures on distributed application development?

9.2 Characteristics of Open Systems

9.2.1 Definitions and Main Concepts

In open systems, users can mix and match computer hardware and software from different suppliers on networks from different suppliers. In his book on open systems, Gary Nutt <1992> states:

> "An open system is one in which the components and their composition are specified in a non-proprietary environment, enabling competing organizations to use these standard components to build competitive systems."

Almost all of the major computer vendors have embraced the concept of open systems for distributed computing under different names. Examples are IBM's Cooperative Processing, DEC's Open Computing Environment, SUN Microsystems's Open Network Computing, Hewlett-Packard's NewWave Computing, and NCR's Open Cooperative Computing. In addition to the differences in names, many differing philosophies and views exist. For example, some feel that a system is "open" as long as the specifications of the system are published. Others are standardizing around the Unix environment. It appears that the definition of an open system is somewhat open to debate. For our purpose, we will use the definition by Gary Nutt with its emphasis on non-proprietary environments.

Theoretically, an open system must exhibit three properties <Nutt 1992>:

- Interoperability
- Portability
- Integration and operability

Interoperability, discussed in Section 9.2.2, is the basic requirement of an open system. As we will see in Sections 9.2.3 and 9.2.4, a system can be open if it is interoperable even if it is not portable or fully integrated. According to a survey conducted by the Open Software Foundation (OSF), the lack of interoperability was cited as the most critical problem facing the open systems industry <OSF 1990>.

The move toward open systems is commonly attributed to the Unix users who insisted on application portability under Unix operating systems across many computers <Moad 1990>. But it is obvious to most information systems managers and practitioners that the Unix environment is just a small part of the open system issue. Open systems need to address portability, interoperability, and integration of many components in an environment with heterogeneous computer hardware, operating systems, data managers, transaction managers, and user interfaces.

9.2.2 Interoperability

Interoperability means that systems ($s_1, s_2,\ldots s_n$) from multiple vendors at multiple vintages can exchange meaningful information through well defined interfaces (see Fig. 9.1). According to Markley <1990>:

> Interoperability provides each user application program, or user process, access to others in network. In the simplest form, it enables a user at one computer to send commands or data to a separate computer (and be understood), and receive, in return, the appropriate response. Interoperability is easier and less expensive if the communications architecture and associated protocols are standard throughout the network, i.e., OSI, DoD Internet, or proprietary.

Specifically, interoperability in an open system involves vendor neutral

- Specification of information sharing and exchange formats
- Rules for synchronized operation of systems which work on common tasks
- Mechanisms for information exchange and synchronization between different components.

Interoperability involves interfaces as well as synchronization between the components of a system. The interfaces and synchronization occurs at various levels, as shown in Fig. 9.1. Examples of the interoperability mechanisms are X.25 protocols, TCP/IP Socket API, LU6.2, RPCs, ASN.1, OSI Remote Database Access (RDA), and Electronic Data Interchange (EDI).

In practice, interoperability is important in three different situations (see Fig. 9.2): between open and proprietary systems, between new and existing systems, and between different parts of an organization.

Standards are essential for interoperability in open systems. The set of standards based on the ISO/OSI Model appear to be the leading force in interoperability.

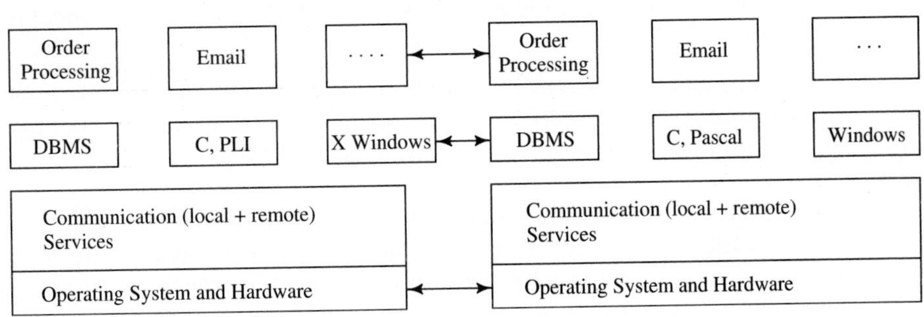

FIGURE 9.1 Interoperable Systems

A. Between Open and Proprietary Systems

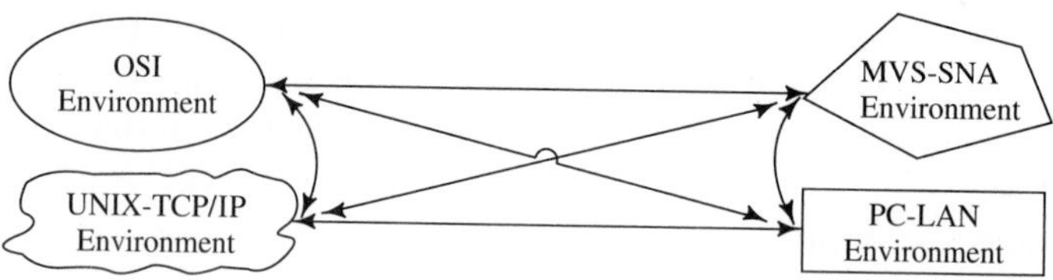

B. Between New and Existing Systems (Vintages)

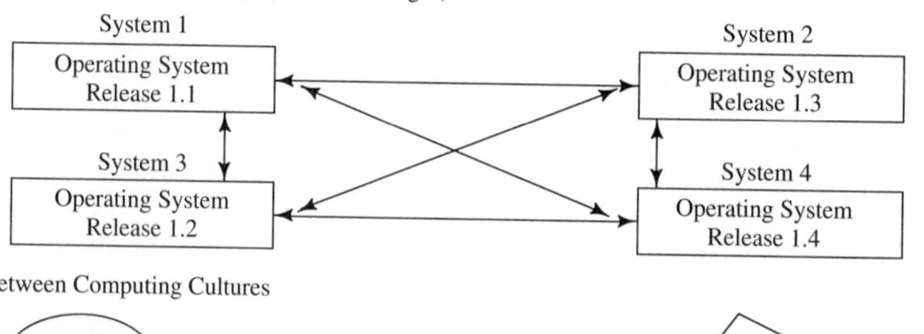

C. Between Computing Cultures

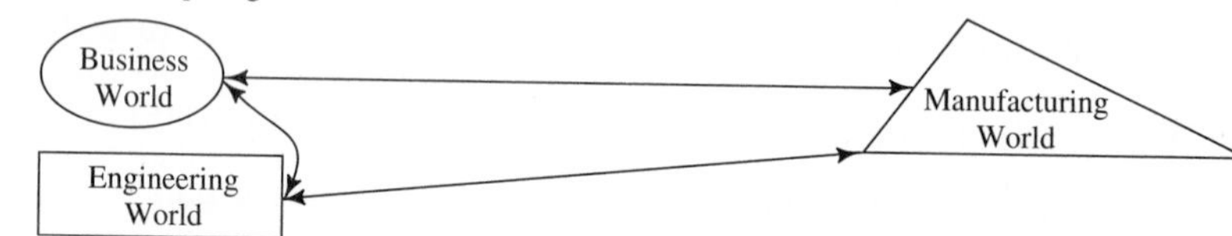

FIGURE 9.2 Interoperability in Practice

However, several de-facto standards have been introduced over the last several years. Some of these standards have been accepted by the standardization bodies. Figure 9.3 lists some of the major interoperability standards. The standards are defined in the following terms:

- Network and device interoperability. These interoperability standards specify the network level information flow and exchange formats. In addition, the physical interfaces between devices and networks are specified (e.g., RS232). This is called "interworking" in the OSI Model.
- Application (high level) interoperability. These standards specify how the applications communicate with each other. Examples are the application interconnectivity and database interoperability standards discussed in Chapters 5 and 6 (e.g., RPCs, RDA).
- Management interoperability. These standards specify how different management applications communicate with each other. Examples are the network management standards discussed in Chapter 4 (e.g., CMIS, SNMP).

Interoperability is of fundamental importance to end users because it concentrates on the "working together" of components which may come from a myriad of sources. As long as the mechanisms for interfaces and synchronization are complied by the vendors, a user has the freedom to mix and match the most competitive products (in terms of price, performance, or service). For example, if the OSI RDA is

Application Interoperability Standards:

Terminal Emulation (Telnet—TCP/IP, VT-OSI)
File Transfer (FTP-TCP/IP, FTAM-OSI)
Client-Server Services

- Berkeley Sockets—TCP/IP
- Remote Operations Service (ROS)—OSI
- Manufacturing Message Specification (MMS)—MAP
- Advanced Program to Program Communications (APPC)—SNA
- Remote Procedure Call (RPC)—TCP/IP Networks
- Connectionless Upper Layers (CUL-OSI)
- Application Programming Interfaces (API)—OSI, TCP/IP, SNA

Distributed Data and Transaction Management

- Network File Services (NFS)—TCP/IP, Token Ring, SNA, OSI
- Remote Data Access (RDA)—OSI
- Distributed Transaction Processing (DTP)—OSI

Miscellaneous Services

- Electronic Mail Protocols (X.400-OSI, SMTP-TCP/IP)
- Directory Services (e.g., X.500)—OSI and TCP/IP
- Distributed Applications Framework/Open Distributed Processing (OSI)
- Network Management Protocols (CMIS-OSI, SNMP-TCP/IP, Netview/SNA)
- Security Services (OSI, TCP/IP)
- Distributed Office Applications (OSI)
- Job Transfer and Management (OSI)

Network and Device Interoperability

- Layer 1 to 3 Standards: X.25 and ISDN Standards
- Layer 1 and 2 Standards: CSMA/CD (IEEE 802.2), Token Bus (IEEE 802.3), Token Bus (IEEE 802.4), FDDI Standard (IEEE 802.6)

FIGURE 9.3 Examples of Interoperability Standards

the remote data access standard for all components in a distributed application system, then different database products from different vendors can be used on different computers. Thus the relational databases from, say, Informix, Oracle, Ingres and Sybase can be accessed from a single client application.

Interoperability plays a key role in client-server applications. Let us assume that we have purchased a DB2 server from vendor X, and that client applications from vendors A, B, C and D need to access DB2. If these clients do not interoperate with vendor X server, then we have a problem; we either do not use these clients or buy additional DB2 severs from vendors A, B, C and D. This may lead to an unacceptable scenario of 10 servers from 10 different vendors accessing the same database (servers, especially on mainframes, are expensive and consume a great deal of memory, CPU and I/O). In another example, if a server uses SUN RPCs, then all clients may have to use the same RPC (i.e., Socket calls and other RPCs may not interoperate). This points out the need for RPC standards.

Interoperability reduces the cost of interconnection and integration. The interoperability standards help in the mass production of the standard products, which reduces the product cost.

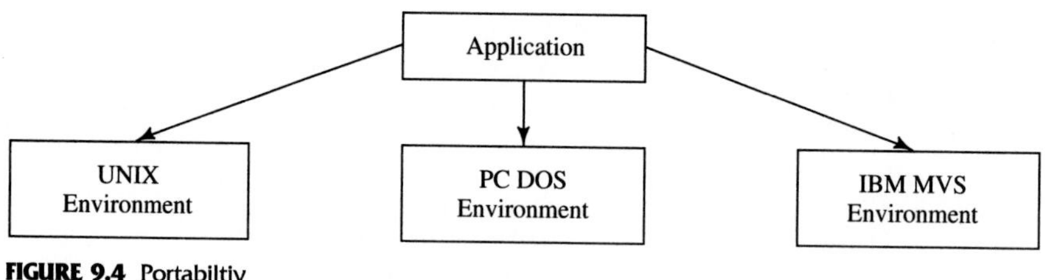

FIGURE 9.4 Portabiltiy

Interoperability is also important for vendors. "Minority" vendors can build pieces of an environment controlled by another vendor. The major vendors can also extend their offerings by selectively including products from smaller vendors. The interoperability specifications are leading to a record number of alliances between different vendors. The eventual beneficiary of this activity is the end user because competition lowers prices and improves vendor service.

Interoperability is a major issue in distributed computing and is discussed widely in the literature. For further discussion of different views, the reader should consult Nutt <1992>, Markley <1990>, Crabb <1989>, Southerton <1989>, Moad <1990>.

9.2.3 Portability

Portability allows a system installed in one environment to be installed at another. In other words, a system is portable between two environments X and Y if it can be moved from environment X to Y, and vice versa, without any modifications (see Fig. 9.4). In reality very few systems are 100 percent portable (i.e., require absolutely no modifications). Ninety percent portability is considered good. What can be portable? Here are some examples:

- *Computing hardware*. A hardware disk is portable between two different computers if the disk can be installed at any of the two computers. A computer is considered portable if it can be plugged in and used in different places. (Most computers are not portable between Europe and the United States due to the differences in power requirements.)
- *Operating systems*. An operating system is portable between two computers if it can be moved from one computer to the other without any modification. An example, although not 100 percent portable, is the Unix operating system. IEEE Posix and AT&T SVID are examples of portable Unix operating systems. Another example is the PC DOS operating system which is portable across many personal computers.
- *Database management systems (DBMS)*. A database management system is portable between two different computers if it can be installed at any of the two computers without any modifications. An example is the Oracle DBMS which is portable between PC-DOS, Unix and MVS environments.
- *Application systems*. An application system is portable between two environments if the processing code, user interface, as well as data access code is portable. Specifically, a 100 percent portable application system requires:

- Program code portability. The same program code should be portable to different computers. The emerging programming standard in this area is C code.
- User interface portability. The same user interface should be portable to different computers. The emerging standard in this area is the XWindow system.
- Database portability. The database definition and access should be portable across many computers. The main standard for database access is SQL. In fact, SQL is becoming the de facto standard for accessing corporate data which may or may not be in relational tables. However, almost all database vendors add "special" features to SQL. SQL Access Group, a consortium of database vendors, is developing SQL standards for portability and interoperability.
- Remote program communication portability. The program to program communications over a heterogeneous network are not completely standardized at present. Examples of de facto standards are SUN RPCs and TCP/IP Sockets.

- *Portable network architecture.* An example is the TCP/IP network architecture which is portable across many networks such as LANs (Ethernet as well as token ring) and WANs (e.g., X.25).
- *Portable knowledge.* The developer knowledge is portable if the same knowledge can be applied to develop applications in different environments. For example, the knowledge of developing applications by using XWindow, SQL and C code is portable across mainframes, minis and PCs/workstations. Similarly, the end-user knowledge is portable as long as the user interface is kept the same.

The leading open effort in portability is the X/Open Portability Guide <X/Open 1989> which addresses many of the portability cases discussed so far.

The primary business pressure behind the portability requirement is to minimize the cost and time spent in application development and application conversion. The highest payoff is in "decoupling" the applications from the computing systems and the networks so that changes in computers and networks do not necessitate modifications of the application systems. For example, an application developed in the IBM MVS-SNA environment should be portable to a Unix-TCP/IP network. The application developers should be shielded from the details of different systems while developing applications. In essence, the environment in which the applications are developed should be transparent (developer transparency) to the developer. While most efforts are directed at source code portability, machine code portability is a much more desirable goal. Standards in this area are also being developed by Xopen.

9.2.4 Integration and Operability

Simply stated, integration refers to the ease with which a system can be used. An integrated system basically minimizes the effort needed to use it. This implies that two systems, S_1 and S_2, are integrated if they

- Share and exchange information without external intervention,
- Are seamless in terms of operations, and
- Show consistency of behavior and presentation.

Operability, a term becoming increasingly popular, refers to the following characteristics of a system:

- Ease of use and operation
- Ease of deployment
- Ease of training
- Reliability and performance.

Thus operability covers a greater range of characteristics (integration can be viewed as a subset of operability). We will primarily concentrate on integration in this section. Other aspects of operability (ease of deployment, training, reliability and performance) will be mentioned where appropriate.

Interest in integration has been around for several years. In the recent years, integration has been brought to the attention of top management due to an emphasis on Computer Integrated Manufacturing (CIM), Computer Integrated Businesses (CIB,) and Computer Integrated Enterprises (CIE) <LaVie 1988, Campbell 1988, Malas 1988, Bray 1988, Ranky 1986, Appleton 1977>. System integration has become a major business with several large companies, including IBM and GE, declaring themselves as "system integrators" <Rapport 1991, Moad 1989>. It is estimated that the system integrator's contracts will exceed $22 billion by 1993 <Rapport 1991>.

Integration can be discussed in terms of user view integration, process integration, and data integration. The most important aspect of integration is concerned with user view integration, also known as end-user transparency. This implies the following <Nutt 1992, p. 21>:

- *Consistency of presentation.* All presentations to the user should be same so that the user does not have to re-learn. For example, all windows should behave similarly (i.e., similar ways to start windows, close windows, redraw, etc.).
- *Consistency of operations.* There should be similar ways to perform similar tasks such as initiating print jobs, sending mail, establishing sessions, saving files, etc.

In addition to the "horizontal" integration where several different systems appear seamless, it is possible to envision "vertical" integration through strong couplings between a transaction manager, a database manager and an operating system. This type of integration leads us into distributed operating systems which we have discussed in Chapter 7.

Standards in user view integration are still evolving. The OSI VT (Virtual Terminal) standard does not provide any windowing operations. OSF/Motif is becoming a de facto GUI standard due to its use in XWindow. However, XWindow and Motif are very tedious to learn and use. Other noticeable developments in GUI are the MS-Window and Apple Terminal Service (ATS) environments. ANSI is now standardizing the X protocol (called a data stream definition in ANSI X3H3.6). This may facilitate OSI window management and graphics efforts based on working implementations.

TABLE 9.2 Views of Integration

Consider two processes, p1 and p2, which share information, i. Are p1 and p2 integrated? What will make them integrated? A brief literature survey has shown that many views and definitions of integration exist. Here are some examples:

1. p1 and p2 are integrated if the information shared by p1 and p2 is consistent. For example, updates between p1 and p2 are coordinated. This appears to be the view of database professionals <Date 1989, Lew 1988, Hsu 1988>.
2. Integrated systems can interact directly. For example, Prolog programs may be considered integrated with a DBMS if the DBMS calls can be directly issued from Prolog <Elmasri 1983, page 652>. This view is held by software engineering professionals <Chappel 1985, Van Nostrand 1986>.
3. Integrated systems provide transparent access to computing resources across many computers. For example, a set of computers managed by a single distributed operating system may give p1 and p2 the impression that p1 and p2 are using the resources of a single computer system. This appears to be the view of computing network professionals <Coulouris 1989, Elliot 1988>.
4. Integrated systems bring together hardware, software, networks, and staff to apply information technology to solve a business problem. This appears to be the view from the system integrator's bench <Rapport 1991>.
5. Integrated systems are synchronized so that the events triggered in one system are detected by and, if needed, controlled by another system. For example, the events occurring in manufacturing devices may be detected and responded/controlled by cell and area controllers in flexible manufacturing systems. This view is prevalent especially in manufacturing engineering <Odrey 1986, Li 1988>.
6. Integrated systems have common focus and goal. This view is held by organizational structure designers <Aulds 1988>.

Processes integration is normally achieved through seamless processes which share and exchange information without human intervention. For example, a computer integrated manufacturing environment is achieved through business processes, manufacturing processes, and engineering processes which automatically share and exchange information to automate production. Database integration combines and interrelates data elements from different sources so that all users can view, access, and manipulate data in a consistent manner. Many systems are integrated around a common database because a database can provide consistency of presentation and operation.

Does everyone agree on what integration is? No (see Table 9.2 for some examples). It is obvious that all these views are correct to some extent. In distributed systems, integration is considerably complicated due to the interconnectivity issues (i.e., how does interconnectivity differ from integration and when do two interconnected systems become integrated?). In general, integration can be viewed in terms of coupling (i.e., interactions between various systems). Simply stated, two loosely coupled systems are connected while two very tightly coupled systems are integrated. As the coupling between two systems increases, they become more and more integrated (see Fig. 9.5). This allows us to describe many loosely coupled and integrated systems. In addition, we can develop a conceptual framework for categorizing and understanding the integration and interconnectivity issues in distributed computing, distributed applications, and distributed enterprise systems. Figure 9.6 shows such a framework.

At the lowest level are the distributed computing platforms (DCPs), which consist of the hardware, operating systems, networks and application support services.

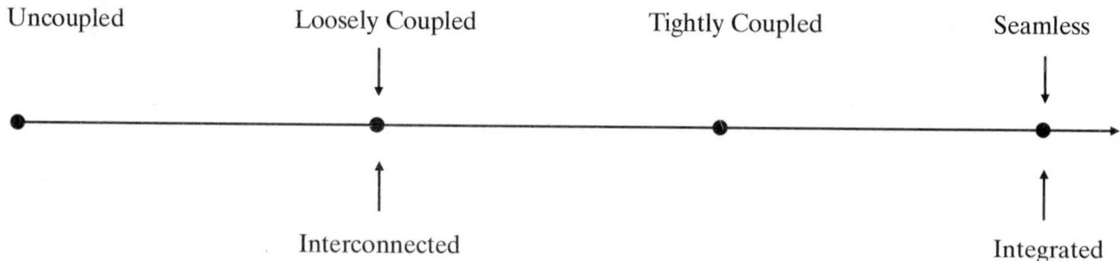

FIGURE 9.5 Coupling and Integration

These platforms can be loosely coupled or integrated as shown in Fig. 9.6. A loosely coupled distributed computing platform represents a network of computers, interconnected through routers and gateways, which exchange information through terminal emulation and file transfer. In these systems, a user needs to know the location of the target resources and is restricted to batch file transfer capabilities. In some of the literature, the term *federated systems* is used to represent loosely coupled autonomous systems. Integrated distributed computing platforms provide strong coupling between computing systems through distributed database managers and client-server facilities (e.g., RPCs). The distributed operating systems, an area of future research discussed in Chapter 7, will integrate DCPs even further by making all of the resources (CPUs, disks, databases, programs, I/O devices, etc.) of a network available to a user as if they were local. This single system image will make the DCPs very tightly coupled (integrated).

At the next level in Fig. 9.6, a distributed application system (DAS) can be loosely coupled, tightly coupled, or integrated. In a loosely coupled DAS, the application system components at different computers exchange information through batch data transfers and remote logons, while in an integrated DAS, the application systems components interact with each other through realtime message exchanges across systems. It is obvious from Fig. 9.6 that it is easy to develop integrated DAS if the underlying DCP is also integrated (an integrated DCP essentially provides the services needed by the integrated DAS).

	Loosely Coupled Systems	*Integrated (Tightly Coupled) Systems*
• Enterprise systems	• Remote activities • Telephones • Human mail • Occasional human contact	• Same-site activities • Tele/videoconferencing • Electronic mail • Increased human contact
• Distributed application systems	• Batch data transfer • Remote logon	• Realtime message exchange and failure/security handling
• Distributed computing platforms	• File transfer packages • Terminal emulation • Network gateways	• Client-server computing • DDBMS • Distributed operating systems

FIGURE 9.6 A Framework for Integration of Distributed Systems

At the highest level, the enterprise system interconnection and integration is needed when the enterprise activities of manufacturing, engineering, finance, etc. are performed at different geographical sites. As shown in Fig. 9.6, the current systems of telephones and mail interconnect remotely located enterprise activities. However, the increased use of corporate-wide networks, electronic mail and videoconferencing could help organizational activities to be integrated across geographical distances. The role of computers in integrating enterprise activities is well recognized as evidenced by the attention on CIM (Computer Integrated Manufacturing) and CIB (Computer Integrated Business). Organizational models such as CIM models (CIM-OSA <LaVie 1988> and CIMA <Campbell 1988>) are also intended to integrate organizational activities. Detailed discussion of this topic is beyond the scope of this book.

9.2.5 Transparency in Open Systems

The issues of portability, integration, and interoperability can be discussed in terms of transparency. We defined the following levels of transparency in Chapters 1 and 7:

- End user transparency (integration)
- Developer transparency (portability)
- Architect/manager transparency (interoperability).

Various components of a distributed computing environment provide these levels of transparency. An open distributed computing environment will exhibit transparencies in a vendor neutral environment. Figure 9.7 shows how these levels of transparency are delivered. (We discussed this figure in Chapter 7. The following discussion highlights the main points.)

End user transparency shows how transparent the user operations are from the underlying networks, operating systems, computer systems and application systems. Ideally, a completely user transparent system should operate as a single system in which the user is not aware of what activities are taking place where in the system. As shown in Fig. 9.7, the network architectures, the application support services (e.g., distributed database managers, client-server computing, distributed operating systems), and application systems cooperate in providing user transparency. If the application support services and network interfaces do not provide adequate transparency to the users, then the needed transparency can be built in the application user interface and processing modules. Theoretically, application code can be developed to provide a nearly complete user transparency. As the platforms become more sophisticated, this code does not need to be implemented in the application systems.

The application developers can be shielded from the details of different systems while developing applications. The application systems developed should be portable to different computers interconnected through different networks. The developer transparency (application portability) can be discussed at three levels: user interface transparency, program code transparency, and data transparency.

In addition, the application systems architects/designers should not have to decide at what location the various application systems components should reside. As

	Network Services (Layers 1 to 4)	*Application Support Services:* Terminal Emulation & File Servers	*Application Support Services:* Distributed Database and Transaction Management	Distributed Operating System	Distributed Application System
User Transparency					
Network hardware transparency	x				
Network services transparency	x	x			
User location (command) transparency	x			x	x
Data location transparency		x	x		
Transaction execution transparency			x		
Processor transparency				x	
I/O device transparency				x	
Fault transparency	x	x	x	x	x
Developer Transparency					
User interface transparency				x	x
Program code transparency	x				x
Data transparency		x	x		x
Architect Transparency					
Interconnectivity transparency	x	x	x	x	
Performance transparency	x	x	x	x	
Availability transparency	x	x	x	x	x
Management Transparency					
Security transparency	x	x	x	x	x
Network management transparency	x	x	x	x	x
Distributed application management transparency	x	x	x	x	x

Note: An x indicates that this type of technology supports the shown transparency level.

FIGURE 9.7 Transparency Support in Distributed Computing

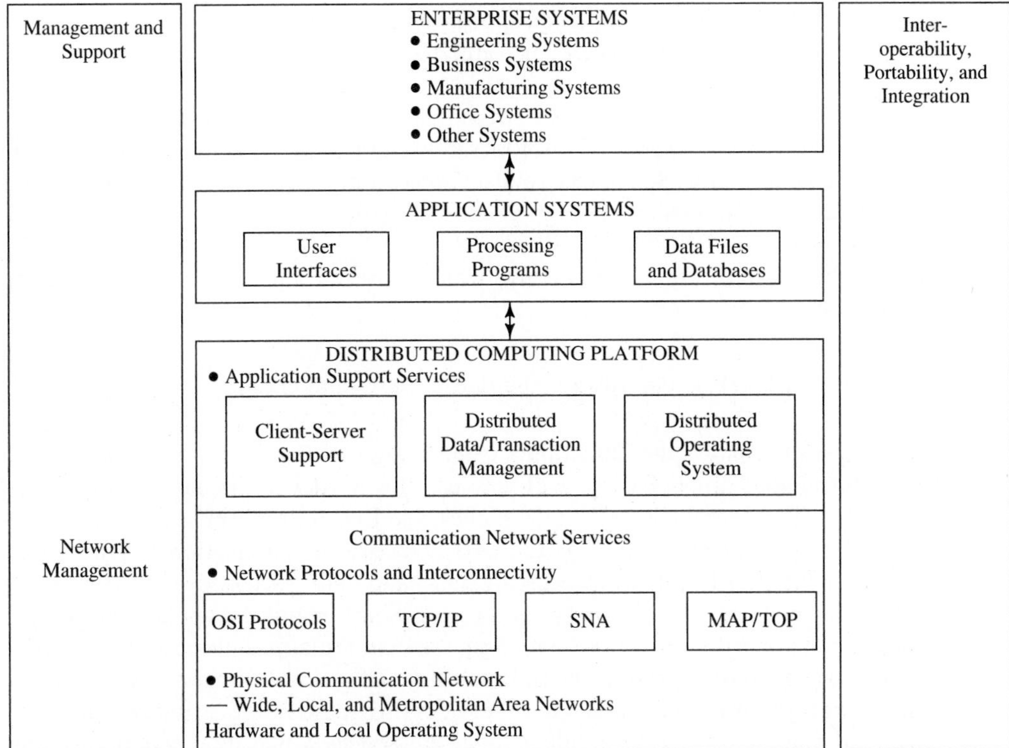

FIGURE 9.8 A Distributed Computing Reference Model

the distributed computing technologies become more sophisticated, it is becoming easier to interconnect applications, and the application system components will be moved automatically to appropriate locations for improvements in performance and availability. As shown in Fig. 9.7, these intelligent facilities can be provided by a combination of network architectures, and application support services. At present, some of these facilities are not state of the market. The management transparency means that the management of distributed computing becomes as simple as the management of centralized systems. As shown in Fig. 9.7, these facilities can be provided by a combination of network architectures and application support services. A great deal of work is still needed in this area.

9.3 Open System Architectures for Distributed Computing

9.3.1 Open System Architecture: A Special Case of Distributed Computing Architecture

An open system architecture consists of a collection of open components such as open hardware and operating systems, open database and transaction managers, open user interfaces, and open networks. According to Gary Nutt <1992>:

"If the architecture is agreed upon by all of the component for the system, then the parts can be interconnected; such architectures are open system architectures."

Open system architecture is a special case of distributed computing architectures which address the general interoperability, portability and integration issues in distributed computing. Specifically, a distributed computing architecture synthesizes two major architectures into a single framework (see Fig. 9.8):

- Distributed application architectures which represent the user interface, data and program architectures.
- Distributed computing platform (DCP) architectures which represent application support, network, and hardware and operating system architectures.

Figure 9.8 shows the Distributed Computing Reference Model which we have used throughout this book. We will now use this Model to discuss the distributed computing architectural issues. At the highest level are the enterprise activities which drive all lower level activities. At the next level are the application systems which consist of the user interfaces, processing logic, and data. At the lowest level are the DCPs on which the application systems reside. Since any of the application components can be distributed across computing systems, the application support services collectively attempt to provide the transparency of data location, transaction processing, processors and I/O devices. These services provide RPCs, distributed data management, naming services (also called directory services, which allow common storage and access of information), and security services. At the next lower level are the communication network services which provide access to local data stores, local communication devices and the network communication over LANS, MANs, and WANs. The computing hardware and operating systems are at the lowest level. Notice that the issues of interoperability, portability, integration, management, and support occur at all levels of this Model.

This Model can represent "closed" (vendor proprietary), open (vendor neutral), or hybrid architectures. For example, a system consisting of many applications operating on a Novell Netware LAN is a closed architecture. Similarly, distributed applications implemented on IBM MVS mainframes, AS/400 minicomputers and PS2 microcomputers, interconnected through SNA, also represent a closed architecture. A hybrid architecture would consist of applications that span IBM mainframes, Unix minicomputers and workstations, and PS2/Macintosh microcomputers interconnected on a TCP/IP or OSI network. In the last few years, the distributed computing architectures have moved from closed to hybrid architectures, with a trend toward completely open architectures.

9.3.2 Illustration of a Distributed Computing Architecture

Figure 9.9 illustrates how a distributed computing architecture may actually be realized. This figure shows how application system components (application programs, user databases and user interfaces) interface with network layers, local I/O,

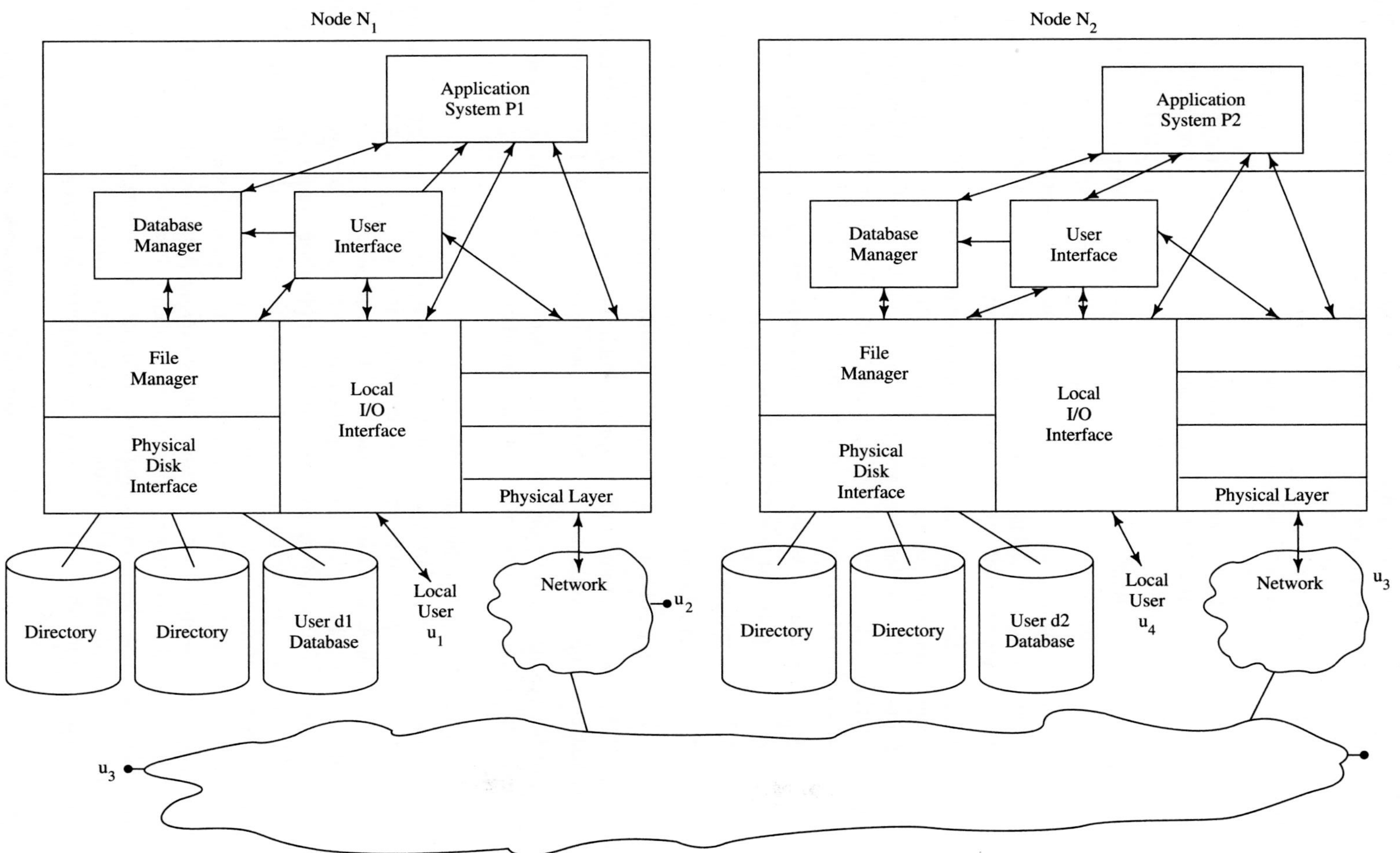

FIGURE 9.9 Distributed Computing Architecture Example

database managers, directories, and local or network users in a distributed environment. For example, an application system consisting of programs p_1, p_2 and datasets d_1, d_2 is distributed to two nodes as shown in Fig. 9.9. Several users (u_1 through u_5) can access portions of this application system from various sites.

Let us consider the following situations:

- *Case 1*: User u_1 can directly access the application system program p_1 to manipulate dataset d_1 through the local I/O interface, the user interface and the database management interface.
- *Case 2*: User u_1 can issue an SQL query against dataset d_1 which does not need to access program p_1.
- *Case 3*: User u_2 can access the program p_1 through a network. The requests are handled by the network layers which translate/transform the user message, send it to p_1, receive the response from p_1, and send it back to u_2.
- *Case 4*: User u_1 can access p_2 and d_2 through a local user interface such as XWindow or a presentation manager which then passes control to a network for remote data access. In this case the local node can assume the role of a client. In addition, the user interface and commands are translated from different network protocols by using the different network architectures that are used at both nodes.
- *Case 5*: User u_3, who is sitting at a wide area network, can access information at node n_1 or n_2 in a similar fashion by going through network interfaces.
- *Case 6*: User u_2 can access d_1, with or without p_1.
- *Case 7*: User u_2 can access d_2, with or without p_2.
- *Case 8*: Users u_3, u_4 and u_5 can access d_1 or d_2 with or without p_1 or p_2.
- *Case 9*: Any user can issue an SQL query which accesses d_1 and d_2. In this case, the database managers at the two nodes may operate through a DDTMS (Chapter 6).
- *Case 10*: Any user may issue a transaction which involves p_1, p_2, d_1 and d_2. Once again, the actual exchanges may be coordinated by a DDTMS.

It is clear that the architecture presented in Fig. 9.9 allows several sets of users to access several application system components in a wide variety of ways. The users can access a local application, they can use a user interface, they can directly issue database calls through a user interface, or they can access a remote application component. This architecture allows application systems to be configured in a wide variety of ways with a combination of standalone applications, remote logons through terminal emulation, batch file transfers, network file services, distributed database management, and client-server systems.

Figures 9.8 and 9.9 serve as a foundation for open system architecture in distributed computing. Open systems architectures, as indicated, are motivated by three interrelated business pressures: interoperability, integration and portability. These architectures also provide increased management control, security, and standardization of applications. Users are realizing that a completely open system must include a nonproprietary environment consisting of the following <Moad 1990>:

- Operating systems that are transportable across computers (e.g., Unix)
- Standard network protocols to manage large as well as small networks (e.g., OSI)
- Industry wide database interface definitions to mix and match relational databases
- A single graphical user interface
- Development tools and CASE (computer aided software engineering) environments that can be ported to different computers
- Standard object management across heterogeneous systems.

Specifically, open architectures require

- Open operating systems such as Unix.
- Open network architectures which specify the vendor transparent network architectures for LANs, MANs, etc. The specifications are prepared for network portability, network interoperability and network integration.
- Open application support architectures which specify the vendor transparent architectures for distributed operating systems, distributed database managers and distributed transaction processing. Open operating systems provide portability of subcomponents, specifications of interfaces for interoperability and integration of components to give user transparency. Users of operating systems are application systems, database management systems and end users. Open database systems provide database portability, database interoperability, and database integration. Open client/server systems provide client/server portability, client/server interoperability, and client/server integration.
- Open application architectures which specify the vendor transparent architectures for distributed data access language, distributed user interfaces, and distributed application processing logic.

Figure 9.10 attempts to relate the open architecture to the OSI Distributed Reference Model. The user application systems are placed at layer 8 which is above the traditional OSI seventh layer. At the highest layer (layer 9) are the business/enterprise processes for which the application systems are developed. Layers 7, 6, and 5 conceptually provide the application support functions and application interconnectivity at the back-end (local) and front-end (remote) interfaces. The back-end local support only consists of three layers (7, 2, and 1) because the local support does not need the functions of routing, transport, session establishment, etc.

9.3.3 Examples of Open System Architectures

Open System Architectures must combine the growing underlying technologies in computing networks and application support services with the new choices, issues and interfaces introduced by distributed applications. Many vendors, large corporations and standardization bodies are announcing standards for distributed systems archi-

- Business Processes Layer (9)
  Function: Enterprise processes
  Examples:
  - Business processes
  - Engineering/scientific processes
  - Manufacturing processes

- User Application Systems (8)
  Function:User programs
  Examples:
  - Business applications
  - Engineering/scientific applications
  - Manufacturing applications
  - Office automation applications
  - Other applications

- Application Support Services (7)
  Function: manage resources across computers
  Examples:
  - Distributed operating systems
  - Distributed database management
  - Distributed transaction management

Back-End (Local) Support	Front-End (Network) Support
Application Interconnection Layer (7) Function: Support/management of local applications Examples: Transaction Management User interface management, Database management	Application Interconnection Layer (7, 6, 5) Function: Support/management of network applications Example: Layer 7 of ISO Model Example: file transfer, terminal emulation
	Network Interconnection Layers (4 and 3) Function: Support/management of network (session establishment, transport, monitoring, etc.) Example: layer 3–6 of ISO Model – Presentation layer (6) – Session layer (5) – Transport layer (4) – Network layer (3)
Physical Interconnection Layers (2, 1) Function: Interconnection of physical local devices Example: Disk, keyboard interfaces • Disks, keyboards	Physical Interconnection Layers (2, 1) Function: Interconnection of physical network devices Example: Layers 1, 2 of ISO Model or other proprietary models – Data link layer (2) – Physical layer (1) • Cables, transmission media

FIGURE 9.10 Distributed Computing Architecture Model (OSI Extention)

tectures. Examples of some of these architectures are as follows <Davis 1992, Moad 1990, DeBoever 1989, Williams 1989-May>:

- OSI's Distributed Applications Framework/Open Distributed Processing (DAF/ODP)
- Open Software Foundation's (OSF) Distributed Computing Environment (DCE)
- Unix International's ATLAS
- IBM's System Application Architecture (SAA)
- DEC's Application Integration Architecture (AIA) and Network Application Support (NAS)
- HP's Distributed Application Architecture (DAA)
- Software AG's Integrated Software Architecture (ISA)
- Data General's Distributed Application Architecture (DAA)
- NCR's Open Cooperative Computing Architecture (OCCA)
- Microsoft Corporation's Windows Open Services Architecture (WOSA)
- Bellcore's OSCA Architecture
- AT&T's Application Operating Environment (AOE).

Although there are many commonalities among these architectures, not all architectures are fully compatible with each other. Sections 9.4 through 9.6 review a few examples to expose the reader to different approaches to essentially the same problem. Section 9.4 reviews the standards from two standardizing bodies: ISO and X/OPEN. Two major vendor initiated architectures (IBM's SAA and Digital's NAS) are presented in Section 9.5 to illustrate how the vendors are moving from proprietary to open system architectures. The two architectures from Unix-based consortiums (Open Software Foundation's Distributed Computing Environments and Unix International's ATLAS) are reviewed in Section 9.6 to outline how some consortiums are trying to mix the proprietary offerings with standards-based products. An analysis of these architectures is presented in Section 9.7.

9.4 Examples of Standards in Open System Architectures

The predominant international/national standards have been introduced by ISO (International Standards Organization). In addition, some proprietary standards have become de facto standards (e.g., SQL) and have been included in the national/international standards. Due to the proliferation of national/international and de facto standards, some consortiums are being formed to analyze and select appropriate standards for different user communities. X/Open is an example of such a consortium. We review here standards being introduced by ISO and outline the guidelines being established by X/Open.

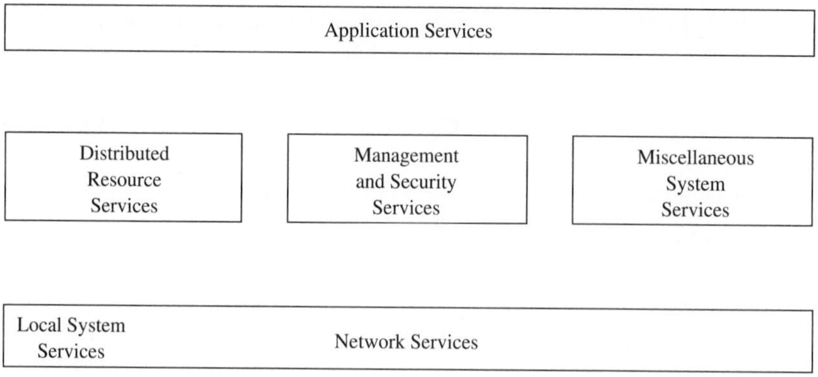

Application Services

Distributed Resource Services	Management and Security Services	Miscellaneous System Services

Local System Services	Network Services

FIGURE 9.11 OSI Standards

9.4.1 OSI's Distributed Applications Framework/Open Distributed Processing (DAF/ODP)

ISO has proposed a series of open systems standards. We have reviewed the seven-layer ISO/OSI Distributed Reference Model previously. Distributed Applications Framework/Open Distributed Processing (DAF/ODP) is the OSI framework and model for open distributed systems. This framework extends the seven-layer model to include a variety of services needed for distributed applications. The services provided by this framework include distributed resource services, management and security services, network services, local system services, and miscellaneous services such as directory services (see Fig. 9.11). This framework corresponds conveniently to our Distributed Computing Reference Model (see Fig. 9.8).

The distributed resource services support applications that span many systems. Examples of these services are as follows:[1]

- *Remote Operations Service (ROS)*: This OSI service and protocol defines the standards for interacting with remote applications as clients-servers. The standard specifies the syntax and semantics about client calls (remote procedure call) to a server and the server responses. The ROS standard is specified in the ISO9072-1 document.
- *Remote Procedure Call (RPC)*: This service, now implemented on many networks, allows an application to call a remotely located procedure (process) as if it was a local process. RPCs are used in the ROS standard. While an OSI RPC standard is

[1]We have included references to the ISO documents which specify the standards at the time of this writing. This information is included for the purpose of illustration. It is natural to assume that some document numbers will change with time.

being developed, many RPCs are becoming commercially available. Examples are the SUN RPC and Open Software Foundation's RPC.

- *Remote Data Access (RDA)*: This SQL-based OSI standard is being developed for update and retrieval of remotely located databases. The RDA standard is specified in the ISO DP 9579 document.
- *Network File Services (NFS)*: This service, initially developed by the SUN Microsystems, has become a de facto standard for transparent access of remote files in a network.
- *Distributed Transaction Processing (DTP)*: These standards are being developed for dialogue services and remote executions needed for transaction processing on multiple sites. DTP controls the exchange of information between remote transactions according to a set of rules which ensure that a number of events are accounted for and completed reliably. The ISO DTP standard is specified in the ISO DIS 10026-1 document.
- *Advanced Program to Program Communications (APPC)*: This protocol, initially developed by IBM, is widely accepted as a standard for developing business distributed applications.
- *Manufacturing Message Standard (MMS)*: This protocol, initially developed for the Manufacturing Automation Protocols (MAP), is widely accepted as a protocol for developing manufacturing applications. The MMS standard is specified in the ISO 9606-1 document.

The miscellaneous application services include standards such as the following:

1. *Directory services protocols:* X.500 is an OSI standard for directory services. The ISO X.500 standard is specified in the ISO 9504-1 document.
2. *Distributed Office Applications (DOA):* This OSI service defines the standards for office automation. The DOA standard is specified in the ISO 10031-1 document.
3. *Job Transfer and Management (JTM)*: This service is used for batch remote job entry (RJE) to a remote computer and receive the results. It permits the users to inquire about the status of the request and to cancel, suspend,or resume processing. The JTM standard is specified in the ISO 8831 document.
4. *Connectionless Upper Layers (CUL)*: These services are being developed for efficient client-server applications.
5. *Application Programming Interfaces (API)*: These OSI services define standardized interfaces for application programs to interface with network services.
6. *Terminal emulators* such as the TCP/IP TELNET and the ISO VT standards.
7. *File transfer standards* such as the OSI FTAM (File Transfer Access Method) and the TCP/IP FTP (File Transfer Protocol).

The OSI network service standards are as follows:

- Layer 1 and 2 standards for LANs, WANs, and MANs specify the communication media used (coaxial cables, twisted pair, optical fiber), transmission techniques employed (broadband, baseband, carrierband), transmission data rates allowed for each standard and data link protocols such as token ring, Ethernet, FDDI, SDLC, etc.
- Layer 1 to 3 standards specify network interconnectivity in connection-oriented and connectionless modes. Examples are the X.25 packet switching standard and the ISDN standard.
- Transport layer standards are defined by the ISO 8072 and ISO 8073 approved standards. The CCITT X.214 and X.224 are equivalent to these standards. Transmission Control Protocol (TCP), part of the DOD Protocol Suite which was developed for the ARPANET project, is one of the best known layer 4 protocols, and runs on top of IP (Internet Protocol), a layer 3 protocol in the DOD Suite.

The OSI management services use the OSI Management Framework. This Framework is based on the Common Management Information Service/Protocol (CMIS/CMIP), which defines the building blocks and bit patterns needed to carry out a network management function. The OSI Management Framework uses the OSI layers to transfer the CMIP data between devices. A network device, called a manager, uses CMIP to send commands or request data from other devices, called agents. An agent can be a single device such as a workstation or a collection of network devices with common properties (e.g., modems). The OSI security protocol defines the standards for secure communications. The ISO security standard is specified in the ISO DP 10181-1 document.

The main operating system standard for open systems is the Unix operating system. However, many versions of Unix exist. The two best known versions are the AT&T's System V and the Berkeley Unix. In addition, DEC has developed ULTRIX and IBM has announced AIX as its Unix versions. Posix, a Unix interface standard, is gaining importance for vendor independent Unix interfaces. Originally, Posix was a project of the IEEE Computer Society to define external specifications for Unix. In the last few years, the IEEE's Posix work has been endorsed and adopted by ANSI (American National Standards Institute), X/Open, and NIST (National Institute for Standards and Technology). The IEEE Posix standards committee at present consists of the following working groups:

1003.0 Open-system architecture
1003.1 Posix application interface
1003.2 Shell and command utilities
1003.3 Testing and verification methods
1003.4 Real-time extensions to Posix
1003.5 Ada language bindings
1003.6 System security extensions
1003.7 System administration
1003.8 Transparent file access

1003.9 Fortran language bindings
1003.10 Supercomputing profile
1003.11 Transaction processing
1003.12 Protocol-independent network access
1003.13 Application environment profiles
1003.14 Multiprocessing application environment profiles
1003.15 Batch services

It is important to distinguish Posix from Unix. Posix is an interface, not an implementation; Unix is an interface and an implementation. The Posix interface consists of conventional Unix system calls and other facilities implemented as library routines in Unix. The Posix interface can be implemented by any kernel to provide Unix services. For example, the Posix interface can be implemented by the Mach kernel, DEC VMS kernel, or even MVS. This allows Unix applications to be ported to non-Unix environments. A detailed description of Posix can be found in the Posix Programmer's Guide <Zlotnick 1991>. An analysis of the Posix interface is given by <Tucker 1990> and the potential of Posix for real-time applications is described in <Stein 1992>.

It should be noted that the OSI standards are shifting focus toward interoperability between functioning areas of organizations. An example is the development of OSI Profiles which define subsets and/or combinations of standards for specific functions (e.g., factory automation) and conformance tests for interoperability. The ISO TR 10000 document describes a framework and taxonomy of international standardized profiles. To illustrate the concept of profiles, let us take the simple example of business versus scientific programming profiles. A business profile would consist of Cobol compiler, sort routines and report generation facilities, and a scientific profile would support Fortran compiler and a mathematical subroutine library.

Many books and commentaries have been written on the evolving OSI standards. Table 9.3 lists the main references. Additional references are listed in Appendix A, Section A.1. A devoted reader may venture into reading the actual ISO standard and draft documents.

TABLE 9.3 OSI Sources of Information

1. Black, U., *OSI: A Model of Computer Communications Standards,* Prentice Hall, 1991.
2. Cameron, D., *OSI: An International Standard for Open Systems,* Computer Technology Research Corporation, Charleston, S.C., 1991.
3. Rose, M., *The Open Book: A Practical Perspective on OSI,* Prentice Hall, 1990.
4. Henshell, J., and Shaw, H., *OSI Explained: End to End Communications Standards,* 2nd ed., Prentice Hall, 1991.
5. *Proceedings of the IEEE,* Special Issue on Open System Interconnection, Dec. 1983.
6. Stallings, W., *Handbook of Computer Communications Standards,* Macmillan, 1987, vol. 1 (ISO Model).
7. Stalling W., *Networks and Data Communications,* 3rd ed., Macmillan, 1991.
8. Tanenbaum, A., *Computing Networks,* 2nd ed., Prentice Hall, 1988.

9.4.2 X/OPEN Platform Architecture

The X/Open Company Limited is an international consortium of computer hardware and operating system vendors. The following statements list the objectives and scope of X/Open <X/Open 1989>:

> "X/Open's objectives are:
>
> - Portability of applications at the source code level so that application porting is a mechanical recompilation process.
> - Connectivity of applications via portable networking services that are independent of underlying protocols, plus support for common protocol stacks to ensure that X/Open machines may be interconnected.
> - A consistent approach to the user interface with the system.
>
> X/Open is not a standard-setting body. It is a joint initiative by members of the business community to adopt and adapt existing standards into a consistent environment. Where there is an agreed official standard, X/Open adopts it; where there is no agreed official standard, X/Open adopts de facto standards where it is necessary to provide the comprehensive environment demanded by users and applications developers."

The members of the consortium are competitors who have agreed to use X/Open as a mechanism to develop portability guidelines. The business pressure for this consortium is the need for third party application software. All hardware and operating system vendors recognize that without adequate software, it is almost impossible to introduce new hardware and operating systems. For example, hardware advances are far outpacing software, especially application software. A hardware manufacturer who controls only a small fraction of computer installed base cannot introduce radically innovative computer hardware. Who will write the software for this unique software? This manufacturer may join X/Open to help define a software layer which serves as a uniform interface between its hardware and commonly available operating systems and application software.

X/Open has published an X/Open Portability Guide (XPG) as a collection of portability standards. These standards define an abstract machine interface, called the Common Application Environment (CAE), to be used by third party software suppliers. CAE, shown in Fig. 9.12, is in practice a subset of commonly accepted standards in the computing industry. For example, X/Open has adopted the IEEE Posix interface for operating systems. The XPGs and other publications by X/Open are listed in Table 9.4.

The evolving standards will use the CAE architecture shown in Fig. 9.12 to define portability guidelines. CAE is an application programming interface (API) at the Tools level. CAE focuses portability at the source code level; no attempt is made for portability at the object (machine) code level. Third party vendors build products that can be compiled and linked into the Tools facilities of CAE without having to know the underlying hardware.

The X/Open Portability Guide (XPG) is a multivolume collection of standards for CAE. The XPG documents contain the evolving portfolio of standards which are

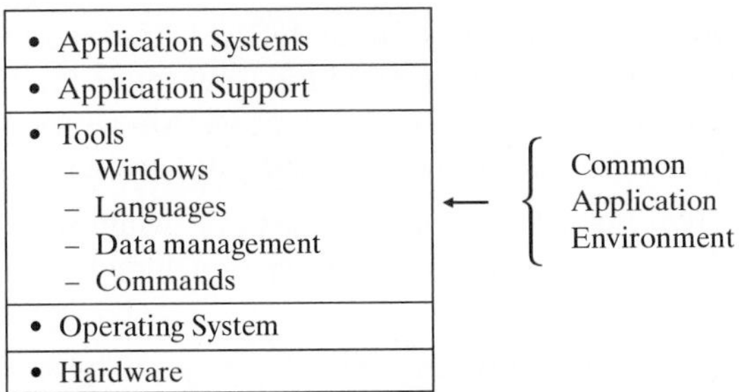

FIGURE 9.12 The X/Open Common Application Environment (CAE)

supported by the X/Open members. The first issue, called XPG1, was published in 1986. XPG2 appeared in 1987, and XPG3 was developed in 1988 and 1989. XPG3 describes CAE in seven volumes:

- *Volume 1: XSI Commands and Utilities*. This part of the Portability Guide defines the commands and utilities of the X/Open System Interface (XSI). These are the set of user commands (e.g., listing a directory) recognized by the command line interpreter. This document, currently in working draft format, will eventually be called the IEEE Standard 1003.2-19xx.
- *Volume 2: XSI System Interfaces and Headers*. This volume describes the application programming interface to the operating system. It essentially describes the X/Open version of Posix (IEEE Standard 1003.1). The X/Open definition is compliant with the IEEE Standard, although it includes a few extensions.
- *Volume 3: XSI Supplementary Definitions*. This volume includes a glossary of terms used at the operating system level and the native (international) language support needed by an X/Open system.
- *Volume 4: Programming Languages*. The CAE includes C and Cobol programming languages. The C specification conforms to the ANSI standard with provisions for portable C code. Resulting C programs conform to the internationalization standards discussed in volume 3. X/Open Cobol also conforms to the ANSI Cobol standard. X/Open has been required to extend languages to support interactive programs.

TABLE 9.4 X/Open Documents

- XPG, *The X/Open Portability Guide,* 7 Volumes, Issue 3, X/Open Company Limited, Prentice Hall, 1989.
- X/Open Company Limited, "Security: Auditing and Authentication," *X/Open Snapshot,* October 1990.
- X/Open Company Limited, *X/Open Systems Mangement: Reference Model,* Draft, June 1991.
- X/Open Company Limited, *The X/Open Reference Model for Distributed Transaction Processing,* November 1991.

- *Volume 5: Data Management.* SQL and ISAM (indexed sequential access method) are included in CAE. X/Open ISAM is a subset of the Informix C-ISAM and is compatible with the Cobol ISAM definition. X/Open SQL is based on the ANSI SQL standard. Differences are discussed in this volume.
- *Volume 6: Window Management.* The CAE window management is based on XWindow Version 11. The Xlib interface is included, but no toolkit or widgets are included.
- *Volume 7: Networking Services.* The CAE networking services are standardized at the Transport Layer (layer 4) interface. This allows support of LANs, WANs, and MANs. The OSI Transport Layer protocols, the TCP, and the UDP protocols are supported.

Future guides will be issued every few years as new standards are introduced. In addition to the X/Open Portability Guides, X/Open has published documents on "Security: Auditing and Authentication," "X/Open Systems Management: Reference Model," and "The X/Open Reference Model for Distributed Transaction Processing." These and other documents listed in Table 9.4 are suggested for the interested reader.

9.5 Examples of Vendor-Based Architectures for Distributed Computing

Many vendors have been announcing architectures for distributed computing, such as the following:

- IBM's System Application Architecture (SAA)
- DEC's Application Integration Architecture (AIA) and Network Application Support (NAS)
- Sun Microsystems' Open Network Computing (ONC)
- NCR's Open Cooperative Computing Architecture (OCCA) and Top End
- HP's Distributed Application Architecture (DAA)
- Software AG's Integrated Software Architecture (ISA)
- Data General's Distributed Application Architecture (DAA)
- Microsoft Corporation's Windows Open Services Architecture (WOSA).

These architectures are significant because they play a major role in the industrial adoption of open systems. We review two major architectures: IBM's SAA and Digital's NAS.

9.5.1 IBM's System Application Architecture (SAA)

IBM's System Application Architecture (SAA), announced in 1987, was one of the first industrial efforts toward application portability and interoperability, albeit within

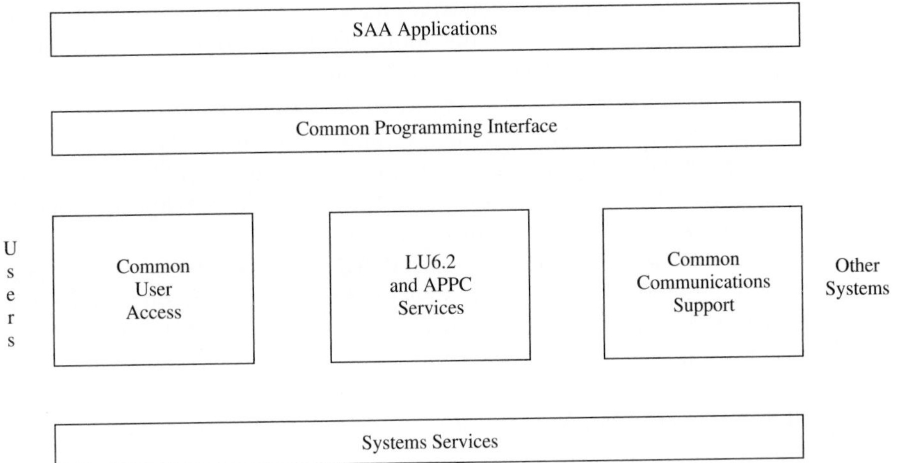

FIGURE 9.13 Systems Application Architecture (SAA)

IBM environments. SAA was announced by IBM primarily to consolidate IBM's product lines on its mainframes, minis and microcomputers. Before SAA, IBM's products were not portable and/or interoperable across IBM mainframes, minis and PCs. The basic System Application Architecture provides a series of standards which apply to the corporate business world. The standards include common user access, programming languages, database accesses, local and remote file accesses, communication protocols, etc. Figure 9.13 shows the basic architectural components of SAA. Examples of some of the most important standards are:

- Common programming interfaces which include ANSI Cobol, Fortran and C programming language and SQL database manipulation language. In addition, a cross services product (CSP) allows programs written on one IBM machine to generate the code for another. In the case of database management systems, SQL is the primary database access language. A user can access local as well as remote data by using SQL. In addition, a user can access local and remote files through what IBM calls a distributed data manager. For dialog management, a product called EZ-VU is available.
- Common user access which defines standard program function (PF) keys for all system access (logon, logoff, help, session end, page up, page down, etc.). This allows a common user access to all of its systems.
- Common communications support based on SNA with APPC, LU6.2, PU2.1, SDLC, token ring, X.25 and SNADS support of DCA and DIA. SAA also supports OSI protocols like FTAM and X.400.
- System services provided by the operating systems of mainframes, AS/400 minicomputers and PS2 personal computers.
- Netview and System View are the main management vehicles in SAA.

Several common applications on SAA have been promised but not all of them are available. Examples of some of the applications that conform to the SAA standards are DISSOS for office automation and Netview for network management.

The main focus of SAA has been on portability. Theoretically, a user can build an application on one SAA compliant computer and run it on another SAA compliant computer. Details about SAA can be found in <Wheeler 1988>. Interested readers should review the *IBM Systems Journal*, Vol 27, No. 3, 1988, Special Issue on Systems Application Architecture for more details on SAA.

In February 1990, IBM announced AIX (IBM's version of Unix), on its RISC processors RS600. The significant aspect of this announcement is that SAA and AIX are expected to coexist. The main features of the AIX/SAA interoperability and interconnection are as follows:

- SQL DBMS for database access
- C, Cobol, Fortran code
- LU6.2, TCP/IP and OSI protocols for communications
- XWindow for user interfaces
- Ethernet, token ring, X.25 for network interconnections.

SAA has been mainly applicable to the corporate and business operations with little impact on plant floors and engineering offices. AIX has opened the Unix and TCP/IP market to IBM. In addition, specific architectures for specialized industries are being integrated into AIX and SAA. For example, Design Automation Edition (DAE), a factory floor architecture, is being integrated into other proprietary and open system architectures. DAE will support OSI and OSF's DCE (see Section 9.6 for a discussion of DCE). DAE will be extended to include support for MVS and AIX. This will include AIX clients serviced by OS2 servers and vice versa.

IBM's corporate strategy appears to be to integrate SAA/AIX into the open standards such as OSI and Open Software Foundation's DCE. IBM has initiated an Open Systems Project which attempts to integrate non-IBM and non-SAA products into a single framework <Scannel 1991>. An "Open Distributed Computing (ODC)" framework has been announced which includes common network services (SNA, TCP/IP, OSI, NetBIOS and Novell IPX), system services (remote procedure calls, directory, security, time), resource managers (file servers, print servers, database servers, transaction managers, etc.), and application development and management services. This framework conforms to OSF DCE. The focus of ODC seems to be interoperability and not necessarily portability, a departure from SAA. Many ODC compliant products are expected to become available in the next few years.

It seems that MVS to Unix interconnectivity is a major area of future focus in SAA, AIX and ODC. For example, the AIX/RS6000 presence in the engineering offices is increasing Unix-based applications on IBM computers. In addition, TCP/IP is becoming an important product in the IBM world. OS/2, AIX and MVS currently support TCP/IP. The ODC framework allows TCP/IP direct access to IMS and DB2 databases. IBM is making improvement in NFS to improve the MVS to Unix interconnectivity. Finally, MVS is being tuned to operate as a backend server <Snell 1992>.

9.5.2 Digital's Network Application Support (NAS)

DEC's open strategy is based on its Network Application Support (NAS) environment in which heterogeneous clients and servers can communicate with each other (see Fig. 9.14). Through this strategy, DEC provides a multivendor integration platform. NAS architectural components use the following ingredients:

- Open client/server computing
- Application Integration Architecture for portable applications in DEC environments
- Interconnectivity technologies and arrangements with other vendors.

Network Application Support (NAS) is a collection of standards for distributed applications in a multivendor environment. It is expected to make a multivendor, distributed computing environment function as a single, integrated unit. The architectural components of NAS are as follows:

- *Applications*: These consist of the processing logic represented in some programming language. The applications use the Application Integration Architecture (AIA) described later.
- *User interfaces*: These specify graphical user interfaces (GUI) such as XWindow and character based user interactions.
- *Data management*: These services include remote data access and file sharing in a network. A Distributed Database Architecture (DDA) defines a global relational database which includes access to data residing in databases on different computers created by different vendors.
- *Communication services*: These are based on Digital's Network Architecture (DNA) which supports communication services such as X.25, Ethernet, ISDN, and OSI protocols. Gateways to other network architectures such as SNA are provided.
- *System services*: These are standardized around Posix.

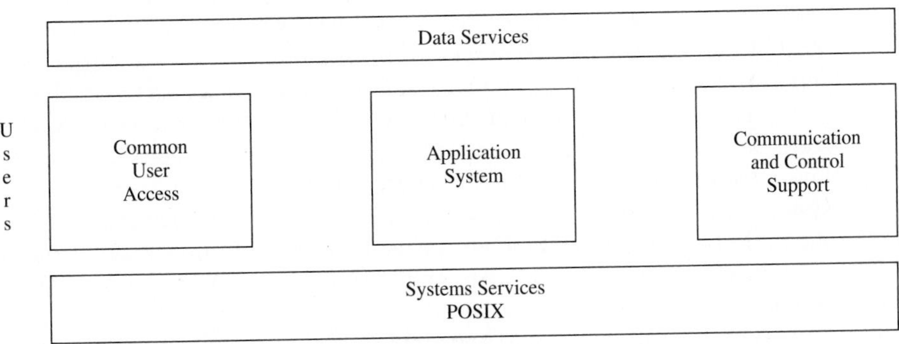

FIGURE 9.14 Digital's Network Application Support (NAS)

- *Management*: The Enterprise Management Architecture (EMA) defines an open model for managing networks and devices.

DEC has introduced a family of open servers to support NAS. These servers, called the VAXserver family, can run on any of the VAX machines to provide the following services:

- *PC LAN servers*: These packaged servers integrate PCs into corporate networks by providing sharing of data, applications and other resources scattered around on a LAN. These servers are marketed as PATHWORKS server packages which follow the Digital's Personal Computing System Architecture. Examples are PATHWORKS for DOS and VMS.
- *Compute servers*: These servers let various clients access high performance vector and parallel processors. An example is the VAX Supercomputer Server which allows a family of VAX supercomputers to be used by clients residing on workstations and PCs.
- *Information servers*: These servers provide shared access to databases, documents and information repositories. Examples are the Database Server for relational SQL databases and the Infoserver 100 which provides CD-ROM, hard disk and magneto-optical disk access to clients over Ethernet.
- *Application servers*: These servers consolidate the common application services (such as word processing) needed by many clients. Examples are the ALL-IN-1 Office Server for documentation and Email, and DECimage Express for conversion of paper-based information into electronic data.
- *Communication servers*: These servers are intended to improve the information flow in organizations. Examples are the ALL-IN-1 Mail Server and the Enterprise Messaging Server.
- *Data integration servers*: These servers contain all the elements included in the Database Server plus the additional software and integration services to provide access to databases on other systems. The databases on other systems may be IBM mainframe data sources such as VSAM, IMS and DB2.

DEC AIA (Application Integration Architecture) is essentially an umbrella architecture. It allows users to mix VAX VMS with non-DEC systems. It includes RISC, Unix, and distributed computing. It strongly encourages a shift to workstations, supports non-DEC systems and is oriented toward a client-server model.

The basic components of AIA are DEC facilities such as VMS, Ultrix, DEC windows, DECNET and SQL and the open interfaces based on OSF (Open Software Foundation). DEC is very heavily reliant on OSF to provide an open architectural system. All AIA interfaces are submitted to OSF and if OSF does not accept them then DEC will adopt the OSF choice as their basic offering. Not all components of AIA are completely defined. DEC is publishing various AIA interfaces and providing training courses in the use of AIA.

Basically, DEC VAX VMS applications have been transportable across all DEC computers. However, DEC needed to consider some architecture to provide independence from VAX. The main motivation for this independence is to support the applications that use ULTRIX (DEC's version of Unix) operating system instead of VMS. The two primary themes of DEC appear to be: interoperability with multi-vendor products and conformance to national and international standards. NAS, active participation in open standards, and numerous gateways are evidence of DEC's continued "open" strategy. It is especially interesting to note that DECNET at present fully supports the OSI Protocol Stack.

9.6 Examples of Consortium Open System Architectures

Many consortiums are being formed to understand and translate the proliferation of standards and vendor architectures into open system products. Two consortiums, Open Software Foundation (OSF) and Unix International (UI), have devoted considerable effort in this area. The result is the emergence of two powerful distributed computing architectures, discussed here, which integrate many of the open system standards and architectures into products. The reader should be warned that, unlike the vendor architectures such as IBM's SAA, the OSF and UI architectures are in their early stages of development. Most of the information discussed next is extracted from the consortium documents, seminars, and early exposure to the products. Use judgement when the description sounds too glorious.

9.6.1 Open Software Foundation's Distributed Computing Environment (DCE)

The Open Software Foundation (OSF) was formed initially by Unix (non-AT&T) vendors to standardize on Unix that could run on many computers. Many vendors, including IBM, DEC and Hewlett-Packard, are participating in OSF. A non-profit company, OSF has gone through many changes in the past few years. While the initial focus of OSF has been on standardizing Unix, it realized that a standardized Unix is not enough to provide transportable distributed applications across computers. OSF is especially concentrating on interoperability between multiple products from multiple vendors. For example, part of applications may reside at mainframes, at Unix minicomputers or OS/2 workstations. The main focus is on distributed cooperative processing and on standards to help connections at many levels.

OSF has proposed a Distributed Computing Environment (DCE) which provides such an environment (see Fig. 9.15). The applications are at the highest level and the OSI transport services are at the lowest level in DCE (at present, DCE uses the TCP/IP transport services). The security and management functions are built at various levels so that one component is not responsible for these two crucial functions. The distributed file access to access remotely located data, naming services for accessing objects across the network, and remote procedure calls (RPCs) and presentation services are at the core of DCE. DCE allows for growth of future services, which will be enabled as future technologies become available.

The DCE offering is composed of a set of services which are organized into two categories: Fundamental Services and Data-Sharing Services. These services are provided by the DCE Servers in a network. Fundamental Services include software

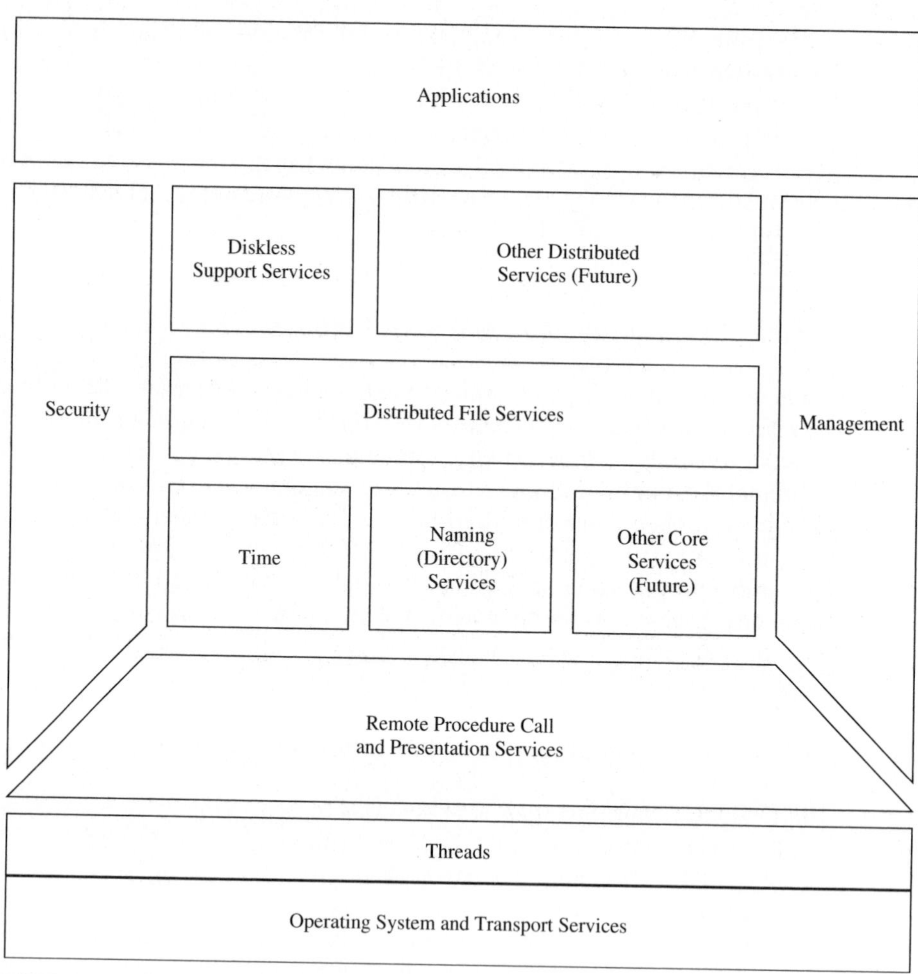

FIGURE 9.15 OSF's Distributed Computing Environment (DCE)

development tools such as RPCs, naming (directory) services, security services, time services, and threads services. Data-Sharing Services provide end user support such as distributed file system and diskless support. These services are built on the Fundamental Services and are integrated into the operating system for use. Figure 9.15 shows how the DCE services are included in the DCE architecture. These services are portable to many computers because they are written in C. The following discussion gives an overview of the DCE services depicted in Fig. 9.15. For additional information, refer to <OSF 1990> and/or consult the OSF documents listed in Table 9.5.

Threads Service. The OSF Threads Service allows application programs to perform many services simultaneously. For example, one thread can be used to issue a remote procedure call while the other can be used to receive input. Each thread is essentially an independent path between a client and a server, thus allowing one client to

TABLE 9.5 Significant Open Software Foundation Documents

- "OSF Distributed Computing Environment Rationale," OSF Document, May 14, 1990
- "Distributed Computing Environment, An Overview," OSF Document, April 1991
- "Remote Procedure Call in a Distributed Computing Environment," OSF White Paper, January, 1991
- "Security in a Distributed Computing Environment," OSF White Paper, April, 1991

These and additional documents can be obtained from

Open Software Foundation
11 Cambridge Center
Cambridge, MA 02142

simultaneously interact with several servers and vice versa. The Threads Service includes operations to create and control multiple threads in a single process and to synchronize global data access. The Threads Service is used by a number of DCE components such as RPCs, Directory, Security and Time Services and the Distributed File System. The main features of the Threads Service are as follows:

- A simple programming method for building concurrent applications. For example, one client can open 5 threads to simultaneously communicate with 5 servers.
- Support for C and other high-level languages
- Transparency of where the threads are executing (one or many processors)
- Threads can be built in an operating system or on top of an operating system.

Remote Produre Call (RPC). OSF's RPC supports direct calls to remote procedures usually on remote systems. RPC presentation services mask the differences between data representation on different computers. This facilitates programs to interact with each other across heterogeneous computers. OSF's RPC provides a compiler that converts high-level interface descriptions of the remote procedures into C source code. The calls to remote procedures behave the same way as local procedure calls. Main features of the OSF RPC are as follows:

- Network and protocol independence by shielding the network transport services from the application programs. Connectionless as well as connection-oriented services are supported.
- Secure RPC communication between clients and servers. Authenticity, integrity, and privacy of communications is guaranteed through integration with DCE Security Service.
- Multiplicity of clients and servers for mutual interactions and location of servers by name. These features are supported by the Threads Service and the Directory Service, respectively, of the DCE.
- Support for large data-processing applications by permitting unlimited argument size and handling bulk data.
- Support of international character sets (e.g., Japanese, Arabic, and Chinese) as specified by the ISO standards.

Distributed Directory and Name Service. The OSF Directory Service allows users to name resources such as servers, files, disks, or print queues, and gain access to them without having to know where they are located in the network. Thus the resource names can stay the same even if their location in the network changes. This also allows scaling of services from small networks to large and vice versa. The main features of this service are as follows:

- Each computer in DCE environment provides directory service. These directories are tied together through X.500.
- Integration of X.500 global naming system with a replicated local naming system. This allows programmers to move transparently from environments supporting full ISO functionality to those supporting only the local naming service. The X/Open Directory Service API (application programming interface) of the Directory Service offers full X.500 functionality.
- Replication of critical data to increase availability and caching of recent lookups to improve performance. Update synchronization mechanisms are provided to assure data consistency.
- Secure communication and authority control through integration with the Security Service.
- Network transport independence by utilizing the OSF RPCs which operate transparently over many LANs and MANs.

Time Service. DCE provides fault tolerant clock synchronization for computers tied together in WANs, MANs and LANs. The Time Service supplies time with a plus/minus range so that close times can be matched. This Service is also integrated with other DCE facilities such as RPCs and Directory Service to locate time servers.

Security Service. The DCE Security Service provides authentication, authorization, and user account management. The basic authentication and authorization is provided by the message corruption detection facility of OSF RPC. In addition, the Kerberos system is used by the Security Service for authentication. The OSF Authorization Tools are well integrated with the Kerberos Authentication System. OSF's User Registery addresses the user account management problems in DCE by maintaining a logical database which contains user IDs, passwords, etc. Following are the main features of this Service:

- The authenticity of requests made across a network are trusted by multiple hosts and operating systems.
- A single repository of user accounts is maintained to avoid conflicts in logins and passwords. This database is replicated across the network for high availability and response.
- Different privileges and authorities are supported.
- Data privacy is ensured through encryption/decryption across networks.

Distributed File System (DFS). OSF DFS makes global file access easy by providing a consistent interface to file systems at individual computers. OSF DFS uses a client-server model to access remotely located files. The main features of OSF DFS are as follows:

- It is based on the Andrew File System but is intended to interoperate with the SUN Network File System (NFS) and other file servers.
- It includes high performance and availability features through file replication and caching of recently used files.
- It is scalable from small users on a LAN to a large number of users across multiple networks.
- It uses OSF's secure RPC and utilizes Access Control Lists for allowing access to appropriate files.

Diskless Support. This support is provided for low cost diskless workstations which need to access disks located on servers. OSF Diskless Support provides well-defined and general-purpose protocols for diskless operations.

Management. A set of management capabilities are included in DCE. These capabilities are bundled with the individual technologies included in DCE. OSF is planning to expand and integrate these capabilities into the OSF Distributed Management Environment (see Chapter 10).

At present, DCE is being developed by active participation of many organizations. It has been deployed on some computers (for example, the Hewlett-Packard 700 Series, IBM RS6000, SUNs). OSF is pricing DCE very competitively and is planning a very wide deployment on many platforms. A process called the Request For Technology (RFT) has been established to introduce new technologies and standards. OSF supports ISO standards, and Internet Standards and is a member of X/Open. In addition, many industrial organizations are active members of OSF. Many vendors, including IBM and DEC, have pledged to include OSF DCE in their environments. There is some controversy on the real impact of OSF due to the potential difficulties of achieving agreement among diverse participants on a large range of issues. The main challenge facing OSF is to balance proprietary versus open systems.

OSF publishes a variety of documents and white papers which explain OSF services and approaches. Table 9.5 lists a few documents. Additional documents can be obtained from the OSF address also shown in Table 9.5.

9.6.2 Unix International's ATLAS for Distributed Computing

Unix International (UI) was formed initially by AT&T Unix vendors to standardize on Unix that could run on many computers. UI has become a large consortium of many users, vendors and standardizing bodies. The UI architectures and frameworks are implemented by the Unix System Laboratory. In 1989, UI announced Unix System V Release 4 (SVR4) as a foundation for open systems. SVR4 essentially merges the AT&T Unix facilities with the Berkeley Unix.

UI-ATLAS is the major offering of UI in open distributed computing. It encompasses enterprise-wide systems by integrating corporate computing, desktop computing and distributed computing. Figure 9.16 shows the five-layered architecture of UI-ATLAS. In addition, two pervasive groups address the security and interoperability at all layers. For each layer, a complete set of application programming interface (API) is specified. ATLAS is based on established technologies such as Unix System V Release 4, TCP/IP and OSI network architectures, IBM's SAA and DEC's NAS, and OSF DCE. The stated purpose of UI-ATLAS is to allow users to:

- View any combination of systems as a single entity.
- Integrate existing and emerging technologies.
- Integrate open and proprietary systems.

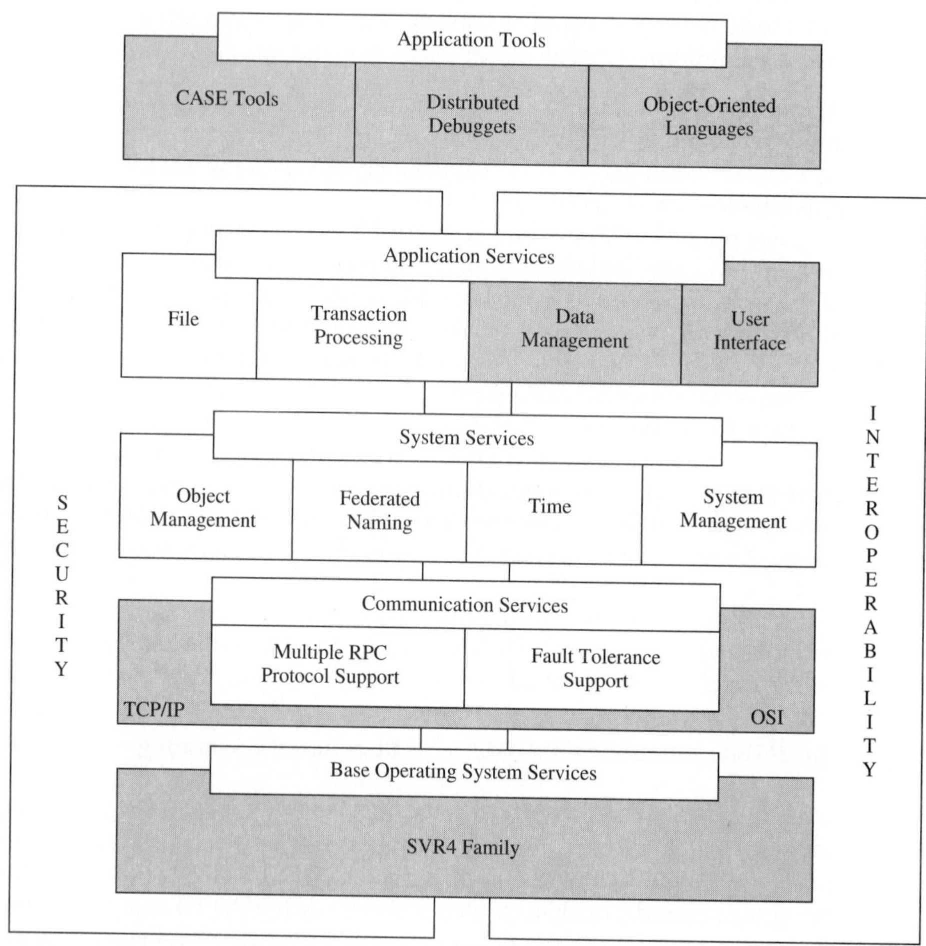

FIGURE 9.16 UNIX International's ATLAS

- Utilize the fullest set of services to manage the network.
- Support development of the next generation of distributed applications.

UI-ATLAS is based on existing and evolving standards (e.g., X/OPEN, Posix, ISO). A distributed object model is used as a foundation to provide transparent global access and processing in a distributed environment. The major layers of the UI-ATLAS, shown in Fig. 9.16, are as follows:

- Base Operating System Services
- Communication Services
- System Services
- Application Services
- Application Tools
- Security
- Interoperability.

These services, described in more detail in the documents listed in Table 9.6, are briefly reviewed here.

Base Operating System Services. Base Operating System Services integrate major variants of Unix systems around the Unix System V Release 4 (SVR4) family. Unix SVR4 is portable across many computers and is upward compatible from many existing releases of Unix. The base operating systems are scalable across computers from PC to mainframes. This is accomplished through a scaled feature set according to computer capabilities and support of multiprocessor implementations. For example, smaller machines can choose fewer features, which can be increased gradually as the machine adds more capabilities.

Communication Services. ATLAS Communication Services support existing and emerging network standards such as TCP/IP and OSI. The main features of these services are:

- Transport independence by supporting OSI and TCP/IP transport services. TCP/IP support includes Telnet, File Transfer protocol (FTP), Domain Naming Services, Simplified Mail Transfer Protocol (SMTP) and Simplified Network Management Protocol (SNMP). The OSI support includes X.400 mail, X.500 Directory Services, CMIP Management Protocol, FTAM and Virtual Terminal.
- RPC independence through an Interface Definition Language (IDL) which can be compiled into different RPC protocols such as the SUN RPC and the OSF DCE RPC. The OSI RPC will be supported as it develops. Multiple RPCs are supported so that a user can choose a suitable RPC facility. This allows the users to build distributed applications independent of one RPC. (There is some question as to the real details of this. For example, it is not clear that ATLAS clients or servers will interoperate with DCE clients and servers.)

- Fault tolerance through replication of services. ATLAS provides high availability through redundant objects which can be viewed consistently and recovered automatically from failures.

System Services. System Services provide the basis for a single image in a distributed environment through object management, composite naming service, time synchronization, and system management.

- The object management system provides a management framework and tools for static and dynamic invocation of services across diverse systems. ATLAS utilizes an object model to provide naming and management services. This model is based on the standards being developed by the Object Management Group (OMG).
- The composite (federated) naming service gives the users choices among a variety of directory services such as X.500, Internet Domain Name Services, NIS (previously known as the Yellow Pages), Cell Directory Services, and specialized name spaces such as files, databases and spreadsheets. The ATLAS naming services integrate these autonomous naming systems into a loosely-coupled federation for object naming anywhere in the network.
- The distributed time synchronization service allows variable as well as constant error bounds across networks. The constant error time service, called Class 1 service, synchronizes the local system clock with Coordinated Universal Time Clock within a small constant error bound. The variable time error bound, called Class 2 service, is also used in OSF DCE time services.
- The system management services provide a variety of services for backup/recovery, system initialization/shutdown, software installation, object definitions, and management of resources such as printers, user profiles and network elements. Network management in UI-ATLAS includes OSI based CMIP and TCP/IP based SNMP network management protocols. ATLAS uses distributed object management to manage the complex and multivendor environment.

Application Services. Application services support transparent file access across heterogeneous systems, distributed database management, distributed transaction management, and consistent user interfaces across multiple computers. The distributed file system, based on NFS, supports data replication in LAN/WAN environments, data caching for recently accessed data, and global naming across multiple systems. The distributed database management supports SQL access across multiple computers with DBMS from different vendors. The DDBMS complies with the X/Open standards. The distributed transaction manager coordinates the execution of distributed transactions and maintains data integrity in a heterogeneous environment. At the time of this writing, UI-ATLAS supports TUXEDO and TOP END Distributed Transaction Management Systems. The user interface supports multiple standards such as Motif and Open Look. These standards are used in an object-oriented desktop manager.

Application Tools. Application tools provide a complete application development environment. This includes distributed object oriented languages such as C++ for object based distributed applications. A computer aided software engineering (CASE) is envisioned to support all phases of distributed applications. This environment is supported through standard libraries and data formats.

Security. UI-ATLAS provides corporate wide security which conforms to government standards. The security is built on top of the secure and modular Unix SVR4 base. A desirable security environment can be configured from a wide variety of packages which support authentication, confidentiality, integrity, digital signature, access control, and encryption. Notice that security is implemented at each layer of UI-ATLAS (Fig. 9.16).

Interoperability. The interoperability services attempt to minimize the impact of the existing base with newer technologies at personal computers, mainframes and departmental computers. As shown in Fig. 9.16, interoperability is required at all levels from network protocols to applications. For example, UI-ATLAS network services support OSI, TCP/IP, SNA, X/Open Distributed Services, and PC Networking. System services include IBM SAA mainframes, departmental computers such as IBM AS/400, DEC NAS machines and DOS/Macintosh's PCs.

In short, the UI-ATLAS environment includes a comprehensive set of facilities for distributed computing. Inclusion of other architectures such as OSF DCE, IBM's SAA and SUN's ONC is especially worth noting. UI-ATLAS includes OSF DCE, thus protecting the investment of users in OSF DCE. It also encompasses corporate mainframe computing which is a weakness in many Unix-based solutions. The Unix workstation users are protected through inclusion of SUN's ONC. A UI Roadmap, listed in Table 9.6, is published in January of every year by UI to show what features will be implemented when by UI.

The heavy utilization of object-oriented technology is a particularly interesting feature of ATLAS. The object model views the entire distributed computing environment as a collection of objects where each object provides a service. For example, each file, printer, and spreadsheet is viewed as an object. The service is defined by an interface, which consists of a set of operations. A requester of the object service is called a client; the object providing the service is called a server. Object interfaces are defined by using the Interface Definition Language (IDL) which can be translated

TABLE 9.6 Main UNIX International ATLAS Documents

- UI-ATLAS Distributed Computing: An Introduction
- UI-ATLAS Distributed Computing Architecture: A Technical Overview
- UI-ATLAS Availability Schedule
- UI-ATLAS Systems Management Requirements: An Overview
- DCE Functionality in UI-ATLAS; A Perspective, June 1991
- Background—UNIX International: Overview
- UI 1991 System V Roadmap

These and additional documents can be obtained from

Unix International, Inc.
20 Waterview Blvd,
Parsipanny, NJ, 07054

into different programming language code, operating system calls and communication services for actual communication. This model conforms to the OMG Model and is described in detail in the UI-ATLAS technical overview document (see Table 9.6).

A major concern about UI-ATLAS is that it promises to do everything for everyone. This may result in an expensive, slow and clumsy product. We will have to see how it all works.

9.7 Analysis of Open System Architectures

Many questions are fundamental to the analysis of open systems: Why so many different approaches to open systems (why not one?), what is the impact of open systems on application architectures, and what is the down side of open systems (if any)?

Figure 9.17 shows a Venn diagram of the various architectures discussed in the previous sections and Table 9.7 lists the main characteristics of the dominant architectures. The features in Table 9.7 include application systems, application support services (RPCs, directory services, security, management and distributed data), network services and operating systems/hardware.

It can be seen that there are several areas of commonality as well as differences. Some of the services that are already common across most distributed systems architecture standards are as follows:

- C, Cobol, Fortran for programming languages
- SQL for local and remote database access
- XWindow and Motif for user access
- X.500 for directory services
- SNMP and CMIP for network management
- TCP/IP and OSI protocols for network transport
- Ethernet, token ring, X.25 for network interconnections
- Unix-compatible (e.g., Posix) operating systems.

Although more commonalities are needed for truly open systems, these standards are beginning to impact the development of distributed applications. The main impact of these standards is that the task of developing distributed application architectures is greatly simplified. For example, an architecture can be developed to best satisfy the user needs without having to be restricted by the vendor offerings. The following simple example, based on my personal experience, will illustrate this point.

In the early 1980s, I was responsible for developing a relatively small application. The application was simple but there was only one complication—we were not sure if the application was a mainframe or PC application (IBM PCs were just becoming popular at that time). This gave us a major headache; the mainframe applications were developed in Cobol and IMS; the PC applications could not be developed in Cobol and IMS (Cobol compiler and IMS data managers

a. 1992 View

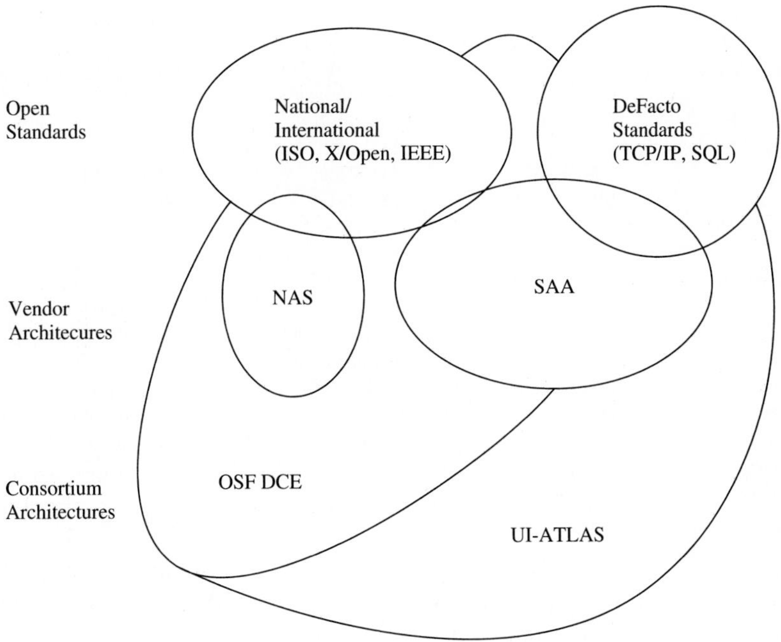

b. Future View (We Hope)

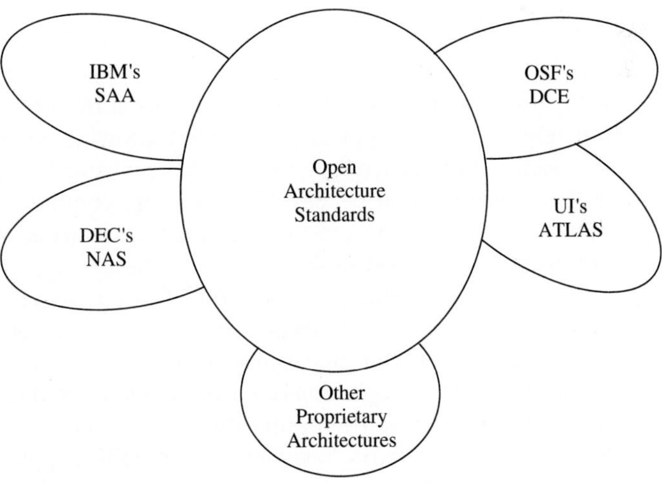

FIGURE 9.17 Relationship between Architectures

TABLE 9.7 Distributed Computing Architecture Analysis (1992)

	OSF's DCE	*IBM's SAA*	*DEC's NAS*	*UI's ATLAS*
Applications Systems Standards				
User Interface	OSF Motif	GDDM X Windows	DEC Windows	OSF Motif, Openlook
Program code	C and other	C, Cobol,	C, Pscal	C and others
Data access	SQL, UNIX, PC files	SQL, MVS file, PC files	SQL, UNIX, VMS files	SQL
Application Support Services				
RPCs	OSF RPC	LU6.2, TCP/IP RPC	SUN RPC, TCP/IP RPC	SUN RPC, OSF RPC
Directory	X.500	Proprietary	X.500	X.500
Distributed data services	OSF DFS	SQL, NFS	SQL, NFS	SQL, NFS
Distributed transaction management	OSF Threads	IMS/ISC, CICS/ISC	Tuxedo	Tuxedo TOP/END
Security	OSF Security	RACF	Kerberos	UNIX-based
Management	Future	Netview	SNMP	SNMP, CMIP
Network Services				
Network transport	OSI, TCP/IP	SNA, OSI, TCP/IP	OSI, TCP/IP DECNET	OSI, TCP/IP
Operating system	Posix, UNIX, OS2, MS-DOS	MVS, UNIX, OS2, MS-DOS AS400	VMS, ULTRIX Posix, OS2	UNIX SVR4
Hardware	Many	309x AS400 PS2	VAX non-DEC	Many

were not available on PCs, PCs had DbaseIII and Pascal compilers). We could not implement the application without knowing where the application was going to reside! Problems of this nature have virtually disappeared because a C and SQL application can be developed on any computer. Although some differences between SQL and C exist on different platforms, 90 percent of the code and design choices are portable across platforms.

The set of standards based on the OSI Model are a leading force in open systems. The other standards discussed above have various degrees of dominance in the industry. It seems that many systems work in Unix to Unix environments. However, true heterogeneous environments which include MVS, Unix and OS/2 are rare. UI's ATLAS is attempting this and will have significant impact if successful. Some of these standards have been accepted by suppliers, others have not. The main reason for the differences is that some standards appeal to one group body and not the others due to

Factors	Choices	
	Proprietary	Open System
Component cost reduction		
Ease of application design and architecture		
Improved performance		
Portability and interoperability		
Diagnostic ease		
Improved vendor support		
Ease of innovation and technology introduction		
Ease of system administration		

FIGURE 9.18 Model for Evaluating Open Systems

- Different views of the standardizing bodies activities
- Different "technical" cultures of the members (Unix world versus the IBM mainframe world)
- Different backgrounds (people from academia not understanding business and vice versa).

Although it is generally accepted that open systems are fundamental to the growth of distributed computing, some criticism should be noted. For example, it is not clear if dealing with too many vendors will be easier than one or two. Many corporations are narrowing down the number of vendors to deal with <Yankee 1990>. In addition, there are questions about the overall system performance, diagnostic ability, vendor support, introduction of latest technology, and administration of systems that are composed of components from many suppliers. Figure 9.18 shows a framework for evaluating the tradeoffs between proprietary and open systems.

It seems that open systems will decrease the component costs and increase common applications that can run on many platforms. In addition, open systems will make the task of development and architecture easier. However, the performance of generalized layered systems versus specialized proprietary systems is an issue. For example, the seven layers of the OSI model have too much overhead for a small three- to four-workstation LAN in a room (this in fact was the reason for introducing MiniMAP which eliminates several layers of MAP). Systems designers also often criticize the standards because they fear that standards will stifle innovation <Nutt 1992, page 22>. For example, a company that is exploring new technology may have to wait a long time for standards—many standards are developed only after a technology matures. Thus it is important to develop architectures and frameworks which allow inclusion of new technologies and standards.

At present, OSF DCE and UI ATLAS are especially focusing on performance and technology innovation by active participation of many vendors and users. Vendor proposed architectures such as IBM's SAA and DEC's NAS are included in these architectures. This protects the user investment because a great deal of money is tied in proprietary systems. This will persist for a while. There is some controversy on the real impact of OSF and ATLAS due to the potential difficulties of achieving agreement on such a large range of issues. The main challenge facing these consortiums is how to balance proprietary versus open systems. Many user groups are being formed to understand the impact of open systems standards <Hayes 1991>. For a user perspective on Open Systems, see <Poole 1991>. <Loven 1989> describes why some corporations are more amenable to open systems.

9.8 Impact on Application Architectures: Bellcore's OSCA™ Architecture

Ideally, open system standards and architectures should minimize the impact of platform and vendor selection/modification on distributed applications. The sequence of activities in an idealized open system would be as follows:

1. Define and analyze application requirements.
2. Develop an application architecture which conforms to the open standards.
3. Choose the target distributed computing platforms and vendors which conform to the standards.
4. Implement the application on the chosen platform.
5. Deploy and operate the application system.
6. Move the application components between computers, if needed.
7. Change platform and vendors if needed.

The most significant aspect of this life cycle is that once an application architecture is chosen based on open standards, the selection and modification of the platforms does not affect the architecture and the implemented application. Thus, an investment in implemented applications is protected despite platform and vendor changes.

The key life cycle activity is the application architecture determination, shown in Fig. 9.19a. It can be seen that too many inputs are involved primarily due to the numerous standards and open architectures we have discussed so far. For large corporations which use many vendor products at different vintages at different sites, several questions arise:

- How can the task of building application architectures be simplified?
- What can the organizations do while open standards are still evolving?
- How can the applications take advantage of existing open standards and architectures?

Figure 9.19b shows an approach in which a corporate group establishes guidelines to simplify the task of application architecture. The approach shown in Fig. 9.19b can effectively provide interoperability, portability, and integration of applications by

a. Current Application Architecture Problem

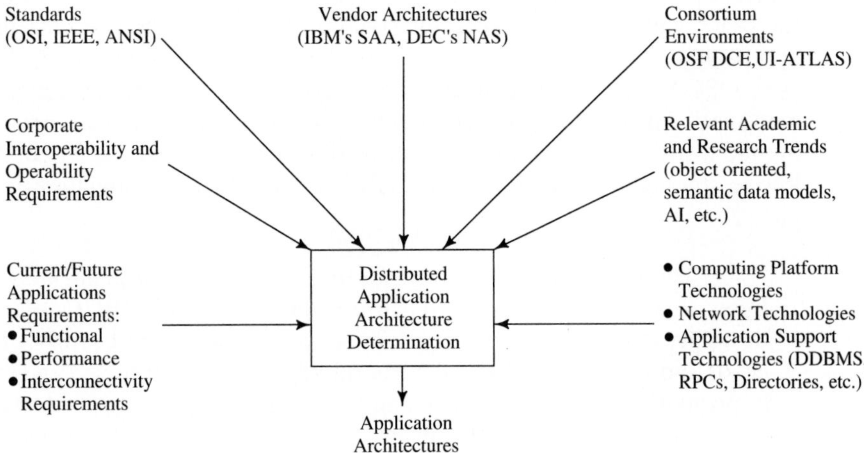

b. Desired Application Architecture Problem

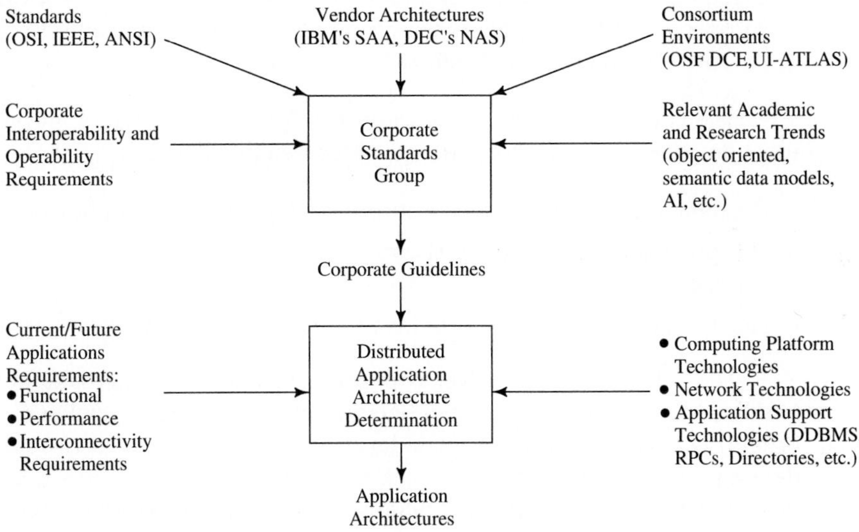

FIGURE 9.19 The Role of Standards in Applicatoin Architectures

imbedding these requirements into the corporate application guidelines. The corporate group could provide overall guidance to the various development groups in an organization. Several organizations are adopting this approach. We briefly describe the Bell Communications Research (Bellcore) OSCA[2] architecture to illustrate this approach.

OSCA architecture concentrates on structuring the application systems (business aware functions) while all other environments discussed so far focus on structuring the distributed computing platforms (business independent functions). The following statements describe the objective of the OSCA architecture <OSCA 1992, page 2>:

> "The OSCA architecture is an *implementation-independent* system design *framework* intended to give Bellcore Client Companies (BCCs) and others the flexibility to combine software products in ways which best satisfy their business needs and to provide access to corporate data by all authorized users. It does this by promoting the interoperability and operability of software products that consist of large numbers of programs, transactions and data bases. *It is not an architecture for programs. Interoperability* is the ability to interconnect business aware software products irrespective of their suppliers and vintages, to provide access to corporate data and functionality by any authorized user, and to maintain that interconnection and access over changes in suppliers and vintages. *Operability* is the ability to efficiently and cost effectively manage and control the deployment, administration, execution, and user access of a loosely coupled collection of software products, irrespective of their suppliers, to meet the performance, availability, reliability, and security objectives of the business."

The OSCA architecture, shown in Fig. 9.20, requires that application systems functions be separated (grouped) into three functional layers:

- The data layer, which shows the corporate data management functionality
- The processing layer, which shows the business aware operations and control functions
- The user layer, which reflects human interaction functionality.

The software in each layer is partitioned into "building blocks" where each building block implements a set of functions related to that layer. For example, in an order processing application, a data layer building block may manage the customer data, a processing layer building block may represent the customer account verification procedure, and a user layer building block may support the interaction of the company representative with the customer. The building blocks must adhere to specific principles, and the interfaces provided by building blocks for other building blocks are well-defined and well-formed (called "contracts"). As shown in Fig. 9.20, many building blocks (BBs) work together in each layer of an OSCA architecture compliant application.

[2]OSCA is a trademark of Bellcore, Inc.

General Building Block Principles:

A. Release independence
B. Infrastructure and resource independence
C. No accessibility assumptions between building blocks
D. Execution in only one recoverable domain
E. Location independence
F. Interactions among building blocks are defined by contracts
G. Secure environment

Contract Principles:

A. Use of standards
B. Restricted set of syntax encodings
C. Isolation from building block internals
D. Release independence
E. Equality of invocation
F. Well-defined interfaces
G. Location independence
H. No contract accessibility assumptions
I. Recognition of authorized humans and building blocks
J. Minimum trust of invoker
K. Maintain identity of invoking human and building block
L. Security audits

DLBB Principles:

Each DLBB must adhere to all of the general building block principles. Each DLBB not part of a cooperative set or each set of cooperating DLBBs:

A. must contain *only* the functionality enumerated in these principles and guarantee support of its contracts over internal changes (separation);
B. must provide sufficient and necessary access so that any piece of data that it stewards need only be updatable and readable via the stewarding DLBB (sufficiently);
C. must allow ad-hoc retrieval of *all* corporate data that it stewards for *all authorized* building blocks via contracts supporting an implementation-independent information model using an industry accepted standard query language; may provide other appropriate predefined retrievals or ad-hoc retrieval access (or both) to any shared redundant data that it has (openness);
D. must ensure the semantic integrity of the data that it stewards; must support inter-DLBB semantic integrity; must maintain well-defined consistency requirements between any shared redundant data that it has and the corresponding stewarded data; and must ensure that the semantic integrity of the shared redundant copy is maintained (semantic integrity);
E. must provide means whereby updates to the corporate data that it stewards can be passed to building blocks having redundant copies of that data; and must *not* propagate updates received from the steward for any of its shared redundant data to other building blocks (managing redundancy).

A DLBB adheres to redundancy management principles:

1. Cooperatively stewarded data or shared redundant data should be used wherever applicable and practical, and in preference to private redundant copies.
2. The stewarded data is assumed to be the correct data.
3. Only updates made to the stewarded data are valid updates.
4. Shared redundant copies are obtained only and directly from the steward.
5. A shared redundant copy does not propagate updates to other private redundant or shared copies.
6. Updates to a shared redundant copy are made only by the steward.
7. A private redundant copy requiring automatic updates must be obtained from the steward; otherwise a private redundant copy may be downloaded from a shared redundant copy.
8. The building block having a redundant copy is responsible for its copy.

PLBB Principles:

A. A PLBB contains any functionality that cannot be construed as infrastructure, data layer, or user layer functionality, and guarantees support of its contracts over internal changes (functionality).

ULBB Principles:

A. Any business aware function that supports interaction with the user, or the understanding of the user and the user's work that is required to support interaction with the user, belongs in a ULBB, and only those functions are allowed in a ULBB (interaction with a human).
B. A ULBB must support the separation of human interaction activities from all other activities (separation).
C. Every ULBB must provide the following *required functionality* (required ULBB functionality)
   - translation of user goals and tasks;
   - presentation structuring;
   - user identification and authentication; and
   - authorization of ULBB services.
D. Functions that provide users with additional flexibility and control during user interactions are *additional functionality* and, when present, they must reside in a ULBB (additional ULBB functionality).
E. A ULBB does not steward any corporate or shared redundant data (private data only).
F. A ULBB may provide contracts that offer user layer business aware functionality but do not presume the human presentation or form. (user layer contracts).

Infrastructure Principles:

A. business independence;
B. release independence;
C. infrastructure and resources independence;
D. location independence and logical addressing for inter-system infrastrucure interface
E. no accessibility assumptions for inter-system infrastructure interfaces
F. isolation from infrastructure internals;
G. no sharability of bound infrastructure;
H. use of standards;
I. equality of invocation;
J. secure environment.

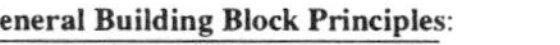

FIGURE 9-20 Summary of OSCA Architecture Principles

Corporate data is viewed as data that is shared across the business processes of a corporation and is partitioned into portions, each of which is *stewarded* by a data layer building block. The corporate data is a corporate resource and is not owned by any DLBB; it can be only stewarded. In addition to the corporate data, each building block may have private data which is not shared and is not visible to other building blocks. Private data may be redundant, permanently stored, or may be working data.

An "infrastructure" provides a platform of generally useful, business independent functions. The infrastructure is synonymous to the distributed computing platform (DCP) discussed in this book. Thus the infrastructure provides functionality such as operating system services, local and distributed data management, directory and naming services, security services, communication services, graphical user interfaces, file transfer/terminal emulation services, etc. The OSCA architecture views the OSCA-based systems as a collection of building blocks and a sharable infrastructure that can be used by many building blocks.

Building blocks and contracts are the major mechanism for applications to interoperate with each other. For example, different BBs may reside on different computers, interconnected through different networks, under different operating systems, and use different database managers. A description of a building block's inputs, outputs, syntax, semantics and pragmatics (e.g., performance and security) unambiguously defines the functions it provides to other building blocks. For a building block to be interoperable, all of its interfaces (and therefore all of its functions) must be documented and fully supported. Other than these interfaces, no building block needs to know the internal logistics of any other building block. Thus a building block can be substituted with another building block with the same interfaces. The functions performed within each building block must show high cohesion with each other and low coupling with the functions of other building blocks. To guarantee interoperability, building blocks must satisfy the following guidelines:

- *Release independence*: Each instance of a building block must be able to be installed and updated without concurrently installing other instances of itself and other building blocks.
- *Infrastructure and resource independence*: Building blocks can share infrastructure and resources as long as no violation of OSCA principles and portability occurs.
- *Unavailability semantics*: Each building block communicating with another building block must be able to respond to the unavailability of the target building block and not itself become unavailable in the process.
- *One recoverable domain*: Each building block is deployed in a single recoverable domain which represents the span of control of a single transaction manager (the transaction manager may be distributed among many computers).
- *Location independence*: Addressable units, such as building blocks and contracts, are identified by logical addresses that are network location independent.
- *Contract independence*: All interactions among building blocks are defined by contracts to attain interoperability. Thus contracts must be defined for general use,

must employ widely used syntax encoding, and infrastructure services used must be based on standards (e.g., OSI or de facto).

- *Secure environment*: A building block must provide a secure environment with full support for authentication and journaling/logging.

All interactions among building blocks are defined by contracts. A contract is the specification of a well-defined set of business functionality and a commitment by the building block to offer that set of functionality to all other building blocks. In other words, a contract specifies how a BB can be invoked by other BBs in an implementation independent format. Thus, even when the underlying computers change, the interoperability is guaranteed through contracts. For example, an inventory control BB may specify at least two contracts: retrieve-inventory-status, and update-inventory-status. The retrieve-inventory-status contract may specify input such as product identification number, and output such as the number of items on stock. The contract does not specify where and how the product information is stored (on a database or a flat file). In essence, a contract is similar to an operation in object oriented systems which adheres to the following principles:

- Use of standards (national, international, and industrial) to specify the contracts
- Isolation from the internals of a building block which provide the contract
- Independence from releases so that changes to a contract are minimized and properly notified to the contract invokers
- Well-defined interfaces and equality of invocation (i.e., a building block must return exactly the same output for exactly the same input every time irrespective of the invoking building block)
- Logical address of the contract which does not tie the contract to a specific location
- Recognition of authorized humans and other building blocks through authority checking before producing outputs
- Provision of audit trails for security audits.

OSCA architecture combines many of the software engineering principles such as structured and object-oriented design with the current distributed computing technologies. The main idea is to imbed many of the interoperability principles into the building blocks and contracts of each application instead of general guidelines. More information about OSCA architecture can be found in the references listed in Table 9.8.

TABLE 9.8 The OSCA™ Architecture Documents

- *The Bellcore OSCA Architecture,* Technical Advisory, TA-STS-000915, Issue 3, March 1992.
- Mills, J., and Ruston, L., "The OSCA Architecture: Enabling Independent Product Software Maintenance," *Proceedings of EUROMICRO '90 Workshop on Real Time,* June 1990.
- Mills, J., "An OSCA Architecture characterization of Network Functionality and Data," *Journal of System Integration,* July 1991.

9.9 Management Summary and Trends

An open system is a vendor transparent environment in which the users can mix and match hardware and software from various vendors on networks from different vendors. An open system provides interoperability, portability and integration at different levels in distributed computing. Many standards are evolving in different sectors of computing industry. Here are some examples:

- OSI's Distributed Applications Framework/Open Distributed Processing (DAF/ODP)
- Open Software Foundation's (OSF) Distributed Computing Environment (DCE)
- Unix International's ATLAS
- Bellcore's OSCA Architecture
- AT&T's Application Operating Environment (AOE)
- IBM's System Application Architecture (SAA)
- DEC's Application Integration Architecture (AIA) and Network Application Support (NAS)
- HP's Distributed Application Architecture (DAA)
- Software AG's Integrated Software Architecture (ISA)
- Data General's Distributed Application Architecture (DAA)
- NCR's Open Cooperative Computing Architecture (OCCA)

We have reviewed the major standards. Although many differences exist between different standards, with time many of these standards will look the same. Some of the services that are already common across most distributed systems architecture standards are as follows:

- SQL for local and remote database access
- C, Cobol, Fortran programming code
- TCP/IP and OSI protocols for communications
- SNMP and CMIP for network management
- Ethernet, token ring, X.25 for network interconnections
- XWindow for user access
- Unix-compatible (e.g., Posix) operating system.

An important trend is the cooperation between various standardizing bodies.

Problems and Excercises

1. Collect at least three different definitions of open systems. What are the differences and commonalities?

2. If you are the MIS manager of a small company, then what are the advantages/disadvantages of adopting open system standards?
3. Assume that you are the MIS manager of a large international company with over 500 applications which reside on many mainframes, minicomputers, workstations and PCs which are dispersed over 3 continents. What are the advantages/disadvantages of adopting open system standards?
4. What are the differences between interoperability, portability, integration, interconnectivity and transparency. Explain your answer through an example.
5. Review the open architectures described in Sections 9.4 through 9.7. Which one is your most and least favorite. Why?
6. Choose an open architecture which has not been discussed in this chapter and describe it in detail.
7. Propose a framework for evaluating the various open architectures.
8. Outline a transition strategy for moving from current systems to open systems. What factors will you consider in this strategy?

CASE Study: Open Systems for XYZCORP

The management at XYZCORP has just returned from a briefing on open systems. As you know, the company has developed an overall application architecture for computer integrated business. The IMCS (integrated manufacturing control system) application discussed in Chapter 8 case study is an example. After a "brain-storming" session, you have been asked to evaluate the impact of open systems on IMCS. Your specific responsibilities are:

1. List the following requirements for IMCS (keep in mind that different portions of IMCS may be purchased from different vendors):
   - interoperability
   - portability
   - integration
2. Select a target open architecture (OSI, OSF DCE, UI-ATLAS) and then evaluate the decision of moving from the current environment to the future environment (advantages/disadvantages). The current system operates under IBM SAA and Unix, MAP.
3. List the standards that can be used in IMCS to protect the investment in IMCS.
4. Recommend an organizational strategy which will simplify the task of developing IMCS while the standards are still being developed. How does this strategy modify the approach being used to develop IMCS at this point?

Hints About the Case Study

IMCS has very serious interoperability requirements because order processing, inventory control, CAD/CAM, CAPP and FMS applications must interoperate with each other. The portability requirements are perhaps not very serious because the need to move the systems between different platforms is minimal (manufacturing applications will perhaps stay on plant floors and business applications will stay at the corporate headquarters). The need for integration are important because the human effort needed to use the system should be minimized through end-user transparency.

The discussion in Section 9.7 (especially Table 9.7 and Fig. 9.18) should help in analyzing and evaluating the transition from the current to an open environment.

The organizational strategy to reduce complexity can be based on Fig. 9.19b. XYZCORP may develop guidelines based on the OSCA principles. The reader should review the life cycle methodology discussed in Chapter 8 and determine how this methodology will be affected by Fig. 9.19b.

References

Appleton, D., "A Strategy for Factory Automation," *Datamation*, Oct. 1977.

Aulds, S., "Organizing for Integration," *Autofact '88 Proc., SME*, ISBN 0-87263-328-4, 1988.

Black, U., *OSI: A Model of Computer Communications Standards*, Prentice Hall, 1991.

Bray, O., "Integration of Configuration Management, MRPII," *Autofact '88 Proceedings, SME*, 1988, pp. 14.31-14.43.

Campbell, R., "An Architecture for Factory Control Automation," *AT&T Technical Journal*, 1988.

Cameron, D., "OSI: An International Standard for Open Systems," Computer Technology Research Corporation, Charleston, S.C., 1991.

Chappell, T., "A Case Study in Software Systems Integration," *CIM Review*, Spring 1985.

Coulouris, G. and Dollimore, J., *Distributed Systems: Concepts and Design*, Addison-Wesley, 1989.

Crabb, D., "The Truth About Interoperability," *UnixWorld*, Special Report on Unix Networking, 1989, pp. 19-28.

Date, C., *An Introduction to Database Systems*, 5th ed., Addison-Wesley, 1989.

Davis, D.B., "Windows for the Mainframe," *Datamation*, July 15, 1992, pp. 28-34.

DeBoever, L., "Emerging Standards in Connectivity," *Software Magazine*, June 1989, pp. 69-75.

Elliot, S., "Local Area Network Integration," *Autofact '88, SME*, 1988.

Elmasri, R. and Navathe, S., *Fundamentals of Database Systems*, Benjamin-Cummings, 1989.

Hayes, F., "The New Users," *UnixWorld*, July 1991, pp. 76-82.

Hsu, C. and Skevington, C., "Integration of Data and Knowledge in Manufacturing Enterprises: A Conceptual Framework," *Journal of Manufacturing Systems*, Vol. 6, No. 4, 1988.

LaVie, R., "The CIM Integrated Data Processing Environment in the European Open Systems Architecture CIM-OSA," *Engineering Network Enterprise Conf. Proc.*, Baltimore, MD., June, 1988, pp. 1-33.

Lew, W. and Machmuller, P., "A Case Study in Database Integration," *CIM Review*, Winter 1985.

Li, R.K. and Bedworth, D., "A Framework for the Integration of Computer-Aided Design and Computer-Aided Process Planning," *Computers and Industrial Engineering*, Vol. 14, No. 4, 1988, pp. 395-413.

Loven, S., "The Road to Open Systems," UnixWorld, Special Report: International Unix, 1989, pp. 21-26.

Malas, D.E., "Integrating Information Flow in a Discrete Manufacturing Enterprise," *Engineering Network Enterprise Conf. Proc.,* Baltimore, Md., June 1988, pp. 1-113.

Markley, R., *Data Communications and Interoperability*, Prentice Hall, 1990.

Martin, R., "The Standards Test for Portability," *Datamation*, May 15, 1989.

Moad, J., "Contracting with Integrators," *Datamation*, May 15, 1989.

Moad, J., "The New Agenda for Open Systems," *Datamation*, April 1, 1990, pp. 22-30.

Negoita, C., *Expert Systems and Fuzzy Sets*, Benjamin-Cummings, 1985.

Nutt, G., *Open Systems*, Prentice Hall, 1992.

Odrey, N. and Nagel, R., "Critical Issues in Integrating Factory Automation Systems," *CIM Review*, Winter 1986, pp. 29-37.

OSCA, "The Bellcore OSCA Architecture," *Technical Advisory*, TA-STS-000915, Issue 3, March 1992.

OSF Document, "OSF Distributed Computing Environment Rationale," May 14, 1990.

Poole, G., "Interview: Walter DeBacker," *UnixWorld,* June 1991, pp. 83-88.

Ranky, Paul, *Computer Integrated Manufacturing*, Prentice Hall International, 1986.

Rapport, D., "Management Perspective on System Integration," *Business Communications Review*, Nov. 1991, pp. 56-60.

Rashid, R., "The Catalyst for Open Systems," *Datamation*, May 15, 1989.

Rose, M., *The Open Book: A Practical Perspective on OSI*, Prentice Hall, 1990.

Runyan, L., "The Open Opportunity," *Datamation*, May 15, 1989.

Scannell, E., "SAA Under Fire; IBM Starts Open Systems Project," *Info World*, May 13, 1991, p. 1.

Sapronov, W., Hunter, J., and Friend, W., "Legal Pitfalls in Integrated Network Management," *Business Communications Review*, Nov. 1990, pp. 46-50.

Sball, N., "The New MVS: Tuned to Serve," *Datamation*, July 15, 1992.

Southerton, A., "The Basics of Networking Open Systems," *UnixWorld*, Special Report on Unix Networking, 1989, pp. 10-18.

Stein, R.M., "Real-Time Posix," *Byte Magazine*, Aug. 1992, pp. 177-182.

Tucker, M., "Paradoxically Posix," *UnixWorld*, Mar. 1990, pp. 85-92.

Van Nostrand, R.C., "A User's Perspective on CAD/CAM and MIS Integration," *CIM Review*, Winter 1986.

Ward, D., "Using Open Systems Interconnection Standards as the Base for a Comprehensive Distributed System," *Engineering Network Enterprise Conf. Proc.*, Baltimore, Md., June 1988, pp. 1-13.

Wheeler, F. and Ganek, A.G., "Introduction to Systems Application Architecture," *IBM Systems Journal*, Vol. 27, No. 3, 1988.

Wilbur, S. and Bacarisse, B., "Building Distributed Systems with Remote Procedure Call," *Software Engineering Journal*, Sept. 1987, pp. 148-159.

Williams, G., "Integrated Computing Environments," *Datamation*, May 1, 1989.

Williams, G., "Digital's Architectural Gamble," *Datamation*, March 1, 1989.

X/Open XPG, *The X/Open Portability Guide*, 7 volumes, Issue 3, X/Open Company Limited, Prentice Hall, 1989.

Yankee Group Report, "Network Computing," Mar. 1990.

Zlotnick, F., *The Posix.1 Standard: A Programmer's Guide*, Benjamin/Cummings Pub. Co., 1991.

Chapter 10

Management and Support Considerations

10.1 Introduction

So far, we have concentrated on the technical issues of the Distributed Computing Reference Model shown in Fig. 10.1. Let us shift our focus to the management and support aspects of distributed computing (the highlighted area in Fig. 10.1). The purpose of this chapter is to address two major issues:

- How to manage and support the distributed computing technologies (i.e., networks, databases, and distributed applications)?
- How to employ some of these technologies to improve the management processes?

These two topics are of crucial importance because as mentioned in Chapter 1, distributed computing technologies are becoming critical to the survival of most organizations. For example, between 25 and 80 percent of companies' cash flow is being processed through online processing networks <Keen 1991>. Table 10.1 lists other examples. It is naturally important to manage these critical technologies wisely and invest in them as business "insurance."

These technologies can also help in the management process. For example, the computer-communication technologies can help in the organization structure design by developing a location independent organizational structure. In other words, the distributed computing platform *is* the organizational structure. The organizational information and decision flow can change without having to move the people. Another example is the development of system management environments (e.g., Open Software Foundation's Distributed Management Environment) which utilize the capabilities of networks and databases to manage the corporate networks and databases. We will visit these topics in Sections 10.3 and 10.5.

It is important for upper management to provide a vision for the management and support of distributed computing technologies. Once a vision has been stated, continued and active support from top management is essential for materializing a vision. The vision must be clearly defined and doable in the given time frame. As noted by a CEO <Charan 1991>:

> "There is a fine line between vision and hallucination."

To avoid "hallucination," the promises and pitfalls of the changing and evolving underlying technologies in networks, distributed databases, client-server systems, and

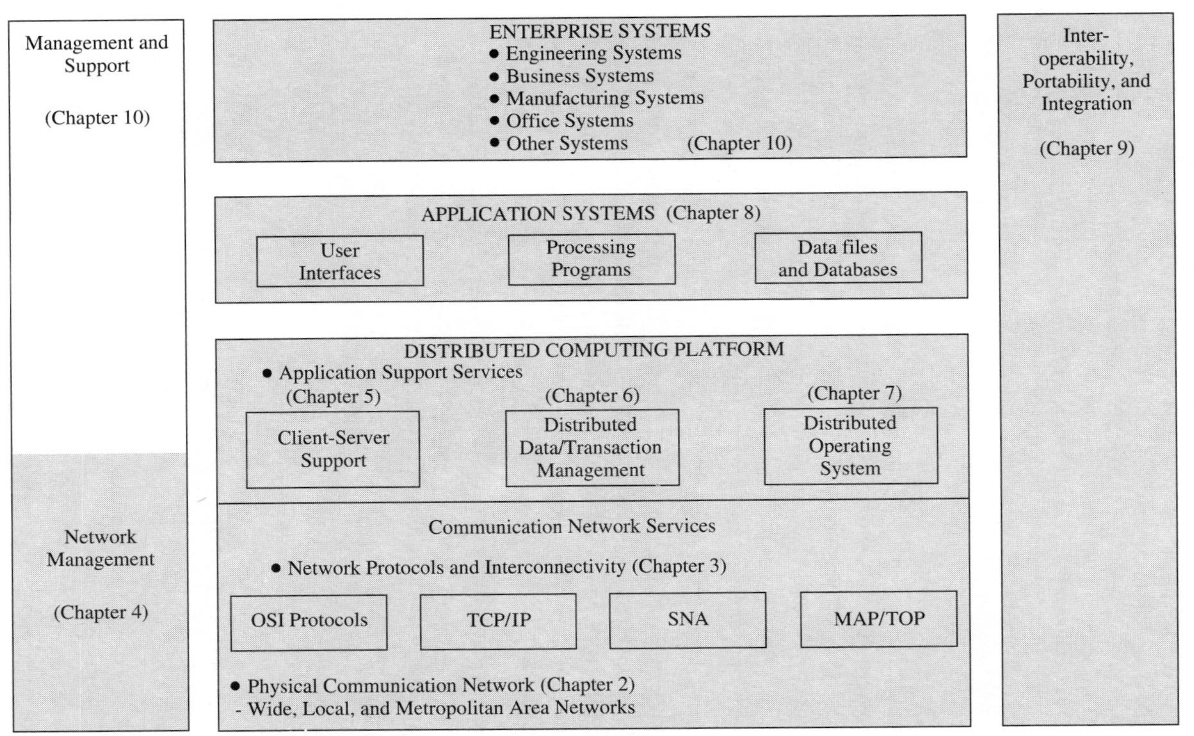

FIGURE 10.1 Distributed Computing Reference Model as Roadmap

TABLE 10.1 Business Realities in the 1990s: Distributed Systems at Work

- $1.5 trillion of financial transactions flowed through New York City's telecommunications systems each day in 1990 (this number is probably higher now).
- When British Airways acquired British Caledonian, the two airlines' operations were meshed over a weekend because they both used the same information architecture and standards.
- EDI (Electronic Data Interchange) has become a "got to have it" technology for eliminating the paper chase of purchase orders, accounts receivable, accounts payable, delivery notices, and so forth. In 1990, the chairman of Sears sent letters to its 5000 suppliers telling them to adopt EDI or be dropped from Sears' suppliers' list.
- Some airlines process ticket orders at about 1500 transactions per second.

Source: Keen, Peter, *Shaping the Future: Business Design Through Information Technology,* Harvard Business School Press, 1991.

distributed application systems must be kept in mind. A quick travel through the well known management cycle of planning, organizing/staffing, development/deployment, and monitoring/control, shown in Fig. 10.2, can be used to solidify visions. In other words, this cycle can be exercised in a small project to develop an understanding of the management processes and the tools needed for distributed computing. The processes of particular interest to us are as follows:

Planning for distributed computing. This process, discussed in Section 10.2, shows how the technologies discussed so far in this book are employed to support corporate visions. Given a business architecture of an enterprise, this process produces a technology architecture which shows the application and network architectures. The objective of the planning process is to exploit the role of this technology to shape a company's future.

Organizing for distributed computing. This process, explained in Section 10.3, produces an organizational structure to support the plan. The centralization/decentralization of organizational activities (e.g., central administration of data, decentralized development) is discussed in this section. As a result of this process, tasks are delegated, responsibilities are assigned, and flow of decisions and information across organizational units is determined.

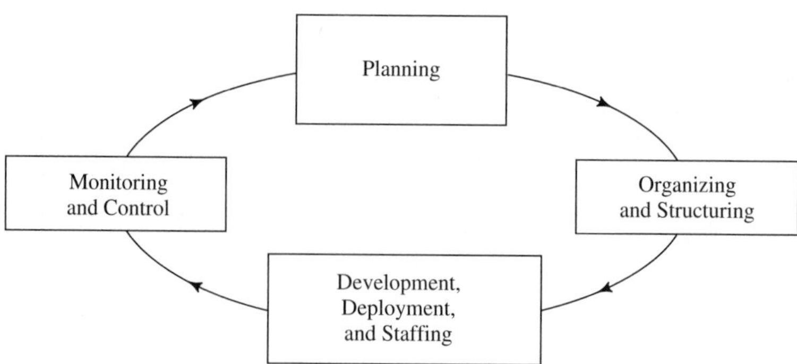

FIGURE 10.2 The Management Cycle

Development and deployment of distributed computing. This process, discussed in Section 10.4, actually delivers the services promised in the planning process. The distributed computing related issues are how to select, purchase/develop and install the diverse array of hardware/software components needed.

Monitoring and control of distributed computing. This process, discussed in Section 10.5, is concerned with the day-to-day administration and support activities needed to assure smooth customer services. These include the tools and environments being developed for distributed systems configuration management, fault management, performance management, security, accounting, etc. Distributed computing introduces the issues of distributed application plus the network management problems.

Section 10.6 illustrates the management processes and associated tools by reviewing a management and support example (XYZCORP, of course).

10.2 Planning for Distributed Computing

10.2.1 Overview of Planning in Enterprises

Planning determines what needs to be done (the objective), outlines the steps and the sequence of steps to accomplish the objective, and lists the time and effort needed to meet the objective. The result of a planning process is a document, a *plan*, which is a repository of information about the approach, the steps, the resources needed and the time frame for an effort. Within this general framework, several levels and types of planning exist in enterprises. Figure 10.3 shows three major levels of planning in enterprises. At the highest level is the enterprise strategic planning which determines the enterprise services to be provided. At the next level, the support services (financial, engineering, manufacturing and application systems) are planned. The resources (facilities, equipments, human and computer-communication systems) needed for the services are planned at the third level. The actual development is conducted at the fourth level. The major planning processes and the interrelationships between the planning processes are displayed in Fig. 10.3 Our main interest is in the information systems related processes (highlighted borders in Fig. 10.3).

10.2.1.1 Enterprise Strategic Planning

The objective of enterprise strategic planning, often simply referred to as strategic planning, is to define and refine the type of business activities an enterprise intends to undertake. Specifically, the type of services and products to be provided to the customers are determined based on external conditions (market conditions, government regulations, economy trends, etc.) and internal conditions (strengths/weaknesses of products and services, staff skills, physical and technical resources available, etc.). As a result of strategic planning, a "business architecture" is developed to define how an enterprise will conduct its business. In most cases, strategic planning is an ongoing process with major periodic revisions (e.g., once a year).

Enterprise strategic planning is specific to the type of enterprise and is beyond the scope of this book. However, information services strategy, which is established

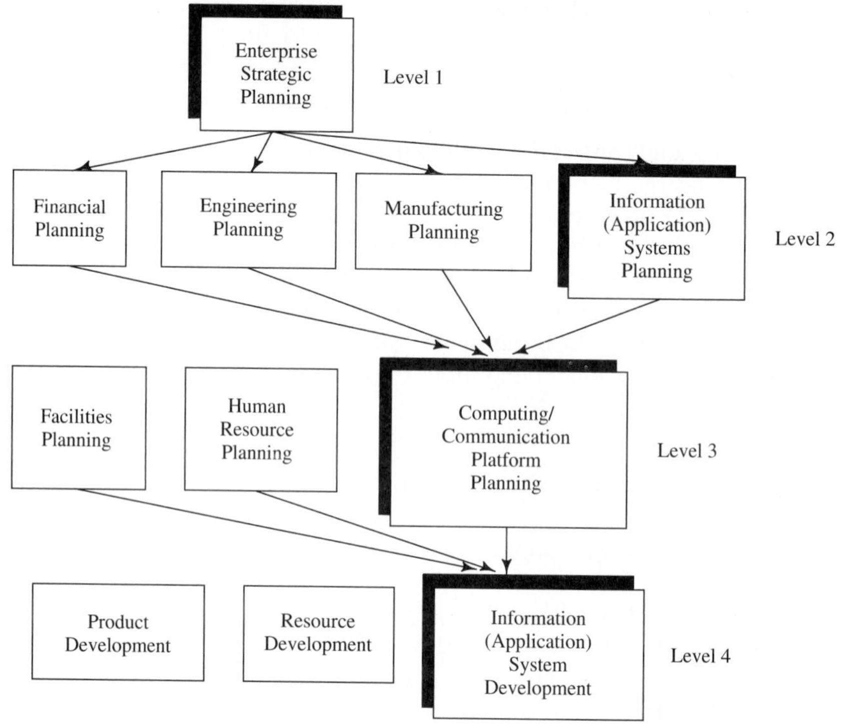

FIGURE 10.3 Planning Levels

in strategic planning, is of particular interest to us. An information services strategy is established to define a short-range and long-range vision of information services in an enterprise. We will discuss this topic in Section 10.2.2.

10.2.1.2 Application Systems Planning

The application systems planning process mainly defines the application systems which satisfy the information services strategy. It also identifies the application system's characteristics in terms of the processes, and data, the required flow of information between the processes, and various response time and application/corporate security restrictions. Several methodologies have been developed for this planning process. Examples of the existing methodologies, also known as information systems planning methodologies, are as follows:

1. IBM's Business Systems Planning <IBM 1978, Zachman 1982>
2. Rockart's Critical Success Factors <Rockart 1982>
3. Nolan's Stage Model <Nolan 1973>
4. Extensions of existing methodologies such as the BSP extensions by Blodgik and Blodgik <Blodijk 1988>, and homegrown methodologies <Highsmith 1987, Hulfnagel 1987, Mushet 1985>.

5. Specialized methodologies and models for particular systems such as the manufacturing information systems <Campbell 1988, LaVie 1988, Jones 1987>.
6. Innovative approaches to plan and design businesses through information technologies. Example is the book, "Shaping the Future: Business Design Through Information Technology," by Peter Keen <Keen 1991>.

There is a need for extension of traditional information systems planning methodologies to handle the additional technical and management issues raised in distributed computing. A major additional decision is the centralization/decentralization of organizational activities as well as the application systems. It is also important to specify the physical sites where the information processing activities will take place. This helps to allocate data, processing programs, and user interfaces. For manufacturing applications, the flow of materials may need to be specified. Examples of the extensions are James Martin's Distributed Application Management (DAM) and Rockarts' Distributed Systems Model <Martin 1985, Rockart 1977>. We will discuss an extended methodology in Section 10.2.2.

10.2.1.3 Platform (Technology) Planning

Platform planning is concerned with determining the most appropriate technology needed to develop and deploy the application systems. This is a crucial activity because computers and communication systems are the basic delivery mechanisms for not only the application systems but also the manufacturing, engineering, and financial services, as shown in Fig. 10.3. Our interest is in distributed computing platforms (DCPs) which, as we already know, focus on the following technologies:

- Computing devices where the application/information systems reside. Examples are microcomputers, mainframes, robots, numerical controllers, cell controllers, automated guided vehicles, CAD/CAM workstations, etc.
- Networks which interconnect the computing devices through a variety of communication devices and communication media.
- System software programs such as the operating systems, database managers, data communications managers, and transaction managers which manage computers and networks so that the users and application programs can communicate with each other.

Examples of DCPs in organizations are research and development networks such as the Internet (an outgrowth of ARPANET); enterprise systems which connect many departmental minicomputers to a host mainframe over wide area networks; factory networks which connect many manufacturing devices to cell and area controllers through broadband cables using, say, the Manufacturing Automation Protocol (MAP); and engineering networks which connect many CAD/CAM workstations on an Ethernet local area network. DCP planning is a much more challenging and crucial task than network planning because the diverse applications in business, engineering, and manufacturing written in different software/database formats which reside on heterogeneous computing devices need to be interconnected through different communication media by using a variety of communication software packages. We will discuss this in the next section.

10.2.2 Enterprise-Wide Information System Planning in Distributed Computing Environments

Let us now synthesize the three levels of planning into an enterprise-wide information system (IS) plan which combines the strategic, application systems and the platform planning into a single procedure. The enterprise-wide IS plan in a distributed computing environment must satisfy the following requirements:

1. Physical network response time, availability, and cost requirements imposed by the end users and management throughout the enterprise.
2. Network growth and interconnectivity requirements between the various computing devices, communication devices, and network transmission mechanisms used in the enterprise.
3. Application interconnectivity requirements, which establish the mechanisms of information exchange between applications at different enterprise sites such as remote logon, file transfer, distributed database management, and cooperative processing.
4. Application functional requirements, which state the things done by the applications being used in different parts of an enterprise.
5. Management control, security, interoperability, portability, and integration requirements to make the applications independent of the underlying distributed computing platforms so that changes in the platforms do not necessitate modifications of the application systems.

Existing literature on network planning primarily focuses on the first two requirements (see, for example, the IEEE Network Special Issue on Network Planning, November 1989; Peck 1988; and the Third International Network Planning Symposium, 1986). Application interconnectivity and interoperability requirements are not commonly discussed in network planning despite their key role in integrated environments. On the other hand, the information system planning literature does not address the first two requirements. This section presents a procedure which can be used to plan the various levels of computing devices, system software, and networks with particular emphasis on interconnectivity and decoupling requirements. This procedure synthesizes high-level strategic requirements with low-level interconnection mechanisms and is based on the Distributed Computing Reference Model shown in Fig. 10.1.

Figure 10.4 shows a high level view of the enterprise-wide IS planning process and defines its interfaces with the individual application system planning and development processes. In practice, the individual application planning processes (already discussed in Chapter 8) need to interact frequently with an enterprise-wide planning unit. This enforces appropriate enterprise-wide information system strategies and policies; ensures conformance to interoperability, integration, and trans-

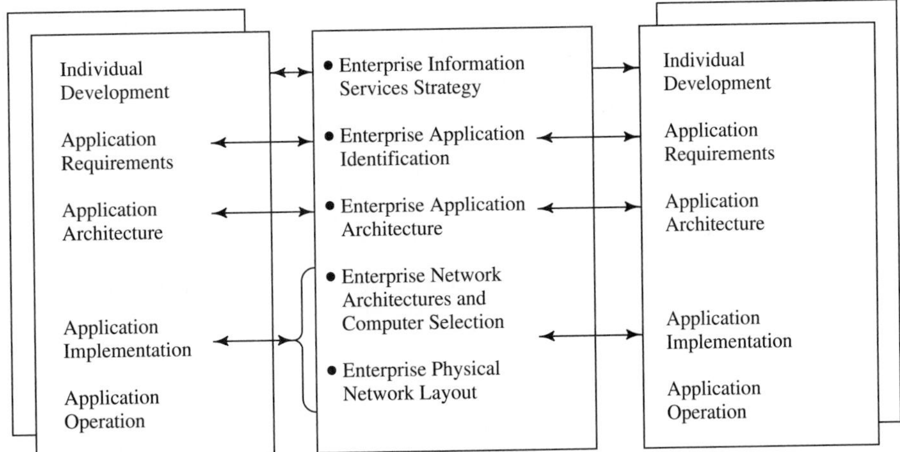

FIGURE 10.4 Enterprise-Wide Information Systems Planning

portability requirements; and takes into account the technical computer and communication platform considerations. The enterprise-wide IS planning may be conducted through a steering committee, a focus group, or a department. The planning group establishes standards (e.g., the open system standards discussed in the previous chapter) and guidelines for interactions between the corporate and individual efforts.

Figure 10.5 shows the stages of the enterprise-wide IS planning process. This process addresses the aforementioned requirements. The IS service strategies and the application system identification address requirements 4 and 5, the application system interconnection is concerned with how the applications will exchange information in an enterprise (requirement 3), and the network architecture planning and physical network address requirements 1 and 2. Sections 10.2.3 through 10.2.8 describe these stages in more detail.

10.2.3 Enterprise-Wide Information Systems Strategy

An information systems strategy outlines the role of information technologies in the business architecture of an enterprise. For example, an enterprise may have the vision to use information technologies as a competitive edge. Typical questions asked in strategic information services planning are as follows:

- Are we doing the right things (i.e., can the information technologies help us to reshape our future, are our information services providing us competitive edge, will they help us to administer our business objectives, will they enable us to adapt to unexpected changes?)?
- Are we doing things right (i.e., are we minimizing the unit costs for each information service, is the value of information service worth the cost?)?

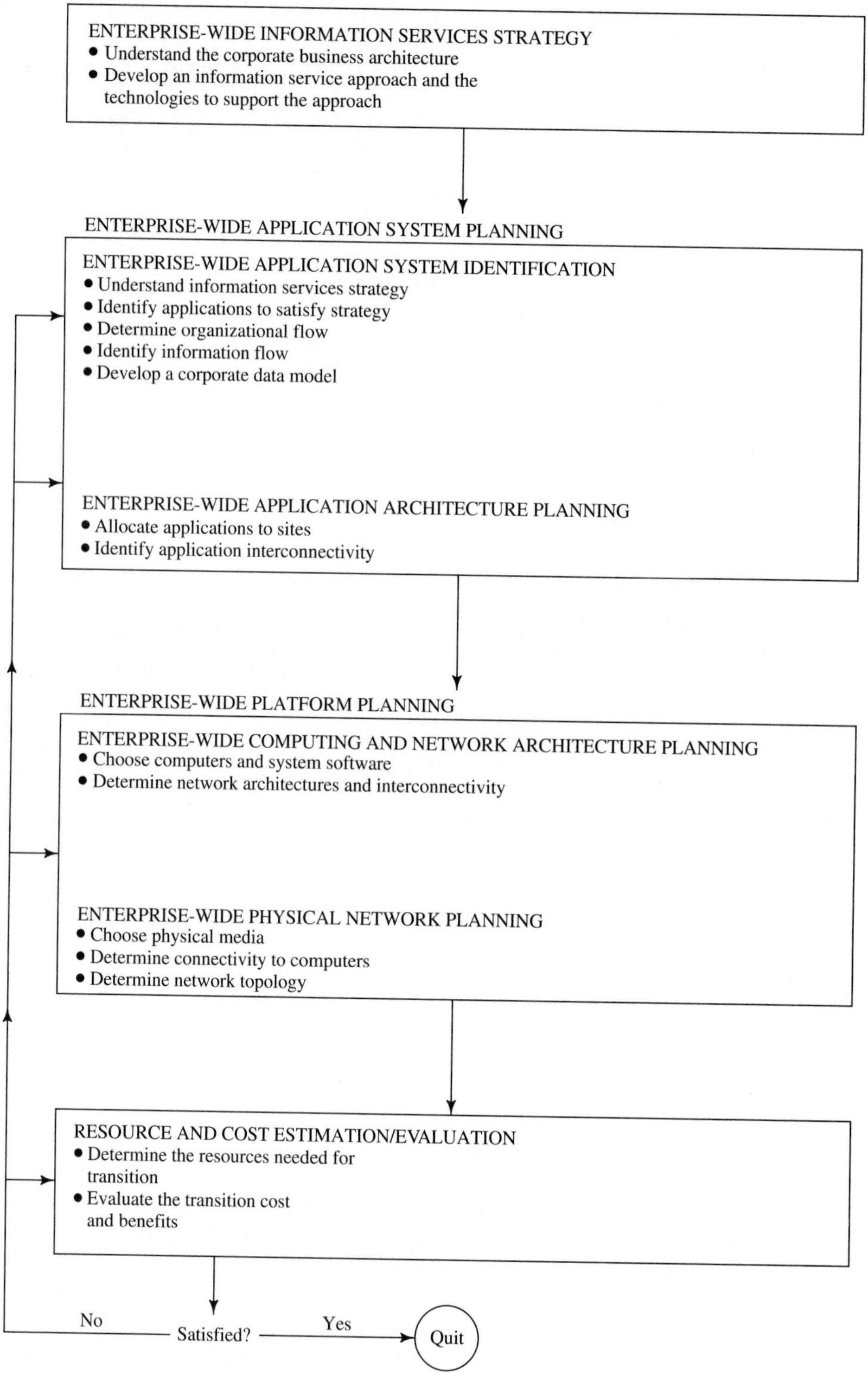

ENTERPRISE-WIDE INFORMATION SERVICES STRATEGY
- Understand the corporate business architecture
- Develop an information service approach and the technologies to support the approach

ENTERPRISE-WIDE APPLICATION SYSTEM PLANNING

ENTERPRISE-WIDE APPLICATION SYSTEM IDENTIFICATION
- Understand information services strategy
- Identify applications to satisfy strategy
- Determine organizational flow
- Identify information flow
- Develop a corporate data model

ENTERPRISE-WIDE APPLICATION ARCHITECTURE PLANNING
- Allocate applications to sites
- Identify application interconnectivity

ENTERPRISE-WIDE PLATFORM PLANNING

ENTERPRISE-WIDE COMPUTING AND NETWORK ARCHITECTURE PLANNING
- Choose computers and system software
- Determine network architectures and interconnectivity

ENTERPRISE-WIDE PHYSICAL NETWORK PLANNING
- Choose physical media
- Determine connectivity to computers
- Determine network topology

RESOURCE AND COST ESTIMATION/EVALUATION
- Determine the resources needed for transition
- Evaluate the transition cost and benefits

Satisfied? No / Yes → Quit

FIGURE 10.5 Enterprise-Wide Information Systems Planning Steps

- Are we heading in the right direction (i.e., are we listening to our customers and paying attention to their information services needs, are we aware of the changing market and government conditions)?
- What are the services we are good at and what are the services we need to improve/ discontinue (are we sinking too much money into older technologies, how confident are we about the new technologies?)?

As a result of these questions, an information services strategy can be established which defines a short range and long range vision of information services in an enterprise. It is the responsibility of management to develop and present a clearly defined and doable vision. Unfounded visions and too many visions ("vision of the day") cause serious problems. Announcing a vision is not enough; continued and visible support from management is essential for the success of a strategy. One possible approach to achieve these objectives is to get the information technology experts involved in strategy formation. These experts can help in making the vision realistic and then work as agents and supporters during the implementation stages.

Developing strategic information services—intended to make a company more flexible, more responsive to customer needs, or more able to adapt to rapidly changing conditions—are fundamentally different from traditional applications developed for expense reduction. A fundamental problem is that there are too many alternatives which are difficult to evaluate. <Clemens 1991> lists the following caveats while evaluating the business case for strategic services, with several case studies to explain these caveats:

1. Rank alternatives even if the ranking is not based on precise values.
2. Work with numbers and use sensitivity analysis to evaluate selected alternatives.
3. Balance many forms of risk and evaluate different approaches to risk management.
4. Actively manage the risk even after the least risky decision is made.
5. Use the technology to leverage the key nontechnological assets of the corporation.
6. Clear competitive edge is difficult to obtain and sustain. It may be better to develop cooperation with other corporations than win-lose situations.
7. Do not forget the down side of strategic systems and do not ignore the long term benefits.

10.2.4 Enterprise-Wide Application System Identification

This stage attempts to translate the information services strategy into specific application systems. Specifically, it consists of identifying the application systems at the enterprise level which can satisfy the information services strategy of an enterprise. For example, this stage would identify the office applications (e.g., voice mail, Email, intelligent documentation retrieval and storage systems, electronic form processing, multimedia systems) to satisfy the vision of a paperless enterprise. In manufacturing enterprises, the applications in business, engineering, and manufacturing are identified to support a computer integrated manufacturing vision.

The identified application systems are defined in terms of the processes, the required flow of information between the processes, and various response time and application/ corporate security restrictions. The application systems identified in this stage are specified in detail later in the application requirement specification phase of the application. This stage essentially identifies the applications which, if approved, are carried through a system life cycle project. Several methodologies have been developed for this stage. Examples are the traditional information systems planning methodologies such as IBM's Business Systems Planning (BSP), Rockart's Critical Success Factors (CSF), and Nolan's Stage Model.

IBM's Business Systems Planning (BSP) is the most widely known and used information system methodology. Gallier <Gallier 1987> quotes a survey which reports that BSP is used 23 percent of the time in organizations. BSP was used by IBM internally and was introduced to customers in the mid-1970s. The main steps in BSP are as follows:

1. Define the organization's business needs and processes.
2. Identify the data classes and applications needed to support the business processes.
3. Chart and analyze how the current applications can meet these needs.
4. Identify and evaluate the new applications that need to be developed.

BSP involves a lengthy procedure in which data is tracked as it flows through various activities (e.g., order processing, inventory control, etc.). The output of one activity is treated as input to the next so that all data flow between all organizational units is studied. BSP generates a large amount of information which can be stored in databases. More information about BSP can be found in IBM 1978, Zachman 1982.

Critical Success Factors (CSF) was introduced by John Rockart at MIT <Rockart 1982>. CSF has been used by many consulting firms and is used by 17 percent of the companies surveyed <Gallier 1987>. The main steps of CSF are as follows:

1. Identify the most critical ingredients of an enterprise which will make the enterprise successful.
2. Define the application systems which will support the critical business functions.
3. Analyze, evaluate, and justify the proposed application systems.

The main difference between CSF and BSP is that CSF points the enterprise toward long-range critical factors without having to analyze all the data and processes.

The Stage Model was introduced by Richard Nolan in 1973 at Harvard and later expanded by the consulting firm of Nolan, Norton and Company <Nolan 1973>. This approach was initially developed to map the growth of the IS (information system) budget over time in relation to the services provided by the information systems. At present, the stage model analyzes the ways in which IS growth affects the information services. This approach compares the stage of each firm with the stages of growth in other similar companies.

In addition to these well-known methodologies, many other methodologies have been proposed <Blodjik 1989, Highsmith 1987, Hulfnagel 1987, Mushet 1985, Campbell 1988, Lavie 1988, Jones 1987>. The traditional requirement definition and analysis techniques are also relevant to this stage <Davis 1982, Davis 1988, Ellis 1988, Zachman 1987>. In addition, the Decision Matrix Approach may be used to build consensus among users with competing requirements <Sheridan 1989>. For distributed computing planning, it is important to specify the various physical sites where the information processing activities will take place.

The following steps generically represent the activities in this stage:

1. Understand the short range and long range critical business needs of the enterprise as stated in the information services strategy.
2. Identify the applications needed to support the business needs.
3. Categorize the needed applications in terms of transaction processing, realtime, integration, organizational level to be used, volume and origin of work, security, autonomy, missions, etc.
4. Evaluate current applications to determine how many new applications will need to be developed and how many existing applications will need to be extended and "revitalized" by using new technologies (i.e., provide multimedia interfaces to existing applications). It may be desirable to determine the applications that may need to be decentralized for better support. This may involve organization politics to assess the effort needed for application conversion (downsizing). This also involves selection of appropriate information technologies, albeit at a high level, which can be used in the future applications.

Which information technologies, in general, can be of key importance for future applications? The answer can vary from corporation to corporation. A careful study by Straub and Wetherbe <Straub 1989> forecasts the dominant technological forces that will affect strategic use of information technologies in the 1990s. The study is based on interviews with 11 experts. These experts synthesize their selections into the following groups:

- The winners, called the "critical information technologies," are human interface technologies and communications technologies. Examples of human interface technologies are speech recognition, voice input, natural language processing, high-end workstations, graphical user interfaces and executive information systems. Examples of the key communication technologies are voice mail, Email, FAX, EDI, ISDN, and LANs. Other technologies, not directly mentioned, in this category can be video conferencing and imaging.
- The technologies with "indirect impact" in the 1990s are CASE, CD-ROM, relational databases, 4GL, prototyping, 32-bit PCs, and hypertext/hypermedia.

- The "limited impact" technologies in the 1990s include expert systems and AI, mainframes and minicomputers, generalized decision support systems, PBX, computerized libraries, calendaring and tickling software, and external database search techniques.

The objective of the study is to help managers focus on the critical technologies. This is their conclusion:

In sum, where management understands the potential of these high return information technologies and takes steps to implement them, they will be able to respond more proactively to the expected turbulence and functional fragmentation of the 1990s.

10.2.5 Enterprise-Wide Application Architecture Planning

This stage is concerned with the following major decisions: (1) assignment of organizational responsibilities to oversee the actual implementation of application systems identified, (2) allocation of applications to the sites of the enterprise, and (3) interconnection between the applications so that information between applications can be exchanged for enterprise-wide integration. As shown in Fig. 10.5, the main inputs to this stage are the application descriptions and the organizational site planning specified in the previous stage. The output produced by this stage shows the various organizational sites where the end users will submit requests, the sites where the programs and data will reside and how the information between the various sites will be exchanged. We discussed the details of distributed application architectures in Chapter 8. Here we highlight and recap the main points from an enterprise-wide management point of view.

The major issue in this stage is the centralization/distribution of the application system components <Pratt 1985>. This issue, discussed in Chapter 8, is also referred to as "downsizing of applications" if centralized applications are moved to minicomputers and workstations. The applications to be centralized/distributed/downsized can be shop floor control systems, office automation systems, business data processing and/or engineering CAD/CAM systems <Mcleod 1986, Malas 1988, Bray 1988, Ranky 1986, Appleton 1977, Dove 1988>. As discussed in Chapter 8, the management advantages of application system distribution across workstations, minicomputers, and mainframes are as follows:

- *Strategic factors*. Customers, suppliers, and companies can be tied together to give the companies competitive edge.
- *Flexibility and configurability*. Performance and reliability can improve through redundant data and processing.
- *Equipment costs*. Distributed applications allow more economic use of computer equipment.
- *Development costs*. Workstation development cost may be lower due to the availability of interactive packages in several areas.

- *User know-how and control.* Distributed applications put data and processing close to the user.
- *User interfaces.* The workstations are especially suitable for sophisticated graphical user interfaces (GUI) with pointing devices (mouse).
- *Exploitation of special hardware.* Each computer can be used as a specialized "server" to satisfy requests from clients.

However, distributed applications present many management challenges:

- *Lack of support and management infrastructure.* At present, many of the management and support issues are not well understood and consequently have not been addressed (this chapter should help).
- *Concerns for security and integrity control.* Distribution of data and programs to multiple sites opens security and integrity control issues which are not easy to address (this chapter should help).
- *Difficulties in large application design.* Breaking applications into pieces where each piece can reside on a separate computer is non-trivial and represents a departure from the traditional application design approaches (the discussion on downsizing in Chapter 8 should help).
- *Lack of standards and tools.* The interconnectivity and interoperability standards are still evolving (discussion of open system standards in Chapter 9 should help). It is hoped that efforts such as OSF DCE (Section 9.6.1, Chapter 9) will help solve these problems.
- *Too many options and confusion.* The availability of a large number of choices makes decision making difficult (the methodology presented in Chapter 8 should help).
- *Application versus network interconnectivity.* Understanding of which application interconnectivity technologies (e.g., client-server systems, distributed data management, distributed transaction management, distributed operating systems) are mature enough is difficult. The discussion of these topics in Chapters 5, 6, and 7 should help. Network interconnectivity choices described in Chapter 3 should be useful.

To distribute/downsize an application, the designers may choose to migrate the entire application to workstations, or gradually downsize portions of applications. Each organization must develop its own cost-benefit ratio for downsizing, upsizing and rightsizing. The following procedure, discussed in Chapter 8, can be used as a starting point:

- Define application and business needs in terms of data sharing, pressures to downsize, flexibility and growth requirements, security and control needs, performance constraints, availability constraints, budgetary constraints (cost, time), user independence needs, and user training level. These are defined as rows in Table 10.2.

- Define the technology choices available and planned in terms of distribution of data, programs, and user interfaces. These are defined as columns in Table 10.2.
- Evaluate the possible configurations against the stated requirements for the specific application(s) by using some criteria as shown in Table 10.2. Table 10.2 suggests a framework for evaluating the centralization/downsizing decisions. The actual requirements and the values assigned will depend on the particular application being distributed. The entries in Table 10.2 have been reviewed in Chapter 8.

General information about downsizing can be found in the Yankee Group Report, "Downsizing Manufacturing Applications through Client-Server Systems," Dec. 1991 and the "Downsizing/Rightsizing Conference," presented by the Boston University Corporate Education Center, April and October, 1992. Many other papers are also beginning to appear on this topic <Edelstein 1992, Radding 1992>.

10.2.6 Enterprise-Wide Network Architecture and Computing Platform Planning

The hardware devices (computers, terminals, I/O devices) and the system software (operating systems and database managers) are chosen and the network architectures for interconnecting various hardware and software components are selected in this

TABLE 10-2 Application Downsizing/Centralization Decision Table

	Application Configurations →				
Enterp. & Appl. Needs	*Data-C Process-C User int. C (Conf.1)*	*Data-C Process-C User int. D (Conf.2)*	*Data-C Process-C User-D (Conf.3)*	*Data-D, U Process-D User-D (Conf.4)*	*Data-D, R Process-D User-D (Conf.5)*
Downsizing pressures	−3	+1	+2	+3	+3
Flexibility & growth	−1	+1	+2	+2	+2
Data sharing needs	+1	+1	+1	−1	−2
Interconnectivity needs	+1	+1	0	−1	−1
Large database needs	+2	+3	+3	−1	−2
Control & security needs	+3	0	−1	−2	−2
Availability needs	−1	−1	−1	1	+3
Performance requirements	−1	+1	+1	+1	+2
User training reqmts.	+3	−1	−2	−3	−3
User independence needs	−2	−1	−1	+3	+3
Development costs	+1	−1	−1	−1	−1
Maintenance & operation costs	+1	−1	−1	−2	−2
Backup and recovery ease	+3	+3	+1	−1	−2
Management & support considerations	+1	−1	−2	−3	−3

Legend: C = centralized, D = distributed, U = unique (only one copy), R = replicated

Evaluation factors (−3 to +3) indicate how well the configurations satisfy the requirements:
−3 = does not satisfy at all
+3 = very well satisfied
0 = no impact

stage. In addition, the subnets in the enterprise and the interconnections between the subnets are chosen to support the application interconnection determined in the previous stage. This stage addresses the layer 3 to 4 issues of the OSI Model and is concerned with interoperability throughout an enterprise.

The choices of the hardware devices and the system software are dependent on the target applications and the application system allocations chosen in earlier stages. In addition, the computing costs, reliability, current equipment, past experience, organizational preferences, growth potential, vendor support and vendor staying power are commonly included in hardware selection. The open systems environments such as UI-ATLAS and OSF DCE provide guidelines for organizations to adopt. We discussed these environments in previous chapters.

One or more network architectures for the business, engineering, manufacturing and office processes may be chosen in this stage. The choice may be based on the application interconnection services provided, the devices supported, and the growth potential of each network architecture. Other factors such as customer support, organizational preferences and past experience, existing networks, and migration costs may be considered. Although it is better to plan for the open systems architectures such as OSI, the products supporting OSI are sparse. The current choices are limited by the available network architectures such as TCP/IP, SNA, DECNET and MAP/TOP. At present, most of the decisions in this stage are based on heuristics, the training/experience of the planners/designers of networks, and state-of-the-market products.

From an enterprise networking point of view, it is important for the organizations to seriously consider the open systems due to the advantages in interoperability, portability and integration. We discussed the various open systems in Chapter 9. Organizations should develop transition strategies from the existing proprietary platforms to future open environments.

10.2.7 Enterprise-Wide Physical Network Planning

This stage evaluates the existing physical network interconnections and takes into account the impact of evolving network technologies such as fiber optic links, broadband networks and Integrated Services Digital Network (ISDN). This stage addresses the layer 1 and 2 issues of the ISO Model.

The most widely used layer 1 and 2 interfaces for local area networks (LANs) at present are the Ethernet and token passing systems at 10 million bits per second (Mbps) and 16 Mbps data rates, respectively. Slower LANs are commonly standardized on RS232 or RS422 interfaces. Faster FDDI LANS using fiber optics are being introduced at 100 Mbps. Most wide area networks (WANs) are packet switching systems with speeds ranging from 1200 bps to 1.53 Mbps over X.25, IBM's SDLC and DEC's DDCMP. The evolving network technologies such as Broadband ISDN, fast packet switching networks and SONET/SMDS will increase the speed of the LAN/MAN/WAN systems to about 100 Mbps with newer interconnection choices.

The choices of physical interconnection are based primarily on the computers and network architectures chosen. For example, if IBM computers and SNA are chosen in the previous stage, then SDLC and token ring are the primary choices for WAN and LAN respectively. Similarly, if MAP is chosen in the previous stage, then the main choice in this stage is broadband versus carrierband MAP. However, development in multiprotocol routers is making it possible to run many different network architecture on the same physical backbone. For example, many TCP/IP backbones are being developed which transport SNA and other non-TCP/IP traffic by using these multiprotocol routers.

The physical media, topology, and layout of the entire organization is chosen (i.e., the broadband backbone, fiber optic networks between several LANs, etc.) based on a large number of factors. This topic has been discussed extensively as the network design problem and can be formulated as follows: given N network components, determine the transmission speeds of L links that interconnect the network components to minimize the cost and to satisfy the response time and availability requirements. Many papers have been written on this topic (see for example the IEEE Network Special Issue on Network Planning, November 1989; and <Bertsekas 1992, Peck 1988, Ellis 1986>).

10.2.8 Resource and Cost Estimation/Evaluation

The time, money, computing, and human resources needed for conversion from the existing platforms to the future platforms are estimated and evaluated in this stage. The major activity is to decide if the transition between the existing networks and the future networks is cost beneficial. (The open systems are intended to minimize the transition costs.) If it appears that the decisions made in the earlier stages are cost beneficial, then the plan is finalized; otherwise one or more of the planning stages are iterated until a satisfactory network configuration is finalized. In each iteration, the stages may be repeated with more details.

Better cost estimation is of key importance in this stage. Over the last 20 years, many cost estimation techniques for information systems have been suggested. Despite a great deal of work, most cost estimates in information systems are based on heuristics and guidelines. Lederer and Prasad <Lederer 1992> suggest the following 9 guidelines for better cost estimation, with numerous examples:

1. Assign the initial estimating task to the final developers.
2. Delay finalizing the initial estimate until the end of a thorough study.
3. Anticipate and control user changes.
4. Monitor the progress of the proposed project.
5. Evaluate proposed project progress by using independent auditors.
6. Use the estimate to evaluate project personnel.
7. Computing management should carefully study and approve the cost estimate.
8. Rely on documented facts, standards, and simple arithmetic formulas rather than guessing, intuition, personal memory, and complex formulas.
9. Do not rely on cost estimating software for an accurate estimate.

In practice, the planning process goes through several iterations with each iteration going into more details. For example, the first iteration may establish an overall configuration which is further refined in the later iterations. This process involves a great deal of information gathering and analysis. At present, most of the tools and techniques used in distributed computing are manual, however the need for capacity planning models which combine queuing, simulation and animation is widely recognized. Expert systems can be used in recording, analyzing, and presenting the information in different formats for participants of planning and provide modeling and reasoning capabilities for what-if situations.

10.3 Organizational Structures and Centralization/Decentralization

Let us now focus on establishing the organizational structure, the information and decision flows, and the management and staff responsibilities to meet the plan developed in Section 10.2. For example, how should an enterprise organize itself in order to integrate the manufacturing, business and engineering information systems. Since the 1958 seminal article "Management in the 1980s" by Leavitt and Whisler <Leavitt 1958>, which predicted the impact of computing on management, many interesting articles have appeared in the management literature on the computer-communication technology based organizations of the future <Applegate 1988, George 1991, Owen 1986, Dearden 1987, Drucker 1988, Burn 1989>. Although a detailed analysis of organizational issues and problems is beyond the scope of this book, it is important for us to review the basic approaches in organizational design and understand the impact of networks and distributed computing on the current practices. Specifically, the following questions need to be addressed:

- What are the basic issues and approaches in organizational structure design (Section 10.3.1)?
- What is the impact of distributed computing technologies on the centralization/decentralization debate (Section 10.3.2)?
- What is the impact of distributed computing on organizational interdependencies (Section 10.3.3)?
- How are the roles of management being impacted by the distributed computing technologies (Section 10.3.4)?

The case study discussed in Section 10.6 illustrates the concepts discussed here.

10.3.1 Overview of Organizational Structure Design

All organizations require a vision and a strategic plan, resources (financial, human, technological) to satisfy the plan, and organizational design to direct the resources to accomplish the plan. Organizational design consists of organizational structures, policies/procedures, reports, performance measurement and evaluation, and rewards/reprimands. Our focus is on organizational structures which defines the division of labor into subunits, subunit work assignments, and controlling the interdependencies and interactions between the subunits. It is important to study organizational structures for two reasons. First, new technology gives more options and raises new issues that must be addressed. Second, bad structures lead to too many conflicts and coordination problems, which result in poor employee morale and eventual failures of organizations <Kotter 1979, Nystrom 1981>.

Design of organizational structures is commonly referred to as structure design in management literature and should not be confused with software structure design. This field has progressed through several stages: the Classical School of Management, the Human Relations School, the Carnegie-Mellon School, and the Integration School <Galbraith 1977>. In addition, the approaches of "one best way" versus "it all depends" are used frequently by management consultants and theorists <Mintzberg 1979>. Much literature has been published on the theoretical as well as empirical aspects of this area. The main idea is to structure subunits by similarity (e.g., function, service/product, geographical location). Organizations are commonly structured by the following (see Fig. 10.6):

- *Function*: Each subunit is responsible for a function (e.g., marketing).
- *Product/service/customer*: Each subunit is responsible for a product.
- *Matrix*: Combination of functional and product structures where work definition is left to workers.
- *Geographic locations*: Subunits are consolidated by country, region, etc.

Table 10.3 shows typical advantages/disadvantages of these "classical" organizational structures. In addition, knowledge workers and researchers are usually organized differently to allow direct interactions and exchange of ideas. A given organization typically uses a combination of organizational structures where functional subunits at one level are decomposed into product subunits at the next level, subunits are grouped within regions for administrative control, and knowledge workers are organized differently than plant floor operations in the same company. In addition, organizations change structures with new products and services.

To illustrate the main concepts, let us review the structure designs for computer integrated environments (CIE) such as computer integrated manufacturing (CIM). Such organizations depend heavily on information technologies for integration of enterprise processes such as manufacturing, engineering, administration, and office processes to produce high quality products/services with minimum cost and in minimum time. CIE/CIM enterprises encounter two sets of organizational problems: (1) the typical manufacturing problems between the product versus functional management, and the engineering/manufacturing/marketing interfaces <Hayes 1978, Dean 1989>, and (2) the information technology related organizational problems of coping with the expectations/implications of technology <Owen 1986, Dearden 1987, Drucker 1988, Burn 1989>. Here is a list of specific challenges in organizational structure design for such systems:

- These systems must satisfy multiple, often conflicting requirements for performance, reliability, flexibility, and maintainability. For example, CIM systems must

a. Functional

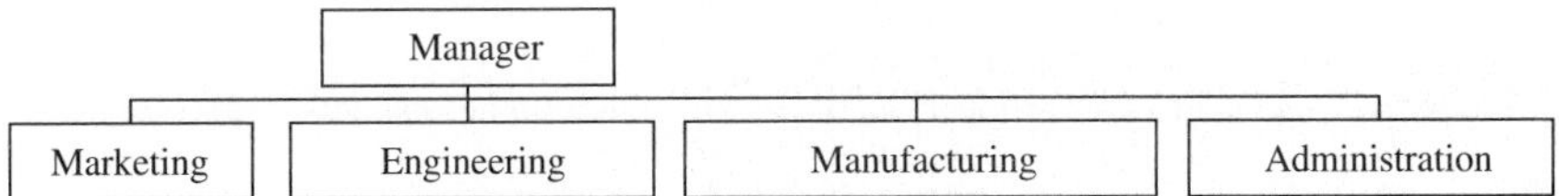

b. Products/Services

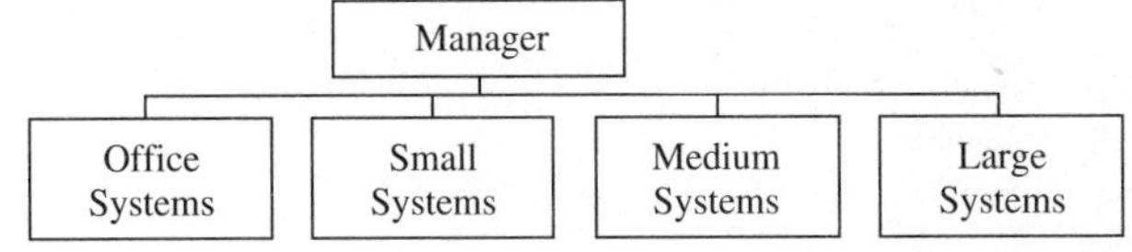

c. Matrix

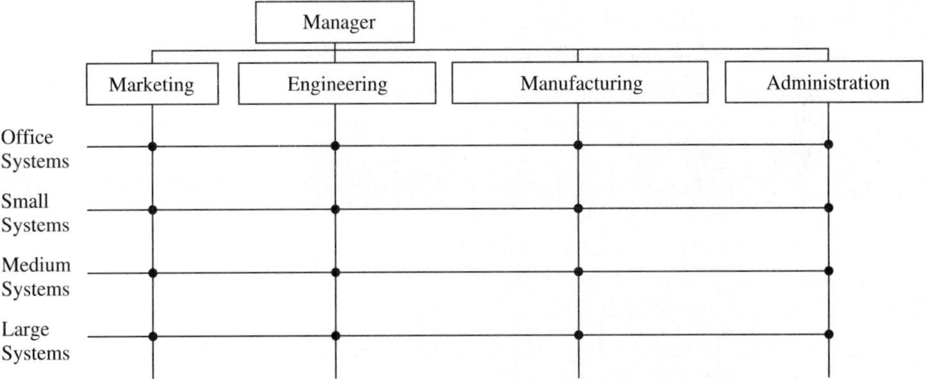

FIGURE 10.6 Typical Organizational Structures

have adaptable architectures for evolving technologies, such as flexible manufacturing systems. In addition, these systems must be easily modifiable to reflect changes in competitive market conditions and national/international standards.

- These systems are dispersed among the enterprise units, which may be located in different cities or countries. Consequently, management of integration requires a great deal of interdisciplinary work among geographically distributed units with potentially different equipments, standards, and policies.
- These systems are developed by professionals (such as process engineers, computer scientists, business programmers, etc.) with diverse backgrounds, training, specialized terminology, and professional outlooks.
- Development of these items requires an understanding and synthesis/application of existing and evolving tools, techniques, standards and models in enterprise

TABLE 10.3 Main Advantages/Disadvantages of Basic Structures

Functional Organizations:
+ Easy and natural for new ventures
+ Good utilization of area specialists
− Not good for many products/services (cannot determine why one product/service is failing)

Product/Service-Oriented Organizations:
+ Good for volatile products/services
+ Good for products/services with varying sizes
− May lead to duplication, lack of standards, and interface problems
+− Develops loyalty toward products/services

Matrix Organizations:
+ Good utilization of personnel
+ Good for volatile industries (i.e., aerospace)
− Two bosses (increase interdependencies)
− Disastrous for new organizations

services (e.g., manufacturing), computing devices, communication technologies, systems engineering, and management. These tools and techniques include growing areas, such as database systems, software engineering, artificial intelligence, operations research, distributed intelligence, organizational behavior, and ergonomics.

The main question is: How can an organization structure itself to introduce enterprise-wide integration? Should this responsibility be assigned to an existing group or should a new group be initiated? Who should this group report to and how should it interface with other organization subunits? How should this group be staffed and trained, etc.? Examples of CIE/CIM organizational structures have been reported by <Aulds 1988, Cloutier 1988, Daner 1988>. A survey of the approaches being adopted by various companies involved in CIM have indicated three main approaches <Umar 1991>:

- Single functional ownership in which a group starts somewhere within a functional department, such as manufacturing, engineering, or finance/administration.
- A project team is introduced to oversee the planning, design, implementation, and management of corporate-wide CIM activities. The project leader may belong to any of the functional areas with team members representing various functions, as well as multiple levels in the organization.
- Top management involvement which is similar to the project team approach. The main difference is that the CIM project manager reports directly to top management. In large organizations, the CIM project manager may report to a top management representative, such as a division vice president.

Other approaches are variants of these three. Our studies suggest that an organization may choose all three approaches or combinations at different stages. For example, the initial investigation may be conducted by a project team to study and evaluate the organizational and technological aspects of integration and to conduct a feasibility study. In the next stage, after management approval, the project team may be elevated to a top management team for detailed planning of the needed tasks. The implementation may be achieved by decomposing the tasks into functional areas which are managed by the functional units. In this stage, the team members may assume the role of agents and advocates of the plan in their respective functional units. A corporate-wide team may still exist, however, both to monitor individual unit progress and to provide an integrative approach.

Figure 10.7 shows a procedure for evaluating various organizational structures which combines many of the existing techniques into a single framework. Our experience has shown that such a procedure allows a systematic approach for a detailed examination and analysis of the proposed organizational structure. It has been especially useful in providing a uniform basis for evaluation: it has led to valuable insights and discussions. It was also found that the model was instrumental in keeping the discussions more focused on appreciation of tradeoffs.

Location Independent Teams: Information technology for organization design. Computer-communication technologies can help in the organization structure design by developing a location independent organizational structure. In such a structure, the distributed computing platform *is* the organizational structure. The platform allows managers and workers to communicate with each other independent of their geographical location. With this structure, the organizational information and decision flows can change (an organization restructure) without moving people's desks. Thus the organization structure is defined through software <Keen 1991>.

10.3.2 Centralization/Decentralization Debate

The impact of computerization on centralization (single site) and decentralization (multiple autonomous sites) management approaches has been debated for over 30 years. At issue is the effect of computerization on organizational decision authority and management control. Emergence of distributed computing technologies has added new dimensions to this debate. The impact of distributed computing on centralization versus decentralization of enterprise activities is being discussed in

1. Identify the problems that need to be addressed (interdependencies, lack of coordination, etc.).
2. Identify the main candidate structures which appear to address the problems identified (should not exceed four, current structure must be a candidate).
3. List the major requirements to be satisfied by the organization:
   - organizational requirements
   - responsiveness to change
   - integration requirements
   - human needs/requirements.
4. Assign importance to the requirements (0 to 5) and choose, if possible, the most important requirements (about 10).
5. Evaluate the candidate structures against the requirements on the scale 0 to 5.
6. Repeat steps 1 through 4, if needed.
7. Analyze the results and make recommendations.

FIGURE 10.7 A Procedure for Organizational Structure Design

trade literature (see, for example, the *Computerworld*, Jan. 1, 1990 Special Issue on Technology Trends, and the *MIS Week*, Dec. 4, 1989 Issue on Downsizing) as well as in business/ information systems literature <Rockart 1977, King 1983, Donovan 1988, George 1991>. Several reference models are being developed, especially in computer integrated manufacturing <Ranky 1986>, for organizations to address the management problems of centralization versus decentralization of activities (see, for example, CIM-OSA <LaVie 1988> and CIMA <Campbell 1988>).

What can be centralized and decentralized? Here is a partial list:

- Management decisions and control
- Application system planning
- Application development
- Application support
- Application operation (i.e., centralization/decentralization of data, programs and user interfaces)
- Computing equipment

Figure 10.8 represents a typical situation in which four application systems (payroll, inventory control, order processing, manufacturing resource planning) are managed, planned, developed, and operated in an environment where the computing equipment is decentralized (i.e., many computers at many sites). For example, all organizational activities related to payroll are centralized while all organizational activities related to manufacturing resource planning are decentralized. It can be seen from Fig. 10.8 that a large number of centralization/decentralization configurations can be envisioned. How can we evaluate the "goodness" of these choices. Here are some factors:

- Computer hardware/software purchase and maintenance costs
- Network hardware/software purchase and maintenance costs
- Security, integrity, and configuration control
- Backup and recovery considerations
- Flexibility of services needed by the users
- End-user autonomy

	Payroll	*Inventory Control*	*Order Processing*	*Manufacturing Resource Planning*
Management	C	D	C	D
Planning	C	D	C	C
Development	C	D	D	D
Operation	C	D	D	D
Equipment	D	D	D	D

Legend: C = centralized, D = decentralized

FIGURE 10.8 Example of Centralization/Decentralization

- Performance of the system
- Availability and reliability of the system
- Organizational politics
- Staff training and morale considerations

A detailed discussion of the various centralization/decentralization choices and the evaluating factors is given by King <King 1983>. To illustrate the key points, we describe the models proposed by Rockart <Rockart 1977>, Donovan <Donovan 1988>, and King <King 1983>. The analysis and examination of this topic by George and King <George 1991> concludes this section.

10.3.2.1 Rockart's Centralization/Decentralization Model

According to this Model, the following three activities can be centralized/decentralized (these are the main decision variables):

- *Development*: The process of designing and implementing a system
- *Operation*: The process of running and using the system
- *Management*: The process of planning, establishing standards, monitoring and controlling the system

These activities can be centralized/distributed for each application system (see Fig. 10.9a). It may be possible to group application systems into what Rockart calls as Logical Application Groups (LAGs), to which the same centralization/ decentralization approach applies. For example, all business applications could be grouped into a single group which is developed, managed, and operated similarly. In addition to the centralization/decentralization of application systems, the computing hardware/software can be managed similarly.

The key points of this model are as follows:

- The separation of management activities from the operation and development activities for centralization/decentralization is crucial. This emphasizes that even though the operation and development may be distributed, the management can be centralized for standards, equipment procurement, etc.
- Application systems or logical application groups can be treated as independent units for separate centralization/decentralization decisions. Thus if one application system is managed centrally, the management of others can be parcelled out.
- Distributed systems can be managed centrally. For example, the planning and standardization of a decentralized inventory control system can be centralized.
- Centralized systems (systems that are developed, operated and managed centrally) can support distributed organizations. For example, a centralized payroll system can support a decentralized organization.

Thus the centralization/decentralization decision can be viewed as a set of decisions - one per application system. The choice of centralization/decentralization is based on

a. Rockart's Model

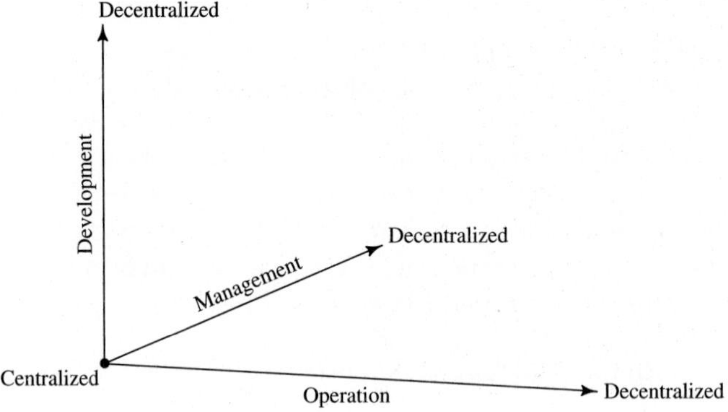

b. Donovan's Model

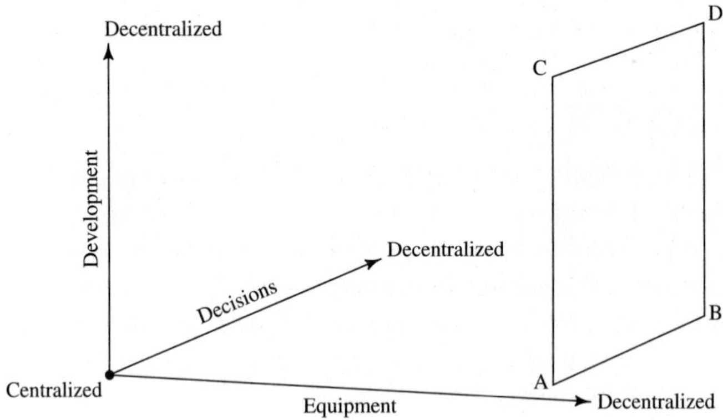

c. King's Model

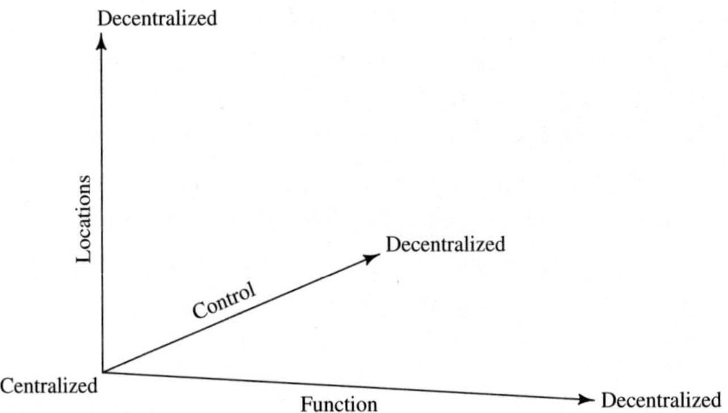

FIGURE 10.9 Frameworks for Centralization/Decentralization

the advantages/disadvantages of the decision. Here are the main advantages of centralization:

- It maximizes use of common resources.
- It makes standardization easier.
- It is easier to monitor and control.

The main advantages of decentralization are as follows:

- It gives local autonomy.
- It makes decision making and product delivery easier.
- It removes the performance bottlenecks.

The question then is of discovering the set of conditions which compel an organization to centralize one application while decentralizing others. For example, a common database between many applications may favor centralization. These conditions can be stated as the aforementioned "givens" or constraints in the generalized problem. Examples of some of these conditions are (Rockart lists almost 50 conditions):

- *Current organizational structure*: A centralized organization tends to choose centralized solutions and vice versa.
- *Size of organization*: Large organizations with several geographically dispersed offices tend to favor decentralization.
- *Staff and management orientation*: Several staff members and managers have grown up on workstations and do not understand why a mainframe exists. (This technology bias may also influence organizational orientation.) These members naturally choose decentralized approaches.
- *Need for uniformity*: High need for uniformity and standards leads to centralized management.
- *Current and planned use of technology*: Large centralized computing centers tend to stay centralized.
- *Current applications*: It is not easy to decentralize a centralized application, however it is possible to centralize a decentralized application.
- *Nature of applications*: Strategic applications (e.g., corporate planning) are usually centralized.
- *Availability requirements*: The applications requiring high availability should be decentralized through redundancy.
- *Performance predictability*: A decentralized system can help in performance by avoiding bottlenecks.

This procedure can be used to systematically evaluate and select appropriate decisions. For example, some organizational structures in information system services departments have been structured around hardware (e.g., mainframe support, PC support, etc.). This structure is not appropriate to support distributed applications which span several computers. The impact of distributed applications is particularly significant on the organizational design for help desks (hotlines). For example, many organizations currently have separate help desks for mainframes, minicomputers, and microcomputers. However, this organizational separation is not suitable to support applications that span mainframes, minicomputers, and microcomputers. Which help desk should a user call if a distributed application fails? The procedure discussed above can be used to centralize/decentralize the help desks.

10.3.2.2 Donovan's Chief Information Officer to Network Manager

John Donovan <Donovan 1988> presents the argument that decentralized computing is unstoppable. One of the consequence of this, according to Donovan, is the emergence of the network manager as a senior information executive. He claims that the growth of network managers in the 1990s will be as dramatic as has been the growth of chief information officers (CIO) in the 1980s. This claim is somewhat substantiated by the growth in the network management tools described in Chapter 5 (network management). According to Donovan:

> "Network managers understand that in a world of accelerating decentralization, the most effective way to oversee a company's computer resources is to relinquish control of them and instead focus on the networks that connect them. Network managers won't merely accept the inevitability of centralized computing. They will encourage it by surrendering authority over hardware purchases and software development while seizing control of communication systems and policies."

Figure 10.9b shows a framework to illustrate the shift of focus from computers to communications. According to this framework, the centralization/decentralization decisions are made at three levels (compare it with Rockarts model):

- Equipment centralization/decentralization (the X axis).
- Development centralization/decentralization (the Y axis).
- Decision making centralization/decentralization (the Z axis).

The point where the three axes meet reflects a completely centralized approach in equipment, development, and decision making (e.g., approval for equipment and development). The four points (A, B, C, D) in Fig. 10.9b represent four different strategies for centralization/decentralization. Point A represents decentralized equipment but centralized development and decision making. Point B represents decentralized equipment and decision-making but centralized development. Point C represents decentralized equipment and development but centralized decision making. Point D represents a completely decentralized environment where equipment, development, and decision-making are decentralized. Although Donovan claims that the CIOs must adopt the D strategy, called the network strategy, several issues need to be resolved before this strategy can be employed. Difficult security, standards and integrity control questions must be addressed.

10.3.2.3 King's Centralization/Decentralization Model

<King 1983> reviewed many centralization/decentralization approaches in computing environments and presented a model to analyze/evaluate various approaches. In his view, there are three main options to centralization/decentralization:

- Extensive centralization
- Intermediate arrangement
- Extensive decentralization

These options can be applied to:

- Control (decision making, policy setting)
- Location (sites for computing resources)
- Functions (operations, installation, development, etc.)

King's model, shown in Fig. 10.9c analyzes the tradeoffs involved in centralization/decentralization of control, location and functions. The options considered are continuums between extensive centralization and extensive decentralization. The intermediate positions indicate a compromise. In case of extreme decentralization, the user departments are free to acquire their own computing capabilities and build their own applications. In the case of extreme centralization, all controls and functions are restricted to one site. In the intermediate situations, some controls and functions are centralized while others are decentralized. For additional information, the reader is referred to King <1983>.

10.3.2.4 Examining the Debate (George and King)

Joey George and John King <George 1991> have published an extensive analysis and examination of the computerization and centralization/decentralization literature published in the last 30 years. They ask: What is the relationship between computerization and organizational centralization/decentralization. They observe that four different positions concerning this question have emerged over the last three decades:

1. Organizational computerization causes centralization of an organization's decision authority structure.
2. Organizational computerization causes decentralization of an organization's decision authority structure. This position contradicts the first position.
3. There is no inherent relationship between computerization and decision authority structure, i.e., the decision authority structure is determined by factors other than computerization.
4. Organizational decision authority structures shape organizational computing and not the other way around. This position reverses the causality between computing and decision structures.

The authors describe and analyze the literature that supports these seemingly contradictory positions. Then they examine the seminal papers in this area to conclude that these four positions can be reconciled by using a different perspective <George 1991, page 69>:

> ". . . decision authority structures in organizations are largely the result of organizing choices made by management. Computers and automation are seen as tools, mechanisms, and means for bringing about the desired ends of management. Computerization is carried out in a way that supports the prevailing choices being made. Since management philosophies differ from organization to organization, one would expect to find evidence of centralization in one place and of decentralization in another. One would also expect to find the aggregate results of a study of many organizations to suggest that there is no inherent relationship, since many organizations would be using computing to reinforce the existing distribution, and not to change the decision authority distribution."

Their main point is that management actions affect computing. For example, computerization led to centralization because management wanted centralization. Similarly, computerization led to decentralization because management wanted decentralization, and used computers to achieve it. The authors agree with those who claim that the debate over computing and centralization is over. However, they point to many research areas concerning the study of organizational dynamics. In the same vein, Burns and McFarland <Burns 1987> state:

> "Technology is organizationally neutral. It does not favor centralization over decentralization. It simply offers top managers choices they have not had before."

The focus has shifted to other issues of the debate. For example, in a banking business, you must have automated teller machines (ATMs) whether you are centralized or not. So the question really is how many ATMs to have and where to locate them.

10.3.3 Interdependency Management and Distributed Computing

Distributed computing increases interdependencies due to several technical as well as organizational factors. Examples of the factors are as follows:

- Distributed application systems, distributed databases and distributed cooperative processing create interdependencies between remotely located computers; and consequently between the staff working on these computers.
- The vagueness of responsibilities and the uncertainty of employee tasks occurs due to the newness of the field.
- The direction of information (simplex, half duplex, full duplex) and the nature of information exchange between organizational units and computer systems is not always predictable.

- The differences in values and attitudes of employees in different subunits and poor human relationships (hidden agendas, suspicion, distrust) surface when different "organizational cultures" have to work together. This can happen, for example, in cases where manufacturing and corporate business systems are integrated.

Increased interdependencies cause increased coordination need, increased response time, more conflicts, and difficulties in integration. The typical problem is: units accomplish individual tasks adequately but the whole doesn't accomplish its goals. Several management as well as technical devices can be used to manage interdependencies <Kotter 1979, Mintzberg 1979, Galbraith 1977>. The main device is to clearly define the interfaces, procedures and guidelines between interacting units (this applies to technical as well as organizational units). Specifically:

- Clearly define the boundaries of the subunits (e.g., who will backup/recover what data at what sites, what exactly will corporate security do).
- Determine how the output of unit A relates to the input of unit B (e.g., what exactly will a corporate data architecture group provide to database designers at different sites).
- Whenever a formal request is received from unit A, how should unit B respond to it (time and form)?
- Define technology utilization such as groupware for collaborative problem solving across units (e.g., tie remote manufacturing and business through group decision support systems for increased interactions)

In some cases, these devices do not produce desirable results. In such cases, perhaps the best organizational device to manage interdependencies is to have the units report to the same manager. This usually clarifies common goals and targets. Additional devices are:

- Changing/swapping personnel and/or positions.
- Meetings, committees and task forces to increase coordination.
- Introduction of coordinators (product manager to coordinate the development, deployment and support of software product A).
- Physical proximity for increased communication (even though electronic mail can help, physical proximity promotes a friendlier atmosphere; people have lunches together, talk about their vacations, etc.).
- Redesign to contain interdependence within a subunit.
- Reward systems to promote teamwork.

Which device is used depends on the situation and on the cost of the device (see Kotter <1979> for general discussion).

The similarities between software systems design and organizational design to manage interdependencies are obvious from this discussion. Blokdijk and Blokdijk <Blokdijk 1987> recognized this similarity. In their book, "Planning and Design of

Information systems," <Blokdijk 1987>, they extensively utilize structured software design principles (e.g., coupling and cohesion) for organizational design. Considerable work is needed in this area.

10.3.4 Impact on Management Roles

Networks and distributed computing are significant in changing the role of management. Many papers have highlighted the impact of information technologies on management roles and organizational change (see <Attewell 1984, Clark 1992, Gurbaxani 1991, Huber 1990, Kling 1989, Markus 1988> for excellent reviews of research in this area). The best known work in this area is the paper by Leavitt and Whisler <Leavitt 1958>. They predicted that by the late 1980s, the combination of management science and information technology would cause middle management ranks to shrink, and top management to take more of the creative functions. Despite a great deal of criticism in the 1960s and 1970s, we have seen that these two predictions became true by the late 1980s. Let us review the changing roles of middle and top management.

The traditional thinking in management has been that the top management makes decisions and the operational staff carries out the decisions <Owen 1986, Drucker 1988>. Thus, in typical organizations the decisions flow down and the information needed for decisions flows up (see Fig. 10.10). The following comments reflect the thinking of many modern management theorists <Drucker 1988>:

> "It turns out that whole layers of management neither make decisions nor lead. Instead, their main, if not only function, is to serve as 'relays.' "

With the availability of corporate wide networks with transparent end-user access to data at any site, top management can directly communicate their decisions to the operational staff and the information from the operational staff can be directly viewed by top management. This raises the question: What will be the role of middle management in such a case? Here are some theories:

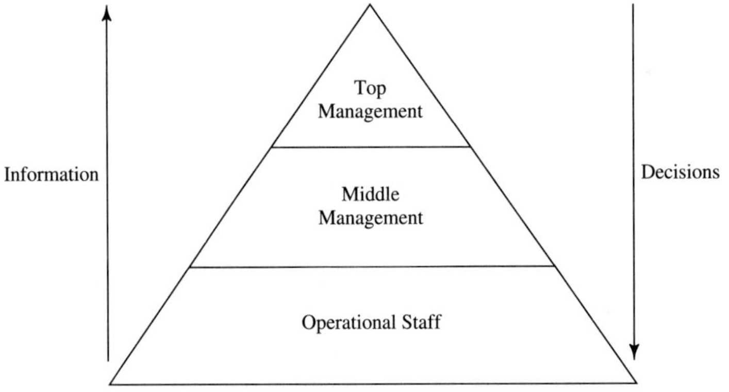

FIGURE 10.10 Traditional Organizational Model

- The number of levels in organizations will decrease leading to more flat organizations. For example, <Daner 1988, Drucker 1988> propose that the typical "pyramid" organizations with 12 to 13 layers of management will evolve into flatter organizational structures (see Fig. 10.11). One estimate indicates that organizations have eliminated more than a million middle management and staff positions since 1979 <Applegate 1988>.
- The operational staff will evolve into a staff of knowledge workers—subject area specialists who work with minimum supervision and who are motivated by feedback and recognition from peers <Drucker 1988>. The knowledge workers will not need a great deal of supervision, and will use "networking" of talent that does not necessarily follow organizational boundaries. The number of middle managers for knowledge workers can be decreased by increasing the span of control of each manager. The span of control principle initially proposed by Lyndall Urwick <Urwick 1952> suggests that no person should supervise more than six direct subordinates whose work interlocks. This classical principle does not apply in the case of knowledge workers.
- Widespread introduction and use of information technology will introduce new interdependencies and responsibilities which will need to be managed by middle managers. For example, the introduction of workstations, LANs, and distributed applications increases the interdependencies between various hardware, software, and organizational units which are becoming the responsibility of middle managers <Owen 1986>.
- The middle managers will take a more active role in leadership, innovation, and stress management of the operational staff because the role of middle management will be more of team leaders and asset managers who are managing the most valuable asset of organizations - their people <Brown 1986, Van DeVen 1981>. The middle managers may be evaluated based on the appreciation/de-appreciation of the human asset in a manner similar to the fixed asset evaluation. For example, a manager is considered a better manager if an asset (e.g., a plant) grows in value under the manager.

The role of top management is also changing due to information technologies <Applegate 1988, Clark 1992, Drucker 1988>:

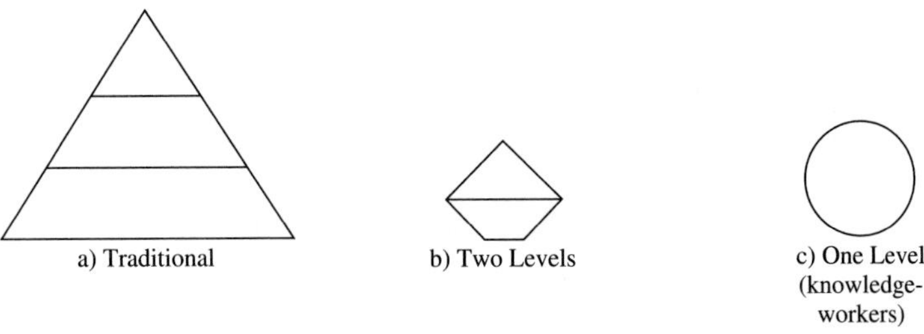

Three forms of organizational structures.

FIGURE 10.11 Evaluation of Organizational Structures

- Distributed computing technologies have become an active tool for top managers to downsize and restructure organizations.
- Due to the availability of information about all aspects of an organization, top managers will have more centralized control.
- The decision making will shift from top management to middle management (decentralized decision making) for more responsiveness.
- Top managers will not just react to technology; they will use it to shape the organization.

What will happen in the next century? While no one is sure, here are some thoughts from Lynda Applegate, James Cash and D. Mills from a *Harvard Business Review* paper "Information Technology and Tomorrow's Manager" <Appelgate 1988>. This paper analyzes the Leavitt and Whisler paper and offers the following predictions for the twenty-first century (this is just an example, you can agree or disagree):

Organizational structure:

- Companies will have the benefits of small scale and large scale simultaneously (large companies will be able to react quickly like small companies).
- Even large organizations will be able to adopt more flexible and dynamic structures.
- The distinctions between centralized and decentralized control will blur.
- The focus will be on projects and processes rather than on tasks and standard procedures.

Management processes:

- Decision making will be better understood.
- Control will be separate from reporting relationships.
- Information and communications systems will retain corporate history, experience, and expertise.

Human resources:

- Workers will be better trained (perhaps some), more autonomous, and more transient.
- The work environment will be exciting and engaging.
- Management will be for some people a part-time activity that is shared and rotated.
- Job descriptions tied to narrowly defined tasks will become obsolete.
- Compensation will be tied more directly to contribution.

10.4 Development, Deployment and Staffing Considerations

10.4.1 Overview

So far, we have discussed how to plan and organize for distributed computing. Let us now turn our attention to the actual task of doing the work for which we have been planning and organizing. This task, the development, acquisition, and deployment of distributed computing, involves two service categories:

- Application development and deployment.
- Platform acquisition and installation.

The organizational aspects of these two service categories are discussed in Sections 10.4.2 and 10.4.3, respectively. Each service category involves three issues:

- *The functions to be supported.* Examples of the functions are software development, software purchasing, leasing, hardware/software installation, etc.
- *Type of components to be developed, acquired, and installed.* Examples are network hardware devices, database managers, network management software, and application system modules.
- *Levels of support to be provided.* Support can be at two main levels: (1) consulting support in which a user is advised on what to order, how to order, and how to configure/install a component, and (2) hands-on support, in which the service center actually orders, configures, and installs a component for a user.

Ideally, an enterprise should support all functions, for all components at all levels. In practice, an enterprise may have to make difficult choices in determining support levels due to resource shortages. Figure 10.12 shows a framework that can be used to analyze and evaluate the acquisition/deployment activities of an enterprise.

Service Categories	*Functions Supported*	*Components Supported*	*Levels of Support*
Application System Development/ Deployment	• Analysis design • Design • Development/ purchase • Installation	• User interfaces • Programs • Databases • Communications	• Consulting • Hands-on • Tools and environments
Platform Acquisition/ Installation	• Analysis • Product evaluation • Pricing/policies • Installation	• Networks • Workstations • System packages • Client-server • Distributed data and transaction managers	• Consulting • Hands-on • Tools and environments

FIGURE 10.12 A Framework for Analyzing Development/Acquisition Support

The rows of Fig. 10.12 show the service categories and the columns indicate the functions, the components and the support levels. This framework will be used to analyze the service categories in more detail in the following sections.

10.4.2 Development and Deployment of Distributed Applications

The development and deployment of distributed applications involves the following generic functions:

- Specification and analysis of application requirements
- Design of an application architecture which conforms to the necessary standards and the interoperability, portability, and integration requirements (Chapter 9)
- Development of application system components (programs, user interfaces, databases) and the application interconnectivity mechanisms
- Purchase and customization of existing application system components (programs, user interfaces, databases)
- Installation and configuration of application system components
- Centralization/decentralization of implementation activities.

These functions can be performed by a centralized development/deployment group or can be decentralized. The main advantage of centralized development/deployment is maximization of developer time. According to the framework shown in Fig. 10.12, these functions can be applied to different application components (user interfaces, application processing programs, databases). The support may include consulting, hands-on support (build the application software), and tools/environment (e..g., CASE tools). The following scenarios illustrate the choices:

- A completely centralized development/deployment group which performs all analysis, evaluation, implementation and installation for all application systems components. This represents a software house which develops/deploys all software in an enterprise. However, this group falls apart quickly if there are no standards and enforceable policies.
- A completely decentralized development/deployment operation where all functions for all application systems at all support levels are conducted by the users. This represents an information center where the end users select and install their own packages (usually word processing and spread sheets) on their own workstations.
- A distributed development/deployment operation which centralizes few functions for few components at few support levels. The rest of the functions are decentralized. For example, the centralized department may provide consulting and guidance on user interface design, software design and database design; leaving the implementation and installation to the users. This represents a technology transfer center which is responsible for overall direction for application development in the enterprise.

10.4.3 Acquisition and Installation of Distributed Computing Platforms

The acquisition and installation of hardware and software needed to support distributed computing involves the following generic functions:

- Analyzing user requirements in distributed computing
- Evaluating and selecting vendor hardware/software which satisfies the user requirements
- Establishing pricing structures (e.g., bulk purchase rates, maintenance prices) with selected vendors
- Establishing procedures for administrative approval before an order is sent to a vendor
- Receiving and verifying ordered components
- Installing and configuring the ordered components.

These functions can be performed by a centralized purchasing/installation center or can be decentralized to end users. The main advantage of centralized acquisition/installation, as mentioned previously, is enforcement of standards and policies. Centralized systems can also direct the users to common software usage across all environments in an enterprise. However, centralized purchasing and installation can be quite slow in large organizations. In such cases, "regional" purchasing and installation may be more appropriate.

In addition, according to the framework shown in Fig. 10.12, these functions can be applied to different types of components and can be provided at different support levels. For example, the components to be ordered and acquired may be workstations (memory, I/O devices, CPU model), network devices (LAN software, cables, modems, routers, bridges, gateways, etc.), and resource sharing software (distributed database managers, client-server packages, etc.). The support can be at the consulting level only where the user receives guidance in selecting the appropriate components to be ordered and then receives instructions on how to install the systems. This may be extended to administration where all the selection, evaluation, installation and configuration is done by a central purchasing/installation group.

Naturally, the choice of centralization/decentralization depends on the type of components and the level of support. The following scenarios illustrate the choices:

- A completely centralized purchasing/installation center, which performs all functions for all components at all support levels. Due to complete centralization of all decisions and activities, this scenario is only appropriate for small enterprises.
- A completely decentralized purchasing/installation operation, where all functions for all components at all support levels are conducted by the users. This scenario is appropriate for large decentralized enterprises.
- A "distributed" purchasing/installation operation, which centralizes a few functions for a few components at few support levels. The rest of the functions are decentralized. For example, the centralized purchasing/installation may just pro-

vide consulting and guidance on LAN acquisition and installation, leaving the actual ordering and installation to the users. This scenario may be appropriate for many enterprises.

10.4.4 Staffing and Training Considerations

A major consideration in developing, deploying, and supporting distributed systems is to determine who needs to know what about distributed systems. This question is not easy to answer. One reason is the plethora of articles, papers, and books on different aspects of distributed computing systems, application systems and enterprise systems. In addition, several positions may need to be redefined in order to emphasize the internode management activities. Specifically, how are the roles and responsibilities of existing personnel (technical support, computing system specialists, application systems designers, database designers, application systems programmers) affected due to the introduction of distributed computing?

A framework, shown in Fig. 10.13, is introduced to answer these questions. The three level model of computer based systems, first introduced in Chapter 1, is used to classify the personnel into the following generic categories (in practice each category can be further subdivided):

1. Analysts who plan, specify, analyze, and evaluate the requirements of a system. An analyst may develop enterprise systems, application systems, or computer systems. For example, financial analysts study the financial aspects of an enterprise, application analysts develop the requirements of application systems, and

Staff Category	*Examples*
Enterprise Systems	
Analysts	• Process analyst, financial analyst
Developers	• Manufacturing engineer, inventory controller
Operators	• Mechanic, machine operators
Users	• Customers
Managers	• Plant managers, corporate managers
Application Systems	
Analysts	• Application systems analysts, application planners
Developers	• Programmers, database designers
Operators	• Operations staff, Help Desks
Users	• Payroll clerks, automated factory workers
Managers	• Business application managers
Computer Systems	
Analysts	• Computer capacity planner, network planner
Developers	• DBMS developer, compiler writer
Operators	• Computer operators, network center operations
Users	• Programmers, analysts, application designers
Managers	• Computer center managers

FIGURE 10.13 A Framework for Staff Classification

network analysts/planners develop the requirements of a network. Many analysts also provide user consulting and customer support.

2. Developers who design, construct, and test a system. A developer may develop enterprise systems, application systems, or computer systems. For example, a manufacturing engineer is a developer of a factory, application programmers/designers/analysts are developers of application systems, and network designers/installers are developers of a distributed computing system.
3. Operators who install, maintain, and run a system. An operator may operate enterprise systems, application systems or computer systems. For example, a factory mechanic installs and maintains factory equipment, application maintenance programmers install and upgrade application systems, and network control center personnel operate install, modify and upgrade networks.
4. Users who utilize a system to support their day-to-day activities. A user may use an enterprise system, an application system, or a computing system. For example, a factory worker uses the factory facilities to develop a product, a payroll clerk uses the payroll application system to print a check, and a technical writer uses the facilities of a computing system (word processing) to develop documentation.
5. Managers who are responsible for the cost and resource administration (e.g., security and access control, availability, user satisfaction) of a system. A manager may manage an enterprise system, an application system, or a computing system. Examples are the factory managers, application system managers, and computing center managers.

In layered systems, the developers/operators of a system at layer n are users of the system at layer $n - 1$. For example, considering the layered architecture in Fig. 10.14, the developers/operators of enterprise systems are users of the application systems and the developers/operators of application systems are users of the computing system.

Figure 10.14 analyzes the impact and training needed by the developers, operators, managers, and users of a system S in terms of the following categories:

- External behavior (E) of S represented by inputs/outputs, environment information, and cost of S. Examples are the externals of a factory (what does it produce, where is it located), externals of an application system (what type of reports does it generate), and externals of a computing system (what commands does it support).
- Architecture (A) of S represented by the physical components (c1,c2,,cn) of S, the functions performed and the interfaces/interactions between (c1, c2,. . . cn) and other related systems S′. Examples are the architecture (layout) of the factory, architecture (high level design) of an application, and network architectures.
- Implementation details (I) about the internal workings of S. Examples are the equipment used in a factory, programming details of an application, and concurrency control algorithms implemented in a distributed database manager.

Figure 10.14 shows that the developers, operators, managers and users of contemporary enterprise, application and computing systems need to have different

Staff	Distributed Computer System (DCS)	Distributed Application System (DAS)	Distributed Enterprise System (DES)
	Systems		
Enterprise System			
Analysts		E	E, A, I
Developers		E	E, A, I
Operators		E	E, A
Users		E	E
Managers	E	E	E, A
Application System			
Analysts	E	E, A	E, A
Developers	E, A	E, A, I	E, A
Operators	E	E, A	E
Users	E	E	E, A
Managers	E	E, A	E, A
Computing System			
Analysts	E, A	E, A	
Developers	E, A, I	E, A	
Operators	E, A	E	
Users	E, A	E, A, I	E, A
Managers	E, A	E	

Legend:

- E: external behavior of the system represented by inputs/outputs, environment and cost information
- A: architecture of the system represented by the physical components of the system, the functions performed, and the interfaces/interactions between the components
- I: implementation details about the internal workings of the system

FIGURE 10.14 Training Model for Staff

levels of knowledge about distributed systems. At the enterprise system level, the enterprise staff does not need to know very much about the distributed computer systems (DCS) being used, external knowledge about the distributed application systems is needed by the staff (e.g., order processing clerks should know the input/output of order processing systems), and the implementation details about the enterprise systems is naturally needed by the enterprise system developers. At the application systems level, the application systems staff needs to know the externals of the DCS on which the applications are residing, they naturally need more detailed knowledge of distributed application characteristics, and they need external knowledge of the enterprise system which is served by the application system. At the computing system level, the implementation details of DCS are primarily of interest to the developers of DCS, such as the employees of a distributed database vendor; the knowledge of DCS externals is needed by the managers, users, and operators of DCS; and the knowledge of DCS architecture is needed by the application system developers, among others.

The information shown in Fig. 10.14 can be used to train personnel in organizations. It can also be used to galvanize the impact of distribution/centralization on staff assignments and responsibilities. Naturally, the computer system staff is greatly affected if an organization moves from centralized to distributed computing. For example, they need to know the issues of network design, network architectures, network protocols, distributed database algorithms, client-server protocols, etc. The application systems staff is affected differently depending on the specific responsibility. The following statements highlight the impact:

- *Application users*: Impact on response time and availability due to centralization/distribution of applications can be significant.
- *Application programmers*: No impact if distributed database managers are used because they provide transparency of data access.
- *Database designers*: Distributed database design is influenced by the partitioning/allocation of data
- *Application designers*: Distributed applications designers will need to partition/allocate programs and will need to understand the tradeoffs between different methods of accessing remote data (file transfer, distributed database managers, client server). In addition, application designers will need to understand the industrial trends in distributed applications architecture such as SAA, OSF-DCE, etc.
- *Database administrators*: Distributed data administration involves local and global data views, local and remote authorities, performance evaluation of data distribution, and the impact of remote joins
- *Application system managers*: Costs/benefits of distribution and impacts on organizational design must be taken into account.

10.5 Monitoring and Control Considerations

Monitoring and control of resources in a distributed environment can be discussed in terms of the three issues introduced in Section 10.4.1:

- *Functions to be supported.* Examples of the functions are configuration management services (defining and monitoring components), fault management (detecting, diagnosing and recovering from faults), performance management (monitoring, controlling and predicting performance), configuration management (defining, changing, monitoring and controlling), accounting (recording usage of resources and generating billing information), security (ensuring authorized access to resources), and operational support (help desks, backup and recovery, and automated operations).
- *Type of components monitored and controlled.* Examples are network hardware devices, resource sharing software and application system software.

- *Level of support to be provided.* Support can be at two main levels: (1) consulting support in which a user is advised on how to monitor and control the resources, and (2) "hands-on" support in which the service center actually monitors and controls the resources for a user.

Figure 10.15 shows a framework that can be used to analyze and evaluate the monitoring and control of computing resources of an enterprise. The rows of Fig. 10.15

Service Categories	*Functions Supported*	*Components Supported*	*Levels of Support*
Fault Management	• Fault detection • Fault isolation • Fault resolution	• Network • Hardware • Application interconnection software • Application software	• Consulting • Hands-on support • Tools and environments
Performance Management	• Performance monitoring • Performance analysis • Performance tuning	• Network • Hardware • Application interconnection software • Application software	• Consulting • Hands-on support • Tools and environments
Accounting and Security	• Encryption and privacy • Authentication • Alarms • Access rights • Audit trails	• Network • Hardware • Application interconnection software • Application software • Computers	• Consulting • Hands-on support • Tools and environments • Administrative control
Configuration Management	• Component description • Access rights • Interrela-tionships • Change management	• Network • Hardware • Application interconnection software • Application software	• Consulting • Hands-on support • Tools and environments
Operational Support	• Helpdesk (hotlines) • Operations • System administration • Customer support	• Network • Hardware • Application interconnection software • Application software	• Consulting • Hands-on support • Tools and environments

FIGURE 10.15 A Framework for Analyzing Monitoring and Control Support

show the functions and the columns indicate the type of components and levels of support. This is very similar to the framework introduced in Fig. 10.12. Sections 10.5.2 through 10.5.6 explain the service categories in more detail. Many network and distributed applications management tools are being developed and integrated into distributed management environments. We discuss these topics first.

10.5.1 Network Management and Distributed Applications Management Tools (OSF DME and UI DSHF)

Network management and distributed applications management are of principal importance in monitoring and control of distributed resources. Network management is concerned primarily with managing layer 1 to 4 activities of the OSI Reference Model. We have discussed network management principles and products in Chapter 4. Distributed applications management concentrates on higher level (layer 5 and above) issues. This is a relatively new area. The particular issues addressed by distributed applications management can also be discussed by using the network management service categories discussed in Chapter 4:

- *Configuration management*: Defining, changing, monitoring, and controlling distributed programs and data
- *Fault management*: Detecting, diagnosing, and recovering from distributed applications faults
- *Performance management*: Monitoring, controlling, and predicting performance
- *Accounting*: Recording usage of application resources and generating billing information
- *Security*: Ensuring only authorized access to resources
- *Resource management/user directory*: Supporting directories for managing system assets.

These service categories can be discussed in terms of the framework introduced in Fig. 10.15. Some environments, discussed below, are combining the network management and distributed application management tools into integrated frameworks.

10.5.1.1 OSF Distributed Management Environment (DME)

The objective of Open Software Foundation's Distributed Management Environment (DME) is to identify a common framework for managing heterogeneous distributed systems in an open environment. Figure 10.16a shows the DME components. The framework provides many application programming interfaces (APIs) which allow programs at several levels to invoke services and to interact with local/remote managed objects.

The user interface provides a character as well as a graphical user interface access to management applications. The management applications perform management tasks, such as remote reconfiguration of parameters of network nodes and remote reinitialization of network nodes. DME intends to include applications that

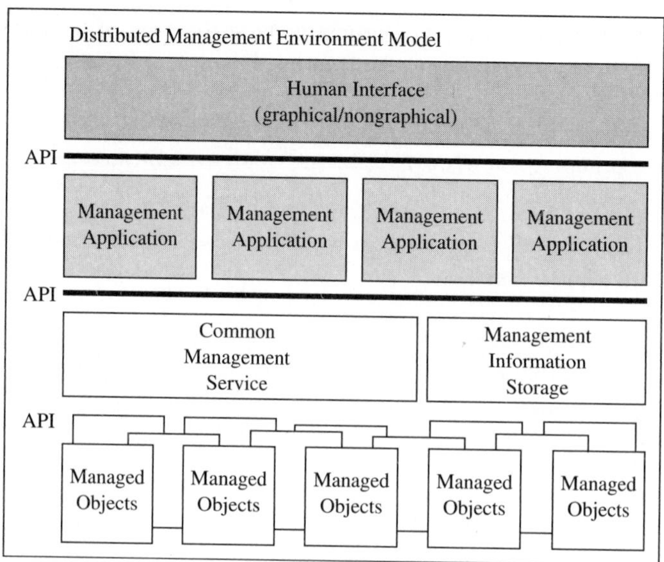

FIGURE 10.16a OSF Distributed Management

provide the basic means to manage any open system (single system or a large heterogeneous network of systems). These applications hide the details of the management procedures from the users. The common management services provide functionalities for communications, event management and logging, and object management. These services enable the development of portable management applications and allow interoperability between applications. The common management information storage services provide APIs for storage and retrieval of information in a uniform manner. A managed object represents a computing resource or an entity in a system. Examples of managed objects are files, printers, users, workstations, and application programs. DME will provide a general interface to the managed objects so that portable, extensible, and adaptable management applications can be built.

DME supports a distributed management architecture in which the management software is broken into pieces that are linked together through some kind of interprocess communications. The management software itself does not know if it is on one computer or on many. This allows for easy scaling, because more computers can be added to maintain performance. In addition, the distributed system is reliable; if one computer fails, the rest of the system can continue to operate.

A network configuration database typically resides on a shared server; another server collects alarms from all network components. The alarms are sent to appropriate processes in the system that request notification of various network events. In large systems, the alarm services may be partitioned and allocated to different servers in the network. The distributed servers communicate with each other through the standard management communication protocol CMIP (see Chapter 4) for a discussion of CMIP). More information about the OSF DME can be found in OSF DME documents (see, for example, the OSF White Paper on DME, January 1991). The analysis by James Herman <Herman 1991, Herman 1992> is recommended.

10.5.1.2 UI Distributed System Management Framework (DSMF)

Unix International has introduced the Distributed System Management Framework (DSMF). DSMF, shown in Fig. 10.16b, has four components:

- Framework/common facilities
- Management applications/application objects
- Application presentation layer
- Application programming interface (API).

The framework/common facilities enable users to access application objects throughout a network via the common facilities, and allow developers and system administrators to create new and modify existing objects. The framework is based on an object oriented model. This paradigm provides access to each application task through a well defined interface. The application objects are combined and recombined to create higher level objects. Application objects are modeled after the typical administrative tasks. For example, the routines of a backup/recovery system are encapsulated as application objects. New backup/recovery systems can now be created by including some of these objects and combining them with newly created objects. This framework also provides a standard way to access objects in a distributed environment through remote object operations. As shown in Fig. 10.16b, this framework provides five common facilities: object management facilities to handle requests to access application objects, naming/location facilities to find objects in the network, authoriza-

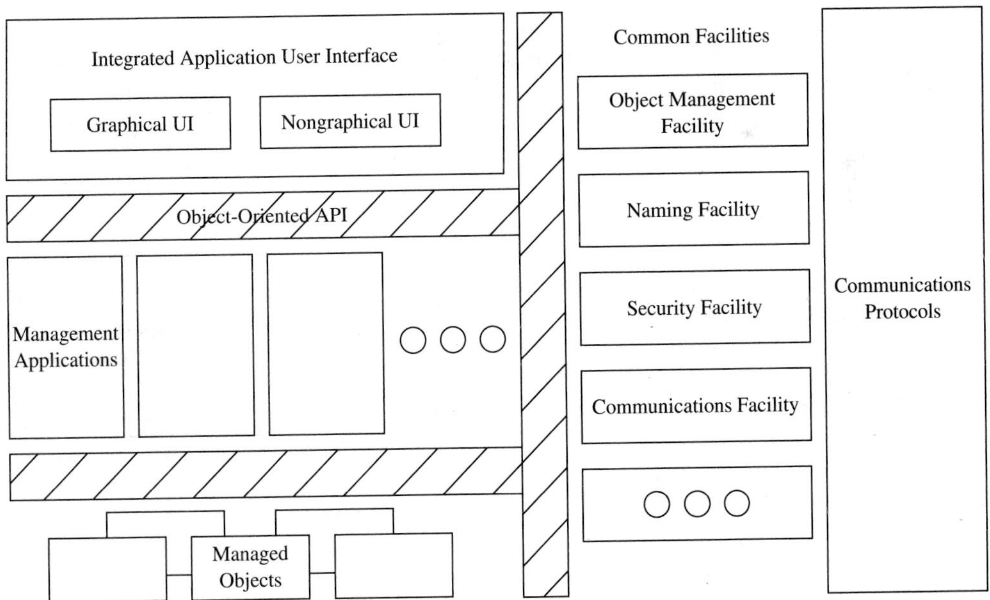

FIGURE 10.16b Unix International's Distributed Systems Management Framework

tion/authentication facilities to control access to application objects, communication facilities for remote object access, and general facilities such as error reporting and event notification.

The management applications/application objects provide solutions to management tasks and problems in distributed systems. Examples of management tasks are network management and distributed application management activities mentioned previously. These application objects may be simple or complex, and may access other application objects. Users of these application objects are system administrators and network operators who need to configure the system, detect and recover from faults, monitor and control the system performance, account/bill for resource consumption, ensure authorized access to system resources, and support system directories. Users can also be other application objects. The users of application objects utilize the framework common facilities for accessing application objects in a network. Existing management applications that are not object oriented can be encapsulated into objects by adding some interface code.

The application presentation layer shields the application developers from the complexities of user interface programming. In an object-oriented model, the object attributes include the presentation information used to display the object. An application object may provide an appropriate method for displaying the object attributes. This provides a great deal of flexibility for presentation. For example, the presentation layer does not need to know how to display different objects—this information is actually embedded in the object.

The application programming interface (API) allows programs to access the application objects and other facilities of the framework. The API defines a set of library routines which can be called from application programs to access the needed facilities.

This framework allows customization of administrative policies, evolution of management applications, distribution of system administrative functions across a network, and scaling up and down of system management for large or small networks. This framework is described in the Unix International Systems Management Work Group documents.

10.5.2 Fault Management

Let us now turn our attention to the system management task of fault management. Fault management in distributed computing is concerned with detecting, isolating, and correcting faults in the networks as well as the application systems. The basic goal of fault management is to provide smooth and fault free operations. The fault management functions needed depend on the nature of applications and the networks being managed. Since down-time is intolerable in most applications, the fault management must be proactive (i.e., it should forecast faults and provide support to prevent fault occurrence). The basic fault management functions are as follows:

- Fault detection, which includes detecting faults in the individual components or the paths between the components, providing notification of the detected faults, and predicting faults before they occur.

- Fault isolation, which includes determining the failing component and/or components which are causing the problem.
- Fault resolution, which includes determining the corrective actions and then executing them if possible.

These functions can be performed by a centralized unit which remotely monitors the system for faults, or can be decentralized to end users. In addition, according to the framework shown in Fig. 10.15, these functions can be applied to different component types and can be provided at different support levels. For example, fault management may detect and correct faults in workstations, network components (LAN hardware/software, cables, modems, routers, bridges, gateways, etc.), resource sharing software (distributed database managers, client-server packages, etc.), and the application systems. Support can be at the consulting level only where the user receives guidance in fault detection and correction. Support may be embedded in software packages which help users diagnose and correct their own problems.

Fault management in distributed computing is a complex activity, especially if all components are to be managed automatically. It requires correlation of a large number of inputs from network devices and application system components to detect trends and isolate problem areas. This is an excellent application area for expert systems. As mentioned in Chapter 4, many expert systems have been and are being built for network fault management. These tools need to be extended to distributed applications management. Open Software Foundation's Distributed Management Environment and Unix International's Distributed System Management Framework, discussed previously, are attempting to combine network management and distributed applications management tools into cohesive environments. The idea is to integrate network management tools such as SNMP, CMIS, and Netview with application programs and data at different sites.

It is important to emphasize the role of management commitment on proactive fault management throughout the enterprise. It is also critical to recognize that a collection of tools, no matter how sophisticated, is of little value without proper management vision and approach. As distributed computing depends to a great degree on network availability, network management tools and policies/procedures become increasingly important. A management approach to use these tools and environments effectively for proactive fault management is essential.

10.5.3 Performance Management

The goal of performance management is to maintain system performance at levels which satisfy user response time requirements. The overall response time of the system should be maintained at acceptable levels even if the workload on individual system components (network cables, bridges, routers, multiplexors, databases, dictionaries, etc.) varies. Performance management includes the following:

- Performance monitoring to measure system activities (e.g., arrival rates, queues being formed, bottlenecks, performance thresholds)

- Analysis/prediction to assess the results and impact of performance measurement on response times
- Tuning to adjust resources (e.g., adjusting network traffic) to improve system performance.

These functions can be performed by a centralized center which remotely monitors the system for performance bottlenecks. According to the framework shown in Fig. 10.15, these functions can be applied to different component types and can be provided at different support levels. For example, performance management may detect and correct performance problems in workstations, network components (LAN hardware/software, cables, modems, routers, bridges, gateways, etc.), resource sharing software (distributed data and transaction management systems, client-server packages, etc.), and application systems. Performance management services can be at the consulting level only where the user receives guidance in performance measurement and correction. These services may be embedded in performance measurement software packages which help users diagnose and correct their own problems. A variety of performance monitoring, tracing, and prediction tools are becoming commercially available.

Performance evaluation in distributed computing systems is complicated due to the large number of interacting components. For example, in a large network, a message goes through several routes before it reaches its destination. It can be delayed at several points due to congestions at any of the intermediate stations or gateways. In addition, a relational database join between two tables residing at two different computers can send a burst of messages across network which can cause network congestion. If many tables in the network are being joined across the network, then it becomes very difficult to predict and tune the system performance. Performance of realtime distributed systems is an area of great importance because in such systems performance degradation can cause serious problems. For example, in a flexible manufacturing systems (FMS), a performance problem can bring a factory to a halt. Performance management in such environments requires a large number of interrelated variables, including communication problems due to noise and heat.

It is desirable to automate the distributed system's performance management as much as possible. Many tools for network performance monitoring are currently available. However, these tools have not been extended to include the issues of distributed applications management such as remote relational joins and client-server performance considerations. This is expected to be an area of future development.

An issue of particular importance is the performance of open systems. In these systems, many components from many vendors interoperate with each other. The standardizing bodies for OSI focus on functionality and not on performance. The vendors of OSI products are also concentrating on developing products which satisfy the functional specifications of the standards. Performance of OSI products is primarily the responsibility of the OSI users. The OSI products provide many options which can be configured to tune and improve the performance of a system. It is the responsibility of the users to properly tune the system, design applications for performance and manage performance through appropriate tools and techniques. This is needed for any system. However, in open systems it is primarily the responsibility of the user. The difficulty is that without automated aids it will be virtually impossible for the users to tune these systems.

10.5.4 Security and Accounting

Security services include the following functions:

- Authentication which verifies and controls the access of resources
- Data confidentiality to assure privacy of data and the access of data
- Data integrity to ensure that information is not altered or corrupted as it flows through a system
- Encryption/decryption which scrambles the data so that unauthorized users cannot understand it
- Security information management which provides administrative tools for creating and managing user profiles for access control
- Security alarm reporting to send alerts about security violations
- Audit trails which record the various security related events.

According to the framework shown in Fig. 10.15, these functions can be applied to different component types and can be provided at different support levels. For example, security may be enforced at workstations, at network access and at the application resource level. The security services can be at the consulting level only, where the user receives guidance in security procedures. The service may be embedded in security software packages which automate the security management. In the absence of adequate software packages, administrative policies are usually introduced with appropriate penalties (if you are caught accessing unauthorized data, you loose your job and/or are subjected to criminal prosecution).

Distributed systems introduce many security risks due to the widespread use of workstations and networks which are accessed by hundreds of users. The information transferred over networks is also quite sensitive because it carries corporate financial and strategic information. Many security and authentication packages are currently available (e.g., Kerberos on Unix and Resource Access Control Facility on IBM mainframes). Some government agencies are attempting to define standards. For example, the National Institute of Standards and Technology (NIST) has proposed a Digital Signature Algorithm (DSA) as the public encryption standard. This standard is being debated at the time of this writing. See, for example, Communications of the ACM, July 1992 issue. Environments such as Open Software Foundation's Distributed Management Environment and Unix International's Distributed System Management Framework are integrating many of the available tools. For example, Open Software Foundation's Distributed Management Environment (DCE) provides the following:

- Kerberos authentication, which allows principals to identify each other through secret key encryption. For example, the two principals exchange their secret keys with each other for authentication before information exchange. In addition, "tickets" are used to identify the name and the location of the principals.
- Secure Remote Procedure Call (RPC), which provides for data privacy. The OSF-DCE RPCs use trusted third party secret key encryption technology which allows a trusted third party to maintain a "key distribution center" for principals to obtain the same secret keys. The RPC automatically encrypts and decrypts data depending on the user choice: private, which encrypts all data, and non-private, which bypasses encryption/decryption.
- Cryptographic checksum, which allows detection of corrupted data for data integrity. The DCE Remote Procedure Call (RPC) uses the checksums so that the receiver can verify if the data was corrupted or modified while passing through the network.
- Registery service, which manages the database of valid principals. The database can be distributed to many sites and can be accessed from any computer in the DCE environment.
- Access control mechanism, which controls access to resources. Access control lists are used to associate users and user operations (read, update) to resources (databases, printers, programs, etc.).

The issue of accounting and billing in distributed computing is concerned with the difficult task of allocating costs based on resource utilization. Most organizations have specialized accounting and billing procedures which need to be extended for distributed computing. The main challenge in this area is to determine the originator of resource utilization and charge him or her for the expenditure. The difficulty is that one exchange between two processes at two stations can generate secondary traffic messages, which are often difficult to associate with the original exchange.

Protocols and standards for security and accounting in distributed computing are evolving. A detailed review of different authentication protocols in distributed systems is given by <Woo 1992>, and some future issues in network security are discussed by <Fireworker 1992>. Standards for open systems security are progressing at two levels: security architectures and application security. The OSI security architecture, originally defined in the ISO document 7498-2 (1984), is being refined for Authentication, Access Control, Confidentiality, Integrity, and Non-repudiation. International Standards in these areas are intended to be registered as OSI Standards by 1994. Standards for application security include Access Control for the Directory (X.500), Access Control for the OSI Management and Security Exchange for Association Service Elements. Other application security standards will be developed in the future.

10.5.5 Configuration Management

Configuration management for distributed computing facilitates the normal and continuous operation of distributed applications and the networks. It works with other management functions, such as fault and performance management, to correct or optimize the system's performance. Configuration management functions include the following:

- Keeping information about the release and version of the various hardware and software components of the environment (workstation software, LAN software, application software)
- Establishing and recording the interrelationships and the interdependencies between the various components of the environment (e.g., network configuration, application configuration)
- Establishing enterprise-wide standards for systems and subsystems to make system integration easier
- Clearly defining the functions and the interfaces between the components
- Specifying the guidelines and responsibilities for change management and control at the local as well as global levels.

These functions can be performed by a centralized configuration management system or can be decentralized to the end users. Some centralized configuration management is essential for the enforcement of standards and policies. However, "regional" configuration management is appropriate for large enterprises. In addition, according to the framework shown in Fig. 10.15, these functions can be applied to different component types and can be provided at different support levels. For example, the components to be managed may be workstation files/programs, LAN software, and/or application files and programs.

The support for configuration management may be at consulting level or enforced through environments such as the Open Software Foundation Distributed Management Environment and Unix International Distributed System Management Framework. Some other models have also been presented. For example, Black <Black 1987> presents a Distributed Automation Model (DAM) which contains detailed information about the hardware/software resources in a distributed environment. At its most general level, DAM contains information on project management, database administration, software inventory, and sources and uses of reports. DAM does not show any tools which can be used to store, retrieve, process, manipulate and transmit the DAM information. More information about DAM can be found in Black <1987, Chapter 10>.

10.5.6 Customer Contact and Operational Support

The customer contact and operational support is concerned with the day-to-day activities needed for a smooth operation. These services include the following:

- Help desk (hotline) support, where the users can call for information and to report problems with the system
- Operations, which involves system startup/shutdown, backup/recovery and failure recovery

- System administration, which involves user profile management and resource utilization monitoring
- Customer support, which shows the customers how they can best utilize the services.

These functions are usually performed by a customer support organizational unit which is the main point of contact between the users and information system services. According to the framework shown in Fig. 10.15, these functions can be applied to different component types and can be provided at different support levels. For example, customer support may be provided for workstations, for networks and for application systems. The customer services can be at the consulting level only where the user receives guidance in day-to-day operations. On the other hand, the customer service may be provided by one or more customer support organizational units, with staff and associated hardware/software tools. In large organizations, the customer service centers resemble control centers in the airline industry, with dozens of consoles and monitors.

These functions are difficult in distributed computing for two reasons: the large number of network and application system configurations to be supported, and the interdependencies between the various systems and subsystems. It is not easy to train and retain the user consultant and operations staff. For example, it may be necessary to consolidate different hotlines (network hotlines, IBM hotline, LAN hotline, Unix hotline, etc.) into a single unit so that the users call one number to get help. The single unit can maximize staff cross-training opportunities and can be used to provide performance and fault management functions.

10.6 An Example: Management and Support for XYZCORP

XYZCORP management needs to develop a management and support approach to completely integrate all business, engineering and manufacturing operations. They are especially frustrated that the IMCS (Integrated Manufacturing Control System) has not gotten off the ground despite a great deal of excitement about this system. This system, introduced in the Chapter 8 case study, receives a customer order and assembles and packs a product for shipping within half an hour of order reception. Figure 10.17 shows a simplified conceptual diagram of IMCS. XYZCORP management wants to use IMCS as a pilot in integrating and automating the order processing, CAD/CAM and the "manufacturing" processes of the company products (radios, TVs, VCRs, calculators, IBM PC clones).

The management feels that all the activities initiated so far have focused on technical issues (e.g., network architecture and layout, distributed databases and distributed applications designs) and not on how to manage and support integration efforts such as IMCS. Consequently, in a moment of brilliance they have developed a management approach which consists of the following:

- A distributed computing systems plan (Section 10.6.1)
- An organization and staffing approach (Section 10.6.2)

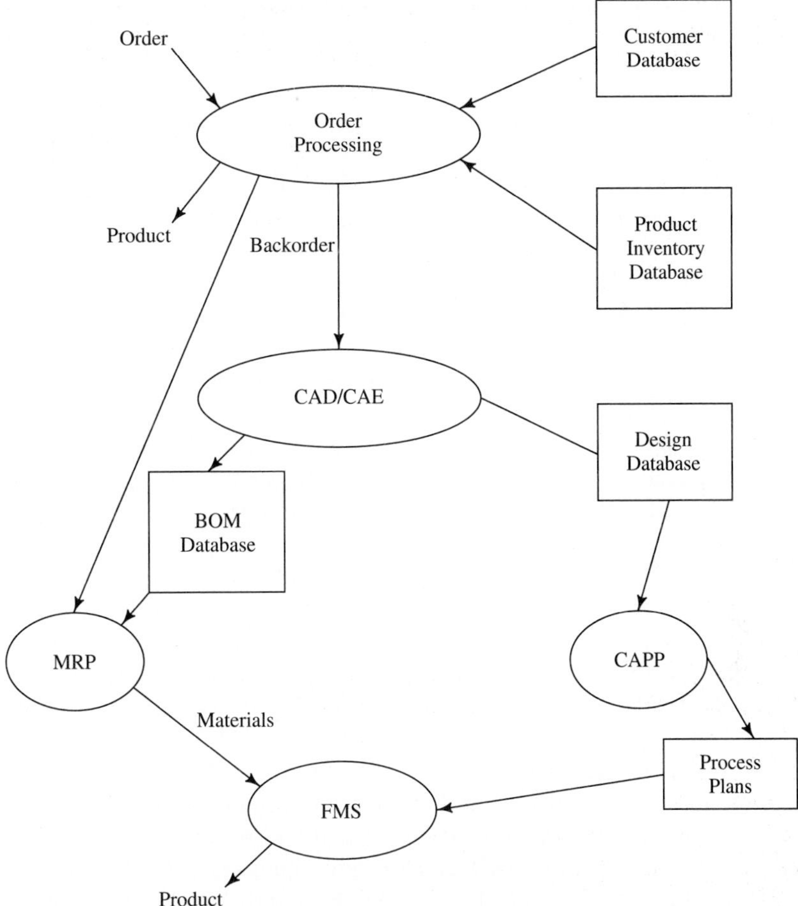

FIGURE 10.17 Integrated Manufacturing Control System (IMCS)

- A development/deployment approach (Section 10.6.3)
- A methodology for monitoring and controlling (Section 10.6.4).

A discussion of these activities will illustrate the main concepts discussed in this chapter. The results shown here reflect a combination of results obtained through consulting assignments and a series of industrial seminars in which this case study was used by the author.

10.6.1 Example of Distributed Computing Plan

The distributed computing plan for IMCS follows the steps of the methodology presented in Section 10.2 (Fig. 10.5).

10.6.1.1 Application Systems Identification

An information services strategy for integration has already been completed and has produced a list of applications. This strategy was developed as a combination of Business Systems Planning (BSP) and Critical Success Factors (CSF) planning methodologies. The strategy is to integrate the business processes (accounts receivable/accounts payable, order processing, marketing information systems, and computerized checkout system), engineering processes (CAD, CAE, computer-aided process planning) and manufacturing processes (material requirement planning, production scheduling and flexible manufacturing systems). The critical component of integration is the IMCS project which will integrate and automate the order processing, CAD/CAM and the "manufacturing" processes of the company products (radios, TVs, VCRs, calculators, IBM PC clones). The information services strategy is to use IMCS as a driving force for the integration process. As stated previously, IMCS will receive a customer order and assemble and pack a product for shipping within half an hour of order reception. In the first year, it will focus on two products and then expand them later. The first year experiment will attempt to exploit the latest technologies (including multimedia applications), if possible.

As shown in Fig. 10.17, the first stage of IMCS is an order processing system which processes orders for a product. If the specified product is in stock and the customer credit is acceptable, the product is shipped to the customer from the finished product inventory. The product inventory is adjusted to show products shipped. For an out of stock product, a CAD/CAE system produces the design based on the customer specification. The design is then downloaded to a Computer Aided Process Planning (CAPP) system where the manufacturing program is automatically created which shows how the product will be assembled. The CAPP system uses the information about available assembly equipment to generate the process plans. An MRP (Material Requirements Planning) system determines the materials needed for the product. MRP systems use sophisticated algorithms to take into account quantity discounts, vendor preferences, various capacity constraints and factory status. The manufacturing program is downloaded to a flexible manufacturing system (FMS), which consists of an area controller, two cells and several manufacturing devices. FMS also receives a production schedule (how many products to manufacture) and needed raw materials. Because FMS is a realtime system, it must conform to the constraints of realtime control on factory floors.

10.6.1.2 Application Architecture Planning

The data and programs of IMCS are allocated to the Chicago/Detroit sites or to the appliance stores in this stage. In addition, the application systems interconnections are determined in terms of file transfer, terminal emulation, distributed databases and cooperative processing. Figure 10.18 shows the result of application architecture planning for IMCS. Existing applications in XYZCORP were not affected in this stage.

The CAD/CAE and FMS systems were allocated, naturally, to the Detroit branch, and the MRP system was allocated to the corporate office due to management

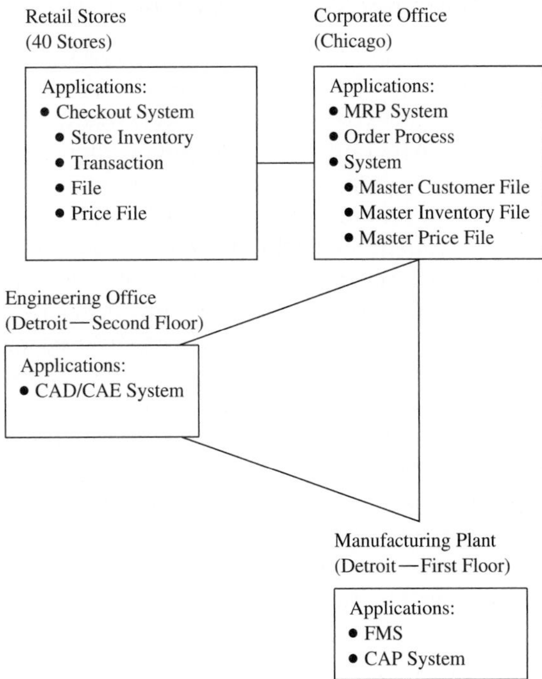

FIGURE 10.18 Application Architecture

restrictions. However, a great deal of discussion and debate ensued for the order processing and checkout system.

The order processing system was initially centralized with a master customer file, a master product inventory file and a master price file. The price file would be sent to the individual stores at the start of the day, and individual store inventory files would be kept at the stores.

The checkout system would operate in the stores where each store processor maintains a database with this store's inventory, a separate database that records each day's transactions and another database with prices of items sold at this store. At checkout, a point-of-sale (POS) terminal would read the code on an item and get the price information from the store's price database. The POS terminal would also post each sale to the transaction database. The processor updates inventory every hour. At the end of each day, the main computer facility in Chicago would read the transaction and inventory files and send a new price file.

The information from different stores would be accessed mainly through client-server and file transfers. A distributed database manager was chosen for the order processing and MRP system because it allows users to allocate the data at different sites and then access and manipulate the information without knowledge of the location. The main application of cooperative processing was the FMS because it required realtime message exchange between processes as peers.

10.6.1.3 Platform and Network Architecture Planning

In this stage, the computing systems at the various sites were chosen and the business, manufacturing and engineering network architectures were determined, keeping the integration in mind. For computing systems, it was decided that mainframes would continue to be used in the corporate office, minicomputers would be used in the stores, workstations would be used in the engineering branch, and different PLCs and robots would be used in the manufacturing plant. The exact vendors and models would be chosen based on compatibility with the existing equipment.

The platform decisions have led to the following choices for network architectures: IBM's SNA will be used in the corporate office and the stores, token ring LANs will be used in the corporate offices, TCP/IP will be used in the engineering office, and MAP will be used in the manufacturing plant. The company will explore the OSI based products in the next two years.

A great deal of discussion has focused on the tradeoffs between the TCP/IP protocol suite, OSI based products and proprietary networks. After some debate, the XYZCORP management has decided to stay with TCP/IP protocol suite and SNA because of their stability and manageability. This situation may change as more reliable products based on open systems become available. With open systems, the same system would run on all sites and the need for gateways would be eliminated.

10.6.1.4 Physical Network Planning

A site planning for XYZCORP for the next five years has been completed. The corporate headquarters will continue to house the data processing (first floor), administration and distribution (second floor) and marketing/corporate planning and management offices (third floor). The Detroit branch will continue to house the manufacturing plant on the first floor, and the research/engineering will be located on the second floor. In short, no major site modifications are planned. Figure 10.19 shows the result of the physical interconnection planning. Due to the long time horizon, detailed physical layouts are not needed.

The physical interconnections between the sites will use the latest in wide and local area networks. Basically, fast packet switching will be used between remote sites and fiber optic LANs will be used for local operations. Due to the emphasis on multimedia applications, ISDN and BISDN are of primary interest. Figure 10.19 also shows the interconnecting gateways between the three sites and the various computers and the application systems at all sites.

10.6.1.5 Resource Estimation and Evaluation

The overall plan to introduce IMCS requires several resources: the computing systems will need to be updated and installed, the network hardware and software will be upgraded, the files and programs will be developed and allocated to various sites, and standards and policies will be needed for smooth operation. In addition to the hardware/software cost, a great deal of human resources will be needed for the installation, operation, and management of IMCS. These are discussed in the next section.

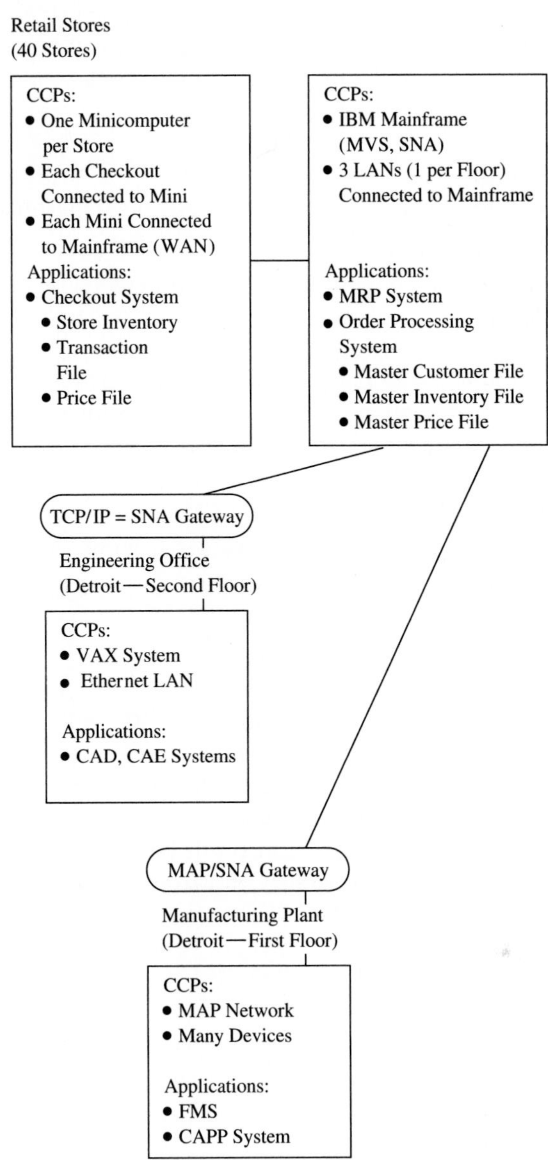

FIGURE 10.19 Physical Interconnection Planning

10.6.2 Example of Organization Structure Design

The current organizational structure of XYZCORP is strictly functional (marketing, engineering, manufacturing, and information services divisions). Each division is subdivided into several departments. Some departments may be subdivided into groups.

This structure needs to be studied to introduce IMCS. An organizational unit is needed to provide leadership in IMCS. This unit will be responsible for taking the overall plan discussed in the previous section and make it a reality within a year. We need to address the following three issues:

- How will the organizational unit be introduced in the organization? Will it be a new department/division or extension of an existing department/division?
- How will the unit be staffed and trained?
- Which IMCS related organizational activities will be centralized and which will be decentralized?

To determine the organizational structure, the procedure shown in Fig. 10.7 is used. The results of applying this procedure are shown in Table 10.4. The organizational unit may be implemented as follows:

- New department within an existing division
- Expansion/modification of an existing department
- Expansion/modification of an existing division (the division may choose to spread the task to many departments)
- An advisory board or a committee

The evaluating factors listed in Table 10.4 are the most important in this situation. Based on what is most important, a decision can now be made. For example, XYZCORP decided to create a new department because it provides a clarity of results and is more conducive to enforcement of standards and responsiveness to management decisions. The new department will be under the Information Technology Division. This division was previously known as the Data Processing Division and has

TABLE 10.4 Evaluation of Organizational Structure

	Alternatives			
Evaluating Factors	*New Department*	*Existing Department*	*Existing Division*	*Committee*
Clear focus/commitment (goal setting)	5	3	2	1
Clear accountability (progress monitoring)	5	3	2	1
Ease of implementation	1	3	5	4
Speed of implementation	2	4	4	2
Time required to make decisions	5	3	2	0
Problem diagnosis ease	5	3	2	1
Openness to innovation	5	4	2	1
Standards of policy enforcement	5	4	4	3

Note: Values range from 0 to 5 (5 means highly satisfactory).

been renamed to emphasize the role of information technology for integration. The role of the new division will be to coordinate all information technology efforts at XYZCORP. The "new and improved" Information Technology Division, shown in Fig. 10.20, consists of departments in software development (business, engineering, and manufacturing software design and construction), user support (helpdesk, user contacts, systems analysis), technical support (database support, network support, technical planning and hardware/software selection, system performance, capacity planning), and operation/maintenance (system startup, diagnostics, equipment maintenance and installation).

The new department, called the Integrated Systems Department, will focus on the distributed computing issues and will be responsible for IMCS. The 10 staff members will work as consultants to other departments in application interconnectivity, distributed data integrity, and distributed application architectures. For example, they work with the technical support department on application versus network interconnectivity issues, with the developers on distributed application architecture issues, with the user support department on the helpdesk for distributed computing, and with operation and maintenance on how to diagnose distributed computing problems. Procedurally, any "local" issues are referred to the existing department while any issues that cross computer systems are first referred to the Integrated Systems Department. These staff members have backgrounds in interconnectivity (application interconnectivity, device interconnectivity, network interconnectivity), distributed databases, client-server systems, and distributed application design.

The first major assignment of this department is to develop an architecture of IMCS and work with a team of analysts, one from each area (manufacturing, engineering, business), and developers who will actually build the system. Six developers have been assigned to the IMCS project. Contractors will be used for additional programming, if needed. This Department will also test the IMCS system before it is deployed. Consequently, all of the design and testing functions are centralized.

10.6.3 A Deployment and Support Program

The Integrated Systems Department (ISD) will serve, as mentioned previously, mainly as a consulting group. Let us review the exact role of this department in the development, deployment and support of the IMCS application systems and the underlying

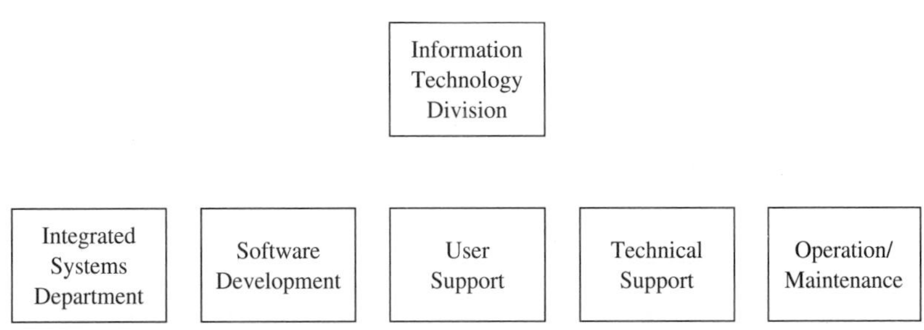

FIGURE 10.20 Organizational Structure for Information Technology Division

platforms. Figure 10.21 shows the development/deployment and Fig.10.22 shows the monitoring and control activities of ISD as they relate to IMCS. It can be seen from Fig. 10.21 that ISD will develop the application system architecture and perform the acceptance tests for IMCS. It will act as a consultant to other departments in the actual application system development and selection/installation of the underlying DCP. Fig. 10.22 shows that ISD will only do fault management, and performance management of the IMCS software. All other functions are performed by other departments with ISD as a consulting resource.

Based on this program, the following steps have been outlined for the Integrated Systems Department for the first year:

1. Hold a planning session to determine who will do what and to work out the logistics of information and decision flow.

Service Categories	*Functions Supported*	*Components Supported*	*Levels of Support*
Application System Development/ Deployment	• Analysis • Development • Purchase • Installation	• All application components	Consulting support
Application System Architecture	• Architecture • Testing	• All application components	Hands-on
Platform Acquisition/ Installation	• Selection • Purchase • Installation	• Computers • Communications	Consulting support

FIGURE 10.21 Example of Development/Acquisition for IMCS

Service Categories	*Functions Supported*	*Components Supported*	*Levels of Support*
Configuration Management	All	IMCS software	Consulting only
Fault Management	All	IMCS software	Consulting and hands-on
Performance Management	All	IMCS software	Consulting and hands-on
Accounting and Security	All	IMCS software	Consulting only
Operational Support	All	IMCS software	Consulting only

FIGURE 10.22 Example of Monitoring and Control Support for IMCS

2. Provide the consulting, administrative, and platform services as determined by the planning session.
3. Develop a training/education plan for the Information Technology Division on distributed computing and IMCS.
4. Explain to the customers the nature of IMCS work.
5. Identify two products on which IMCS can be tried.
6. Consult literature and visit other plants for outside perspectives on IMCS.
7. Develop an architecture of IMCS and test IMCS when completed.
8. Help in the installation/configuration of IMCS.

At the end of year, ISD will document the observations, problems encountered, approaches used, and lessons learned, etc. (technical plus organizational). It will then prepare, present and defend a proposal for continuation/ discontinuation/modification of IMCS and identify additional products for IMCS, if possible.

10.7 Management Summary and Trends

The support and management challenges in distributed systems can be analyzed by using the planning, organizing/staffing, development, and monitoring control cycle as a framework. We have used this framework in this chapter to review the major issues and to outline the main approaches. In general, the following key points and trends can be observed:

- Distributed computing technology does not change business needs, it just gives additional choices to satisfy those needs.
- There are more questions than answers in this area. Many opportunities for leadership and original work exist in this area because very little good literature exists.
- It is essential to tie the distributed computing technologies with the corporate information systems strategy by extending the scope of the planning process.
- The management and support activities are complicated due to the changing and evolving underlying technologies in networks, distributed databases, client-server systems, distributed application systems, and distributed application systems. These technologies create interdependencies which must be carefully managed.
- The distributed environments such as the OSF DME and UI DSMF are combining many of the tools, techniques, and standards into integrated environments for management control.
- Special attention needs to be paid to the evolving standards in management for the open systems. Most of these standards will be established by the mid 1990s.
- It is important for managers to develop a vision about how to utilize the tools effectively. Distributed systems may require increased centralized control in several areas.

- Broad staff training and perspective is important in order to understand the wide variety of issues to be addressed while managing distributed systems.

As a final comment, management and support of distributed computing is becoming more important and needs more attention because many technical problems are being solved but the management problems are not being addressed. While tools to assist management are beginning to appear, these tools cannot succeed by themselves without proper management philosophy and approach.

Problems and Exercises

1. Develop a table to show the main management processes and the tools available for each process.
2. Describe different levels of planning in organizations and describe the levels which are of importance in distributed systems.
3. Compare and contrast an information systems planning methodology (e.g., IBM's BSP) with the methodology shown in Fig. 10.5.
4. List the major issues in organizing for distributed computing.
5. List the major issues and approaches in centralization/decentralization of distributed systems.
6. Describe the acquisition and deployment policies of a company that you are familiar with.
7. Compare and contrast the OSF DCE and UI DSMF.
8. Describe the monitoring and control policies of a company that you are familiar with.
9. Consider an information system that you are familiar with and work through it as shown in Section 10.6.
10. List the management issues, in order of priority, that have not been addressed adequately.

References

Applegate, L., et al., "Information Technology and Tomorrow's Manager," *Harvard Business Review*, Nov.-Dec., 1988, pp. 128-136.

Appleton, D., "State of CIM," *Datamation*, Dec. 15, 1984.

Appleton, D., "A Strategy for Factory Automation," *Datamation,* Oct. 1977.

Attewell, P. and Rule, J., "Computing and Organizations: What We Know and What We Don't Know," *Comm. of ACM*, Dec. 1984, pp. 1184-1192.

Aulds, S., "Organizing for Integration," *Autofact '88 Proc., SME*, ISBN 0-87263-328-4, 1988, pp. 1.57-1.70.

Bertsekas and Gallager, *Data Networks*, 2nd ed., Prentice Hall, 1992.

Bray, O., "Integration of Configuration Management, MRPII," *Autofact '88 Proc., SME*, 1988, pp. 14.31-14.43.

Bruns, W., and McFarland, F., "Information Technology Puts Power in Control Systems," *Harvard Business Review,* Sept.-Oct., 1987, pp. 89-94.

Black, U., *Data Communications, Networks and Distributed Processing,* 2nd ed., Reston Publishing, 1987.

Blokdijk, A. and Blokdijk, P., *Planning and Design of Information Systems*, Academic Press, 1987.

Brown, O., and Hendrick, H., "Symposium on Human Factors in Organizational Design and Management II," North Holland, 1986.

Burn, J., "The Impact of Information Technology on Organizational Structures," *Information and Management,* Vol. 16, No. 1, Jan. 1989, pp. 1-10.

Campbell, R., "An Architecture for Factory Control Automation," *AT&T Technical Journal*, 1988.

Charan, R., "How Networks Reshape Organizations—For Results," *Harvard Business Review*, Sept-Oct., 1991, pp. 104-115.

Clark, T., "Corporate Systems Management: An Overview and Research Perspective," Comm. of ACM, Feb. 1992, pp. 50-59.

Clemens, E., "Evaluation of Strategic Investments in Information Technology," *Comm. of ACM*, Jan. 1992, pp. 22-37.

Cloutier, E., "Top Management Experiences in Applying CIM," *Engineering Network Enterprise Conf. Proc.*, Baltimore, Md., June, 1988, pp. 1-57.

Daner, S., "Organizing for CIM: the Evolution of Organizational Structure," *Autofact '88 Proc., SME*, 1988, pp. 1.43-1.70

Davis, G.B., "Strategies for Information Requirements Determination," *IBM Systems Journal*, Vol. 21, No. 1, 1982, pp. 4-30.

Dean, J.W., and Susman, G.I., "Organizing for Manufacturable Design," *Harvard Business Review*, Jan.-Feb. 1989, pp. 28-36.

Dearden, J., "The Withering Away of the IS Organization," *Sloan Management Review*, Summer 1987, pp. 87-92.

Donovan, J., "Beyond Chief Information Officer to Network Manager," *Harvard Business Review*, Sept.-Oct. 1988, pp. 134-140.

Dove, R.K., "Process Design Automation," *Autofact '88 Proc., SME*, 1988, pp. 10.13-10.30.

Drucker, P., "The Coming of the New Organization," *Harvard Business Review*, Jan.-Feb., 1988.

Edelstein, H., "Lions, Tigers, and Downsizing," *Database Programming and Design*, Mar. 1992, pp. 39-45.

Ellis, R., *Designing Data Networks*, Prentice Hall, 1986.

Fireworker, R.B., "Comments: Network Security Precautions," *Computer Communications Journal*, Vol. 15, No. 5, June 1992, pp. 283-285.

Galbraith, J.R., *Organization Design*, Addison-Wesley, 1977.

Gallier, R., "Information Systems Planning: A Manifesto for Australian-Based Research," *The Australian Computer Journal*, May 1987, pp. 55-69.

George, J. and King, J., "Examining the Computing and Centralization Debate," *Comm. of ACM*, July 1991, pp. 63-72.

Gurbaxani, V. and Whang, S., "The Impact of Information Systems on Organizations and Markets," *Comm. of ACM*, Jan. 1992, pp. 59-73.

Halevi, G., "CIM—The Future Technology," *IFIP*, 1986, pp. 1035-1041.

Hayes, R. and Schemer, R., "How Should You Organize Manufacturing?" *Harvard Business Review*, Jan.-Feb. 1978, pp. 105-118.

Herman, J., "The Move Towards Distributed Management Systems," *Business Communications Review,* Oct. 1991, pp. 74-76.

Herman, J., "OSF's Distributed Management Environment," *Business Communications Review*, May 1992, pp. 59-69.

Heyel, C., Ed., *The Encyclopedia of Management*, Van Nostrand-Reinhold, 1982.

Highsmith, J., "Structured Systems Planning," *Information Systems Management*, Vol. 4, No. 2, Spring 1987.

Huber, G., "A Theory of the Effects of Advanced Information Technologies on Organizational Design, Intelligence, and Decision Making," *Academic Management Review*, Jan. 1990, pp. 47-71.

Hulfnagel, E.M., "Information Systems Planning: Lessons from Strategic Planning," *Information and Management*, Vol. 12, No. 5, 1987, pp. 263-270.

IBM Corporation, "Business Systems Planning," 1978, GE20-0527.

Jones, A. and Mclean, C., "A Proposed Hierarchical Control Model for Automated Manufacturing Systems," *Jour. of Manufacturing Systems*, Vol. 5, No. 1, 1987.

Keen, P., *Shaping the Future: Business Design Through Information Technology*, Harvard Business School Press, 1991.

King, L., "Centralization/Decentralization in Computing Environments," *ACM Computing Surveys*, 1983.

King, W.R. and Premkumar, G., "Key Issues in Telecommunications Planning," *Information and Management,* Dec. 1989, pp. 255-266.

Kling, R., "Social Analysis of Computing: Theoretical Perspectives in Recent Empirical Research," *Computing Surveys*, Mar. 1980, pp. 61-110.

Kotter, J., Schlesinger, L. and Sathe, V., *Organization: Text, Cases and Readings,* Irwin, 1979.

LaVie, R., "The CIM Integrated Data Processing Environment in the European Open Systems Architecture CIM-OSA," *Engineering Network Enterprise Conf. Proc.,* Baltimore, Md., June 1988, pp. 1-33.

Leavitt, H. and Whisler, T., "Management in the 1980s," *Harvard Business Review*, Nov.-Dec., 1958.

Lederer, A. and Prasad, J., "Nine Management Guidelines for Better Cost Estimating," *Comm. of ACM*, Feb. 1992, pp. 34-49.

Malas, D.E., "Integrating Information Flow in a Discrete Manufacturing Enterprise," *Engineering Network Enterprise Conf. Proc.*, Baltimore, Md., June 1988, pp. 1-113.

Markus, L. and Robey, D., "Information Technology and Organizational Change: Causal Structure in Theory and Research," *Management Science*, May 1988, pp. 585-598.

Martin, James, *Distributed Data Processing Strategies*, Prentice Hall, 1985.

Martin, J.M, "CIM: What the Future Holds," *Manufacturing Engineering*, Jan. 1988. Mcleod, Raymond, "Management Information Systems," SRA, 1986.

Melkanoff, M., "The 'I' in CIM," *IFIP*, 1986, pp. 915-920.

Mintzberg, H., *The Structuring of Organizations*, Prentice Hall, 1979.

Mushet, M., "Application Systems Planning," *Information Systems Management*, Winter 1985.

Nolan, R., "Managing the Computer Resource: A Stage Hypothesis," *Communications of the ACM*, Vol. 16, No. 7, July 1973, pp. 399-405. NSF report, *A Research Agenda for CIM—Information Technology*, National Research Council, National Academy Press, 1988.

Nystrom, P. and Starbuck, W., *Handbook of organizational Design*, Oxford University Press, 1981.

Owen, D., "Information Systems Organizations—Keeping Pace with the Pressures," *Sloan Management Review*, Spring 1986, pp. 59-68.

Peck, R., "Planning Guide," *DataPro,* 1988.

Pratt, S., "Applicability of Decentralized/Centralized Control Procedures in Distributed Processing System Development and Operation," *IEEE Trans. on Engineering Management*, Vol. EM32, No. 3, Aug. 1985, pp. 116-123.

Ranky, Paul, *Computer Integrated Manufacturing*, Prentice Hall International, 1986.

Radding, A., "Dirty Downsizing," *Computerworld*, Aug. 10, 1992, pp. 65-68.

Rockart, J., "The Changing Role of the Information Systems Executive: A Critical Success Factors Perspective," *Sloan Management Review*, Vol. 24, No. 1, 1982, pp. 3-13.

Rockart, John, "Distributed Data Processing Model," *SHARE 48*, Mar. 4-11, 1977.

Straub, D. and Wetherbe, J., "Information Technologies for the 1990s: An Organizational Impact Perspective," *Communications of ACM*, 32, 11, Nov. 1989, pp. 1328-1339.

Umar, A., Krackenburg, R. and Lyons, T., "Organizing for Computer Integrated Manufacturing," *Information and Management Journal*, 20, 1991, pp. 355-362.

Umar, A. and Teorey, T.J., "A Generalized Procedure for Program and Data Allocation," Proc. of First Pacific Conference in Computer Communications, Seoul, Korea, Oct. 1985.

Urwick, L., *Notes on the Theory of Organization*, American Management Association, 1952.

Van De Ven, A. and Joyce, W., *Perspectives on Organization Design and Behavior*, Wiley, 1981.

Woo, T.Y.C. and Lam, S.S., "Authentication for Distributed Systems," *IEEE Computer*, Jan. 1992, pp. 39-53.

Zachman, J.A., "Business Systems Planning and Business Information Control Study," *IBM Systems Journal*, Vol. 21, No. 1, 1982, pp. 31-53.

Concluding Comments

Let us conclude by highlighting the main concepts, outlining the trends and listing open issues. Figure 1.1 in Chapter 1 shows the typical jargon, concepts, interrelationships, models, frameworks, products and techniques associated with distributed computing systems (DCS). Review this diagram to see if you have learned something (if not, how about starting all over again!). We have attempted to answer questions such as:

- What exactly is distributed computing, what are its advantages/disadvantages and what are the impediments to its growth?
- What are the underlying technologies in distributed computing and what approaches can be used to develop/acquire, utilize, support and manage these technologies?
- What do the commonly used terms such as Ethernet, TCP/IP, SNA, LU6.2, OSI, FTP, NFS, sockets, X.25, client-server systems, and distributed databases mean; how are these terms related to each other; and why/when should anybody worry about them?
- What are different levels of interconnectivity in distributed computing? Why network connectivity is not enough?
- What is the role of open systems in the current and future technologies? How do the current and proposed standards help in interoperability, portability and integration?

- What are the key issues in the management and support of distributed applications and the networks on which these applications reside?

We hope that we have answered these questions. You should be able to architect and design distributed computing services and mesh diverse networks, databases, user interfaces, applications and management services to meet the enterprise needs. We introduced a Distributed Computing Reference Model (DCRM) in Chapter 1 and used it throughout this book to introduce different topics. Numerous references for additional study have been provided. To illustrate the key points, a single case study has been used throughout the book.

Let us outline major observations and trends:

- The network technologies and facilities are moving toward wide, local and metropolitan area networks with data rates more than 100 Mbps.
- Newer applications in multimedia, graphics, video conferencing, and collaborative computing will demand higher bandwidths from the networks.
- The open network architectures such as OSI are becoming popular, however the proprietary networks such as SNA will be around for a number of years. TCP/IP Protocol Suite is becoming a de facto standard for heterogeneous system interconnection. For many years to come, interoperability between different networks will continue to be a major issue, and OSI will play a major role in this respect.
- Network management is gaining momentum in terms of tools, standards and corporate visibility. Major emphasis is shifting toward enterprise-wide network management.
- Client-server systems are becoming increasingly popular. The availability of off-the-shelf client-server support software and applications will further fuel this popularity. These systems will provide the major shift for moving some of the application logic and data away from mainframes. These systems will utilize the power of desktop computers.
- Workstations and mainframes have, and will continue to, coexist as information clients and information servers, respectively.
- Distributed data and transaction management systems (DDTMSs) need major work to support heterogeneous data sources and to manage transactions across multiple computers connected through diverse networks and operating systems. Standards such as the OSI Remote Data Access (OSI-RDA) and OSI Transaction Processing (OSI-TP) will play a key role in this area.
- Distributed operating systems are still in the state of the art stage and could transition to state of the market and state of the practice in the next four to five years. Many interesting and challenging research topics are open in this area (e.g., distributed workflow management and distributed fault management).
- The distributed computing platforms (DCPs) which combine computing hardware, local operating systems, communication hardware and software, distributed data managers, distributed operating systems, and client-server facilities will become

more and more available. These platforms will provide the following enabling technologies for distributed application development, management, and support:

- RPCs (remote procedure calls)
- RDAs (remote data accesses)
- Global naming services
- Object oriented approaches to hide internal details
- Transparent access to distributed data
- Management of distributed transactions
- Distributed work flow management
- Network management and security/authentication services
- Presentation services (e.g., graphical user displays)
- Network services across WANs, MANs, LANs.

• Major challenges exist in structuring and designing distributed application systems which best utilize the sophisticated DCPs. The main challenge will be to develop methodologies to build successful and cost-effective applications which utilize this technology.

• Future distributed applications could increasingly use the sophisticated DCP facilities mentioned previously for peer-to-peer cooperative processing. These cooperative processors will operate as human cells which cooperate with each other for problem solving.

• Management and support of distributed computing is becoming more important and needs more attention because many technical problems are being solved but the management problems are not being addressed. The management challenges will include planning issues, organizational structures, evaluation of computing versus communication tradeoffs, system security, and backup/recovery in networks. In addition, the focus will shift from network to systems management.

• The management need for transition strategies will grow. The need for piloting new technologies, monitoring the growth of standards, developing infrastructures for transition, and coexistence with existing technologies will grow.

• Standards will play more important role in the "open systems" with increased cooperation and coexistence between standardization bodies (OSI, IEEE, ANSI, OSF) and vendors. The OSF approach of developing interoperability by cooperation between developers by IBM, DEC, HP, and others will provide good foundation for portability and interoperability.

• The combined effect of many advancing technologies will be to provide transparency at the following levels:
  - End user transparency
  - Developer transparency
  - Designer transparency
  - Manager transparency

In other words, the designers, users, developers and managers will view distributed computing as a single large computer system. At such a point, the need to distinguish between distributed computing and just computing will disappear.

Naturally, there are several open questions. Here is an interesting one: What will be the real business need for distributed computing if very fast communication links can get information from any site instantly? What will be the business case for centralization/decentralization in such situations? One school of thought is that we will find ourselves back in the traditional mainframe model because centralized servers with terminals may eventually prove to be cheaper and easier to manage. For example, consider the following arguments. First, some studies are showing that Xterminals with servers are cheaper than workstations with servers. Second, the transparency of services means that a user does not know the service providers (there may be one or hundreds of servers). Third, if it does not make any difference to the user who is providing the service, why not use one computer to provide all the services?

Here are two other topics worth considering: Network supercomputing and neural networking. It is technically feasible at present to tie supercomputers through Gigabit per second networks. These high speed computers tied to high speed networks have a great deal of potential. Developments in neural computing are attempting to simulate the physical thought processes of human brain. Basically, a human brain can be thought of as a network (a neural network) in which billions of neurons are interconnected in a variety of ways. However, the individual neurons are slow (about 100 Hertz). Supercomputers connected through very fast networks create fast neural networks for developments in artificial intelligence.

What is missing? Applications. There is a need for imaginative and creative applications in business, management, engineering, manufacturing, medicine, education, and many other walks of life to fully take advantage of these powerful technologies. Although many applications in multimedia, video conferencing, and collaborative computing are being discussed frequently, there is a need for innovative thinking in this area. Such applications can usher a totally new information age for all of us.

We will just have to wait and see what happens. There is one thing for certain: as more technologies emerge, there will be an increased need to synthesize these technologies into products which help solve real problems of today and tomorrow. This book has, hopefully, discussed the concepts, the vocabulary, and the basic building blocks. Additional sources of information, listed in Chapter 1, Table 1.1, may be consulted for more information (more specific references have been given in each chapter). It is important for the readers to keep an eye on state of the art, state of the market, and state of the practice aspects of technologies for a complete picture. Good luck.

APPENDICES

Tutorials on Selected Topics

Appendix **A**

Tutorial on Communication Protocols and the OSI Stack

A.1 Introduction

The OSI Model, introduced in Chapter 3, defines many standards in its 7 layers (Fig. A.1 shows a few). The first compilation of the OSI standards, published in 1978, contained 99 standards. The 1990 compilation <Folts 1990> has more than 1000 standards and is published in six volumes. The objective of this tutorial is to give a few examples of the OSI standards which are relevant to distributed computing.

Section A.2 describes the principles of communication protocols which are used in protocol standards for OSI or any other network architecture. Section A.3 gives examples of layer 1 to 3 protocols which concentrate on the physical aspects of communication networks. The Transport Layer and the upper layers are reviewed in Section A.4. The options in network interconnectivity and interworking are discussed in Section A.5.

This short tutorial is intended primarily as an overview of the OSI standards. More details about the OSI Model can be found in the following books:[1]

1. Black, U., *OSI: A Model of Computer Communications Standards*, Prentice Hall, 1991.
2. Black, U., *The X Series Recommendations*, McGraw-Hill, 1992.
3. Black, U., *The V Series Recommendations*, McGraw-Hill, 1992.
4. Cameron, D., *OSI: An International Standard for Open Systems*, Computer Technology Research Corporation, Charleston, S.C., 1991.
5. Henshell, J. and Shaw, S., *OSI Explained: End to End Communications Standards*, 2nd ed., Prentice Hall, 1991.
6. Jain, B. and Agrawala, A., *Open Systems Interconnection: Its Architecture and Protocols*, Elsevier, 1990.
7. MacKinnon, D., McCrum, W., and Sheppard, D., *An Introduction to Open Systems Interconnection*, Computer Science Press, 1990.
8. McClain, G., *The Open Systems Interconnection Handbook*, McGraw-Hill, 1992.
9. Rose, M., *The Open Book: A Practical Perspective on OSI*, Prentice Hall, 1990.

A.1.1 OSI Terms and Definitions

The OSI Model is based on a large vocabulary of terms and definitions. Let us, once again, review the three basic terms: service, protocol and standard. A *service* represents the functions performed by layer N for layer N+1. Layer N can be viewed as a "service provider" for layer N+1. Layer N+1 is a "service user" of layer N. A *protocol* specifies the precise rules of information exchange between two peers. A protocol specifies the message format (e.g., bit pattern) and the rules to interpret and react to the messages. Protocols are the basis for interconnection and interworking of different

[1]If these books do not satisfy you, then by all means read the six volumes published by McGraw-Hill <Folts 1990>.

Layer 7—Application Layer

User-level formats and procedures, programs, operators, devices
Examples: Virtual Terminal, FTAM, X.400 e mail,
CMISE (Common Management Information Service Element),
EDI (Electronic Data Interchange),
ODA (Office Document Architecture),
X.409 (Message Handling Systems),
X.500 (Directory Services)
TP (Transaction Processing)

Layer 6—Presentation Layer

Management of entry, exchange, display, & control of data; interface transformation and application

Example: ISO 8822 (Connection-Oriented Presentation)

Layer 5—Session Layer

Session administration services, control of data exchange; delineating/synchronizing data operations

Examples: X.215 and X.225 (Session Service and Protocol Definition), accepted as ISO 8326 and 8327

Layer 4—Transport Layer

Transparent transfer of data between sessions; optimize use of available communications services

Examples: X.214 (Transport Service Definition) and X.224 (Transport Service Definition) equivalent to ISO8072 and ISO8073

Layer 3—Network Layer

Form and route packets across networks of networks

Examples: X.25, X.75, ISDN interfaces (I.450/I.451), subnetworks (ISO 8473)

Layer 2—Link Layer

Data flow initialization, control, termination, recovery

Examples: HDLC, IEEE 802.3, IEEE 802.4, IEEE 802.5, IEEE 802.6
FDDI frames, ISDN frames (1.441)

Layer 1—Physical Layer

Electrical/mechanical interfaces to communication media

Examples: RS232, RS449, X.21, ISDN interfaces (I.430, I.431), FDDI physical interface

FIGURE A.1 OSI Reference Model: Functions and Services

systems and are thus the "visible" aspect of OSI. *Interworking* here means the exchange of meaningful information to support distributed processing tasks. Protocols can be tested and verified for conformance. A *standard* is an agreed upon formal specification of the protocols and/or the services. International standards are very much like treaties between different parties—they specify high level goals as well as detailed procedures. The OSI standards specify the OSI Reference Model, the services to be provided by the different layers of the Model and the protocols for exchange of information between peers.

The following definitions will also help our discussion:

- An *entity* implements functions of each layer and also the protocol for communicating with peer entities in other systems. Examples of an entity are a process implemented on a chip or a software subroutine. There are one or more entities in each layer of the OSI open system.
- A *service access point (SAP)* is an interface (port) used by each entity to communicate with entities in the layers above and below it.
- *Primitives*: An entity at layer N requests the services of layer N-1 via invocation of primitives. An example of a primitive is a subroutine call.
- An *intermediate system* only performs functions related to the lowest three layers of the Reference Model (e.g., routing and bit transmission).
- An *end system* provides the functions above the Network Layer: Transport, Session, Presentation, and Application. Examples of end systems are computers on which applications reside. End system is a synonym of "host," a term commonly used to refer to computers where applications reside.

We will capitalize the first letter (e.g., Network, Application, Session) to refer to the OSI layers.

A.2 Principles of Communications Protocols

A.2.1 Classification of Protocols

Communication protocols, the protocols used in communication networks, can be classified in terms of services such as access initiation, flow control, acknowledgement handling, failure handling mechanisms, and error checking. These services are performed at different layers of the OSI Model, some more often than the others.

The access initiation of a protocol decides how two entities in two different systems establish and control the information exchange. There are several methods of access initiation.

- Polling/selection schemes in which a master asks (polls) the other entities (slaves) if any of them want to send any data. If they do want to respond, they send the message to the master, otherwise they pass. Most polling systems use a circular list to ask the slaves. If the master wants to send a message to a slave, then it selects (i.e., tells a slave to get ready to receive data). This scheme is used in many terminal handling systems where the mainframe acts as a master.
- Contention schemes do not use a master. Instead, the sender sends the message if the communication facility (e.g., a line) is free. If the facility is not free or the

message collides with another, the sender waits and attempts to send again. In this scheme, the receivers check to see if the message is for them. This scheme is used in peer to peer systems such as CSMA/CD.

- The time slot scheme uses time slots to send messages at given times. If no message is sent in the time slot, then the sender has to wait for the next time slot.

The flow control feature of a protocol decides if the two entities will communicate with each other in simplex (one way, always), half duplex (two ways, one at a time) and full duplex (two ways, simultaneously). Full duplex protocols are not trivial to implement because the two entities can send and receive information simultaneously. Full duplex protocols can use two channels (one for sending, one for receiving) or they can intermix data and control in same message. Special "framing" bits are employed to indicate message type (data, control).

The acknowledgement control schemes can employ the following schemes:

- *Acknowledgement Ignore*: The sender just keeps on sending the message and does not wait for any acknowledgement from the receiver.
- *Stop and Wait*: The sender waits for an acknowledgement before sending the next message. The positive acknowledgement (ACK) indicates that the message has been received properly on the other side. The negative acknowledgement (NACK) indicates that the message has not been received properly due to sequencing or frame check error. Sometime, this protocol is also referred to as the "ACK-NACK" protocol.
- *Sliding Window*: Instead of waiting for ACK-NACK for each message, the sender transmits up to n messages (n is the window size) before waiting for an acknowledgement. The receiver remembers the next message to be received within the window. In case of an error, the sender may retransmit all n messages. This facility greatly improves the speed and efficiency of the network and is especially useful in global networks where waiting for response of each message is too slow due to turnaround delays. Many protocols, such as TCP and SDLC, use a sliding window.
- *Piggybacking*: When two entities are operating at full or half duplex, a common situation in interactive computing, then the acknowledgements can be sent (piggybacked) with messages instead of a separate message which only carries the acknowledgement. For example, the acknowledgement from message i, system A, can be sent with the next data for system A. Piggybacking is also used in many protocols, such as SDLC.

The failure handling schemes commonly use a timeout mechanism where the sender waits for an ACK-NACK for a while (timeout period) and then resends the message. Thus if a message is lost on its way, it is resent. However, timeout mechanisms may resend a message which was properly delivered and processed but for which the acknowledgement was lost. In this case, the same message will be reprocessed erroneously (for example, this could withdraw the same amount twice). To circumvent this situation, the sender attaches a sequence number to each message before it is sent. The receiver checks for the sequence number with an expected sequence number to verify that the correct message has arrived. Sequence numbers are useful to detect and recover from many types of errors. For example, consider that message number 5 is being sent:

- If the message is lost before it is received and processed, the timeout mechanism resends the same message. The sequence number checking finds no jump in sequence numbers (message 5 received after message 4, 5 is resent but the receiver does not know).
- If an acknowledgement is lost on its way back after being processed, then the receiver will resend message 5. However, the receiver will find that this is a duplicate message and throw it away.

The error control schemes are used by communication protocols to detect if the data in a message has been distorted due to communication media errors. Examples of error control schemes are the vertical redundancy checks (VRC), which add a parity bit per byte of each data byte sent; cyclic redundancy checks (CRC), which add parity bits per block; and the combined VRC and CRC schemes. Most of the current protocols use the combined VRC and CRC schemes. The sender builds a CRC frame check sequence (FCS) by using some predetermined algorithm and sends FCS with the message. The receiver applies the same algorithm on the received message and builds a received message FCS. The receiver then compares the two FCSs and indicates an error (NACK) if the two do not match.

A.2.2 Generic Protocols

Let us review a few generic protocols to illustrate how the aforementioned classification can be applied. The simplest information exchange protocol is the *contention-based, simplex, acknowledgement-ignored protocol* in which the sender keeps on sending the information and the receiver keeps on receiving the information. This protocol (known as the unrestricted simplex protocol), displayed in Fig. A.2, is based on the following assumptions:

1. Sender and receiver are always ready.
2. There are no errors on the communication channel.
3. There are infinite buffers on both sides or the processors at both sides are of the same speed.
4. Transmission is always in one direction (sender always sends, receiver always receives).

These assumptions are naturally very simplistic and are not satisfied in most communication systems. Let us remove the first three assumptions for a more realistic protocol. A *Stop and Wait, Timeout Half-Duplex Protocol with Sequence Numbers*, is

```
Procedure, Sender              Procedure, Receiver

begin                          begin
  repeat                         repeat
                                   wait for message
    send message                   receive message
  until end                        process message
                                 until end
```

FIGURE A.2 Unrestricted Simplex Protocol

used commonly to handle initial handshaking, communication channel errors and the different machine capabilities of the senders and receivers. A simplified version of this protocol is shown in Fig. A.3. Although this protocol satisfies many practical situations, the computer to computer communications protocols commonly employ full duplex, sliding window, and piggybacking schemes.

Remember that as more functions are added in a protocol, the message format as well as the rules of the protocol become more complicated. For example, in the unrestricted simplex protocol the message format is very simple (data only). However, message formats for a full duplex protocol with piggybacking, sliding windows and sequencing must provide bits to clearly identify the message type (ACK versus data), control information (session initiation/termination commands) and sequence numbers. We will see some formats when we discuss various protocols. A generic message format is shown in Fig. A.4.

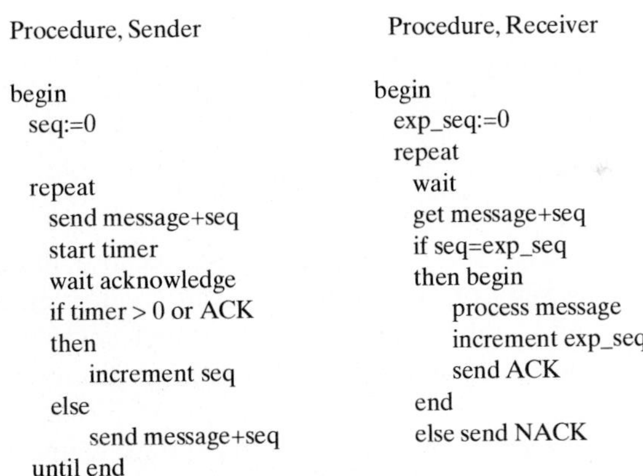

```
Procedure, Sender              Procedure, Receiver

begin                          begin
  seq:=0                         exp_seq:=0
                                 repeat
  repeat                           wait
    send message+seq               get message+seq
    start timer                    if seq=exp_seq
    wait acknowledge               then begin
    if timer > 0 or ACK                process message
    then                               increment exp_seq
        increment seq                  send ACK
    else                           end
        send message+seq           else send NACK
  until end
```

FIGURE A.3 Stop and Wait, Timeout Protocol with Sequence Numbers

Header	Flags	Data	Trailer

FIGURE A.4 A Generic Message Format

The header identifies the start of a message and usually shows the sender/receiver addresses. The flag fields are used to show if the data is application data, control, or an acknowledgement. The flags are used to carry several other pieces of information such as sequence number and command category and/or priority. The data field contains the application data, acknowledgement and/or commands being sent. The trailer field shows the end of message delimiters and error detection fields (checksums). A good discussion of generic protocols can be found in <Tannenbaum 1988>. An early discussion of various protocols is given by <Davies 1979>.

A.2.3 Connection-Based and Connectionless Protocols

The protocols discussed so far are generic in nature and are applicable to OSI as well as non-OSI systems. Let us now concentrate on the OSI connection-based and connectionless services and protocols.

In connection-based services, two entities at layer N communicate, using a protocol, by means of an N-1 connection. This logical connection is provided by the entities in the N-1 layers on both ends. A connection can exist at any layer of the hierarchy. In the abstract, a connection is established between two N entities by identifying an N-1 service access point for each N entity. The basic idea of connection-based service, also called a reliable service, is that before any communication between two entities at layer N takes place, a connection between layers at N-1 must be established. The basic primitives of connection-based service are as follows:

- Establish connection
- Transfer data
- Break connection

This makes the service reliable and robust because the lower level layers can take the responsibility of establishing a clean connection and can also take care of out of sequence and lost messages. Thus the entities at layer N can assume that a correct message has arrived. This reduces the processing requirements at layer N.

In connectionless services, there is no need for connection establishment prior to data transfer. Each transmission carries all the information needed. The basic primitive of connectionless service is:

- Transfer data

Connectionless protocols are more efficient because the needed control information is in one data unit and not spread over the network in different data units. The main disadvantage of these protocols is that they do not guarantee that a message will be delivered in sequence or delivered at all. It is the responsibility of participating entities to verify that the message is properly sent and received.

A.2.4 Protocol Efficiency

It is natural to observe that the processing logic increases as the message format and protocol sophistication increases. This is why the adaptor cards and software routines which support sophisticated protocols are more expensive. An issue of particular interest to us is the efficiency versus functionality of protocols, e.g., when to choose rigorous and sophisticated protocols and when not to. Basically, the rigor of protocols chosen depends on the type of applications. For example, the protocols employed for financial transactions are much more rigorous than the ones employed to transfer files in academic environments.

A common measure of protocol efficiency is the communication channel utilization given by the (data bits/total bits) per message of a protocol <Tannenbaum 1988>. For an error free line, the channel utilization is given by

utilization = data bits/(data bits + header + acknowledgement + idle bits)

where idle bits = 2*idletime*capacity(bps) and the idletime = interrupt + propagation delay. This measure does not include the processing overhead at the sender/receiver stations. This measure assumes that the communication channel is the most valuable resource; an assumption not necessarily true in fiber optic networks with slower processors.

Protocol verification tries to find if a protocol will produce correct results under errors and unscheduled events. The common approach to protocol verification is to build detailed analytical models. More information about protocol efficiency and verification can be found in <Tannenbaum 1988, pp.239-252>. A comprehensive discussion of this topic can be found in <Schwartz 1987>. For a mathematical and formal analysis, the reader should refer to <Bertsekas 1987, Davies 1979>. The IEEE Software Magazine, January 1992, is a special issue on network protocols and contains excellent articles on the protocol design, protocol validation for large-scale applications, testing communication protocols, and the use of AI in protocol design.

A.3 Examples of Layer 1 to 3 Protocols: Physical Communication Networks

The protocols in the first three layers are concerned with the physical communication network (also referred to as network) characteristics. A network provides data transfer service between stations attached to the network. The network can be a simple LAN or a collection of subnetworks which are interconnected to form a network. The protocols in this category are layer 1 and 2 protocols for LANs and WANs (Section A.3.1). Examples of protocols which span the first three layers (X.25 and ISDN) are discussed in Sections A.3.2 and A.3.3.

A.3.1 Layer 1 and 2 Protocols for Subnetworks

Many LAN protocols have been specified and are used in the first two layers. Examples of these protocols are the IEEE 802 protocols such as the IEEE 802.3, IEEE 802.4, IEEE 802.5 and the FDDI Protocols. Figure A.5 shows the main LAN standards, with information about communication media used (coaxial cables, twisted pair, optical fiber), transmission techniques employed (broadband, baseband, carrierband), and transmission data rates allowed for each standard. We discussed these topics in Chapter 2.

ISO uses the High-level Data Link Control (HDLC) protocol in layer 2 for WANs. HDLC includes Synchronous Data Link Control (SDLC), the layer 2 protocol used by IBM's SNA. (HDLC is a general term for OSI data link control; you choose options to use SDLC and/or X.25 data link controls.) The basic characteristics of SDLC are as follows:

- It uses synchronous data transmission which transmits data in blocks. On the other hand, the asynchronous transmission, used in many data link protocols, transfers one character at a time, separated by start and stop bits.
- It is bit-oriented because the control characters are bit strings and not character strings. In byte oriented protocols, the control characters are EBCDIC/ASCII characters.
- It uses polling/selection for access initiation.
- It supports full duplex operations so that both parties can send and receive information simultaneously. It can, however, be used on half duplex lines.
- It uses sliding window and piggybacking for acknowledgements.

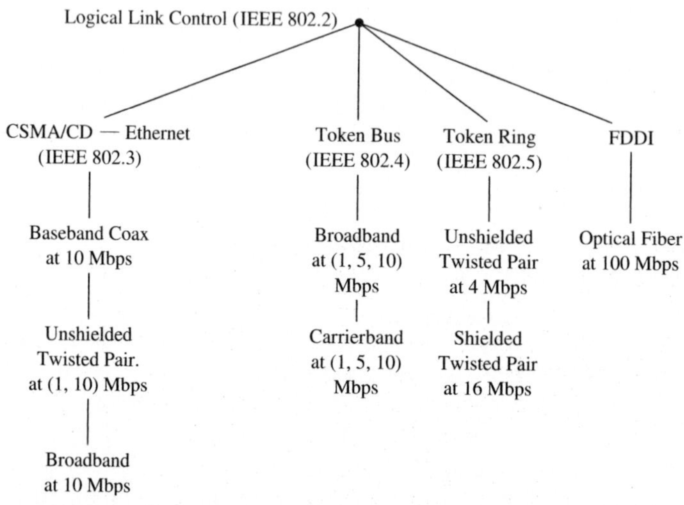

FIGURE A.5 Example of LAN Lower-Level Standards and Protocols

- It uses timeout and sequencing for failure handling.
- It uses cyclic redundancy checks (CRC) for error checking and control.

A.3.2 X.25 Packet Switching Protocol

X.25 is the best known packet switching protocol. Initially proposed by the CCITT in 1974 to standardize the packet switching systems, X.25 has been revised several times (e.g., 1976, 1980, 1984, 1988). X.25 is a collection of the following layer 1, 2, and 3 protocols for packet switching systems.

- Layer 1 physical interface specified as X.21.
- Layer 2 link level LAPB (Link Access Protocol Balanced).
- Layer 3 protocol, sometimes referred to as the X.25 PLP (Packet Layer Protocol).

ISO has adopted the X.25 PLP for the packet switched network interface (ISO standard 8208). The X.25 PLP, henceforth referred to as X.25, is widely used as the connection-based network layer protocol in the OSI model.

As stated previously, the objective of layer 3 is to break up messages (network service data units) into packets for layer 2 and find routes for the packets. The major decisions made in this layer are packet size, packet format, packet routing, and flow control. X.25 uses specific packet formats and routing algorithms. Before discussing these formats and processing rules, we should note the following CCITT terminology:

- A host (computer) is called a DTE (data terminal equipment).
- The carrier equipment (e.g., modems) is called DCE (data circuit-terminating equipment).
- Connections are called virtual calls.
- A byte is called an octet.

A.3.2.1 X.25 Packet Format

Figure A.6 shows a typical X.25 packet format. Other packet formats are variants of this format. The first 3 bytes of the packet comprise the packet header. The group and channel fields together form a 12 bit virtual circuit number where a virtual circuit is essentially a logical channel to send packets. The virtual circuit is independent of the physical channels and circuits that a packet actually traverses. Each user is assigned a virtual circuit for a virtual call. Due to the 12 bits in the X.25 packets, a host (DTE) can choose any of the 4095 virtual circuits and can have up to 4095 virtual circuits open simultaneously. The type field in the packet identifies the packet type. A control bit in this field is turned on to indicate that this is a control packet (command) and is turned off to indicate that this is a data packet. The calling and called fields are used when a call is initially made. These addresses are represented as decimal digits, 4 bits per digit, and use the public switched telephone format (country code, network code, address within a network). The facilities field specifies special facilities such as reverse charging ("collect calls").

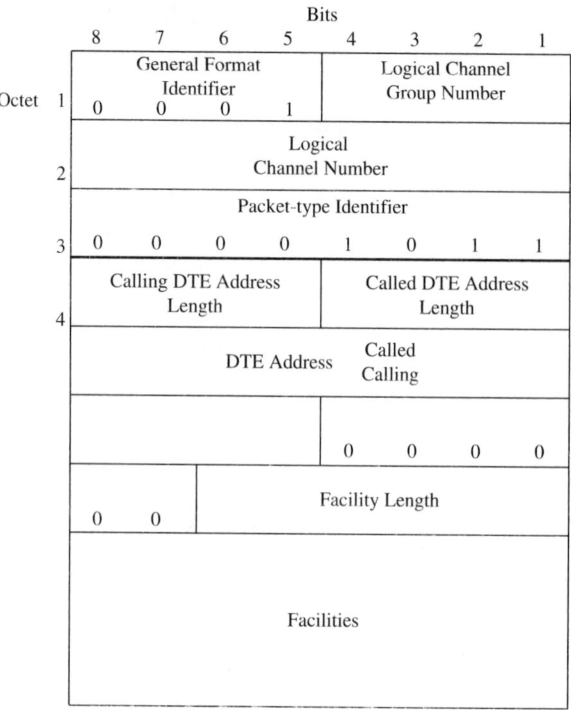

FIGURE A.6 X.25 Packet Format

A.3.2.2 X.25 Processing Flow

X.25 uses the concept of a virtual call to establish connections and transfer data. The virtual call goes through three phases (see Fig. A.7):

- *Call Setup Phase*: In this phase a connection is established. This is similar to dialing a telephone number. The DTE builds a Call Request packet which is sent to its DCE. The DCE then sends this message to the DCE on the other side, which in turn delivers it to the destination DTE. If the destination DTE wishes to accept the call, it sends a Call Accepted packet back. At this point, the originating DTE receives this packet and establishes a virtual circuit.
- *Data Transfer Phase*: In this phase, both DTEs exchange data in full duplex mode by sending data packets back and forth across the network.
- *Call Clearing Phase*: In this phase, the virtual call is terminated by either side sending a Clear Request packet. The receiving party causes disconnection by sending a Clear Confirmation acknowledgement.

The similarity between virtual calls and telephone calls is intentional (remember, X.25 was introduced by CCITT). It is obvious that for applications which need to send short bursts of data, the three phase approach adopted by X.25 adds too much

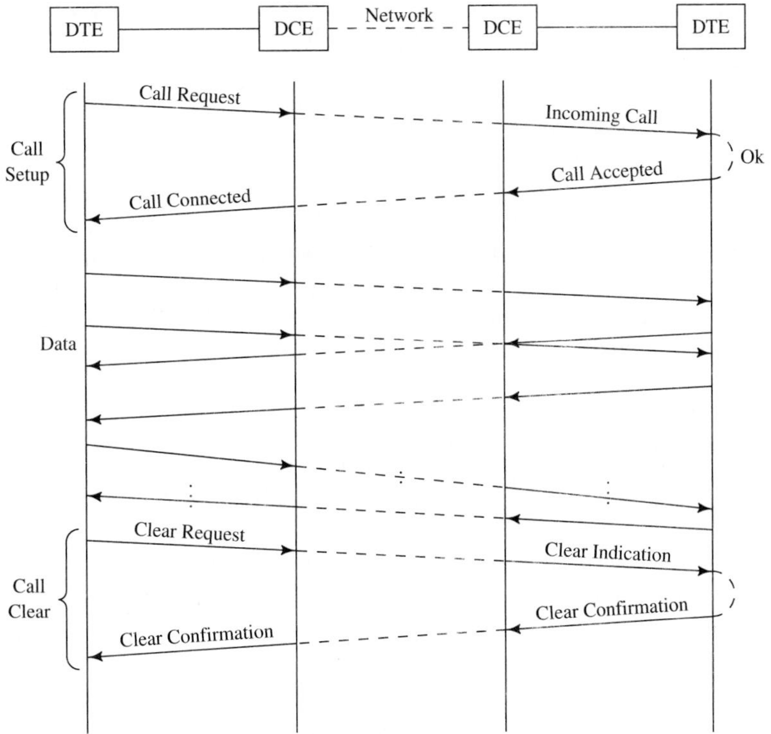

FIGURE A.7 X.25 Flow

overhead. For such applications, a "fast select" datagram protocol is used where a datagram is a single packet which consists of call request, data, and clear request information. In this case, a datagram packet establishes a connection, transfers the data, and disconnects—all in one exchange. This protocol, also called the "connectionless" protocol discussed previously, is in the DOD Internet Protocol (IP) and in the ISO8473 Connectionless Network Layer Protocol (CLNP).

In addition to a virtual circuit, X.25 supports permanent virtual circuits which are preassigned logical channels. Permanent virtual circuits are similar to the leased lines while the virtual call circuits are similar to the dial up lines. Permanent virtual circuits are used to transfer high volumes of data. X.25 also supports several special features, such as call barring and throughput classes.

The network layer protocols, such as X.25, use host to host as well as host to switching node (node) dialogues. The principal dialogue is between the host and its node; the host sends addressed packets to the node for delivery across the network. It requests a virtual circuit connection, uses the connection to transmit data, and terminates the connection. All of this is done by means of a host-node protocol. However, because packets are exchanged and virtual circuits are set up between two hosts, there are aspects of a host-host protocol as well. For this reason, X.25 includes layers 1, 2, and 3 protocols because a switching node may implement all three layers of X.25. The X.25 layer 3 protocol may reside on any two layers. A detailed explanation of X.25 can be found in Deasington <1989>.

A.3.3 ISDN Standards and Protocols

ISDN (Integrated Services Digital Network) is a set of CCITT standards for building advanced end-to-end digital networks. We discussed ISDN in Chapter 2. Our objective here is to show how ISDN standards fit within the OSI Model. Figure A.8 shows the ISDN standards in the OSI Model.

The CCITT recommended standards for ISDN are recorded as I.nnn, where nnn is a decimal number with the following values:

- The I.100 series of recommendations are concerned with general concepts and structural concepts of ISDN.
- The I.200 and I.300 series describe the service aspects and the network aspects of ISDN.
- The I.400 series describe the user-network interface aspects of ISDN. These standards are of direct interest to us and are used in Fig. A.8.

Layer 7 — Application Layer	
Layer 6 — Presentation Layer	
Layer 5 — Session Layer	
Layer 4 — Transport Layer	
Layer 3 — Network Layer	
ISDN D Channel I.451 and X.25 Packet	ISDN B Channel X.25 Packet
Layer 2 — Link Layer	
ISDN D Channel LAP=D Frames (I.441)	ISDN B Channel X.25 LAP=B
Layer 1 — Physical Layer	
ISDN Basic Service I.430 for Basic	ISDN Primary Service I.431 for Primary

FIGURE A.8 ISDN Standards in the OSI Model

The Physical Layer standards for ISDN specify I.430 for ISDN basic rate services and I.431 for ISDN primary rate services. The basic services are intended for domestic use and small businesses because they provide three channels: two 64 Kbps (Kilo bits per second) channels (B channels) and one 16 Kbps channel (D channel). The ISDN primary services are intended for business offices with 23 B or 30 B channels, and one D channel. The layer 2 and 3 standards for ISDN are specified for B and D channels, as shown in Fig. A.8. For example, I.441 LAP-D (Logical Access Protocol for D) is used for D channels, and X.25 LAP-B is used for B channels at layer 2. At layer 3, the X.25 packet can be used for B and D channels, or the I.451 is used for call control.

A detailed discussion of these standards and protocols is beyond the scope of this book (see the book by Kessler <Kessler 1991> for a detailed coverage of this topic). However, this discussion illustrates that ISDN can be easily included in the lower level ISO layers and thus can be used to support common higher level applications. It is also obvious that ISDN and X.25 networks can coexist well. For these reasons, many vendor network architectures such as IBM's SNA and DEC's DECNET support ISDN at their lower layers through gateways.

A.4 Transport Layer and Higher Layer Protocols

The Transport Layer provides overall integrity of the networking services of layers 1 through 3. Because of its end-to-end responsibility, the Transport Layer is only active in end systems. The upper layers of the OSI Model (Session, Presentation and Application) are responsible for ensuring successful interworking between Application processes at the end systems. The three upper layers are driven by the application semantics specified in the Application Layer. The Session and Presentation Layers perform functions under the control of the Application Layer.

A.4.1 Transport Layer Overview

The OSI Transport Layer operates in a connection-based as well as connectionless mode.

The connection-based services and supporting protocols for the Transport Layer are defined by the ISO 8072 and ISO 8073 standards. The CCITT X.214 and X.224 are equivalent to these standards. These Transport Service Definitions define three types of networks:

- Type A networks provide acceptable residual (user data) error rate and acceptable rate of signalled failures (e.g., resetting of network connections).
- Type B networks provide acceptable residual (user data) error rate but unacceptable rate of signalled failures (e.g., network connections are reset too many times).
- Type C networks provide unacceptable residual (user data) error rates.

The following five classes of Transport Services, referred to as TP0 through TP4, are defined for these three network types:

- Class 0 provides the simplest mechanisms for Type A networks.
- Class 1 provides an error recovery mechanism for lost data in Type B networks.
- Class 2 provides multiplexing and flow control without the Class 1 error recovery for Type A networks.
- Class 3 provides a combination of Class 1 and 2 services for Type B networks.
- Class 4 provides full detection and error recovery for Type C networks. This service can run over connectionless Network Layers with the added provisions of ISO 8073/Add.2.

All these classes can be used for different types of networks. Lower class services work well with reliable (Type A) networks and higher class services are needed for less reliable (Type C) networks. The reason for this is simple: more reliable networks do not need sophisticated Transport Services while less reliable networks need sophisticated end-to-end Transport Services to assure reliable communications. Class 4 Transport Services (TP4) are very powerful and are well suited for less reliable networks. TP4 ensures that all blocks or packets of data have been received without any error, i.e. data units are delivered in sequence, with no losses or duplications. In essence, TP4 Services are very similar to the ARPANET Transmission Control Protocol (TCP) services. The main power of TP4 is its ability to run on connectionless lower layers. Thus TP4 can run on many end systems and provide the basis for interworking (the higher level layers communicate with TP4 and TP4 deals with the underlying physical network routing and transmissions).

The connectionless transport service (CLTP), specified in ISO 8602, can operate on connectionless as well as connection-based Network services. Selection of the appropriate Network service depends on the availability of these services (some networks may only provide connectionless services) and the quality of service needed. For example, a connectionless Network service is likely to have less delays and costs but higher error rates than a connection-based Network service. For a connectionless Network service, CLTP sends the data unit directly to the Network service. However, for a connection-based Network service, the data unit is not sent until a connection has been established.

At present, many transport layer protocols are being developed for newer technologies. For example, see the transport protocols for multimedia communications <Shepherd 1990>.

A.4.2 The Session Layer

The Session Layer provides a means for two application processes to establish and use a connection, called a session. In addition to session establishment and release, it may provide services such as the following:

- Normal and expedited data transfer
- Token management to exercise the right to use certain functions
- Dialogue control at full or half duplex

- Error recovery and control through synchronization/resynchronization points and
- Exception reporting for unanticipated situations.

It is important to remember that the Session Layer provides these services only as a service provider. It is the responsibility of application designers to invoke appropriate services. For example, the Session Layer does not handle resynchronization automatically; it just provides this service when invoked. Examples of Session Layer standards and protocols are X.215 and X.225 (Session Service Protocol Definition), which have been accepted as ISO 8326 and 8327.

A.4.3 The Presentation Layer

The Presentation Layer is only concerned with the syntax (the representation) and not the semantics (meaning) of the data. It performs functions such as encryption, compression, terminal screen formatting, and conversion from one transmission code to another (such as EBCDIC to ASCII). Many file/code conversion and virtual terminal protocols are supported by this layer.

The main function of the Presentation Layer is syntax transformation. It is thus responsible for abstract syntax (e.g., data types) and transfer syntax (bit patterns while in transit). ISO has defined Abstract Syntax Notation One (ASN.1) (ISO 824) for specifying abstract syntax of data. A set of encoding rules (ISO 8825) is associated with ASN.1 for generating transfer syntax. The CCITT X.409 (Message Handling Systems) and ISO 8822 (Connection Oriented Presentation) are examples of other standards specified for this layer.

A.4.4 The Application Layer

The Application Layer provides all the services needed by the application processes (programs or humans) that are not already being provided by the lower layers. A large number of Application Layer services and protocols have been developed for a wide variety of application processes and continue to emerge rapidly. Some of the Application Layer services are "complete services" (e.g., file transfer, electronic mail) while others are basic building blocks from which other complete services can be developed. Two important basic services are as follows:

Association Control Service Element (ACSE). This service is designed to manage connections, called associations, between applications.

Commitment, Concurrency, and Recovery (CCR). This service is designed to coordinate multiapplication interactions in the face of failures.

The OSI basic stack consists of the ACSE plus the Presentation and Session Layer functions. This stack can be used to provide basic data transfer between any applications in the OSI Model.

The complete services may use any of the basic building blocks. Here are some examples of the protocols associated with these services:

Virtual Terminal Protocols. Many terminal emulators have been developed and are currently available in the application layer. An example is TCP/IP Telnet. The ISO VT service and protocol are developed for character-oriented, line-oriented, and page-oriented terminals. This standard is specified in the ISO 9040 document.

File Transfer Protocols. Many file transfer protocols have been developed and are currently available in layer 7. The best known file transfer protocols are: FTAM (File Transfer Access Method)—the OSI Model standard, and FTP (File Transfer Protocol)—the TCP/IP file transfer protocol. The ISO FTAM standard is specified in the ISO 8571-1 document. FTAM is based on the concept of a virtual filestore which is the common basis within OSI environment to perform file related operations (open, close, read, write) across systems.

Electronic Mail Protocols. The electronic mail protocols are growing rapidly due to the growth in the electronic mail applications. Examples of the electronic mail protocols are X.400 of the OSI and simplified mail transfer protocol (SMPTP) of the DOD Suite. The X.400 family of protocols is specified in the CCITT X.400 through X.420 documents. Some other applications, such as the Electronic Data Interchange (EDI), have been built on top of X.400 for business applications (e.g., billing, purchase orders). The EDI standard is specified in the ISO 9735 document.

Network Management Protocols. In most enterprises, the issue of managing large networks is gaining importance. Many network management protocols have been developed and are currently in use. Examples are the Common Management Information Protocol (CMIP) of OSI and the Simplified Network Management Protocol (SNMP) of the TCP/IP Suite. The CMIP standard is specified in the ISO DIS 9595 document.

Distributed Applications Protocols. Due to the increase in distributed applications, many protocols have been introduced to support access of remotely located data and interprocess communications between remotely located operations. Examples of some of the best known application layer protocols for distributed applications are as follows (due to the importance of these protocols in distributed systems, details about these protocols are given in the chapters indicated):

- *Distributed Applications Framework/Open Distributed Processing (DAF/ODP)*: This is an OSI framework and model for distributed applications. This framework is described in Chapter 9.
- *Remote Operations Service (ROS)*: This OSI service and protocol defines the standards for interacting with remote applications as peer-to-peer and clients-servers. The standard specifies the syntax and semantics about client calls to a server and the server responses. The ROS standard is specified in the ISO 9072-1 document and is reviewed in Chapter 5.
- *Remote Procedure Call (RPC)*: This family of protocols, now implemented on many networks, allows an application to call a remotely located procedure

(process) as if it were a local process. SUN RPC, Netwise RPC and OSF RPC are examples. An OSI RPC standard is being developed at present. RPCs are described in Chapter 5.

- *Remote Data Access (RDA)*: This is an OSI standard for update and retrieval of remotely located databases. The RDA standard is specified in the ISO DP 9579 document and briefly described in Chapter 6.
- *Transaction Processing (TP)*: These protocols are being developed for dialogue services and remote executions needed for transaction processing on multiple sites. The OSI TP controls the exchange of information between remote transactions according to a set of rules which ensure that a number of events are accounted for and completed reliably. The ISO TP standard is specified in the ISO DIS 10026-1 document and is reviewed in Chapter 6.

Miscellaneous Application Services and Protocols. Many other application layer protocols have been developed. Here are some examples:

- *Directory services protocols*: X.500 is an OSI standard for directory services. The ISO X.500 standard is specified in the ISO DIS9504-1 document.
- *OSI Security*: This OSI standard defines the protocols for secure communications. The ISO security standard is specified in the ISO DP 10181-1 document.
- *Distributed Office Architecture (DOA)*: This OSI framework defines the standards for office automation. DOA has defined a standard Office Document Interchange Format (ODIF) for document transfer. The DOA standard is specified in the ISO 10031-1 document.
- *Job Transfer and Management (JTM)*: This service is used for batch remote job entry (RJE) to a remote computer and for receiving the results. It permits users to inquire about the status of the request and to cancel, suspend, or resume processing. The JTM standard is specified in the ISO 8831 document.
- *Connectionless Upper Layers (CUL)*: These services have been developed for efficient client-server applications
- *Application Programming Interfaces (API)*: These OSI services define standardized interfaces for application programs to interface with network services.

A.5 Interworking (Interoperability) in Networks

Large communication networks are usually formed by interconnecting two or more similar, or dissimilar, communication subnetworks. Difficulties arise in interconnecting the subnetworks if they use different protocols. For example, it is not easy to interconnect TCP/IP, OSI, X.25, IBM Token Ring, Novell Netware and Appletalk subnetworks. In addition, two OSI conformant subnetworks cannot interconnect ("interwork") directly if one uses connection-based while the other uses connectionless Network services. Gateways, called "interworking units" in OSI, are needed for appropriate conversions. Approaches used in interworking units can exist at Application Layer, Transport Layer or Network Layer level.

A.5.1 Interworking (Interoperability) at Application Layers

Figure A.9 shows two major options used for Application Layer interworking. The dual stack approach, shown in Fig. A.9a, includes two stacks in end system X. The application in the end system X interfaces with both stacks. For example, this application can communicate to OSI applications through the OSI stack and to non-OSI applications through the non-OSI stack. The dual stack approach can be used to gradually phase out non-OSI applications. However, this option can lead to performance problems because the host with two stacks can become a bottleneck. Instead of dual stacks, protocol conversion can be used at Application Layer level. Figure A.9b shows an example of this approach in which a "mail gateway," translates TCP/IP

a. Dual Stack

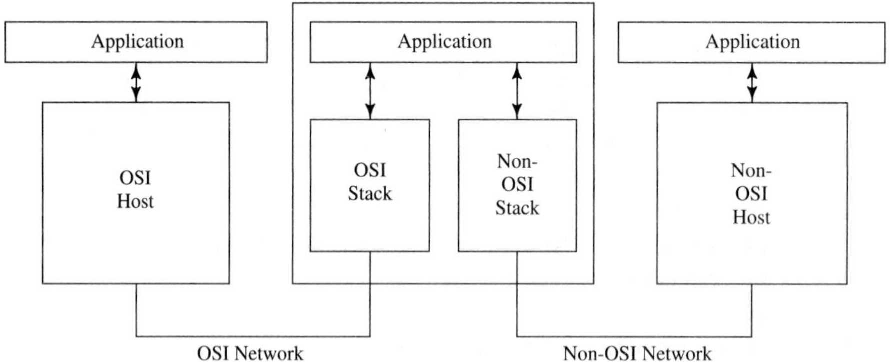

b. Application Layer Conversion

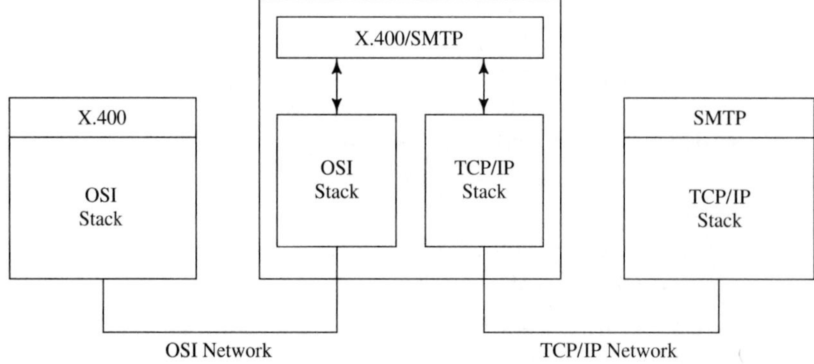

FIGURE A.9 Application Gateways

Simplified Mail Transfer Protocol (SMTP) to OSI X.400 mail protocol. This approach is implemented in many gateways at present.

A.5.2 Interworking (Interoperability) at Transport Layers

Figure A.10 shows examples of Transport Layer interworking. Figure A.10a shows TP4 running on many end systems and thus providing the basis for interworking. The "ubiquotous" TP4 layer is the basis for this type of interworking. Fig. A.10b shows a situation when TP4 cannot run in all subnetworks. For example, consider the case when a TCP/IP subnetwork needs to interwork with an OSI connectionless (CLNP) subnetwork. In this case, TP4 will run in OSI but is not supported on TCP/IP. Fig. A.10b shows a Transport Service Bridge for the interworking of TCP/IP and OSI networks at the Transport Layer level. These bridges use the Request For Comments (RFC1006). This RFC describes how the OSI upper layers (Session,

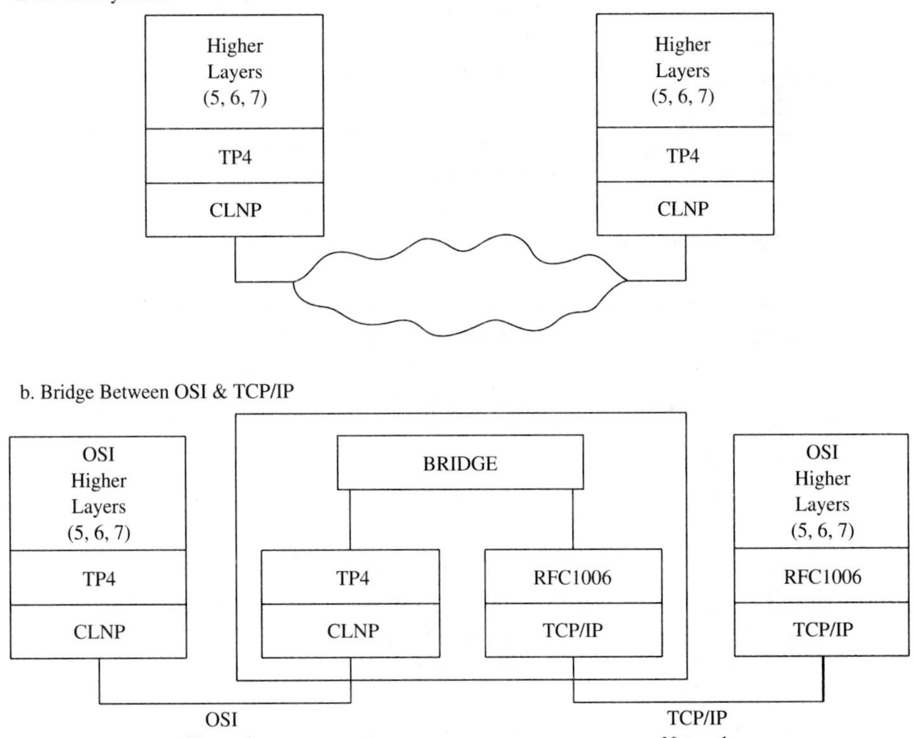

FIGURE A.10 Transport Layer Interworking

Presentation and Application) can operate on TCP/IP. As shown in Fig. A.10b, RFC1006 procedures are implemented in the TCP/IP end system and also in the Transport Service Bridge.

We should note here that RFC1006 can be used to run OSI on a TCP/IP network. This approach has the advantage that the very rich higher layers (5, 6, 7) of OSI can be used on top of the existing installed base of TCP/IP networks.

A.5.3 Interworking at Network Layers (Multiprotocol Routers)

Figure A.11 shows examples of Network Layer interworking. Fig. A.11a shows how X.25 PLP at layer 3 can be used for LAN-LAN and WAN-LAN interworking. X.25 PLP serves well at this level because it can be implemented on layer 2 of local and/or wide area networks. The network layer gateway is straightforward to implement in these cases because the same layer 3 protocol can be implemented on layer 2 of each subnetwork ("a ubiquotous layer 3"). This is an example of connection-based interworking.

Multiple protocol routers are used in the case where the same layer 3 protocol cannot be implemented on different subnetworks. This happens when a common communication medium (e.g., a backbone cable) is used by many different networks (Appletalks, Novells, SNA, TCP/IP, etc). Consider, for example, the situation where a corporate Ethernet backbone cable is used to interconnect many TCP/IP LANs. The routers on this backbone will be "single" protocol routers which will use IP (TCP is higher level and is not included in routers) to route the traffic betweeen senders and receivers. Now let us suppose that two Novell LANs also need to be connected to the same backbone. In this case, multiple protocol routers can be used to pass along Novell data over the IP backbone.

A technique called "encapsulation" or tunnelling is used in many multiprotocol routers. By using this technique, a multiple protocol router inserts the entire protocol "A" data units as a user data of protocol "B." For example, Novell IPX protocol is treated as user data and shuffled around the network as IP packets.[2]

A Novell-TCP/IP router would operate as follows:

- Encapsulate (insert) the IPX data at the sender before passing it to the TCP/IP network.
- The data unit is passed to different routers.
- The destination router (another Novell LAN interface) will "decapsulate" (remove the TCP/IP headers) the data unit and pass it to a Novell LAN.

This principal can be used to route OSI, token-ring, and Appletalk data over the same communication medium.

It should be noted that the ISO 8473 connectionless network protocol (CLNP) can be encapsulated over X.25 as well as the Internet Protocol (IP) of TCP/IP. A "convergence function" (CF) is used to provide an interface between CLNP and IP.

[2]IPX is the layer 3 and above protocol used in the Novell Netware LANs.

a. X-25 PLP Everywhere

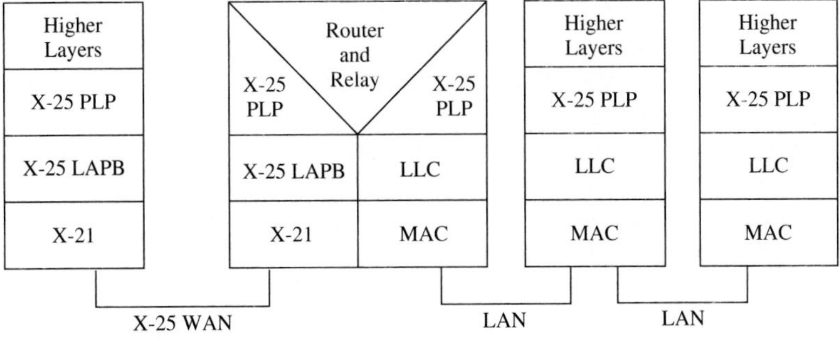

b. Multiprotocol Routers

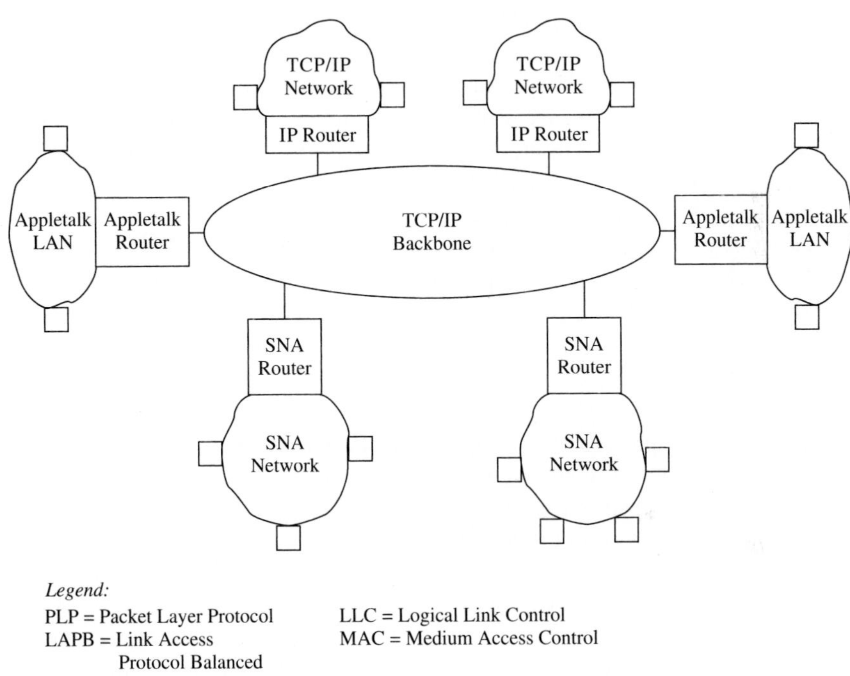

Legend:
PLP = Packet Layer Protocol
LAPB = Link Access Protocol Balanced
LLC = Logical Link Control
MAC = Medium Access Control

FIGURE A.11 Network Layer Interworking

The OSI 8473 Connectionless Network Protocol (CLNP) is referred to as an internetwork protocol. CLNP is intended to be implemented by end systems to provide end-to-end connectionless Network service. CLNP may be used across one subnetwork or on interconnection of a number of subnetworks. Logical Link Control Class 1 (LLC1) provides such a service in LANs.

Some multiprotocol routers do not use encapsulation. They send native protocols over the backbone by setting special flags in the message to indicate protocol type. For example, consider an Ethernet backbone which carries TCP/IP, Novell and

Appletalk traffic. A router can use the frame-type field of Ethernet frames to indicate what type of data is being carried. For example, a Novell data unit would be indicated by a special code in the Ethernet frame by the sending router. The receiver router will recognize this code and send it to the destination Novell LAN. This technique is used frequently by multiprotocol routers from Cisco, Inc.

Multiprotocol routers give organizations a great deal of flexibility in interconnecting different network architectures over the same physical wires. Figure A.11b shows a corporate backbone with many multiple protocol routers. These routers are extremely valuable in transitioning towards OSI by running OSI protocols (e.g., ISO 8473 Connectionless protocols) on TCP/IP LANs. Many routers can handle multiple protocols by adding a few software routines which encapsulate/decapsulate the data. It is important to remember that multiprotocol routers do not translate one protocol to another; they just allow different network protocols to share the same communication medium. A gateway is needed for protocol conversion, in addition to a router, if a TCP/IP end system needs to communicate with an OSI or SNA end system.

In the last few years, a multitude of multiprotocol routers have become available (see Hinden <1992> for a state of the market review). The Data Communications magazine publishes frequent articles on multiprotocol routers. An example of a multiprotocol router is the IBM 6611 Network Processor which allows equal coexistence of SNA, TCP/IP, DECnet, Novell and Appletalk layer-3 protocols. Another example is the DECNIS Router which allows coexistence of TCP/IP, OSI and DECnet networks. Details about multiprotocol routers can be found in <Cypser 1991, Perlman 1992, Rose 1990>.

A.5.4 Analysis

Which approach is better: Application Layer, Transport Layer or Network Layer interworking? Application Layer gateways, although used frequently, raise concerns about human resources which are needed to develop/maintain dual stacks and provide translation functions. The Transport Layer interworking has the advantage that it needs to be implemented only between the end systems (Transport Layers only exist at the end systems). However, this approach leads to several administrative and security problems as well as a single point of failure (if the interworking unit fails, then the end systems cannot communicate). The Network Layer interworking provides many alternate paths and makes automated management of routing tables easier. This interworking option is preferable. In addition, many multiple protocol routers which operate at the Network Layer are becoming commercially available.

We should note the following limitation of protocol conversion for interworking. When one protocol is converted to another, only those protocol elements, and associated services, that are common to both protocols are available end-to-end. This becomes a major concern for Transport Service Bridges between connectionless and connection-based systems because very few protocol elements are common between these two systems.

Many research and development efforts are being directed towards interworking between OSI and non-OSI networks. <Janson 1992> describes the results of a research project at IBM to interwork OSI with SNA and shows various interworking examples and tradeoffs. Additional information can be found in <Cypser 1992, Cypser 1991, Perlman 1992>.

A.6 Management Summary and Trends

Communication protocols are used in communication networks to provide services between peers such as access initiation, flow control, acknowledgement handling, failure handling mechanisms and error checking. These services are performed at different layers of the OSI Model. The OSI Model services and protocols have evolved at a very rapid rate to keep pace with the evolving network technologies, computing devices and the application requirements. Examples are the standards for LANs, ISDN, electronic mail, network management, distributed transaction processing and remote data access. One of the main issues at present is internetworking (or interworking): how to connect non-OSI (e.g., TCP/IP) end systems on OSI networks, and how to connect OSI end systems on non-OSI (e.g., TCP/IP) networks. Many "interworking units" are being developed at present to achieve these goals.

The main trend in OSI is that the interest in open systems and OSI will continue to increase. This interest will be driven by the user requirements in portability, integration and interoperability. It is hoped that more vendors will actively announce and support OSI products in the future.

We have attempted to expose the reader to the main services and protocols. For more details, the books listed in the beginning of this tutorial should be consulted.

CASE STUDY: OSI for XYZCORP

The investigation of an open network for XYZCORP (see the case study at the end of Chapter 3, project C) has stirred interest in OSI. You have been asked especially to show what role OSI should play in XYZCORP and to highlight the benefits of the OSI Protocol Stack.

Hints About the Case Study

Since it is not possible for XYZCORP to convert to OSI overnight, two approaches can be taken. First, XYZCORP could use OSI as a backbone to support non-OSI end systems such as SNA and TCP/IP. For example, X.25 networks (X.25 is OSI-based) can be used as a starter backbone which could be expanded later. The discussion in Section A.5, this chapter, and the case study at the end of Chapter 3, project C, should be consulted. The main strength of OSI protocols is the wide array of application layer services available (see Chapter 5, Section 5.2, and this appendix, Section A.4). The second possible approach for XYZCORP is to implement and provide the OSI higher layer services over non-OSI networks. For example, OSI higher layer services such as electronic mail and distributed transaction processing could be supported on a corporate wide TCP/IP network.

References

Belisle, P. and Janson, H., "OSI—What Is Next?" Enterprise Conference Proc., June 1988, pp. 4-1–4-28.

Bertsekas, D., and Gallager, R., *Data Networks,* Prentice Hall, 1987.

Black, U., *OSI: A Model of Computer Communications Standards*, Prentice Hall, 1991.

Cameron, D., *OSI: An International Standard for Open Systems,* Computer Technology Research Corporation, Charleston, S.C., 1991.

Chapin, A.L., "Connections and Connectionless Data Transmission," *Proc. of the IEEE*, Vol. 71, Dec. 1983, pp. 1365-1371.

Comer, D., *Internetworking with TCP/IP*, Prentice Hall, 1988.

Conard, J.W., "Services and Protocols of the Data Link Layer," *Proc. of the IEEE*, Vol. 71, Dec. 1983, pp. 1378-1383.

Cypser, R.J, "Evolution of an Open Communication Architecture," *IBM Systems Journal,* Vol. 31, No. 2, 1992, pp. 161-188.

Cypser, R.J., *Communications for Cooperative Systems*, Addison-Wesley, 1991.

Davies, D.W., et al., *Computer Networks and Their Protocols*, Wiley, 1979.

Deasington, R,J., *X.25 Explained: Protocols for Packet Switching Networks*, Prentice Hall, 1989.

Folts, H.C. (Ed.), *Compilation of Open System Standards*, McGraw-Hill, Ed. IV, Vols. 1 to 6, 1990.

Hayes, V., "Standardization Efforts for Wireless LANs," *IEEE Network,* Nov. 1991, pp. 19-20.

Henshell, J. and Shaw, H., *OSI Explained: End to End Communications Standards*, 2nd ed., Prentice Hall, 1991.

Hinden, E., "Multiprotocol Routers: Small Is Getting Big," *Data Communizations*, May 21, 1992, pp. 79-92.

Janson, P., Molva, R., and Zatti, S., "Architectural Directions for Opening IBM Networks: The Case of OSI," *IBM Systems Journal*, Vol. 31, No. 2, 1992, pp. 313-335.

Kaminski, M., "Manufacturing Automation Protocol (MAP)—OSI for Factory Communications," *87 International Symposium on Interoperable Information Systems: ISIS Conf. Proc.*, 1987.

Kessler, G., *ISDN,* McGraw Hill, 1991.

Perlman, R., "A Comparison Between Two Routing Protocols: OSPF and IS-IS," *IEEE Network Magazine*, Sep. 1991, pp. 18-24.

Proc. of the IEEE, Special Issue on Open System Interconnection, Dec. 1983.

Rose, M., *The Open Book: A Practical Perspective on OSI*, Prentice Hall, 1990.

Schwartz, M., *Telecommunications Networks: Protocols, Modelling and Analysis,* Addison-Wesley, 1987.

Sanders, R., and Weaver, A., "The Xpress Transfer Protocol (XTP)—A Tutorial," *ACM Computer Communication Review,* Oct. 1990, pp. 67-80.

Shepherd, D., and Salmony, M., "Extending OSI to Support Synchronization Required by Multimedia Applications," *Computer Communications*, Vol. 13, No. 7, Sept. 1990, pp. 399-406.

Seiffert, W.M., "Bridges and Routers," *IEEE Network Magazine*, Vol. 2, Jan. 1988, pp. 57-64.

Stallings, W., *Handbook of Computer Communications Standards*, Mcmillan, 1987, Vol. 1 (ISO Model).

Tannenbaum, A., *Computing Networks*, 2nd ed., Prentice Hall, 1988.

Appendix B

Tutorial on TCP/IP Protocol Suite

B.1 Introduction

TCP/IP (Transmission Control Protocol/Internet Protocol), briefly introduced in Chapter 3 (Section 3.4.2), was developed in the late 1960s and early 1970s by the Defense Advanced Research Projects Agency (DARPA) for interconnecting many computers in the ARPANET (Advanced Research Projects Agency Network). ARPANET initially consisted of the following protocols:

- Internet Protocol (IP)
- Transmission Control Protocol (TCP)
- File Transfer Protocol (FTP)
- Simplified Mail Transfer Protocol (SMTP)
- Terminal Emulator (Telnet).

Transmission Control Protocol (TCP) and Internet Protocol (IP) are the best known protocols in this suite (they operate roughly at layer 3 and 4 of OSI). Over the years, the entire ARPANET Protocol Suite has become known as the *TCP/IP Protocol Suite.* TCP/IP has dramatically grown in popularity in the last 20 years and has become the de facto standard for large heterogeneous networks. This Suite is available on almost all computing systems today including micro-computers, minicomputers and mainframes. For example, TCP/IP can be used to transfer files between IBM, DEC, SUN, PRIME, Macintosh and several other computers. TCP/IP also supports the "INTERNET" (note the capital letters) which is a very large network with over 60,000 interconnected computers around the globe. IP, the lowest protocol in this Suite, can reside on a very wide variety of physical networks such as Ethernets, FDDI based fiber optic LANs, dial up lines, X.25-based packet switching networks, or ISDN digital networks. TCP, the layer above IP, supports a very wide variety of higher level (application) protocols which allow users to emulate terminals, transfer files, and send/receive mail between different computers.

Due to its popularity, the TCP/IP Protocol Suite continues to evolve. The Internet Activities Board (IAB) provides a framework and focus for most of the research and development of these protocols. A series of technical reports, called Internet Request for Comments (RFC), describe the protocol proposals and standards. Actually, RFC is a formal document which can become a standard. For example, many of the current TCP/IP protocols are specified as RFCs.

The reader of this short tutorial should be able to answer the following questions:

- What are the basic components and facilities of the TCP/IP Suite?
- What type of applications can be run on top of TCP/IP?
- Why is TCP/IP so popular?
- How does TCP/IP compare and contrast with the OSI Model as an open system?

Before proceeding with this tutorial, the reader is advised to review the OSI Model and the TCP/IP overview in Chapter 3.

B.2 The TCP/IP Protocol Suite

The TCP/IP Suite originally consisted of five basic protocols: IP, TCP, FTP, Telnet, and SMTP. At present, Domain Naming Services (DNS) and Simple Network Management Protocol (SNMP) have been added to the TCP/IP basic protocols. In addition, many other protocols and user applications have been developed around TCP/IP. Figure B.1 shows the major protocols in the TCP/IP Suite and their relationships to each other. The TCP/IP Suite addresses the layer 3 and above issues. The Application Layer of this network architecture provides a rich set of file transfer, terminal emulation, network file access, and electronic mail services. It is important to note that a user application may choose to use any of the TCP/IP layers or may directly communicate with the physical network.

B.2.1 The Internet Protocol (IP)

The Internet Protocol (IP) is the lowest layer protocol defined in the TCP/IP Suite. It runs on top of whatever protocols are in use in the physical network (Ethernet, X.25, token ring, serial, etc). IP connects hosts across multiple networks (Internet) and provides a way of moving a block of data from one host machine to another through the Internet. This block of data is known as a datagram.

The delivery of datagrams is made possible by assigning an IP address to every host in the Internet. These addresses are 32 bits in length and are commonly denoted as four decimal numbers separated by periods (e.g., 21.152.214.2). The first part of the address shows which network the host resides on, and the rest of the address shows where within that network the host can be found.

IP is an unreliable (connectionless) protocol. This means that datagrams sent from one host to another may not be delivered in the order in which they were sent, may be delivered more than once, or may not be delivered at all. Higher layer protocols are expected to correct this deficiency. Unreliable protocols are much

User Applications	
Telnet FTP SMTP X Windows	TFTP NFS Sun RPC SNMP
Transmission Control Protocol (TCP)	User Datagram Protocol (UDP)
Internet Protocol (IP)	
Physical Network	

FIGURE B.1 TCP/IP Protocol Suite

simpler and cleaner to implement and facilitate dynamic routing (route around problems) of datagrams within the networks.

B.2.2 The Transmission Control Protocol (TCP)

The Transmission Control Protocol (TCP) runs on top of IP. It provides a reliable, ordered connection between processes on different hosts. One host may run many processes, so a process to process connection is needed. This means that application processes can establish a TCP connection and expect that data will arrive successfully and in order.

A TCP connection is essentially an error-free pipe from one host process to another. There is no inherent meaning at this layer to the data sent over this pipe. This generality allows a variety of higher layer protocols to run on top of TCP. The fact that this protocol is connection based means that some overhead is incurred at connection setup and disconnect. This is appropriate for applications that need to send large amount of data to one place, but it might not be so appropriate for quick, short exchanges.

B.2.3 The User Datagram Protocol (UDP)

The User Datagram Protocol (UDP) also runs on top of IP and is an alternative to using TCP. Like IP, UDP is an unreliable protocol. In fact, the major function that UDP adds to IP is a way to differentiate more than one stream of data going to or from a host (IP addresses only identify the hosts and not the processes within a host). Due to the unreliability of UDP, it is up to higher layer protocols running on top of UDP to provide reliability if it is needed.

UDP is appropriate for applications which exchange a small amount of information, such as a single request and a reply to it. In such applications, the overhead of establishing a connection is unnecessary. UDP may also be appropriate in applications requiring the exchange of data with more than one host. Since every UDP datagram is individually addressed, a host can talk to as many other hosts as necessary without having to establish a TCP connection to every one of them.

B.2.4 Higher (Application) Layer Protocols

Many higher layer protocols run on top of TCP and UDP. It is also possible to define private application protocols as long as both hosts agree on the protocol. The following protocols (the first three belong to the original DOD Suite) are among the best known application protocols defined in the TCP/IP Suite.

- *Telnet*: This protocol is used to provide terminal access to hosts and runs on top of TCP.
- *File Transfer Protocol (FTP)*: This TCP based protocol provides a way to transfer files between hosts on the Internet.

- *Simple Mail Transfer Protocol (SMTP)*: This TCP based protocol is the Internet electronic mail exchange mechanism.
- *Trivial File Transfer Protocol (TFTP)*: This UDP based protocol also transfers files between hosts, but with less functionality (e.g., no authorization mechanism). This protocol is used typically for "booting" over the network.
- *Network File System (NFS) Protocol*: This UDP based protocol has become a de facto standard for use in building distributed file systems through transparent access.
- *X Window*: This is a windowing system that provides uniform user views of several executing programs and processes on bit-mapped displays. Although X Window is supposedly network independent, it has been implemented widely on top of TCP.
- *SUN Remote Procedure Call (RPC)*: This protocol allows programs to execute subroutines that are actually at remote sites. RPCs, like X Window are, supposedly network independent but have been implemented widely on top of TCP. SUN RPC is one of the oldest RPCs. Examples of other RPCs are Netwise RPC and OSF RPC. RPCs are described in detail in Chapter 5.
- *Domain Naming Services*: This protocol defines hierarchical naming structures which are much easier to remember than the IP addresses. The naming structures define the organization type, organization name, etc.
- *Time and Daytime Protocol*: This provides a machine readable time and day information.
- *SNMP (Simple Network Management Protocol)*: This is a protocol defined for managing (monitoring and controlling) networks.
- *Kerberos*: This is a security authentication protocol developed at MIT.

Other frequently used services in TCP/IP are Ping (an echo command), Netstat (command to display the network status of the local host, e.g., active TCP connection and IP routing tables), and Finger (displays information about users of a remote host, e.g., list of all users logged on to the remote host). In addition, the OSI upper layers can be implemented on TCP/IP as specified in the RFC1006.

B.3 Operational Characteristics of Internet Protocol (IP)

The purpose of IP is to deliver messages over an Internet. Sections B.3.1 and B.3.2 give an overview of the Internet architecture, gateways and addressing schemes. This background is useful in understanding IP, which is described in Section B.3.3.

B.3.1 Internet Architecture and Gateways

An Internet, as stated previously, consists of several physical networks that are interconnected together. The physical networks, also called local networks or subnets, may be LANS, WANS or MANs. An example of an Internet is shown in Fig. B.2. An Internet connects many disparate physical networks into a coordinated unit and hides

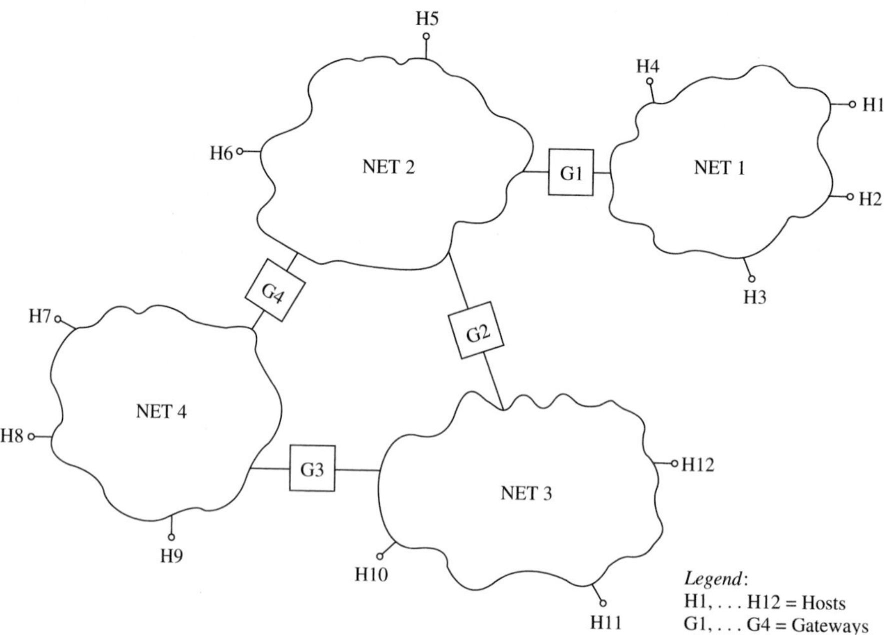

FIGURE B.2 Example of an Internet

the details of the physical network hardware; it allows computers to communicate independent of their physical network connections.

Internet gateways, simply termed as gateways, are used between physical networks of an Internet and perform the functions of an ISO intermediate system (relay). Gateways are computers that shuffle messages between physical networks. For example, the gateway G1 shown in Fig. B.2 passes the messages from NET1 to NET2 and vice versa. In general, an outgoing message from a host first checks to see if its destination is on the same physical network. If its destination is not on the physical network, then it goes to a gateway for routing.

The role of a gateway becomes more complex as the complexity of an Internet grows. In a complex network, the gateways must understand the network topology and must know how to get to the next gateway. For example, gateway G1 in Fig. B.2 must know how to pass messages from NET1 to NET4 through the intermediate gateways. In all cases, Internet gateways are responsible for routing messages to a destination network and not to a destination host. In most cases, Internet gateways are dedicated computers which house the routing tables. The size of the routing table depends on the number of physical networks and not on the number of computers in an Internet.

A gateway may be a core gateway which is maintained by a recognized authority. An example of a core gateway is the gateway that connects Internet to local nets. Most core gateways are operated by the Internet Network Operations Center (INOC). Other gateways can be introduced by owners of a private Internet or other groups of the Internet Community (IC). The IC spans the United States and extends to some foreign countries as well. At present, many networks using TCP/IP, including most university networks, are part of the IC. The IC connection allows the exchange of files and mail as well as terminal connections for all IC users. There are many ways to establish a connection between a local area network and the IC, and these communications options are expanding rapidly. For example, IC links for IBM PC, Macintosh LANs, and IBM mainframes are currently available.

Several algorithms for routing between gateways have been proposed and are currently operational. Some of these algorithms are used in the core gateways while others are used by private gateways. Discussion of these algorithms is beyond the scope of this book. The interested reader can find more information on this topic in several RFCs (e.g., RFC 823 and RFC 891). A good overview is presented in <Comer 1991, Comer 1988>.

B.3.2 Internet Addressing

An addressing scheme allows different networks, hosts and applications to identify the sources and destination of messages in a network. The addressing scheme in an Internet has three levels (see Fig. B.3):

- The network attachment point address, which identifies the physical location (e.g., an Ethernet controller address) where the host is connected to a physical network. This address is unique within a physical network and conforms to the addressing scheme of the physical network (e.g., 48 bit for Ethernet, 16 or 48 bit for a token ring, and 10 decimal digits in a packet switching network).
- The Internet address, also called the global network address, which shows the (network ID, host ID) pair for identifying hosts attached to different physical networks in an Internet. The Internet address is a 32 bit address commonly denoted as four decimal numbers separated by periods, e.g., 25.102.112.5. This address identifies the location of the host within an Internet: the first part of the address

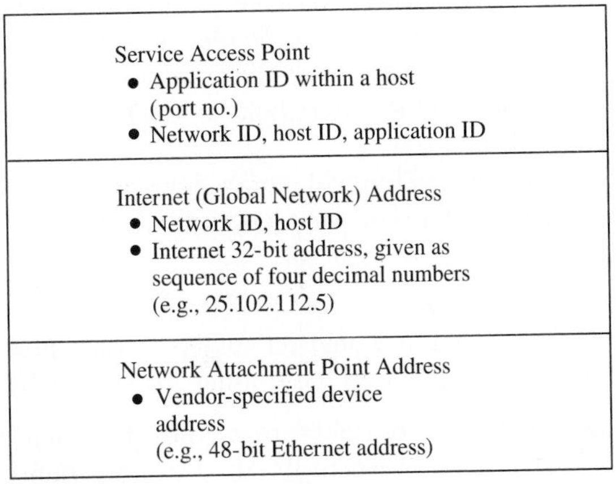

Service Access Point • Application ID within a host (port no.) • Network ID, host ID, application ID
Internet (Global Network) Address • Network ID, host ID • Internet 32-bit address, given as sequence of four decimal numbers (e.g., 25.102.112.5)
Network Attachment Point Address • Vendor-specified device address (e.g., 48-bit Ethernet address)

FIGURE B.3 Address Levels in IP

tells which network the host resides on, and the rest of the address shows where within that network the host can be found. A registration authority, Network Information Center, is responsible for assigning the IP addresses on the Internet.

- The service access point (SAP), which identifies an application process within a host connected to the Internet. An SAP allows a complete application to application communication through a three level address (network ID, host ID, application ID). Thus an application A1 on host H1 connected to NET1 can send a message to an application A2 on host H2 connected to NET2. Many applications at H1 can simultaneously communicate with applications at H2. In practice, an SAP appears as a port number in TCP (e.g., TCP port for FTP and Telnet) or UDP.

Schemes are needed to map the higher level addresses to lower addresses. The mapping of an Internet address to a network attachment address is commonly done by an address resolution protocol (ARP). A common method used by ARP includes tables at each machine which contain pairs of Internet and network attachment addresses. An address table is created by the installer of IP software at a host. Other methods encode physical addresses in the Internet address. Details about ARP can be found in RFC826. The translation from SAP to Internet address is performed by the TCP software. TCP pre-assigns some port numbers for commonly used applications (e.g., FTP, Telnet) and allows other applications to use "free" ports for communications.

B.3.3 Internet Protocol

The Internet uses a connectionless (unreliable) delivery protocol. This protocol is called unreliable because delivery is not guaranteed. The packets may be lost, duplicated, or delivered out of order, but the Internet will not detect such conditions. The protocol is called connectionless because it does not rely on an already established connection. It is the responsibility of higher layer protocols to establish connections and to verify the correct delivery of messages.

The IP sends each message as a *datagram*, which is its basic unit of information transfer. Each datagram contains a header and data areas. The datagram header contains the IP addresses of the sender and receiver. Figure B.4 shows a typical datagram format. Some of the main fields in the datagram are as follows:

- Two different fields, version and length fields, show the IP version and the length of the datagram header. The total length field gives the total size of the datagram in bytes.
- The service type fields are used to choose the quality of routing service needed: low delay, high throughput and high reliability. Setting these bits does not guarantee this type of service, it just tells the routing algorithm what your preferences are.
- The fragmentation control fields are used to show if you, or a gateway along the path to the destination, wish to break your datagram into fragments (packets), which can be assembled on the other side. You can choose to avoid fragmentation

0	8	16	31
Version and Length	Type of Service	Total Datagram Length (bytes)	
Identifier		Flags and Fragment Offset	
Fragmentation Control Fields			
Time		Header Checksum	
Source IP Address			
Destination IP Address			
Options and Padding			
Data			
Data			

FIGURE B.4 Format of an Internet Datagram (in Bits)

altogether. Fragmentation allows you to send long datagrams (longer than the maximum transmission unit of any single physical network along the path).

- The time field shows the maximum time a datagram can survive in the network. This field, usually represented as the maximum number of gateway hops, forces datagrams to be deleted from the Internet so that they do not roam around forever (a datagram may be roaming around due to problems with a routing protocol).
- The checksum is used to ensure the integrity of header values.
- The source and destination IP addresses obviously show the sender and receiver of the datagram. These addresses use the 32 bit Internet addresses which show the network and host IDs.

IP supports several service options for security, performance and fault management. For example, IP allows security labeling (classification level, handling restrictions, etc.) for security control, route recording (gateways encountered) for debugging, and timestamping (time trace of a datagram) for performance monitoring. These choices are specified in the options field of the datagram.

The datagrams are routed through the Internet by using a variety of routing algorithms. The choice of the routing algorithm depends on the nature and complexity of the Internet. The IP routing occurs at a higher level (global) than the physical network routing in a subnet. The IP routing is responsible for transferring messages between the physical networks of an Internet. The physical networks (subnets) are interconnected through gateways. The routing of a message within a physical network (e.g., an Ethernet) is the responsibility of network routing (the data link protocol) mechanism of the network.

The route can be direct (within a physical network) or indirect (between networks through gateways). Internet routing algorithms usually employ routing tables, which show possible destinations. An example of a routing table for a simple Internet is given in Fig. B.5. A typical routing algorithm used in IP is as follows:

- Extract the destination address DA from the datagram.
- Find the route for DA from the routing table.

a. A Simple Internet

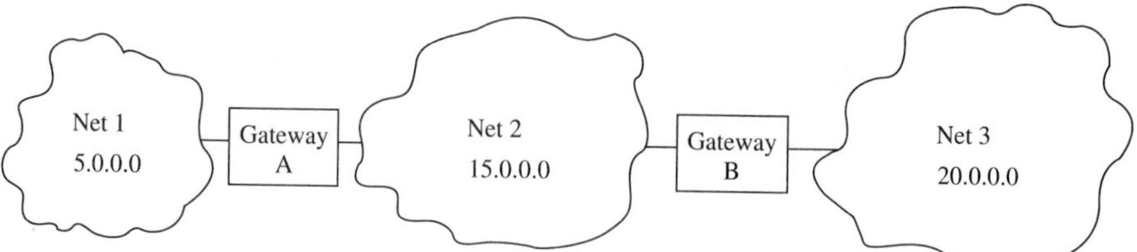

b. Routing Table for Gateway A

Destination Network	*Route Information*
5.0.0.0.	Direct
15.0.0.0.	Direct
20.0.0.0.	Route to gateway B (address = 15.0.0.8)

FIGURE B.5 Example of a Routing Table

- If DA is a direct path (within this subnet), send the message directly.
- If DA is an indirect path, send the message to the proper subnet or gateway.
- If none, then give a routing error.

Briefly, the Internet datagrams travel from gateway to gateway until they reach a gateway that can deliver them directly to the destination host. At present, many different routing protocols are used in TCP/IP. Examples of gateway protocols can be found in RFC 904 (April 1984) and RFC 1131 (1989).

If a gateway cannot route or deliver a datagram due to an addressing problem or congestion, it needs to instruct the host to take action. The mechanism commonly employed to communicate the errors is the Internet Control Messages Protocol (ICMP). ICMP messages travel across the Internet in the data portion of the datagram just like all other traffic. The destination of an ICMP message is the IP software on the destination machine and not the application process. Basically, ICMP provides a communication mechanism between the IP software at various machines (hosts and/or gateways) in the networks. ICMP is considered a required part of IP. More details about ICMP can be found in the DARPA standard RFC 792 by Postel.

B.4 Operational Characteristics of Transmission Control Protocol (TCP)

TCP is a reliable and connection-based protocol that resides above IP. Although TCP is usually discussed as a protocol on top of IP, TCP is a general purpose protocol that can be used on other delivery systems. For example, TCP can directly run on top of an Ethernet LAN, dial up telephone lines, a high speed fiber optic network, a packet switching system or a slow speed serial connection. The main strength of TCP is the large number of delivery systems it can run on (this, however, requires global addressing). It should be emphasized that TCP is a protocol and not a software package. Basically, TCP defines a set of rules and message formats for reliable service which have been implemented in the TCP software packages.

TCP allows many applications on one host to communicate concurrently with other applications on another host. The concept of a *port* is introduced to specify an endpoint in a host. Each port is a unique address within a host. Thus the TCP traffic sender and receiver address is given by the host Internet address plus the port number within the host. TCP has many ports reserved for specific services while other ports are assigned dynamically to the applications. Figure B.6 shows some common port numbers in TCP. It can be seen that FTP, SMTP, Telnet, and several other applications have preassigned TCP port numbers.

The two endpoints (ports) are essential in TCP because TCP is a connection oriented protocol (UDP also has ports). The applications on both sides must establish a connection between the two ports before TCP traffic can be initiated. Communication between two applications using TCP commonly involves the following steps:

1. Application A at host H1 performs a "passive open" by indicating that it will accept an incoming connection. This request is sent to the operating system at H1 which assigns a port number at H1. The passive open can be specific (listen for a specific user) or unspecific (listen to any user such as print or file user).
2. Application B at host H2 performs an "active open" to establish a connection with A at H1.
3. The TCP software modules at H1 and H2 establish and verify the connection.
4. The application A can now send and/or receive data from B.

TCP divides the application data into segments, where each segment has a sequence number and travels as an Internet datagram. To ensure reliable communi-

Prt No.	*Keyword*	*Description*
0		Reserved
1–4		Not assigned
5	RJE	Remote Job Entry
7	Echo	Echo port
11	Users	No. of active users
13	Daytime	Daytime
15	Netstat	Network status
20	FTP-Data	FTP—data send/receive
21	FTP	FTP—session management
23	TELNET	Terminal logon/logoff
25	SMTP	Simple Mail Transport Protocol
42	NAMESERVER	Host name server
53	Domain	Domain name server
69	TFTP	Trivial File Transfer
79	Finger	Finger

FIGURE B.6 Examples of Assigned TCP Port Numbers

cation, TCP uses a positive acknowledgement with timeout algorithm. This algorithm consists of the following steps:

1. The sender sends a message.
2. The receiver receives a message and sends an acknowledgement.
3. The sender receives the acknowledgement and sends the next message.
4. If the sender does not get an acknowledgement within a specified time period, it times out and resends the message.

To improve efficiency of network communication, TCP uses a sliding window protocol. Simply stated, a sliding window allows the sender to keep on sending n data units (n is the sliding window size) before waiting for an acknowledgement. Figure B.7 illustrates the difference between a positive acknowledgement (stop-and-wait) and sliding window protocol. This is a much more efficient protocol because the sender does not have to wait for acknowledgement of a message before sending the next message. In the limiting case when the window size is 1, the sliding window protocol becomes a simple positive acknowledgement algorithm.

TCP uses a variable size sliding window for flow control (see Appendix A). For example, if the receiver buffer is getting full, it may give the sender a small window size to minimize incoming traffic. In the limiting case, a sliding window size of zero stops incoming traffic. Adequate flow control is essential in an Internet environment because in such an environment several machines with different speeds and capacities are interconnected.

As stated previously, TCP uses segments as the basic unit of information transfer between TCP modules. Segments are exchanged to establish connection, to send data, to send acknowledgements, to send window size, and to close a connection. The format of a TCP segment is shown in Fig. B.8. The main fields of interest in the TCP segment are as follows:

- The Source Port and Destination Port show the sender and receiver application programs.
- The Sequence Number shows the starting position of data in sender's segment and the Acknowledgement Number shows the position of the last byte received (next byte expected). These two fields are used to synchronize the positions of data sent and received.
- The Flags are used to show the type of data being sent in the segment (information data, acknowledgement, command, etc.).
- The Window parameter is used for flow control. This parameter sets the sliding window size and is used to tell the sender how much data to send.
- The Urgent indicator is used to tell TCP to deliver this segment before others.

TCP does leave several issues for implementers of TCP software. For example, an implementer can choose to use piggybacking of acknowledgements with data, use timers to retransmit unacknowledged data and send one byte at a time instead of maxi-

a. Simple Positive Acknowledgment Protocol

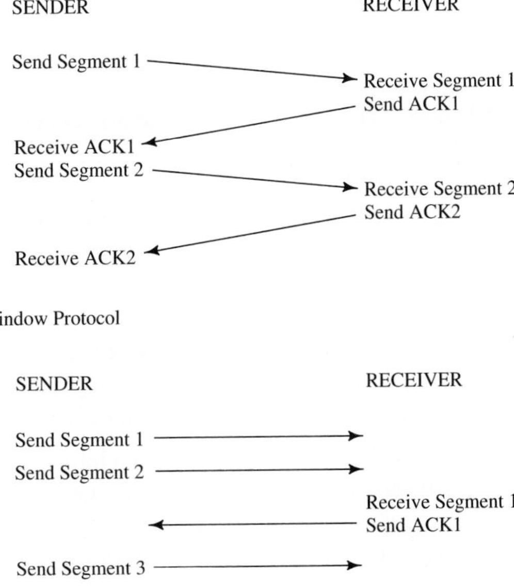

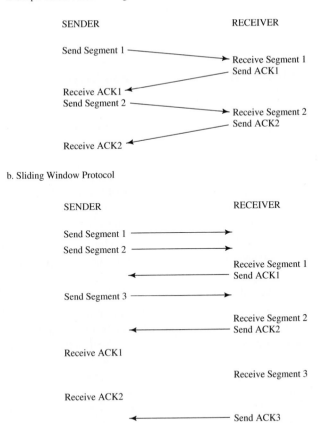

b. Sliding Window Protocol

FIGURE B.7 Sliding Window versus Simple Acknowledgment

0 · 8	16 · 31
Source Port	Destination
Sequence Number	
Acknowledgement Number	
Flags	Window
Checksum	Urgent Pointer
Options and Padding	
Data	
Data	

FIGURE B.8 Format of a TCP Segment

mum segment size. Additional technical details about TCP are given in the DARPA RFC793 by Postel. A quick overview of TCP is given by Davidson <1988>. For detailed coverage, the books by Comer <Comer 1988, Comer 1991> are recommended.

B.5 Operational Characteristics of Application Layer Protocols

A rich set of higher-level (application) protocols can run on top of TCP or UDP. All higher-level protocols have some common characteristics:

- They can be standardized and shipped with the TCP/IP product. For example, the TCP/IP Suite includes application protocols such as Telnet, FTP, and SMTP. These are the most widely implemented application protocols, but many others exist. Each particular TCP/IP implementation includes a set of application protocols.
- They use UDP or TCP as a transport mechanism. Recall that UDP is unreliable and offers no flow-control; so in this case, the application has to provide its own error recovery and flow-control routines. It is easier to build applications on top of TCP, a reliable, connection-oriented protocol.
- Most application protocols use TCP, but many applications are built on UDP especially for higher performance of connectionless services. Most use the client-server model of interaction in which one host acts as a client and the other as a server. The client hosts send a request over the Internet that is received and processed by the server. The tasks performed by a server can be simple or complex. For example, a time-of-day server simply returns the current time whenever it receives a client request; a file server receives requests to perform file reads/writes and returns the results.

A few operational details of the TCP/IP application protocols that are important in distributed computing are given next.

B.5.1 Telnet

Telnet is the protocol used to provide terminal access to hosts. Telnet runs on top of TCP and provides minimal terminal support. Telnet client software usually allows the user to specify the server address as Internet address or domain names. This capability allows users to use Telnet with or without the domain naming services.

Figure B.9 shows a generic Telnet session. It should be emphasized that Telnet implementations vary slightly between systems. As shown in Fig. B.9, the user activates Telnet by typing "telnet" on a terminal or workstation. Telnet software prompts the user to identify a host and then goes through a logon process. After the logon process, the user workstation or terminal behaves as a terminal connected to the remote host.

Figure B.10 shows how Telnet actually operates. The Telnet client reads the keyboard data, passes it to the server and concurrently receives the server response and displays it on the user display unit. The Telnet server basically reads the client

```
>Telenet
>  Telenet initiated
>  Type the system name
>host1
>  Connection to host1 established.
>  Enter logon
>logon user1
>  Enter password
>pw
>  Logon completed
>
>do work
>
>quit
>  Session completed
```

Note: The responses from the server are indented for the sake of clarification

FIGURE B.9. Sample TELENET Session

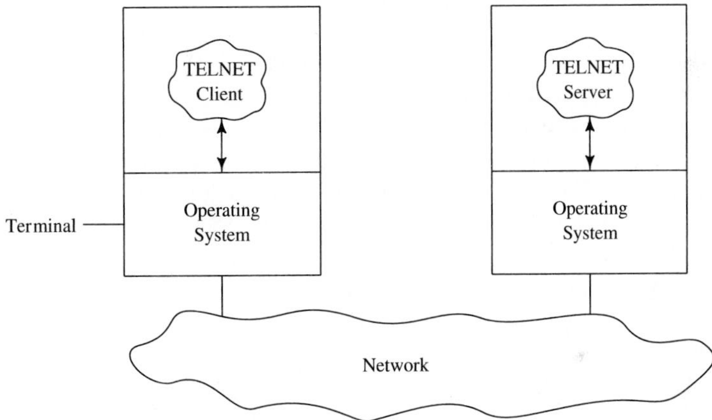

FIGURE B.10. Example of TELENET Operation

requests (keyboard data) and passes them to the local operating system. However, the Telnet server must have the capability to handle multiple, concurrent sessions. Usually, a main server monitors the new connections and initiates new programs to handle the new connections.

The Telnet protocol is based on three ideas: the concept of a Network Virtual Terminal (NVT), the principle of negotiated options, and a symmetric view of terminals and processes. An NVT is a virtual device, which provides the basic functionalities of a standard terminal. Each host maps its own terminal characteristics to an NVT and assumes that the other host will do the same. Telnet uses the principle of negotiated options because most hosts provide many services beyond those available with the NVT. Servers and clients negotiate the options to establish their Telnet connection (e.g., an option controls whether data passed across the connection is binary or ASCII text). The symmetry of the terminals or processes allows every host to negotiate options. To begin the negotiation, hosts verify their mutual understanding, using standard syntax. After a minimum of understanding, they can use sub-negotiation under free syntax. This allows Telnet to connect two application programs, where one acts as a client and the other as a server.

B.5.2 The File Transfer Protocol (FTP)

The File Transfer Protocol (FTP) provides a way to transfer files between hosts on the Internet. Copying files from one machine to another is one of the most frequently used operations. To support this essential function, a reliable end-to-end protocol like TCP is used. The data transfer between client and server can be in either direction. The client may send a file to the server machine, it may also request a file from this server. FTP can also be used to exchange files between programs. Many FTP implementations provide statistics on file transfer rates.

FTP allows authorized users to log into a remote machine, identify themselves, list remote directories, copy files to and from the remote system, and execute a few simple commands. FTP understands a few basic file formats and translates between different types of character codes such as ASCII and EBCDIC texts. It gives the ability to require IDs and passwords in order to access files, thereby making it practical to use with private files. To access remote files, the user must provide identification to the server which is responsible for authenticating the client before it allows the file transfer. Figure B.11 shows a typical FTP session. It can be seen that the FTP initiation is similar to Telnet (logging on to remote host, etc.). We have used a different logon format for purpose of illustration (FTP as well as Telnet can directly establish a session with a host in the activation command such as "Telnet Host1" and "FTP Host1"). After logon, the FTP commands of GET and PUT are used to transfer files.

The FTP link is connection-oriented; TCP/IP must be up and running on both hosts in order to establish a file transfer. FTP uses two connections: one for login to the remote host and one for managing the data transfer. The login connection employs Telnet protocol. To use the login connection, the user must have a user name and a password to access remote files and directories. The user who initiates the connection becomes a client and the remote host assumes the server function.

Figure B.12 shows a typical FTP connection. The client establishes two connections with the server: one to transfer the file data and the other to pass the control information (e.g., file name). The server waits for the connection at the FTP port (a preassigned TCP port 21). When a connection arrives on this port, the server initiates a control process C to handle this connection and goes back to wait for the connection. The process C communicates with the client over the control connection for logon authentication and for control commands such as list remote directories and specify the file name to be transferred. After the authentication and identification of file name to be transferred, C opens another process T to actually transfer the file selected. This transfer is conducted over the other connection.

```
>ftp host1
>  FTP initiated
>  Connection to host1 established.
>  Enter logon
>logon user1
>  Enter password
>pw
>  Logon completed
>put file1.sys1 file1.sys2
>  File transfer initiated
>  File transfer completed
>get file1.sys2 file1.sys1
>  File transfer initiated
>  File transfer completed
>quit
>  Session completed
```

FIGURE B.11 Sample FTP Session

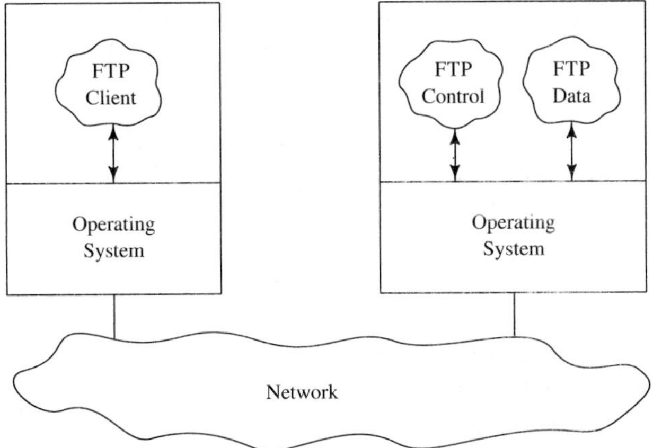

FIGURE B.12 Example of FTP Operation

The examples shown in Figs. B.11 and B.12 present a conceptual overview of FTP operations. The FTP software commonly provides a wide variety of options, as illustrated by the following sequence of operations:

- *Login to Foreign Host.* To execute a file transfer, the user has to start with a login operation. Login may allow change of the data representation during the transfer.
- *Define a Directory.* After the login is complete, the user may have to execute a change directory (CD) in order to manage space for data (e.g., CD userid).
- *Define the File to be Transferred.* The DIR subcommand of FTP displays the filenames within a directory. The most frequent operations performed on the files are copying a file from the remote host into the local file system, using the GET subcommand; and copying a file from the local system file to the remote host, using the PUT subcommand.

- *Define Mode of Transfer.* FTP subcommands allow transformation of data representation between dissimilar systems. The user can decide on: 1) the way the bits will be moved from one place to another and 2) the different representations of data upon the system's architecture. Examples of the subcommands are as follows:
  - Block mode parameter preserves the logical record boundaries of the file. Stream mode parameter, the default transfer mode, is the most efficient mode of transfer because no data block of information is transferred. Any type of data representation can be transferred in stream mode.
  - TYPE with ASCII, EBCDIC, IMAGE parameters shows the data representation. ASCII, the default transfer type, is normally used between ASCII hosts and EBCDIC is used for transferring data between hosts using this data representation. IMAGE data is sent as contiguous bits packed in 8-bit bytes. This transfer type is the most efficient for transferring and storing binary data.
- *Site Command.* The SITE subcommand is used with PUT to specify how data is to be stored on the remote host. The parameters of this subcommand are used by the foreign host system. Sending information to the remote system may be accomplished with the subcommands SENDSITE and SITE.
- *End the Transfer Session.* Issue a QUIT, which will disconnect the hosts running FTP. When issuing a CLOSE subcommand, FTP stays active and you can OPEN a new session.

B.5.3 The SUN Network File System (NFS) Protocol

This protocol, originally developed by the SUN Microsystems, has become a de facto standard for use in building distributed file systems. NFS runs on top of UDP; however, a few implementations of NFS on TCP also exist. NFS provides the ability for host computers and workstations running NFS to transparently share files across the entire Internet. For example, an IBM PC could logically have files resident on a mainframe, Apollo, or Sun; however, the file location is totally transparent to the user. In general, an NFS user at computer C1 can access a file F in the network without knowing the location of F. The user also accesses a remote file as if it were local.

Figure B.13 shows a sample NFS session. The user of NFS basically issues a MOUNT command to mount a remote directory from a remote host to the local host. The user can search the remote directories by using the LOOKUP command and can retrieve and delete remote files by using GET and REMOVE commands. The user can also display the attributes of remotely located files and access them as local files. An UNMOUNT makes the remotely located files unavailable to the local host.

Figure B.14 shows the operational view of NFS. The NFS client C sends the file access commands to the NFS server. The server at host H receives requests from authorized clients at C to access the files at H as if they were local to C. The server at H must have the facilities to concurrently receive and process many client requests. The server at H also provides the facilities for file creation at H. The files at H appear as extensions to the local disk at C.

```
>mount host1 dir1
>  directory dir1 mounted
>lookup file1
>  f1 is the file handle for file1
>showattr f1
>  attributes of file1 displayed
>get f1
>  file1 retrieved
>remove f1
>  file1 deleted
>unmount
>  directory unmounted
```

FIGURE B.13 Sample NFS Session

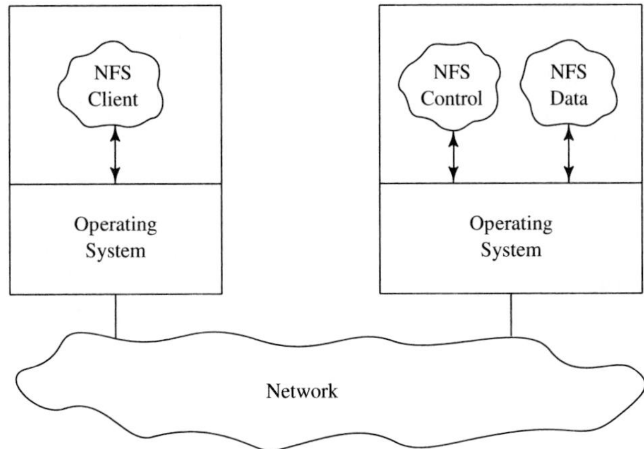

FIGURE B.14 Example of NFS Operation

The steps in using NFS are as follows:

- Assume that the client site C has files F1, F2, F3
- Logon to remote site H from the client
- Issue a MOUNT command to make a remote directory at H available. Assume that the remote directory contains files F4, F5. The remote directory is mounted to C and can be accessed as a local directory.
- Issue reads to F1, F2, F3, F4, and F5 from C. The read requests do not have to specify the location of any of these files.

Chapter 5 shows how NFS can be used in client-server computing environments. Let us review some of the NFS protocols. NFS uses two basic protocols: the MOUNT protocol and the NFS Protocol.

The MOUNT protocol specifies the remote host and the file system to be accessed. This protocol supports a MOUNT command which mounts a remote directory and returns a file handle pointing to the directory. This file handle is used later by the client to access the remote files. Some implementations may encrypt the file handle for security reasons. Other commands supported by this protocol are UNMOUNT and UNMTALL to unmount one or all remote directories, respectively.

The NFS protocol performs the actual file operations after it has been requested through a MOUNT command. Some of the commands supported by NFS are as follows:

- LOOKUP: searches for a file in the mounted directory and, if found, returns a file handle
- READ and WRITE: basic file I/O operations
- RENAME: rename a file
- REMOVE: delete a file
- MKDIR and RMDIR: creation/deletion of subdirectories
- GET and SET-ATTR: retrieve and set file attributes.

These commands correspond to the local file operations. If the file to be accessed is a remote file, the operating system just reroutes these calls to a remote host. This makes all file operations look alike, independent of the site where they are located.

NFS is designed to be machine, operating systems, and transport protocol independent. This independence is achieved by using the Remote Procedure Call (RPC) facility on top of the UDP. NFS is currently available on most TCP/IP based mini and microcomputer systems. IBM has announced NFS support on its mainframes under MVS operating systems. This announcement has expanded the availability of NFS to all ranges of computing systems.

B.5.4 XWindow

XWindow is a windowing system that provides simultaneous views of several executing programs and processes on bit-mapped displays. It is an interface designed to enhance the overall system usability. The user should be able to control all of his sessions from one screen, with applications either running in a window, or in separate machine. The purpose of this discussion is to expose the reader to the overall characteristics of XWindow. The physical programming aspects of XWindow (e.g., setting the screen sizes) are beyond the scope of this book. Chapter 5 discusses Xwindow in a client-server environment.

XWindow provides the capability to manage both local and remote windows. Remote windows are established through TCP/IP, local windows through the use of BSD (Berkeley Unix) Sockets. Basically, there are two parts communicating with each other.

1. The user's terminal, running a display-managing software which receives/sends data from/to the application and is called the X-Server.
2. The application, called the X-Client, which gets input from the user, executes code and sends output back to the user. Instead of reading and writing directly to a display, the application uses the XLIB programming interface to send data to and receive data at the user's terminal.

The main functionalities of XWindow are as follows:

- X-Client and X-Server can be on different hosts, communicating over the network by using the TCP/IP protocol. They can also be on the same machine, using IPC (interprocess communication) to communicate (through sockets).
- There is only one X-Server per terminal. Multiple X-Client applications can communicate with this one X-Server. The X-Server displays the application windows and sends the user input to the appropriate X-Client application.
- It is up to the X-Client to maintain the created windows. It is notified by events from X-Server whenever something is changed on the display for other clients. However, they do not have to care about which part of their windows is visible or not when they are drawing or redrawing their windows.
- The X-Server keeps track of the visibility of the windows, by maintaining stacks. A stack contains all "first generation" children of a parent window. A child window can also be a parent window by having one or more child windows itself, which are again held in a substack. The primary stack is the stack which holds all windows located directly below the root. Subwindows can only be fully visible when their parent is on the top of its respective stack and mapped to the display.
- X-Server itself has no management functions; it only performs window clipping according to its stacks. Every client is responsible for its own windows. There is a Window Manager which manipulates the top level windows of all the clients. The Window Manager prevents the clients from putting their windows on top of each other and thus avoids obscuring of windows. Window Manager is not part of X-Server but is itself a client. As soon as Window Manager changes something on the screen (for instance, resizing a window), it makes X-Server send out an exposure event to all the other clients.

B.5.5 TCP/IP Berkeley Sockets

Recent versions of Unix (BSD4.3, Unix System V Version 4 and higher) support many client-server Application Layer protocols and services. Here are some examples:

- Unix InterProcess Communication (IPC) systems, which provide many Unix processes to communicate with each other. Examples are pipes, FIFOs or named pipes, semaphores, and shared memory.
- Berkeley Sockets, available on Unix BSD4.3 and above which use TCP or UDP
- TLI (Transport Layer Interfaces) available on Unix System V, which also uses TCP and UDP
- RPC (Remote Procedure Calls), which are available on several Unix systems.

Berkley Sockets, simply called sockets, and RPCs are the best known Unix-TCP/IP client-server services. We will discuss the Berkley Sockets here. RPCs are described in Chapter 5. For a detailed discussion of other Unix communication services, the reader is referred to the book by Stevens, *Networking with Unix* <Stevens 1990>.

Berkeley Sockets are application programming interfaces (APIs). Sockets support two main domains: the Unix domain and the Internet domain. The Internet domain allows communication between machines, whereas the Unix domain only allows communication between processes in the same Unix system. The Internet domain is a necessary choice for communication within a network and is discussed here.

A socket is an addressed endpoint of communication which conceptually resides above TCP. The addresses associated with the sockets are commonly the IP physical addresses (32 bit host number, 16 bit port number). These machine-specific addresses have raised concerns about the transportability of Unix applications <Quarterman 1985>. There are several types of sockets, grouped according to the services they provide. The services include stream sockets, which provide duplex, sequenced flow of data, with no record boundaries; datagram sockets which transfer messages of different sizes in both directions and which are not promised to be reliable and sequenced; and sequenced packet sockets which are similar to stream sockets, with the difference that record boundaries are preserved. Applications in Unix environments are written by using stream (reliable connection) or datagram mode, by using forking which allows several processes to be initiated by one process and/or by mailboxes, which allow an intermediate file for message transmission.

Table B.1 shows a summary of the socket commands for stream or datagram services. The commands, available as Unix system calls, are shown generically because different versions of Unix support different command verbs for the same activity through different facilities. It can be seen that sockets support relatively few commands. The first five commands are initialization commands. SOCKET creates a socket; BIND is used by the servers to register their well-known address to the system so that the clients can connect and transfer information; CONNECT is used by the client to establish a connection with the server after the server has issued a BIND; and LISTEN and ACCEPT are issued by the server to indicate that it is willing to accept connections from the clients and then to queue the connections on a queue for later processing. Commands 6 and 7 are the main information transfer commands for connection-based (TCP) client-server systems and commands 8 and 9 are the main information transfer commands for connectionless (UDP) client-server systems.

Figure B.15a shows the code for a TCP based socket code and the UDP based socket code is shown in Fig. B.15b.

TABLE B-1. Berkley Socket Command Summary (Basic Commands)

1. SOCKET—Creates a socket and specifies socket type (TCP, UDP)
2. BIND—Assigns a name to an unnamed socket (handle)
3. CONNECT—Establishes a connection between local and remote server
4. LISTEN—Server is willing to accept connections
5. ACCEPT—Accept a connection and put it on queue
6. WRITE—Send data on TCP socket
7. READ—Read data from TCP socket
8. SENDTO—Send data on UDP socket
9. RECVFROM—Read data from UDP socket

a. TCP-based code

Server	Client
1. SOCKET	
2. BIND	
3. LISTEN	
4. ACCEPT	5. SOCKET
	6. CONNECT
	• Read local data
	7. WRITE (to socket)
8. READ (from socket)	
• process request	
9. WRITE (to socket)	10. READ (from socket)
	11. CLOSE, EXIT

b. UDP code

Server	Client
1. SOCKET	
2. BIND	
3. RECVFROM (socket)	4. SOCKET
	• Read local data
	5. SENDTO (socket)
• process request	
6. SENDTO (socket)	7. RECVFROM (socket)
	8. CLOSE, EXIT

Comments:

- Code does not use any locking or failure recovery.
- No synchronization and backout is provided.
  - If systems fail, then restart.
  - Data is sent as records to show sequencing control.

FIGURE B.15 Pseudo Code of Program in Berkeley Sockets

For the connection-based code shown in Fig. B.15a, commands 1 through 4 represent the Initiation State of the server by using the SOCKET, BIND and LISTEN commands. Instruction 1 is used to create a socket. A socket number is chosen which is not already being used by the standard Internet services such as FTP and Telnet. The BIND command is used to make the address of the server available to the Internet ("register the server socket with the network") and LISTEN and ACCEPT indicate that the server is willing and waiting for a client to issue a connect. Instruction 4 processes a CONNECT instruction from the client and puts it on a queue for processing. Instructions 5 and 6 create a socket and issue a CONNECT from the client (Initiation State of the client), which is "ACCEPTed" by the server. After this, a connection between the two processes to pass messages is established. Basically, the server process specifies half of the association by issuing an ACCEPT system call and then passively listening on its socket for a CONNECT. The association is completed by the client process when it issues a CONNECT call to the server's socket. The next commands are used to send and receive information in the Information Transfer State.

In this state, the data is sent and received by using the READ and WRITE commands. The CLOSE and EXIT commands constitute the Termination State of the data transfer phase of the application.

In the connectionless datagram code, also called the lightweight protocol, the SOCKET and BIND commands are used in the client and server Initiation State. Note that the LISTEN, CONNECT, and ACCEPT commands are not used in the datagram services. Due to the unreliable nature of the datagram, it is the responsibility of the programmer to assure that the clients and servers properly synchronize their operations by using the RECVFROM command and sending positive and negative acknowledgements through the SENDTO commands. The information transfer commands in the connection-less UDP services are different from the connection-based TCP commands because UDP uses record sockets (each send is transferred) while TCP uses stream sockets (many sends are accumulated in a socket and are transferred when the socket is full). Additional code may be needed for sequence checking and control to handle lost messages.

This pseudo code can be translated into programs by using C, ADA, or assembler compilers with proper support libraries on Unix. The main limitation with socket API is that it does not provide any primitives for command controls such as locking, commit, roll-backs, etc. Each programmer designs his/her own control verbs, which are sent as data by Unix through the READ/WRITE and RECVFROM/SENDTO commands. This can lead to applications that are not portable across Unix networks.

A detailed description of Berkeley Sockets with numerous C examples is given in Chapter 5 of Stevens book, *Unix Network Programming* <Stevens 1990>.

B.5.6 Miscellaneous Application Layer Protocols

In addition to the aforementioned protocols, many other application protocols are available on TCP/IP Suite. Some of these protocols are described here briefly.

The Trivial File Transfer Protocol. The Trivial File Transfer Protocol (TFTP) also transfers files between hosts, but with less functionality. TFTP is much less complex to implement than FTP, it runs on top of UDP, and it avoids the complexities of TCP. TFTP does not provide any authorization mechanism, so it typically can only be used with publicly available files.

The Simple Mail Transfer Protocol. The Simple Mail Transfer Protocol (SMTP) is the Internet electronic mail exchange mechanism. This TCP based protocol provides a way for dissimilar hosts to exchange mail. It is responsible for transporting mail and is not concerned with mail format. An SMTP implementation is usually built beneath the native mail system in the host. SMTP manages the mail connection such as establishing sender's credentials and ensures recipient mailbox. It provides forwarding and deferred delivery and supports a variety of message formats and native mail systems.

The Domain Name Services. The Domain Naming service can be used to assign symbolic names to the Internet addresses. Symbolic names are preferable to Internet addresses because they are easier for humans to work with, and because an address may change if a host is moved or a network is reorganized. The Domain Naming system defines a hierarchical naming structure. At the highest level is the organization type (EDU for educational, COM for commercial, GOV for governmental, etc.). Below that is the organization name. Further levels may be needed in large organizations. For example, EE.MIT.EDU identifies an educational computer that resides in the EE department of MIT. The mapping between a domain name and an Internet address is performed by name server machines in each domain. For example, one name server at MIT may contain the mapping between domain names and IP addresses in the MIT domain. This avoids proliferation of independent address tables in every host. A protocol, run on top of UDP, is used to query the name server, to determine the IP address for a particular domain name. The name server may in turn ask another name server if it does not know. This distribution of names means that each server need not know all of the hosts in an Internet. In addition, if a host is assigned a new IP address, only the name server local to that host needs to be updated. The change will then be available to other name servers and hosts as needed.

The Simple Network Management Protocol (SNMP). This network management protocol reflects the DARPA/OSI short range approach to network management. The focus of this protocol is on the network monitoring and control functions of networks. The OSI based network management standard CMIP (Common Management Information Protocol) includes many other network management functions such as network performance, accounting and security. SNMP uses polling where the manager repeatedly polls the components about their status. SNMP is based on a series of RFCs (e.g., RFC 1067, August, 1988) and is available from a substantial number of vendors. Due to its simplicity and vendor support, SNMP has furthered the popularity of TCP/IP in managing heterogeneous networks. In addition, it is being considered as a transition path to CMIP by using the following scenario: (1) install SNMP over TCP/IP for network management, (2) convert to CMOT (CMIS over TCP/IP) by changing the application layer, and (3) convert to CMIP by replacing the underlying TCP/IP with OSI. A detailed discussion of SNMP, CMIP and CMOT is given in Chapter 4.

B.6 TCP/IP as an Open System: TCP/IP versus the OSI Model

The use of TCP/IP Suite is expanding rapidly. Vendors are making it available for their machines, and more and more networks are using TCP/IP as a way of interconnecting diverse computing. TCP/IP provides the first instance of widely-available integration of all ranges of machines. Although not perfect, it makes possible a level of functionality that was not achievable previously. This kind of interconnection will lay the foundation for the network environment envisioned for the future.

The ISO Open Systems Interconnection (OSI) Reference Model, commonly referred to as the OSI Model, was developed to provide open interconnections between many computers; however, TCP/IP has become a de facto interconnectivity standard. The key question is: What are the tradeoffs and differences between TCP/IP and OSI? The following statements encapsulate some of the differences between the two standards:

- TCP/IP was developed in the late 1960s to meet the specific needs of information exchange between research communities. However, OSI was defined in 1977 to provide a framework for open systems connections for conceivably every type of computer system. The differences between the two systems are due to the origin (TCP/IP originated from research and development community and not from a standards committee) and vintage (1969 versus 1977).
- Most of the TCP/IP protocols are developed (coded and tested) before being described in an RFC (usually by the implementers). This ensures feasibility of the TCP/IP protocols. In contrast, many of the OSI protocols and standards are drafted before implementation; thus there is no guarantee of their feasibility.
- The TCP/IP layering concepts are similar to the OSI layers but the two systems are different. TCP/IP protocol software is organized into four conceptual layers and not the seven OSI layers (Fig. B.16) which reside on top of a hardware layer. The Application Layer runs the application protocols such as NFS, FTP; the Transport Layer provides application-to-application connectivity (e.g., TCP); the Internet Layer is responsible for delivering the datagrams; and the network interface provides the physical network connection. It is important to note that a user application may choose to use any of the TCP/IP layers or may directly communicate with the physical network. TCP/IP does not require the applications to go through all intermediate layers.
- In TCP/IP Suite, a layer represents a reasonable "packaging" of functionality. For example, TCP and UDP exist at same layer in the Internet even though they provide different services (one is reliable, the other is not). The OSI layers, on the other hand, reflect narrow functionalities. The modularity in OSI is achieved through

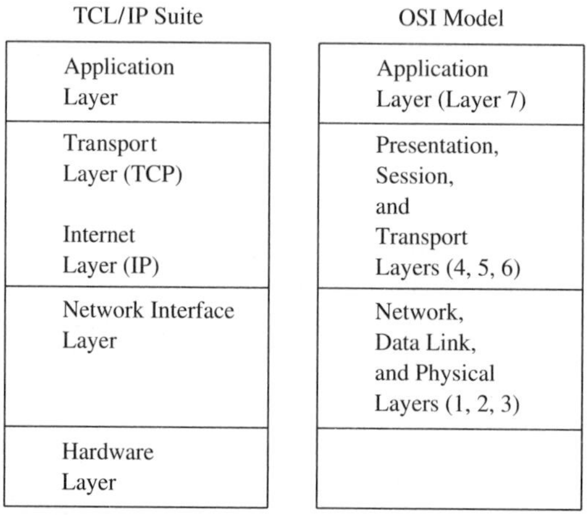

TCL/IP Suite	OSI Model
Application Layer	Application Layer (Layer 7)
Transport Layer (TCP) Internet Layer (IP)	Presentation, Session, and Transport Layers (4, 5, 6)
Network Interface Layer	Network, Data Link, and Physical Layers (1, 2, 3)
Hardware Layer	

FIGURE B.16 TCP/IP versus the OSI Model Layers

additional layers for additional functionality. In addition, the TCP/IP Suite allows a protocol to use another protocol at the same layer (for example, FTP uses Telnet). However, OSI forces a mechanism where a high level layer can only use (call) lower level functionalities.

Many of the differences between TCP/IP and OSI are disappearing because OSI also supports connectionless services at present. An area of active discussion is the migration from TCP/IP to OSI. It is well known that the number of TCP/IP based networks is growing dramatically, mainly due to the availability of products. On the other hand, many vendors are announcing or are pledging to announce OSI products. The DOD has published a statement on OSI in January, 1988, based on the Government OSI Profile (GOSIP) of April 22, 1987. This statement has been published as RFC 1039 - "A DOD Statement on OSI." Here is an excerpt from this statement:

> "... It is intended to adopt the OSI protocols as a full *co-standard* with the DOD protocols when GOSIP is formally approved as a Federal Information Processing Standard. Two years thereafter, the OSI protocols would become the sole mandatory interoperable protocol suite; however, a capability for interoperation with DOD protocols would be provided for the expected life of systems supporting the DOD protocols ..."

The Internet community is spending a great deal of time and effort on studying the possible transitions and co-existence of the ISO and TCP/IP Protocol Suite. Examples of some of the RFCs in this area are as follows:

- RFC 1006: ISO upper layers on top of TCP
- RFC 1066 : ISO Transport Services on top of TCP
- RFC 1069 : Guidelines for the use of Internet IP addresses in the ISO Connectionless -Mode Network Protocol.
- RFC 1085: ISO: Presentation Services on top of the TCP/IP based Internets
- RFCC 1086: ISO-TP0 bridge between TCP and X.25
- RFC 1090: SMTP on X.25.

Independent of the work being done by various standardizing bodies, the migration from TCP/IP to OSI is not easy to predict. For example, given a company which uses TCP/IP to communicate among heterogeneous private networks, what is the advantage of migrating to the OSI products?Although OSI is the accepted international standard for networks, in essence the decision to migrate from TCP/IP to OSI depends on the following factors:

- Tangible benefits of migrating to OSI
- Availability of OSI products on as many machines as TCP/IP
- Reliability of the OSI products

- User dissatisfaction with current TCP/IP systems to motivate the migration (e.g., shortage of address space in TCP/IP networks)
- Price/performance ratio for TCP/IP versus OSI products
- User requirements in security and reliability of data exchange.

The Open Book by Marshall Rose <Rose 1990> provides a good reference on TCP/IP, and OSI co-existence and transition.

B.7 Interconnectivity Through TCP/IP

Consider a simple situation in which file F on a SUN workstation needs to be transferred to an IBM PC and a Mac. We have the following two options:

- Connect the three computers by using serial RS232 cables and then transfer the file by using a serial file transfer package such as Kermit.
- Connect the three computers through Ethernet; run TCP/IP on all three computers, and transfer the file by using FTP.

The first choice is inexpensive but slow. The main advantage of using the second choice is that it allows fast file transfer (Ethernet runs at 10 million bits per second). Thus a user can choose a proper option depending on the speed requirements and financial constraints. In fact, whenever files need to be transferred between heterogeneous computers, serial file transfer or TCP/IP based file transfers are the two main choices.

Let us now consider a company that has three sites (a corporate office, an engineering office and a manufacturing plant). Let us assume that the corporate office uses an IBM SNA network, the engineering office uses DECNET, and the manufacturing plant uses MAP. To interconnect these three sites, the company has the following choices (see Fig. B.17):

- Purchase gateways to translate from SNA to DECNET, DECNET to MAP, and MAP to SNA (Fig. B.17a).
- Use a TCP/IP backbone and purchase gateways to translate from SNA to TCP/IP, DECNET TO TCP/IP and MAP to TCP/IP (Fig. B.17b).
- Install and use TCP/IP at all sites for all backbone traffic but keep the native "private" networks such as SNA and DECNET, (Fig. B.17c). In this case, the applications at each computer communicate with TCP/IP and may need to do some conversions (limited gateway functionality).
- Install and use TCP/IP at all sites and eliminate all private networks.
- Repeat these steps but use OSI instead of TCP/IP.

The first option involves purchase of gateways. Although many gateways are commercially available between different type of networks, gateways can become serious performance bottlenecks. The second choice provides a good strategy by slowly

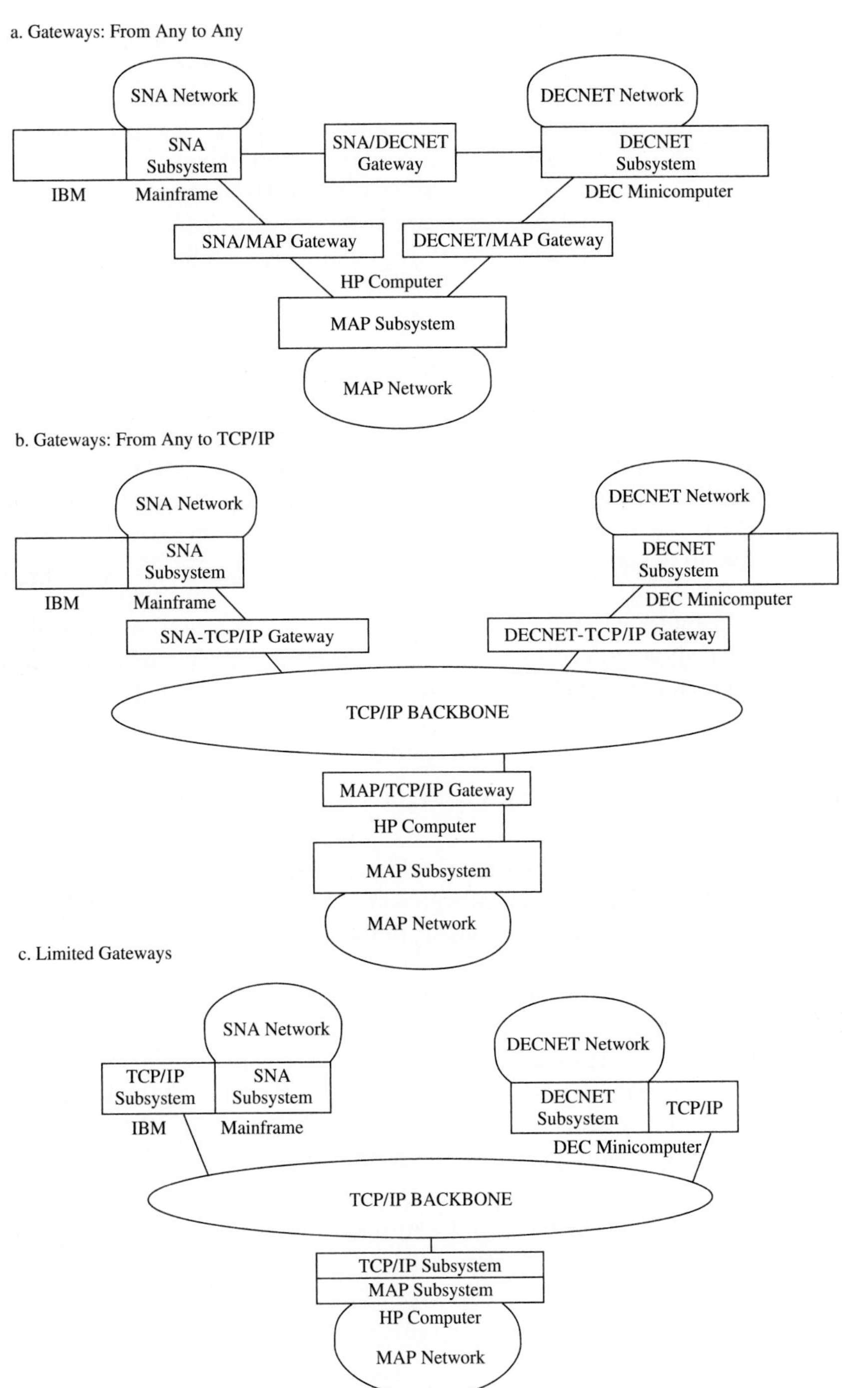

FIGURE B.17 Network Interconnectivity through TCP/IP

eliminating gateways and moving to choice 3. The third choice is currently doable because TCP/IP can be installed on all systems. However, the question is how to convert existing SNA and DECNET applications to communicate with TCP/IP. The fourth option, although theoretically possible, requires disruption and conversion of existing network applications which may be too expensive and/or infeasible. For example, conversion from SNA to TCP/IP on IBM mainframes is not feasible at present because the IBM database applications are primarily accessible through SNA. The fifth family of choices is contingent on the availability of OSI based products.

B.8 Common TCP/IP Implementations

TCP/IP has been implemented on most computers under the Unix operating system. In many Unix systems such as SUN, TCP/IP is shipped as part of the operating system. TCP/IP is also becoming available on many other operating systems. An interesting example is the availability of TCP/IP on IBM mainframes. The IBM mainframes use two operating systems: MVS and VM. TCP/IP is currently available on MVS as well as VM. These implementations provide NFS and Xwindow support. in addition to the common Internet Application Layer protocols. MVS-NFS is especially interesting because it allows MVS files to be accessed transparently from Unix workstations. This is a major step toward file transparency in most corporations.

B.9 Management Summary and Trends

The TCP/IP Protocol Suite is a set of de facto standards developed for the Department of Defense (DOD) for interconnecting computer networks and hosts on those networks. The TCP/IP Suite consists of the following major protocols:

- *IP (Internet Protocol)*. This protocol provides roughly the OSI layer 3 type facilities for interconnecting devices in a network. IP is the lowest protocol in this Suite. It can reside on a very wide variety of physical networks such as Ethernets, FDDI based fiber optic LANs, dial up lines , X.25 based packet switching networks or ISDN digital networks. The Internet technology used by IP allows communication across many computers across many networks.
- *TCP (Transmission Control Protocol)*. This protocol roughly provides the layer 4 facilities of the OSI Model for end-to-end transmissions between devices on the network. TCP, the layer above IP, supports a very wide variety of higher level (application) protocols which allow users to emulate terminals, transfer files, and send/receive mail between different computers.
- *Telnet*. This application protocol is used to provide terminal access to hosts and runs on top of TCP. A diverse set of terminals and computers can use Telnet.
- *File Transfer Protocol (FTP)*. This TCP based application protocol provides a way to transfer files between hosts on the Internet.

- *Simple Mail Transfer Protocol (SMTP).* This TCP based application protocol is the Internet electronic mail exchange mechanism.

Many application protocols and user applications have been developed around TCP/IP. Examples of the significant protocols are as follows:

- *Network File System (NFS) Protocol.* This UDP based protocol has become a de facto standard for use in building distributed file systems through transparent access.
- *Xwindow.* This is a windowing system that provides uniform user views of several executing programs and processes on bit-mapped displays. Although Xwindow is supposedly network independent, it has been implemented widely on top of TCP.
- *SUN Remote Procedure Call (RPC).* This protocol allows programs to execute subroutines that are actually at remote sites. RPCs, like Xwindow are, supposedly network independent but have been implemented widely on top of TCP.
- *SNMP (Simple Network Management Protocol).* This protocol has been defined for managing (monitoring and controlling) networks.

In the last few years these protocols have dramatically grown in popularity and have become the de facto standards for large heterogeneous networks. The TCP/IP Suite is available on almost all computing systems today including microcomputers, minicomputers and mainframes (it is estimated that there were about 200 TCP/IP vendors in 1990). For example, TCP/IP can be used to transfer files between IBM, DEC, SUN, PRIME, Macintosh and several other machines. In addition, TCP/IP is closely associated with the Unix operating system and all Unix vendors support TCP/IP. For example, the SUN Microsystems Unix includes TCP/IP in its software package.

TCP/IP Suite is competing with the OSI Model for interoperability and open systems to cooperate in solving computational problems. Unlike OSI, most of the TCP/IP protocols are implemented before becoming standards. This ensures feasibility and availability of products for interoperability. In addition, Simplified Network Management Protocol (SNMP), a TCP/IP-based network management protocol, has become widely accepted by vendors and users for network management in heterogeneous networks. Due to the growing importance of network management, SNMP has furthered the popularity of TCP/IP Suite over OSI as the glue between disparate networks and devices.

The following major trends in TCP/IP are worth noting:

- This protocol suite will continue to evolve on almost all computing systems including microcomputers, minicomputers and mainframes. The display of TCP/IP products and projections in the Interop Shows in the last few years is indicating strong support in favor of TCP/IP as an interoperability platform (see Scott <1990>).
- A great deal of research and development activity in Internet protocols is being conducted. The Internet Activities Board (IAB) provides a framework and focus

for most of the research and development of these protocols. It will be interesting to see how the future TCP/IP protocol development will be shaped by the IAB.

- The decision of DOD to include OSI as full-costandards will perhaps eliminate the differences between OSI and TCP/IP. It will be interesting to see if the TCP/IP protocol and OSI will compete or merge for open systems interconnection.

CASE STUDY: TCP/IP in XYZCORP

The management at XYZCORP has just come back from a presentation on TCP/IP and how TCP/IP can be used as a basis for interconnecting heterogeneous systems. You have been asked to investigate this issue and present a strategic plan about the role of TCP/IP in XYZCORP. The management is especially interested in the following questions:

- Should the management consider TCP/IP instead of OSI in its long range plans?
- How do the TCP/IP services and products differ from OSI? In what cases is OSI superior to TCP/IP?

The engineers in the Detroit branch already have some experience with TCP/IP local area networks. They are especially interested in developing an overall architecture of the engineering office by using TCP/IP. The management has asked that while you are investigating TCP/IP as a strategic network platform, you might as well get your feet wet with the details of TCP/IP implementation in the engineering plant. Figure B.18 shows the layout of the engineering office. All stations in the office have Ethernet

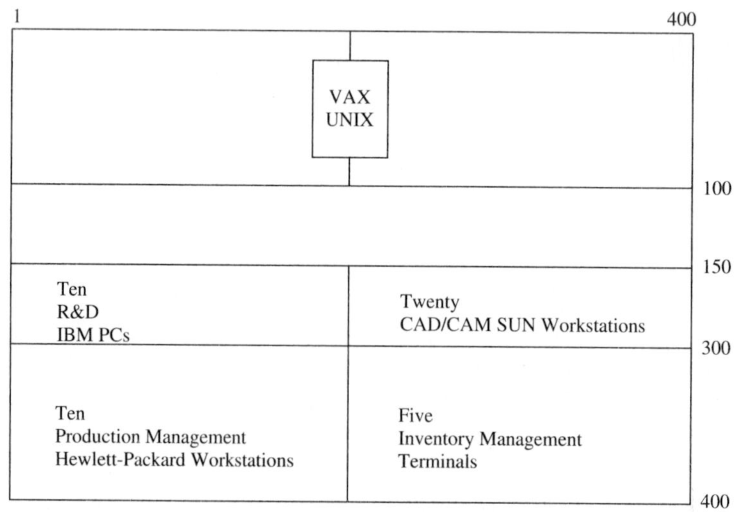

FIGURE B.18 Floor Two Layout—Detroit Branch

cards. You are to recommend how TCP/IP can be used in this plant to provide terminal emulation and file transfer capabilities.

Deliverables

- A management report which describes a strategic plan about the role of TCP/IP in XYZCORP. This report should answer the management questions listed above.
- A TCP/IP based local area network in the engineering office. The LAN should show:
  - the location of one or more servers and the functions performed by the servers (print server, file server, etc)
  - the network topology which shows how the stations will be connected through Ethernet cables
  - a user manual which describes how the users can use the network to perform the following basic functions:
    terminal emulation
    file transfer
    electronic mail
    how NFS and any other high level protocols can be of value in the engineering office

Hints About the Case Study

Sections B.6 and B.7 should be consulted to compare OSI with TCP/IP. The TCP/IP LAN for the engineering office should connect the PCs, SUNs, HPs and terminals through an Ethernet LAN. The VAX Unix minicomputer can be used as a server for common files and printers. The IBM PCs can connect to Ethernet TCP/IP LANs through off-the-shelf software. All workstations and terminals can use Telnet to logon to any of the computers in this network. In addition, FTP and NFS can be used to download engineering drawings and access remote files transparently. An SNA gateway can allow these users to also access the corporate data at the XYZCORP headquarters.

References

Comer, D., *Internetworking with TCP/IP: Principles, Protocols, Architectures*, Prentice Hall, 1988.

Comer, D., *Internetworking with TCP/IP*, 2 volumes, Prentice Hall, 1991.

Cerf, V. and Cain, E., "The DOD Internet Architecture Model," *Computer Networks*, Oct. 1983.

Davidson, J., *An Introduction to TCP/IP*, Springer-Verlag, 1988. IBM User's Guide, "Transmission Control Protocol/Internet Protocol for MVS," IBM Manual No. SC09-1255-00.

Green, P. (Ed), *Computer Network Architectures and Protocols,* Plenum Press, 1982.

Postel, J., "Internetwork Protocol Approaches," *IEEE Trans. on Communications*, Apr. 1980.

Rose, M., *The Open Book: A Practical Perspective on OSI*, Prentice Hall, 1990.

Scott, K. and Greenfield, D., "Interop 90 Show Preview: Not Just TCP/IP," *Data Communications*, Oct. 1990, pp. 99-114.

Stallings, W., *Handbook of Computer Communications Standards*, Mcmillan, 1987, Vol. 3 (DOD Protocol Suite).

Stalling, W., *Networks and Data Communications*, 2nd ed., McMillan, 1988.

Stevens, R., *Unix Network Programming,* Prentice Hall, 1990.

Tannenbaum, A., *Computing Networks*, 2nd ed., Prentice Hall, 1988.

Appendix C

Tutorial on IBM's SNA and APPC/LU6.2

C.1 Introduction

The objective of this appendix is to give the reader an overview of System Network Architecture (SNA) concepts and terminology, and to explain the LU6.2/APPC communication protocol. The reader should be able to answer the following questions (see Chapter 3, Section 3.4.3, for a quick review of SNA):

- What is SNA and what are its major components?
- How does SNA fit within the IBM computing environments?
- What is LU6.2 and APPC?
- How has SNA evolved in the last two decades?
- How does SNA compare and contrast with OSI?

We explain the concepts and terms of SNA in Section C.2, describe the IBM environments in which SNA operates (Section C.3), describe the Advanced Program to Program Communication (APPC) protocol which is used for cooperative processing in SNA (Section C.4), and highlight the evolution of SNA and compare it SNA with OSI (Section C.5).

This appendix contains many terms that are used commonly in IBM environments. The reader who is not familiar with IBM systems is advised to read Sections C.2 and C.3 to develop an overall understanding of the SNA concepts, environments and trends, and Section C.4 to understand the IBM application layer protocols such as the Advanced Program to Program Communications (APPC). This section is particularly important for distributed application developers in SNA environments. It is advised that the reader review the OSI Model (Chapter 3) before reading this tutorial because the OSI Model is used as a framework, where appropriate, to explain the functions of various SNA components.

C.2 SNA Overview

C.2.1 Motivation for SNA

SNA was introduced in 1973 to consolidate IBM's communication products and services. In 1973, IBM was supporting 35 communication software systems and 15 data link protocols to provide communications between IBM mainframes, communications controllers (front end processors), a wide variety of terminals, several types of cluster controllers (terminal servers), minicomputers, and batch remote job entry (RJE) workstations. Due to the IBM philosophy of supporting hierarchical data processing operations, the IBM mainframes were the centralized controllers/masters of the communication networks. IBM introduced SNA as the main architecture for all current and future computer communications between mainframes and devices. The main objectives of SNA as defined by the architects of SNA are <Martin 1987>:

1. *Unification.* SNA must unify IBM's communication products so that all products employ a standard set of protocols.
2. *Diversity.* SNA formats and protocols must allow diverse hardware and software products to be interconnected. SNA must provide migration and evolution of devices and applications.
3. *Ease of use and modification.* SNA must free users and application programmers from concerns about the network structure. In addition, SNA software must be divided into independent layers so that each layer can evolve independently without affecting other layers.
4. *Computer to computer communications.* SNA must support generalized program-to-program communication needed in computer communication networks. This architecture must support the creation of distributed processing applications.

The first two objectives made it possible to combine the 15 link protocols into a single data link protocol (SDLC) and reduced the 35 software systems into two packages: VTAM (Virtual Telecommunications Access Method) and NCP (Network Control Program). The third objective allowed layers of protocols and services (this concept was later adopted by the OSI Model). The fourth objective introduced peer-to-peer communications, interactive distributed computing, and communications between multiple hosts to support large networks and distributed processing. In 1973, when most computing was terminal to mainframe oriented, SNA provided a major shift toward computer to computer communications and layered architectures (initial implementations of SNA only supported mainframe to terminal communications; however, the "hooks" were introduced to include computer to computer communications).

C.2.2 SNA Concepts, Terms and Components

The three architectural components of SNA are as follows (see Fig. C.1):

- VTAM (Virtual Telecommunications Access Method) which resides in the mainframe and manages the end-to-end sessions between application programs, terminals, workstations, etc. VTAM, also called a systems services control point (SSCP), interfaces with applications at the mainframe and roughly performs the functions of layers 6 and 5 of the OSI Model.
- NCP (Network Control Program) resides in the communications controller and is responsible for network routing and transport control. NCP roughly performs the functions of layers 4 and 3 of the OSI Model.
- SDLC (Synchronous Data Link Control) is the link protocol of SNA and performs the functions of layer 2 of the OSI Model.

Every network user is assigned a logical unit (LU) as shown in Fig. C.1 in SNA. A network user is an end-point in a network and may be a program or a terminal. For example, in Fig. C.1, LUa, LUb, LUc, LUd and LUe represent the

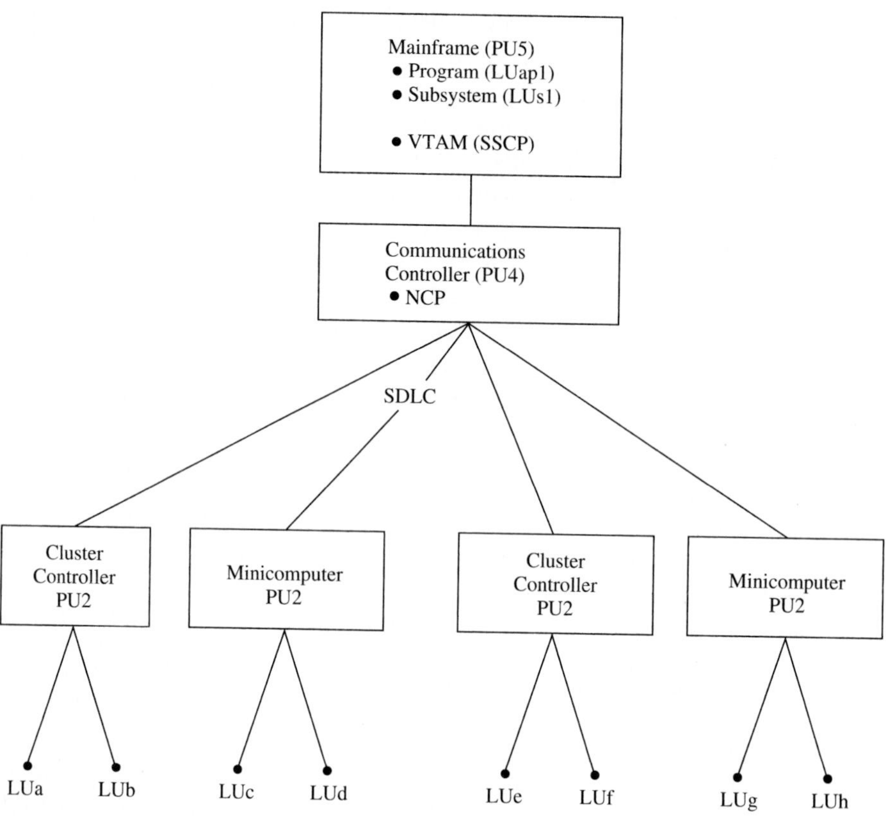

FIGURE C.1 SNA Components

terminals connected to the cluster controllers and minicomputers; LUap1 represents an application program and LUs1 represents a subsystem (e.g., a transaction manager) in the mainframe. SNA has introduced different LU types to represent different capabilities of end-points. For example, LU type 0 to 4, written as LU0 to LU4, were introduced in the 1970s to represent different terminal types. LU6 was introduced to represent programs and LU6.2 represents a program capable of peer-to-peer communications. A session between two end-points is called an LU-LU session. For example, the following session types are used in SNA to emulate terminals, transfer files, and exchange messages between remotely located programs:

- *LU type 1 session*: Program to non-programmable terminals/printers
- *LU type 2 session*: Program to programmable terminal

- *LU type 3 session*: Program to printer
- *LU type 6 session*: Generalized program to program.

LU6.2 is an application layer protocol developed by IBM which allows application programs to exchange messages for distributed cooperative processing (see Section C.5 for details). Advanced Program to Program Communications (APPC) is an implementation of LU6.2 on different computing platforms. The applications in SNA are typical IBM software packages such as IMS (Information Management System), TSO (Time Sharing Option), CICS (Customer Information Control System), office automation/electronic mail systems, and user written applications that directly communicate with VTAM (see Section C.4 for details).

The hardware devices in SNA (mainframes, communication controllers, workstations, minicomputers, cluster controllers, terminals, etc.) are represented as physical units (PUs). Because different SNA devices have different capabilities, SNA defines several PU types. For example, as shown in Fig. C.1, a host is PU type 5, a communications controller is PU type 4, and a cluster controller/minicomputer is PU type 2. New PU types have been introduced for new hardware devices. For example, PU type 2.1 (known as T2.1) has been introduced to define minicomputers and microcomputers for peer-to-peer networking.

An SNA network is a collection of domains, where a mainframe is at the top of hierarchy in each domain. Every domain is subdivided into subareas, where each subarea consists of a communications controller and all the devices (workstations, minicomputers, cluster controllers, terminals, etc.) connected to the communications controller. In addition, the mainframe VTAM is also a subarea (Fig. C.2). A communications controller is at the top of hierarchy in a subarea and is responsible for managing the subarea activities. For example, Fig. C.2 shows a one domain SNA network with three subareas: the host subarea, the subarea controlled by communication controller 1, and the subarea controlled by communications controller 2. In SNA, each subarea can support up to 32,000 devices.

Complex networks can be built in SNA by using multiple domain networks. A single domain network has only one host and is limited to simple networks. Fig. C.3 shows a two domain system. Note that a mainframe is at the top hierarchy of each domain. SNA uses "cross domain" services for LUs in one domain to communicate with an LU in another domain. By using these services, a program running on one mainframe computer can communicate with another program or a device on another host processor. Multiple domain services are used heavily in large SNA networks for communications between mainframes.

The initial versions of SNA allowed peer-to-peer communications only at the communications controller level; two users within a subarea could not directly communicate with each other without having to go through the host subarea. A new feature, called the Advanced Peer to Peer Networking (APPN), allows cluster controllers/minicomputers to communicate directly with each other.

SNA supports many interconnectivity options through SNA gateways. Examples are SNA-LAN gateways to connect local area networks to hosts and gateways to connect DECNet, TCP/IP and MAP networks to SNA. Most of these interconnectivity products have been developed by other network vendors who wish to communicate with SNA due to its market dominance.

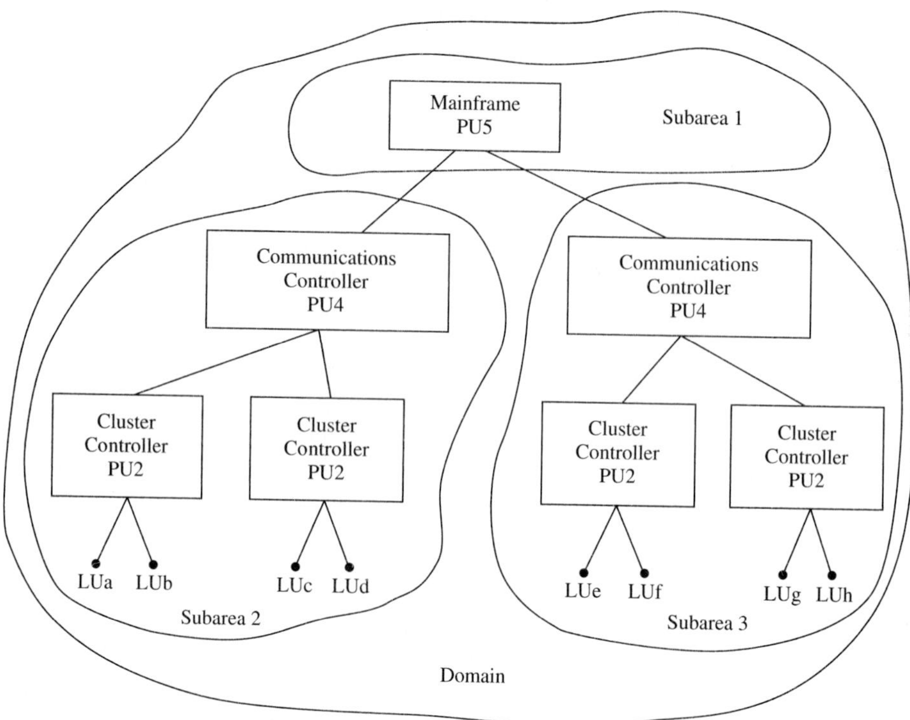

FIGURE C.2 SNA Network as Domains and Subareas

C.2.3 SNA Layers

SNA supports a layered model, although the SNA layers do not conform exactly to the OSI Model layers. Examples of the SNA layers are as follows (see Fig. C.4):

- The end user and network services layer is similar to the application and presentation layers of the OSI Model. This layer provides end user services such as format conversion, compression/decompression and connections between programs. It may provide session network services such as operator commands, activation/deactivation of lines and conversion of LU names into physical addresses.
- The data flow control layer performs functions similar to the Session and Transport Layers of ISO. It primarily sets flow control between LUs by defining three type of responses: definite response, exception response (error only), and no response.
- The transmission control layer is similar to the Transport Layer of OSI. This layer limits buffer overruns, sets the number of messages received simultaneously (message window) and encryption/decryption.
- The path control layer is similar to the network control layer of ISO. This layer is responsible for routing and flow control. Routing determines the path from the origin LU to destination LU, handles multiple domains, constructs packets from

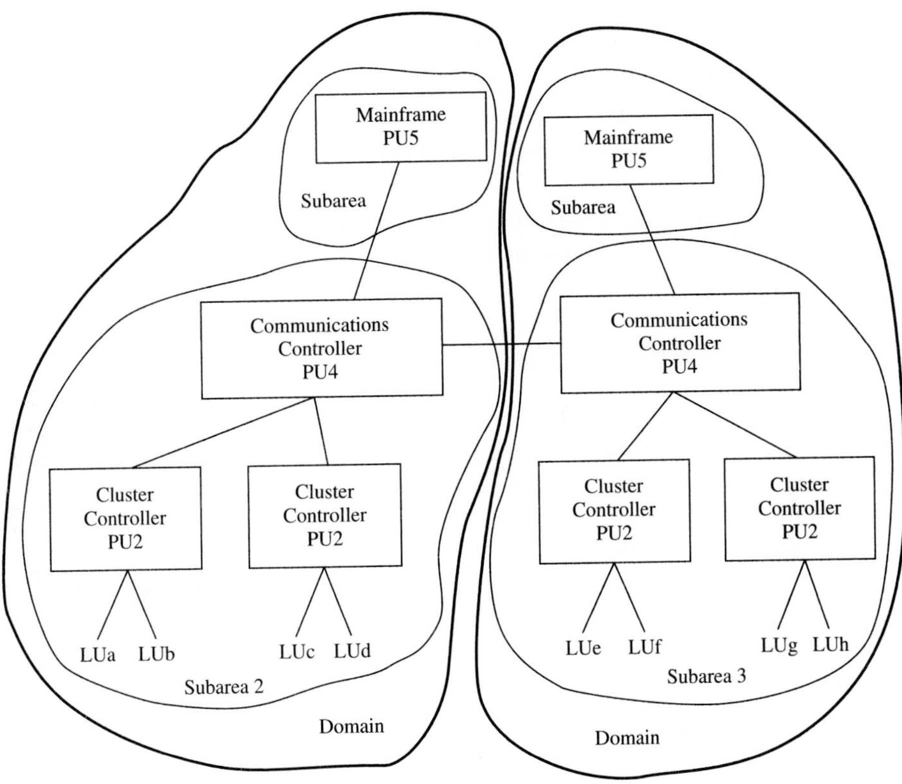

FIGURE C.3 A Multiple Domain System

Network Users	
End User and Network Services Layer	VTAM
Presentation Services Layer	
Data Flow Control Layer	
Transmission Control Layer	NCP
Path Control Layer	
Data Link Control Layer	SDLC
Physical Layer	

FIGURE C.4 SNA Layers

messages and vice/versa, and sets the message priorities at high, low, or medium. Flow control is responsible for message pacing and slowdown.

- The data link control corresponds to the ISO data link layer and supports SDLC (synchronous data link control). SDLC is a synchronous, bit-oriented (control characters are bit strings) data transmission protocol used in IBM wide area networks.
- The physical layer corresponds to the OSI physical layer and supports the RS232-C and X.21 physical interfaces.

C.3 Overview of SNA Environments

SNA is the data communication portion of an IBM computing environment. The IBM environments involve mainframes, minicomputers, microcomputers, LANs, terminals and many other I/O devices which operate under different operating systems and utilize a plethora of database managers, transaction managers, compilers, utilities, etc. This section is intended to familiarize the "non-IBM" reader with the hardware, systems software, and application processing environments in which SNA operates.

C.3.1 SNA Hardware

A variety of IBM's hardware products can be used as components in an SNA network. Fig. C.5 shows some of these components.

- *Host processors (mainframes)*: The IBM mainframes are large scale computing systems equipped with extensive processing, storage and input/output (I/O) capabilities. The mainframes play a central role in SNA networks: they control the peripheral equipment connected to the mainframe and they house large scale applications and databases which are accessed by the network users. Examples of the host processors are the IBM large scale ES/9000 and 30xx systems such as the 309x and 308x series and the medium range 4300 series.[1] The host processors operate under the MVS (Multiple Virtual System) operating system <Clark 1989>.
- *Distributed processors*: Many minicomputers operate in SNA environments to perform database lookups, message routing and specialized computation. Perhaps the best known IBM distributed processors are the Application System/400 (AS/400) processors which are mid-range computers with many connectivity options in SNA environments. AS/400 systems operate under the OS/400 operating system <Baritz 1991, Schneider 1989>.
- *Communications controllers*: The communication controllers are specialized computers which are programmed to control communication devices. The communication controllers, also called the front-end processors (FEPs), are used extensively

[1]The "x" in these computers represents model numbers and usually range from 0 to 9 to represent different hardware configurations. For example, the 309x series can appear as 3090, 3091, 3092, etc (usually higher numbers mean more capabilities).

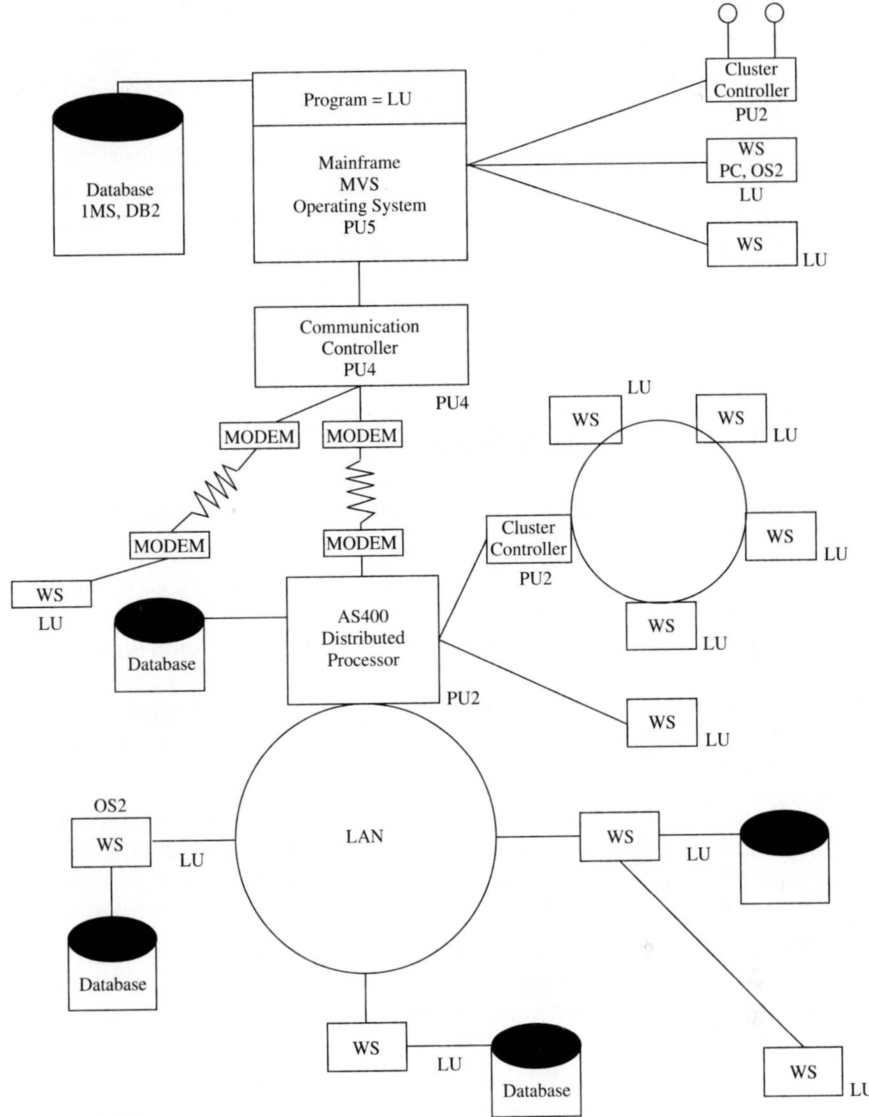

Legend:
IMS = Information Managment System
DB2 = Database 2
MVS = Multiple Virtual System
WS = Workstation
LU = Logical Unit
PU = Physical Unit

FIGURE C.5 SNA Hardware Environment

in SNA to manage portions of SNA networks. The NCP (network control program) resides in the communication controllers. Examples of the communication controllers are the IBM 3720, 3725, and 3745 controllers. These models differ by capabilities (speed, number of ports supported, memory size, etc.) and price.

- *Cluster controllers*: These devices, known as the terminal servers in the non-IBM world, control many terminals, workstations, printers, etc. An example of a cluster controller is the IBM 3x74 local cluster controller. With proper software, a workstation or a minicomputer can emulate a cluster controller.
- *Workstations*: These devices are used by the network users to send and receive messages. Examples of workstations are microcomputers such as PCs/PS2s or IBM 3270 information display systems.

C.3.2 Network Addressable Units

SNA consists of hardware, software, and microcode components. These components are grouped into two major types:

- Network Addressable Units (NAUs), which include all logical units, all physical units, all system service control points, and communication links that connect them. Each network addressable unit has a network address that identifies it to the other NAUs in the network. The NAUs provide services to move information through the network from one user to another and allow the network to be controlled and managed.
- Path Control Network, which consists of lower-level components that control routing and flow of data through the network. It handles physical transmission of data from one SNA node in the network to another.

This section gives more details about the network addressable units and how do they relate to each other. The path control network is not explained here due to the space shortage. Details can be found in <Ranade 1989>.

C.3.2.1 Logical Units and SNA Users

An SNA user can be a person who interacts directly with the network through a terminal or an application program which can be located at different points within the network (in the user workstation, in the workstation server or in a mainframe computer). Basically, an application program may provide services to people or to other application programs. A logical unit is an end-point in SNA and is used to represent the SNA user. Each user accesses the SNA network through a logical unit. Consequently, an LU may be a program, a terminal, a workstation, or a printer. All communications in SNA are between LUs (called LU to LU sessions). LUs reside on various SNA network devices in the form of software or microcode. Seven major LU types have been defined so far. LU types 0 through 4 are used to represent terminals, and LU type 6 is used to represent programs. Examples of the LU types are as follows:

- LU Type 0 represents non-SNA devices and protocols (e.g., BSC).
- LU Type 1 represents a terminal cluster (printers, readers, CRTs) such as an IBM 8100 system.
- LU Type 2 represents a single workstation/terminal (e.g., IBM 3277).
- LU Type 3 represents a printer.
- LU Type 4 can be used to represent a word processor (e.g., IBM 6670).
- LU Type 6 represents a program for peer-to-peer communications. Programs are subdivided into two categories:
- LU 6.1 represents subsystem communication, i.e. IMS to CICS.
- LU 6.2 is used for generalized, any-to-any communication between programs.
- LU Type 7 can be used between host application and a midrange system (e.g., system 36).

The LU code provides transmission capabilities and a set of services related to a user type and converts information it receives from a physical device to simulate the logical terminal/workstation it represents. The complexity of the LU code depends on the type of device or program it represents. This allows the users to communicate without knowing characteristics of each other's physical device. Thus network and users are isolated from hardware changes. The LU types are used by SNA application programmers. The programmer chooses an LU type and then codes the primitives allowed by the particular LU type. Details about SNA programming can be found in the IBM Manual "VTAM Programming," SC23-0115.

During an LU to LU session, data may pass through several intermediate points on its way through the network. The transfer of data may involve functions that are transparent to the network users. Examples of these functions are operations that enable data to travel more efficiently through the network and data conversion from one form to another.

C.3.2.2 Physical Units (PUs)

A physical unit (PU) represents the actual hardware devices in an SNA network. Examples of PUs are computing systems, various types of controllers and terminal devices. PUs are implemented with some combination of hardware, software, and microcode within the actual device represented. A PU provides services to manage and use a particular type of device and to handle physical resources (e.g., communications links). Each physical unit in the network is one of five possible types:

- PU type 1: a non-programmable terminal
- PU type 2: a programmable terminal and a cluster controller
- PU type 2.1: a distributed processor with peer-to-peer capabilities
- PU type 4: a communication controller
- PU type 5: a mainframe.

The architectural definitions of the various physical unit types have been enhanced as SNA has evolved. The type 2 physical unit that implements the most comprehensive set of functions is now known as PU type 2.1, or PU 2.1. This is the physical unit that is used in conjunction with LU 6.1 in implementing Advanced Program-to-Program Communication (APPC) facilities.

C.3.2.3 System Service Control Point (SSCP)

The SSCP provides the central management and control services in SNA. An SSCP resides in every mainframe and manages an SNA network or portion of a complex network. It also establishes and controls interconnections for communications between network users. The functions of SSCP are much broader than a logical unit, which represents a single user, and a physical unit, which represents a physical device and its resources. SSCP instead manages all the hardware resources (PUs) and users (LUs) in the network domain. An SSCP

- Manages the bringing up and shutting down of the network
- Manages network resources
- Coordinates the interconnection of logical and physical units required for communication between network users
- Converts symbolic names employed by network users to internal network addresses
- Manages the recovery of communication without the loss of data when failures occur on the network Interacts with the network operations personnel and executes their commands
- Collects measurement data on the usage of the network
- Acts on physical components of the network when necessary to establish interconnection (e.g., causing a telephone number to be dialed).

The counterpart of an SSCP is a PUCP (a physical unit control point). A PUCP implements a subset of SSCP functions that are needed to activate or deactivate controllers, workstations, and terminals. PUCP resides in the subareas.

C.3.3 SNA Application Processing Environments

SNA applications interface with many transaction managers, database managers, terminal handlers, and remote job spoolers at various levels. Fig. C.6 shows a sample SNA environment consisting of a mainframe (e.g., an IBM 3090), a communications front-end controller (e.g. an IBM 3725), a dial up PC, a LAN and a minicomputer. (e.g., IBM AS400 Processor). An IMS (Information Management System) or DB2 (Database 2) database resides in the mainframe. The database manager is responsible for access to the database and maintains a data dictionary. Let us assume that the database in the mainframe is accessed by the various workstations through the applications programs P1 through P5. VTAM resides in the mainframe and is responsible for all SNA sessions. The applications in the mainframe can be of many types:

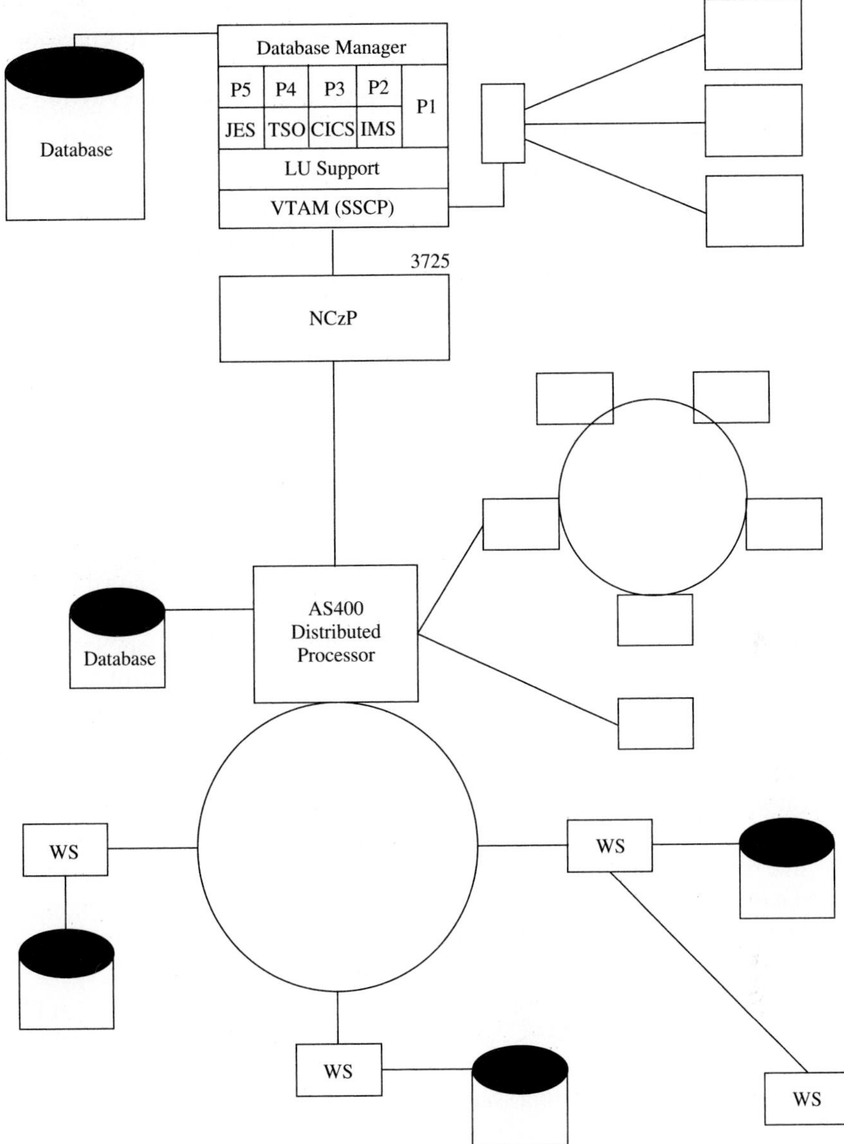

FIGURE C.6 SNA Application Processing

- A *Native* application program, P1, which directly interfaces with VTAM by issuing APPC calls to communicate with an application running on the minicomputer or any of the workstations in the network. Examples of native application programs may be specialized applications (e.g., an order processing system) or commercial systems such as Netview and SNA electronic mail services. Netview is the network manager in SNA environments and is discussed in Chapter 4.

- Transaction programs which interactively access the database. These programs are processed under the IBM transaction managers such as CICS (Customer Information Control System) and IMS (Information Management System) Data Communication Manager. The IMS or CICS programs (P2 and P3) issue IMS and CICS calls respectively to access SNA facilities and the databases. See Section C.3.4 for more discussion of IMS and CICS.
- A time sharing program P4 which runs under TSO (Time Sharing Option) to allow users to write interactive applications against databases. TSO does not have sophisticated transaction management capabilities comparable to CICS and IMS (e.g., transaction locking, backup/recovery, logging and audit trails). For this reason, TSO is not used frequently for transactions. More information about TSO can be found in <Janossy 1989>.
- A batch program, say P5, which gets input as a batch job from a remote site. This job runs under a batch processor, JES (Job Entry Subsystem), which spools, schedules, and prints the batch jobs.

These programs and transactions/database managers run under the mainframe operating system MVS (Multiple Virtual Systems). MVS is not shown in Fig. 3.2 because in essence it controls all processes (VTAM, JES, CICS, application programs) in the mainframe. In practice, IMS, TSO, CICS, JES and VTAM run as subsystems under MVS. Each subsystem manages its own tasks. The main role of MVS is to schedule, dispatch and pass requests between subsystems. For example, if a workstation needs to read the database through an application program P2, then MVS passes the VTAM data to the IMS transaction manager which in turn passes the data to P2. More information about MVS can be found in <Johnson 1989, Clark 1989>.

In addition to the mainframe, the AS/400 distributed processor can run interactive applications under a transaction manager which allows access to relational database management systems. The AS/400 runs under the OS/400 operating system. Details about the AS/400 distributed processor can be found in the *IBM Systems Journal*, Vol. 28, No.3, Special Issue on Applications System/400, 1989.

The workstations and terminals in Fig. 3.6 may run standalone applications such as word processing, CAD/CAM or behave as user interfaces to the data that is located at the AS/400 or the IBM mainframe. The workstations use OS2, DOS, or AIX (IBM version of Unix) operating systems. These workstations may run terminal emulations (e.g., 3270 emulation) to access mainframes.

C.3.4 Mainframe Database and Transaction Management Systems

The IBM mainframes are designed to handle a large number of business transactions which concurrently access and manipulate large centralized databases. The main products are: IMS, CICS and DB2. Figure C.7 shows the conceptual relationships between SNA and these IBM database/ transaction management systems. It can be seen that an SNA user can access flat files, IMS and/or DB2 relational databases through CICS, IMS, and/or native (homegrown) transaction management systems.

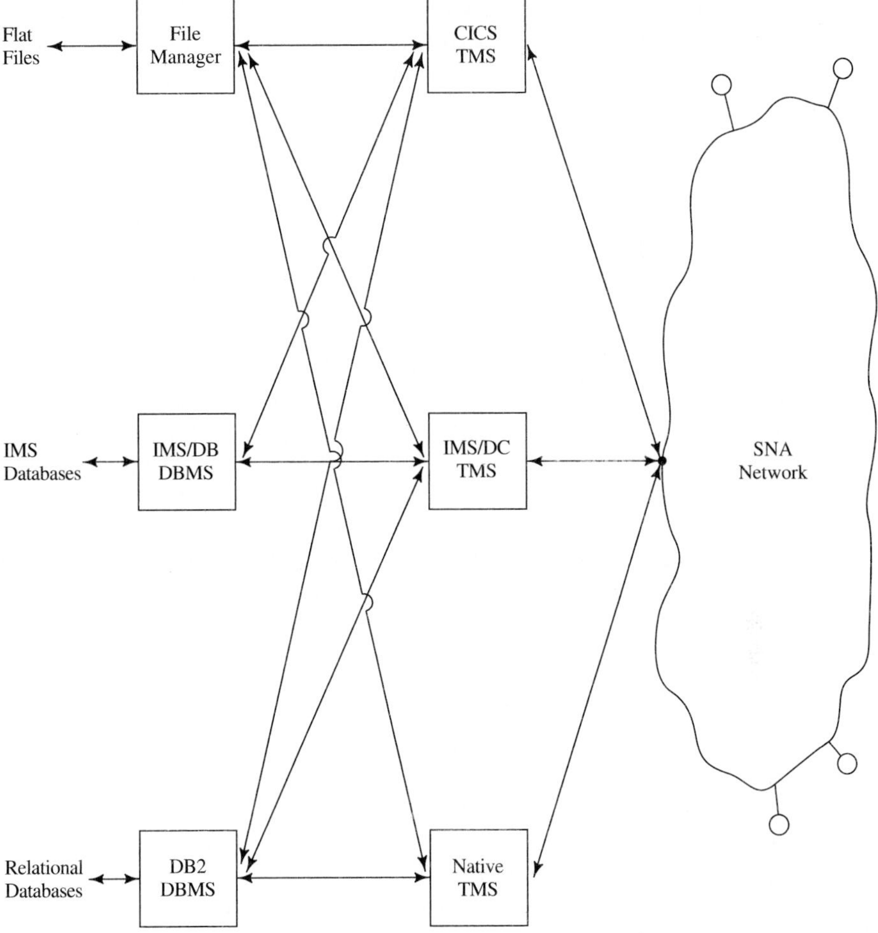

FIGURE C.7 Relationship of SNA with Host Database/Transaction Managers

IBM's main database management system (DBMS) for the last 20 years has been IMS (Information Management System). IMS was originally announced in 1969 as a hierarchical database management system and was referred to as DL1 (Data Language 1). The IMS applications were mainly batch applications until 1972 when a transaction manager, called IMS DC (Data Communications), was integrated with the IMS database manager. At present, the IMS DB/DC system provides database management and transaction management facilities with extensive SNA connections, locking, backup/recovery and logging/audit trail systems. Despite the current shift towards relational database management systems, a large number of business applications in IBM environments continue to be IMS based. One of the primary reasons is that over the years many performance and functional improvements in IMS have made it a reliable and well performing system <Geller 1989>.

As opposed to IMS, which was a DBMS with transaction management added later, CICS was introduced in 1972 as a transaction manager with no database facilities. CICS applications could read and manipulate flat files and could access IMS databases through DL1 calls (IMS database calls). Several organizations at present run IMS DB, without the IMS DC, and use CICS to manage online interactive transactions which issue IMS database calls. CICS also provides connections to SNA networks. See Nirmal <1992> for more information on CICS.

DB2 is IBM's entry into relational database management systems. DB2 allows users to define relational databases on mainframes which can be manipulated by SQL. The relational databases defined under DB2 can be accessed through the IMS/DC or CICS transaction managers. DB2 does not have its own transaction manager. The *IBM Systems Journal*, Vol. 23, No. 2, Special Issue on Database2, 1984, contains many papers on different aspects of DB2. The paper by Harderle <Harderle 1984> gives a good overview. Appendix E describes the relational database concepts.

The following steps illustrate how an IMS application program P1 accesses a database D1 for an SNA user LU1.

1. A database administrator (a human being) defines the structure (schema) of database D1 by using the IMS/DB facilities.
2. The administrator defines the program P1 view of the database, called the Program Specification Block (PSB). A PSB defines the following two pieces of information, among others:
   - The SNA user id: LU1
   - The database that is going to be accessed: D1.
3. A programmer writes the code for program P1. The pseudo code of this program is as follows:
   - Call IMS/DC to read from LU1.
   - Process the input received.
   - Call IMS/DB to read from D1.
   - Process the database record read.
   - Call IMS/DB to update D1.
   - Call IMS/DC to write to LU1.

C.3.5 System Application Architecture (SAA) Overview

SNA is the primary communications support system for IBM's System Application Architecture (SAA) which provides an overall framework for building applications that can be transported between various IBM computing systems. IBM introduced SAA in 1987 to consolidate applications across mainframes, minicomputers (distributed processors) and workstations. For example, the IBM environments before 1987 fell into three categories:

- Mainframes with IMS, CICS, DB2 and TSO subsystems under the MVS operating system.
- Minicomputers with a very wide range of hardware/software systems. Examples are the systems 34/36/38, Series1, 8100 and 3790 minicomputers all running under different operating systems and with different database/transaction management systems.
- Workstations such as the IBM PCs under the DOS operating system.

The main problems with these environments was that migration of an application developed in one environment to an another environment was a major undertaking: a majority of software had to be redeveloped and redesigned, the developers had to be retrained and the users often had to be re-educated. As a matter of fact, an application developed on one IBM minicomputer could not be ported to another IBM minicomputer (e.g., System 36 to System 8100).

The primary objective of SAA is to provide application portability across all IBM environments. SAA essentially consists of a set of standards (interfaces, conventions, protocols, APIs) to guarantee transportable applications across all "major" mainframes, minicomputers and workstations. Examples of some of the most important standards are as follows:

- Common programming interfaces, which include ANSI Cobol, Fortran, REXX and C programming languages and the SQL database manipulation language
- Common communications support based on SNA with LU6.2, PU2.1, SDLC, token ring, X.25, and SNA Distribution Services support for Document Interchange Architecture and Document Content Architecture.
- Common user access which defines standard program function (PF) keys for system access (logon, logoff, help, session end, page up, page down, etc.).

The environments supported by SAA consist of IBM's main current and future offerings. Several applications which conform to SAA are also being announced by IBM. The initial focus is on office applications. Other industry specific applications are expected to appear in the future.

SAA has greatly affected the business data processing industry in defining distributed application architectures which provide systems connectivity, portability, consistency, uniform programming and user access. We discuss the role of SAA in open systems in Chapter 9. A quick overview of SAA can be found in Wheeler <1988>.

C.3.6 Distributed Relational Database Architecture and Information Warehouse

SAA provides a wide array of specifications and conventions. Distributed Relational Database Architecture (DRDA) is the SAA Common Communication Service for distributed relational databases in an enterprise. It specifies the protocols and conventions that govern the interactions between database clients and a database server. DRDA consists of four building blocks:

- Distributed Data Management describes the commands for passing requests and replies across systems.
- SNA LU6.2 communication protocol between data clients and servers.
- Character Data Representation describes how characters are recognized across systems.
- Formatted Data Object Content Architecture specifies the way to describe transmitted data.

Many vendors have pledged to support DRDA. Details about DRDA can be found in IBM Manuals such as DRDA Connectivity Guide (SC26-4783-00) and DRDA Planning Guide (SC26-4650).

Information Warehouse, introduced in September 1991, extends the scope of DRDA to corporate wide information access. This information may be in non-relational format. For example, this framework views computers as warehouse cells which contain different type of information stored in different formats in different physical locations. From this point of view, DRDA is a part of the Information Warehouse. Details about the Information Warehouse can be found in the IBM Programming Announcement, September 11, 1991, and "Information Warehouse: An Introduction" (GC26-4876).

C.4 Advanced Program to Program Communications (APPC) and LU6.2

In the IBM SNA environments, most applications in the past have been master-slave applications in which a mainframe application receives input from remotely located users, processes the input and sends responses back. IBM provides extensive transaction and database management systems such as IMS which make it easier for the users to write master-slave applications. However, with the need for business applications which could cooperate between different sites, IBM developed the LU6.2 protocol, for any-to-any communications among remotely located applications. LU6.2 is IBM's strategic protocol for interprogram communications for its SNA networks and has been used in IBM's Customer Information Control System (CICS) to access remote data. A large number of local and wide area networks are already supporting or planning to support LU6.2.

APPC (Advanced Program to Program Communication), is an *implementation* of LU6.2. It provides the application programming interfaces (APIs) for applications to use LU6.2. Most of the literature does not differentiate between LU6.2 and APPC. We will use the term APPC/LU6.2 when it is not necessary to differentiate between the two. Examples of APPC support in IBM environments are APPC/SNA and APPC/PC. IBM has also announced APPC/MVS which provides extensive scheduling and management facilities for APPC applications. In addition, APPC is a central offering in IBM's System Application Architecture (SAA) which was reviewed earlier. Other vendors have also implemented APPC/LU6.2 as part of their network offering. Examples are DEC/APPC on DECNet, APPC/SUN for SUN Microsystems

TCP/IP networks, Novell's Netware APPC for Novell LANs and MAC/APPC for Apple networks. Due to its strategic position and commercial acceptance, APPC/LU6.2 is emerging as a client-server standard for business distributed applications <Davis 1989, Griswald 1988>.

Every APPC package consists of two parts: LU6.2 and PU2.1. As mentioned previously, a LU session type defines the characteristics of an SNA session and a PU defines the characteristics of physical devices that participates in a session. LU6.2 defines a distributed application and manages sessions between applications. PU2.1 represents a special distributed processor which can communicate directly with another processor. Basically, PU 2.1 has the physical characteristics of a workstation to support peer-to-peer operations for LU 6.2. PU2.1, commonly known as T2.1, allows APPC to assume that intelligence is distributed around the network, thus the network nodes can communicate without having to go through a host. In addition to PU2.1, LU6.2 can also be implemented on mainframes (PU5). Because a PU is of almost no consequence to application developers, managers and users, we will not mention PU2.1 unless necessary (there are enough terms already).

LU6.2 is a common program to program protocol which encourages compatible distributed programs. It coordinates the processes on different nodes and may also involve distributed databases. LU 6.2 allows both LUs to be masters so that any LU can be responsible for error recovery. The other LU types in SNA (e.g., LU type 0 to 4) are master-slave and are not suitable for distributed cooperative applications. LU 6.2 introduces the concept of conversation between two programs. A conversation is a short interaction, usually a transaction. Conversations are efficient for short data transfers.

Fig. C.8 shows a conceptual view of LU6.2 communications. Note that two transaction programs P1 and P2 issue LU6.2 calls which are passed through the SNA network. P1 and P2 may be written in any language which may use other subsystems such as IMS, for database retrieval. The following LU 6.2 commands represent the basic command verbs which can be issued by the transaction programs P1 and P2:

- ALLOCATE: initiate a conversation
- DEALLOCATE: terminate a conversation
- SEND-DATA: send data
- RECEIVE-AND-WAIT: receive
- REQUEST-TO-SEND: program wants to send
- PREPARE-TO-RECEIVE: ready to receive
- SEND-ERROR: program error
- CONFIRM: send a confirmation request
- CONFIRMED: response to confirm
- GET-ATTRIBUTE: read conversation type.

These commands are actually the LU6.2 verbs which are sent across the network. How does an application program use these verbs? This is where APPC comes in.

FIGURE C.8 Conceptual View of APPC

APPC provides an application programming interface to invoke these verbs. The APPC calls are mapped to the LU6.2 verbs. For example, APPC/MVS allows the programmers to invoke the ALLOCATE, DEALLOCATE and SEND verbs by the following CALL statements:

- CALL ATBALLC (parameters,,,)
- CALL ATBDEAL (parameters,,,,)
- CALL ATBSEND (parameters,,,)

The application programs issue these calls with appropriate parameters. The programs can be IMS or CICS transactions. In the simplest case, an APPC program would only use the ALLOCATE, SEND-DATA, RECEIVE-AND-WAIT, and DEALLOCATE commands for a simple conversation. Fig. C.9 shows example of such an application. The first two commands show how a conversation is established between P1 and P2 by using an ALLOCATE and GET-ATTRIBUTE commands. Commands 3, 4, and 5 show a data sent, received and responded operation. Command 6 terminates the conversation by issuing a DEALLOCATE.

The request-to-send command is used to indicate that a sender wants to send (selects) to a receiver. The confirm and confirmed commands are used to verify that a command has been received by the receiver. Figure C.10 shows an example using these commands. In this example, the first two statements establish a conversation and P1 sends data in statement 3. Statement 4 issues a request from P1 that the data received be confirmed. P2 confirms the data received in statement 6, and then processes the data and sends a response back in statement 8. Statement 9 requests that P2 be given a chance to send data and thus reverse the information

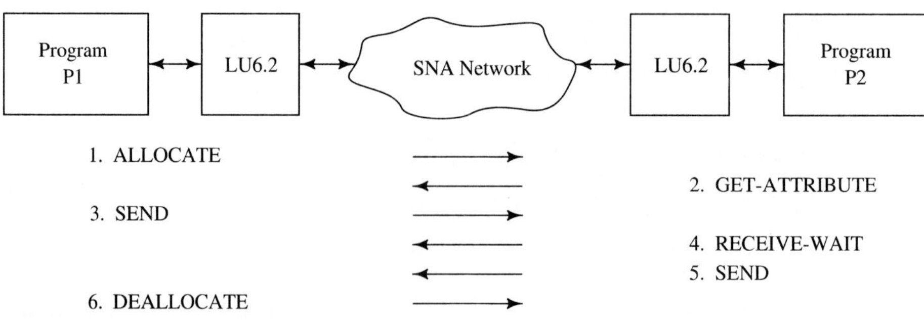

FIGURE C.9 Simple Example of APPC/LU6.2

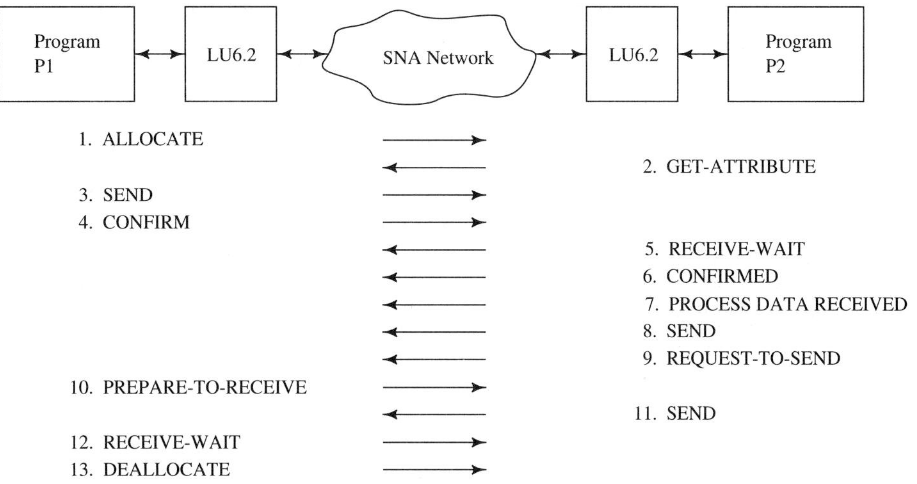

FIGURE C.10 Example of APPC/LU6.2 with Confirmation

exchange. Statement 10 indicates to P2 that P1 is prepared to receive. After this P2 sends and P1 receives data.

So far, we have only looked at simple applications of APPC/LU6.2. However, LU6.2 is a complex protocol and is suitable for complex distributed applications where the two applications frequently need to exchange data (e.g., DDBMS and cooperative processing). LU6.2 allows peer-to-peer communications in SNA and supports a large number of command primitives so that the applications can be standardized across various systems. LU6.2 provides three categories of commands for communications: control commands, conversation (basic and mapped) commands and system services commands (see Table C.1). Control commands are used by application subsystems to request services from or provide services to APPC. These services are normally not seen by end users and include the definition of the LU and PU, and the control of sessions. These commands are used in the Initialization State. Conversation commands include basic and mapped verbs and are used by transaction programs for information exchange. Before a conversation can take place, a session must be activated between two LUs. With mapped conversations, transaction programs are not concerned with ensuring that all data that form part of a conversation are converted into a standard format—the generalized data stream (GDS). With basic conversations, the programmer must at least build and interpret the logical length (LL) field of the GDS header. System services commands are used for tasks such as network management and ASCII/EBCDIC conversions.

APPC includes optional features to support data security and data integrity. The level of data security is decided on when a conversation is requested. Data security provides for data encryption, use of passwords, restricted areas to transaction programs, etc. Data integrity protection is provided in terms of synchronization. Synchronization levels are as follows:

TABLE C.1 LU6.2 Command Summary

Command	Description
a. Control Commands	
ACTIVATE	Opens the adapters designated during APPC configuration.
ATTACH-LU	Defines each local LU an its characteristics, the potential partner LUs, and the modes.
ATTACH-PU	Defines and establishes APPC conversations for the PU.
CHANGE-LU	Alters parameters for an existing local LU.
CNOS	Sets active number of sessions.
DETACH-LU	Terminates the local LU.
DETACH-PU	Terminates the local PU.
DISPLAY	Makes current values of operating parameters of local LU available.
GET-ALLOCATE	Checks queue for incoming ALLOCATEs.
TP-STARTED	Resources for a transaction program are requested locally.
TP-ENDED	Indicates end of transaction program.
b. Conversation Commands	
ALLOCATE	Establishes conversation between local and remote transaction programs.
BACKOUT	Rollback the changes made back to the previous synchpoint.
CONFIRM	Sends confirmation request to remote TP and waits for reply.
CONFIRMED	Sends confirmation reply to a confirmation request.
DEALLOCATE	Ends the conversation with the remote TP.
FLUSH	Sends all buffered information to remote LU.
GET-ATTRIBUTES	Returns information about specified conversation.
GET-TYPE	Indicates whether conversation is basic or mapped.
POST-ON-RECEIPT	Posts specified conversation when information is available for TP to receive.
PREPARE-TO-RECEIVE	Changes state of conversation from send to receive.
RECEIVE-AND-WAIT	Waits for information from remote TP and receives it on arrival.
RECEIVE-IMMEDIATE	Receives an information that is available, without waiting for information to arrive.
REQUEST-TO-SEND	Local TP notifies remote TP that it wants to enter state.
SEND-DATA	Sends data to remote TP.
SEND-ERROR	Local TP informs remote TP that an error was detected.

TABLE C.1 (Continued)

SYNCPT	Indicates that all changes are committed at this synchpoint and new changes after this synchpoint can be rolled back.
TEST	Tests a conversation for a particular condition.
WAIT	Waits for posting to occur.
c. System Service Commands	
TRANSFER-MS-DATA	Provides management services information to a network management services function.
CONVERT	Provides service for ASCII/EBCDIC conversion.

- *No Synchronization*: LU provides no synchronization services.
- *Confirm Synchronization*: A definite response is required by each cohort (cooperating program) when it receives data correctly.
- *Syncpoint Synchronization*: This implements two phase commit. Some resources are defined as protected. The LU rolls back any changes to these resources in case of an error.

Fig. C.11 shows pseudo code for a realistically complex business application in which program P1 at C1 downloads data segment D to computer C2. Then program P1 connects with program P2 at C2 and sends messages to P2. This application uses synchronization and failure handling facilities to illustrate the data integrity features of APPC. This is a complex program. You may want to skip it unless you need to know how two-phase commit is implemented in APPC/LU6.2. The steps are as follows:

1. The application subprogram performs a loop while waiting for an incoming ALLOCATE.
2. Program P1 issues a user-defined verb to indicate that the local transaction program has begun.
3. P1 issues an ALLOCATE to set up a conversation with SYNCPT synchronization level. This automatically implements the two phase commit processing. This statement also creates a SYNCPT record to indicate the program state to restart from in case of failure.
4. The application subsystem is informed of the receipt of an ALLOCATE and it is requested to initiate a new transaction program (program P2).
5. Application subsystem issues TP-VALID to give an indication of the status of the new transaction program (whether it has been validated and loaded).
6. The application subsystem issues verb to indicate start of remote transaction program.

Program P1 LU (local)	Program P2 LU (remote)
	1. GET-ALLOCATE
2. TP-INITIATE (local)	
3. ALLOCATE SYNC-LEVEL (SYNCPT)	
	4. CREATE-TP
	5. TP-VALID
	6. TP-INITIATE (remote)
	7. RECEIVE-AND-WAIT w-recv = data-incomplete
8. SEND-DATA	
9. FLUSH	
	10. RECEIVE-AND-WAIT w-recv = data-incomplete
11. CONFIRM	
	12. CONFIRMED
	13. Do local processing
14. SEND-DATA	
15. FLUSH	
	16. RECEIVE-AND-WAIT w-recv = data-incomplete
17. DEALLOCATE SYNC_LEVEL(SYNCPT)	
	18. Perform commit processing
	19. TP-ENDED
20. TP-ENDED	

Note: This pseudo code has been simplified for the purpose of illustration.

FIGURE C.11 LU6.2 Example

7. Since P2 was remotely initiated, it is initially in a receive state. Its first verb it issues is RECEIVE-AND-WAIT which causes it to receive information. The w-recv parameter (what received) indicates that an incomplete message was received. In this case no data was received.
8. P1 issues a SEND-DATA to send a message to P2. The message will consist of a complete data segment D. The message is put into a buffer, and unless the buffer is full nothing happens.
9. P1 issues a FLUSH, which causes the LU to empty its buffer by sending all information to the remote LU.
10. P2 again issues a RECEIVE-AND-WAIT. This time w-recv indicates that a complete message was received.
11. P1 issues a CONFIRM to ensure that the data segment D was successfully received before starting a conversation.
12. P2 issues a CONFIRMED, which returns an acknowledgement to the conversation partner indicating that the data D has been received.
13. Program P2 now processes the data received.

14. P1 issues a SEND-DATA to send another message to P2. This message may tell P2 what to do with the results of processing D and is put into a buffer. Unless the buffer is full nothing happens.
15. FLUSH causes the LU to empty its buffer by sending all information to the remote LU.
16. Since the state of the connection has not been changed, P2 is still in a receive state. The first verb it issues is RECEIVE-AND-WAIT, which causes it to receive information. The w-recv parameter (what received) indicates that a complete message was received.
17. P1 issues a DEALLOCATE to take down the conversation with P2 and indicates a SYNCPT to commit the data sent so far. This statement initiates the two phase commit process.
18. P2 performs the actual two phase commit processing. This is usually done through a transaction manager such as CICS. APPC/LU6.2 does not actually perform the two phase commit because commit processing needs to have knowledge of data management which is beyond the scope of APPC/LU6.2.
19. P2 indicates that the transaction program is complete (complete).
20. P1 indicates that the transaction program is complete.

The point at which the programmer interacts with the LU is called the protocol boundary and describes the users' responsibilities (e.g., valid verbs that may be issued will depend on the current state of the conversation). Transaction programs need not concern themselves with the details of communications (e.g., session initiation and packet creation) because LU6.2 provides an interface to the sixth layer (SNA presentation services layer).

To develop an LU6.2 based server on IBM mainframes, the client requests must be scheduled properly. The latest IBM announcement, APPC/MVS, provides a scheduler which makes it easier to develop servers on the mainframes by using LU6.2. APPC/MVS provides a complete run-time environment for distributed transaction processing where each application program manages an LU-to-LU session just as another resource. In essence, SNA can be viewed as a distributed operating system in which LUs perform the roles of loosely coupled processors.

Details about APPC characteristics and programming can be found in the book, *APPC: Introduction to LU6.2*, by Alex Berson <Berson 1990>. A good overview can be found in Gray <1983>. Additional information can be found in the following IBM manuals:

- *SNA Transaction Programmer's Reference Manual for LU Type 6.2*, IBM Manual Number SC30-3084.
- *SNA Format and Protocol Reference Manual: Architecture Logic for LU Type 6.2*, IBM Manual Number SC30-3269. IBM (International Business Machines), *Advanced Program-to-Program Communication for the IBM Personal Computer*, Programming Guide, February 1986.

C.5 Evolution of SNA

SNA has been IBM's main strategic network architecture since the mid 1970s. SNA has evolved gradually into a robust system and has added a great deal of functionality and reliability since its introduction in 1973. The shift towards program-to-program communications to support distributed computing (i.e. LU6.2 support) and peer-to-peer networking is especially worth noticing. Due to the new features of SNA, in contrast to the strictly hierarchical single mainframe system introduced in 1973, some consultants are calling it the "neo-SNA" and "not your father's SNA" <Guruge January 1992>. The major enhancements have been in the following areas:

- Multiple systems support: The initial SNA systems were single host systems. The support for multiple domains was added later for large networks with many mainframes.
- Distributed cooperative processing: APPC is a major step in SNA toward cooperative distributed processing. APPC allows peer-to-peer support for application processes because the cooperating processes do not need a master-slave relationship. Before APPC, all SNA sessions required master-slave relationships. APPC itself has also evolved. It was first introduced for cooperative processing between mainframes. However, it has been extended for cooperative processing between any SNA nodes (mainframes, minicomputers, workstations). This allows distributed cooperative processing where portions of an application may be split across one or more mainframes, minicomputers and/or microcomputers.
- Peer-to-peer support: SNA has made a major shift towards peer-to-peer operations through APPN (Advanced Peer-to-Peer Networking). APPN allows distributed processors (IBM minicomputers) to communicate with each other directly without the help of a mainframe. Before APPN, all SNA sessions required mainframe control and fixed routing. What is the difference between APPC and APPN? APPC defines protocols for communicating between network applications, regardless of how network routing is performed. APPN defines how the network routing between applications is controlled. An APPC application can use APPN network to route data or it can use a traditional SNA network to route data. APPN appears to be a major area of future development in SNA <Guruge May 1992>.
- *Transmission technology support*: Initial versions of SNA only supported SDLC lines. In 1981, an X.25 interface to SNA was introduced at the NCP level. This allowed X.25 based packet switching systems to be used at lower layers instead of or in addition to SDLC. SNA gateways for LANs and multiple domains were introduced to extend SNA to local area networks. In addition, SNA now supports token ring and Ethernet LANs attached directly to the communications controllers. Many other enhancements have also been introduced in SNA. For example, voice, data and image application support through IDNX has been announced so that an LU can be a voice unit.
- *Large network support*: The original 16 bit SNA address was extended to a 23 bit address to support larger networks. At present, SNA is being extended to 31 bit and 48 bit addressing.

- *Routing*: Initial SNA versions used point to point fixed routes. SNA has added options for dynamic routing.
- *Network management support*: All SNA diagnostics and operational features have been integrated into Netview, IBM's strategic network management platform. Netview has evolved into an extensive network management system with facilities for network monitoring, diagnostics, error recovery and network control.
- *Interconnectivity to other networks*: The SNA gateways are growing rapidly in the market to allow SNA networks to be interconnected to LANs, DECNet, MAP and TCP/IP. Many routers are providing mechanisms to allow SNA and non-SNA traffic to be transmitted on a common backbone. In addition, extensive support is available to interconnect many SNA networks together.
- *Strategic position*: SNA has moved into a strategic position in all IBM environments. For example, SNA is a key component of the systems application architecture (SAA). This is primarily due to the evolving architecture of SNA.

C.6 SNA versus OSI

SNA and the OSI Model have evolved and coexisted in roughly the same time period (SNA was introduced four years before OSI). Let us now compare the OSI Model with SNA.

SNA and OSI belong to two entirely different schools: SNA was initially developed for proprietary centrally controlled networks while OSI was developed for open peer-to-peer environments. The main advantages of SNA are its high installed base, excellent vendor and third-party support and good connectivity options (gateways) to most proprietary and open networks. The main disadvantages of SNA are the lack of conformance with the open standards and the hardware/software dependence of applications on SNA. The main advantages of the OSI Model are its international connectivity and hardware/software application independence. The main disadvantage of OSI is that the complete OSI Suite is not widely available.

Although the overall services provided by SNA and OSI are the same and they both have seven layers, the manner in which the functions are implemented is quite different. Figure C.12 compares the OSI layers with the SNA layers and lists the main functions in each layer of the two models. Mainly the functions of the top two layers are similar but not exactly the same. For example, data encryption is handled at the presentation layer in OSI and at a lower layer in SNA. In addition, the OSI network layer divides the data into packets; SNA does not use this concept in any layer, although a similar operation (message segmentation) is performed in the SNA transmission control layer. Also the broadband/baseband issues of the OSI physical layer do not have a direct counterpart in SNA. Despite some of these differences, both architectures use upper layers for application interfaces and lower layers for physical network interfaces. A detailed comparison of the OSI layers with SNA layers can be found in <Martin 1987, Raynade 1989>.

Due to the large SNA user-installed base, it is not likely that the SNA users will throw away their investment in favor of OSI. Perhaps the most practical option is to

	OSI	SNA
7	Application Layer • Interface to application	End User and Network Services Layer • Data exchange between LUs
6	Presentation Layer • Syntax and format	Presentation Services Layer
5	Session Layer • User dialogue management	Data Flow Control Layer • User dialogue management
4	Transport Layer • End-to-end error control	Transmission Control Layer • Data pacing, encryption
3	Network Layer • Packet formation routing	Path Control Layer • Message segmentation routing
2	Data Link Layer • Manage data flow on a link	Data Link Control Layer • Manage data flow on a link
1	Physical Layer • Physical interface to network	Physical Layer • Physical interface to network

FIGURE C.12 Comparison between OSI and SNA Suite

interwork the SNA network with OSI. We have discussed the general principles of interworking with OSI in appendix A. Let us now review some specific examples. A detailed description of SNA to ISO connectivity with examples for LAN and WAN is given by Tilleman <1990>. The suggested strategies are:

- Direct conversion through gateways, protocol converters or device emulators which directly convert one or more layers of SNA to OSI and vice versa. An example of such a device is an OSI-SNA gateway shown in Fig. C.13a. The main advantage of this strategy is the end-user transparency of any conversions and translations taking place in between. However, this option is expensive (gateways are expensive) and leads to deeper entrenchment of proprietary architectures.
- Indirect conversion through an intermediate network architecture which complies to OSI. An example is to use DECNet because DECNet Phase IV is OSI compliant and there are many DECNet-SNA gateways in the market (Fig. C.13b). The main advantage of this approach is the wide range of products that can serve as intermediaries. Examples are DEC, Hewlett-Packard, Data General and Tymnet. The main disadvantage is the performance delay incurred due to the additional conversion.
- Mixed conversion where some layers are converted directly while the others are converted through an intermediary. Mixed conversions are suitable when the lower layers are compatible. For example, SNA and OSI can both use X.25 at layers 1 to 3 and use conversions at higher layers (Fig. C.13c). This approach has the advantage that it increases the interoperability of layers.

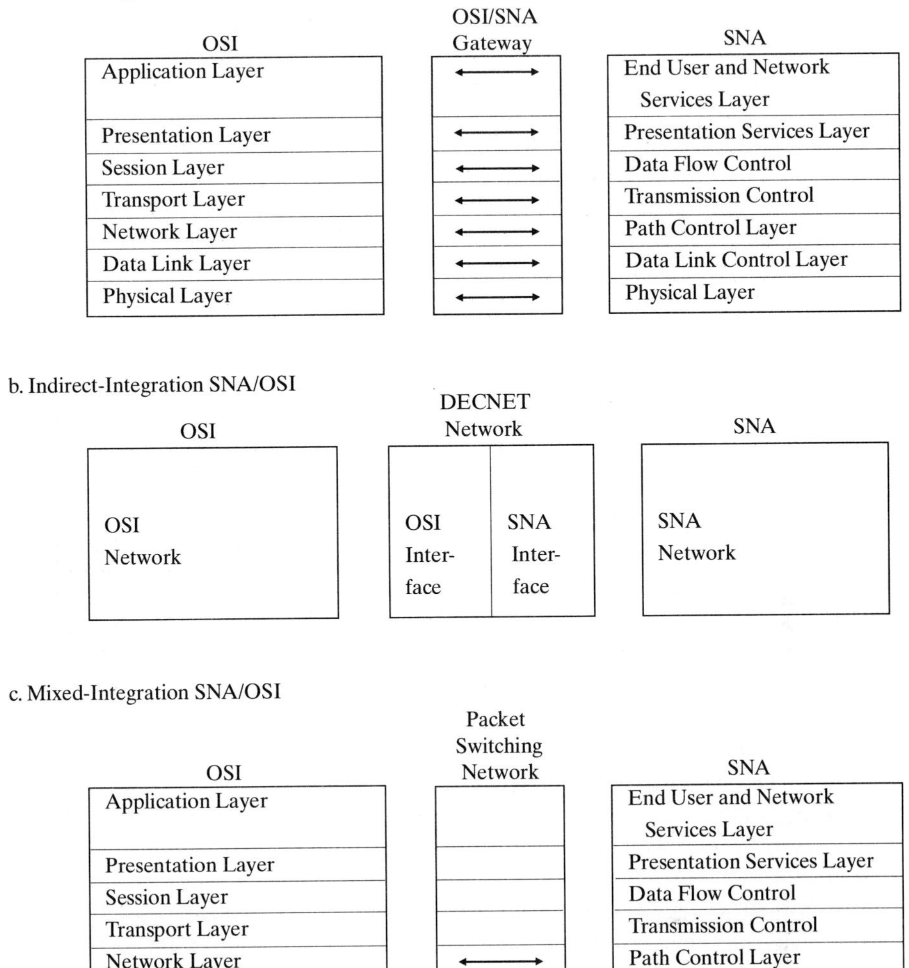

FIGURE C-13 SNA to OSI

<Janson 1992> describes two different approaches in detail: how to run OSI protocols over an SNA backbone, and how to run SNA over an OSI backbone. A common technique is "encapsulation" in which the OSI protocol data unit is inserted as data in SNA and then moved around an SNA network. Similarly, SNA protocol data units can be encapsulated inside OSI data and moved around an OSI network. The considerations of interworking at application, transport and network layer discussed in Section A.5, appendix A, should be consulted for more details.

The book by Cypser, "Communications for Cooperating Systems: OSI, SNA and TCP/IP" <Cypser 1991>, gives a detailed technical discussion of SNA versus OSI and

TCP/IP. The results of an IBM research project to open SNA to OSI networks is described in <Janson 1992>. Cypser <1992> describes evolution of opening SNA.

C.7 Management Summary and Trends

IBM announced System Network Architecture (SNA) in 1973 to consolidate network offerrings and to provide long range direction for computer to computer communications. The objectives of SNA as defined by IBM are as follows:

- Versatility
- Ease of use
- Distributed processing orientation
- Ease of modification
- Reliability
- Use of current technology
- Modularity
- Ease of implementation
- Unification.

At present, SNA is the most widely used private network architecture. with over 40,000 registered SNA licenses around the globe <Guruge January 1992>. Although SNA is also arranged in seven layers, the seven layers of SNA do not correspond exactly to the seven layers of the OSI Model. The components of SNA are:

- Synchronous data link control (SDLC) is used in layer 2 of IBM's wide area networks. SNA at present also uses X.25 in the first three layers and token ring in the first two layers of LANs.
- The Network Control Program (NCP) roughly performs the layer 4 and some layer 3 functions and resides in a front-end communications controller (e.g., IBM's 3725, 3745 or 3705).
- Layers 5 and 6 of SNA are handled by the Virtual Telecommunications Access Method (VTAM) which resides in IBM-compatible mainframes. VTAM controls the SNA network.
- SNA applications may be database applications which use the IMS hierarchical or DB2 relational databases. IMS and DB2 are not part of SNA, but these databases are commonly accessed through SNA networks.
- The main application layer protocol offered by IBM is the LU6.2 protocol. The Advanced Program to Program Communications (APPC) protocol is an application program interface (API) to LU6.2. APPC/LU6.2 allows two remotely located programs to engage in conversations.

- The SNA nodes can be mainframes, minicomputers, workstations and/or personal computers. The mainframes operate under the MVS (Multiple Virtual Operating System) operating system, the minicomputers operate under different minicomputer operating systems (e.g., AS400), and workstations/personal computers operate under the OS/2 or PC DOS operating systems.

An end-point in SNA is a logical unit (LU). An LU can be a terminal, a workstation, a printer, a large computer or an application program. Sessions between end-points are established as LU-LU sessions and can be of the following types:

- *LU type 1 session*: Program to non-programmable terminal
- *LU type 2 session*: Program to programmable terminal
- *LU type 3 session*: Program to printer
- *LU type 6 session*: Generalized program to program.

These session types are used in SNA to emulate terminals, transfer files and exchange messages between remotely located programs. These sessions types also provide rules for information exchange. For example, LU type 3 sessions have predefined rules which are applicable to printer operations. LU type 6 sessions provide sophisticated rules for remote program to program communications. A well known example is the LU6.2 protocol, which has become a de facto standard for interactions between remotely located business applications.

The initial versions of SNA did not provide any peer-to-peer communications. The new versions of SNA have added peer-to-peer communications. SNA supports many interconnectivity options through SNA gateways. Examples are SNA-LAN gateways to connect local area networks to hosts and gateways to connect DECNet, TCP/IP and MAP networks to SNA. Most of these interconnectivity products have been developed by other network vendors who wish to communicate with SNA due to its market dominance.

Although most of the SNA knowledge is embedded in IBM manuals (see a partial list in Table C.2), some books and magazines are beginning to appear in the open literature. For example, the books by James Martin <Martin 1987> and Ranade and Sackett <Ranade 1989, Ranade 1990> cover SNA in great detail. James Martin gives a more architectural and user perspective while Ranade and Sackett describe SNA from a systems programmer point of view. The *IBM Systems Journal*, Vol. 22, No.4, 1983, is an original issue on SNA directions with many good articles on SNA architecture, routing, APPC, SNA interconnections, etc.

The following trends in SNA are worth noting:

- There will be expansion of SNA capabilities to support more devices, larger networks, newer transmission technologies, peer-to-peer support and distributed applications.
- There will be increased interoperabilty and connectivity with other network s through gateways, protocol converters, etc. Coexistence with international standards will be attempted. For example, IBM has announced the OSI/CS product which provides OSI support.

TABLE C.2 Relevant IBM Publications

SAA Publications
SAA: An overview (SC26-4341)
Writing Applications: A Design Guide (SC26-4362)
Application Generator Reference (SC26-4355)
C Reference (SC26-4353)
COBOL Reference (SC26-4354)
Communications Reference (SC26-4348)
Database Reference (SC26-4348)
Dialog Reference (SC26-4356)
Presentation Reference (SC26-4359)
Procedures Language Reference (SC26-4358)
Query Reference (SC26-4349)
SNA Publications
SNA Concepts and Products (GC30-3072)
SNA Technical Overview (GC30-3073)
SNA Format and Protocol Reference Manual: Architectural Logic (SC30-3112)
SNA Reference Summary (GA27-3136)
SNA—Sessions Between Logical Units (GC20-1868)
IBM SDLC General Information (GA27-3093)
SNA Network Product Formats (LY43-0081)
SNA Format and Protocol Reference Manual: Distribution Services (SC30-3098)
LU6.2 Publications
SNA Format and Protocol Reference Manual: Architecture Logic for LU Type 6.2 (SC30-3269)
SNA Transaction Programmer's Reference Manual for LU Type 6.2 (SC30-3084)
AS/400 Communications Publications
AS/400 Communications: Programmer's Guide (SC21-9590)
AS/400 Communications: User's Guide (SC21-9601)
AS/400 Communications: Advanced Program-to-Program Communications and Advanced Peer-to-Peer Networking User's Guide (SC21-9598)
OS/2 Communications Publications
OS/2 Information and Planning Guide (G360-2650)
OS/2 Extended Edition System Administrator's Guide for Communications (90X7808)
OS/2 Extended Edition User's Guide
OS/2 Extended Edition APPC Programming Reference (90X7910)
OS/2 Extended Edition Programming Services and Advanced Problem Determination for Communications (90X7906)
CICS/VS Intersystem Communications Publications
CICS/VS General Information (GC33-0155)
CICS/VS Release Guide (GC-0132)
CICS/VS Facilities and Planning Guide (SC33-0202)
CICS/VS Intercommunication Facilities Guide (SC33-0230)
CICS/VS Resource Definition (Online) (SC33-0186)
CICS/VS Resource Definition (Macro) (SC33-0237)
CICS/VS Application Programmer's Reference Manual (Command Level) (SC33-0241)

- SNA will become even more reliable with time. At present, the mean time between SNA failures due to an SNA fault is reportedly one year.

It will be interesting to see if SNA will continue its market share even with the emergence of open network architecture standards.

CASE STUDY: SNA for XYZCORP

The corporate office is planning to use SNA as the main network architecture to support the corporate administrative processing. The corporate headquarters, a three floor 300 feet × 500 feet building, will house the data processing (first floor), administration and distribution (second floor) and marketing / corporate planning and management offices on the third floor. Each floor will have the office layout as shown in Fig. C.14. Each person in the office wants a desktop computer. You are to develop a recommendation for SNA implementation which should contain:

1. A layout of the SNA hardware (mainframe, 3745/3725, minis, micros) in the corporate office. Does any floor need any minicomputer to do departmental processing?
2. A layout of how the 40 stores are connected to the MVS mainframe through an SNA network.
3. A configuration which shows where the main files and data processing activities will take place in the corporate office. Files may be on host, on PCs or on a mini.
4. All gateways and bridges needed to connect the SNA network with the LANS in the engineering and manufacturing plants
5. The SNA software components (MVS, VTAM, NCP) with an identification of main LUs and PUs.
6. An evaluation of where System Application Architecture (SAA) can be useful
7. An evaluation of where APPC can be used in this environment.

While designing the hardware layout, you need to keep the following factors in mind:

1. Some people in the DP department do not like IBM PCs and insist on Macs for "quality" word processing and graphics. Three Macs, indicated by M, will be placed as indicated in Fig. C.14.
2. Some stations, indicated by E in Fig. C.14, need to emulate IBM 3270-SDLC terminals when communicating with IBM host. An IRMA board (cost $800) can emulate a PC as an IBM 3270 terminal connected to an IBM 3274 Terminal Controller (shown in Fig. C.14).
3. Every station needs to transfer files (upload/download) from the host.

Floor One Layout — Chicago Office

Note: Each regular office room is assumed to be 10 feet × 10 feet.
Each double office room is assumed to be 20 feet × 30 feet.

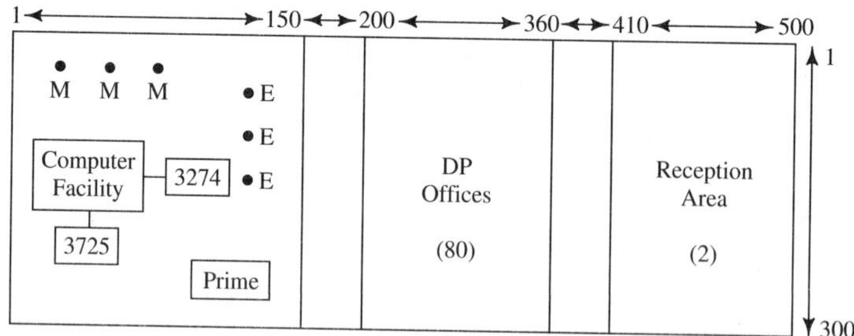

Floor Two Layout — Chicago Office

Payroll AR/AP

(20)

Order Processing

(10)

Personnel

(5)

Floor Three Layout — Chicago Office

Top Management Offices

(10)

Marketing Offices

(10)

Meeting Halls

Note: The number of workstations in each area is indicated in parentheses. The workstations are assumed to be equally distributed in each area.

FIGURE C.14. Corporate Office Layout

4. A PRIME system that was used by the ECI stores will also be placed in the Data Processing Department to "help out" in processing additional workload. PRIME uses Ethernet and TCP/IP and will need to upload/download from the host.

Hints About the Case Study

This case study builds on the LAN/WAN design conducted for XYZCORP at the end of Chapter 2. The suggested solution in Chapter 2 has already outlined a hardware layout. The PCs in the office can be connected directly to the headquarter LAN. If a Novell LAN is used, then Macs can be directly connected to the LAN. Otherwise, a small Appletalk LAN can be setup and connected through a gateway. The mainframe is defined as PU5, the 3725 is defined as PU4, and each minicomputer in the corporate office and the stores is defined as PU2. Essentially, each workstation is defined as an LU. In addition, each program on the mainframe which is accessed from these LUs is also defined as an LU (SNA supports LU to LU communications). The IBM mainframe can be connected to the corporate TCP/IP backbone through a multiple protocol router and an SNA to TCP/IP gateway.

References

Baritz, T. and David, D., *AS/400 Concepts and Facilities*, McGraw-Hill, 1991.

Berson, A., *APPC: Introduction to LU6.2*, McGraw-Hill, 1990.

Benjamin, J.H., "Interconnecting SNA Networks," *IBM Systems Journal*, Vol. 22, No. 4, Special Issue on SNA, 1983, pp. 344-366.

Booker, E., "Latest IBM Product Avalanche Embraces OSI Compatibility," *Telephony*, Sept. 1988.

Clark, C.E., "The Facilities and Evolution of MVS/ESA," *IBM Systems Journal*, Vol. 28, No. 1, Special Issue on Large Systems, 1989, pp. 104-123.

Comer, D., *Internetworking with TCP/IP: Principles, Protocols, Architectures*, Prentice Hall, 1988.

Cypser, R.J., *Communications for Cooperating Systems: OSI, SNA and TCP/IP,* Addison-Wesley, 1991.

Cypser, R.J, "Evolution of an Open Communication Architecture," *IBM Systems Journal*, Vol. 31, No. 2, 1992, pp. 161-188.

Davis, Ralph, "A Logical Choice," *BYTE*, Jan. 1989, pp. 309-315.

Geller, J., *IMS Administration, Programming and Database Design*, Wiley, 1989.

Gray, J., et al., "Advanced Program to Program Communications in SNA," *IBM Systems Journal*, Vol. 22, No. 4, Special Issue on SNA, 1983, pp. 298-318.

Griswold, C., "LU6.2: A View from the Database," *Database Programming and Design*, May 1988, pp 34-39.

Guruge, A., "SNA: The Dawn of the Next Era," *Enterprise Systems Journal,* Jan. 1992, pp. 16-27.

Guruge, A., "SNA is Dead; Long Live APPN?" *Business Communications Review*, May 1992, pp. 53-58. IBM "Advanced Program-to-Program Communication for the IBM Personal Computer," *Programming Guide*, Feb. 1986.

Harderle, D.J., "IBM Database 2 Review," *IBM Systems Journal*, Vol. 23, No. 2, Special Issue on Database2, 1984, pp. 112-125.

IBM Systems Journal, Special Issue on SNA, Vol. 22, No. 4, 1983.

Jaffe, J.M., et al., "SNA Routing: Past, Present and Possible Future," *IBM Systems Journal*, Special Issue on SNA, Vol. 22, No. 4, 1983.

Janosy, J., *Practical TSO/ISPF for Programmers and the Information Center*, Wiley, 1989.

Janson, P., Molva, R., and Zatti, S., "Architectural Directions for Opening IBM Networks: The Case of OSI," *IBM Systems Journal*, Vol. 31, No. 2, 1992, pp. 313-335.

Johnson, R., *MVS Concepts and Facilities*, McGraw-Hill, 1989.

Kapoor, A., *SNA: Architecture, Protocols, and Implementation*, McGraw-Hill, 1991.

Martin, James, *SNA: IBM's Networking Solution*, Prentice Hall, 1987.

Nirmal, B., "CICS Applications and System Programming," QED, 1992.

Pickens, J.R., "Which Way is SNA Moving," *Computer Decisions,* Jan 1987, pp. 45-46.

Ranade, J. and Sackett, G.C., *Introduction to SNA Networking Using VTAM/NCP,* McGraw-Hill, 1989.

Ranade, J. and Sackett, G.C., *Advanced SNA Networking: A Professional's Guide to VTAM/NCP*, McGraw-Hill, 1990.

Routt, T.J., "SNA Network Management: What Makes Netview Tick?" *Data Communications,* June 1988.

Routt, T.J., "SNA to OSI—IBM Building Upper Layer Gateways," *Data Communications,* May 1987.

Schneider, D.L. and Taylor, R.L, "System Overview of the Applications Systems/400," *IBM Systems Journal*, Vol. 28, No. 3, Special Issue on Applications System/400, 1989, pp. 360-375.

Sundstrom, R.J., "SNA Current Requirements and Direction," *IBM Systems Journal*, Vol. 26, No. 1, 1987. "Systems Network Architecture—Concepts and Products," IBM Technical Manual, Reference No. SC30-3112.

Tillman, M. and Yen, D., "SNA and OSI: Three Strategies for Interconnection," *CACM*, Feb. 1990, pp. 214-224.

Wheeler, E.F. and Ganek, A.G., "Introduction to Systems Application Architecture," *IBM Systems Journal*, Vol. 27, No. 3, Special Issue on Systems Applications Architecture, 1988, pp. 250-263.

Appendix D

Tutorial on MAP and Top

D.1 Introduction

This appendix reviews some network architectures that are well known in a few industry segments. MAP (Manufacturing Automation Protocol), discussed in Section D.2, is an ISO based standard for computer integrated manufacturing. TOP (Technical and Office Protocol), reviewed in Section D.3, is also an ISO based standard for business, engineering and office systems. After reading this appendix, the reader should be able to answer the following questions:

- What are the interrelationships between different network architectures which are popular in different segments of the industry.
- What is the motivation for so many different network architectures, and why do these architectures continue to exist?

The discussion in this tutorial uses OSI terminology since MAP and TOP are based on the OSI Model. The reader should quickly review the OSI terms (Appendix A, Section A.1) before proceeding.

D.2 Manufacturing Automation Protocol (MAP)

D.2.1 Motivation for MAP

The Manufacturing Automation Protocol (MAP) was introduced to meet the distributed computing communication needs of manufacturers. The manufacturing enterprises rely on automation to improve the control and analysis of current business and technological data and to reduce the design and development cycles for sophisticated products. However, increased automation on the plant floors makes communication between devices a major bottleneck. The following comments by Mike Kaminski, Manager of General Motors (GM) Manufacturing Automation Protocol (MAP) describe a typical situation faced by many large manufacturing enterprises <Kaminski 1986>:

> "Only 15 percent of the 40,000 programmable tools, instruments, controls and systems already installed at General Motors facilities are able to communicate with one another. When such communication does occur, it is costly, accounting for up to 50 percent of the total expense of automation because of the special wiring and the custom hardware and software interfaces needed.
>
> "Wiring costs are incurred whenever new systems are installed and again each time a production process changes. In the automotive business, where retooling for new models occurs annually, the rewiring costs are significant. Specialized interfaces are necessitated by supplier-unique communication methods. Custom software is usually required to interface two process applications. To make matters worse, incompatible software performing similar functions may exist for different process applications.
>
> "With installed programmable equipment in GM plants expected to increase by 400 to 500 percent over the next five years, the communications problem would rapidly get out of hand if no solution were found."

MAP has been specifically oriented toward the computer communication needs of manufacturing enterprises. It supports the application layer protocols (e.g., the Manufacturing Messaging Specification (MMS)) which are intended for communications between the factory devices such as robots, numerical controllers, cell controllers, and area controllers.

The primary pressure behind automation in manufacturing, and hence behind MAP, is Computer Integrated Manufacturing (CIM). CIM is concerned with integration of four functional areas: business data processing, computer aided design (CAD), computer aided manufacturing (CAM), and flexible manufacturing systems (FMS). A discussion of CIM is beyond the scope of this book. Interested readers are referred to Ranky <1986>, Cad <1988>, Cain <1988>, Malas <1988>, Despotakis <1988> for general information and to Campbell <1988>, LaVie <1988> for CIM reference models. Simply stated, the four functional areas contain a wide variety of related activities which are usually performed in different locations by using diverse computing devices that need to communicate with each other. The following communications requirements for CIM have been identified McGuffin <1988>:

- Lower-level communications support is needed to transport data between machines reliably. The data must be delivered to the correct machine within an expected time frame and in an intended format despite the factory floor conditions of heat, noise and electrical fluctuations.
- Network access and system support is needed to connect different geographically distributed devices through a network. The CIM network must be able to satisfy the requirements of dynamic configuration, realtime performance restrictions, and manageability of network errors.
- Information formatting and sharing is needed between various machines which contain different internal data representation. For example, the special graphical data representations of CAD and CAM systems and different file systems must be taken into account.
- Machine control and monitoring is needed for automated manufacturing. This includes automated operations, diagnostics, error recovery, and automated status and problem reporting.

The MAP specification was developed to address these, among other, requirements.

D.2.2 Overview of Manufacturing Automation Protocol (MAP)

MAP was defined by a General Motors (GM) task force on " Manufacturing Automated Protocol (MAP)." The task force was initiated in November, 1980, by the engineering and manufacturing computer coordination (EMCC) of GM to facilitate information exchange among shop-floor devices (robots, numerical controllers, program logic controllers, etc.). The specific motivating factors for introducing MAP are as follows:

- GM has thousands of shop-floor devices which are growing rapidly. These devices are built by different vendors.
- GM recognized the need to purchase devices from different vendors. This presents the problems of lack of connectivity between vendors, the need for many software packages to accommodate incompatibilities and many physical media needed to connect.

- The upgrade costs must be minimized. Most of these costs are due to communication between devices from different vendors.
- Provide a framework for upgrading the old equipment so that the new releases provide new functions but are compatible with older versions.

The main philosophy of MAP is to use the ISO/ANSI Reference Model as a framework and to coordinate with TOP (Technical and Office Protocol) and other standards. The MAP committee chose a cost-effective and stable subset of OSI and introduced specifications at each layer aimed at the manufacturing environment. MAP specification, shown in Fig. D.1, has used either international standards (IS) or draft international standards (DIS) of the International Standards Organization (ISO). The committee decided to add network management facilities in MAP at a later stage.

The major decisions and milestones in MAP development are as follows:

1. First document was prepared in October 1982. This document specified the OSI Model as a general framework and adopted a token bus broadband network at 10 Mbps as a basis of MAP.
2. Version 1.0 was announced in April 1984 and expanded the first document.
3. Version 2.0 was introduced in February 1985 and defined the upper layers.
4. Version 2.1 and 2.2 introduced the file transfers, bridges, etc., in MAP. In MAP 2.1 and 2.2, the MAP layer 6 (presentation) was null. MAP 2.2 introduced 5 Mbps carrierband networks and Mini-MAP which supports only three layers (application, data link, physical) for small and simple networks.
5. MAP 3.0 was introduced in 1988 and was demonstrated in a large demonstration at the Enterprise Network Event held in Baltimore, Maryland. The main features of MAP 3.0 are as follows:
   - The specifications are frozen for six years to allow vendors to build products based on 3.0 specifications.

ISO Layers	*MAP Specifications*
Application	• ACSE (Association Control Service Element) • FTAM (File Transfer Access Method) • Naming and Directory Services (X.500) • MMS (Manufacturing Message Specification)
Presentation	ISO Presentation Service
Session	ISO Connection Oriented Service
Transport	ISO Class 4 Transport (TP4)
Network	X.25
Data Link	IEEE 802.2 LLC IEEE 802.4 Token Passing Bus
Physical	10 MBPS Broadband (802.4) 5 MBPS Carrierband

FIGURE D.1. Manufacturing Network Architecture

- Manufacturing Message Specification (MMS) is introduced in the Application Layer for realtime manufacturing applications.
- Carrierband and Min-MAP are fully supported.
- GM formally transferred the control of MAP to SME (Society of Manufacturing Engineers).

6. Most computing vendors have announced MAP products.
7. The current and future activities of MAP are naming and addressing issues in media, user interfaces, and distributed database/distributed processing protocols.

MAP protocols consist of low level physical protocols for device interconnection and high level protocols for application interconnection. Manufacturing Message Specification (MMS) is the main Application Layer protocol for manufacturing applications. MMS is currently available on IBM PC under MS-DOS and will be available on DEC, HP, Tandem, Apollo and several other computer systems which are supporting MAP. MMS is being developed for non-MAP networks also. For example, MMS has been implemented on RS232 (see <Bryant 1988>). Thus MMS may become an Application Layer protocol which is available, like APPC and TCP/IP, on many networks.

In November of 1985, TOP and MAP networks were demonstrated at AUTOFACT '85. Since that time, the MAP Steering Committee has been expanded to become the MAP/TOP Steering Committee. Under its direction, the MAP and TOP user groups coexist. Most importantly, however, is the coordinated technical direction that these two efforts now have to realize the goal of interoperable computing communications in any environment. Any individual/company can submit requests for changes to MAP/TOP specifications. Formal submittal procedures have been instituted to introduce changes.

As types of communication supported by MAP/TOP have expanded, so have the number of vendors who supply or intend to supply MAP/TOP communications capabilities within their product lines. Beginning in 1984, an ever-expanding number of vendors committed to providing and supporting computing equipment with MAP?TOP communications interfaces. Figure D.2 shows a simple MAP network where a 10 Mbps broadband cable connects two area controllers. A cell consisting of a cell controller, a robot and a numerical control device uses a 5 Mbps carrierband cable. The area controller uses full MAP (all seven layers) and the cell devices support Mini-MAP (three layers). A bridge connects the carrierband network to the broadband cable.

D.2.3 Layers of MAP

MAP uses an overall peer to peer and full duplex architecture based on the OSI Model. Due to the direct relationship with OSI, it is easy to describe the MAP facilities in terms of the OSI layers (Fig. D.3).

D.2.3.1 Physical Layer

MAP consists of a backbone cable which is connected to other networks through gateways, routers, bridges, etc. A broadband coaxial cable (75 ohm, amplitude modu-

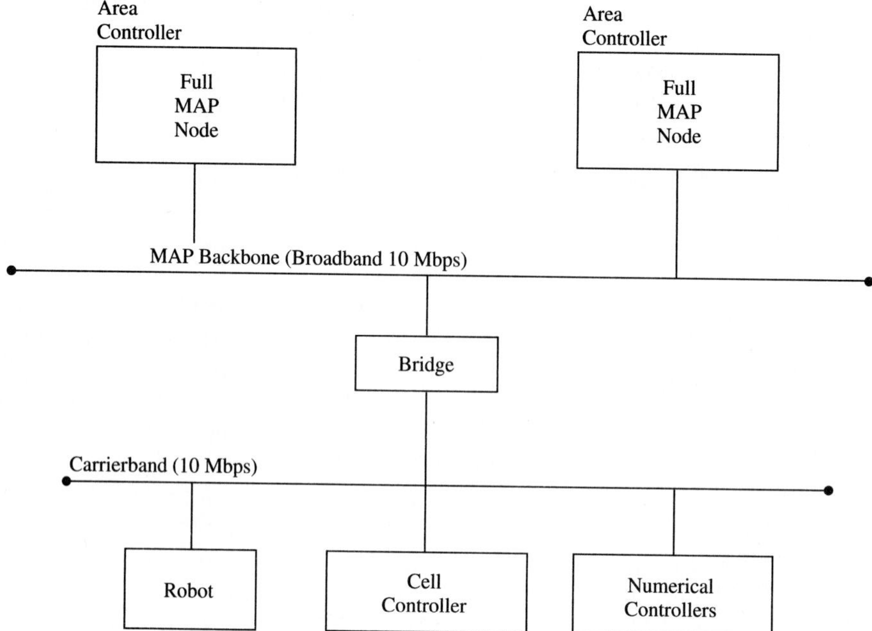

FIGURE D.2. A Simple MAP Network Example

lated/phase shift keyed, duobinary) at 10 MBPs is recommended as the standard media for backbone. The interfacing devices follow IEEE 802.4 standard. In addition to the broadband 10 MBPs cable, MAP version 2.2 introduced a 5 MBPs carrier band coaxial cable for small networks or subnets (e.g., cell networks) which can be connected to the broadband backbone.

Basically, the Physical Layer of MAP specifies the 10 Mbps IEEE 802.4 Broadband and the 5 Mbps IEEE 802.4 Carrierband technologies. The broadband technology was chosen because it allows multiple networks (channels) on same media, and it supports voice and video applications (e.g., teleconferencing). The broadband technology is especially suitable for manufacturing environments because of its

ISO Layer	Protocols Chosen
Application	• ACSE, FTAM, NM/DS, MMS
Presentation	• ISO Presentation Service
Session	• ISO Connection-Oriented Service
Transport	• ISO Class 4 Transport
Network	• X.25
Data Link	• IEEE 802.2 LLC • IEEE 802.4 Token Passing Bus
Physical	• 10-Mbps Broadband • 5-Mbps Carrierband

FIGURE D.3. MAP Specification

excellent noise immunity characteristics and larger area/distance coverage. The broadband technology is also supported for the IEEE 802.4 (token bus) and 802.3 (CSMA/CD) Link Layer protocols. The carrierband technology was chosen as a lower cost solution for smaller manufacturing systems and sub-networks. Recall that carrierband is essentially a broadband system which only supports one channel. The single channel support makes the modems cheaper. Carrierband is also more reliable than broadband due to its simplicity. However, carrierband systems support few stations and shorter distances (1000 meters between stations and up to 32 stations per carrierband cable).

D.2.3.2 Data Link Layer

IEEE 802 subdivided the Data Link Layer into two sublayers: the Media Access Control Layer which manages access of the physical media, and the Logical Link Control (LLC) Layer, which performs error checking and addressing.

MAP chose Token Passing on a bus configuration for its Medium Access Control Layer. The Token Bus protocol was chosen for two reasons: 1) it is believed to be the most robust for a realtime manufacturing environment, and 2) it uses deterministic network access delay. In addition, Token Bus is supported on broadband and carrierband cables and is supported by many vendors.

MAP specifies the IEEE 802.2 Logical Link Control (LLC), which supports multipoint and peer to peer interactions. There are three different types of LLC. LLC Type 1 is unacknowledged connectionless; LLC Type 2 is connection oriented; LLC Type 3 is acknowledged connectionless. MAP recommends the use of LLC Type 1, and if acknowledgements are necessary, LLC Type 3. LLC supports data transfer at high rates on multiple media.

D.2.3.3 Network Layer

The Network Layer converts global addresses to routing information, maintains message routing tables and algorithms, and maintains routing and network directories. The MAP choices can be specified in terms of the following four major sublayers of the Network Layer.

- The Internet Sublayer (3.4), which shows end-node to end-node exchange. Sublayer 3.4 represents the highest sublayer in layer 3. MAP endorses use of the Connectionless-Mode Network Service, ISO 8473, also called CLNS with its corresponding protocol (CLNP) for this sublayer. CLNS is used with the LAN specifications. CLNS uses static routing in which the network directory is not modified. The user multiplexing is left to the Transport Layer. MAP also specifies the End System to Intermediate System routing and relaying protocol, the ES-IS Exchange Protocol (ISO 9542). This protocol supports services which perform dynamic routing and update table information in end and intermediate systems.
- The Harmonizing Sublayer (3.3) provides uniform support to the internet sublayer. This sublayer allows a local network as a link in the larger MAP network by translating internetwork (MAP) addresses into intranetwork (local) addresses. This sublayer may be null or implementation dependent.

- The Intranetwork Routing Sublayer (3.2) routes in an "immediate local network" by using a common protocol (e.g., X.25). MAP allows this sublayer to be null by letting the sublayer 3.4 to do the routing.
- The Link Access Interface Sublayer (3.1) interfaces with Data Link Control Layer (layer 2). If the Data Link is connection oriented and sublayer 3.4 is connection-less, then this sublayer does the conversion (e.g., MAP to X.25).

D.2.3.4 Transport Layer

The Transport Layer is responsible for two types of services between sessions:

- Transport-connection management to create/maintain paths and connect/disconnect services.
- Transfer of data between endpoints (normal and expedited).

MAP standard for the Transport Layer is the Class 4 ISO Transport Protocol. This standard is the ISO 8072, the Transport Service, and it defines four levels of service (Class 1 through Class 4). The MAP choice is Class 4 service, which provides a connection oriented service, with flow control and the ability to multiplex upper layer connections over the same transport connection. The companion standard to ISO 8072 is ISO 8073, the connection oriented transport protocol definition. Class 4 is supported by most U.S. manufacturers and provides extensive error detection and recovery. The ISO Class 4 services are slightly different from the NIST (National Institute of Standards and Technology) Class 4 services: NIST supports datagram and graceful close of session while OSI does not. The main features of the ISO Class 4 transport service chosen for MAP are as follows:

- 7-bit and 31-bit sequence numbers are supported.
- Expedited data is supported.
- Checksum is required for error detection and recovery.
- Version number may be included by the sender.
- Concurrent use of multiple connections is supported.

The main source of information for the Class 4 transport service is the ISO/DIS 8073, "Transport Protocol Specification."

D.2.3.5 Session Layer

The Session Layer establishes half duplex, simplex or full duplex sessions. MAP supports full duplex transmission. The chosen standards are the ISO 8326, the Basic Connection Oriented Session Service Definition, and ISO 8327, the Basic Connection Oriented Session Protocol Definition. These standards support the following session services:

- Session connect is confirmed.
- Session-data is non-confirmed.
- Session-release is confirmed.

D.2.3.6 Presentation Layer

The Presentation Layer allows many data representations to be used for the same application programs. This helps in system integration by relieving the applications of data reformatting functions, thus satisfying some requirements of CIM information formatting and sharing. MAP 2.0 recommended a null Presentation Layer. Later, ISO 8822 and ISO 8823 were chosen as the standards for the presentation services and protocol, respectively, for MAP 3.0. Only the Presentation Kernel functional unit is used for all MAP Application Layer standards and provides for the negotiation of abstract syntax and transfer syntax pairs.

D.2.3.7 Application Layer

The MAP Application Layer provides the most interesting and diverse services because the Application Layer is the "glue" between MAP user programs and MAP network services. Due to the diverse and evolving manufacturing applications, it is difficult to define protocols for manufacturing applications. The GM specifications for the Application Layer are based on the Saginaw Steering Gear (SSG) Factory of the Future. The major Application Layer standards for MAP are as follows:

- *Association Control Service Elements (ACSE)*: ISO 8649/2 and ISO 8650/2 provide services for the establishment and termination of application associations. ACSEs are used to communicate names and addresses of Application Layer objects. ACSEs also satisfy some of the CIM network access requirements.
- *File Transfer Access and Management (FTAM)*: MAP supports the ISO file transfer and access method (FTAM). Especially, ISO 8571/1-4 is chosen to provide the transfer, access and management services of filestores. MAP supports binary and ASCII text files. For binary and text files, the services include the ability to create files, delete files, transfer files between end systems, read and change file attributes, etc. FTAM supports remote creation and deletion of files and stores a "transferred" file for access on a local system under several formats. FTAM supports the fundamental information exchange in CIM. For example, FTAM can be used to move formatted graphic, office, and product data between engineering workstations and business data processing systems. FTAM can also be used to move production schedules and manufacturing operations related data among computer systems on a MAP network.
- *Network Management (NM) and Directory Services (DS)*: Network Management (ISO DP 9595—Service and ISO DP 9596—Protocol) provides services for managing the performance, security and configurations of many aspects of a MAP network. The Directory Services (ISO 9594/1-8) provide the management of logical names used for identifying systems and applications on a network. These services help to fulfill the network access and system support requirements for CIM.
- *Manufacturing Message Specification (MMS)*: This standard (ISO 9506) provides the messaging services needed between programmable devices (robot controllers,

computer numerical controllers, etc.) and cell controllers in a CIM environment. MMS is considered the most important standard in the MAP architecture because its services are designed specifically for manufacturing devices, thus fulfilling CIM machine monitoring and control requirements. MMS is a complex protocol which supports over 80 different services. We will discuss MMS in more detail in Section D.2.4.

D.2.3.8 Other Capabilities

Beyond the Application Layer, many common data representation schemes for different applications in CIM have been specified in MAP and its companion standard, TOP. Examples of some of these formats are as follows:

- Product Definition Interchange Format (PDIF)
- Initial Graphics Exchange Specification (IGES)
- Computer Graphics Metafile Interchange Format (CGMIF)
- Office Document Interchange Format (ODIF)

MAP/TOP specifies use of the CGMIF, PDIF, and ODIF over the FTAM services to fulfill the CIM requirements of information format and sharing. The CGMIF and PDIF formats can be used in CAD/CAM operations where product parts must be drawn, analyzed, and in some cases, translated into numerical control (NC) part programs. The ODIF format is useful for business data processing tasks such as word processing and spreadsheet exchange. These common formats allow computer systems and application packages from different vendors to perform data operations without requiring extensive data conversions in a multivendor operation.

MAP specifications in the future are expected to enhance the Application Layer protocols and services. In particular, the standards for distributed databases and distributed transaction processing are of particular interest. The Remote Database Access (RDA) Application Layer standard is presently being developed at the national and international levels for distributed databases. RDA will allow remote databases to be accessed for CIM applications. The Distributed Transaction Processing service and protocol is being developed by the ANSI ASC X3T5.5 committee on the national level and the ISO SC21 committee on the international level. Similar to RDA, the distributed transaction processing service would greatly expand the communication services in the Application Layer of MAP.

D.2.4 Manufacturing Message Services (MMS): Application Protocol for Manufacturing

The Application Layer protocols for manufacturing applications must be able to handle unique manufacturing application requirements. For example, the distributed software for manufacturing applications should satisfy the following requirements <Barr 1988>:

- Manufacturing device software for robots, machining, and drilling devices must respond to stimuli within extremely short realtime constraints.
- Workstation software must be able to communicate with lower level manufacturing devices and the higher level cell controllers.
- Cell controller software must provide control mechanisms for remote programs at the workstations and must also provide for human interactions.

Manufacturing Message Specification (MMS) is the MAP Application Layer protocol for manufacturing applications. These applications utilize generic manufacturing devices such as robots, computerized numerical controllers (CNC), programmable logic controllers (PLCs), and cell/area controllers. MAP and MMS are currently available on IBM PC under MS-DOS and are expected to be available on DEC, HP, Tandem, Apollo, and several other computer systems. However, MMS has been developed for non-MAP networks also. For example, MMS has been implemented on RS232 (see <Bryant 1988>). Thus MMS may become an Application Layer protocol which is available on many networks. Due to its wide acceptance, MMS is becoming the most important standard in the MAP architecture because its services are designed specifically for manufacturing devices, thus fulfilling CIM machine monitoring and control requirements. MMS supports over 80 different services which are grouped to perform the following functions <McGuffin 1988>:

- *Connection management*: These services manage the MMS application associations.
- *Device information sharing*: These services support collection of status and other information stored within the programmable devices.
- *Program upload and download*: These services upload and download programs and data between a cell controller and a programmable device.
- *Program management*: These services support remote program control, (e.g., Start, Stop, Reset, Resume, Kill) on device controllers.
- *Variable access*: These services are for the creation, deletion, reading, and writing of remote variables on device controllers.
- *Resource management*: These services are used to control access to device and network resources among many different controllers.
- *Operator communication*: These services allow remote terminal access to MMS devices for the input and output of display data.
- *Event management*: These services provide an environment for setting up timed events (actions performed when a particular condition occurs such as machine failure) on remote devices. Different event notification and acknowledge mechanisms are supported.
- *Journal management*: These services write device specific information to journals (files with a predefined data structure) for chronological recording of activities.

MMS is used for interprocess communication and provides distributed operating system type facilities. MMS uses a server and client model for interprocess communication. The client issues MMS calls and the server performs the task on a "virtual" manufacturing device (VMD). A unique feature of the MMS client-server model is that in MMS, one client may control many servers while in non-MMS systems one server usually serves many clients. This has been introduced to facilitate manufacturing control devices (e.g. cell controllers) to monitor and review the status of manufacturing devices.

MMS is developed to support a wide number of manufacturing devices and services by using an object-oriented approach (see Appendix E, Section E.5 for a review of object-oriented approach). The manufacturing devices and services are represented by 16 object classes (see Table D.1). The best known object class is a VMD (virtual manufacturing device), which is a generic factory floor device and contains the generic attributes of manufacturing devices. Companion standards for specific devices with special attributes are being developed. Examples of companion standards are robots, CNCs, process control devices, and PLCs.

MMS contains services to create objects, delete objects and change states (values of attributes) of objects. These services may be categorized into general messages (alarm, log, status), program messages (download, upload, directory, delete), cycle messages (start, stop, resume), part/pallet messages (load, unload, examine), tool messages (load, unload, examine) and move messages (move from a to b). These services are available to the users through an extensive set of commands shown in Table D.2. Some of the commands shown in Table D.2 are group commands (e.g., define event, trigger event, check event, etc are indicated by / EVENT COMMANDS) which represent several related commands. These services have syntax and semantics. The syntax has been defined by ASN.1 (Abstract Syntax Notation). An overview of MMS is presented below; details can be found elsewhere <Rhein 1988, MMS 1988>.

TABLE D.1 MMS Objects

- Virtual Manufacturing Device (VMD): Represents a real manufacturing device, which includes the status and capabilities of the device
- Transaction: Represents information pertaining to an MMS confirmed service processing
- Domain: Represents a subset of VMD capabilities such as application program modules and memory
- Program invocation: Represents an executable program
- Unnamed variable: Represents data in some memory location
- Named variable: Represents data identified by a name
- Scattered access variable: Represents data which has components at several memory locations
- Named variable list: Represents a list of variables with identical type specifications
- Named type: Represents a variable type description similar to structure definitions in program languages
- Semaphore: Represents a controlling agent or entity, similar to a queue processor, which manages the resources of a VMD
- Semaphore entry: Represents an agent or entity wishing to use resources within a VMD
- Operator station: Represents an input/output device that can be used by a human operator to issue commands and view responses
- Event condition: Represents a set of object states. An event occurs whenever these states change.
- Event action: Represents an action that is executed whenever an event occurs
- Event enrollment: Represents an agent or entity wishing to be notified when a particular event condition occurs
- Journal: Represents an information log of MMS requests, object state changes, etc.

TABLE D.2 MMS Command Summary (main commands)

• INITIATE	=	Establish connection between two MMS users
• CONCLUDE	=	Terminate connection between two MMS users
• ABORT	=	Abruptly terminate connection
• CANCEL	=	Terminate a previous MMS service
• REJECT	=	Reject an unauthorized/invalid request
• READ	=	Read from a remote MMS user
• WRITE	=	Write to a remote MMS user
• STATUS	=	Check the condition of a server
• IDENTIFY	=	Obtain identifying information about a server (vendor name, model, revision)
• START	=	Start a program from the idle state
• STOP	=	Temporarily stop a program
• RESUME	=	Restart a program
• RESET	=	Put a program in the idle state
• KILL	=	Put a program in the unrunnable state
• INPUT/OUTPUT	=	Read/write from operator's console
/ SEMAPHORE COMMANDS	=	Create, delete, and verify seMAPhores
/ DOWNLOAD/ UPLOAD COMMANDS	=	Download/upload programs and/or data files
/ EVENT COMMANDS	=	Define, delete, check, trigger, and notify events
/ ALARM COMMANDS	=	Extract, report, and reset alarm conditions
/ JOURNAL COMMANDS	=	Initialize, read, and write journal entries

VMD is a key object type in MMS. VMD contains all the server capabilities of a real device and the semantics of these services is defined in terms of state changes of associated VMD-specific objects. VMD consists of several attributes (vendor names, etc). Two specific objects are explicitly defined for VMD: Program Invocations and Domains. Program Invocations (PI) are abstractions of programs and are bound to Domains which represent the program algorithms or data or combinations. PIs and Domains allow modelling of several situations in manufacturing systems. For example, shared code can be represented by allowing Program Invocations P1 and P2 to use Algorithm Domain A, and shared data can be represented by allowing Program Invocations P1 and P2 to use Data Domain D.

In addition to the VMD Object, MMS Variable Objects allow data collection and support operations. MMS Variable Objects can be directly mapped to data on real devices by V-Put and V-Get operations. The dynamic behavior of manufacturing devices is modeled through the Event Condition and Event Action Objects. In addition, Journaling Objects are provided for logging, Semaphore Objects are provided for synchronizing access to shared resources, and Operator Station Objects are provided for operator communications. Most application programs for MMS are written in C. The C programs issue calls by using the MMS verbs.

MMS may not be needed for all of the manufacturing applications. The terminal emulation and file transfer can be accomplished through the Virtual Terminal and

FTAM support of MAP. The file server facilities can be achieved through the Program Invocation and Domain facilities of MMS. At present, DDBMS facilities are not available on MAP. The next standard of MAP (Remote Data Access) will address this issue. MMS does provide extensive facilities for message passing and client-server models. The MMS Objects, as briefly described earlier, can be used to download programs, control remote programs, perform logging, data collection, asynchronous event handling, and network resource management through Semaphores.

Figure D.4 shows a pseudo code of a manufacturing application where a cell controller downloads a program to a robot and then activates the program in the robot. Instructions 1 through 3 are in the Initiation State, steps 4 and 5 download the program and step 6 invokes the remotely located program in robot, steps 7 through 10 exchange information between the robot and the cell controller, and steps 11 through 13 terminate this session after reviewing the Alarm and Journal data.

The main advantage of MMS for this example is that explicit commands are available for download/upload and program invocation at remote sites. In addition, MMS provides a large number of commands for status checking, error detection, alarm detection and journaling, etc. Implementation of these commands using Unix IPC and APPC would be difficult and yield non transportable code.

D.2.5 MAP Enhanced Performance Architecture (MAP/EPA and Mini-MAP)

During the early stages of MAP specifications, it was found that the full MAP can be slow, cumbersome and expensive due to too many layers of sophisticated processing. The overhead is unnecessary for the following cases:

- Manufacturing cells, which consist of robots, numerical controllers, automated guided vehicles, etc linked together for machining/assembling with little or no human intervention. In the manufacturing cells, 70 to 95 percent of the traffic is local. Due to this, a simple, inexpensive network with very fast local response is needed.

Cell Controller	*Robot*
1. INITIATE	2. INITIATE
3. STATUS	
4. INITIATEDOWNLOAD	
5. TERMINATEDOWNLOAD	
6. CREATEPROGRAMINVOCATION	
	7. START
8. SEND	9. RECEIVE
	10. STOP
11. ALARM	
12. JOURNAL	
13. CONCLUDE	

FIGURE D.4 Sample Program Pseudo Code in MMS

- Process control systems with distributed control of manufacturing processes. The process controllers (specialized computers) need to communicate with each other to automate their processes on very fast networks for quick response.

A MAP Enhanced Performance Architecture (MAP/EPA commonly referred to as Mini-MAP) was introduced as a tradeoff between MAP functionality and response time. The requirements of MAP/EPA are as follows:

- Rapid response for short messages from "local" nodes (less than 50 msec response for 16 to 20 byte long messages from less than 32 nodes at 5 Mbps)
- High reliability and access security
- Network can connect through bridges to main factory network

The main idea of Mini-MAP is to bypass layers 3 to 6 of MAP (see Fig. D.5). The Mini-Map architecture allows applications to interface directly with the data link layer. The EPA data link is a subset of the full MAP data link (IEEE 802.2) and provides a single frame, connectionless service with immediate response of frame delivery. This limits the maximum data size to less than 1 kbytes. The media access control (MAC) sublayer is 802.4 token passing with priority options and immediate response. Most importantly, the EPA physical layer is commonly 5 Mbps carrier band. Due to these architectural choices, the Mini-MAP does not

- Guarantee message delivery (it uses connectionless services)
- Handle indefinite message length (1 kbyte is the maximum length allowed)
- Provide synchronized dialogs between applications because the session layer does not exist
- Allow more than one unacknowledged message at one time.

In most practical cases, Mini-MAP is used for manufacturing cells over 5 Mbps carrierband cables (see Fig. D.6). Mini-MAP connects to full MAP through gateways and bridges. The MAP standardizing bodies (General Motors, Society of Manufacturing Engineers) recommend that Mini-MAP should be used only for limited situations and if Mini-MAP is not enough then the users should use full MAP instead of extending Mini-MAP. This avoids the undesirable emergence of several versions of Mini-MAP.

Mini-MAP Layers	Full-MAP Layers
Application	Application
Null	Presentation
Null	Session
Null	Transport
Null	Network
Data Link	Data Link
Physical	Physical

FIGURE D.5 Full-MAP versus Mini-MAP

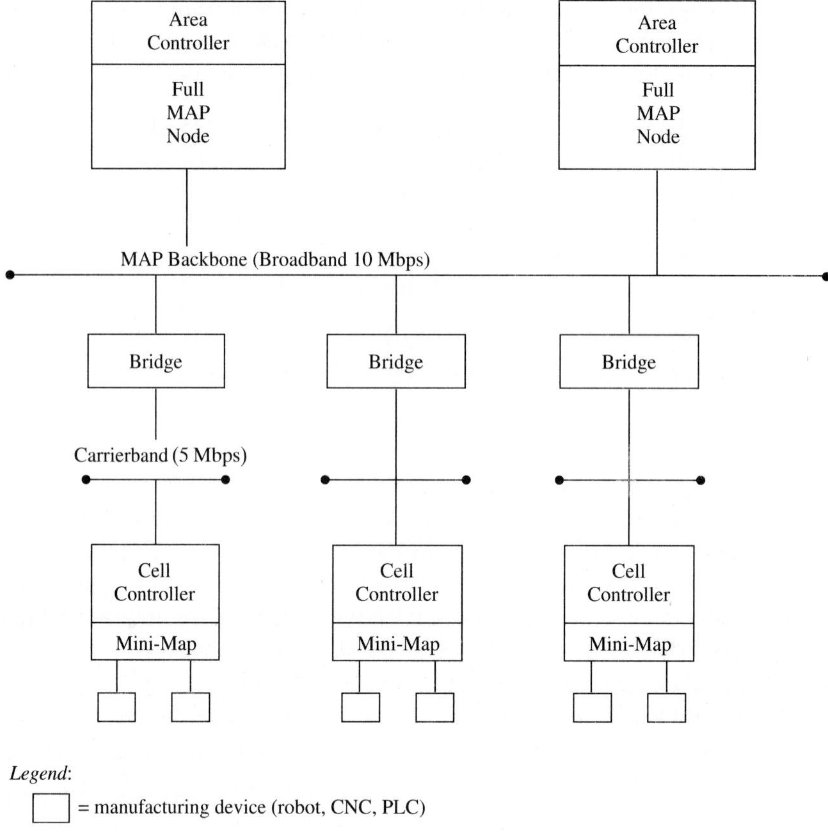

FIGURE D.6 Mini-MAP in Manufacturing Plants

D.2.6 MAP Devices and Examples

A MAP network consists of four type of devices (see Fig. D.6):

- Full nodes, which implement all MAP layers. Detailed guidelines and specifications for device design have been supplied to vendors. Many vendors are providing or intend to provide full MAP, direct attachment, support for programmable controllers, robots, CNCs, etc. A directory of MAP products with vendor names and prices is published annually by the Society of Manufacturing Engineers. Examples of some of the products are Ungermann-Bass MAP Interface, Concord series 1200 Full MAP Card and GMF Robotics MAP Interface.[1]
- Mini nodes, which only implement three layers (physical, data link, application). Several vendors support layers 1 and 2 of MAP. An example is the Token Interface

[1]These vendor products are mentioned here for illustration purpose only and do not constitute endorsement.

Module (TIM) by Concord, Inc., which has been used to interface many manufacturing devices to MAP networks (see, for example, the John Deere and Co. sheet metal facility described in the MAP/TOP Interface, SME, Vol. 3, No. 3, Summer, 1987).

- Bridges, which consist of physical and link layer, and are used to connect similar networks. Examples are the broadband to carrierband MAP bridges (e.g., Concord Series 4200 Backbone Bridge).
- Routers (switches), which consist of physical, data link and network layer and are used to route messages between nodes. For example, the MAP to PBX switches provide WAN support for MAP. A PBX can be used as a router between several MAP LANs or as a gateway between MAP backbone and PBX. Detailed specifications for MAP PBX require that MAP PBX must support ISO connectionless internetworking protocol.
- Gateways, which convert one full node to another (e.g., MAP to SNA gateways). MAP gateways are viewed as interim before all devices implement full MAP. Detailed software specifications for MAP gateways have been published <MAP 1986, MAP 1988>.

MAP gateways are viewed essential for migration plans to go from non-MAP to MAP. This is because: (i) many vendors do not support MAP and (ii) MAP specifications use standards that are not fully implemented. The first step in MAP migration plan is installation of a backbone broadband coaxial cable to communicate at 10 Mbps. The devices that support full MAP are connected directly to the MAP backbone and non-MAP devices (e.g., an Allen Bradley shop floor system running under the Allen-Bradley Data Highway Plus) are connected to the backbone through gateways (see Fig. D.7a). This allows non-MAP devices to behave as full MAP nodes. When a non-MAP device implements MAP functions, the gateway is not needed (see Fig. D.7b).

An Example. Let us consider the example of implementing a MAP network in a factory which assembles electronic products such as calculators. The steps in developing a factory network are as follows:

1. Develop a layout of the plant which shows the area controllers, cell controllers, and manufacturing devices.
2. Develop a cable layout (network topology) which shows how the backbone cable will be spread across the factory floor and where the devices will be connected.
3. Allocate the channels for the broadband cable, showing what transmit and receive frequencies will be used.
4. Make choices about device interconnectivity and carrierband versus broadband.
5. Make choices about applications interconnectivity to show what application services (e.g., FTAM, MMS) will be needed at what point.

a. A MAP Network with Non-MAP Nodes (robot and CNC are non-MAP)

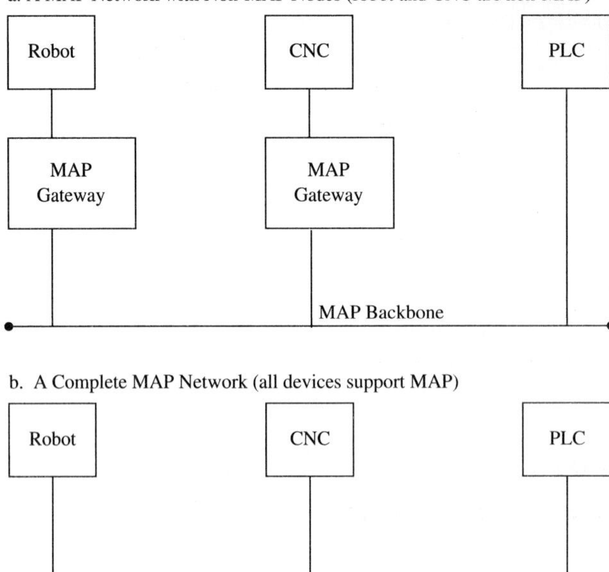

FIGURE D.7 MAP Migration Plan

Figure D.8a shows the conceptual factory floor layout as an area which consists of two cells. The first cell builds the circuit board and the second cell assembles and packs the calculator for shipment. This layout represents a simplified flexible assembly system which is suitable for our discussion (details of manufacturing operations can be found in Ranky <1986>). We assume that each cell consists of two programmable devices (e.g., robots) and one cell controller (a specialized computer). The area controller (a minicomputer) receives the specifications of the calculator to be built and sends the appropriate programs to the two cell controllers. The cell controllers examine the programs, divide and allocate the programs to cell devices, and then initiate and monitor the assembly process through completion.

Figure D.8B shows the MAP layout for this factory floor after the aforementioned steps. The backbone is a 10 Mbps broadband cable which directly connects the area controller with the cell controllers and monitoring terminals (this is one of many choices and is used here for illustration purposes only). The following 12 MHZ full duplex channels can be assigned to this cable based on the IEEE 802.4 recommendation:

Transmit Frequency	*Receive Frequency*
59.75 to 71.75 MHZ	252 to 264 MHZ
71.5 to 83.75 MHZ	264 to 276 MHZ
83.75 to 85.75 MHZ	276 to 288 MHZ

a. A Conceptual Factory Layout

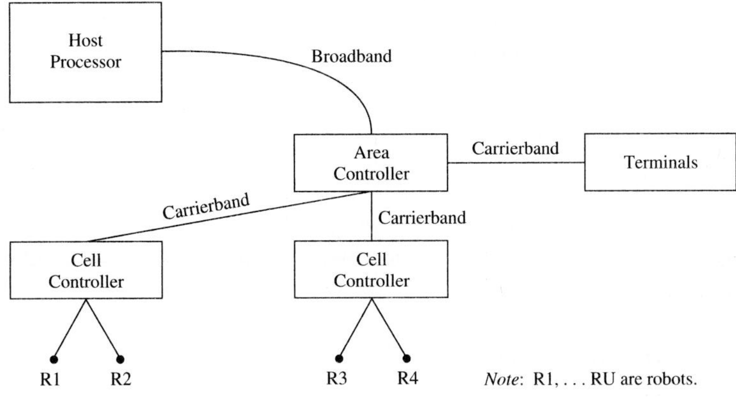

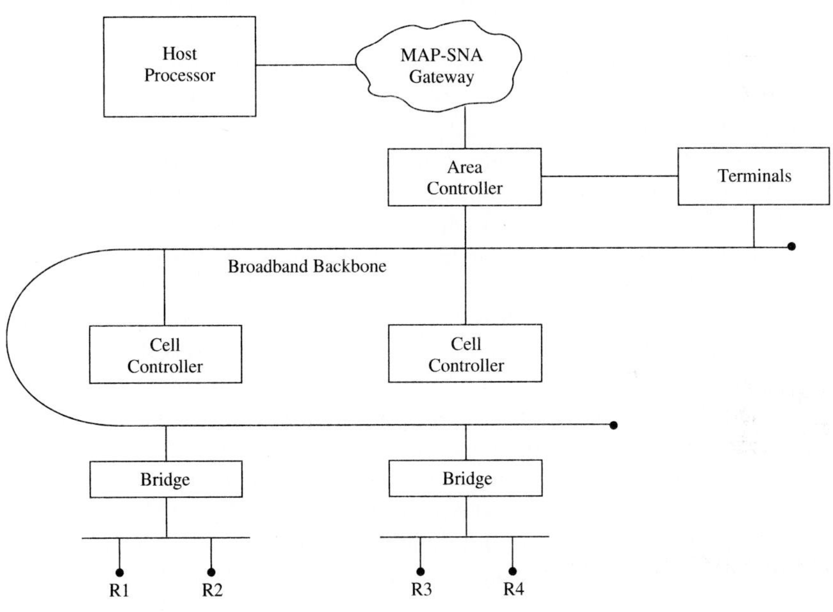

FIGURE D.8 An Example

This channel allocation can support three 10 MBS networks and leaves enough room for other applications (e.g., video). To support full duplex operations, a head-end modulator is needed which transmits at one frequency and receives at another. The cell devices in Fig. D.8B are connected through carrierbands. The tradeoffs between the carrierband and broadband networks are as follows:

Broadband	Carrierband
1. Long distance (10 KM) at 10 Mbps	1 KM at 5 Mbps, 7 KM at 1Mbps
2. Allows hundreds of taps (devices)	30-40 taps
3. Expensive modems	Cheaper modems
4. Head-end modulator needed	Head-end modulator not needed

The files are exchanged between the nodes by using FTAM. It is possible to develop an MMS application which runs in each cell controller to produce the calculator.

D.2.7 MAP Summary

MAP (Manufacturing Automation Protocol) has been developed as a standard to support the manufacturing applications, especially Computer Integrated Manufacturing. MAP is based on the OSI Reference Model and is intended to replace and/or interconnect the numerous proprietary network architectures that are currently being used in manufacturing.

MAP was originally developed for GM product integration and has evolved into an open architecture for manufacturing applications. MAP provides a subset of OSI, a Mini-Map for fast response, network management standards, a manufacturing message protocol, and gradual migration paths from non-MAP to MAP. It supports CIM designers and implementers through protocols which are intended to provide more than a reliable transfer of bits from machine to machine. These protocols define types and meanings for messages which are common to many CIM organizations.

The acceptance of MAP is high and the MAP products are arriving in the marketplace. Widespread vendor support of the MAP/TOP communications architecture provides maximum flexibility, performance, and cost benefits needed for CIM. Despite the high acceptance and heavy industrial participation, many small to medium companies have not migrated to MAP for two reasons <Roach 1988>. First, the cost of MAP hardware/software is higher than the competing proprietary networks (for example, in 1990, the cost per MAP node was about $5000 as compared to about $800 per DEC/Ethernet node). In addition, the competing network architectures on factory floors such as DECnet have a very loyal and long following which is not easy to dislodge.

D.3 Technical and Office Protocol (TOP)

Technical and Office Protocol (TOP) was developed by the Boeing Company at the same time when GM was defining MAP. TOP's principal goal is to accelerate the availability of multi vendor off-the-shelf computing systems, devices and components for business systems, engineering and design systems and publishing systems. TOP explicitly excludes manufacturing systems because these systems are addressed by MAP. As mentioned previously, TOP and MAP technical directions and user groups are closely coordinated by the MAP/TOP Steering Committee. This coordination, initiated in 1985, is promoting open systems for CIM which span manufacturing, engineering, business data processing, and office automation functions.

TOP, like MAP, is also based on OSI. The first version, TOP 1.0, announced in November, 1985, was a full seven-layer specification. TOP 2.0 was skipped so that the MAP and TOP release 3.0 could be announced together in the summer of 1987. Fig. D.9 shows a comparison of TOP 3.0 with MAP 3.0. Basically, MAP and TOP differ at the application layer and the physical and data link layers. All other layers between MAP and TOP are the same. This commonality of protocols at several layers makes it easier for the TOP and MAP subcommittees to work together. We will briefly describe the differences between MAP and TOP.

TOP's primary recommendation for layer 1 LANs is the IEEE 802.3 Baseband. Additional choices for TOP layer 1 include IEEE 802.5 Shielded Twisted Pair, and IEEE 802.4 Broadband. TOP allows the use of IEEE 802.4 so that the MAP applications can be better integrated with TOP. For WANs, TOP layer 1 specifies the use of the CCITT Recommendation X.21. These protocols are used in point-to-point links. Recall that MAP uses the IEEE 802.4 Broadband specification.

For the Link Layer, TOP permits CSMA/CD and token passing on either a bus or ring configuration (as compared to MAP which uses token passing only). Both MAP and TOP specify the IEEE 802.2 Logical Link Control (LLC) Type 1 (unacknowledged connectionless). For WANs, TOP requires the CCITT Recommendation X.25 LAPB. As mentioned previously, X.25 is a connection oriented point-to-point protocol, providing flow control, error recovery, error detection, message sequencing, and ordered delivery for packet switching systems.

TOP and MAP essentially use the same protocols at layers 3, 4, 5, and 6.

The application layer of TOP includes MAP standards such as File Transfer, Access, and Management, supporting the transfer of files between different machines in the production and office environments. The Virtual Terminal (VT) —ISO 9040 Virtual Terminal Service — Basic Class and the ISO 9041 Virtual Terminal Protocol

ISO Layers	*MAP*	*TOP*
Application	ACSE, FTAM, NM/DS, MMS	ACSE, VT, FTAM, MHS
Presentation	ISO Presentation Service	ISO Presentation Service
Session	ISO Connection-Oriented Service	ISO Connection-Oriented Service
Transport	ISO Class 4 Transport	ISO Class 4 Transport
Network	X.25	X.25
Data Link	IEEE 802.2 LLC IEEE 802.4 Token Passing Bus	IEEE 802.2 LLC IEEE 802.3 CSMA/CS IEEE 802.4 Token Passing Bus
Physical	10 MBPS Broadband (802.4) 5 MBPS Carrierband	Broadband (802.4) Baseband

FIGURE D.9 MAP versus TOP

— Basic Class have been developed for the TOP network. VT provides a remote, interactive terminal service between host systems in heterogeneous environments, with many different terminal types and different host systems. The main TOP application layer service is the Message Handling Service (MHS). MHS consists of two types of service: Message Transfer Service and Interpersonal Messaging (electronic mail). TOP only requires implementation of Interpersonal Messaging. Thus, MHS is commonly referred to as the electronic mail system. MHS is based on the CCITT Recommendation X.400. It supports interpersonal mail and application independent message transfer. Creation and displaying of mail are local functions and are not included in MHS.

Above the application layer, TOP specifies data formats which are used for common data representation schemes in many applications. Examples of these formats are as follows:

- Product Definition Interchange Format (PDIF)
- Initial Graphics Exchange Specification (IGES)
- Computer Graphics Metafile Interchange Format (CGMIF)
- Office Document Interchange Format (ODIF).

TOP and MAP specify use of the CGMIF, PDIF, and ODIF for CIM applications. These formats define data of a product over its life cycle (design data, manufacturing data, user instructions, financial data, etc.). These formats facilitate exchange of product data among heterogeneous computers by standardizing the format and content of data exchanged. The actual data is transferred by using the FTAM protocol.

For TOP, the developing standards for distributed databases and distributed transaction processing are of particular interest. The Remote Database Access (RDA) standard and the distributed transaction processing standard, discussed in MAP, can be very useful in TOP for distributed applications.

We have briefly reviewed TOP by using MAP as a framework for describing the TOP facilities. Detailed TOP specifications can be found in the MAP/TOP User Group Document, "Technical and Office Protocol Specification," Version 3.0, Implementation Release, August, 1987. The industrial acceptance of TOP is not as high as MAP and, compared to MAP, very few vendors have announced TOP products. A listing of TOP products and vendors can be obtained from the SME MAP/TOP Committee.

D.4 Management Summary and Trends

Many layered network architectures have been developed for different industry segments. MAP and TOP are examples of such architectures, for manufacturing and office systems, respectively. The most important aspect of the layered architectures is that the relative issues addressed by most networks can be analyzed. For example, lower layers are always concerned with station attachment and higher layers connect applications to the network services. The advancements in communication technology are hidden from higher layers. For example, most network architectures are planning to support fiber optics and ISDN services at the first two layers without having to modify the higher level layers. In addition, vendors can provide layer 7 protocols and services without having to provide all of the lower layers. For example, MMS (Manufacturing Message Specification) was originally developed for MAP but is now available on DECnet, Ethernet LANs and Tandem TCP/IP networks. The implications of same layer 7 protocols on many networks are:

- Specific application layer protocols can be used for specific application types independent of the network. For example, manufacturing applications residing on any network can use MMS for sending/receiving messages.
- Applications using the same application layer protocols can interoperate across networks. For example, an application residing on DECNET can exchange messages with an application residing on TCP/IP by using the well defined syntax of MMS.

MAP has gone through an evolutionary process in which different capabilities have been introduced since the mid-1980s. It is expected that more options and facilities will be added to meet the growing demands of computer integrated manufacturing.

CASE STUDY: XYZCORP Manufacturing Network Architecture

XYZCORP has completed its corporate office and business operations network layout as described previously. Now it is time to devote some attention to the manufacturing plant.

The manufacturing/engineering plant is developing a layout for an automated factory. The conceptual layout of the 400 ft $\times$ 400 ft factory floor with planned equipment is shown in Fig. D.10.

The people in corporate planning insist that MAP is the "in thing" and must be adopted to provide a corporate wide integrated environment. They have read the literature on MAP products and are convinced that anything other than MAP is out of the question. A group in the manufacturing plant believes that TCP/IP is quite appropriate for the plant in Detroit. It can be assumed that MAP as well as TCP/IP products and interfaces are available for the devices shown in Fig. D.10.

You have been asked to prepare the two plans and comment on the tradeoffs.

Deliverables:

1. The MAP layout with interconnection hardware and software which includes
   - A layout of the MAP cables (choice between broadband/baseband/carrierband)

Note: The manufacturing factory is on the first floor. The second floor houses the engineering and research groups.

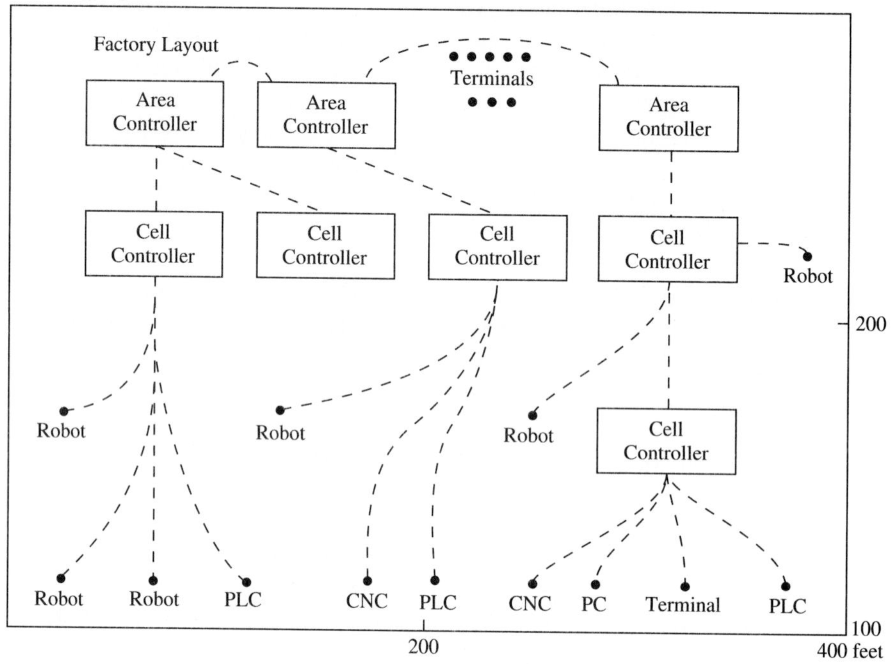

Legend: Dotted line (- - - -) = Conceptual Connection.

FIGURE D.10 Manufacturing Plant Layout

- Full MAP nodes wherever possible
- Mini MAP nodes with justification
- Migration plan to full MAP
- All gateways and bridges needed in the factory

2. The TCP/IP layout with all of the interconnection hardware and software.
3. A list of tradeoffs between the two plans.
   - What do you see as advantages of MAP?
   - What do you see as advantages of a widely supplied network solution such as TCP/IP and DECnet?

Hints About the Case Study

For MAP Layout, a broadband cable can be used to connect all area controllers and cell controllers in a bus topology. The various manufacturing devices (robots, CNCs, PCs) can be directly connected to the respective cell controllers by using carrierband cables. The bridges between broadband and carrierband may be needed. (See Fig. D.8.)

The TCP/IP, or DECNet, layout for this plant can use roughly the same layout (TCP/IP as well as DECNet use Ethernet bus topologies). Although TCP/IP and

DECNet may be cheaper, MAP offers many advantages because it is specifically designed for manufacturing applications.

References

Barr, J., "Connectivity in the Factory," *Unix Review,* June 1987, pp. 33-42.

Bryant, S., "Implementation of Cell Control Using MMS," *MAP/TOP Interface*, Vol. 4, No. 4, Fall 1988.

Byers, T.J., "MAPping the Islands of Automation," *PC World*, Dec. 1986.

Cad, G., "Plant-Wide Communications: A Hierarchical Model and Solution," *Autofact '88 Proceedings, SME*, 1988, pp. 25.31-25.51.

Cain, D., "The Evolution of CIM at the John Deere Harvester Works," *Autofact '88 Proceedings, SME*, 1988, pp. 6.19-6.31.

Campbell, R., "An Architecture for Factory Control Automation," *AT&T Technical Journal*, 1988.

Cloutier, E., "Top Management Experiences in Applying CIM," *Engineering Network Enterprise Conf. Proc.,* Baltimore, Md., June 1988, pp. 1-57. DEC Handbook, "Networks and Communications Buyer's Guide," Sept. 1990.

Despotakis, J., "Shop Floor Control Systems—Changing Times—Changing Requirements," *Autofact '88 Proceedings, SME*, 1988, pp. 19.1-19.14.

Digital Technical Journal, Sept. 1986.

Foley, J. and Weon-Yoon, Y., "The Current Status of MAP," ACM Conference on Network Protocols and Architectures, 1986. GOSIP: Government Open Systems Interconnection Profile, U.S. Department of Commerce, Federal Inf. Process. Standards Publication 146, Aug. 15, 1988.

Hamilton, D. and L. Main, "In Concert, How MAP will Harmonize Computing," *Business Software Review*, Apr. 1986.

Herrin, G. E., "What MAP Means to You," Modern Machine Shop, Apr. 1986.

Kaminski, M.A., "Manufacturing Automation Protocol (MAP)—OSI for Factory Communications," in 87 International Symposium on Interoperable Information Systems: ISIS Conference Proceedings, 1987.

LaVie, R., "The CIM Integrated Data Processing Environment in the European Open Systems Architecture CIM-OSA," *Engineering Network Enterprise Conf. Proc.*, Baltimore, Md., June 1988, pp. 1-33.

Leben, J., "DEC's Naming Service: Directory Assistance for DECnet," *Data Communications*, Sept. 1990, pp. 99-100.

Malas, D.E., "Integrating Information Flow in a Discrete Manufacturing Enterprise," *Engineering Network Enterprise Conf. Proc.*, Baltimore, Md., June 1988, pp. 1-113.

Malmud, C., *DEC Networks and Architectures*, McGraw-Hill, 1989.

MAP: General Motor's Manufacturing Automation Protocol, Version 2.1, Aug. 1, 1986 MAP 3.0 Specifications, SME, 1988. MAP/TOP User Group, "Manufacturing Automation Protocol Specification," Version 3.0, Implementation Release, Aug. 1987.

MAP Handbook, INI Corporation, June 1988.

MAP/TOP User Group, "Technical and Office Protocol Specification," Version 3.0, Implementation Release, Aug. 1987.

McGuffin, L., "MAP/TOP in CIM Distributed Computing," *IEEE Network*, May 1988.

MMS Programmer's Guide, Concord Communications, Inc., 1988. "Networks and Communications Buyer's Guide," *Digital Publication*.

Ranky, Paul, *Computer Integrated Manufacturing*, Prentice Hall International, 1986.

Rhein, V., "Manufacturing Message Specification," *Engineering Network Enterprise Conf. Proc.*, Baltimore, Md., June 1988, pp. 611-657.

Roach, M., "LANS and MAP: The Past, Present and Future," *Autofact '88 Proceedings, SME*, 1988, pp. 20.1-20.7.

Rhein, V.V., "Manufacturing Message Specification," *Enterprise Con. Proceedings*, June 1988.

Sanders, R., and Weaver, A., "The Xpress Transfer Protocol (XTP)—A Tutorial," *ACM Computer Communication Review,* Oct. 1990, pp. 67-80.

Shapiro, S. F., "Automaker's MAP Leads the Way to Factory Automation," *Computer Design*, May 1985.

Shepherd, D., and Salmony, M., "Extending OSI to Support Synchronization Required by Multimedia Applications," *Computer Communications,* Vol. 13, No. 7, Sept. 1990, pp. 399-406.

Shirey, R., "Defense Data Network Security Administration," *Computer Communication* Review, Vol. 20, No. 2, Apr. 1990, pp. 66-71.

Singer, L.M., "Closing the MAP Gap," *Manufacturing Systems*, Sept. 1987. TOP 3.0 Specifications, SME, 1988.

Appendix E

Tutorial on Database Technologies and SQL

E.1 Introduction

Databases are used for business, engineering, office automation, expert systems/AI, and statistical/scientific applications. These databases may use different database management systems from different vendors and may reside on different computers (microcomputers, minicomputers, mainframes) which are interconnected through different networks. In distributed computing, transparent access to databases located anywhere in the network is needed. We discussed this issue in Chapter 6.

The focus of this tutorial is primarily on how different databases are used for different applications in contemporary enterprises. In this short and informal tutorial, we will give a broad perspective and highlight the database concepts and technologies as they relate to distributed computing. Due to the space limitations, it is not possible to include many details. The interested reader is referred to several books <Date 1990, Elmasri 1989, Ullman 1988, Martin 1986, Vasta 1985, Teorey 1982> for additional information.

E.2 Database Management Concepts

E.2.1 Files and Databases

At the lowest level, a *data item* is the smallest unit of data which cannot be subdivided. Examples of data items are part_no, part_name, weight, cost, etc. A *data record* is a collection of data items. An example of a data record is a part record which is a collection of part_no, part_name, weight and cost of a part. A *file* is a collection of similar data records. For example, a customer file consists of customer records and a parts-file consists of part records. Figure E.1 shows a typical file environment in which different files are created and maintained for batch programs, spreadsheets, simulations and other activities. Most of the file systems were developed in the 1960s for business data processing applications.

Conceptually, a *database* is a collection of files (dissimilar records). For example, a manufacturing database is a collection of data records and files associated with manufacturing activities (e.g., finished goods inventory, bill of materials, equipment),

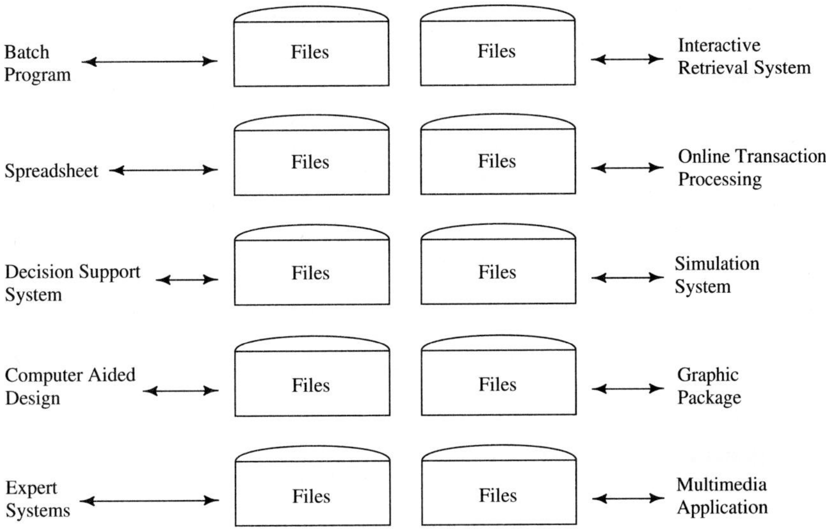

FIGURE E.1 A File Environment

and a financial database consists of payroll data, accounts receivable, general ledger, etc. It is common to assign additional properties to a database definition. For example, according to Elmasri and Navathe <Elmasri 1989>:

> "A database has the following implicit properties:
> - A database is a logically coherent collection of data with some inherent meaning. A random assortment of data cannot be referred to as a database.
> - A database is designed, built, and populated with data for a specific purpose. It has an intended group of users and some preconceived applications in which these users are interested.
> - A database represents some aspect of the real world. Changes to the miniworld are reflected in the database."

Figure E.2 shows a typical database environment in which different users can view, access and manipulate the data in a database. The database may be a business database for financial and administrative applications; a manufacturing database containing bills of material, goods inventory and scheduling data; an office database consisting of memos and proposals; and a knowledge base for artificial intelligence and expert system applications. The database technologies, developed in the 1970s, have evolved into a multibillion dollar industry in the last 20 years.

E.2.2 Database Management System (DBMS)

Database access and manipulation are controlled by a database management system (DBMS). A DBMS, shown in Fig. E.3, is a software package which is designed to

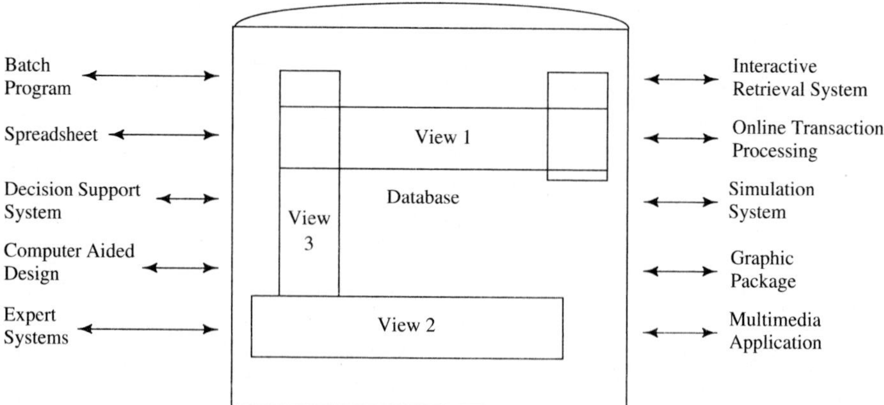

FIGURE E.2 Ideal View of a Database

- Manage logical views of data so that different users can access and manipulate the data without having to know the physical representation of data
- Manage concurrent access to data by multiple users, enforcing logical isolation of transactions
- Enforce security to allow access to authorized users only
- Provide integrity controls and backup/recovery of a database.

These functions of a DBMS are described later. As shown in Fig. E.3, a typical database management system (DBMS) uses a database dictionary/directory to store the data views, data relationships, data formats and security restrictions; database logs to record the activities of transactions; and lock tables to allow synchronous concurrent access to the database by several users.

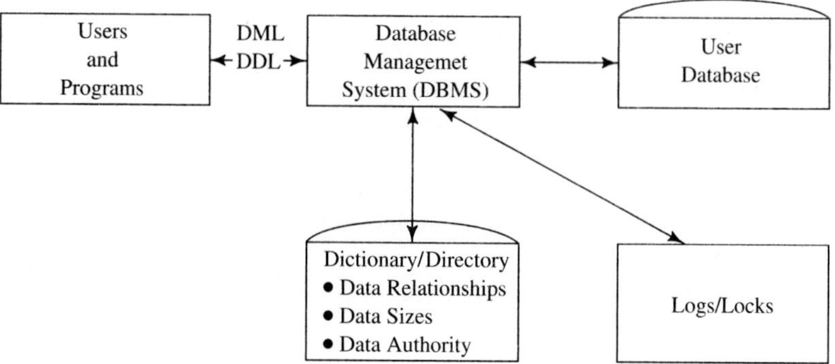

FIGURE E.3 Architectural View of a Database Management System

E.2.3 Data Models and Categories of DBMS.

A data model is a conceptual representation of data that does not include many of the details of how the data is physically stored. Database management systems have traditionally supported the following data models (see Fig. E.4):

- *Hierarchical*: the data model supports one to many relationships (i.e. each record has only one parent). The DBMSs which are based on this data model are called hierarchical DBMSs. IBM's IMS <Kapp 1978> is an example of a hierarchical DBMS.
- *Network*: Many to many relationships among logical data records are supported. An example of a network database management system is Cullinets's IDMS <IDMS 1981>.
- *Relational*: the data is viewed as tables (relations). An example of a relational DBMS is IBM's DB2 <Larson 1988, Date 1984>.

Two other data models gained importance since the early 1980s: Entity-Relationship-Attribute (ERA) and Semantic data models. In the ERA data model, the data is viewed in terms of entities (objects), attributes of entities and relationships between the entities. This model is used to build a conceptual view of data in an organization (called logical data model). Semantic data model is an extension of the ERA model. The main difference is that the relationships carry meanings and the objects can inherit properties from other objects. "Object-oriented databases," discussed in Section E.5, use the semantic data model for storage and retrieval of objects and rules for complex engineering, business and expert systems applications.

Although database management systems can be categorized in a wide variety of ways, the categorization by data models is the most common. The network and hierarchical DBMS, not discussed in this tutorial, are older systems (these DBMSs flourished in the 1970s). We will concentrate more on the relational and object-oriented DBMSs (Sections E.3 through E.5).

E.2.4 Data View Support

A DBMS allows different users to view the same data differently. For example, information about an employee can be viewed differently by different users. The term *schema* is used in database literature to represent a data view. In a DBMS, schema

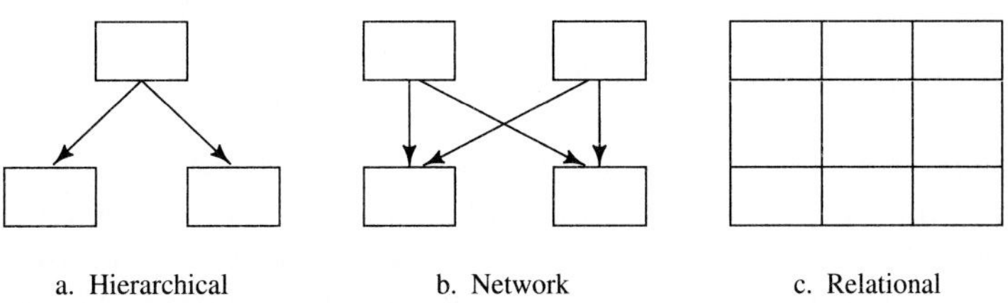

FIGURE E.4 Traditional Data Models

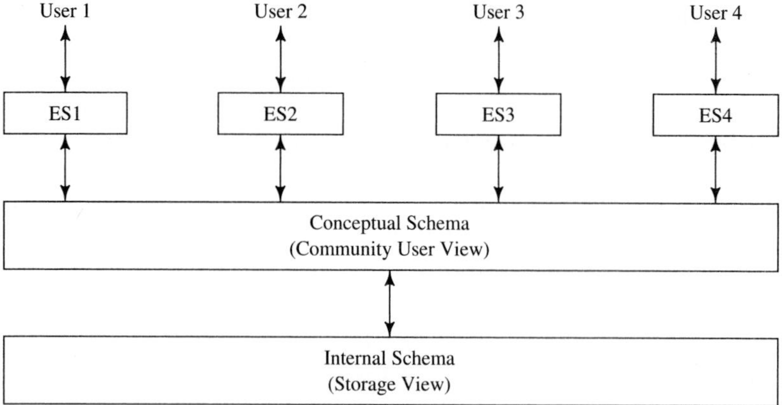

Legend: ES = external schema (individual user view).

FIGURE E.5 Views (Schemas) in a Database Environment

exist at three levels: internal, conceptual and external (see Fig. E.5). The internal schema shows the physical format (e.g., linked list) in which the data are stored on a storage medium. The *conceptual schema* shows the logical layout and the relationships between data records of a database (it is also referred to as the logical data model). Database management systems have traditionally supported the conceptual schemas based on the hierarchical, network and relational data models. An *external schema*, also called a *subschema*, shows a user view of data. This view can be hierarchical, network, relational or object-oriented. In most cases, the external schema is a subset of the conceptual schema. However, relational views can be created from a hierarchical and/or network conceptual views.

E.2.5 Data Definition Facilities

Data definition facilities allow creation of databases. A *Data Definition Language (DDL)* is used to define the data formats and data relationships. DDL allows data definitions at the conceptual as well as external schema levels. In addition, security and authority information is defined. DDLs can be interactive commands or batch programs. Results of DDL commands are stored in the database dictionary. In many corporations, a database administrator controls the data definition facilities for corporate-wide views, access rights, and enforcement of standards.

E.2.6 Data Manipulation Facilities

A *Data Manipulation Language (DML)* allows a user to access, manipulate and modify the database. The power and capability of DMLs depends on the underlying DBMS. Most of the modern DMLs, such as SQL, support ad hoc queries which select information and display answers on demand. DML statements may be embedded in programs written in third generation languages such as C and Cobol, and/or fourth generation languages such as Focus. A DML may support report generators which produce reports with headings on special forms with appropriate printer controls. Some specialized packages such as spreadsheets and expert system shells may provide interfaces with database DMLs. For example, the Lotus Data Lens allows Lotus-123 spreadsheets to access relational databases through SQL. In addition, special features, such as graphics, can be built around a DML. As we will see in Section E.5, the DMLs of object-oriented databases support some of the artificial intelligence features such as inheritance.

E.2.7 Operational Facilities

The operational facilities of a DBMS provide security, integrity and backup/recovery of a database. This includes authentication, audit trails, data consistency (the data must correctly reflect the state of a system even after failures), and concurrency (the data must be simultaneously accessible by different users). Operational facilities of a large, centralized DBMS must be comprehensive enough to allow simultaneous access of hundreds of users to large centralized databases. On the other hand, extensive operational facilities may not be needed for single user microcomputer databases.

Different commercial DBMSs provide different levels of data views, data definitions, data manipulation, and operational support.

E.2.8 Overview of Database Design

Database design attempts to provide consistent and current information to the end users in a speedy fashion. The design process goes through the following general steps (see Elmasri <1989>, Teorey <1982> for details):

1. *Build a Logical Data Model (LDM).* An LDM represents user data requirements and contains the following pieces of information:
   - Entities (objects) such as customers, parts, products, students
   - Attributes of entities such as the name and address of customer
   - Relationships between objects such as customers buy products.

   Different people may develop different views of LDM (user view, management view, programmer view). These views are usually integrated to create a common corporate LDM. In addition, the LDM is cleaned up to remove synonyms, homonyms, and derived data. The resultant LDM can be represented as an ERA diagram.
2. *Develop a Logical Database Design.* This step creates a "normalized" database structure. Normalization is a procedure for decomposing large data entities to remove update anomaly (should not have to update more than is needed) and delete anomaly (should not delete more than is needed). Normalization, not needed for retrieval only data, should be in 1st, 2nd and 3rd normal forms. Discussion of normalization is beyond the scope of this book (see Date <1990>).
3. *Physical Database Design.* This translates the normalized logical data model into a DBMS supported physical structure. The physical design depends on the DBMS

type. In case of a relational database system, the physical design shows the tables, the attributes of each table, and the indexes (see Section E.3). Detailed discussion of this topic is also beyond the scope of this book.

E.3 Overview of Relational Databases

The relational database technology, introduced by E.F. Codd <Codd 1970> at IBM, views all data as tables; all database operations are on tables; and all outputs produced are also tables. A relational database is a collection of tables. Fig. E.6 shows a relational database which consists of two tables: EMPLOYEE and OFFICE. The following terms are used in relational DBMSs (RDBMSs):

A relation is a table in which each row is unique. In addition, a relation must have a fixed number of columns. A table which satisfies these two properties is known to be in the "First Normal Form." The EMPLOYEE and OFFICE tables represent two relations in First Normal Form. A tuple of a relation is synonymous to a row in a table. For example, the EMPLOYEE relation has 5 tuples. An attribute of a relation is a table column. For example, the OFFICE relation has 3 attributes: Location, Manager and Employee-ID. The degree of a relation represents the number of attributes in a table. For example, the degree of OFFICE relation is 3. The domain of an attribute represents the range of values for an attribute. For example, the domain for the age attribute is 0 to, say, 120 years.

The relational DBMSs allow a user to access information from the database with only three basic operations:

- Selection
- Projection
- Join

Selection chooses rows of a table based on a criteria. For example, selection on EMPLOYEE for Age > 30 produces the rows for Joe, Warner and Donna. Projection chooses columns of a table based on a criteria. For example, projection on EMPLOYEE for the Name column lists the names: Joe, Sam, Bruce, Warner and Donna. Join combines two different tables on a common attribute. For example, join of the EMPLOYEE and OFFICE tables on the Employee-ID is shown in Fig. E.7. Theoret-

EMPLOYEE

Name	*ID*	*Age*	*Salary*
Joe	001	32	24K
Sam	002	28	27K
Bruce	003	25	22K
Warner	004	40	45K
Donna	005	37	42K

OFFICE

Location	*Manager*	*Employee-ID*
NY	Pat	005
NY	Pat	004
NY	Pat	002
Chicago	Pete	001
Chicago	Pete	003

FIGURE E.6 A Sample Relational Database

Name	*ID*	*Age*	*Salary*	*Location*	*Manager*	*Employee-ID*
Joe	001	32	24K	NY	Pat	005
Sam	002	28	27K	NY	Pat	004
Bruce	003	25	22K	NY	Pat	002
Warner	004	40	45K	Chicago	Pete	001
Donna	005	37	42K	Chicago	Pete	003

FIGURE E.7 Result of a Join between EMPLOYEE and OFFICE on the Employee-ID

ically, a join between two relations r1 and r2 on the joining condition r1.a1 = r2.a2 involves the following steps (a1 and a2 represent two attributes):

1. Form product of r1 and r2 to produce r3′. In a product (cartesian), every tuple of r1 is concatenated with every tuple of r2 so that r3′ has m x n tuples if r1 has m tuples and r2 has n tuples.
2. Perform a selection on r3′ where the joining attributes a1 and a2 are the same. This produces r3″, known as *equijoin*.
3. Eliminate duplicate attributes from r3″ with a projection. This produces r3, known as *natural join,* or just a join. r3 is the normal result of a join.

Joins are implemented differently by different DBMSs for efficiency. In addition to the natural joins, other forms of joins are supported in relational DBMSs. Examples are the theta and outer joins. In theta joins, also known as nonequijoins, the joining condition is r1.a1 <> r2.a2. The outer joins retrieve rows that may not meet the join conditions. This allows retrieval of data that may be lost (e.g., if joining columns have null values).

In addition to the basic operations of selection, projection and join, relational DBMSs allow unions, differences and intersections. A union concatenates the tuples from r1 with r2 and produce r3. Duplicate relations are eliminated from r3 as a result of union. In addition, r1 and r2 must have same number of attributes and attributes must be from same domain (union compatible). After a difference between r1 and r2, the result r3 has tuples which occur in r1 and not in r2. After an intersection between r1 and r2, the result r3 has tuples that are common in r1 and r2. Unions, intersection, differences, and products can be performed with selection, projection, and join.

In addition to these operations, some manipulation operations are introduced specifically for distributed systems. For example, the semi-join is introduced to minimize the internode traffic while performing a join of two remotely located tables <Bernstein 1981>.

Relational DBMS's provide a number of attractive features:

- The relational model is simple and easy to understand.
- Desired data can be reached through a series of joins. If two tables do not have a joining column, then an "index table" can be created to facilitate joins.
- A standard query language, SQL, is used by all relational DBMS.

- Many commercial relational DBMSs are currently available for mainframes, minicomputers and workstations. Due to the popularity of relational DBMSs and SQL, many tools in business and engineering are developing interfaces to access the relational tables. This is leading to a corporate-wide database concept illustrated in Fig. E.2.
- The relational model supports "data independence" (i.e. the queries are non-procedural and do not have to know the physical data organization such as indexes and pointers).
- Relational database searches are based on data values and not on the position of data in the database. This makes data access easier.
- Relational databases and SQL are used in almost all of the currently available distributed database management systems (DDBMS).

However, relational DBMSs have a number of limitations:

- Relationships between tables cannot be modeled directly; each relationship is implicitly modeled by the inclusion of "foreign keys" as attributes. Simply stated, a foreign key enables a join between two relations. For example, the Employee-ID in the OFFICE table in Fig. E.6 is a foreign key.
- It is very difficult to represent complex design information in relational database model because relational tables do not lend themselves easily to complex data relationships, design versions and views <Spooner 1986, Ketabchi 1987>.
- The user may be responsible for the semantic integrity of a query and completeness of an update. "Referential integrity," which ensures that all tables are modified correctly when a tuple is inserted or deleted, is not implemented in all relational DBMSs.
- The performance of queries depends on an "optimizer" which knows the internal structure of a database. It is difficult to know how well an optimizer is doing its job or if it is doing it at all.

E.4 SQL

Structured Query Language (SQL) is the standard query language for relational databases. SQL, initially also referred to as "SEQUEL," was developed at the IBM San Jose Research Laboratories in 1974. It provides interactive ad hoc queries as well as program interfaces in C, Cobol, Fortran, ADA and PL1. The SQL language consists of a set of facilities for defining, manipulating, and controlling data in a relational database.

E.4.1 Data Definition

SQL data definition language (DDL) is used to create tables by using a CREATE TABLE command. The following two SQL statements are used to create a parts and a customers table:

```
CREATE TABLE parts (part_no char(4), part_name char(5)), price nu-
meric(5))
CREATE TABLE customers (cust_name char(30) not null, address
char(30) not null,
cust_id char(12) unique not null, part_no char(4))
```

E.4.2 Data Retrieval

The main power of SQL lies in its data manipulation facilities. There are four basic SQL operations: SELECT, UPDATE, INSERT, and DELETE. All data retrievals are invoked by a SELECT command, which has the following general syntax:

```
SELECT <a1,a2,a3,...,an> FROM <t1,t2,...,tm> WHERE <conditions>;
```

where a1, a2,,, an are the attributes; t1, t2,, tm, are the tables; and the conditions, if specified, indicate the retrieval criteria. Conditions are specified by the "attribute op value" pairs, which can be combined through logical operators such as AND, OR, NOT. An op indicates predicates such as =,<,>,<=,>=,and <>. Examples of conditions are "age > 30," "age < 30 AND salary > 50K," etc. An SQL statement is terminated either by a ";" or by another SQL command. The SQL statements can be coded in upper or lower case. We will use uppercase letters to indicate the keywords in SQL.

The selection, projection and join operations of relational databases are performed by the SELECT statement. For example, the following statement performs relational selection (i.e., shows all columns):

```
SELECT * FROM t1 WHERE attribute op value
```

For example, "`SELECT * FROM parts WHERE price > 100;`" would display the rows of the parts table for prices more than 100. The statement, "`SELECT * FROM parts;`" would display the entire table. The projection and selection can be combined by using the following statement:

```
SELECT a1, a2,...,an FROM t1 WHERE attribute op value
```

For example, "`SELECT part_no, part_name FROM parts WHERE price > 100`" would display the part_no and part_name from the parts table for prices more than 100. The joins are also performed by the select statement. The following statement causes an equijoin, where the joining condition is equality and the result include duplicates:

```
SELECT t1.*, t2.* FROM t1, t2 WHERE t1.a1 = t2.a2 op value;
```

The following statement invokes a natural join, an equijoin, which eliminates duplicates:

```
SELECT a1, a2, a3,...,an FROM t1, t2 WHERE t1.a1 = t2.a2 op value;
```

For example, " SELECT part_no, part-price, cust_name FROM parts, customers WHERE customer.part_no = parts_no " lists the customer names who have ordered certain parts. Additional conditions can be included in joins. For example, "SELECT part-price, cust_name FROM parts, customers WHERE part_no.customer = part_no.parts and part-price >200 " would list the names of the customers who have ordered parts which cost more than $200. A product between two tables is formed by ignoring the joining condition. For example, the following statement forms a product between the parts and customers tables: " SELECT * FROM parts, customers ." Theta joins are performed by the following statement:

```
SELECT a1, a2,...,an FROM t1, t2 WHERE a1.t1 <> a2.t1 op value
```

More than two tables can be joined in a single statement:

```
SELECT a1, a2,...,an FROM t1, t2,...,tm WHERE condition1 AND con-
dition2 AND condition3;
```

A table can be joined with itself. Aliases can be used to avoid confusion. For example, the following statement produces a list of salesmen in the same city: " SELECT first.name, second.name FROM salesperson first = salesperson second WHERE first.city = second.city AND first.ss# <> second.ss# ." In this statement, first and second are assigned as aliases. You can build complex queries by nesting queries within other queries by using the following format:

```
SELECT a1, a2,...,an FROM t1 WHERE an IN (SELECT a5,a6,...,am
FROM t2 WHERE am op value)
```

For example, the statement "SELECT part_no, part_name FROM parts WHERE part_no in (SELECT cust_name FROM customers WHERE city='Detroit')" would display part numbers and names ordered by the customers who live in Detroit. The innermost query is executed first; the outer query operates on the results of the inner query.

SQL provides a powerful set of built-in functions such as ORDER, AVG, SUM, COUNT, and GROUP BY. The statement " SELECT part_no, part_name FROM parts ORDER BY part_no; " lists the part_no and part_name, sorted by part_no. The statement " SELECT AVG (price), MIN(price), MAX(price), SUM (price), COUNT DISTINCT, COUNT (*) FROM parts; " lists the average, minimum, maximum, and sum of prices. This statement will also list the distinct and total count of records in the parts table. The statement " SELECT AVG(salary) FROM employees GROUP BY title; " will produce the following display:

```
  Title          Avg(salary)
secretary           1300
programmer          2500
manager             3400
```

The MINUS produces a difference (this operator is supported by some DBMSs). For example, " `SELECT * FROM parts MINUS (SELECTFROM parts WHERE price <1000)` " produces the list of parts with price greater than or equal to 1000.

The predicates, used in the where clause of the select statement, provide many options, such as the following:

- Comparison: =, <, >, <=, >= , <>
- BETWEEN/NOT BETWEEN: An example is "where price between 5 and 20;"
- IN/NOT IN: example is "where price not in (5, 7, 10);"
- LIKE/NOT LIKE: these are used for pattern recognition. A "_" is used for single characters, and "%" is used for 0 to n char length. For example, "select cust_name from customers where cust_name like 'B%';" displays the names of all customers whose name starts with a B. Like/not like predicates can be used with character or graphic data.
- NULL: An example is "where part_no is null;"

E.4.3 Data Modification

SQL data modification statements allow insertion, deletion and update of data in tables through the INSERT, DELETE and UPDATE statements. Here are some (hopefully) self explanatory examples:

```
INSERT INTO parts(part_no, part_name, price) (xy22, rods, 100);
INSERT INTO parts(part_no, part_name, price) (xy22, rods, null);
INSERT INTO parts-high(part_no, part_name, price) (select
part_no, part_name, price FROM parts WHERE price >1000);
DELETE FROM parts where part_no = xy20;
UPDATE PARTS set price=120 where part_no=xy22;
```

E.4.4 View Support

Views may be used to operate on portions of tables. For example, " `CREATE VIEW salesperson AS SELECT name, number FROM employees WHERE job='salesperson';` " creates a portion of the employees table populated with salesmen. The " DROP VIEW salesperson; " deletes the view. One view can be created to contain columns from several tables. Views are treated as tables in SQL and can be used in any of the SQL statements. For example, views can be created from joins and can be joined with tables or with other views. Views are created temporarily; the operations are performed on actual tables. Thus updates are performed on the tables from which the views are created. Views can be used to restrict user access and handle subqueries for intermediate tables. You may create a table for more permanent operations by using statements such as: " `CREATE TABLE temp1 (name, part#, price) AS (SELECT name, part#, price FROM suppliers WHERE price > = 1000);.` "

E.4.5 Administrative Facilities

SQL provides two data control statements for administrators:

```
GRANT access-type ON tablename TO id;
REVOKE access-type FROM id;
```

where access-type specifies: all privileges, update, select and insert. In addition, programmers can issue "commit work" command to make changes available to others. Before the commit command, only the person entering changes sees the changes. The "rollback work" command can be used to undo changes before commit. You can modify table structure (add columns, change column width) by using the following statements (these statements are not supported by ANSI SQL):

- `ALTER TABLE tablename ADD column-name datatype;`
- `ALTER TABLE tablename MODIFY column-name datatype new-width;`

E.4.6 Embedded SQL

SQL statements can be embedded in host programs written in several languages such as C, Cobol, Fortran, and PL1. The SQL statements in programs are embedded by using the EXEC SQL statements in a program:

```
EXEC SQL sql statements
```

Two unique problems are concerned with embedded SQL: connecting the SQL variables with programming language (host) variables and handling of multiple rows returned from SQL statements. Connection with host variables is established by reading the selected attributes INTO a set of host program variables:

```
EXEC SQL SELECT a1, a2,,,, an
INTO :p1, :p2,,,,,:pn
FROM t1 WHERE condition;
```

The host variables p1, p2,,, pn are indicated by a ":." For example, the statement "`EXEC SQL SELECT part_no part_name INTO :pnumber, :pname FROM parts`" will store the part_number and part_name attributes from table parts into host variables pnumber and pname.

A "cursor" is used to handle multiple rows returned from SQL. The problem is that the traditional procedural languages are record oriented; they process one record at a time. However, SQL may return many rows as the result of a single embedded select statement. A cursor is first declared for an SQL statement to be executed. It is then opened in a manner similar to a file open. The program then issues FETCH statements to retrieve the rows returned. SQLCODE, a flag, is checked to see if any rows are left to be retrieved. The following code is an example:

```
EXEC SQL DECLARE cs CURSOR FOR <SQL statements>
EXEC SQL OPEN cs
EXEC SQL FETCH cs INTO <host variables>
CHECK SQLCODE for end of fetch
```

Figure E.8 shows a sample Cobol code which illustrates how embedded SQL can be used to extract information from the parts table that we have used in this section. This code has three segments. The first segment shows how the host variables are defined by using a DECLARE statement. The inclusion of SQLCA brings many of the SQL flags and variables (e.g., the SQLCODE which shows return codes) into

```
...
...
DATA DIVISION.
WORKING-STORAGE SECTION.
EXEC SQL BEGIN DECLARE SECTION.
01 PART-RECORD.
  05 PNUMBER  PICTURE X(4).
  05 PNAME    PICTURE A(5).
  05 PPRICE   PICTURE 99999.
EXEC SQL  END DECLARE SECTION.

EXEC SQL  INCLUDE SQLCA.

PROCEDURE DIVISION.
    ..
    ..
    MOVE 'XY20' TO PNUMBER.
    EXEC SQL SELECT PART_NO, PART_NAME, PRICE
         INTO :PNUMBER, :PNAME, :PPRICE
         FROM PARTS WHERE PRICE > :PNUMBER.
    DISPLAY 'RECORD IS ' PNUMBER, PNAME, PPRICE.
     ..
     ...
    EXEC SQL DECLARE CURRENT CURSOR FOR
         SELECT PART_NO, PART_NAME, PRICE
         FROM PARTS WHERE PRICE > 200.
    EXEC SQL OPEN CURRENT.
    EXEC SQL FETCH CURRENT INTO :PNUMBER, PNAME, :PPRICE.
    PERFORM PROCESS-FETCH UNTIL SQLCODE NOT = 0.
    EXEC SQL CLOSE CURRENT.

PROCESS-FETC H.
    ... code to process PNUMBER, PNAME, PPRICE
    EXEC SQL FETCH CURRENT INTO :PNUMBER, PNAME, :PPRICE.
```

FIGURE E.8 Sample SQL Embedded Code in Cobol

the program code. The second segment of the code, in the PROCEDURE DIVISION, shows how the information for part number 'xy20' is displayed. The third part of the code shows how multiple rows are processed by using the cursor statement. The reader should understand that the code shown here is given for illustrative purposes only. Slight differences exist between different languages and vendors.

E.4.7 Performance

SQL query optimization is the responsibility of DBMS which parses the query and then executes it in an appropriate manner. Clever techniques which rely on internal organization are not recommended. A user can create an index for fast access. For example, if the parts table needs to be accessed by part_no frequently, then an index on this column will speed up the performance. The following statements create and drop an index:

```
CREATE INDEX indexname ON tablename (column-name);
DROP INDEX indexname ON tablename;
```

Many indices can be created on one table. The user does not specify when and how the index will be used. SQL determines when to use an index (recall that a SELECT statement does not include any reference to an index). An index is not used if a WHERE clause is absent in queries. The use of the index to satisfy a query is decided by the query optimizer.

E.4.8 SQL Products

At present, SQL is supported on a very large number of relational as well as non-relational database products. Here are examples of the DBMSs which support SQL:

- SQL/DS, part of DB2, IBM's major relational DBMS
- Oracle from Oracle, Inc.
- Informix SQL from Informix Corp.
- Ingres/SQL from INGRES Corp.
- Sybase from Sybase Corp.
- DbaseIV from Ashton Tate.
- SQL Server from Gupta Technologies.

In addition to the relational DBMS, SQL interfaces have been developed to read information from non-relational databases. An example is the EDA/SQL product from Information Builders, Inc., which uses SQL to retrieve information from more than 30 data sources such as ADABAS, IMS, VSAM, IDMS/R, Model 204, Supra, TOTAL, and OS/400 DB. SQL is also generated from a variety of tools to provide access to relational databases. Here are some examples:

- Data Lense, which provides access to SQL databases from spreadsheets (e.g., the Lotus Data Lens from Lotus Corp)
- Executive information systems, which access data through SQL (e.g., the Data Access Language for Command Center from Pilot Software)
- Expert systems, which use SQL to access relational databases (e.g., the SQL interface for ART/IM System from Inference Corp.)
- CASE (computer aided software engineering) tools from Oracle, which are built around relational databases.

E.4.9 Strengths and Weaknesses

SQL has many strengths:

- SQL is easy to learn and use. It is based on relational algebra and allows a user to perform all retrievals by using a single verb (SELECT).
- SQL is the standard query language for all relational databases. An ANSI SQL standard has been published.
- At present, almost all relational database vendors support ANSI SQL. Due to its popularity, an application using ANSI SQL is portable across different database vendors running on different computer systems under different operating systems.
- SQL is used as the global query language for distributed heterogeneous databases. A user issues an SQL call which is translated to other data manipulation language, if needed.
- Due to the popularity of SQL, many tools and aids are being developed around SQL.

A practical limitation of SQL is that SQL queries can become quite complex when information from many tables is needed requiring many joins and nested queries. In addition, ad hoc SQL queries from inexperienced users can cause serious system performance problems. For example, a user may inadvertantly issue a join between 4 to 5 tables, causing thousands of messages in the system. E.F. Codd has discussed many weaknesses of SQL in his papers entitled "Fatal Flaws in SQL" <Codd 1988>. The main flaws discussed by Codd are as follows:

- SQL allows duplicate rows in tables,
- SQL supports an inadequately defined nesting of queries within queries, and
- SQL's support of third and fourth value logic (the logic that evaluates three and four conditions) is not adequate.

Suggested Readings. We have highlighted the main features of SQL. For a quick tutorial on SQL, refer to Dowgiallo <1988>. SQL is an extensive query language with many features that are beyond the scope of this book. The following books are recommended for additional details:

- Date, D.J., *A Guide to The SQL Standard*, Addison-Wesley, 1987
- Hursch, C. and Hursch, J., *SQL The Structured Query Language*, Tab Books, 1988
- Date, C.J., *A Guide to DB2*, Addison-Wesley, 1984

E.5 Object-Oriented Systems and Databases

E.5.1 Introduction

Relational databases are suitable for many applications. However, it is not easy to represent complex information in terms of relational tables. For example, a car design, a computing network layout, and software design of an airline reservation system cannot be represented easily in terms of tables. For these cases, we need to represent complex interrelationships between data elements, retrieve several versions of design, represent the semantics (meaning) of relationships, and utilize the concepts of similarities to reduced redundancies.

The next generation of database systems, commonly known as the object-oriented database management systems (OODBMSs), have been developed to support applications in computer aided design and computer-aided manufacturing (CAD/CAM), expert systems, computer-aided software engineering (CASE), and office automation. Simply stated, OODBMSs combine and extend the features of database management systems, artificial intelligence, and "object oriented programming" for these and other future applications. What exactly is object-oriented programming? Consider the following statements by Tim Rentsh <Rentsh 1982>:

> "Object-oriented programming will be in the 1980s what structured programming was in the 1970s. Everyone will be in favor of it. Every manufacturer will promote his products as supporting it. Every manager will pay lip service to it. Every programmer will practice it differently. And no one will know what it is."

It seems that we are in the middle of an object-oriented "revolution." There is object-oriented analysis, object-oriented design, object-oriented programming, object-oriented databases, and so on. Due to too many object-oriented "things," many groups are trying to figure out what to do. An example is the Object Management Group (OMG) which has been formed as a non-profit consortium of more than 110 software and systems manufacturers and technology information providers. OMG is building a set of standard interfaces for interoperable software by using the object-oriented concepts. OMG is attempting to use the object-oriented technology to maximize the portability, interoperability, and reusability of computer software.

For our purpose, we focus on OODBMS. However, many OODBMSs are very closely related to, or are extensions of, object-oriented programming languages. Section E.5.2 introduces the basic concepts which underlie object-oriented databases and programming. The principles of object-oriented design and programming are discussed in Section E.5.3 for background information. The main characteristics of OODBMS are defined in Section E.5.4.

E.5.2 Object-Oriented Concepts

The five key concepts of the object-oriented paradigm are object, method, message, class, and instance. Let us use an example of cars to quickly illustrate these concepts (more details can wait).

- A car is an object. The attributes of this object are model, year, color, etc.
- The behavior of a car is given by start, stop, go-left, go-right, forward, reverse. These are the methods of the object.
- Turning the ignition key and putting the car in the reverse gear represent the messages which invoke the methods of start and reverse, respectively.
- All cars have several common properties. For example, a vehicle can be used to represent the common properties of objects such as cars, trucks, buses, and taxis. Vehicle is the class.
- Buick is an instance of the vehicle class.

Now, let us describe these concepts in more details.

Object. An object, according to the Webster's Dictionary, is something mental or physical toward which thought, feeling, or action is directed. In computing, an object is something that can be represented in computer memory. Examples of objects are a program variable, a robot, a car, an employee, a factory, and a company. Different objects can be defined in different problem areas. In distributed computing, for example, each file, printer, spreadsheet, program, user, communication line, workstation, and device can be viewed as an object.

An object can be defined in a program or in a database stored on a permanent medium such as disks. The objects in a database are referred to as *persistent* and the ones in a program storage are referred to as *non-persistent*. The data access is the same if the objects are non-persistent or persistent.

Methods and Attributes. An object is represented by at least two properties: attributes and methods. Attributes uniquely identify an object. For example, attributes of an employee object are name, social security number, etc. A method shows the object behavior (what it can do) and is a list of detailed instructions that define how an object responds to a message. A method hides the implementation details from the users of an object. A method typically receives a message, performs some operations, and sends messages to other objects. An object essentially is a collection of attributes and the valid methods that manipulate the data elements. For example, consider the following object definitions:

1. Object Name = employee name
   Attributes = character string
   Methods = read, change, compare insert, delete
2. Object Name = employee
   Attributes = employee name, employee address, employee pay
   Methods = add employee, retrieve employee, update employee

3. Object Name = workstation
   Attributes = workstation type, vender name, cost, operating system used, etc.
   Methods = boot, restart, login, use, logout, etc.
4. Object Name = network
   Attributes = network type, network vendor, number of nodes, etc.
   Methods = boot, login, print service, file service, etc.

Message. An object knows the list of messages to which it can respond to and how it will respond to each. A message is represented by an identifier, or a combination of identifiers that implies an action to be taken by an object. The way an object responds to a message may be affected by the value of its attributes.

Classes, Instances, and Inheritance. A class is a template which represents the properties that are common among many objects. For example, the class *vehicle* can be used to represent the common properties of objects such as cars, trucks, busses and taxis. An object is an instance of a class. Objects can inherit common properties from a class. The properties that can be inherited can be attributes as well as methods. A class hierarchy can be constructed where lower level classes (subclasses) inherit the properties from higher level classes (superclass). Figure E.9 illustrates a class hierarchy.

An object can possess unique (specialized) properties which are not inherited from a class. For example, the taxi object has the specialized property of a meter. Inheritance comes in two flavors: single inheritance in which an object can only inherit from one class, and multiple inheritance in which an object can inherit from many classes. Multiple inheritance allows creation of new objects from existing objects. Inheritance is based on the "is-a" relationship in artificial intelligence (see Fig. E.9).

E.5.3 Object-Oriented Design and Programming

Object-oriented systems are intended to maximize information hiding (through methods) and reusability (through inheritance). The following steps are used to design a system by using an object-oriented paradigm <Booch 1991, Booch 1986>:

- Decompose a given system in terms of objects in the system and not the operations (functions) performed.
- For each object, identify the attributes and the methods. Make sure that the methods hide internal information.
- Develop an initial hierarchy of classes.
- Enforce reusability by inheriting attributes and methods from existing systems. Attempt to maximize inheritance.
- List the messages which invoke methods. These messages establish relationships between objects.

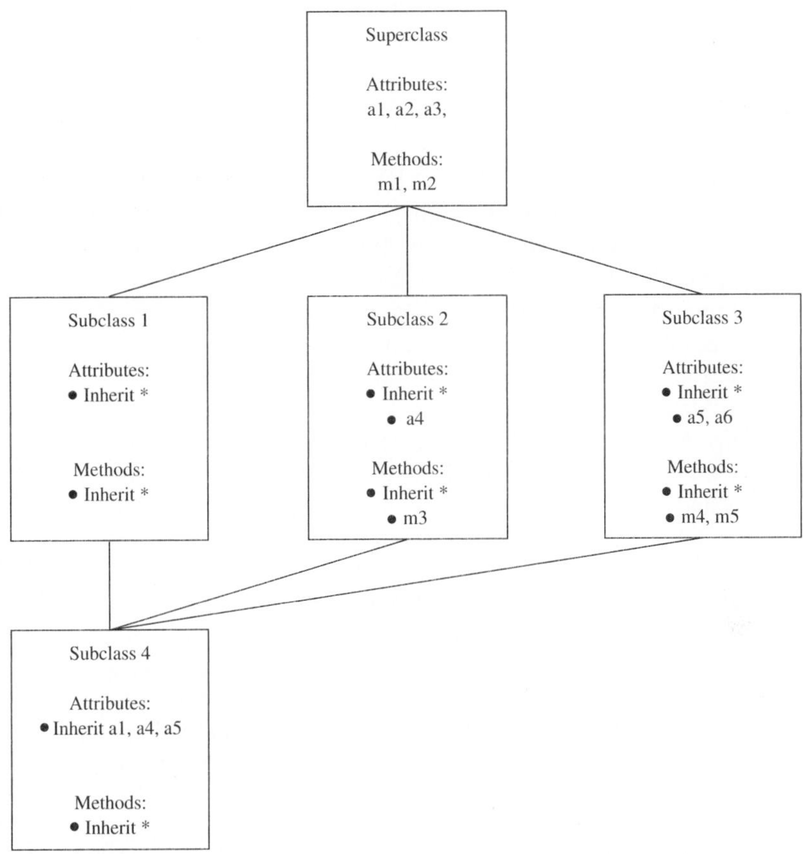

Notes:

- The superclass defines the attributes a1, a2, a3 and the methods m1, m2, which are inherited by all immediate subclasses (and objects) in this system. "Inherit *" means that all properties of a superclass are inherited. If these properties are changed in the superclass, then all other classes inherit these changes.
- The subclass 1 inherits all properties (methods and attributes) from the superclass. It does not define any of its own properties.
- The subclass 2 inherites all properties (methods and attributes) from the superclass. In addition, it defines its own properties (attribute a4 and method m3).
- The subclass 3 inherites all properties (methods and attributes) from the superclass. In addition, it defines its own properties (attributes a5, a6 and methods m4, m5).
- The subclass 4 inherites attributes and methods from different subclasses. This is an example of multiple inheritance.

FIGURE E.9 A Class Hierarchy

- Develop a prototype solution approach which maps each object into a module. Some of these modules may be implemented as program modules or as database objects (see the discussion later).
- Evaluate and refine the design iteratively.

Object-oriented design is translated into code by using object-oriented or object-based programming languages. An object-based programming language supports objects as a language feature but does not support the concept of inheritance. ADA and Modula-2 are examples. Our interest here is in the object-oriented programming languages (OOPL) which support inheritance. OOPL support classes, objects, methods, messages, and inheritance. Other properties supported by OOPL include abstraction, encapsulation, and polymorphism.

Abstraction represents the properties without attention to implementation details. Methods as well as messages support abstraction by hiding unnecessary implementation details. Encapsulation leads to distinct border, well-defined interfaces and a protected internal representation. Object is the basic unit of encapsulation. Objects are called encapsulated abstractions. Polymorphism is defined as the quality or state of being able to assume different forms. Polymorphism can be displayed in messages and/or objects. An example is sending the same message, "print," to different objects which respond to it differently. An example of object polymorphism is a car object, which also serves as a vehicle object (i.e., a subclass behaves as a class).

Several object-oriented programming languages have been introduced. The first object oriented language, Simula, was introduced in the 1960s. Since then, OOPLs have evolved as follows:

- Extensions of procedural languages to support inheritance and other features of OOP. Examples are C++ <Stroustrup 1986>, Objective C <Pinsen 1991>, and Object Pascal <Pascal 1989>.
- Extensions of AI languages to include object-oriented concepts. Examples are Lisp extensions such as Loops and the Common Lisp Object System <Alpert 1990>.
- Languages which are fundamentally based on object-oriented concepts and provide basic building blocks for object-oriented systems. Eiffel <Meyer 1988> and Smalltalk-80 <Goldberg 1989> are examples.

A detailed review of these and many other OOPLs can be found in the OOPL survey by Saunders <1989>. For developments in OOPL, the *Journal of Object-Oriented Programming Languages* should be consulted. The main advantages of object oriented programming and design are:

- Most changes in software systems are related to objects in real life. Thus object-oriented systems are easier to maintain.
- New objects can be created from existing objects by using inheritance thus allowing clustering of similar objects and reducing the complexity of the system.

- The modules can encapsulate (i.e., hide internal details) by allowing external objects to appropriate methods (the external objects invoke methods but do not know how the methods are implemented).

The combined effect is that OOPL can improve code reusability and maintainability.

E.5.4 Object-Oriented Databases

Object-oriented databases allow storage and retrieval of nontraditional data types such as bitmaps, icons, text, polygons, sets, arrays and lists. The objects can be simple or complex, can be related to each other through complex relationships, and can inherit properties from other objects. Object-oriented database management systems (OODBMSs), which can store, retrieve, and manipulate objects, have been an area of active research and exploration since the mid 1980s. Most of the work in OODBMSs has been driven by the computer aided design and computer aided manufacturing (CAD/CAM) applications <Spooner 1986>.

Not everybody has always agreed on exactly what an OODBMS is. The debate over defining an OODBMS has continued since the mid 1980s. In 1989, a group of computer scientists got together and established "The Object-Oriented Database Manifesto" <Atkinson 1989>. This Manifesto, displayed in Table E.1, establishes the basic properties of OODBMS by combining conventional database functionalities with object-oriented functionalities. We have discussed most of these properties in our previous discussions. Let us highlight the most significant properties of OODBMSs in terms of the following features mentioned in the Manifesto:

Complex Objects. Data may be stored, retrieved and manipulated as complex objects which consist of sets, lists, arrays or relational tuples. For example, a relational table represents a simple object while a composite of many tables represents a complex object. A complex object may represent a plant which consists of simple objects such as personnel, buildings, and equipment. In addition, many plant objects can be combined to form a corporation object, and so on. OODBMSs provide data definition and manipulation facilities for complex objects.

Inheritance. OODBMSs allow creation of objects from existing objects by using inheritance of properties. This greatly simplifies the description of complex data. A DDL, for example, would allow creation of a new object which inherits its properties from existing objects in the database. Single or multiple inheritances may be used.

Procedural Encapsulation (Passive and Active Databases). Procedures can be stored as objects in the database. These procedures can be used as methods to encapsulate object semantics. Two types of object-oriented databases are commonly discussed: passive databases which only store the data attributes and active databases which store the data plus the methods associated with the object. Passive databases represent a more conventional view of the database, where the data is stored in the databases and the procedures are embedded in the programs. Procedural encapsulation implies active databases where the code associated with the object is stored in the database. Active databases have the attractive feature that entire systems can be stored and

TABLE E.1 The Object-Oriented Database Manifesto, <Atkinson1989>.

Object-Oriented Features	*Database Management Features*
• Complex objects • Object identity • Encapsulation • Types and classes • Inheritance • Overriding, overloading, and late binding • Computational completeness • Extensibility	• Persistence • Secondary storage management • Concurrency • Recovery • Ad hoc queries

retrieved as objects. Gemstone, Starburst, and POSTGRES are examples of active OODBMSs (see discussion later about these DBMSs).

Links. The relationships between objects can be complex, many to many relationships. In OODBMS, objects are related to other objects through relationships which carry semantic information. The syntax of relationships is much more convenient than the relational joins. For example, relationships between objects can be assigned names such as SUBPART_OF, CREATED_BY, COMPONENTS_ARE, DOCUMENTATION_IS, etc. The DDL allows definition of such relationships and the DML allows retrieval and manipulation of objects by using these relationships. For example, an OODBMS query could say: RETRIEVE SUBPARTS_OF CAR.

Multimedia data. Objects can contain very large values to store pictures, voice or text. Most OODBMS provide facilities to store and retrieve multimedia data. In some relational DBMS, multimedia data is referred to as BLOB (Binary Large Objects). A BLOB appears as any other object in the database and can be retrieved and displayed. This allows integration of multimedia applications around a database.

Versions. Most OODBMSs provide facilities to track multiple versions of an object. Many versions can be linked with one object. A user can issue queries such as retrieve all versions of design and retrieve the documentation associated with version 3.1 of the design.

Integration with programming languages. In many OODBMSs, the data manipulation language is closely related to the programming language. In some object-oriented systems, it is difficult to say if a system is a database or a programming system. This leads to powerful DML capabilities such as use of AI and pattern matching for data manipulation. In addition, same operations can be used to operate on persistent or non-persistent data. For example, let us assume that we need to evaluate the expression C=A+B. In conventional programming systems, we will use a statement such as "C:=A+B;" in a program if A, B, and C were all in main memory (not-persistent). But if these three variables were on persistent storage, say a relational table, then different statements (e.g., SQL SELECT) would be needed before the addition. Thus the language syntax depends on where the data is. OODBMS programming languages attempt to eliminate this difference by providing a common syntax independent of where the data is: non-persistent, persistent, or remotely located.

Categories and Examples. The OODBMS systems generally fall into two categories:

- Extensions of the object-oriented programming languages (OOPL) to include the features of DBMS. Examples are O2 and Gemstone systems.
- Extensions of the relational DBMS to include the features of OOPL. Examples are Starburst and POSTGRESS.

OODBMSs are moving from state of the art to state of the market. Among the earliest OODBMSs are Gemstone (Servio Logic Corp) and Vbase (Antalogic Corp), announced in 1988. It is beyond the scope of this book to discuss detailed features of existing OODBMS. A quick synopsis of a few OODBMSs in the aforementioned categories is included here.

- The O2 System <Deux 1991> is an OODBMS with a complete development environment and a set of user interface tools. The core of O2 is the O2 Engine which stores structures and multimedia objects. O2 Engine handles disk management, transaction management, concurrency, recovery, security, and data administration. The O2 Engine can support two types of interfaces: language interfaces (C and C++ at present) and the O2 environment. The O2 environment provides a complete set of tools such as a query language, a user interface generator, an object-oriented 4th generation language, and a graphical programming environment consisting of graphical editors and database browsers. More information about O2 can be found in Deux <1991, 1990>.
- Gemstone <Butterworth 1991> is a commercially available OODBMS intended for the business as well as the engineering market. The facilities provided by Gemstone include C++ and other language support, active object storage and retrieval, and a variety of development tools. Gemstone consists of two architectural pieces: the Gem server process and the Stone monitor. Gem server is responsible for execution of the object behavior as specified in the Gemstone DML. Requests to store and query the objects are executed in the server. The Stone monitor coordinates the commit activity and allocates new object identifiers. More information about Gemstone can be found in Bretl <1989>, Butterworth <1991>.
- Starburst is being extended to handle OODBMS functionalities such as objects, types, functions and rules <Lohman 1991>. Starburst is being developed by IBM as an extensible DBMS to support new applications and to serve as a testbed for exploring new DBMS technology. Starburst currently executes all the standard SQL statements plus extensions of SQL for retrieval, storage and manipulation of objects. A complex object can be stored either entirely in a "long field" or as a view composed of many rows from many tables. In addition, Starburst supports an "active" database by storing rules in the database. Details about Starburst can be found in Haas <1990> and Lohman <1991>.
- POSTGRES, an extension of the INGRES DBMS, handles object management and knowledge management <Stonebraker 1991>. The POSTGRES data model is

based on the class concept and its query language, POSTQUEL, is a set-oriented query language that resembles a superset of a relational query language. POSTGRES supports complex data objects for object-oriented applications. The rule system of POSTGRES allows storage and execution of rules in the database. Thus POSTGRES supports an "active" database. POSTGRES does not support separate logs as found in the extant DBMSs. Instead, it keeps the old records in the database as logs. Details about POSTGRES can be found in Kemnitz <1991> and Stonebraker <1991>.

Advantages/Disadvantages of OODBMSs. OODBMSs have emerged due to the limitations of relational DBMSs in handling complex relationships and semantics. In addition, OODBMSs attempt to include desirable features from AI and software engineering to improve application reusability and maintainability. Despite several potential advantages of OODBMSs, a few concerns should be noted. First, no standard query language for OODBMS has been defined. Groups like the Object Management Groups and other standardizing bodies will play a key role in this area. In addition, the performance characteristics of OODBMSs are not well understood. This problem is expected to be addressed by performance improvements in the OODBMSs. We have to see how OODBMSs operate in large applications with thousands of users.

E.6 Emerging Database Applications

The network, hierarchical and relational database technologies were developed in the 1970s for business applications. The databases for such applications need static data (the schema does not change frequently) and require extensive reporting capabilities. Relational databases seem to handle these requirements quite well. In the 1980s, requirements for databases in engineering, artificial intelligence, scientific, statistical, office and realtime applications have emerged. DBMSs for these applications require storage and retrieval of objects (digitized voice, digitized images, sets, arrays), specification and validation of constraints, inferences from rules, and realtime performance. Object oriented databases are suitable for a few but not all of these applications. We briefly introduce the database technologies being developed for these applications. Our purpose, once again, is to expose the reader to the various issues and approaches which are relevant in distributed computing (different applications at different sites may utilize different databases). The reader is referred to Catteli <1991> for more details.

E.6.1 Databases for Expert Systems

Databases for expert system applications need to:

- Represent and retrieve/modify facts. Examples of facts are as follows: Buick is a car, Joe is a project manager, project due date is Sept. 20, today is Nov. 10, etc. The collection of facts, known as a factbase, can be easily stored in relational tables.

- Represent a set of rules, which may appear in the following formats:
  - if cond then action
  - if cond1 then cond2
- Process rules, (i.e., parse rules) and draw conclusions (inference). For example, consider the following rules:
  - 1. if a project is past due-date then the project is late
  - 2. if a project is past due-date then hire more people
  - 3. if a project is late then notify manager

If a user asks "should Joe be notified?," then the inference engine will infer from the rules and the factbase and respond with a "yes."

Databases which include facts and rules are referred to as knowledgebases. The main challenge in developing knowledgebases is to support rule processing. Figure E.10 shows two common approaches. In the first approach, shown in Fig. E.10a, the facts are stored in a relational database. The user program contains the rules which are processed by the inference engine of the expert system shell. The shell interfaces with the DBMS to retrieve the facts from the database. Many existing expert system shells (for example ART from the Inference Corp.) interface with relational tables by issuing SQL calls to retrieve data. The second approach involves extension of the DBMS to include an inference engine in addition to the conventional data search (see Fig. E.10). This approach utilizes an "active" database in which the rules are stored as procedures in the database. This approach, used in the POSTGRES and Starbusrst DBMSs, is much more attractive.

E.6.2 Databases for Engineering and Manufacturing Applications

Engineers need databases for representing and analyzing designs, representing and extracting data for projects, inventories, and materials, and supporting manufacturing operations. Engineering databases need to represent long (several megabytes) variable length records, graphic data, complex relationships, version control/archiving of portions of designs, and constraints on the data (restrict data values, monitor the correctness of data item values, and specify standards and relationships).

The relational model can be extended for engineering applications by adding a constraint management system <Rasdorf 1987>. The constraint management system specifies constraints and checks if constraints are satisfied for integrity. For example, consider an inventory table with attributes item-no, item-price and on-hand. The main constraint is that item-price must be more than $100. Constraints can involve one or many rows (avg, max, min). For example, "maximum price of parts must not exceed 1000" specifies a constraint on all rows of the price table. Similarly, constraints can involve one or many attributes, or one or many relations.

Instead of extending the relational model to handle constraints, engineering applications may use OODBMS for complex object manipulation and versioning control. Many articles were written in the late 1980s to demonstrate the use of OODBMS for computer-aided design (see, for example, Spooner <1986>, Hardwick

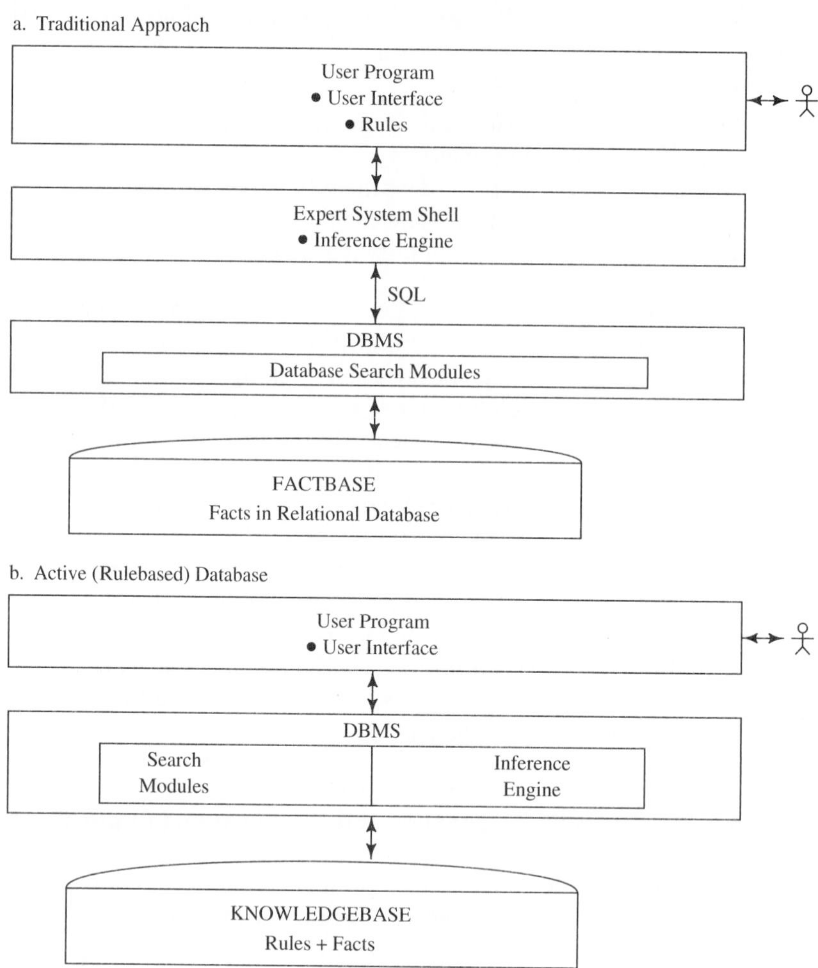

FIGURE E.10 Approaches in Knowledge Processing

<1987>, Ketabchi <1987>). More attention is also being paid to databases for Computer Integrated Manufacturing (CIM) which require integration of business, engineering, manufacturing and office databases <Bray 1987>. The conceptual view of CIM databases, presented in Fig. E.11, can be materialized through distributed database managers and client-server systems, described in Chapters 5 and 6.

E.6.3 Databases for Realtime Applications

Real-time databases are designed for applications with stringent performance constraints. These applications heavily use "in-core" databases to eliminate the disk access delays. The real-time database management systems use algorithms which

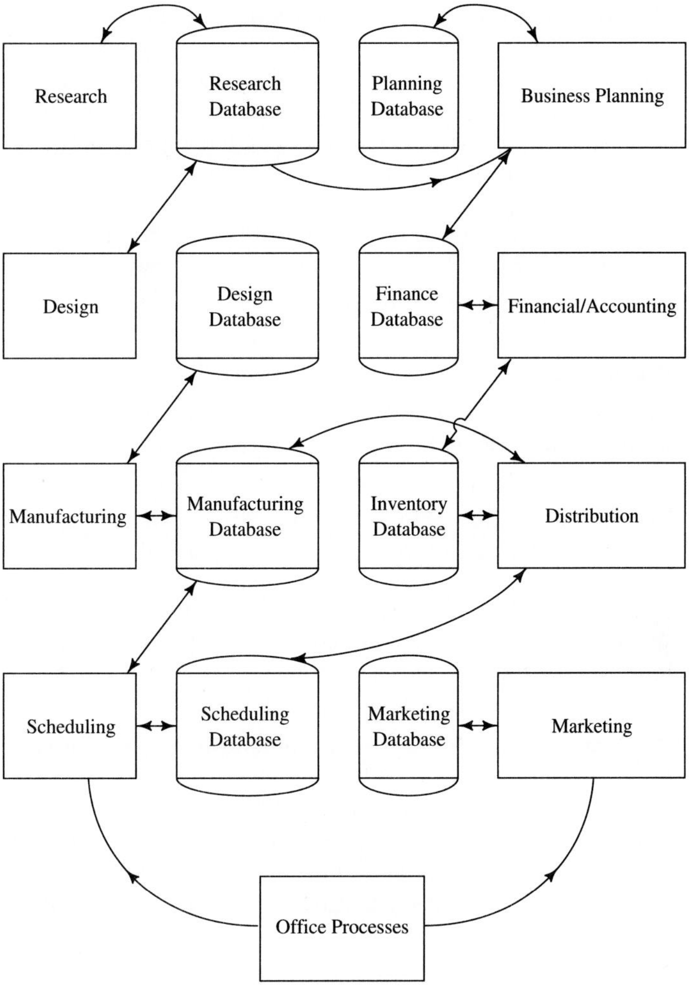

Note: All interrelationships and interactions
are not shown to reduce graphical complexity.

FIGURE E.11 CIM Databases: Conceptual View

minimize I/O and maximize CPU utilization. Another consideration for realtime databases is that ad hoc query facilities and "user-friendly" interfaces are not needed because most realtime databases are used by other machines. For example, in a flexible manufacturing system many robots and controllers may access a realtime database. From what I can remember, robots do not issue many ad hoc queries! Real-time databases are still largely in the research and exploration stage. For a state of the art review of real-time databases, the reader is referred to the ACM SIGMOD Record, March 1988, Special Issue on Real-Time Databases. This reference, although somewhat dated, is quite good.

E.6.4 Databases for Office Information Systems

Office information systems (OISs) are one of the fastest growing applications. Databases for OISs provide storage and retrieval/manipulation of letters, memos, drawings, and other artifacts. Designers of databases for OIS must keep the following characteristics of OIS in mind <Elmasri 1989, pp. 645-647>:

- The office data tends to be semantically rich with unstructured information (e.g., messages, chains of forwarding addresses, oral communications) and "stereotypical information groupings" such as business letters and progress reports.
- Timing information is needed for different activities such as schedules, expected arrival time for products, purchase orders, document transmission, etc.
- The information is usually incomplete and irregular, is highly interconnected because it represents human interactions as individuals and groups, and evolves rapidly.
- OISs are highly interactive, have built-in hierarchies for information routing and approval, and have different priorities associated with information.

It is not easy to design a database at the core of such a system. OODBMSs show a great deal of promise in this area. However, production-quality OISs based on this technology are not currently available.

E.6.5 Databases for Statistical and Scientific Applications

Statistical and scientific databases (SSDBs) exist at two levels <Wong 1984>: micro SSDBs for individual entries and raw events such as consensus data, and macro SSDBs for summary information derived from the former after regressions and other statistical operations. The special features of SSDBs are as follows <Elmasri 1989, pp. 647-648>):

- *Data definition.* Micro SSDBs tend to have hundreds of attributes per record, field sizes vary widely over a record, and attributes need to be added and deleted frequently.
- *Data manipulation.* Micro SSDBs need statistical operations such as cross tabulations, regressions and sampling. Macro SSDBs need many aggregations by different attributes.
- *User interfaces.* Facilities to remember hundreds of attribute names and their abbreviations are essential.
- *Operational support.* Large SSDBs require extensive data dictionary support. However, the need for different levels of locking is minimal because most databases are read-only.

A few SSDBs are commercially available. The SSDB yearly workshops at the Lawrence Livermore Laboratories, initiated in 1981, contain many useful articles in this area.

E.7 Management Summary and Trends

Different databases are used for different applications in a distributed computing environment. As stated previously, relational database technology is state of the market and state of the practice. SQL, the query language for relational DBMS has become a de-facto standard for enterprise-wide data access, even for non-relational data sources. However, relational DBMSs are not suitable for many engineering and other emerging applications discussed in the previous section. Object-oriented DBMSs are state of the market but not state of the practice at the time of this writing.

The main question is which database technologies are suitable for which applications? Figure E.12 attempts to answer this question by using the data and process complexity of applications as a measure. For example, the x-axis shows the complexity of the data model (one to one versus many to many relationships) and the y-axis shows the complexity of the processes (simple retrieval and storage versus complex computations). This figure, based on a diagram produced by Ontologic Corp., shows the regions where some of the database technologies can be most effective. For example, it shows that the older network and hierarchical DBMSs are more suited for complex data but relatively simple processing type applications while the relational DBMSs are more suitable for applications with

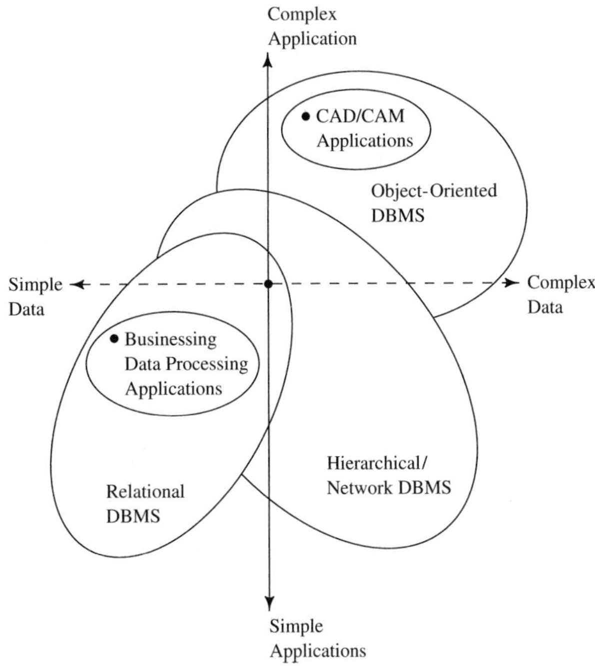

FIGURE E.12 A Model for Evaluating Database Technologies

relatively simple data models. Theoretically, OODBMSs are intended for the complex data and complex processing type applications. A few applications are shown in Fig. E.12 for illustrative purposes.

The following are database research trends <Silberschatz 1991>:

- The next generation of DBMS will support data, objects and rules to support a wide variety of applications.
- Research in multimedia databases and user interfaces will be pursued actively.
- Work in database machines (specialized machines that are designed for handling all DBMS processing) will show its application in database servers.
- More work in distributed databases, especially the object-oriented distributed databases, is needed.

CASE STUDY: Databases for XYZCORP

XYZCORP has embarked on a corporate-wide database effort. As a result of this effort, you have been assigned the following three projects.

Project A: Define the databases needed for the IMCS (Integrated Manufacturing Control System) project described in Chapter 8 Case Study. For each database, you should:

- Define the logical data model for IMCS
- Define the main attributes of the database in IMCS
- Describe at least 5 queries, in English, against the database
- Choose an appropriate data model

Project B: Assume that the following databases have been defined for the stores and the products sold in different stores in IMCS:

- `STORE (S-NAME, S-ID, S-ADDRESS, S-MANAGER, PROD-ID)`
- `PRODUCT (PROD-ID, PROD-NAME, PROD-TYPE, PROD-DESCRIPTION)`

Create these two databases by using SQL Translate the following simple queries to SQL:

1. List the store names in Michigan
2. List the names and ids of product type = "PC"
   - List the names of the stores that carry product type = "PC"
   - Count the total number of stores
   - Count the total number of distinct products
   - Delete the product type "radio" from the products
3. Create indices on PROD-ID and S-ID

Project C: Design a Bill of Materials (BOM) database for the IBM PC compatible desktop computers. You must include all materials (connectors, adapters) in this database. Create the BOM database by using SQL statements and issue at least 5 SQL queries against the BOM database. What are the limitations of the relational data model, if any, for this database.

The administration has also asked you to create a database which describes the XYZCORP network. The backbone network used by XYZCORP has been described in other chapters. This database will be used for different purposes: to maintain an inventory of the network devices, to provide information for network management and to support expert systems. List the main attributes of this database and choose an appropriate data model for this database.

Hints About the Case Study

Project A: The LDM for IMCS would show business entities (customers, bills, inventory, etc), engineering entities (designs, test results, etc.) and manufacturing entities (robots, cells,e tc). Many of these entities can be represented as relational or object-oriented databases.

Project B: This is a straightforward application of SQL (Section E.4).

Project C: The BOM database can be a relational database. However, the network configuration database should be an object-oriented database. This database is very similar to the network configuration database described in Chapter 4 (see Section 4.7.2 and Case Study of Chapter 4). You should also review Section E.6 of this appendix to complete this project. You should especially view this database as a knowledgebase for many tools in XYZCORP.

References

Alpert, S., et al., "Guest Editor's Introduction: Object-Oriented Programming in AI," *IEEE Expert*, Dec. 1990, Special Issue on Object-Oriented Programming.

Atkinson, M., et al., "The Object-Oriented Database Manifesto," *Proceedings of the International Conference on Deductive and Object-Oriented Databases*, Kyoto, Japan, Dec. 1989.

Bernstein, P.A. and Chu, D.W., "Using Semi_joins to Solve Relational Queries," *Journal of ACM*, Jan. 1981.

Bic, L. and Gilbert, J., "Learning from AI: New Trends in Database Technology," *IEEE Computer*, Mar. 1986.

Booch, G., "Object-Oriented Design," *IEEE Trans. on Software Eng.*, Feb. 1986.

Booch, G., *Object Oriented Design with Applications*, Benjamins Cummings, 1991.

Bray, O., *CIM: The Data Management Strategy*, Digital Press, 1988.

Bretl, B., et al., *The Gemstone Data Management System: Object-Oriented Concepts, Applications, and Databases*, Addison-Wesley, 1989.

Browning, D., "Database Design Techniques," *PC Tech Journal*, July 1987.

Butterworth, P., et al., "The Gemstone Object Database Management System," *Comm. of ACM*, Oct. 1991, pp. 64-77.

Catteli, R.G.G, "Introduction to The Next Generation Database Systems," *Comm. of ACM*, Oct. 1991, pp. 33-33.

Codd, E.F., "A Relational Model of Data in Large Shared Databanks," *Comm. of ACM*, June 1970.

Codd, E.F., "Fatal Flaws in SQL," *Datamation*, Aug. 15 and Sept. 1, 1988.

Date, C.J., *An Introduction to Database Systems,* 5th ed., Vols. 1 and 2, Addison-Wesley, 1990.

Date, C.J., *A Guide to DB2*, Addison-Wesley, 1984.

Date, D.J., *A Guide to The SQL Standard*, Addison-Wesley, 1987.

Delisle, N., "Neptune: A Hypertext System for CAD Applications," 1986 ACM.

Deux, G., et al., "The O2 System," Comm. of ACM, Oct. 1991, pp. 34-49.

Deux, G., et al., "The Story of O2," *IEEE Trans. on Knowledge and Data Engineering,* Mar. 1990.

Dowgiallo, E., "An Introduction to SQL," Micro Systems, Sept. 1988.

Elmasri, R. and Navathe, S., *Fundamentals of Database Systems*, Benjamin-Cummings, 1989.

Goldberg, A., and Robson, D., *Smalltalk-80: The Language*, Addison-Wesley, 1989.

Gray, J., "Notes on Database Operating Systems," in *Operating Systems: An Advanced Course*, Springer-Verlag, 1979, pp. 393-481.

Gray, J., "The Transaction Concept: Virtues and Limitations," *Proc. of Conf. Very Large Databases*, Sept. 1981, pp. 144-154.

Gray, J., "Transparency in Its Place," *Unix Review*, May 1987.

Haas, L., et al., "Starburst Mid-Flight: As the Dust Clears," *IEEE Trans. on Knowledge and Data Engineering*, Mar. 1990.

Hardwick, M., and D.L. Spooner, "Comparison of Some Data Models for Engineering Objects," *IEEE CG&A*, Mar. 1987

Hursch, C. and Hursch, J., "SQL: The Structured Query Language," *TAB Books*, 1988.

Inmon, W., "Optimizing Performance with Denormalization," *Database Programming and Design*, Premier Issue, 1987.

IDMS System Overview, Westwood, Mass., Cullinane Database Systems, 1981.

Kapp, D., and Leben, J., *IMS Programming Techniques*, Van Nostrand-Reinhold Company, 1978.

Kemnitz, G. and Stonebraker, M., "The POSTGRES Tutorial," Electronics Research Laboratory, Memo M91/82, UC Berkeley, Feb. 1991.

Ketabchi, M., and Berzins, V., "Modeling and Managing CAD Databases," *IEEE Computer,* Feb. 1987, pp. 93-102.

Kroenke, D., "Database Processing," *SRA*, 1977.

Larson, B., *The Database Experts' Guide to DB2*, McGraw Hill, 1988.

Larson, J. A., "A Flexible Reference Architecture for Distributed Database Management," *Proceedings of ACM 13th Annual Computer Science Conference*, Mar. 1985, New Orleans, pp. 58-72.

Lim, P.A., *CICS/VS Command Level with ANS Cobol Examples,* Van Nostrand Reinhold, 1982.

Lohman, G.M. et al., "Extensions to Starburst: Objects, Types, Functions, and Rules," *Comm. of ACM*, Oct. 1991, pp. 94-109.

Martin, D., *Advanced Database Techniques,* MIT Press, 1986.

Meyer, Bertrand, *Object-Oriented Software Construction*, Prentice Hall, 1988.

Pascal, *Macintosh Programmer's Workshop Pascal 3.0 Reference*, Apple Computer, 1989.

Pinsen, L.J., and Weiner, R.S., *Objective-C*, Addison-Wesley, 1991.

Rasdorf, M., "Extending DBMSs for Engineering Applications," *Computers in Mechanical Engineering*, March 1987, pp. 62-69.

Rentsh, T., Sigplan Notices, Vol. 17, No. 9, 1982.

Saunders, J., "A Survey of Object-Oriented Programming Languages," *Journal of Object-Oriented Programming Languages*, Mar./Apr. 1989.

Silberschatz, A., Stonebraker, M., and Ullman, J., "Database Systems: Achievements and Opportunities," *Comm. of ACM*, Oct. 1991, pp. 110-129.

Silberschatz, A., et al., "Database Systems: Achievements and Opportunities," *Comm. of ACM*, Oct. 1991, pp. 110-120.

Spooner, D., "An Object Oriented Data Management System for Mechanical CAD," *IEEE*, 1986 Conf. on Graphics Stroustrup, B., "The C++ Programming Language," Addison-Wesley, 1986.

Stonebraker, M. and Kemnitz, G., "The POSTGRES Next Generation Database System," *Comm. of ACM*, Oct. 1991, pp. 78-93.

Teorey, T.J and Fry, J.P *Design of Database Structures*, Prentice Hall, 1982.

Turk, T.A., "Using Data Normalization Techniques for Effective Data Base Design," *Journal of Information Systems Management*, Winter, 1985.

Ullman, J., *Principles of Database Systems*, John Wiley, 1982.

Ullman, J., *Principles of Database and Knowledge-Base Systems,* Computer Science Press, 1988.

Vasta, J., *Understanding Database Management Systems*, Wardsworth, 1985.

Vinzant, D., "SQL Database Servers," *Data Communications*, Jan. 1990, pp. 72-88.

Wirfs-Brock, R., Wilkerson, B. and Wiener, L., *Designing Object-Oriented Software*, Prentice-Hall, 1990.

Wong, H., "Micro and Macro Statistical/Scientific Database Management," in Data Engineering Conference, 1984.

Index